The Walter Lippmann Reader

Hardcover ISBN 13: 978-1-5154-4955-3
Trade Paperback ISBN 13: 978-1-5154-4956-0
E-book ISBN 13: 978-1-5154-4957-7

The Walter Lippmann Reader

by Walter Lippmann

A Preface to Politics
Liberty and the News
Public Opinion
The Phantom Public

A Preface to Politics

Table of Contents

Introduction

The most incisive comment on politics to-day is indifference. When men and women begin to feel that elections and legislatures do not matter very much, that politics is a rather distant and unimportant exercise, the reformer might as well put to himself a few searching doubts. Indifference is a criticism that cuts beneath oppositions and wranglings by calling the political method itself into question. Leaders in public affairs recognize this. They know that no attack is so disastrous as silence, that no invective is so blasting as the wise and indulgent smile of the people who do not care. Eager to believe that all the world is as interested as they are, there comes a time when even the reformer is compelled to face the fairly widespread suspicion of the average man that politics is an exhibition in which there is much ado about nothing. But such moments of illumination are rare. They appear in writers who realize how large is the public that doesn't read their books, in reformers who venture to compare the membership list of their league with the census of the United States. Whoever has been granted such a moment of insight knows how exquisitely painful it is. To conquer it men turn generally to their ancient comforter, self-deception: they complain about the stolid, inert masses and the apathy of the people. In a more confidential tone they will tell you that the ordinary citizen is a "hopelessly private person."

The reformer is himself not lacking in stolidity if he can believe such a fiction of a people that crowds about tickers and demands the news of the day before it happens, that trembles on the verge of a panic over the unguarded utterance of a financier, and founds a new religion every month or so. But after a while self-deception ceases to be a comfort. This is when the reformer notices how indifference to politics is settling upon some of the most alert minds of our generation, entering into the attitude of men as capable as any reformer of large and imaginative interests. For among the keenest minds, among artists, scientists and philosophers, there is a remarkable inclination to make a virtue of political indifference. Too passionate an absorption in public affairs is felt to be a somewhat shallow performance, and the reformer is patronized as a well-meaning but rather dull fellow. This is the criticism of men engaged in some genuinely creative labor. Often it is unexpressed, often as not the artist or scientist will join in a political movement. But in the depths of his soul there is, I suspect, some feeling which says to the politician, "Why so hot, my little sir?"

Nothing, too, is more illuminating than the painful way in which many people cultivate a knowledge of public affairs because they have a conscience and wish to do a citizen's duty. Having read a number of articles on the tariff and ploughed through the metaphysics of the currency question, what do they do? They turn with all the more zest to some spontaneous human interest. Perhaps they follow, follow, follow Roosevelt everywhere, and live with him through the emotions of a great battle. But for the affairs of statecraft, for the very policies that a Roosevelt advocates, the interest is largely perfunctory, maintained out of a sense of duty and dropped with a sigh of relief.

That reaction may not be as deplorable as it seems. Pick up your newspaper, read the Congressional Record, run over in your mind the "issues" of a campaign, and then ask yourself whether the average man is entirely to blame because he smiles a bit at Armageddon and refuses to take the politician at his own rhetorical valuation. If men find statecraft uninteresting, may it not be that statecraft is uninteresting? I have a more or less professional interest in public affairs; that is to say, I have had opportunity to look at politics from the point of view of the man who is trying to get the attention of people in order to carry through some reform. At first it was a hard confession to make, but the more I saw of politics at first-hand, the more I respected the indifference of the public. There was something monotonously trivial and irrelevant about our reformist enthusiasm, and an appalling justice in that half-conscious criticism which refuses to place politics among the genuine, creative activities of men. Science was valid, art was valid, the poorest grubber in a laboratory was engaged in a real labor, anyone who had found expression in some beautiful object was truly centered. But politics was a personal drama without meaning or a vague abstraction without substance.

Yet there was the fact, just as indisputable as ever, that public affairs do have an enormous and intimate effect upon our lives. They make or unmake us. They are the foundation of that national vigor through which civilizations mature. City and countryside, factories and play, schools and the family are powerful influences in every life, and politics is directly concerned with them. If politics is irrelevant, it is certainly not because its subject matter is unimportant. Public affairs govern our thinking and doing with subtlety and persistence.

The Walter Lippmann Reader

The trouble, I figured, must be in the way politics is concerned with the nation's interests. If public business seems to drift aimlessly, its results are, nevertheless, of the highest consequence. In statecraft the penalties and rewards are tremendous. Perhaps the approach is distorted. Perhaps uncriticised assumptions have obscured the real uses of politics. Perhaps an attitude can be worked out which will engage a fresher attention. For there are, I believe, blunders in our political thinking which confuse fictitious activity with genuine achievement, and make it difficult for men to know where they should enlist. Perhaps if we can see politics in a different light, it will rivet our creative interests.

These essays, then, are an attempt to sketch an attitude towards statecraft. I have tried to suggest an approach, to illustrate it concretely, to prepare a point of view. In selecting for the title "A Preface to Politics," I have wished to stamp upon the whole book my own sense that it is a beginning and not a conclusion. I have wished to emphasize that there is nothing in this book which can be drafted into a legislative proposal and presented to the legislature the day after to-morrow. It was not written with the notion that these pages would contain an adequate exposition of modern political method. Much less was it written to further a concrete program. There are, I hope, no assumptions put forward as dogmas.

It is a preliminary sketch for a theory of politics, a preface to thinking. Like all speculation about human affairs, it is the result of a grapple with problems as they appear in the experience of one man. For though a personal vision may at times assume an eloquent and universal language, it is well never to forget that all philosophies are the language of particular men.

W. L.

46 East 80th Street, New York City, January 1913.

Routineer and Inventor

Politics does not exist for the sake of demonstrating the superior righteousness of anybody. It is not a competition in deportment. In fact, before you can begin to think about politics at all you have to abandon the notion that there is a war between good men and bad men. That is one of the great American superstitions. More than any other fetish it has ruined our sense of political values by glorifying the pharisee with his vain cruelty to individuals and his unfounded approval of himself. You have only to look at the Senate of the United States, to see how that body is capable of turning itself into a court of preliminary hearings for the Last Judgment, wasting its time and our time and absorbing public enthusiasm and newspaper scareheads. For a hundred needs of the nation it has no thought, but about the precise morality of an historical transaction eight years old there is a meticulous interest. Whether in the Presidential Campaign of 1904 Roosevelt was aware that the ancient tradition of corporate subscriptions had or had not been followed, and the exact and ultimate measure of the guilt that knowledge would have implied—this in the year 1912 is enough to start the Senate on a protracted man-hunt.

Now if one half of the people is bent upon proving how wicked a man is and the other half is determined to show how good he is, neither half will think very much about the nation. An innocent paragraph in the New York Evening Post for August 27, 1912, gives the whole performance away. It shows as clearly as words could how disastrous the good-and-bad-man theory is to political thinking:

"Provided the first hearing takes place on September 30, it is expected that the developments will be made with a view to keeping the Colonel on the defensive. After the beginning of October, it is pointed out, the evidence before the Committee should keep him so busy explaining and denying that the country will not hear much Bull Moose doctrine."

Whether you like the Roosevelt doctrines or not, there can be no two opinions about such an abuse of morality. It is a flat public loss, another attempt to befuddle our thinking. For if politics is merely a guerilla war between the bribed and the unbribed, then statecraft is not a human service but a moral testing ground. It is a public amusement, a melodrama of real life, in which a few conspicuous characters are tried, and it resembles nothing so much as schoolboy hazing which we are told exists for the high purpose of detecting a "yellow streak." But even though we

9

desired it there would be no way of establishing any clear-cut difference in politics between the angels and the imps. The angels are largely self-appointed, being somewhat more sensitive to other people's tar than their own.

But if the issue is not between honesty and dishonesty, where is it?

If you stare at a checkerboard you can see it as black on red, or red on black, as series of horizontal, vertical or diagonal steps which recede or protrude. The longer you look the more patterns you can trace, and the more certain it becomes that there is no single way of looking at the board. So with political issues. There is no obvious cleavage which everyone recognizes. Many patterns appear in the national life. The "progressives" say the issue is between "Privilege" and the "People"; the Socialists, that it is between the "working class" and the "master class." An apologist for dynamite told me once that society was divided into the weak and the strong, and there are people who draw a line between Philistia and Bohemia.

When you rise up and announce that the conflict is between this and that, you mean that this particular conflict interests you. The issue of good-and-bad-men interests this nation to the exclusion of almost all others. But experience shows, I believe, that it is a fruitless conflict and a wasting enthusiasm. Yet some distinction must be drawn if we are to act at all in politics. With nothing we are for and nothing to oppose, we are merely neutral. This cleavage in public affairs is the most important choice we are called upon to make. In large measure it determines the rest of our thinking. Now some issues are fertile; some are not. Some lead to spacious results; others are blind alleys. With this in mind I wish to suggest that the distinction most worth emphasizing to-day is between those who regard government as a routine to be administered and those who regard it as a problem to be solved.

The class of routineers is larger than the conservatives. The man who will follow precedent, but never create one, is merely an obvious example of the routineer. You find him desperately numerous in the civil service, in the official bureaus. To him government is something given as unconditionally, as absolutely as ocean or hill. He goes on winding the tape that he finds. His imagination has rarely extricated itself from under the administrative machine to gain any sense of what a human, temporary contraption the whole affair is. What he thinks is the heavens above him is nothing but the roof.

He is the slave of routine. He can boast of somewhat more spiritual cousins in the men who reverence their ancestors' independence, who feel, as it were, that a disreputable great-grandfather is necessary to a family's respectability. These are the routineers gifted with historical sense. They take their forefathers with enormous solemnity. But one mistake is rarely avoided: they imitate the old-fashioned thing their grandfather did, and ignore the originality which enabled him to do it.

If tradition were a reverent record of those crucial moments when men burst through their habits, a love of the past would not be the butt on which every sophomoric radical can practice his wit. But almost always tradition is nothing but a record and a machine-made imitation of the habits that our ancestors created. The average conservative is a slave to the most incidental and trivial part of his forefathers' glory—to the archaic formula which happened to express their genius or the eighteenth century contrivance by which for a time it was served. To reverence Washington they wear a powdered wig; they do honor to Lincoln by cultivating awkward hands and ungainly feet.

It is fascinating to watch this kind of conservative in action. From Senator Lodge, for example, we do not expect any new perception of popular need. We know that probably his deepest sincerity is an attempt to reproduce the atmosphere of the Senate a hundred years ago. The manners of Mr. Lodge have that immobility which comes from too much gazing at bad statues of dead statesmen.

Yet just because a man is in opposition to Senator Lodge there is no guarantee that he has freed himself from the routineer's habit of mind. A prejudice against some mannerism or a dislike of pretensions may merely cloak some other kind of routine. Take the "good government" attitude. No fresh insight is behind that. It does not promise anything; it does not offer to contribute new values to human life. The machine which exists is accepted in all its essentials: the "goo-goo" yearns for a somewhat smoother rotation.

Often as not the very effort to make the existing machine run more perfectly merely makes matters worse. For the tinkering reformer is frequently one of the worst of the routineers. Even machines are not altogether inflexible, and sometimes what the reformer regards as a sad deviation from the original plans is a poor rickety attempt to adapt the machine to changing conditions. Think what would have happened had we actually remained stolidly faithful to every intention of the Fathers. Think what would happen if every statute were enforced. By the sheer force of circumstances we have twisted constitutions and laws to some approximation of our needs. A changing country has managed to live in spite of a static government machine. Perhaps Bernard Shaw was right when he said that "the famous Constitution survives only because whenever any corner of it gets into the way of the accumulating dollar it is pettishly knocked off and thrown away. Every social development, however beneficial and inevitable from the public point of view, is met, not by an intelligent adaptation of the social structure to its novelties but by a panic and a cry of Go Back."

I am tempted to go further and put into the same class all those radicals who wish simply to substitute some other kind of machine for the one we have. Though not all of them would accept the name, these reformers are simply utopia-makers in action. Their perceptions are more critical than the ordinary conservatives'. They do see that humanity is badly squeezed in the existing mould. They have enough imagination to conceive a different one. But they have an infinite faith in moulds. This routine they don't believe in, but they believe in their own: if you could put the country under a new "system," then human affairs would run automatically for the welfare of all. Some improvement there might be, but as almost all men are held in an iron devotion to their own creations, the routine reformers are simply working for another conservatism, and not for any continuing liberation.

The type of statesman we must oppose to the routineer is one who regards all social organization as an instrument. Systems, institutions and mechanical contrivances have for him no virtue of their own: they are valuable only when they serve the purposes of men. He uses them, of course, but with a constant sense that men have made them, that new ones can be devised, that only an effort of the will can keep machinery in its place. He has no faith whatever in automatic governments. While the routineers see machinery and precedents revolving with mankind as puppets, he puts the deliberate, conscious, willing individual at the center of his philosophy. This reversal is pregnant with a new outlook for statecraft. I hope to show that it alone can keep step with life; it alone is humanly relevant; and it alone achieves valuable results.

Call this man a political creator or a political inventor. The essential quality of him is that he makes that part of existence which has experience the master of it. He serves the ideals of human feelings, not the tendencies of mechanical things.

The difference between a phonograph and the human voice is that the phonograph must sing the song which is stamped upon it. Now there are days—I suspect the vast majority of them in most of our lives—when we grind out the thing that is stamped upon us. It may be the governing of a city, or teaching school, or running a business. We do not get out of bed in the morning because we are eager for the day; something external—we often call it our duty—throws off the bed-clothes, complains that the shaving water isn't hot, puts us into the subway and lands us at our office in season for punching the time-check. We revolve with the business for three or four hours, signing letters, answering telephones, checking up lists, and perhaps towards twelve o'clock the prospect of lunch puts a touch of romance upon life. Then because our days are so unutterably the same, we turn to the newspapers, we go to the magazines and read only the "stuff with punch," we seek out a "show" and drive serious playwrights into the poorhouse. "You can go through contemporary life," writes Wells, "fudging and evading, indulging and slacking, never really hungry nor frightened nor passionately stirred, your highest moment a mere sentimental orgasm, and your first real contact with primary and elementary necessities the sweat of your death-bed."

The world grinds on: we are a fly on the wheel. That sense of an impersonal machine going on with endless reiteration is an experience that imaginative politicians face. Often as not they disguise it under heroic phrases and still louder affirmation, just as most of us hide our cowardly submission to monotony under some word like duty, loyalty, conscience. If you have ever been an office-holder or been close to officials, you must surely have been appalled by the grim way in which committee-meetings, verbose reports, flamboyant speeches, requests, and delegations hold the statesman in a mind-destroying grasp. Perhaps this is the reason why it has been necessary to retire Theodore Roosevelt from public life every now and then in order to give him a chance to learn something new. Every statesman like every professor should have his sabbatical year.

The revolt against the service of our own mechanical habits is well known to anyone who has followed modern thought. As a sharp example one might point to Thomas Davidson, whom William James called "individualist à outrance".... "Reprehending (mildly) a certain chapter of my own on 'Habit,' he said that it was a fixed rule with him to form no regular habits. When he found himself in danger of settling into even a good one, he made a point of interrupting it."

Such men are the sparkling streams that flow through the dusty stretches of a nation. They invigorate and emphasize those times in your own life when each day is new. Then you are alive, then you drive the world before you. The business, however difficult, shapes itself to your effort; you seem to manage detail with an inferior part of yourself, while the real soul of you is active, planning, light. "I wanted thought like an edge of steel and desire like a flame." Eager with sympathy, you and your work are reflected from many angles. You have become luminous.

The Walter Lippmann Reader

Some people are predominantly eager and wilful. The world does not huddle and bend them to a task. They are not, as we say, creatures of environment, but creators of it. Of other people's environment they become the most active part—the part which sets the fashion. What they initiate, others imitate. Theirs is a kind of intrinsic prestige. These are the natural leaders of men, whether it be as head of the gang or as founder of a religion.

It is, I believe, this power of being aggressively active towards the world which gives man a miraculous assurance that the world is something he can make. In creative moments men always draw upon "some secret spring of certainty, some fundamental well into which no disturbing glimmers penetrate." But this is no slack philosophy, for the chance is denied by which we can lie back upon the perfection of some mechanical contrivance. Yet in the light of it government becomes alert to a process of continual creation, an unceasing invention of forms to meet constantly changing needs.

This philosophy is not only difficult to practice: it is elusive when you come to state it. For our political language was made to express a routine conception of government. It comes to us from the Eighteenth Century. And no matter how much we talk about the infusion of the "evolutionary" point of view into all of modern thought, when the test is made political practice shows itself almost virgin to the idea. Our theories assume, and our language is fitted to thinking of government as a frame—Massachusetts, I believe, actually calls her fundamental law the Frame of Government. We picture political institutions as mechanically constructed contrivances within which the nation's life is contained and compelled to approximate some abstract idea of justice or liberty. These frames have very little elasticity, and we take it as an historical commonplace that sooner or later a revolution must come to burst the frame apart. Then a new one is constructed.

Our own Federal Constitution is a striking example of this machine conception of government. It is probably the most important instance we have of the deliberate application of a mechanical philosophy to human affairs. Leaving out all question of the Fathers' ideals, looking simply at the bias which directed their thinking, is there in all the world a more plain-spoken attempt to contrive an automatic governor—a machine which would preserve its balance without the need of taking human nature into account? What other explanation is there for the naïve faith of the Fathers in the "symmetry" of executive, legislature, and judiciary; in the fantastic attempts to circumvent human folly by balancing it with vetoes and checks? No

14

insight into the evident fact that power upsets all mechanical foresight and gravitates toward the natural leaders seems to have illuminated those historic deliberations. The Fathers had a rather pale god, they had only a speaking acquaintance with humanity, so they put their faith in a scaffold, and it has been part of our national piety to pretend that they succeeded.

They worked with the philosophy of their age. Living in the Eighteenth Century, they thought in the images of Newton and Montesquieu. "The Government of the United States," writes Woodrow Wilson, "was constructed upon the Whig theory of political dynamics, which was a sort of unconscious copy of the Newtonian theory of the universe.... As Montesquieu pointed out to them (the English Whigs) in his lucid way, they had sought to balance executive, legislative and judiciary off against one another by a series of checks and counterpoises, which Newton might readily have recognized as suggestive of the mechanism of the heavens." No doubt this automatic and balanced theory of government suited admirably that distrust of the people which seems to have been a dominant feeling among the Fathers. For they were the conservatives of their day: between '76 and '89 they had gone the usual way of opportunist radicals. But had they written the Constitution in the fire of their youth, they might have made it more democratic,—I doubt whether they would have made it less mechanical. The rebellious spirit of Tom Paine expressed itself in logical formulæ as inflexible to the pace of life as did the more contented Hamilton's. This is a determinant which burrows beneath our ordinary classification of progressive and reactionary to the spiritual habits of a period.

If you look into the early utopias of Fourier and Saint-Simon, or better still into the early trade unions, this same faith that a government can be made to work mechanically is predominant everywhere. All the devices of rotation in office, short terms, undelegated authority are simply attempts to defeat the half-perceived fact that power will not long stay diffused. It is characteristic of these primitive democracies that they worship Man and distrust men. They cling to some arrangement, hoping against experience that a government freed from human nature will automatically produce human benefits. To-day within the Socialist Party there is perhaps the greatest surviving example of the desire to offset natural leadership by artificial contrivance. It is an article of faith among orthodox socialists that personalities do not count, and I sincerely believe I am not exaggerating the case when I say that their ideal of government is like Gordon Craig's ideal of the theater—the acting is to be done by a row of supermarionettes. There is a myth among socialists to which all are expected to subscribe, that initiative springs anonymously out of the mass of the people,—that there are no "leaders," that the conspicuous figures are no more influential than the figurehead on the prow of a ship.

This is one of the paradoxes of the democratic movement—that it loves a crowd and fears the individuals who compose it—that the religion of humanity should have had no faith in human beings. Jealous of all individuals, democracies have turned to machines. They have tried to blot out human prestige, to minimize the influence of personality. That there is historical justification for this fear is plain enough. To put it briefly, democracy is afraid of the tyrant. That explains, but does not justify. Governments have to be carried on by men, however much we distrust them. Nobody has yet invented a mechanically beneficent sovereign.

Democracy has put an unfounded faith in automatic contrivances. Because it left personality out of its speculation, it rested in the empty faith that it had excluded it from reality. But in the actual stress of life these frictions do not survive ten minutes. Public officials do not become political marionettes, though people pretend that they are. When theory runs against the grain of living forces, the result is a deceptive theory of politics. If the real government of the United States "had, in fact," as Woodrow Wilson says, "been a machine governed by mechanically automatic balances, it would have had no history; but it was not, and its history has been rich with the influence and personalities of the men who have conducted it and made it a living reality." Only by violating the very spirit of the constitution have we been able to preserve the letter of it. For behind that balanced plan there grew up what Senator Beveridge has called so brilliantly the "invisible government," an empire of natural groups about natural leaders. Parties are such groups: they have had a power out of all proportion to the intentions of the Fathers. Behind the parties has grown up the "political machine"—falsely called a machine, the very opposite of one in fact, a natural sovereignty, I believe. The really rigid and mechanical thing is the charter behind which Tammany works. For Tammany is the real government that has defeated a mechanical foresight. Tammany is not a freak, a strange and monstrous excrescence. Its structure and the laws of its life are, I believe, typical of all real sovereignties. You can find Tammany duplicated wherever there is a social group to be governed—in trade unions, in clubs, in boys' gangs, in the Four Hundred, in the Socialist Party. It is an accretion of power around a center of influence, cemented by patronage, graft, favors, friendship, loyalties, habits,—a human grouping, a natural pyramid.

Only recently have we begun to see that the "political ring" is not something confined to public life. It was Lincoln Steffens, I believe, who first perceived that fact. For a time it was my privilege to work under him on an investigation of the "Money Power." The leading idea was different from customary "muckraking." We were looking not for the evils of Big Business, but for its anatomy. Mr. Steffens came to the subject with a first-hand knowledge of politics. He knew the "invisible government" of cities, states, and the nation. He knew how the boss worked, how he organized his power. When Mr. Steffens approached the vast confusion and complication of big business, he needed some hypothesis to guide him through that maze of facts. He made a bold and brilliant guess, an hypothesis. To govern a life insurance company, Mr. Steffens argued, was just as much "government" as to run a city. What if political methods existed in the realm of business? The investigation was never carried through completely, but we did study the methods by which several life and fire insurance companies, banks, two or three railroads, and several industrials are controlled. We found that the anatomy of Big Business was strikingly like that of Tammany Hall: the same pyramiding of influence, the same tendency of power to center on individuals who did not necessarily sit in the official seats, the same effort of human organization to grow independently of legal arrangements. Thus in the life insurance companies, and the Hughes investigation supports this, the real power was held not by the president, not by the voters or policy-holders, but by men who were not even directors. After a while we took it as a matter of course that the head of a company was an administrative dummy, with a dependence on unofficial power similar to that of Governor Dix on Boss Murphy. That seems to be typical of the whole economic life of this country. It is controlled by groups of men whose influence extends like a web to smaller, tributary groups, cutting across all official boundaries and designations, making short work of all legal formulæ, and exercising sovereignty regardless of the little fences we erect to keep it in bounds.

A glimpse into the labor world revealed very much the same condition. The boss, and the bosslet, the heeler—the men who are "it"—all are there exercising the real power, the power that independently of charters and elections decides what shall happen. I don't wish to have this regarded as necessarily malign. It seems so now because we put our faith in the ideal arrangements which it disturbs. But if we could come to face it squarely—to see that that is what sovereignty is—that if we are to use human power for human purposes we must turn to the realities of it, then we shall have gone far towards leaving behind us the futile hopes of mechanical perfection so constantly blasted by natural facts.

The invisible government is malign. But the evil doesn't come from the fact that it plays horse with the Newtonian theory of the constitution. What is dangerous about it is that we do not see it, cannot use it, and are compelled to submit to it. The nature of political power we shall not change. If that is the way human societies organize sovereignty, the sooner we face that fact the better. For the object of democracy is not to imitate the rhythm of the stars but to harness political power to the nation's need. If corporations and governments have indeed gone on a joy ride the business of reform is not to set up fences, Sherman Acts and injunctions into which they can bump, but to take the wheel and to steer.

The corruption of which we hear so much is certainly not accounted for when you have called it dishonesty. It is too widespread for any such glib explanation. When you see how business controls politics, it certainly is not very illuminating to call the successful business men of a nation criminals. Yet I suppose that all of them violate the law. May not this constant dodging or hurdling of statutes be a sign that there is something the matter with the statutes? Is it not possible that graft is the cracking and bursting of the receptacles in which we have tried to constrain the business of this country? It seems possible that business has had to control politics because its laws were so stupidly obstructive. In the trust agitation this is especially plausible. For there is every reason to believe that concentration is a world-wide tendency, made possible at first by mechanical inventions, fostered by the disastrous experiences of competition, and accepted by business men through contagion and imitation. Certainly the trusts increase. Wherever politics is rigid and hostile to that tendency, there is irritation and struggle, but the agglomeration goes on. Hindered by political conditions, the process becomes secretive and morbid. The trust is not checked, but it is perverted. In 1910 the "American Banker" estimated that there were 1,198 corporations with 8,110 subsidiaries liable to all the penalties of the Sherman Act. Now this concentration must represent a profound impetus in the business world—an impetus which certainly cannot be obliterated, even if anyone were foolish enough to wish it. I venture to suggest that much of what is called "corruption" is the odor of a decaying political system done to death by an economic growth.

The Walter Lippmann Reader

It is our desperate adherence to an old method that has produced the confusion of political life. Because we have insisted upon looking at government as a frame and governing as a routine, because in short we have been static in our theories, politics has such an unreal relation to actual conditions. Feckless—that is what our politics is. It is literally eccentric: it has been centered mechanically instead of vitally. We have, it seems, been seduced by a fictitious analogy: we have hoped for machine regularity when we needed human initiative and leadership, when life was crying that its inventive abilities should be freed.

Roosevelt in his term did much to center government truly. For a time natural leadership and nominal position coincided, and the administration became in a measure a real sovereignty. The routine conception dwindled, and the Roosevelt appointees went at issues as problems to be solved. They may have been mistaken: Roosevelt may be uncritical in his judgments. But the fact remains that the Roosevelt régime gave a new prestige to the Presidency by effecting through it the greatest release of political invention in a generation. Contrast it with the Taft administration, and the quality is set in relief. Taft was the perfect routineer trying to run government as automatically as possible. His sincerity consisted in utter respect for form: he denied himself whatever leadership he was capable of, and outwardly at least he tried to "balance" the government. His greatest passions seem to be purely administrative and legal. The people did not like it. They said it was dead. They were right. They had grown accustomed to a humanly liberating atmosphere in which formality was an instrument instead of an idol. They had seen the Roosevelt influence adding to the resources of life—irrigation, and waterways, conservation, the Panama Canal, the "country life" movement. They knew these things were achieved through initiative that burst through formal restrictions, and they applauded wildly. It was only a taste, but it was a taste, a taste of what government might be like.

The opposition was instructive. Apart from those who feared Roosevelt for selfish reasons, his enemies were men who loved an orderly adherence to traditional methods. They shivered in the emotional gale; they obstructed and the gale became destructive. They felt that, along with obviously good things, this sudden national fertility might breed a monster—that a leadership like Roosevelt's might indeed prove dangerous, as giving birth may lead to death.

What the methodically-minded do not see is that the sterility of a routine is far more appalling. Not everyone may feel that to push out into the untried, and take

The Walter Lippmann Reader

risks for big prizes, is worth while. Men will tell you that government has no business to undertake an adventure, to make experiments. They think that safety lies in repetition, that if you do nothing, nothing will be done to you. It's a mistake due to poverty of imagination and inability to learn from experience. Even the timidest soul dare not "stand pat." The indictment against mere routine in government is a staggering one.

For while statesmen are pottering along doing the same thing year in, year out, putting up the tariff one year and down the next, passing appropriation bills and recodifying laws, the real forces in the country do not stand still. Vast changes, economic and psychological, take place, and these changes demand new guidance. But the routineers are always unprepared. It has become one of the grim trade jokes of innovators that the one thing you can count upon is that the rulers will come to think that they are the apex of human development. For a queer effect of responsibility on men is that it makes them try to be as much like machines as possible. Tammany itself becomes rigid when it is too successful, and only defeat seems to give it new life. Success makes men rigid and they tend to exalt stability over all the other virtues; tired of the effort of willing they become fanatics about conservatism. But conditions change whether statesmen wish them to or not; society must have new institutions to fit new wants, and all that rigid conservatism can do is to make the transitions difficult. Violent revolutions may be charged up to the unreadiness of statesmen. It is because they will not see, or cannot see, that feudalism is dead, that chattel slavery is antiquated; it is because they have not the wisdom and the audacity to anticipate these great social changes; it is because they insist upon standing pat that we have French Revolutions and Civil Wars.

But statesmen who had decided that at last men were to be the masters of their own history, instead of its victims, would face politics in a truly revolutionary manner. It would give a new outlook to statesmanship, turning it from the mere preservation of order, the administration of political machinery and the guarding of ancient privilege to the invention of new political forms, the prevision of social wants, and the preparation for new economic growths.

Such a statesmanship would in the '80's have prepared for the trust movement. There would have been nothing miraculous in such foresight. Standard Oil was dominant by the beginning of the '80's, and concentration had begun in sugar, steel and other basic industries. Here was an economic tendency of revolutionary significance—the organization of business in a way that was bound to change the

20

The Walter Lippmann Reader

outlook of a whole nation. It had vast potentialities for good and evil—all it wanted was harnessing and directing. But the new thing did not fit into the little outlines and verbosities which served as a philosophy for our political hacks. So they gaped at it and let it run wild, called it names, and threw stones at it. And by that time the force was too big for them. An alert statesmanship would have facilitated the process of concentration; would have made provision for those who were cast aside; would have been an ally of trust building, and by that very fact it would have had an internal grip on the trust—it would have kept the trust's inner workings public; it could have bent the trust to social uses.

This is not mere wisdom after the event. In the '80's there were hundreds of thousands of people in the world who understood that the trust was a natural economic growth. Karl Marx had proclaimed it some thirty years before, and it was a widely circulated idea. Is it asking too much of a statesman if we expect him to know political theory and to balance it with the facts he sees? By the '90's surely, the egregious folly of a Sherman Anti-Trust Law should have been evident to any man who pretended to political leadership. Yet here it is the year 1912 and that monument of economic ignorance and superstition is still worshiped with the lips by two out of the three big national parties.

Another movement—like that of the trust—is gathering strength to-day. It is the unification of wage-workers. We stand in relation to it as the men of the '80's did to the trusts. It is the complement of that problem. It also has vast potentialities for good and evil. It, too, demands understanding and direction. It, too, will not be stopped by hard names or injunctions.

What we loosely call "syndicalism" is a tendency that no statesman can overlook to-day without earning the jeers of his children. This labor movement has a destructive and constructive energy within it. On its beneficent side it promises a new professional interest in work, self-education, and the co-operative management of industry. But this creative power is constantly choked off because the unions are compelled to fight for their lives—the more opposition they meet the more you are likely to see of sabotage, direct action, the grève perlée—the less chance there is for the educative forces to show themselves. Then, the more violent syndicalism proves itself to be, the more hysterically we bait it in the usual vicious circle of ignorance.

But who amongst us is optimistic enough to hope that the men who sit in the mighty positions are going to make a better show of themselves than their predecessors did over the trust problem? It strains hope a little too much. Those

21

men in Washington, most of them lawyers, are so educated that they are practically incapable of meeting a new condition. All their training plus all their natural ossification of mind is hostile to invention. You cannot endow even the best machine with initiative; the jolliest steam-roller will not plant flowers.

The thought-processes in Washington are too lumbering for the needs of this nation. Against that evil muckraking ought to be directed. Those senators and representatives are largely irrelevant; they are not concerned with realities. Their dishonesties are comparatively insignificant. The scorn of the public should be turned upon the emptiness of political thought, upon the fact that those men seem without even a conception of the nation's needs. And while they maunder along they stifle the forces of life which are trying to break through. It was nothing but the insolence of the routineer that forced Gifford Pinchot out of the Forest Service. Pinchot in respect to his subject was a fine political inventor. But routine forced him out—into what?—into the moil and toil of fighting for offices, and there he has cut a poor figure indeed. You may say that he has had to spend his energy trying to find a chance to use his power. What a wanton waste of talent is that for a civilized nation! Wiley is another case of the creative mind harassed by the routineers. Judge Lindsey is another—a fine, constructive children's judge compelled to be a politician. And of our misuse of the Rockefellers and Carnegies—the retrospect is appalling. Here was industrial genius unquestionably beyond the ordinary. What did this nation do with it? It found no public use for talent. It left that to operate in darkness—then opinion rose in an empty fury, made an outlaw of one and a platitudinous philanthropist of the other. It could lynch one as a moral monster, when as a matter of fact his ideals were commonplace; it could proclaim one a great benefactor when in truth he was a rather dull old gentleman. Abused out of all reason or praised irrelevantly—the one thing this nation has not been able to do with these men is to use their genius. It is this life-sapping quality of our politics that should be fought—its wanton waste of the initiatives we have—its stupid indifference.

We need a new sense of political values. These times require a different order of thinking. We cannot expect to meet our problems with a few inherited ideas, uncriticised assumptions, a foggy vocabulary, and a machine philosophy. Our political thinking needs the infusion of contemporary insights. The enormous vitality that is regenerating other interests can be brought into the service of politics. Our primary care must be to keep the habits of the mind flexible and adapted to the movement of real life. The only way to control our destiny is to work with it. In politics, at least, we stoop to conquer. There is no use, no heroism, in butting against the inevitable, yet nothing is entirely inevitable. There is always some choice, some opportunity for human direction.

It is not easy. It is far easier to treat life as if it were dead, men as if they were dolls. It is everlastingly difficult to keep the mind flexible and alert. The rule of thumb is not here. To follow the pace of living requires enormous vigilance and sympathy. No one can write conclusively about it. Compared with this creative statesmanship, the administering of a routine or the battle for a platitude is a very simple affair. But genuine politics is not an inhuman task. Part of the genuineness is its unpretentious humanity. I am not creating the figure of an ideal statesman out of some inner fancy. That is just the deepest error of our political thinking—to talk of politics without reference to human beings. The creative men appear in public life in spite of the cold blanket the politicians throw over them. Really statesmanlike things are done, inventions are made. But this real achievement comes to us confused, mixed with much that is contradictory. Political inventors are to-day largely unconscious of their purpose, and, so, defenceless against the distraction of their routineer enemies.

Lacking a philosophy they are defenceless against their own inner tendency to sink into repetition. As a witty Frenchman remarked, many geniuses become their own disciples. This is true when the attention is slack, and effort has lost its direction. We have elaborate governmental mechanisms—like the tariff, for example, which we go on making more "scientific" year in, year out—having long since lost sight of their human purpose. They may be defeating the very ends they were meant to serve. We cling to constitutions out of "loyalty." We trudge in the treadmill and call it love of our ancient institutions. We emulate the mule, that greatest of all routineers.

The Taboo

Our government has certainly not measured up to expectations. Even chronic admirers of the "balance" and "symmetry" of the Constitution admit either by word or deed that it did not foresee the whole history of the American people. Poor bewildered statesmen, unused to any notion of change, have seen the national life grow to a monstrous confusion and sprout monstrous evils by the way. Men and women clamored for remedies, vowed, shouted and insisted that their "official servants" do something—something statesmanlike—to abate so much evident wrong. But their representatives had very little more than a frock coat and a slogan as equipment for the task. Trained to interpret a constitution instead of life, these statesmen faced with historic helplessness the vociferations of ministers, muckrakers, labor leaders, women's clubs, granges and reformers' leagues. Out of a tumultuous medley appeared the common theme of public opinion—that the leaders should lead, that the governors should govern.

The trusts had appeared, labor was restless, vice seemed to be corrupting the vitality of the nation. Statesmen had to do something. Their training was legal and therefore utterly inadequate, but it was all they had. They became panicky and reverted to an ancient superstition. They forbade the existence of evil by law. They made it anathema. They pronounced it damnable. They threatened to club it. They issued a legislative curse, and called upon the district attorney to do the rest. They started out to abolish human instincts, check economic tendencies and repress social changes by laws prohibiting them. They turned to this sanctified ignorance which is rampant in almost any nursery, which presides at family councils, flourishes among "reformers"; which from time immemorial has haunted legislatures and courts. Under the spell of it men try to stop drunkenness by closing the saloons; when poolrooms shock them they call a policeman; if Haywood becomes annoying, they procure an injunction. They meet the evils of dance halls by barricading them; they go forth to battle against vice by raiding brothels and fining prostitutes. For trusts there is a Sherman Act. In spite of all experience they cling desperately to these superstitions.

It is the method of the taboo, as naïve as barbarism, as ancient as human failure.

There is a law against suicide. It is illegal for a man to kill himself. What it means in practice, of course, is that there is punishment waiting for a man who doesn't succeed in killing himself. We say to the man who is tired of life that if he bungles

24

we propose to make this world still less attractive by clapping him into jail. I know an economist who has a scheme for keeping down the population by refusing very poor people a marriage license. He used to teach Sunday school and deplore promiscuity. In the annual report of the president of a distilling company I once saw the statement that business had increased in the "dry" states. In a prohibition town where I lived you could drink all you wanted by belonging to a "club" or winking at the druggist. And in another city where Sunday closing was strictly enforced, a minister told me with painful surprise that the Monday police blotter showed less drunks and more wife-beaters.

We pass a law against race-track gambling and add to the profits from faro. We raid the faro joints, and drive gambling into the home, where poker and bridge whist are taught to children who follow their parents' example. We deprive anarchists of free speech by the heavy hand of a police magistrate, and furnish them with a practical instead of a theoretical argument against government. We answer strikes with bayonets, and make treason one of the rights of man.

Everybody knows that when you close the dance halls you fill the parks. Men who in their youth took part in "crusades" against the Tenderloin now admit in a crestfallen way that they succeeded merely in sprinkling the Tenderloin through the whole city. Over twenty years ago we formulated a sweeping taboo against trusts. Those same twenty years mark the centralization of industry.

The routineer in a panic turns to the taboo. Whatever does not fit into his rigid little scheme of things must have its head chopped off. Now human nature and the changing social forces it generates are the very material which fit least well into most little schemes of things. A man cannot sleep in his cradle: whatever is useful must in the nature of life become useless. We employ our instruments and abandon them. But nothing so simply true as that prevails in politics. When a government routine conflicts with the nation's purposes—the statesman actually makes a virtue of his loyalty to the routine. His practice is to ignore human character and pay no attention to social forces. The shallow presumption is that undomesticated impulses can be obliterated; that world-wide economic inventions can be stamped out by jailing millionaires—and acting in the spirit of Mr. Chesterton's man Fipps "who went mad and ran about the country with an axe, hacking branches off the trees whenever there were not the same number on both sides." The routineer is, of course, the first to decry every radical proposal as "against human nature." But the stand-pat mind has forfeited all right to speak for human nature. It has devoted the centuries to torturing men's instincts, stamping on them, passing laws against them, lifting its eyebrows at the thought of them—doing everything but trying to understand them. The same people who with daily insistence say that innovators ignore facts are in the absurd predicament of trying to still human wants with petty taboos. Social systems like ours, which do not even feed and house men and women, which deny pleasure, cramp play, ban adventure, propose celibacy and grind out monotony, are a clear confession of sterility in statesmanship. And politics, however pretentiously rhetorical about ideals, is irrelevant if the only method it knows is to ostracize the desires it cannot manage.

Suppose that statesmen transferred their reverence from the precedents and mistakes of their ancestors to the human material which they have set out to govern. Suppose they looked mankind in the face and asked themselves what was the result of answering evil with a prohibition. Such an exercise would, I fear, involve a considerable strain on what reformers call their moral sensibilities. For human nature is a rather shocking affair if you come to it with ordinary romantic optimism. Certainly the human nature that figures in most political thinking is a wraith that never was—not even in the souls of politicians. "Idealism" creates an abstraction and then shudders at a reality which does not answer to it. Now statesmen who have set out to deal with actual life must deal with actual people. They cannot afford an inclusive pessimism about mankind. Let them have the consistency and good sense to cease bothering about men if men's desires seem intrinsically evil. Moral judgment about the ultimate quality of character is dangerous to a politician. He is too constantly tempted to call a policeman when he disapproves.

We must study our failures. Gambling and drink, for example, produce much misery. But what reformers have to learn is that men don't gamble just for the sake of violating the law. They do so because something within them is satisfied by betting or drinking. To erect a ban doesn't stop the want. It merely prevents its satisfaction. And since this desire for stimulants or taking a chance at a prize is older and far more deeply rooted in the nature of men than love of the Prohibition Party or reverence for laws made at Albany, people will contrive to drink and gamble in spite of the acts of a legislature.

A man may take liquor for a variety of reasons: he may be thirsty; or depressed; or unusually happy; he may want the companionship of a saloon, or he may hope to forget a scolding wife. Perhaps he needs a "bracer" in a weary hunt for a job.

The Walter Lippmann Reader

Perhaps he has a terrible craving for alcohol. He does not take a drink so that he may become an habitual drunkard, or be locked up in jail, or get into a brawl, or lose his job, or go insane. These are what he might call the unfortunate by-products of his desire. If once he could find something which would do for him what liquor does, without hurting him as liquor does, there would be no problem of drink. Bernard Shaw says he has found that substitute in going to church when there's no service. Goethe wrote "The Sorrows of Werther" in order to get rid of his own. Many an unhappy lover has found peace by expressing his misery in sonnet form. The problem is to find something for the common man who is not interested in contemporary churches and who can't write sonnets.

When the socialists in Milwaukee began to experiment with municipal dances they were greeted with indignant protests from the "anti-vice" element and with amused contempt by the newspaper paragraphers. The dances were discontinued, and so the belief in their failure is complete. I think, though, that Mayor Seidel's defense would by itself make this experiment memorable. He admitted freely the worst that can be said against the ordinary dance hall. So far he was with the petty reformers. Then he pointed out with considerable vehemence that dance halls were an urgent social necessity. At that point he had transcended the mind of the petty reformer completely. "We propose," said Seidel, "to go into competition with the devil."

Nothing deeper has come from an American mayor in a long, long time. It is the point that Jane Addams makes in the opening pages of that wisely sweet book, "The Spirit of Youth and the City Streets." She calls attention to the fact that the modern state has failed to provide for pleasure. "This stupid experiment," she writes, "of organizing work and failing to organize play has, of course, brought about a fine revenge. The love of pleasure will not be denied, and when it has turned into all sorts of malignant and vicious appetites, then we, the middle-aged, grow quite distracted and resort to all sorts of restrictive measures."

For human nature seems to have wants that must be filled. If nobody else supplies them, the devil will. The demand for pleasure, adventure, romance has been left to the devil's catering for so long a time that most people think he inspires the demand. He doesn't. Our neglect is the devil's opportunity. What we should use, we let him abuse, and the corruption of the best things, as Hume remarked, produces the worst. Pleasure in our cities has become tied to lobster palaces, adventure to exalted murderers, romance to silly, mooning novels. Like the flower

27

The Walter Lippmann Reader

girl in Galsworthy's play, we have made a very considerable confusion of the life of joy and the joy of life. The first impulse is to abolish all lobster palaces, melodramas, yellow newspapers, and sentimentally erotic novels. Why not abolish all the devil's works? the reformer wonders. The answer is in history. It can't be done that way. It is impossible to abolish either with a law or an axe the desires of men. It is dangerous, explosively dangerous, to thwart them for any length of time. The Puritans tried to choke the craving for pleasure in early New England. They had no theaters, no dances, no festivals. They burned witches instead.

We rail a good deal against Tammany Hall. Reform tickets make periodic sallies against it, crying economy, efficiency, and a business administration. And we all pretend to be enormously surprised when the "ignorant foreign vote" prefers a corrupt political ring to a party of well-dressed, grammatical, and high-minded gentlemen. Some of us are even rather downcast about democracy because the Bowery doesn't take to heart the admonitions of the Evening Post.

We forget completely the important wants supplied by Tammany Hall. We forget that this is a lonely country for an immigrant and that the Statue of Liberty doesn't shed her light with too much warmth. Possessing nothing but a statistical, inhuman conception of government, the average municipal reformer looks down contemptuously upon a man like Tim Sullivan with his clambakes and his dances; his warm and friendly saloons, his handshaking and funeral-going and baby-christening; his readiness to get coal for the family, and a job for the husband. But a Tim Sullivan is closer to the heart of statesmanship than five City Clubs full of people who want low taxes and orderly bookkeeping. He does things which have to be done. He humanizes a strange country; he is a friend at court; he represents the legitimate kindliness of government, standing between the poor and the impersonal, uninviting majesty of the law. Let no man wonder that Lorimer's people do not prefer an efficiency expert, that a Tim Sullivan has power, or that men are loyal to Hinky Dink. The cry raised against these men by the average reformer is a piece of cold, unreal, preposterous idealism compared to the solid warm facts of kindliness, clothes, food and fun.

You cannot beat the bosses with the reformer's taboo. You will not get far on the Bowery with the cost unit system and low taxes. And I don't blame the Bowery. You can beat Tammany Hall permanently in one way—by making the government of a city as human, as kindly, as jolly as Tammany Hall. I am aware of the contract-grafts, the franchise-steals, the dirty streets, the bribing and the blackmail, the

28

vice-and-crime partnerships, the Big Business alliances of Tammany Hall. And yet it seems to me that Tammany has a better perception of human need, and comes nearer to being what a government should be, than any scheme yet proposed by a group of "uptown good government" enthusiasts. Tammany is not a satanic instrument of deception, cleverly devised to thwart "the will of the people." It is a crude and largely unconscious answer to certain immediate needs, and without those needs its power would crumble. That is why I ventured in the preceding chapter to describe it as a natural sovereignty which had grown up behind a mechanical form of government. It is a poor weed compared to what government might be. But it is a real government that has power and serves a want, and not a frame imposed upon men from on top.

The taboo—the merely negative law—is the emptiest of all the impositions from on top. In its long record of failure, in the comparative success of Tammany, those who are aiming at social changes can see a profound lesson; the impulses, cravings and wants of men must be employed. You can employ them well or ill, but you must employ them. A group of reformers lounging at a club cannot, dare not, decide to close up another man's club because it is called a saloon. Unless the reformer can invent something which substitutes attractive virtues for attractive vices, he will fail. He will fail because human nature abhors the vacuum created by the taboo.

An incident in the international peace propaganda illuminates this point. Not long ago a meeting in Carnegie Hall, New York, to forward peace among nations broke up in great disorder. Thousands of people who hate the waste and futility of war as much as any of the orators of that evening were filled with an unholy glee. They chuckled with delight at the idea of a riot in a peace meeting. Though it would have seemed perverse to the ordinary pacificist, this sentiment sprang from a respectable source. It had the same ground as the instinctive feeling of nine men in ten that Roosevelt has more right to talk about peace than William Howard Taft. James made it articulate in his essay on "The Moral Equivalent of War." James was a great advocate of peace, but he understood Theodore Roosevelt and he spoke for the military man when he wrote of war that: "Its 'horrors' are a cheap price to pay for rescue from the only alternative supposed, of a world of clerks and teachers, of co-education and zo-ophily, of 'consumers' leagues' and 'associated charities,' of industrialism unlimited, and feminism unabashed. No scorn, no hardness, no valor any more! Fie upon such a cattleyard of a planet!"

The Walter Lippmann Reader

And he added: "So far as the central essence of this feeling goes, no healthy minded person, it seems to me, can help to some degree partaking of it. Militarism is the great preserver of our ideals of hardihood, and human life with no use for hardihood would be contemptible. Without risks or prizes for the darer, history would be insipid indeed; and there is a type of military character which everyone feels that the race should never cease to breed, for everyone is sensitive to its superiority."

So William James proposed not the abolition of war, but a moral equivalent for it. He dreamed of "a conscription of the whole youthful population to form for a certain number of years a part of the army enlisted against Nature.... The military ideals of hardihood and discipline would be wrought into the growing fibre of the people; no one would remain blind, as the luxurious classes now are blind, to man's relations to the globe he lives on, and to the permanently sour and hard foundations of his higher life." Now we are not concerned here over the question of this particular proposal. The telling point in my opinion is this: that when a wise man, a student of human nature, and a reformer met in the same person, the taboo was abandoned. James has given us a lasting phrase when he speaks of the "moral equivalent" of evil. We can use it, I believe, as a guide post to statesmanship. Rightly understood, the idea behind the words contains all that is valuable in conservatism, and, for the first time, gives a reputable meaning to that tortured epithet "constructive."

"The military feelings," says James, "are too deeply grounded to abdicate their place among our ideals until better substitutes are offered ... such a conscription, with the state of public opinion that would have required it, and the many moral fruits it would bear, would preserve in the midst of a pacific civilization the manly virtues which the military party is so afraid of seeing disappear in peace.... So far, war has been the only force that can discipline a whole community, and until an equivalent discipline is organized I believe that war must have its way. But I have no serious doubt that the ordinary prides and shames of social man, once developed to a certain intensity, are capable of organizing such a moral equivalent as I have sketched, or some other just as effective for preserving manliness of type. It is but a question of time, of skilful propagandism, and of opinion-making men seizing historic opportunities. The martial type of character can be bred without war."

To find for evil its moral equivalent is to be conservative about values and radical about forms, to turn to the establishment of positively good things instead of trying simply to check bad ones, to emphasize the additions to life, instead of the restrictions upon it, to substitute, if you like, the love of heaven for the fear of hell. Such a program means the dignified utilization of the whole nature of man. It will recognize as the first test of all political systems and moral codes whether or not they are "against human nature." It will insist that they be cut to fit the whole man, not merely a part of him. For there are utopian proposals made every day which cover about as much of a human being as a beautiful hat does.

Instead of tabooing our impulses, we must redirect them. Instead of trying to crush badness we must turn the power behind it to good account. The assumption is that every lust is capable of some civilized expression.

We say, in effect, that evil is a way by which desire expresses itself. The older moralists, the taboo philosophers believed that the desires themselves were inherently evil. To us they are the energies of the soul, neither good nor bad in themselves. Like dynamite, they are capable of all sorts of uses, and it is the business of civilization, through the family and the school, religion, art, science, and all institutions, to transmute these energies into fine values. Behind evil there is power, and it is folly,—wasting and disappointing folly,—to ignore this power because it has found an evil issue. All that is dynamic in human character is in these rooted lusts. The great error of the taboo has been just this: that it believed each desire had only one expression, that if that expression was evil the desire itself was evil. We know a little better to-day. We know that it is possible to harness desire to many interests, that evil is one form of a desire, and not the nature of it.

This supplies us with a standard for judging reforms, and so makes clear what "constructive" action really is. When it was discovered recently that the boys' gang was not an unmitigated nuisance to be chased by a policeman, but a force that could be made valuable to civilization through the Boy Scouts, a really constructive reform was given to the world. The effervescence of boys on the street, wasted and perverted through neglect or persecution, was drained and applied to fine uses. When Percy MacKaye pleads for pageants in which the people themselves participate, he offers an opportunity for expressing some of the lusts of the city in the form of an art. The Freudian school of psychologists calls this "sublimation." They have brought forward a wealth of material which gives us every reason to believe that the theory of "moral equivalents" is soundly based, that much the same energies produce crime and civilization, art, vice, insanity, love, lust, and religion. In each individual the original differences are small. Training and opportunity decide in the main how men's lust shall emerge. Left to themselves, or ignorantly tabooed, they break forth in some barbaric or morbid form. Only by supplying our passions with civilized interests can we escape their destructive force.

I have put it negatively, as a counsel of prudence. But he who has the courage of existence will put it triumphantly, crying "yea" as Nietzsche did, and recognizing that all the passions of men are the motive powers of a fine life.

For the roads that lead to heaven and hell are one until they part.

The Changing Focus

The taboo, however useless, is at least concrete. Although it achieves little besides mischief, it has all the appearance of practical action, and consequently enlists the enthusiasm of those people whom Wells describes as rushing about the country shouting: "For Gawd's sake let's do something now." There are weight and solidity in a policeman's club, while a "moral equivalent" happens to be pale like the stuff of which dreams are made. To the politician whose daily life consists in dodging the thousand and one conflicting prejudices of his constituents, in bickering with committees, intriguing and playing for the vote; to the business man harassed on four sides by the trust, the union, the law, and public opinion,—distrustful of any wide scheme because the stupidity of his shipping clerk is the most vivid item in his mind, all this discussion about politics and the inner life will sound like so much fine-spun nonsense.

I, for one, am not disposed to blame the politicians and the business men. They govern the nation, it is true, but they do it in a rather absentminded fashion. Those revolutionists who see the misery of the country as a deliberate and fiendish plot overestimate the bad will, the intelligence and the singleness of purpose in the ruling classes. Business and political leaders don't mean badly; the trouble with them is that most of the time they don't mean anything. They picture themselves as very "practical," which in practice amounts to saying that nothing makes them feel so spiritually homeless as the discussion of values and an invitation to examine first principles. Ideas, most of the time, cause them genuine distress, and are as disconcerting as an idle office boy, or a squeaky telephone.

I do not underestimate the troubles of the man of affairs. I have lived with politicians,—with socialist politicians whose good-will was abundant and intentions constructive. The petty vexations pile up into mountains; the distracting details scatter the attention and break up thinking, while the mere problem of exercising power crowds out speculation about what to do with it. Personal jealousies interrupt co-ordinated effort; committee sessions wear out nerves by their aimless drifting; constant speech-making turns a man back upon a convenient little store of platitudes—misunderstanding and distortion dry up the imagination, make thought timid and expression flat, the atmosphere of publicity requires a mask which soon becomes the reality. Politicians tend to live "in character," and many a public figure has come to imitate the journalism which describes him. You cannot blame politicians if their perceptions are few and their thinking crude.

Football strategy does not originate in a scrimmage: it is useless to expect solutions in a political campaign. Woodrow Wilson brought to public life an exceedingly flexible mind,—many of us when he first emerged rejoiced at the clean and athletic quality of his thinking. But even he under the stress of a campaign slackened into commonplace reiteration, accepting a futile and intellectually dishonest platform, closing his eyes to facts, misrepresenting his opponents, abandoning, in short, the very qualities which distinguished him. It is understandable. When a National Committee puts a megaphone to a man's mouth and tells him to yell, it is difficult for him to hear anything.

If a nation's destiny were really bound up with the politics reported in newspapers, the impasse would be discouraging. If the important sovereignty of a country were in what is called its parliamentary life, then the day of Plato's philosopher-kings would be far off indeed. Certainly nobody expects our politicians to become philosophers. When they do they hide the fact. And when philosophers try to be politicians they generally cease to be philosophers. But the truth is that we overestimate enormously the importance of nominations, campaigns, and office-holding. If we are discouraged it is because we tend to identify statecraft with that official government which is merely one of its instruments. Vastly over-advertised, we have mistaken an inflated fragment for the real political life of the country.

For if you think of men and their welfare, government appears at once as nothing but an agent among many others. The task of civilizing our impulses by creating fine opportunities for their expression cannot be accomplished through the City Hall alone. All the influences of social life are needed. The eggs do not lie in one basket. Thus the issues in the trade unions may be far more directly important to statecraft than the destiny of the Republican Party. The power that workingmen generate when they unite—the demands they will make and the tactics they will pursue—how they are educating themselves and the nation—these are genuine issues which bear upon the future. So with the policies of business men. Whether financiers are to be sullen and stupid like Archbold, defiant like Morgan, or well-intentioned like Perkins is a question that enters deeply into the industrial issues. The whole business problem takes on a new complexion if the representatives of capital are to be men with the temper of Louis Brandeis or William C. Redfield. For when business careers are made professional, new motives enter into the situation; it will make a world of difference if the leadership of industry is in the hands of men interested in production as a creative art instead of as a brute exploitation. The economic conflicts are at once raised to a plane of research, experiment and honest deliberation. For on the level of hate and mean-seeking no solution is possible. That subtle fact,—the change of business motives, the demonstration that industry can be conducted as medicine is,—may civilize the whole class conflict.

Obviously statecraft is concerned with such a change, extra-political though it is. And wherever the politician through his prestige or the government through its universities can stimulate a revolution in business motives, it should do so. That is genuinely constructive work, and will do more to a humane solution of the class struggle than all the jails and state constabularies that ever betrayed the barbarism of the Twentieth Century. It is no wonder that business is such a sordid affair. We have done our best to exclude from it every passionate interest that is capable of lighting up activity with eagerness and joy. "Unbusinesslike" we have called the devotion of craftsmen and scientists. We have actually pretended that the work of extracting a living from nature could be done most successfully by short-sighted money-makers encouraged by their money-spending wives. We are learning better to-day. We are beginning to know that this nation for all its boasts has not touched the real possibilities of business success, that nature and good luck have done most of our work, that our achievements come in spite of our ignorance. And so no man can gauge the civilizing possibilities of a new set of motives in business. That it will add to the dignity and value of millions of careers is only one of its blessings. Given a nation of men trained to think scientifically about their work and feel about it as craftsmen, and you have a people released from a stupid fixation upon the silly little ideals of accumulating dollars and filling their neighbor's eye. We preach against commercialism but without great result. And the reason for our failure is: that we merely say "you ought not" instead of offering a new interest. Instead of telling business men not to be greedy, we should tell them to be industrial statesmen, applied scientists, and members of a craft. Politics can aid that revolution in a hundred Ways: by advocating it, by furnishing schools that teach, laboratories that demonstrate, by putting business on the same plane of interest as the Health Service.

The indictment against politics to-day is not its corruption, but its lack of insight. I believe it is a fact which experience will sustain that men steal because they haven't anything better to do. You don't have to preach honesty to men with a creative purpose. Let a human being throw the energies of his soul into the making of something, and the instinct of workmanship will take care of his honesty. The writers who have nothing to say are the ones that you can buy: the others have too high a price. A genuine craftsman will not adulterate his product: the reason isn't because duty says he shouldn't, but because passion says he couldn't. I suggested in an earlier chapter that the issue of honesty and dishonesty was a futile one, and I placed faith in the creative men. They hate shams and the watering of goods on a more trustworthy basis than the mere routine moralist. To them dishonesty is a contradiction of their own lusts, and they ask no credit, need none, for being true. Creation is an emotional ascent, which makes the standard vices trivial, and turns all that is valuable in virtue to the service of desire.

When politics revolves mechanically it ceases to use the real energies of a nation. Government is then at once irrelevant and mischievous—a mere obstructive nuisance. Not long ago a prominent senator remarked that he didn't know much about the country, because he had spent the last few months in Washington. It was a profound utterance as anyone can testify who reads, let us say, the Congressional Record. For that document, though replete with language, is singularly unacquainted with the forces that agitate the nation. Politics, as the contributors to the Congressional Record seem to understand it, is a very limited selection of well-worn debates on a few arbitrarily chosen "problems." Those questions have developed a technique and an interest in them for their own sake. They are handled with a dull solemnity quite out of proportion to their real interest. Labor receives only a perfunctory and largely disingenuous attention; even commerce is handled in a way that expresses neither its direction nor its public use. Congress has been ready enough to grant favors to corporations, but where in its wrangling from the Sherman Act to the Commerce Court has it shown any sympathetic understanding of the constructive purposes in the trust movement? It has either presented the business man with money or harassed him with bungling enthusiasm in the pretended interests of the consumer. The one thing Congress has not done is to use the talents of business men for the nation's advantage.

If "politics" has been indifferent to forces like the union and the trust, it is no exaggeration to say that it has displayed a modest ignorance of women's problems, of educational conflicts and racial aspirations; of the control of newspapers and magazines, the book publishing world, socialist conventions and unofficial political groups like the single-taxers.

Such genuine powers do not absorb our political interest because we are fooled by the regalia of office. But statesmanship, if it is to be relevant, would obtain a new perspective on these dynamic currents, would find out the wants they express and the energies they contain, would shape and direct and guide them. For unions and trusts, sects, clubs and voluntary associations stand for actual needs. The size of their following, the intensity of their demands are a fair index of what the statesman must think about. No lawyer created a trust though he drew up its charter; no logician made the labor movement or the feminist agitation. If you ask what for political purposes a nation is, a practical answer would be: it is its "movements." They are the social life. So far as the future is man-made it is made of them. They show their real vitality by a relentless growth in spite of all the little fences and obstacles that foolish politicians devise.

There is, of course, much that is dead within the movements. Each one carries along a quantity of inert and outworn ideas,—not infrequently there is an internally contradictory current. Thus the very workingmen who agitate for a better diffusion of wealth display a marked hostility to improvements in the production of it. The feminists too have their atavisms: not a few who object to the patriarchal family seem inclined to cure it by going back still more—to the matriarchal. Constructive business has no end of reactionary moments——the most striking, perhaps, is when it buys up patents in order to suppress them. Yet these inversions, though discouraging, are not essential in the life of movements. They need to be expurgated by an unceasing criticism; yet in bulk the forces I have mentioned, and many others less important, carry with them the creative powers of our times.

It is not surprising that so many political inventions have been made within these movements, fostered by them, and brought to a general public notice through their efforts. When some constructive proposal is being agitated before a legislative committee, it is customary to unite the "movements" in support of it. Trade unions and women's clubs have joined hands in many an agitation. There are proposals to-day, like the minimum wage, which seem sure of support from consumers' leagues, women's federations, trade unions and those far-sighted business men who may be called "State Socialists."

In fact, unless a political invention is woven into a social movement it has no importance. Only when that is done is it imbued with life. But how among

The Walter Lippmann Reader

countless suggestions is a "cause" to know the difference between a true invention and a pipe-dream? There is, of course, no infallible touchstone by which we can tell offhand. No one need hope for an easy certainty either here or anywhere else in human affairs. No one is absolved from experiment and constant revision. Yet there are some hypotheses that prima facie deserve more attention than others.

Those are the suggestions which come out of a recognized human need. If a man proposed that the judges of the Supreme Court be reduced from nine to seven because the number seven has mystical power, we could ignore him. But if he suggested that the number be reduced because seven men can deliberate more effectively than nine he ought to be given a hearing. Or let us suppose that the argument is about granting votes to women. The suffragist who bases a claim on the so-called "logic of democracy" is making the poorest possible showing for a good cause. I have heard people maintain that: "it makes no difference whether women want the ballot, or are fit for it, or can do any good with it,—this country is a democracy. Democracy means government by the votes of the people. Women are people. Therefore women should vote." That in a very simple form is the mechanical conception of government. For notice how it ignores human wants and human powers—how it subordinates people to a rigid formula. I use this crude example because it shows that even the most genuine and deeply grounded demands are as yet unable to free themselves entirely from a superficial manner of thinking. We are only partially emancipated from the mechanical and merely logical tradition of the Eighteenth Century. No end of illustrations could be adduced. In the Socialist party it has been the custom to denounce the "short ballot." Why? Because it reduces the number of elective offices. This is regarded as undemocratic for the reason that democracy has come to mean a series of elections. According to a logic, the more elections the more democratic. But experience has shown that a seven-foot ballot with a regiment of names is so bewildering that a real choice is impossible. So it is proposed to cut down the number of elective offices, focus the attention on a few alternatives, and turn voting into a fairly intelligent performance. Here is an attempt to fit political devices to the actual powers of the voter. The old, crude form of ballot forgot that finite beings had to operate it. But the "democrats" adhere to the multitude of choices because "logic" requires them to.

This incident of the "short ballot" illustrates the cleavage between invention and routine. The socialists oppose it not because their intentions are bad but because on this issue their thinking is mechanical. Instead of applying the test of human need, they apply a verbal and logical consistency. The "short ballot" in itself is a slight affair, but the insight behind it seems to me capable of revolutionary development. It is one symptom of the effort to found institutions on human nature. There are many others. We might point to the first experiments aimed at remedying the helter-skelter of careers by vocational guidance. Carried through successfully, this invention of Prof. Parsons' is one whose significance in happiness can hardly be exaggerated. When you think of the misfits among your acquaintances—the lawyers who should be mechanics, the doctors who should be business men, the teachers who should have been clerks, and the executives who should be doing research in a laboratory—when you think of the talent that would be released by proper use, the imagination takes wing at the possibilities. What could we not make of the world if we employed its genius!

Whoever is working to express special energies is part of a constructive revolution. Whoever is removing the stunting environments of our occupations is doing the fundamentals of reform. The studies of Miss Goldmark of industrial fatigue, recuperative power and maximum productivity are contributions toward that distant and desirable period when labor shall be a free and joyous activity. Every suggestion which turns work from a drudgery to a craft is worth our deepest interest. For until then the labor problem will never be solved. The socialist demand for a better distribution of wealth is of great consequence, but without a change in the very nature of labor society will not have achieved the happiness it expects. That is why imaginative socialists have shown so great an interest in "syndicalism." There at least in some of its forms, we can catch sight of a desire to make all labor a self-governing craft.

The handling of crime has been touched by the modern impetus. The ancient, abstract and wholesale "justice" is breaking up into detailed and carefully adapted treatment of individual offenders. What this means for the child has become common knowledge in late years. Criminology (to use an awkward word) is finding a human center. So is education. Everyone knows how child study is revolutionizing the school room and the curriculum. Why, it seems that Mme. Montessori has had the audacity to sacrifice the sacred bench to the interests of the pupil! The traditional school seems to be vanishing—that place in which an ill-assorted band of youngsters was for a certain number of hours each day placed in the vicinity of a text-book and a maiden lady.

The Walter Lippmann Reader

I mention these experiments at random. It is not the specific reforms that I wish to emphasize but the great possibilities they foreshadow. Whether or not we adopt certain special bills, high tariff or low tariff, one banking system or another, this trust control or that, is a slight gain compared to a change of attitude toward all political problems. The reformer bound up in his special propaganda will, of course, object that "to get something done is worth more than any amount of talk about new ways of looking at political problems." What matters the method, he will cry, provided the reform be good? Well, the method matters more than any particular reform. A man who couldn't think straight might get the right answer to one problem, but how much faith would you have in his capacity to solve the next one? If you wanted to educate a child, would you teach him to read one play of Shakespeare, or would you teach him to *read*? If the world were going to remain frigidly set after next year, we might well thank our stars if we blundered into a few decent solutions right away. But as there is no prospect of a time when our life will be immutably fixed, as we shall, therefore, have to go on inventing, it is fair to say that what the world is aching for is not a special reform embodied in a particular statute, but a way of going at all problems. The lasting value of Darwin, for example, is not in any concrete conclusion he reached. His importance to the world lies in the new twist he gave to science. He lent it fruitful direction, a different impetus, and the results are beyond his imagining.

In that spiritual autobiography of a searching mind, "The New Machiavelli," Wells describes his progress from a reformer of concrete abuses to a revolutionist in method. "You see," he says, "I began in my teens by wanting to plan and build cities and harbors for mankind; I ended in the middle thirties by desiring only to serve and increase a general process of thought, a process fearless, critical, real-spirited, that would in its own time give cities, harbors, air, happiness, everything at a scale and quality and in a light altogether beyond the match-striking imaginations of a contemporary mind...."

This same veering of interest may be seen in the career of another Englishman. I refer to Mr. Graham Wallas. Back in the '80's he was working with the Webbs, Bernard Shaw, Sidney Olivier, Annie Besant and others in socialist propaganda. Readers of the Fabian Essays know Mr. Wallas and appreciate the work of his group. Perhaps more than anyone else, the Fabians are responsible for turning English socialist thought from the verbalism of the Marxian disciples to the actualities of English political life. Their appetite for the concrete was enormous;

40

their knowledge of facts overpowering, as the tomes produced by Mr. and Mrs. Webb can testify. The socialism of the Fabians soon became a definite legislative program which the various political parties were to be bulldozed, cajoled and tricked into enacting. It was effective work, and few can question the value of it. Yet many admirers have been left with a sense of inadequacy.

Unlike the orthodox socialists, the Fabians took an active part in immediate politics. "We permeated the party organizations," writes Shaw, "and pulled all the wires we could lay our hands on with our utmost adroitness and energy.... The generalship of this movement was undertaken chiefly by Sidney Webb, who played such bewildering conjuring tricks with the Liberal thimbles and the Fabian peas that to this day both the Liberals and the sectarian Socialists stand aghast at him." Few Americans know how great has been this influence on English political history for the last twenty years. The well-known Minority Report of the Poor Law Commission bears the Webb signature most conspicuously. Fabianism began to achieve a reputation for getting things done—for taking part in "practical affairs." Bernard Shaw has found time to do no end of campaigning and even the parochial politics of a vestryman has not seemed too insignificant for his Fabian enthusiasm. Graham Wallas was a candidate in five municipal elections, and has held an important office as member of the London County Council.

But the original Fabian enthusiasm has slackened. One might ascribe it to a growing sense that concrete programs by themselves will not insure any profound regeneration of society. H. G. Wells has been savage and often unfair about the Fabian Society, but in "The New Machiavelli" he touched, I believe, the real disillusionment. Remington's history is in a way symbolic. Here was a successful political reformer, coming more and more to a disturbing recognition of his helplessness, perceiving the aimlessness and the unreality of political life, and announcing his contempt for the "crudification" of all issues. What Remington missed was what so many reformers are beginning to miss—an underlying philosophical habit.

Mr. Wallas seems to have had much the same experience. In the midst of a bustle of activity, politics appeared to have no center to which its thinking and doing could be referred. The truth was driven home upon him that political science is a science of human relationship with the human beings left out. So he writes that "the thinkers of the past, from Plato to Bentham and Mill, had each his own view of human nature, and they made these views the basis of their speculations on government." But to-day "nearly all students of politics analyze institutions and avoid the analysis of man." Whoever has read the typical book on politics by a professor or a reformer will agree, I think, when he adds: "One feels that many of the more systematic books on politics by American University professors are useless, just because the writers dealt with abstract men, formed on assumptions of which they were unaware and which they have never tested either by experience or by study."

An extreme example could be made of Nicholas Murray Butler, President of Columbia University. In the space of six months he wrote an impassioned defense of "constitutional government," beginning with the question, "Why is it that in the United States the words politics and politician have associations that are chiefly of evil omen," and then, to make irony complete, proceeded at the New York State Republican Convention to do the jobbery of Boss Barnes. What is there left but to gasp and wonder whether the words of the intellect have anything to do with the facts of life? What insight into reality can a man possess who is capable of discussing politics and ignoring politicians? What kind of naïveté was it that led this educator into asking such a question?

President Butler is, I grant, a caricature of the typical professor. Yet what shall we say of the annual harvest of treatises on "labor problems" which make no analysis of the mental condition of laboring men; of the treatises on marriage and prostitution which gloss over the sexual life of the individual? "In the other sciences which deal with human affairs," writes Mr. Wallas, referring to pedagogy and criminology, "this division between the study of the thing done and the study of the being who does it is not found."

I have in my hands a text-book of six hundred pages which is used in the largest universities as a groundwork of political economy. This remarkable sentence strikes the eye: "The motives to business activity are too familiar to require analysis." But some sense that perhaps the "economic man" is not a self-evident creature seems to have touched our author. So we are treated to these sapient remarks: "To avoid this criticism we will begin with a characterization of the typical business man to be found to-day in the United States and other countries in the same stage of industrial development. *He has four traits which show themselves more or less clearly in all of his acts.*" They are first "self-interest," but "this does not mean that he is steeped in selfishness ..."; secondly, "the larger self," the family, union, club, and "in times of emergency his country"; thirdly, "love of independence," for "his ambition is to stand on his own feet"; fourthly, "business ethics" which "are not usually as high as the standards professed in churches, but they are much higher than current criticisms of business would lead one to think." Three-quarters of a page is sufficient for this penetrating analysis of motive and is followed by the remark that "these four characteristics of the economic man are readily explained by reference to the evolutionary process which has brought industrial society to its present stage of development."

If those were the generalizations of a tired business man after a heavy dinner and a big cigar, they would still seem rather muddled and useless. But as the basis of an economic treatise in which "laws" are announced, "principles" laid down, reforms criticized as "impracticable," all for the benefit of thousands of college students, it is hardly possible to exaggerate the folly of such an exhibition. I have taken a book written by one eminent professor and evidently approved by others, for they use it as a text-book. It is no queer freak. I myself was supposed to read that book pretty nearly every week for a year. With hundreds of others I was supposed to found my economic understanding upon it. We were actually punished for not reading that book. It was given to us as wisdom, as modern political economy.

But what goes by the name to-day is a potpourri in which one can distinguish descriptions of legal forms, charters and institutions; comparative studies of governmental and social machinery; the history of institutions, a few "principles" like the law of rent, some moral admonitions, a good deal of class feeling, not a little timidity—but almost no attempt to cut beneath these manifestations of social life to the creative impulses which produce them. The Economic Man—that lazy abstraction—is still paraded in the lecture room; the study of human nature has not advanced beyond the gossip of old wives.

Graham Wallas touched the cause of the trouble when he pointed out that political science to-day discusses institutions and ignores the nature of the men who make and live under them. I have heard professors reply that it wasn't their business to discuss human nature but to record and interpret economic and political facts. Yet if you probe those "interpretations" there is no escaping the conclusion that they rest upon some notion of what man is like. "The student of politics," writes Mr. Wallas, "must, consciously or unconsciously, form a conception of human nature, and the less conscious he is of his conception the more likely he is to be dominated by it." For politics is an interest of men—a tool which they fabricate and use—and no comment has much value if it tries to get along without mankind. You might as well try to describe food by ignoring the digestion.

Mr. Wallas has called a halt. I think we may say that his is the distinction of having turned the study of politics back to the humane tradition of Plato and Machiavelli—of having made man the center of political investigation. The very title of his book—"Human Nature in Politics"—is significant. Now in making that statement, I am aware that it is a sweeping one, and I do not mean to imply that Mr. Wallas is the only modern man who has tried to think about politics psychologically. Here in America alone we have two splendid critics, a man and a woman, whose thought flows from an interpretation of human character. Thorstein Veblen's brilliant descriptions penetrate deeply into our mental life, and Jane Addams has given new hope to many of us by her capacity for making ideals the goal of natural desire.

Nor is it just to pass by such a suggestive thinker as Gabriel Tarde, even though we may feel that his psychology is too simple and his conclusions somewhat overdriven by a favorite theory. The work of Gustav Le Bon on "crowds" has, of course, passed into current thought, but I doubt whether anyone could say that he had even prepared a basis for a new political psychology. His own aversion to reform, his fondness for vast epochs and his contempt for current effort have left most of his "psychological laws" in the region of interesting literary comment. There are, too, any number of "social psychologies," such as those of Ross and McDougall. But the trouble with them is that the "psychology" is weak and uninformed, distorted by moral enthusiasms, and put out without any particular reference to the task of statesmanship. When you come to special problems, the literature of the subject picks up. Crime is receiving valuable attention, education is profoundly affected, alcoholism and sex have been handled for a good while on a psychological basis.

But it remained for Mr. Wallas to state the philosophy of the matter—to say why the study of human nature must serve politics, and to point out how. He has not produced a political psychology, but he has written the manifesto for it. As a result, fragmentary investigations can be brought together and applied to the work of statecraft. Merely by making these researches self-conscious, he has made clearer their goal, given them direction, and kindled them to practical action. How necessary this work is can be seen in the writing of Miss Addams. Owing to keen insight and fine sympathy her thinking has generally been on a human basis. Yet

The Walter Lippmann Reader

Miss Addams is a reformer, and sympathy without an explicit philosophy may lead to a distorted enthusiasm. Her book on prostitution seems rather the product of her moral fervor than her human insight. Compare it with "The Spirit of Youth" or "Newer Ideals of Peace" or "Democracy and Social Ethics" and I think you will notice a very considerable willingness to gloss over human need in the interests of an unanalyzed reform. To put it bluntly, Miss Addams let her impatience get the better of her wisdom. She had written brilliantly about sex and its "sublimation," she had suggested notable "moral equivalents" for vice, but when she touched the white slave traffic its horrors were so great that she also put her faith in the policeman and the district attorney. "A New Conscience and an Ancient Evil" is an hysterical book, just because the real philosophical basis of Miss Addams' thinking was not deliberate enough to withstand the shock of a poignant horror.

It is this weakness that Mr. Wallas comes to remedy. He has described what political science must be like, and anyone who has absorbed his insight has an intellectual groundwork for political observation. No one, least of all Mr. Wallas, would claim anything like finality for the essay. These labors are not done in a day. But he has deliberately brought the study of politics to the only focus which has any rational interest for mankind. He has made a plea, and sketched a plan which hundreds of investigators the world over must help to realize. If political science could travel in the direction suggested, its criticism would be relevant, its proposals practical. There would, for the first time, be a concerted effort to build a civilization around mankind, to use its talent and to satisfy its needs. There would be no more empty taboos, no erecting of institutions upon abstract and mechanical analogies. Politics would be like education—an effort to develop, train and nurture men's impulses. As Montessori is building the school around the child, so politics would build all of social life around the human being.

That practical issues hang upon these investigations can be shown by an example from Mr. Wallas's book. Take the quarrel over socialism. You hear it said that without the private ownership of capital people will lose ambition and sink into sloth. Many men, just as well aware of present-day evils as the socialists, are unwilling to accept the collectivist remedy. G. K. Chesterton and Hilaire Belloc speak of the "magic of property" as the real obstacle to socialism. Now obviously this is a question of first-rate importance. If socialism will destroy initiative then only a doctrinaire would desire it. But how is the question to be solved? You cannot reason it out. Economics, as we know it to-day, is quite incapable of answering such a

45

The Walter Lippmann Reader

problem, for it is a matter that depends upon psychological investigation. When a professor says that socialism is impracticable he begs the question, for that amounts to assuming that the point at issue is already settled. If he tells you that socialism is against human nature, we have a perfect right to ask where he proved the possibilities of human nature.

But note how Mr. Wallas approaches the debate: "Children quarrel furiously at a very early age over apparently worthless things, and collect and hide them long before they can have any clear notion of the advantages to be derived from individual possession. Those children who in certain charity schools are brought up entirely without personal property, even in their clothes or pocket handkerchiefs, show every sign of the bad effect on health and character which results from complete inability to satisfy a strong inherited instinct.... Some economist ought therefore to give us a treatise in which this property instinct is carefully and quantitatively examined.... How far can it be eliminated or modified by education? Is it satisfied by a leasehold or a life-interest, or by such an arrangement of corporate property as is offered by a collegiate foundation, or by the provision of a public park? Does it require for its satisfaction material and visible things such as land or houses, or is the holding, say, of colonial railway shares sufficient? Is the absence of unlimited proprietary rights felt more strongly in the case of personal chattels (such as furniture and ornaments) than in the case of land or machinery? Does the degree and direction of the instinct markedly differ among different individuals or races, or between the two sexes?"

This puts the argument upon a plane where discussion is relevant. This is no trumped-up issue: it is asked by a politician and a socialist seeking for a real solution. We need to know whether the "magic of property" extends from a man's garden to Standard Oil stocks as anti-socialists say, and, conversely, we need to know what is happening to that mass of proletarians who own no property and cannot satisfy their instincts even with personal chattels.

For if ownership is a human need, we certainly cannot taboo it as the extreme communists so dogmatically urge. "Pending ... an inquiry," writes Mr. Wallas, "my own provisional opinion is that, like a good many instincts of very early evolutionary origin, it can be satisfied by an avowed pretense; just as a kitten which is fed regularly on milk can be kept in good health if it is allowed to indulge its hunting instinct by playing with a bobbin, and a peaceful civil servant satisfies his instinct of combat and adventure at golf."

The Walter Lippmann Reader

Mr. Wallas takes exactly the same position as William James did when he planned a "moral equivalent" for war. Both men illustrate the changing focus of political thought. Both try to found statesmanship on human need. Both see that there are good and bad satisfactions of the same impulse. The routineer with his taboo does not see this, so he attempts the impossible task of obliterating the impulse. He differs fundamentally from the creative politician who devotes himself to inventing fine expressions for human needs, who recognizes that the work of statesmanship is in large measure the finding of good substitutes for the bad things we want.

This is the heart of a political revolution. When we recognize that the focus of politics is shifting from a mechanical to a human center we shall have reached what is, I believe, the most essential idea in modern politics. More than any other generalization it illuminates the currents of our national life and explains the altering tasks of statesmanship.

The old effort was to harness mankind to abstract principles—liberty, justice or equality—and to deduce institutions from these high-sounding words. It did not succeed because human nature was contrary and restive. The new effort proposes to fit creeds and institutions to the wants of men, to satisfy their impulses as fully and beneficially as possible.

And yet we do not begin to know our desires or the art of their satisfaction. Mr. Wallas's book and the special literature of the subject leave no doubt that a precise political psychology is far off indeed. The human nature we must put at the center of our statesmanship is only partially understood. True, Mr. Wallas works with a psychology that is fairly well superseded. But not even the advance-guard to-day, what we may call the Freudian school, would claim that it had brought knowledge to a point where politics could use it in any very deep or comprehensive way. The subject is crude and fragmentary, though we are entitled to call it promising.

Yet the fact had better be faced: psychology has not gone far enough, its results are still too vague for our purposes. We know very little, and what we know has hardly been applied to political problems. That the last few years have witnessed a revolution in the study of mental life is plain: the effects are felt not only in psychotherapy, but in education, morals, religion, and no end of cultural interests. The impetus of Freud is perhaps the greatest advance ever made towards the understanding and control of human character. But for the complexities of politics it is not yet ready. It will take time and endless labor for a detailed study of social problems in the light of this growing knowledge.

47

What then shall we do now? Must we continue to muddle along in the old ruts, gazing rapturously at an impotent ideal, until the works of the scientists are matured?

The Golden Rule and After

It would indeed be an intolerably pedantic performance for a nation to sit still and wait for its scientists to report on their labors. The notion is typical of the pitfalls in the path of any theorist who does not correct his logic by a constant reference to the movement of life. It is true that statecraft must make human nature its basis. It is true that its chief task is the invention of forms and institutions which satisfy the inner needs of mankind. And it is true that our knowledge of those needs and the technique of their satisfaction is hazy, unorganized and blundering.

But to suppose that the remedy lies in waiting for monographs from the research of the laboratory is to have lost a sense of the rhythm of actual affairs. That is not the way things come about: we grow into a new point of view: only afterwards, in looking back, do we see the landmarks of our progress. Thus it is customary to say that Adam Smith dates the change from the old mercantilist economy to the capitalistic economics of the nineteenth century. But that is a manner of speech. The old mercantilist policy was giving way to early industrialism: a thousand unconscious economic and social forces were compelling the change. Adam Smith expressed the process, named it, idealized it and made it self-conscious. Then because men were clearer about what they were doing, they could in a measure direct their destiny.

That is but another way of saying that great revolutionary changes do not spring full-armed from anybody's brow. A genius usually becomes the luminous center of a nation's crisis,—men see better by the light of him. His bias deflects their actions. Unquestionably the doctrine-driven men who made the economics of the last century had much to do with the halo which encircled the smutted head of industrialism. They put the stamp of their genius on certain inhuman practices, and of course it has been the part of the academic mind to imitate them ever since. The orthodox economists are in the unenviable position of having taken their morals from the exploiter and of having translated them into the grandiloquent language of high public policy. They gave capitalism the sanction of the intellect. When later, Carlyle and Ruskin battered the economists into silence with invective and irony they were voicing the dumb protest of the humane people of England. They helped to organize a formless resentment by endowing it with intelligence and will.

So it is to-day. If this nation did not show an unmistakable tendency to put men at the center of politics instead of machinery and things; if there were not evidence to prove that we are turning from the sterile taboo to the creation of finer environments; if the impetus for shaping our destiny were not present in our politics and our life, then essays like these would be so much baying at the moon, fantastic and unworthy pleas for some irrelevant paradise. But the gropings are there,—vastly confused in the tangled strains of the nation's interests. Clogged by the confusion, half-choked by stupid blockades, largely unaware of their own purposes, it is for criticism, organized research, and artistic expression to free and to use these creative energies. They are to be found in the aspirations of labor, among the awakened women, in the development of business, the diffusion of art and science, in the racial mixtures, and many lesser interests which cluster about these greater movements.

The desire for a human politics is all about us. It rises to the surface in slogans like "human rights above property rights," "the man above the dollar." Some measure of its strength is given by the widespread imitation these expressions have compelled: politicians who haven't the slightest intention of putting men above the dollar, who if they had wouldn't know how, take off their hats to the sentiment because it seems a key to popular enthusiasm. It must be bewildering to men brought up, let us say, in the Hanna school of politics. For here is this nation which sixteen years ago vibrated ecstatically to that magic word "Prosperity"; to-day statistical rhetoric about size induces little but excessive boredom. If you wish to drive an audience out of the hall tell it how rich America is; if you wish to stamp yourself an echo of the past talk to us young men about the Republican Party's understanding with God in respect to bumper crops. But talk to us about "human rights," and though you talk rubbish, we'll listen. For our desire is bent that way, and anything which has the flavor of this new interest will rivet our attention. We are still uncritical. It is only a few years since we began to center our politics upon human beings. We have no training in that kind of thought. Our schools and colleges have helped us hardly at all. We still talk about "humanity" as if it were some strange and mystical creature which could not possibly be composed of the grocer, the street-car conductor and our aunts.

That the opinion-making people of America are more interested in human welfare than in empire or abstract prosperity is an item that no statesman can disregard in his thinking. To-day it is no longer necessary to run against the grain of the deepest movements of our time. There is an ascendant feeling among the people that all achievement should be measured in human happiness. This feeling has not always existed. Historians tell us that the very idea of progress in well-being is not much older than, say, Shakespeare's plays. As a general belief it is still more recent. The nineteenth century may perhaps be said to mark its popularization. But as a fact of immediate politics, as a touchstone applied quickly to all the acts of statecraft in America it belongs to the Twentieth Century. There were any number of people who long before 1900 saw that dollars and men could clash. But their insight had not won any general acceptance. It is only within the last few years that the human test has ceased to be the property of a small group and become the convention of a large majority. A study of magazines and newspapers would confirm this rather broad generalization. It would show, I believe, how the whole quality of our most impromptu thinking is being influenced by human values.

The statesman must look to this largely unorganized drift of desire. He will find it clustering about certain big revolts—the unrest of women, for example, or the increasing demands of industrial workers. Rightly understood, these social currents would, I believe, lead to the central issues of life, the vital points upon which happiness depends. They come out of necessities. They express desire. They are power.

Thus feminism, arising out of a crisis in sexual conditions, has liberated energies that are themselves the motors of any reform. In England and America voting has become the symbol of an aspiration as yet half-conscious and undefined. What women want is surely something a great deal deeper than the privilege of taking part in elections. They are looking for a readjustment of their relations to the home, to work, to children, to men, to the interests of civilized life. The vote has become a convenient peg upon which to hang aspirations that are not at all sure of their own meaning. In no insignificant number of cases the vote is a cover by which revolutionary demands can be given a conventional front. The ballot is at the utmost a beginning, as far-sighted conservatives have guessed. Certainly the elimination of "male" from the suffrage qualifications will not end the feminist agitation. From the angle of statecraft the future of the movement may be said to depend upon the wise use of this raw and scattered power. I do not pretend to know in detail how this can be done. But I am certain that the task of leadership is to organize aspiration in the service of the real interests of life. To-day women want—what? They are ready to want something: that describes fairly the condition of most suffragettes. Those who like Ellen Key and Olive Shreiner and Mrs. Gilman give them real problems to think about are drafting that energy into use. By real problems I mean problems of love, work, home, children. They are the real interests of feminism because they have produced it.

The yearnings of to-day are the symptoms of needs, they point the course of invention, they are the energies which animate a social program. The most ideally conceived plan of the human mind has only a slight interest if it does not harness these instinctive forces. That is the great lesson which the utopias teach by their failure—that schemes, however nicely arranged, cannot be imposed upon human beings who are interested in other things. What ailed Don Quixote was that he and his contemporaries wanted different things; the only ideals that count are those which express the possible development of an existing force. Reformers must never forget that three legs are a Quixotic ideal; two good legs a genuine one.

In actual life, yes, in the moil and toil of propaganda, "movements," "causes" and agitations the statesman-inventor and the political psychologist find the raw material for their work. It is not the business of the politician to preserve an Olympian indifference to what stupid people call "popular whim." Being lofty about the "passing fad" and the ephemeral outcry is all very well in the biographies of dead men, but rank nonsense in the rulers of real ones. Oscar Wilde once remarked that only superficial people disliked the superficial. Nothing, for example, could on the surface be more trivial than an interest in baseball scores. Yet during the campaign of 1912 the excitement was so great that Woodrow Wilson said on the stump he felt like apologizing to the American people for daring to be a presidential candidate while the Giants and the Red Sox were playing for the championship. Baseball (not so much for those who play it), is a colossal phenomenon in American life. Watch the crowds in front of a bulletin board, finding a vicarious excitement and an abstract relief from the monotony of their own lives. What a second-hand civilization it is that grows passionate over a scoreboard with little electric lights! What a civilization it is that has learned to enjoy its sport without even seeing it! If ever there was a symptom that this nation needed leisure and direct participation in games, it is that poor scrawny substitute for joy—the baseball extra.

It is as symptomatic as the labor union. It expresses need. And statesmanship would find an answer. It would not let that passion and loyalty be frittered away to drift like scum through the nation. It would see in it the opportunity of art, play, and religion. So with what looks very different—the "syndicalist movement." Perhaps it seems preposterous to discuss baseball and syndicalism in the same paragraph. But that is only because we have not accustomed ourselves to thinking of social events as answers to human needs. The statesman would ask, Why are there syndicalists? What are they driving at? What gift to civilization is in the impetus behind them? They are human beings, and they want human things. There is no reason to become terror-stricken about them. They seem to want things badly. Then ostriches disguised as judges cannot deal with them. Anarchism—men die for that, they undergo intolerable insults. They are tarred and feathered and spat upon. Is it possible that Republicans, Democrats and Socialists clip the wings more than free spirits can allow? Is civilization perhaps too tightly organized? Have the irreconcilables a soul audacious and less blunted than our domesticated ones? To put it mildly, is it ever safe to ignore them entirely in our thinking?

We shall come, I think, to a different appraisal of agitations. Our present method is to discuss whether the proposals are right and feasible. We do this hastily and with prejudice. Generally we decide that any agitation foreign to our settled habits is wrong. And we bolster up our satisfaction by pointing to some mistake of logic or some puerility of statement. That done, we feel the agitation is deplorable and can be ignored unless it becomes so obstreperous that we have to put it in jail. But a genuine statecraft would go deeper. It would know that even God has been defended with nonsense. So it could be sympathetic to agitations. I use the word sympathetic literally. For it would try to understand the inner feeling which had generated what looks like a silly demand. To-day it is as if a hungry man asked for an indigestible food, and we let him go hungry because he was unwise. He isn't any the less hungry because he asks for the wrong food. So with agitations. Their specific plans may be silly, but their demands are real. The hungers and lusts of mankind have produced some stupendous follies, but the desires themselves are no less real and insistent.

The important thing about a social movement is not its stated platform but the source from which it flows. The task of politics is to understand those deeper demands and to find civilized satisfactions for them. The meaning of this is that the statesman must be more than the leader of a party. Thus the socialist statesman is not complete if he is a good socialist. Only the delusion that his truth is the whole truth, his party the human race, and his program a panacea, will produce that singleness of vision.

The moment a man takes office he has no right to be the representative of one group alone. He has assumed the burden of harmonizing particular agitations with the general welfare. That is why great agitators should not accept office. Men like

Debs understand that. Their business is to make social demands so concrete and pressing that statesmen are forced to deal with them. Agitators who accept government positions are a disappointment to their followers. They can no longer be severely partisan. They have to look at affairs nationally. Now the agitator and the statesman are both needed. But they have different functions, and it is unjust to damn one because he hasn't the virtues of the other.

The statesman to-day needs a large equipment. The man who comes forward to shape a country's policy has truly no end of things to consider. He must be aware of the condition of the people: no statesman must fall into the sincere but thoroughly upper class blunder that President Taft committed when he advised a three months' vacation. Realizing how men and women feel at all levels and at different places, he must speak their discontent and project their hopes. Through this he will get power. Standing upon the prestige which that gives he must guide and purify the social demands he finds at work. He is the translator of agitations. For this task he must be keenly sensitive to public opinion and capable of understanding the dynamics of it. Then, in order to fuse it into a civilized achievement, he will require much expert knowledge. Yet he need not be a specialist himself, if only he is expert in choosing experts. It is better indeed that the statesman should have a lay, and not a professional view. For the bogs of technical stupidity and empty formalism are always near and always dangerous. The real political genius stands between the actual life of men, their wishes and their needs, and all the windings of official caste and professional snobbery. It is his supreme business to see that the servants of life stay in their place—that government, industry, "causes," science, all the creatures of man do not succeed in their perpetual effort to become the masters.

I have Roosevelt in mind. He haunts political thinking. And indeed, why shouldn't he? What reality could there be in comments upon American politics which ignored the colossal phenomenon of Roosevelt? If he is wholly evil, as many say he is, then the American democracy is preponderantly evil. For in the first years of the Twentieth Century, Roosevelt spoke for this nation, as few presidents have spoken in our history. And that he has spoken well, who in the perspective of time will deny? Sensitive to the original forces of public opinion, no man has had the same power of rounding up the laggards. Government under him was a throbbing human purpose. He succeeded, where Taft failed, in preventing that drought of invention which officialism brings. Many people say he has tried to be all things to all men—that his speeches are an attempt to corral all sorts of votes. That is a left-handed way of stating a truth. A more generous interpretation would be to say that he had tried to be inclusive, to attach a hundred sectional agitations to a national program. Crude: of course he was crude; he had a hemisphere for his canvas. Inconsistent: yes, he tried to be the leader of factions at war with one another. A late convert: he is a statesman and not an agitator—his business was to meet demands when they had grown to national proportions. No end of possibilities have slipped through the large meshes of his net. He has said some silly things. He has not been subtle, and he has been far from perfect. But his success should be judged by the size of his task, by the fierceness of the opposition, by the intellectual qualities of the nation he represented. When we remember that he was trained in the Republican politics of Hanna and Platt, that he was the first President who shared a new social vision, then I believe we need offer no apologies for making Mr. Roosevelt stand as the working model for a possible American statesman at the beginning of the Twentieth Century.

Critics have often suggested that Roosevelt stole Bryan's clothes. That is perhaps true, and it suggests a comparison which illuminates both men. It would not be unfair to say that it is always the function of the Roosevelts to take from the Bryans. But it is a little silly for an agitator to cry thief when the success of his agitation has led to the adoption of his ideas. It is like the chagrin of the socialists because the National Progressive Party had "stolen twenty-three planks," and it makes a person wonder whether some agitators haven't an overdeveloped sense of private property.

I do not see the statesman in Bryan. He has been something of a voice crying in the wilderness, but a voice that did not understand its own message. Many people talk of him as a prophet. There is a great deal of literal truth in that remark, for it has been the peculiar work of Bryan to express in politics some of that emotion which has made America the home of new religions. What we know as the scientific habit of mind is entirely lacking in his intellectual equipment. There is a vein of mysticism in American life, and Mr. Bryan is its uncritical prophet. His insights are those of the gifted evangelist, often profound and always narrow. It is absurd to debate his sincerity. Mr. Bryan talks with the intoxication of the man who has had a revelation: to skeptics that always seems theatrical. But far from being the scheming hypocrite his enemies say he is, Mr. Bryan is too simple for the task of statesmanship. No bracing critical atmosphere plays about his mind: there are no cleansing doubts and fruitful alternatives. The work of Bryan has been to express

The Walter Lippmann Reader

a certain feeling of unrest—to embody it in the traditional language of prophecy. But it is a shrewd turn of the American people that has kept him out of office. I say this not in disrespect of his qualities, but in definition of them. Bryan does not happen to have the naturalistic outlook, the complete humanity, or the deliberative habit which modern statecraft requires. He is the voice of a confused emotion.

Woodrow Wilson has a talent which is Bryan's chief defect—the scientific habit of holding facts in solution. His mind is lucid and flexible, and he has the faculty of taking advice quickly, of stating something he has borrowed with more ease and subtlety than the specialist from whom he got it. Woodrow Wilson's is an elegant and highly refined intellect, nicely balanced and capable of fine adjustment. An urbane civilization produced it, leisure has given it spaciousness, ease has made it generous. A mind without tension, its roots are not in the somewhat barbarous under-currents of the nation. Woodrow Wilson understands easily, but he does not incarnate: he has never been a part of the protest he speaks. You think of him as a good counsellor, as an excellent presiding officer. Whether his imagination is fibrous enough to catch the inwardness of the mutterings of our age is something experience alone can show. Wilson has class feeling in the least offensive sense of that term: he likes a world of gentlemen. Occasionally he has exhibited a rather amateurish effort to be grimy and shirt-sleeved. But without much success: his contact with American life is not direct, and so he is capable of purely theoretical affirmations. Like all essentially contemplative men, the world has to be reflected in the medium of his intellect before he can grapple with it.

Yet Wilson belongs among the statesmen, and it is fine that he should be in public life. The weakness I have suggested is one that all statesmen share in some degree: an inability to interpret adequately the world they govern. This is a difficulty which is common to conservative and radical, and if I have used three living men to illustrate the problem it is only because they seem to illuminate it. They have faced the task and we can take their measurement. It is no part of my purpose to make any judgment as to the value of particular policies they have advocated. I am attempting to suggest some of the essentials of a statesman's equipment for the work of a humanly centered politics. Roosevelt has seemed to me the most effective, the most nearly complete; Bryan I have ventured to class with the men who though important to politics should never hold high executive office; Wilson, less complete than Roosevelt, is worthy of our deepest interest because his judgment is subtle where Roosevelt's is crude. He is a foretaste of a more advanced statesmanship.

The Walter Lippmann Reader

Because he is self-conscious, Wilson has been able to see the problem that any finely adapted statecraft must meet. It is a problem that would hardly occur to an old-fashioned politician: "Though he (the statesman) cannot himself keep the life of the nation as a whole in his mind, he can at least make sure that he is taking counsel with those who know...." It is not important that Wilson in stating the difficulty should put it as if he had in a measure solved it. He hasn't, because taking counsel is a means to understanding the nation as a whole, and that understanding remains almost as arduous and requires just as fibrous an imagination, if it is gleaned from advisers.

To think of the whole nation: surely the task of statesmanship is more difficult to-day than ever before in history. In the face of a clotted intricacy in the subject-matter of politics, improvements in knowledge seem meager indeed. The distance between what we know and what we need to know appears to be greater than ever. Plato and Aristotle thought in terms of ten thousand homogeneous villagers; we have to think in terms of a hundred million people of all races and all traditions, crossbred and inbred, subject to climates they have never lived in before, plumped down on a continent in the midst of a strange civilization. We have to deal with all grades of life from the frontier to the metropolis, with men who differ in sense of fact, in ideal, in the very groundwork of morals. And we have to take into account not the simple opposition of two classes, but the hostility of many,—the farmers and the factory workers and all the castes within their ranks, the small merchants, and the feudal organization of business. Ours is a problem in which deception has become organized and strong; where truth is poisoned at its source; one in which the skill of the shrewdest brains is devoted to misleading a bewildered people. Nor can we keep to the problem within our borders. Whether we wish it or not we are involved in the world's problems, and all the winds of heaven blow through our land.

It is a great question whether our intellects can grasp the subject. Are we perhaps like a child whose hand is too small to span an octave on the piano? Not only are the facts inhumanly complicated, but the natural ideals of people are so varied and contradictory that action halts in despair. We are putting a tremendous strain upon the mind, and the results are all about us: everyone has known the neutral thinkers who stand forever undecided before the complications of life, who have, as it were, caught a glimpse of the possibilities of knowledge. The sight has paralyzed them. Unless they can act with certainty, they dare not act at all.

That is merely one of the temptations of theory. In the real world, action and thought are so closely related that one cannot wait upon the other. We cannot wait in politics for any completed theoretical discussion of its method: it is a monstrous demand. There is no pausing until political psychology is more certain. We have to act on what we believe, on half-knowledge, illusion and error. Experience itself will reveal our mistakes; research and criticism may convert them into wisdom. But act we must, and act as if we knew the nature of man and proposed to satisfy his needs.

In other words, we must put man at the center of politics, even though we are densely ignorant both of man and of politics. This has always been the method of great political thinkers from Plato to Bentham. But one difference we in this age must note: they made their political man a dogma—we must leave him an hypothesis. That is to say that our task is to temper speculation with scientific humility.

A paradox there is here, but a paradox of language, and not of fact. Men made bridges before there was a science of bridge-building; they cured disease before they knew medicine. Art came before æsthetics, and righteousness before ethics. Conduct and theory react upon each other. Hypothesis is confirmed and modified by action, and action is guided by hypothesis. If it is a paradox to ask for a human politics before we understand humanity or politics, it is what Mr. Chesterton describes as one of those paradoxes that sit beside the wells of truth.

We make our picture of man, knowing that, though it is crude and unjust, we have to work with it. If we are wise we shall become experimental towards life: then every mistake will contribute towards knowledge. Let the exploration of human need and desire become a deliberate purpose of statecraft, and there is no present measure of its possibilities.

In this work there are many guides. A vague common tradition is in the air about us—it expresses itself in journalism, in cheap novels, in the uncritical theater. Every merchant has his stock of assumptions about the mental habits of his customers and competitors; the prostitute hers; the newspaperman his; P. T. Barnum had a few; the vaudeville stage has a number. We test these notions by their results, and even "practical people" find that there is more variety in human nature than they had supposed.

The Walter Lippmann Reader

We forge gradually our greatest instrument for understanding the world—introspection. We discover that humanity may resemble us very considerably—that the best way of knowing the inwardness of our neighbors is to know ourselves. For after all, the only experience we really understand is our own. And that, in the least of us, is so rich that no one has yet exhausted its possibilities. It has been said that every genuine character an artist produces is one of the characters he might have been. By re-creating our own suppressed possibilities we multiply the number of lives that we can really know. That as I understand it is the psychology of the Golden Rule. For note that Jesus did not set up some external fetich: he did not say, make your neighbor righteous, or chaste, or respectable. He said do as you would be done by. Assume that you and he are alike, and you can found morals on humanity.

But experience has enlarged our knowledge of differences. We realize now that our neighbor is not always like ourselves. Knowing how unjust other people's inferences are when they concern us, we have begun to guess that ours may be unjust to them. Any uniformity of conduct becomes at once an impossible ideal, and the willingness to live and let live assumes high place among the virtues. A puzzled wisdom remarks that "it takes all sorts of people to make a world," and half-protestingly men accept Bernard Shaw's amendment, "Do not do unto others as you would that they should do unto you. Their tastes may not be the same."

We learn perhaps that there is no contradiction in speaking of "human nature" while admitting that men are unique. For all deepening of our knowledge gives a greater sense of common likeness and individual variation. It is folly to ignore either insight. But it is done constantly, with no end of confusion as a result. Some men have got themselves into a state where the only view that interests them is the common humanity of us all. Their world is not populated by men and women, but by a Unity that is Permanent. You might as well refuse to see any differences between steam, water and ice because they have common elements. And I have seen some of these people trying to skate on steam. Their brothers, blind in the other eye, go about the world so sure that each person is entirely unique, that society becomes like a row of packing cases, each painted on the inside, and each containing one ego and its own.

Art enlarges experience by admitting us to the inner life of others. That is not the only use of art, for its function is surely greater and more ultimate than to furnish us with a better knowledge of human nature. Nor is that its only use even to statecraft. I suggested earlier that art enters politics as a "moral equivalent" for evil, a medium by which barbarous lusts find civilized expression. It is, too, an ideal for labor. But my purpose here is not to attempt any adequate description of the services of art. It is enough to note that literature in particular elaborates our insight into human life, and, therefore, enables us to center our institutions more truly.

Ibsen discovers a soul in Nora: the discovery is absorbed into the common knowledge of the age. Other Noras discover their own souls; the Helmers all about us begin to see the person in the doll. Plays and novels have indeed an overwhelming political importance, as the "moderns" have maintained. But it lies not in the preaching of a doctrine or the insistence on some particular change in conduct. That is a shallow and wasteful use of the resources of art. For art can open up the springs from which conduct flows. Its genuine influence is on what Wells calls the "hinterland," in a quickening of the sense of life.

Art can really penetrate where most of us can only observe. "I look and I think I see," writes Bergson, "I listen and I think I hear, I examine myself and I think I am reading the very depths of my heart.... (But) my senses and my consciousness ... give me no more than a practical simplification of reality ... in short, we do not see the actual things themselves; in most cases we confine ourselves to reading the labels affixed to them." Who has not known this in thinking of politics? We talk of poverty and forget poor people; we make rules for vagrancy—we forget the vagrant. Some of our best-intentioned political schemes, like reform colonies and scientific jails, turn out to be inhuman tyrannies just because our imagination does not penetrate the sociological label. "We move amidst generalities and symbols ... we live in a zone midway between things and ourselves, external to things, external also to ourselves." This is what works of art help to correct: "Behind the commonplace, conventional expression that both reveals and conceals an individual mental state, it is the emotion, the original mood, to which they attain in its undefiled essence."

This directness of vision fertilizes thought. Without a strong artistic tradition, the life and so the politics of a nation sink into a barren routine. A country populated by pure logicians and mathematical scientists would, I believe, produce few inventions. For creation, even of scientific truth, is no automatic product of logical thought or scientific method, and it has been well said that the greatest discoveries in science are brilliant guesses on insufficient evidence. A nation must, so to speak, live close to its own life, be intimate and sympathetic with natural events. That is what gives understanding, and justifies the observation that the intuitions of scientific discovery and the artist's perceptions are closely related. It is perhaps not altogether without significance for us that primitive science and poetry were indistinguishable. Nor is it strange that latter-day research should confirm so many sayings of the poets. In all great ages art and science have enriched each other. It is only eccentric poets and narrow specialists who lock the doors. The human spirit doesn't grow in sections.

I shall not press the point for it would lead us far afield. It is enough that we remember the close alliance of art, science and politics in Athens, in Florence and Venice at their zenith. We in America have divorced them completely: both art and politics exist in a condition of unnatural celibacy. Is this not a contributing factor to the futility and opacity of our political thinking? We have handed over the government of a nation of people to a set of lawyers, to a class of men who deal in the most verbal and unreal of all human attainments.

A lively artistic tradition is essential to the humanizing of politics. It is the soil in which invention flourishes and the organized knowledge of science attains its greatest reality. Let me illustrate from another field of interests. The religious investigations of William James were a study, not of ecclesiastical institutions or the history of creeds. They were concerned with religious experience, of which churches and rituals are nothing but the external satisfaction. As Graham Wallas is endeavoring to make human nature the center of politics, so James made it the center of religions. It was a work of genius, yet no one would claim that it is a mature psychology of the "Varieties of Religious Experience." It is rather a survey and a description, done with the eye of an artist and the method of a scientist. We know from it more of what religious feeling is like, even though we remain ignorant of its sources. And this intimacy humanizes religious controversy and brings ecclesiasticism back to men.

Like most of James's psychology, it opens up investigation instead of concluding it. In the light even of our present knowledge we can see how primitive his treatment was. But James's services cannot be overestimated: if he did not lay even the foundations of a science, he did lay some of the foundations for research. It was an immense illumination and a warming of interest. It threw open the gates to the whole landscape of possibilities. It was a ventilation of thought. Something similar will have to be done for political psychology. We know how far off is the profound and precise knowledge we desire. But we know too that we have a right to hope for an increasing acquaintance with the varieties of political experience. It would, of course, be drawn from biography, from the human aspect of history and daily observation. We should begin to know what it is that we ought to know. Such a work would be stimulating to politician and psychologist. The statesman's imagination would be guided and organized; it would give him a starting-point for his own understanding of human beings in politics. To the scientists it would be a challenge—to bring these facts under the light of their researches, to extend these researches to the borders of those facts.

The statesman has another way of strengthening his grip upon the complexity of life. Statistics help. This method is neither so conclusive as the devotees say, nor so bad as the people who are awed by it would like to believe. Voting, as Gabriel Tarde points out, is our most conspicuous use of statistics. Mystical democrats believe that an election expresses the will of the people, and that that will is wise. Mystical democrats are rare. Looked at closely an election shows the quantitative division of the people on several alternatives. That choice is not necessarily wise, but it is wise to heed that choice. For it is a rough estimate of an important part of the community's sentiment, and no statecraft can succeed that violates it. It is often immensely suggestive of what a large number of people are in the future going to wish. Democracy, because it registers popular feeling, is at least trying to build truly, and is for that reason an enlightened form of government. So we who are democrats need not believe that the people are necessarily right in their choice: some of us are always in the minority, and not a little proud of the distinction. Voting does not extract wisdom from multitudes: its real value is to furnish wisdom about multitudes. Our faith in democracy has this very solid foundation: that no leader's wisdom can be applied unless the democracy comes to approve of it. To govern a democracy you have to educate it: that contact with great masses of men reciprocates by educating the leader. "The consent of the governed" is more than a safeguard against ignorant tyrants: it is an insurance against benevolent despots as well. In a rough way and with many exceptions, democracy compels law to approximate human need. It is a little difficult to see this when you live right in the midst of one. But in perspective there can be little question that of all governments democracy is the most relevant. Only humane laws can be successfully enforced; and they are the only ones really worth enforcing. Voting is a formal method of registering consent.

But all statistical devices are open to abuse and require constant correction. Bribery, false counting, disfranchisement are the cruder deceptions; they

The Walter Lippmann Reader

correspond to those enrolment statistics of a large university which are artificially fed by counting the same student several times if his courses happen to span two or three of the departments. Just as deceptive as plain fraud is the deceptive ballot. We all know how when the political tricksters were compelled to frame a direct primary law in New York they fixed the ballot so that it botched the election. Corporations have been known to do just that to their reports. Did not E. H. Harriman say of a well-known statistician that he could make an annual report tell any story you pleased? Still subtler is the seven-foot ballot of stupid, good intentions—the hyperdemocratic ballot in which you are asked to vote for the State Printer, and succeed only in voting under the party emblem.

Statistics then is no automatic device for measuring facts. You and I are forever at the mercy of the census-taker and the census-maker. That impertinent fellow who goes from house to house is one of the real masters of the statistical situation. The other is the man who organizes the results. For all the conclusions in the end rest upon their accuracy, honesty, energy and insight. Of course, in an obvious census like that of the number of people personal bias counts for so little that it is lost in the grand total. But the moment you begin inquiries into subjects which people prefer to conceal, the weakness of statistics becomes obvious. All figures which touch upon sexual subjects are nothing but the roughest guesses. No one would take a census of prostitution, illegitimacy, adultery, or venereal disease for a statement of reliable facts. There are religious statistics, but who that has traveled among men would regard the number of professing Christians as any index of the strength of Christianity, or the church attendance as a measure of devotion? In the supremely important subject of literacy, what classification yet devised can weigh the culture of masses of people? We say that such a percentage of the population cannot read or write. But the test of reading and writing is crude and clumsy. It is often administered by men who are themselves half-educated, and it is shot through with racial and class prejudice.

The statistical method is of use only to those who have found it out. This is achieved principally by absorbing into your thinking a lively doubt about all classifications and general terms, for they are the basis of statistical measurement. That done you are fairly proof against seduction. No better popular statement of this is to be found than H. G. Wells' little essay: "Skepticism of the Instrument." Wells has, of course, made no new discovery. The history of philosophy is crowded with quarrels as to how seriously we ought to take our classifications: a large part of

The Walter Lippmann Reader

the battle about Nominalism turns on this, the Empirical and Rational traditions divide on it; in our day the attacks of James, Bergson, and the "anti-intellectualists" are largely a continuation of this old struggle. Wells takes his stand very definitely with those who regard classification "as serviceable for the practical purposes of life" but nevertheless "a departure from the objective truth of things."

"Take the word chair," he writes. "When one says chair, one thinks vaguely of an average chair. But collect individual instances, think of armchairs and reading-chairs, and dining-room chairs and kitchen chairs, chairs that pass into benches, chairs that cross the boundary and become settees, dentists' chairs, thrones, opera stalls, seats of all sorts, those miraculous fungoid growths that cumber the floor of the Arts and Crafts Exhibition, and you will perceive what a lax bundle in fact is this simple straightforward term. In co-operation with an intelligent joiner I would undertake to defeat any definition of chair or chairishness that you gave me." Think then of the glib way in which we speak of "the unemployed," "the unfit," "the criminal," "the unemployable," and how easily we forget that behind these general terms are unique individuals with personal histories and varying needs.

Even the most refined statistics are nothing but an abstraction. But if that truth is held clearly before the mind, the polygons and curves of the statisticians can be used as a skeleton to which the imagination and our general sense of life give some flesh and blood reality. Human statistics are illuminating to those who know humanity. I would not trust a hermit's inferences about the statistics of anything.

It is then no simple formula which answers our question. The problem of a human politics is not solved by a catch phrase. Criticism, of which these essays are a piece, can give the direction we must travel. But for the rest there is no smooth road built, no swift and sure conveyance at the door. We set out as if we knew; we act on the notions of man that we possess. Literature refines, science deepens, various devices extend it. Those who act on the knowledge at hand are the men of affairs. And all the while, research studies their results, artists express subtler perceptions, critics refine and adapt the general culture of the times. There is no other way but through this vast collaboration.

There is no short cut to civilization. We say that the truth will make us free. Yes, but that truth is a thousand truths which grow and change. Nor do I see a final state of blessedness. The world's end will surely find us still engaged in answering riddles. This changing focus in politics is a tendency at work all through our lives. There are many experiments. But the effort is half-conscious; only here and there does it rise to a deliberate purpose. To make it an avowed ideal—a thing of will and intelligence—is to hasten its coming, to illumine its blunders, and, by giving it self-criticism, to convert mistakes into wisdom.

Well Meaning but Unmeaning: the Chicago Vice Report

In casting about for a concrete example to illustrate some of the points under discussion I hesitated a long time before the wealth of material. No age has produced such a multitude of elaborate studies, and any selection was, of course, a limiting one. The Minority Report of the English Poor Law Commission has striking merits and defects, but for our purposes it inheres too deeply in British conditions. American tariff and trust investigations are massive enough in all conscience, but they are so partisan in their origin and so pathetically unattached to any recognized ideal of public policy that it seemed better to look elsewhere. Conservation had the virtue of arising out of a provident statesmanship, but its problems were largely technical.

The real choice narrowed itself finally to the Pittsburgh Survey and the Chicago Vice Report. Had I been looking for an example of the finest expert inquiry, there would have been little question that the vivid and intensive study of Pittsburgh's industrialism was the example to use. But I was looking for something more representative, and, therefore, more revealing. I did not want a detached study of some specially selected cross-section of what is after all not the typical economic life of America. The case demanded was one in which you could see representative American citizens trying to handle a problem which had touched their imaginations.

Vice is such a problem. You can always get a hearing about it; there is no end of interest in the question. Rare indeed is that community which has not been "Lexowed," in which a district attorney or a minister has not led a crusade. Muckraking began with the exposure of vice; men like Heney, Lindsey, Folk founded their reputations on the fight against it. It would be interesting to know how much of the social conscience of our time had as its first insight the prostitute on the city pavement.

We do not have to force an interest, as we do about the trusts, or even about the poor. For this problem lies close indeed to the dynamics of our own natures. Research is stimulated, actively aroused, and a passionate zeal suffuses what is perhaps the most spontaneous reform enthusiasm of our time. Looked at externally it is a curious focusing of attention. Nor is it explained by words like "chivalry," "conscience," "social compassion." Magazines that will condone a thousand cruelties to women gladly publish series of articles on the girl who goes wrong;

The Walter Lippmann Reader

merchants who sweat and rack their women employees serve gallantly on these commissions. These men are not conscious hypocrites. Perhaps like the rest of us they are impelled by forces they are not eager to examine. I do not press the point. It belongs to the analyst of motive.

We need only note the vast interest in the subject—that it extends across class lines, and expresses itself as an immense good-will. Perhaps a largely unconscious absorption in a subject is itself a sign of great importance. Surely vice has a thousand implications that touch all of us directly. It is closely related to most of the interests of life—ramifying into industry, into the family, health, play, art, religion. The miseries it entails are genuine miseries—not points of etiquette or infringements of convention. Vice issues in pain. The world suffers for it. To attack it is to attack as far-reaching and real a problem as any that we human beings face.

The Chicago Commission had no simple, easily measured problem before it. At the very outset the report confesses that an accurate count of the number of prostitutes in Chicago could not be reached. The police lists are obviously incomplete and perhaps corrupt. The whole amorphous field of clandestine vice will, of course, defeat any census. But even public prostitution is so varied that nobody can do better than estimate it roughly. This point is worth keeping in mind, for it lights up the remedies proposed. What the Commission advocates is the constant repression and the ultimate annihilation of a mode of life which refuses discovery and measurement.

The report estimates that there are five thousand women in Chicago who devote their whole time to the traffic; that the annual profits in that one city alone are between fifteen and sixteen million dollars a year. These figures are admittedly low for they leave out all consideration of occasional, or seasonal, or hidden prostitution. It is only the nucleus that can be guessed at; the fringe which shades out into various degrees of respectability remains entirely unmeasured. Yet these suburbs of the Tenderloin must always be kept in mind; their population is shifting and very elastic; it includes the unsuspected; and I am inclined to believe that it is the natural refuge of the "suppressed" prostitute. Moreover it defies control.

The 1012 women recognized on the police lists are of course the most easily studied. From them we can gather some hint of the enormous bewildering demand that prostitution answers. The Commission informs us that this small group alone receives over fifteen thousand visits a day—five million and a half in the year. Yet these 1012 women are only about one-fifth of the professional prostitutes in

67

Chicago. If the average continues, then the figures mount to something over 27,000,000. The five thousand professionals do not begin to represent the whole illicit traffic of a city like Chicago. Clandestine and occasional vice is beyond all measurement.

The figures I have given are taken from the report. They are said to be conservative. For the purposes of this discussion we could well lower the 27,000,000 by half. All I am concerned about is in arriving at a sense of the enormity of the impulse behind the "social evil." For it is this that the Commission proposes to repress, and ultimately to annihilate.

Lust has a thousand avenues. The brothel, the flat, the assignation house, the tenement, saloons, dance halls, steamers, ice-cream parlors, Turkish baths, massage parlors, street-walking—the thing has woven itself into the texture of city life. Like the hydra, it grows new heads, everywhere. It draws into its service the pleasures of the city. Entangled with the love of gaiety, organized as commerce, it is literally impossible to follow the myriad expressions it assumes.

The Commission gives a very fair picture of these manifestations. A mass of material is offered which does in a way show where and how and to what extent lust finds its illicit expression. Deeper than this the report does not go. The human impulses which create these social conditions, the human needs to which they are a sad and degraded answer—this human center of the problem the commission passes by with a platitude.

"So long as there is lust in the hearts of men," we are told, "it will seek out some method of expression. Until the hearts of men are changed we can hope for no absolute annihilation of the Social Evil." But at the head of the report in black-faced type we read:

"Constant and persistent repression of prostitution the immediate method; absolute annihilation the ultimate ideal."

I am not trying to catch the Commissioners in a verbal inconsistency. The inconsistency is real, out of a deep-seated confusion of mind. Lust will seek an expression, they say, until "the hearts of men are changed." All particular expressions are evil and must be constantly repressed. Yet though you repress one form of lust, it will seek some other. Now, says the Commission, in order to change the hearts of men, religion and education must step in. It is their business to eradicate an impulse which is constantly changing form by being "suppressed."

The Walter Lippmann Reader

There is only one meaning in this: the Commission realized vaguely that repression is not even the first step to a cure. For reasons worth analyzing later, these representative American citizens desired both the immediate taboo and an ultimate annihilation of vice. So they fell into the confusion of making immediate and detailed proposals that have nothing to do with the attainment of their ideal.

What the commission saw and described were the particular forms which a great human impulse had assumed at a specific date in a certain city. The dynamic force which created these conditions, which will continue to create them—lust—they refer to in a few pious sentences. Their thinking, in short, is perfectly static and literally superficial. In outlining a ripple they have forgotten the tides.

Had they faced the human sources of their problem, had they tried to think of the social evil as an answer to a human need, their researches would have been different, their remedies fruitful. Suppose they had kept in mind their own statement: "so long as there is lust in the hearts of men it will seek out some method of expression." Had they held fast to that, it would have ceased to be a platitude and have become a fertile idea. For a platitude is generally inert wisdom.

In the sentence I quote the Commissioners had an idea which might have animated all their labors. But they left it in limbo, they reverenced it, and they passed by. Perhaps we can raise it again and follow the hints it unfolds.

If lust will seek an expression, are all expressions of it necessarily evil? That the kind of expression which the Commission describes is evil no one will deny. But is it the only possible expression?

If it is, then the taboo enforced by a Morals Police is, perhaps, as good a way as any of gaining a fictitious sense of activity. But the ideal of "annihilation" becomes an irrelevant and meaningless phrase. If lust is deeply rooted in men and its only expression is evil, I for one should recommend a faith in the millennium. You can put this Paradise at the beginning of the world or the end of it. Practical difference there is none.

No one can read the report without coming to a definite conviction that the Commission regards lust itself as inherently evil. The members assumed without criticism the traditional dogma of Christianity that sex in any manifestation outside of marriage is sinful. But practical sense told them that sex cannot be confined within marriage. It will find expression—"some method of expression" they say. What never occurred to them was that it might find a good, a positively beneficent method. The utterly uncriticised assumption that all expressions not legalized are

69

sinful shut them off from any constructive answer to their problem. Seeing prostitution or something equally bad as the only way sex can find an expression they really set before religion and education the impossible task of removing lust "from the hearts of men." So when their report puts at its head that absolute annihilation of prostitution is the ultimate ideal, we may well translate it into the real intent of the Commission. What is to be absolutely annihilated is not alone prostitution, not alone all the methods of expression which lust seeks out, but lust itself.

That this is what the Commission had in mind is supported by plenty of "internal evidence." For example: one of the most curious recommendations made is about divorce—"The Commission condemns the ease with which divorces may be obtained in certain States, and recommends a stringent, uniform divorce law for all States."

What did the Commission have in mind? I transcribe the paragraph which deals with divorce: "The Vice Commission, after exhaustive consideration of the vice question, records itself of the opinion that divorce to a large extent is a contributory factor to sexual vice. No study of this blight upon the social and moral life of the country would be comprehensive without consideration of the causes which lead to the application for divorce. These are too numerous to mention at length in such a report as this, but the Commission does wish to emphasize the great need of more safeguards against the marrying of persons physically, mentally and morally unfit to take up the responsibilities of family life, including the bearing of children."

Now to be sure that paragraph leaves much to be desired so far as clearness goes. But I think the meaning can be extracted. Divorce is a contributory factor to sexual vice. One way presumably is that divorced women often become prostitutes. That is an evil contribution, unquestionably. The second sentence says that no study of the social evil is complete which leaves out the *causes* of divorce. One of those causes is, I suppose, adultery with a prostitute. This evil is totally different from the first: in one case divorce contributes to prostitution, in the other, prostitution leads to divorce. The third sentence urges greater safeguards against undesirable marriages. This prudence would obviously reduce the need of divorce.

How does the recommendation of a stringent and uniform law fit in with these three statements? A strict divorce law might be like New York's: it would recognize few grounds for a decree. One of those grounds, perhaps the chief one, would be adultery. I say this unhesitatingly for in another place the Commission informs us that marriage has in it "the elements of vested rights."

A strict divorce law would, of course, diminish the number of "divorced women," and perhaps keep them out of prostitution. It does fit the first statement—in a helpless sort of way. But where does the difficulty of divorce affect the causes of it? If you bind a man tightly to a woman he does not love, and, possibly prevent him from marrying one he does love, how do you add to his virtue? And if the only way he can free himself is by adultery, does not your stringent divorce law put a premium upon vice? The third sentence would make it difficult for the unfit to marry. Better marriages would among other blessings require fewer divorces. But what of those who are forbidden to marry? They are unprovided for. And yet who more than they are likely to find desire uncontrollable and seek some other "method of expression"? With marriage prohibited and prostitution tabooed, the Commission has a choice between sterilization and—let us say—other methods of expression.

Make marriage difficult, divorce stringent, prostitution impossible—is there any doubt that the leading idea is to confine the sex impulse within the marriage of healthy, intelligent, "moral," and monogamous couples? For all the other seekings of that impulse what has the Commission to offer? Nothing. That can be asserted flatly. The Commission hopes to wipe out prostitution. But it never hints that the success of its plan means vast alterations in our social life. The members give the impression that they think of prostitution as something that can be subtracted from our civilization without changing the essential character of its institutions. Yet who that has read the report itself and put himself into any imaginative understanding of conditions can escape seeing that prostitution to-day is organic to our industrial life, our marriage sanctions, and our social customs? Low wages, fatigue, and the wretched monotony of the factory—these must go before prostitution can go. And behind these stand the facts of woman's entrance into industry—facts that have one source at least in the general poverty of the family. And that poverty is deeply bound up with the economic system under which we live. In the man's problem, the growing impossibility of early marriages is directly related to the business situation. Nor can we speak of the degradation of religion and the arts, of amusement, of the general morale of the people without referring that degradation to industrial conditions.

The Walter Lippmann Reader

You cannot look at civilization as a row of institutions each external to the other. They interpenetrate and a change in one affects all the others. To abolish prostitution would involve a radical alteration of society. Vice in our cities is a form of the sexual impulse—one of the forms it has taken under prevailing social conditions. It is, if you please, like the crops of a rude and forbidding soil—a coarse, distorted thing though living.

The Commission studied a human problem and left humanity out. I do not mean that the members weren't deeply touched by the misery of these thousands of women. You can pity the poor without understanding them; you can have compassion without insight. The Commissioners had a good deal of sympathy for the prostitute's condition, but for that "lust in the hearts of men," and women we may add, for that, they had no sympathetic understanding. They did not place themselves within the impulse. Officially they remained external to human desires. For what might be called the élan vital of the problem they had no patience. Certain sad results of the particular "method of expression" it had sought out in Chicago called forth their pity and their horror.

In short, the Commission did not face the sexual impulse squarely. The report is an attempt to deal with a sexual problem by disregarding its source. There are almost a hundred recommendations to various authorities—Federal, State, county, city, police, educational and others. I have attempted to classify these proposals under four headings. There are those which mean forcible repression of particular manifestations—the taboos; there are the recommendations which are purely palliative, which aim to abate some of the horrors of existing conditions; there are a few suggestions for further investigation; and, finally, there are the inventions, the plans which show some desire to find moral equivalents for evil—the really statesmanlike offerings.

The palliative measures we may pass by quickly. So long as they do not blind people to the necessity for radical treatment, only a doctrinaire would object to them. Like all intelligent charities they are still a necessary evil. But nothing must be staked upon them, so let us turn at once to the constructive suggestions: The Commission proposes that the county establish a "Permanent Committee on Child Protection." It makes no attempt to say what that protection shall be, but I think it is only fair to let the wish father the thought, and regard this as an effort to give children a better start in life. The separation of delinquent from semi-delinquent girls is a somewhat similar attempt to guard the weak. Another is the recommendation to the city and the nation that it should protect arriving immigrants, and if necessary escort them to their homes. This surely is a constructive plan which might well be enlarged from mere protection to positive hospitality. How great a part the desolating loneliness of a city plays in seductions the individual histories in the report show. Municipal dance halls are a splendid proposal. Freed from a cold and over-chaperoned respectability they compete with the devil. There, at least, is one method of sexual expression which may have positively beneficent results. A municipal lodging house for women is something of a substitute for the wretched rented room. A little suggestion to the police that they send home children found on the streets after nine o'clock has varied possibilities. But there is the seed of an invention in it which might convert the police from mere agents of repression to kindly helpers in the mazes of a city. The educational proposals are all constructive: the teaching of sex hygiene is guardedly recommended for consideration. That is entirely justified, for no one can quarrel with a set of men for leaving a question open. That girls from fourteen to sixteen should receive vocational training in continuation schools; that social centers should be established in the public schools and that the grounds should be open for children—all of these are clearly additions to the positive resource of the community. So is the suggestion that church buildings be used for recreation. The call for greater parental responsibility is, I fear, a rather empty platitude, for it is not re-enforced with anything but an ancient fervor.

How much of this really seeks to create a fine expression of the sexual impulse? How many of these recommendations see sex as an instinct which can be transmuted, and turned into one of the values of life? The dance halls, the social centers, the playgrounds, the reception of strangers—these can become instruments for civilizing sexual need. The educational proposals could become ways of directing it. They could, but will they? Without the habit of mind which sees substitution as the essence of statecraft, without a philosophy which makes the invention of moral equivalents its goal, I for one refuse to see in these recommendations anything more than a haphazard shooting which has accidentally hit the mark. Moreover, I have a deep suspicion that I have tried to read into the proposals more than the Commission intended. Certainly these constructions occupy an insignificant amount of space in the body of the report. On all sides of them is a mass of taboos. No emotional appeal is made for them as there is for the repressions. They stand

The Walter Lippmann Reader

largely unnoticed, and very much undefined—poor ghosts of the truth among the gibbets.

An inadvertent platitude—that lust will seek an expression—and a few diffident proposals for a finer environment—the need and its satisfaction: had the Commission seen the relation of these incipient ideas, animated it, and made it the nerve center of the study, a genuine program might have resulted. But the two ideas never met and fertilized each other. Nothing dynamic holds the recommendations together—the mass of them are taboos, an attempt to kill each mosquito and ignore the marsh. The evils of prostitution are seen as a series of episodes, each of which must be clubbed, forbidden, raided and jailed.

There is a special whack for each mosquito: the laws about excursion boats should be enforced; the owners should help to enforce them; there should be more officers with police power on these boats; the sale of liquor to minors should be forbidden; gambling devices should be suppressed; the midwives, doctors and maternity hospitals practicing abortions should be investigated; employment agencies should be watched and investigated; publishers should be warned against printing suspicious advertisements; the law against infamous crimes should be made more specific; any citizen should have the right to bring equity proceedings against a brothel as a public nuisance; there should be relentless prosecution of professional procurers; there should be constant prosecution of the keepers, inmates, and owners of bawdy houses; there should be prosecution of druggists who sells drugs and "certain appliances" illegally; there should be an identification system for prostitutes in the state courts; instead of fines, prostitutes should be visited with imprisonment or adult probation; there should be a penalty for sending messenger boys under twenty-one to a disorderly house or an unlicensed saloon; the law against prostitutes in saloons, against wine-rooms and stalls in saloons, against communication between saloons and brothels, against dancing in saloons—should be strictly enforced; the police who enforce these laws should be carefully watched, grafters amongst them should be discharged; complaints should be investigated at once by a man stationed outside the district; the pressure of publicity should be brought against the brewers to prevent them from doing business with saloons that violate the law; the Retail Liquor Association should discipline law-breaking saloon-keepers: licenses should be permanently revoked for violations; no women should be allowed in a saloon without a male escort; no professional or paid escorts should be permitted; no soliciting should be allowed in saloons; no immoral or vulgar dances should be permitted in saloons; no intoxicating liquor should be allowed at any public dance; there should be a municipal detention home for women, with probation officers; police inspectors who fail to report law-violations should be dismissed; assignation houses should be suppressed as soon as they are reported; there should be a "special morals police squad"; recommendation IX "to the Police" says they "should wage a relentless warfare against houses of prostitution, immoral flats, assignation rooms, call houses, and disorderly saloons in all sections of the city"; parks and playgrounds should be more thoroughly policed; dancing pavilions should exclude professional prostitutes; soliciting in parks should be suppressed; parks should be lighted with a searchlight; there should be no seats in the shadows....

To perform that staggering list of things that "should" be done you find—what?—the police power, federal, state, municipal. Note how vague and general are the chance constructive suggestions; how precise and definite the taboos. Surely I am not misstating its position when I say that forcible suppression was the creed of this Commission. Nor is there any need of insisting again that the ultimate ideal of annihilating prostitution has nothing to expect from the concrete proposals that were made. The millennial goal was one thing; the immediate method quite another. For ideals, a pious phrase; in practice, the police.

Are we not told that "if the citizens cannot depend upon the men appointed to protect their property, and to maintain order, then chaos and disorganization resulting in vice and crime must follow?" Yet of all the reeds that civilization leans upon, surely the police is the frailest. Anyone who has had the smallest experience of municipal politics knows that the corruption of the police is directly proportionate to the severity of the taboos it is asked to enforce. Tom Johnson saw this as Mayor of Cleveland; he knew that strict law enforcement against saloons, brothels, and gambling houses would not stop vice, but would corrupt the police. I recommend the recent spectacle in New York where the most sensational raider of gambling houses has turned out to be in crooked alliance with the gamblers. And I suggest as a hint that the Commission's recommendations enforced for one year will lay the foundation of an organized system of blackmail and "protection," secrecy and underground chicanery, the like of which Chicago has not yet seen. But the Commission need only have read its own report, have studied its own cases. There is an illuminating chapter on "The Social Evil and the Police." In the summary, the Commission says that "officers on the beat are bold and open in their neglect of duty, drinking in saloons while in uniform, ignoring the solicitations by prostitutes in rear rooms and on the streets, selling tickets at dances frequented by professional and semi-professional prostitutes; protecting 'cadets,' prostitutes and saloon-keepers of disorderly places."

Some suspicion that the police could not carry the burden of suppressing the social evil must have dawned on the Commission.

It felt the need of re-enforcement. Hence the special morals police squad; hence the investigation of the police of one district by the police from another; and hence, in type as black as that of the ideal itself and directly beneath it, the call for "the appointment of a morals commission" and "the establishment of a morals court." Now this commission consists of the Health Officer, a physician and three citizens who serve without pay. It is appointed by the Mayor and approved by the City Council. Its business is to prosecute vice and to help enforce the law.

Just what would happen if the Morals Commission didn't prosecute hard enough I do not know. Conceivably the Governor might be induced to appoint a Commission on Moral Commissions in Cities. But why the men and women who framed the report made this particular recommendation is an interesting question. With federal, state, and municipal authorities in existence, with courts, district attorneys, police all operating, they create another arm of prosecution. Possibly they were somewhat disillusioned about the present instruments of the taboo; perhaps they imagined that a new broom would sweep clean. But I suspect an inner reason. The Commission may have imagined that the four appointees—unpaid—would be four men like themselves—who knows, perhaps four men from among themselves? The whole tenor of their thinking is to set somebody watching everybody and somebody else to watching him. What is more natural than that they should be the Ultimate Watchers?

Spying, informing, constant investigations of everybody and everything must become the rule where there is a forcible attempt to moralize society from the top. Nobody's heart is in the work very long; nobody's but those fanatical and morbid guardians of morality who make it a life's specialty. The aroused public opinion which the Commission asks for cannot be held if all it has to fix upon is an elaborate series of taboos. Sensational disclosures will often make the public flare up spasmodically; but the mass of men is soon bored by intricate rules and tangles of red tape; the "crusade" is looked upon as a melodrama of real life—interesting, but easily forgotten.

The Walter Lippmann Reader

The method proposed ignores the human source: by a kind of poetic justice the great crowd of men will ignore the method. If you want to impose a taboo upon a whole community, you must do it autocratically, you must make it part of the prevailing superstitions. You must never let it reach any public analysis. For it will fail, it will receive only a shallow support from what we call an "enlightened public opinion." That opinion is largely determined by the real impulses of men; and genuine character rejects or at least rebels against foreign, unnatural impositions. This is one of the great virtues of democracy—that it makes alien laws more and more difficult to enforce. The tyrant can use the taboo a thousand times more effectively than the citizens of a republic. When he speaks, it is with a prestige that dumbs questioning and makes obedience a habit. Let that infallibility come to be doubted, as in Russia to-day, and natural impulses reassert themselves, the great impositions begin to weaken. The methods of the Chicago Commission would require a tyranny, a powerful, centralized sovereignty which could command with majesty and silence the rebel. In our shirt-sleeved republic no such power exists. The strongest force we have is that of organized money, and that sovereignty is too closely connected with the social evil, too dependent upon it in a hundred different ways, to undertake the task of suppression.

For the purposes of the Commission democracy is an inefficient weapon. Nothing but disappointment is in store for men who expect a people to outrage its own character. A large part of the unfaith in democracy, of the desire to ignore "the mob," limit the franchise, and confine power to the few is the result of an unsuccessful attempt to make republics act like old-fashioned monarchies. Almost every "crusade" leaves behind it a trail of yearning royalists; many "good-government" clubs are little would-be oligarchies.

When the mass of men emerged from slavish obedience and made democracy inevitable, the taboo entered upon its final illness. For the more self-governing a people becomes, the less possible it is to prescribe external restrictions. The gap between want and ought, between nature and ideals cannot be maintained. The only practical ideals in a democracy are a fine expression of natural wants. This happens to be a thoroughly Greek attitude. But I learned it first from the Bowery. Chuck Connors is reported to have said that "a gentleman is a bloke as can do whatever he wants to do." If Chuck said that, he went straight to the heart of that democratic morality on which a new statecraft must ultimately rest. His gentleman is not the battlefield of wants and prohibitions; in him impulses flow freely through beneficent channels.

The same notion lies imbedded in the phrase: "government must serve the people." That means a good deal more than that elected officials must rule for the majority. For the majority in these semi-democratic times is often as not a cloak for the ruling oligarchy. Representatives who "serve" some majorities may in reality order the nation about. To serve the people means to provide it with services—with clean streets and water, with education, with opportunity, with beneficent channels for its desires, with moral equivalents for evil. The task is turned from the damming and restricting of wants to the creation of fine environments for them. And the environment of an impulse extends all the way from the human body, through family life and education out into the streets of the city.

Had the Commission worked along democratic lines, we should have had recommendations about the hygiene and early training of children, their education, the houses they live in and the streets in which they play; changes would have been suggested in the industrial conditions they face; plans would have been drawn for recreation; hints would have been collected for transmuting the sex impulse into art, into social endeavor, into religion. That is the constructive approach to the problem. I note that the Commission calls upon the churches for help. Its obvious intention was to down sex with religion. What was not realized, it seems, is that this very sex impulse, so largely degraded into vice, is the dynamic force in religious feeling. One need not call in the testimony of the psychologists, the students of religion, the æstheticians or even of Plato, who in the "Symposium" traced out the hierarchy of love from the body to the "whole sea of beauty." Jane Addams in Chicago has tested the truth by her own wide experience, and she has written what the Commission might easily have read,—that "in failing to diffuse and utilize this fundamental instinct of sex through the imagination, we not only inadvertently foster vice and enervation, but we throw away one of the most precious implements for ministering to life's highest needs. There is no doubt that this ill-adjusted function consumes quite unnecessarily vast stores of vital energy, even when we contemplate it in its immature manifestations which are infinitely more wholesome than the dumb swamping process. All high school boys and girls know the difference between the concentration and the diffusion of this impulse, although they would be hopelessly bewildered by the use of terms. They will declare one of their companions to be 'in love' if his fancy is occupied by the image of a single person about whom all the new-found values gather, and without whom his solitude is an eternal melancholy. But if the stimulus does not appear as a definite image, and the values evoked are dispensed over the world, the young person suddenly seems to have discovered a beauty and significance in many things—he responds to poetry, he becomes a lover of nature, he is filled with religious devotion or with philanthropic zeal. Experience, with young people, easily illustrates the possibility and value of diffusion."

It is then not only impossible to confine sex to mere reproduction; it would be a stupid denial of the finest values of civilization. Having seen that the impulse is a necessary part of character, we must not hold to it grudgingly as a necessary evil. It is, on the contrary, the very source of good. Whoever has visited Hull House can see for himself the earnest effort Miss Addams has made to treat sex with dignity and joy. For Hull House differs from most settlements in that it is full of pictures, of color, and of curios. The atmosphere is light; you feel none of that moral oppression which hangs over the usual settlement as over a gathering of missionaries. Miss Addams has not only made Hull House a beautiful place; she has stocked it with curious and interesting objects. The theater, the museum, the crafts and the arts, games and dances—they are some of those "other methods of expression which lust can seek." It is no accident that Hull House is the most successful settlement in America.

Yet who does not feel its isolation in that brutal city? A little Athens in a vast barbarism—you wonder how much of Chicago Hull House can civilize. As you walk those grim streets and look into the stifling houses, or picture the relentless stockyards, the conviction that vice and its misery cannot be transmuted by policemen and Morals Commissions, the feeling that spying and inspecting and prosecuting will not drain the marsh becomes a certainty. You want to shout at the forcible moralizer: "so long as you acquiesce in the degradation of your city, so long as work remains nothing but ill-paid drudgery and every instinct of joy is mocked by dirt and cheapness and brutality,—just so long will your efforts be fruitless, yes even though you raid and prosecute, even though you make Comstock the Czar of Chicago."

But Hull House cannot remake Chicago. A few hundred lives can be changed, and for the rest it is a guide to the imagination. Like all utopias, it cannot succeed, but it may point the way to success. If Hull House is unable to civilize Chicago, it at least shows Chicago and America what a civilization might be like. Friendly,

The Walter Lippmann Reader

where our cities are friendless, beautiful, where they are ugly; sociable and open, where our daily life is furtive; work a craft; art a participation—it is in miniature the goal of statesmanship. If Chicago were like Hull House, we say to ourselves, then vice would be no problem—it would dwindle, what was left would be the Falstaff in us all, and only a spiritual anemia could worry over that jolly and redeeming coarseness.

What stands between Chicago and civilization? No one can doubt that to abolish prostitution means to abolish the slum and the dirty alley, to stop overwork, underpay, the sweating and the torturing monotony of business, to breathe a new life into education, ventilate society with frankness, and fill life with play and art, with games, with passions which hold and suffuse the imagination.

It is a revolutionary task, and like all real revolutions it will not be done in a day or a decade because someone orders it to be done. A change in the whole quality of life is something that neither the policeman's club nor an insurrectionary raid can achieve. If you want a revolution that shall really matter in human life—and what sane man can help desiring it?—you must look to the infinitely complicated results of the dynamic movements in society. These revolutions require a rare combination of personal audacity and social patience. The best agents of such a revolution are men who are bold in their plans because they realize how deep and enormous is the task.

Many people have sought an analogy in our Civil War. They have said that as "black slavery" went, so must "white slavery." In the various agitations of vigilance committees and alliances for the suppression of the traffic they profess to see continued a work which the abolitionists began.

In A. M. Simons' brilliant book on "Social Forces in American History" much help can be found. For example: "Massachusetts abolished slavery at an early date, and we have it on the authority of John Adams that:—'argument might have had some weight in the abolition of slavery in Massachusetts, but the real cause was the multiplication of laboring white people, who would not longer suffer the rich to employ these sable rivals so much to their injury.'" No one to-day doubts that white labor in the North and slavery in the South were not due to the moral superiority of the North. Yet just in the North we find the abolition sentiment strongest. That the Civil War was not a clash of good men and bad men is admitted by every reputable historian. The war did not come when moral fervor had risen to the exploding point; the moral fervor came rather when the economic interests of the

The Walter Lippmann Reader

South collided with those of the North. That the abolitionists clarified the economic interests of the North and gave them an ideal sanction is true enough. But the fact remains that by 1860 some of the aspirations of Phillips and Garrison had become the economic destiny of this country.

You can have a Hull House established by private initiative and maintained by individual genius, just as you had planters who freed their slaves or as you have employers to-day who humanize their factories. But the fine example is not readily imitated when industrial forces fight against it. So even if the Commission had drawn splendid plans for housing, work conditions, education, and play it would have done only part of the task of statesmanship. We should then know what to do, but not how to get it done.

An ideal suspended in a vacuum is ineffective: it must point a dynamic current. Only then does it gather power, only then does it enter into life. That forces exist to-day which carry with them solutions is evident to anyone who has watched the labor movement and the woman's awakening. Even the interests of business give power to the cause. The discovery of manufacturers that degradation spoils industrial efficiency must not be cast aside by the radical because the motive is larger profits. The discovery, whatever the motive, will inevitably humanize industry a good deal. For it happens that in this case the interests of capitalism and of humanity coincide. A propaganda like the single-tax will undoubtedly find increasing support among business men. They see in it a relief from the burden of rent imposed by that older tyrant—the landlord. But the taxation of unimproved property happens at the same time to be a splendid weapon against the slum.

Only when the abolition of "white slavery" becomes part of the social currents of the time will it bear any interesting analogy to the so-called freeing of the slaves. Even then for many enthusiasts the comparison is misleading. They are likely to regard the Emancipation Proclamation as the end of chattel slavery. It wasn't. That historic document broke a legal bond but not a social one. The process of negro emancipation is infinitely slower and it is not accomplished yet. Likewise no statute can end "white slavery." Only vast and complicated changes in the whole texture of social life will achieve such an end. If by some magic every taboo of the commission could be enforced the abolition of sex slavery would not have come one step nearer to reality. Cities and factories, schools and homes, theaters and games, manners and thought will have to be transformed before sex can find a better expression. Living forces, not statutes or clubs, must work that change. The power

The Walter Lippmann Reader

of emancipation is in the social movements which alone can effect any deep reform in a nation. So it is and has been with the negro. I do not think the Abolitionists saw facts truly when they disbanded their organization a few years after the civil war. They found too much comfort in a change of legal status. Profound economic forces brought about the beginning of the end of chattel slavery. But the reality of freedom was not achieved by proclamation. For that the revolution had to go on: the industrial life of the nation had to change its character, social customs had to be replaced, the whole outlook of men had to be transformed. And whether it is negro slavery or a vicious sexual bondage, the actual advance comes from substitutions injected into society by dynamic social forces.

I do not wish to press the analogy or over-emphasize the particular problems. I am not engaged in drawing up the plans for a reconstruction or in telling just what should be done. Only the co-operation of expert minds can do that. The place for a special propaganda is elsewhere. If these essays succeed in suggesting a method of looking at politics, if they draw attention to what is real in social reforms and make somewhat more evident the traps and the blind-alleys of an uncritical approach, they will have done their work. That the report of the Chicago Vice Commission figures so prominently in this chapter is not due to any preoccupation with Chicago, the Commission or with vice. It is a text and nothing else. The report happens to embody what I conceive to be most of the faults of a political method now decadent. Its failure to put human impulses at the center of thought produced remedies valueless to human nature; its false interest in a particular expression of sex—vice—caused it to taboo the civilizing power of sex; its inability to see that wants require fine satisfactions and not prohibitions drove it into an undemocratic tyranny; its blindness to the social forces of our age shut off the motive power for any reform.

The Commission's method was poor, not its intentions. It was an average body of American citizens aroused to action by an obvious evil. But something slipped in to falsify vision. It was, I believe, an array of idols disguised as ideals. They are typical American idols, and they deserve some study.

Some Necessary Iconoclasm

The Commission "has kept constantly in mind that to offer a contribution of any value such an offering must be, first, moral; second, reasonable and practical; third, possible under the Constitutional powers of our Courts; fourth, that which will square with the public conscience of the American people."—The Vice Commission of Chicago—Introduction to Report on the Social Evil.

Having adjusted such spectacles the Commission proceeded to look at "this curse which is more blasting than any plague or epidemic," at an evil "which spells only ruin to the race." In dealing with what it regards as the greatest calamity in the world, a calamity as old as civilization, the Commission lays it down beforehand that the remedy must be "moral," constitutional, and satisfactory to the public conscience. I wonder in all seriousness what the Commission would have done had it discovered a genuine cure for prostitution which happened, let us say, to conflict with the constitutional powers of our courts. I wonder how the Commission would have acted if a humble following of the facts had led them to a conviction out of tune with the existing public conscience of America. Such a conflict is not only possible; it is highly probable. When you come to think of it, the conflict appears a certainty. For the Constitution is a legal expression of the conditions under which prostitution has flourished; the social evil is rooted in institutions and manners which have promoted it, in property relations and business practice which have gathered about them a halo of reason and practicality, of morality and conscience. Any change so vast as the abolition of vice is of necessity a change in morals, practice, law and conscience.

A scientist who began an investigation by saying that his results must be moral or constitutional would be a joke. We have had scientists like that, men who insisted that research must confirm the Biblical theory of creation. We have had economists who set out with the preconceived idea of justifying the factory system. The world has recently begun to see through this kind of intellectual fraud. If a doctor should appear who offered a cure for tuberculosis on the ground that it was justified by the Bible and that it conformed to the opinions of that great mass of the American people who believe that fresh air is the devil, we should promptly lock up that

83

doctor as a dangerous quack. When the negroes of Kansas were said to be taking pink pills to guard themselves against Halley's Comet, they were doing something which appeared to them as eminently practical and entirely reasonable. Not long ago we read of the savage way in which a leper was treated out West; his leprosy was not regarded as a disease, but as the curse of God, and, if I remember correctly, the Bible was quoted in court as an authority on leprosy. The treatment seemed entirely moral and squared very well with the conscience of that community.

I have heard reputable physicians condemn a certain method of psychotherapy because it was "immoral." A woman once told me that she had let her son grow up ignorant of his sexual life because "a mother should never mention anything 'embarrassing' to her child." Many of us are still blushing for the way America treated Gorki when it found that Russian morals did not square with the public conscience of America. And the time is not yet passed when we punish the offspring of illicit love, and visit vengeance unto the third and fourth generations. One reads in the report of the Vice Commission that many public hospitals in Chicago refuse to care for venereal diseases. The examples are endless. They run from the absurd to the monstrous. But always the source is the same. Idols are set up to which all the living must bow; we decide beforehand that things must fit a few preconceived ideas. And when they don't, which is most of the time, we deny truth, falsify facts, and prefer the coddling of our theory to any deeper understanding of the real problem before us.

It seems as if a theory were never so active as when the reality behind it has disappeared. The empty name, the ghostly phrase, exercise an authority that is appalling. When you think of the blood that has been shed in the name of Jesus, when you think of the Holy Roman Empire, "neither holy nor Roman nor imperial," of the constitutional phrases that cloak all sorts of thievery, of the common law precedents that tyrannize over us, history begins to look almost like the struggle of man to emancipate himself from phrase-worship. The devil can quote Scripture, and law, and morality and reason and practicality. The devil can use the public conscience of his time. He does in wars, in racial and religious persecutions; he did in the Spain of the Inquisition; he does in the American lynching.

For there is nothing so bad but it can masquerade as moral. Conquerors have gone forth with the blessing of popes; a nation invokes its God before beginning a campaign of murder, rape and pillage. The ruthless exploitation of India becomes the civilizing fulfilment of the "white man's burden"; not infrequently the missionary, drummer, and prospector are embodied in one man. In the nineteenth century church, press and university devoted no inconsiderable part of their time to proving the high moral and scientific justice of child labor and human sweating. It is a matter of record that chattel slavery in this country was deduced from Biblical injunction, that the universities furnished brains for its defense. Surely Bernard Shaw was not describing the Englishman alone when he said in "The Man of Destiny" that "... you will never find an Englishman in the wrong. He does everything on principle. He fights you on patriotic principles; he robs you on business principles...."

Liberty, equality, fraternity—what a grotesque career those words have had. Almost every attempt to mitigate the hardships of industrialism has had to deal with the bogey of liberty. Labor organization, factory laws, health regulations are still fought as infringements of liberty. And in the name of equality what fantasies of taxation have we not woven? what travesties of justice set up? "The law in its majestic equality," writes Anatole France, "forbids the rich as well as the poor to sleep in the streets and to steal bread." Fraternity becomes the hypocritical slogan by which we refuse to enact what is called "class legislation"—a policy which in theory denies the existence of classes, in practice legislates in favor of the rich. The laws which go unchallenged are laws friendly to business; class legislation means working-class legislation.

You have to go among lawyers to see this idolatrous process in its most perfect form. When a judge sets out to "interpret" the Constitution, what is it that he does? He takes a sentence written by a group of men more than a hundred years ago. That sentence expressed their policy about certain conditions which they had to deal with. In it was summed up what they intended to do about the problems they saw. That is all the sentence means. But in the course of a century new problems arise—problems the Fathers could no more have foreseen than we can foresee the problems of the year two thousand. Yet that sentence which contained their wisdom about particular events has acquired an emotional force which persists long after the events have passed away. Legends gather about the men who wrote it: those legends are absorbed by us almost with our mothers' milk. We never again read that sentence straight. It has a gravity out of all proportion to its use, and we call it a fundamental principle of government. Whatever we want to do is hallowed

The Walter Lippmann Reader

and justified, if it can be made to appear as a deduction from that sentence. To put new wine in old bottles is one of the aims of legal casuistry.

Reformers practice it. You hear it said that the initiative and referendum are a return to the New England town meeting. That is supposed to be an argument for direct legislation. But surely the analogy is superficial; the difference profound. The infinitely greater complexity of legislation to-day, the vast confusion in the aims of the voting population, produce a difference of so great a degree that it amounts to a difference in kind. The naturalist may classify the dog and the fox, the house-cat and the tiger together for certain purposes. The historian of political forms may see in the town meeting a forerunner of direct legislation. But no housewife dare classify the cat and the tiger, the dog and the fox, as the same kind of animal. And no statesman can argue the virtues of the referendum from the successes of the town meeting.

But the propagandists do it nevertheless, and their propaganda thrives upon it. The reason is simple. The town meeting is an obviously respectable institution, glorified by all the reverence men give to the dead. It has acquired the seal of an admired past, and any proposal that can borrow that seal can borrow that reverence too. A name trails behind it an army of associations. That army will fight in any cause that bears the name. So the reformers of California, the Lorimerites of Chicago, and the Barnes Republicans of Albany all use the name of Lincoln for their political associations. In the struggle that preceded the Republican Convention of 1912 it was rumored that the Taft reactionaries would put forward Lincoln's son as chairman of the convention in order to counteract Roosevelt's claim that he stood in Lincoln's shoes.

Casuistry is nothing but the injection of your own meaning into an old name. At school when the teacher asked us whether we had studied the lesson, the invariable answer was Yes. We had indeed stared at the page for a few minutes, and that could be called studying. Sometimes the head-master would break into the room just in time to see the conclusion of a scuffle. Jimmy's clothes are white with dust. "Johnny, did you throw chalk at Jimmy?" "No, sir," says Johnny, and then under his breath to placate God's penchant for truth, "I threw the chalk-eraser." Once in Portland, Maine, I ordered iced tea at an hotel. The waitress brought me a glass of yellowish liquid with a two-inch collar of foam at the top. No tea I had ever seen outside of a prohibition state looked like that. Though it was tea, it might have been beer. Perhaps if I had smiled or winked in ordering the tea, it would have been beer. The two looked alike in Portland; they were interchangeable. You could drink tea and fool yourself into thinking it was beer. You could drink beer and pass for a tea-toper.

It is rare, I think, that the fraud is so genial and so deliberate. The openness cleanses it. Advertising, for example, would be nothing but gigantic and systematic lying if almost everybody didn't know that it was. Yet it runs into the sinister all the time. The pure food agitation is largely an effort to make the label and the contents tell the same story. It was noteworthy that, following the discovery of salvarsan or "606" by Dr. Ehrlich, the quack doctors began to call their treatments "606." But the deliberate casuistry of lawyers, quacks, or politicians is not so difficult to deal with. The very deliberation makes it easier to detect, for it is generally awkward. What one man can consciously devise, other men can understand.

But unconscious casuistry deceives us all. No one escapes it entirely. A wealth of evidence could be adduced to support this from the studies of dreams and fantasies made by the Freudian school of psychologists. They have shown how constantly the mind cloaks a deep meaning in a shallow incident—how the superficial is all the time being shoved into the light of consciousness in order to conceal a buried intention; how inveterate is our use of symbols.

Between ourselves and our real natures we interpose that wax figure of idealizations and selections which we call our character. We extend this into all our thinking. Between us and the realities of social life we build up a mass of generalizations, abstract ideas, ancient glories, and personal wishes. They simplify and soften experience. It is so much easier to talk of poverty than to think of the poor, to argue the rights of capital than to see its results. Pretty soon we come to think of the theories and abstract ideas as things in themselves. We worry about their fate and forget their original content.

For words, theories, symbols, slogans, abstractions of all kinds are nothing but the porous vessels into which life flows, is contained for a time, and then passes through. But our reverence clings to the vessels. The old meaning may have disappeared, a new one come in—no matter, we try to believe there has been no change. And when life's expansion demands some new container, nothing is more difficult than the realization that the old vessels cannot be stretched to the present need.

It is interesting to notice how in the very act of analyzing it I have fallen into this curious and ancient habit. My point is that the metaphor is taken for the reality: I have used at least six metaphors to state it. Abstractions are not cloaks, nor wax figures, nor walls, nor vessels, and life doesn't flow like water. What they really are you and I know inwardly by using abstractions and living our lives. But once I attempt to give that inwardness expression, I must use the only weapons I have—abstractions, theories, phrases. By an effort of the sympathetic imagination you can revive within yourself something of my inward sense. As I have had to abstract from life in order to communicate, so you are compelled to animate my abstractions, in order to understand.

I know of no other method of communication between two people. Language is always grossly inadequate. It is inadequate if the listener is merely passive, if he falls into the mistake of the literal-minded who expect words to contain a precise image of reality. They never do. All language can achieve is to act as a guidepost to the imagination enabling the reader to recreate the author's insight. The artist does that: he controls his medium so that we come most readily to the heart of his intention. In the lyric poet the control is often so delicate that the hearer lives over again the finely shaded mood of the poet. Take the words of a lyric for what they say, and they say nothing most of the time. And that is true of philosophers. You must penetrate the ponderous vocabulary, the professional cant to the insight beneath or you scoff at the mountain ranges of words and phrases. It is this that Bergson means when he tells us that a philosopher's intuition always outlasts his system. Unless you get at that you remain forever foreign to the thinker.

That too is why debating is such a wretched amusement and most partisanship, most controversy, so degrading. The trick here is to argue from the opponent's language, never from his insight. You take him literally, you pick up his sentences, and you show what nonsense they are. You do not try to weigh what you see against what he sees; you contrast what you see with what he says. So debating becomes a way of confirming your own prejudices; it is never, never in any debate I have suffered through, a search for understanding from the angles of two differing insights.

And, of course, in those more sinister forms of debating, court trials, where the stakes are so much bigger, the skill of a successful lawyer is to make the atmosphere as opaque as possible to the other lawyer's contention. Men have been hanged as a result. How often in a political campaign does a candidate suggest that behind the platforms and speeches of his opponents there might be some new and valuable understanding of the country's need?

The Walter Lippmann Reader

The fact is that we argue and quarrel an enormous lot over words. Our prevailing habit is to think about phrases, "ideals," theories, not about the realities they express. In controversy we do not try to find our opponent's meaning: we examine his vocabulary. And in our own efforts to shape policies we do not seek out what is worth doing: we seek out what will pass for moral, practical, popular or constitutional.

In this the Vice Commission reflected our national habits. For those earnest men and women in Chicago did not set out to find a way of abolishing prostitution; they set out to find a way that would conform to four idols they worshiped. The only cure for prostitution might prove to be "immoral," "impractical," unconstitutional, and unpopular. I suspect that it is. But the honest thing to do would have been to look for that cure without preconceived notions. Having found it, the Commission could then have said to the public: "This is what will cure the social evil. It means these changes in industry, sex relations, law and public opinion. If you think it is worth the cost you can begin to deal with the problem. If you don't, then confess that you will not abolish prostitution, and turn your compassion to softening its effects."

That would have left the issues clear and wholesome. But the procedure of the Commission is a blow to honest thinking. Its conclusions may "square with the public conscience of the American people" but they will not square with the intellectual conscience of anybody. To tell you at the top of the page that absolute annihilation of prostitution is the ultimate ideal and twenty lines further on that the method must be constitutional is nothing less than an insult to the intelligence. Calf-worship was never more idolatrous than this. Truth would have slept more comfortably in Procrustes' bed.

Let no one imagine that I take the four preconceived ideas of the Commission too seriously. On the first reading of the report they aroused no more interest in me than the ordinary lip-honor we all do to conventionality—I had heard of the great fearlessness of this report, and I supposed that this bending of the knee was nothing but the innocent hypocrisy of the reformer who wants to make his proposal not too shocking. But it was a mistake. Those four idols really dominated the minds of the Commission, and without them the report cannot be understood. They are typical idols of the American people. This report offers an opportunity to see the concrete results of worshiping them.

The Walter Lippmann Reader

A valuable contribution, then, must be moral. There is no doubt that the Commission means sexually moral. We Americans always use the word in that limited sense. If you say that Jones is a moral man you mean that he is faithful to his wife. He may support her by selling pink pills; he is nevertheless moral if he is monogamous. The average American rarely speaks of industrial piracy as immoral. He may condemn it, but not with that word. If he extends the meaning of immoral at all, it is to the vices most closely allied to sex—drink and gambling.

Now sexual morality is pretty clearly defined for the Commission. As we have seen, it means that sex must be confined to procreation by a healthy, intelligent and strictly monogamous couple. All other sexual expression would come under the ban of disapproval. I am sure I do the Commission no injustice. Now this limited conception of sex has had a disastrous effect: it has forced the Commission to ignore the sexual impulse in discussing a sexual problem. Any modification of the relationship of men and women was immediately put out of consideration. Such suggestions as Forel, Ellen Key, or Havelock Ellis make could, of course, not even get a hearing.

With this moral ideal in mind, not only vice, but sex itself, becomes an evil thing. Hence the hysterical and minute application of the taboo wherever sex shows itself. Barred from any reform which would reabsorb the impulse into civilized life, the Commissioners had no other course but to hunt it, as an outlaw. And in doing this they were compelled to discard the precious values of art, religion and social life of which this superfluous energy is the creator. Driven to think of it as bad, except for certain particular functions, they could, of course, not see its possibilities. Hence the poverty of their suggestions along educational and artistic lines.

A valuable contribution, we are told, must be *reasonable* and *practical*. Here is a case where words cannot be taken literally. "Reasonable" in America certainly never even pretended to mean in accordance with a rational ideal, and "practical,"—well one thinks of "practical politics," "practical business men," and "unpractical reformers." Boiled down these words amount to something like this: the proposals must not be new or startling; must not involve any radical disturbance of any respectable person's selfishness; must not call forth any great opposition; must look definite and immediate; must be tangible like a raid, or a jail, or the paper of an ordinance, or a policeman's club. Above all a "reasonable and practical" proposal must not require any imaginative patience. The actual proposals have all these qualities: if they are "reasonable and practical" then we know by a good demonstration what these terms meant to that average body of citizens.

To see that is to see exposed an important facet of the American temperament. Our dislike of "talk"; the frantic desire to "do something" without inquiring whether it is worth doing; the dollar standard; the unwillingness to cast any bread upon the waters; our preference for a sparrow in the hand to a forest of song-birds; the naïve inability to understand the inner satisfactions of bankrupt poets and the unworldliness of eccentric thinkers; success-mania; philistinism—they are pieces of the same cloth. They come from failure or unwillingness to project the mind beyond the daily routine of things, to play over the whole horizon of possibilities, and to recognize that all is not said when we have spoken. In those words "reasonable and practical" is the Chinese Wall of America, that narrow boundary which contracts our vision to the moment, cuts us off from the culture of the world, and makes us such provincial, unimaginative blunderers over our own problems. Fixation upon the immediate has made a rich country poor in leisure, has in a land meant for liberal living incited an insane struggle for existence. One suspects at times that our national cult of optimism is no real feeling that the world is good, but a fear that pessimism will produce panics.

How this fascination of the obvious has balked the work of the Commission I need not elaborate. That the long process of civilizing sex received perfunctory attention; that the imaginative value of sex was lost in a dogma; that the implied changes in social life were dodged—all that has been pointed out. It was the inability to rise above the immediate that makes the report read as if the policeman were the only agent of civilization.

For where in the report is any thorough discussion by sociologists of the relations of business and marriage to vice? Why is there no testimony by psychologists to show how sex can be affected by environment, by educators to show how it can be trained, by industrial experts to show how monotony and fatigue affect it? Where are the detailed proposals by specialists, for decent housing and working conditions, for educational reform, for play facilities? The Commission wasn't afraid of details: didn't it recommend searchlights in the parks as a weapon against vice? Why then isn't there a budget, a large, comprehensive budget, precise and informing, in which provision is made for beginning to civilize Chicago? That wouldn't have been "reasonable and practical," I presume, for it would have cost millions and millions of dollars. And where would the money have come from? Were the single-taxers, the

Socialists consulted? But their proposals would require big changes in property interests, and would that be "reasonable and practical"? Evidently not: it is more reasonable and practical to keep park benches out of the shadows and to plague unescorted prostitutes.

And where are the open questions: the issues that everybody should consider, the problems that scientists should study? I see almost no trace of them. Why are the sexual problems not even stated? Where are the doubts that should have honored these investigations, the frank statement of all the gaps in knowledge, and the obscurities in morals? Knowing perfectly well that vice will not be repressed within a year or prostitution absolutely annihilated in ten, it might, I should think, have seemed more important that the issues be made clear and the thought of the people fertilized than that the report should look very definite and precise. There are all sorts of things we do not understand about this problem. The opportunities for study which the Commissioners had must have made these empty spaces evident. Why then were we not taken into their confidence? Along what lines is investigation most needed? To what problems, what issues, shall we give our attention? What is the debatable ground in this territory? The Commission does not say, and I for one, ascribe the silence to the American preoccupation with immediate, definite, tangible interests.

Wells has written penetratingly about this in "The New Machiavelli." I have called this fixation on the nearest object at hand an American habit. Perhaps as Mr. Wells shows it is an English one too. But in this country we have a philosophy to express it—the philosophy of the Reasonable and the Practical, and so I do not hesitate to import Mr. Wells's observations: "It has been the chronic mistake of statecraft and all organizing spirits to attempt immediately to scheme and arrange and achieve. Priests, schools of thought, political schemers, leaders of men, have always slipped into the error of assuming that they can think out the whole—or at any rate completely think out definite parts—of the purpose and future of man, clearly and finally; they have set themselves to legislate and construct on that assumption, and, experiencing the perplexing obduracy and evasions of reality, they have taken to dogma, persecution, training, pruning, secretive education; and all the stupidities of self-sufficient energy. In the passion of their good intentions they have not hesitated to conceal facts, suppress thought, crush disturbing initiatives and apparently detrimental desires. And so it is blunderingly and wastefully, destroying with the making, that any extension of social organization is at present achieved.

The Walter Lippmann Reader

Directly, however, this idea of an emancipation from immediacy is grasped, directly the dominating importance of this critical, less personal, mental hinterland in the individual and of the collective mind in the race is understood, the whole problem of the statesman and his attitude toward politics gains a new significance, and becomes accessible to a new series of solutions...."

Let no one suppose that the unwillingness to cultivate what Mr. Wells calls the "mental hinterland" is a vice peculiar to the business man. The colleges submit to it whenever they concentrate their attention on the details of the student's vocation before they have built up some cultural background. The whole drift towards industrial training in schools has the germs of disaster within it—a preoccupation with the technique of a career. I am not a lover of the "cultural" activities of our schools and colleges, still less am I a lover of shallow specialists. The unquestioned need for experts in politics is full of the very real danger that detailed preparation may give us a bureaucracy—a government by men divorced from human tradition. The churches submit to the demand for immediacy with great alacrity. Look at the so-called "liberal" churches. Reacting against an empty formalism they are tumbling over themselves to prove how directly they touch daily life. You read glowing articles in magazines about preachers who devote their time to housing reforms, milk supplies, the purging of the civil service. If you lament the ugliness of their churches, the poverty of the ritual, and the political absorption of their sermons, you are told that the church must abandon forms and serve the common life of men. There are many ways of serving everyday needs,—turning churches into social reform organs and political rostra is, it seems to me, an obvious but shallow way of performing that service. When churches cease to paint the background of our lives, to nourish a Weltanschauung, strengthen men's ultimate purposes and reaffirm the deepest values of life, then churches have ceased to meet the needs for which they exist. That "hinterland" affects daily life, and the church which cannot get a leverage on it by any other method than entering into immediate political controversy is simply a church that is dead. It may be an admirable agent of reform, but it has ceased to be a church.

A large wing of the Socialist Party is the slave of obvious success. It boasts that it has ceased to be "visionary" and has become "practical." Votes, winning campaigns, putting through reform measures seem a great achievement. It forgets the difference between voting the Socialist ticket and understanding Socialism. The vote is the tangible thing, and for that these Socialist politicians work. They get the votes,

The Walter Lippmann Reader

enough to elect them to office. In the City of Schenectady that happened as a result of the mayoralty campaign of 1911. I had an opportunity to observe the results. A few Socialists were in office set to govern a city with no Socialist "hinterland." It was a pathetic situation, for any reform proposal had to pass the judgment of men and women who did not see life as the officials did. On no important measure could the administration expect popular understanding. What was the result? In crucial issues, like taxation, the Socialists had to submit to the ideas,—the general state of mind of the community. They had to reverse their own theories and accept those that prevailed in that unconverted city. I wondered over our helplessness, for I was during a period one of those officials. The other members of the administration used to say at every opportunity that we were fighting "The Beast" or "Special Privilege." But to me it always seemed that we were like Peer Gynt struggling against the formless Boyg—invisible yet everywhere—we were struggling with the unwatered hinterland of the citizens of Schenectady. I understood then, I think, what Wells meant when he said that he wanted "no longer to 'fix up,' as people say, human affairs, but to devote his forces to the development of that needed intellectual life without which all his shallow attempts at fixing up are futile." For in the last analysis the practical and the reasonable are little idols of clay that thwart our efforts.

The third requirement of a valuable contribution, says the Chicago Commission, is the constitutional sanction. This idol carries its own criticism with it. The worship of the constitution amounts, of course, to saying that men exist for the sake of the constitution. The person who holds fast to that idea is forever incapable of understanding either men or constitutions. It is a prime way of making laws ridiculous; if you want to cultivate *lèse-majesté* in Germany get the Kaiser to proclaim his divine origin; if you want to promote disrespect of the courts, announce their infallibility.

But in this case, the Commission is not representative of the dominant thought of our times. The vital part of the population has pretty well emerged from any dumb acquiescence in constitutions. Theodore Roosevelt, who reflects so much of America, has very definitely cast down this idol. Now since he stands generally some twenty years behind the pioneer and about six months ahead of the majority, we may rest assured that this much-needed iconoclasm is in process of achievement.

Closely related to the constitution and just as decadent to-day are the Sanctity of Private Property, Vested Rights, Competition the Life of Trade, Prosperity (at any

94

cost). Each one of these ideas was born of an original need, served its historical function and survived beyond its allotted time. Nowadays you still come across some of these ancient notions, especially in courts, where they do no little damage in perverting justice, but they are ghost-like and disreputable, gibbering and largely helpless. He who is watching the ascendant ideas of American life can afford to feel that the early maxims of capitalism are doomed.

But the habit of mind which would turn an instrument of life into an immutable law of its existence—that habit is always with us. We may outgrow our adoration of the Constitution or Private Property only to establish some new totem pole. In the arts we call this inveterate tendency classicalism. It is, of course, a habit by no means confined to the arts. Politics, religion, science are subject to it,—in politics we call it conservative, in religion orthodox, in science we describe it as academic. Its manifestations are multiform but they have a common source. An original creative impulse of the mind expresses itself in a certain formula; posterity mistakes the formula for the impulse. A genius will use his medium in a particular way because it serves his need; this way becomes a fixed rule which the classicalist serves. It has been pointed out that because the first steam trains were run on roads built for carts and coaches, the railway gauge almost everywhere in the world became fixed at four feet eight and one-half inches.

You might say that genius works inductively and finds a method; the conservative works deductively from the method and defeats whatever genius he may have. A friend of mine had written a very brilliant article on a play which had puzzled New York. Some time later I was discussing the article with another friend of a decidedly classicalist bent. "What is it?" he protested, "it isn't criticism for it's half rhapsody; it isn't rhapsody because it is analytical.... What is it? That's what I want to know." "But isn't it fine, and worth having, and aren't you glad it was written?" I pleaded. "Well, if I knew what it was...." And so the argument ran for hours. Until he had subsumed the article under certain categories he had come to accept, appreciation was impossible for him. I have many arguments with my classicalist friend. This time it was about George Moore's "Ave." I was trying to express my delight. "It isn't a novel, or an essay, or a real confession—it's nothing," said he. His well-ordered mind was compelled to throw out of doors any work for which he had no carefully prepared pocket. I thought of Aristotle, who denied the existence of a mule because it was neither a horse nor an ass.

The Walter Lippmann Reader

Dramatic critics follow Aristotle in more ways than one. A play is produced which fascinates an audience for weeks. It is published and read all over the world. Then you are treated to endless discussions by the critics trying to prove that "it is not a play." So-and-so-and-so constitute a play, they affirm,—this thing doesn't meet the requirements, so away with it. They forget that nobody would have had the slightest idea what a play was if plays hadn't been written; that the rules deduced from the plays that have already been written are no eternal law for the plays that will be.

Classicalism and invention are irreconcilable enemies. Let it be understood that I am not decrying the great nourishment which a living tradition offers. The criticism I am making is of those who try to feed upon the husks alone. Without the slightest paradox one may say that the classicalist is most foreign to the classics. He does not put himself within the creative impulses of the past: he is blinded by their manifestations. It is perhaps no accident that two of the greatest classical scholars in England—Gilbert Murray and Alfred Zimmern—are political radicals. The man whom I call here the classicalist cannot possibly be creative, for the essence of his creed is that there must be nothing new under the sun.

The United States, you imagine, would of all nations be the freest from classicalism. Settled as a great adventure and dedicated to an experiment in republicanism, the tradition of the country is of extending boundaries, obstacles overcome, and pioneering exploits in which a wilderness was subdued to human uses. The very air of America would seem to be a guarantee against formalism. You would think that self-government finds its surest footing here—that real autonomy of the spirit which makes human uses the goal of effort, denies all inhuman ideals, seeks out what men want, and proceeds to create it. With such a history how could a nation fail to see in its constitution anything but a tool of life, like the axe, the spade or the plough?

The West has in a measure carried its freedom over into politics and social life generally. Formalism sets in as you move east and south into the older and more settled communities. There the pioneering impulse has passed out of life into stupid history books, and the inevitable classicalism, the fear of adventure, the superstition before social invention, have reasserted themselves. If I may turn for a moment from description to prophecy, it is to say that this equilibrium will not hold for very long. There are signs that the West after achieving the reforms which it needs to-day—reforms which will free its economic life from the credit monopolies of the East, and give it a greater fluidity in the marketing of its products—will follow the way of all agricultural communities to a rural and placid conservatism. The spirit of the pioneer does not survive forever: it is kept alive to-day, I believe, by certain unnatural irritants which may be summed up as absentee ownership. The West is suffering from foreignly owned railroads, power-resources, and an alien credit control. But once it recaptures these essentials of its economic life, once the "progressive" movement is victorious, I venture to predict that the agricultural West will become the heart of American complacency. The East, on the other hand, with its industrial problem must go to far more revolutionary measures for a solution. And the East is fertilized continually by European traditions: that stream of immigration brings with it a thousand unforeseeable possibilities. The great social adventure of America is no longer the conquest of the wilderness but the absorption of fifty different peoples. To-day perhaps, it is still predominantly a question for the East. But it means that America is turning from the contrast between her courage and nature's obstacles to a comparison of her civilization with Europe's. Immigration more than anything else is drawing us into world problems. Many people profess to see horrible dangers in the foreign invasion. Certainly no man is sure of its conclusion. It may swamp us, it may, if we seize the opportunity, mean the impregnation of our national life with a new brilliancy.

I have said that the West is still moved by the tapering impulse of the pioneer, and I have ventured to predict that this would soon dwindle into an agricultural toryism. That prediction may very easily be upset. Far-reaching mechanical inventions already threaten to transform farming into an industry. I refer to those applications of power to agriculture which will inevitably divorce the farmer from the ownership of his tools. An industrial revolution analogous to that in manufacture during the nineteenth century is distinctly probable, and capitalistic agriculture may soon cease to be a contradiction in terms. Like all inventions it will disturb deeply the classicalist tendency, and this disturbance may generate a new impulse to replace the decadent one of the pioneer.

Without some new dynamic force America, for all her tradition, is not immune to a hardening formalism. The psychological descent into classicalism is always a strong possibility. That is why we, the children of frontiersmen, city builders and immigrants, surprise Europe constantly with our worship of constitutions, our social and political timidity. In many ways we are more defenceless against these deadening habits than the people of Europe. Our geographical isolation preserves us from any vivid sense of national contrast: our imaginations are not stirred by different civilizations. We have almost no spiritual weapons against classicalism: universities, churches, newspapers are by-products of a commercial success; we have no tradition of intellectual revolt. The American college student has the gravity and mental habits of a Supreme Court judge; his "wild oats" are rarely spiritual; the critical, analytical habit of mind is distrusted. We say that "knocking" is a sign of the "sorehead" and we sublimate criticism by saying that "every knock is a boost." America does not play with ideas; generous speculation is regarded as insincere, and shunned as if it might endanger the optimism which underlies success. All this becomes such an insulation against new ideas that when the Yankee goes abroad he takes his environment with him.

It seems at times as if our capacity for appreciating originality were absorbed in the trivial eccentricities of fads and fashions. The obvious novelties of machinery and locomotion, phonographs and yellow journalism slake the American thirst for creation pretty thoroughly. In serious matters we follow the Vice Commission's fourth essential of a valuable contribution—*that which will square with the public conscience of the American people.*

I do not care to dilate upon the exploded pretensions of Mr. and Mrs. Grundy. They are a fairly disreputable couple by this time because we are beginning to know how much morbidity they represent. The Vice Commission, for example, bowed to what might be called the "instinctive conscience" of America when it balked at tracing vice to its source in the over-respected institutions of American life and the over-respected natures of American men and women. It bowed to the prevailing conscience when it proposed taboos instead of radical changes. It bowed to a traditional conscience when it confused the sins of sex with the possibilities of sex; and it paid tribute to a verbal conscience, to a lip morality, when, with extreme irrelevance to its beloved police, it proclaimed "absolute annihilation" the ultimate ideal. In brief, the commission failed to see that the working conscience of America is to-day bound up with the very evil it is supposed to eradicate by a relentless warfare.

It was to be expected. Our conscience is not the vessel of eternal verities. It grows with our social life, and a new social condition means a radical change in conscience. In order to do away with vice America must live and think and feel differently. This is an old story. Because of it all innovators have been at war with the public conscience of their time. Yet there is nothing strange or particularly disheartening about this commonplace observation: to expect anything else is to

The Walter Lippmann Reader

hope that a nation will lift itself by its own bootstraps. Yet there is danger the moment leaders of the people make a virtue of homage to the unregenerate, public conscience.

In La Follette's Magazine (Feb. 17, 1912) there is a leading article called "The Great Issue." You can read there that "the composite judgment is always safer and wiser and stronger and more unselfish than the judgment of any one individual mind. The people have been betrayed by their representatives again and again. The real danger to democracy lies not in the ignorance or want of patriotism of the people, but in the corrupting influence of powerful business organizations upon the representatives of the people...."

I have only one quarrel with that philosophy—its negativity. With the belief that government is futile and mischievous unless supported by the mass of the people; with the undeniable fact that business has corrupted public officials—I have no complaint. What I object to is the emphasis which shifts the blame for our troubles from the shoulders of the people to those of the "corrupting interests." For this seems to me nothing but the resuscitation of the devil: when things go wrong it is somebody else's fault. We are peculiarly open to this kind of vanity in America. If some wise law is passed we say it is the will of the people showing its power of self-government. But if that will is so weak and timid that a great evil like child labor persists to our shame we turn the responsibility over to the devil personified as a "special interest." It is an old habit of the race which seems to have begun with the serpent in the Garden of Eden.

The word demagogue has been frightfully maltreated in late years, but surely here is its real meaning—to flatter the people by telling them that their failures are somebody else's fault. For if a nation declares it has reached its majority by instituting self-government, then it cannot shirk responsibility.

These "special interests"—big business, a corrupt press, crooked politics—grew up within the country, were promoted by American citizens, admired by millions of them, and acquiesced in by almost all of them. Whoever thinks that business corruption is the work of a few inhumanly cunning individuals with monstrous morals is self-righteous without excuse. Capitalists did not violate the public conscience of America; they expressed it. That conscience was inadequate and unintelligent. We are being pinched by the acts it nourished. A great outcry has arisen and a number of perfectly conventional men like Lorimer suffer an undeserved humiliation. We say it is a "moral awakening." That is another dodge by which we pretend that we were always wise and just, though a trifle sleepy. In reality we are witnessing a change of conscience, initiated by cranks and fanatics, sustained for a long time by minorities, which has at last infected the mass of the people.

The danger I spoke of arises just here: the desire to infect at once the whole mass crowds out the courage of the innovator. No man can do his best work if he bows at every step to the public conscience of his age. The real service to democracy is the fullest, freest expression of talent. The best servants of the people, like the best valets, must whisper unpleasant truths in the master's ear. It is the court fool, not the foolish courtier, whom the king can least afford to lose.

Hostile critics of democracy have long pointed out that mediocrity becomes the rule. They have not been without facts for their support. And I do not see why we who believe in democracy should not recognize this danger and trace it to its source. Certainly it is not answered with a sneer. I have worked in the editorial office of a popular magazine, a magazine that is known widely as a champion of popular rights. By personal experience, by intimate conversations, and by looking about, I think I am pretty well aware of what the influence of business upon journalism amounts to. I have seen the inside working of business pressure; articles of my own have been suppressed after they were in type; friends of mine have told me stories of expurgation, of the "morganization" of their editorial policy. And in the face of that I should like to record it as my sincere conviction that no financial power is one-tenth so corrupting, so insidious, so hostile to originality and frank statement as the fear of the public which reads the magazine. For one item suppressed out of respect for a railroad or a bank, nine are rejected because of the prejudices of the public. This will anger the farmers, that will arouse the Catholics, another will shock the summer girl. Anybody can take a fling at poor old Mr. Rockefeller, but the great mass of average citizens (to which none of us belongs) must be left in undisturbed possession of its prejudices. In that subservience, and not in the meddling of Mr. Morgan, is the reason why American journalism is so flaccid, so repetitious and so dull.

The people should be supreme, yes, its will should be the law of the land. But it is a caricature of democracy to make it also the law of individual initiative. One thing it is to say that all proposals must ultimately win the acceptance of the majority; it is quite another to propose nothing which is not immediately acceptable. It is as true of the nation as of the body that one leg cannot go forward very far unless the whole body follows. That is a different thing from trying to move both legs forward at the same time. The one is democracy; the other is—demolatry.

It is better to catch the idol-maker than to smash each idol. It would be an endless task to hunt down all the masks, the will-o'-the-wisps and the shadows which divert us from our real purpose. Each man carries within himself the cause of his own mirages. Whenever we accept an idea as authority instead of as instrument, an idol is set up. We worship the plough, and not the fruit. And from this habit there is no permanent escape. Only effort can keep the mind centered truly. Whenever criticism slackens, whenever we sink into acquiescence, the mind swerves aside and clings with the gratitude of the weary to some fixed idea. It is so much easier to follow a rule of thumb, and obey the constitution, than to find out what we really want and to do it.

A great deal of political theory has been devoted to asking: what is the aim of government? Many readers may have wondered why that question has not figured in these pages. For the logical method would be to decide upon the ultimate ideal of statecraft and then elaborate the technique of its realization. I have not done that because this rational procedure inverts the natural order of things and develops all kinds of theoretical tangles and pseudo-problems. They come from an effort to state abstractly in intellectual terms qualities that can be known only by direct experience. You achieve nothing but confusion if you begin by announcing that politics must achieve "justice" or "liberty" or "happiness." Even though you are perfectly sure that you know exactly what these words mean translated into concrete experiences, it is very doubtful whether you can really convey your meaning to anyone else. "Plaisante justice qu'une rivière borne. Vérité, au deçà des Pyrénées, erreur au de là," says Pascal. If what is good in the world depended on our ability to define it we should be hopeless indeed.

This is an old difficulty in ethics. Many men have remarked that we quarrel over the "problem of evil," never over the "problem of good." That comes from the fact that good is a quality of experience which does not demand an explanation. When we are thwarted we begin to ask why. It was the evil in the world that set Leibniz the task of justifying the ways of God to man. Nor is it an accident that in daily life misfortune turns men to philosophy. One might generalize and say that as soon as we begin to explain, it is because we have been made to complain.

The Walter Lippmann Reader

No moral judgment can decide the value of life. No ethical theory can announce any intrinsic good. The whole speculation about morality is an effort to find a way of living which men who live it will instinctively feel is good. No formula can express an ultimate experience; no axiom can ever be a substitute for what really makes life worth living. Plato may describe the objects which man rejoices over, he may guide them to good experiences, but each man in his inward life is a last judgment on all his values.

This amounts to saying that the goal of action is in its final analysis æsthetic and not moral—a quality of feeling instead of conformity to rule. Words like justice, harmony, power, democracy are simply empirical suggestions which may produce the good life. If the practice of them does not produce it then we are under no obligation to follow them, we should be idolatrous fools to do so. Every abstraction, every rule of conduct, every constitution, every law and social arrangement, is an instrument that has no value in itself. Whatever credit it receives, whatever reverence we give it, is derived from its utility in ministering to those concrete experiences which are as obvious and as undefinable as color or sound. We can celebrate the positively good things, we can live them, we can create them, but we cannot philosophize about them. To the anæsthetic intellect we could not convey the meaning of joy. A creature that could reason but not feel would never know the value of life, for what is ultimate is in itself inexplicable.

Politics is not concerned with prescribing the ultimate qualities of life. When it tries to do so by sumptuary legislation, nothing but mischief is invoked. Its business is to provide opportunities, not to announce ultimate values; to remove oppressive evil and to invent new resources for enjoyment. With the enjoyment itself it can have no concern. That must be lived by each individual. In a sense the politician can never know his own success, for it is registered in men's inner lives, and is largely incommunicable. An increasing harvest of rich personalities is the social reward for a fine statesmanship, but such personalities are free growths in a cordial environment. They cannot be cast in moulds or shaped by law. There is no need, therefore, to generate dialectical disputes about the final goal of politics. No definition can be just—too precise a one can only deceive us into thinking that our definition is true. Call ultimate values by any convenient name, it is of slight importance which you choose. If only men can keep their minds freed from formalism, idol worship, fixed ideas, and exalted abstractions, politicians need not worry about the language in which the end of our striving is expressed. For with the removal of distracting idols, man's experience becomes the center of thought. And if we think in terms of men, find out what really bothers them, seek to supply what they really want, hold only their experience sacred, we shall find our sanction obvious and unchallenged.

The Making of Creeds

My first course in philosophy was nothing less than a summary of the important systems of thought put forward in Western Europe during the last twenty-six hundred years. Perhaps that is a slight exaggeration—we did gloss over a few centuries in the Middle Ages. For the rest we touched upon all the historic names from Thales to Nietzsche. After about nine weeks of this bewildering transit a friend approached me with a sour look on his face. "You know," he said, "I can't make head or tail out of this business. I agree with each philosopher as we study him. But when we get to the next one, I agree with him too. Yet he generally says the other one was wrong. They can't all be right. Can they now?" I was too much puzzled with the same difficulty to help him.

Somewhat later I began to read the history of political theories. It was a less disinterested study than those sophomore speculations, for I had jumped into a profession which carried me through some of the underground passages of "practical politics" and reformist groups. The tangle of motives and facts and ideas was incredible. I began to feel the force of Mr. John Hobson's remark that "if practical workers for social and industrial reforms continue to ignore principles ... they will have to pay the price which short-sighted empiricism always pays; with slow, hesitant, and staggering steps, with innumerable false starts and backslidings, they will move in the dark along an unseen track toward an unseen goal." The political theorists laid some claim to lighting up both the track and the goal, and so I turned to them for help.

Now whoever has followed political theory will have derived perhaps two convictions as a reward. Almost all the thinkers seem to regard their systems as true and binding, and none of these systems are. No matter which one you examine, it is inadequate. You cannot be a Platonist or a Benthamite in politics to-day. You cannot go to any of the great philosophers even for the outlines of a statecraft which shall be fairly complete, and relevant to American life. I returned to the sophomore mood: "Each of these thinkers has contributed something, has had some wisdom about events. Looked at in bulk the philosophers can't all be right or all wrong."

But like so many theoretical riddles, this one rested on a very simple piece of ignorance. The trouble was that without realizing it I too had been in search of the philosopher's stone. I too was looking for something that could not be found. That happened in this case to be nothing less than an absolutely true philosophy of politics. It was the old indolence of hoping that somebody had done the world's thinking once and for all. I had conjured up the fantasy of a system which would contain the whole of life, be as reliable as a table of logarithms, foresee all possible emergencies and offer entirely trustworthy rules of action. When it seemed that no such system had ever been produced, I was on the point of damning the entire tribe of theorists from Plato to Marx.

This is what one may call the naïveté of the intellect. Its hope is that some man living at one place on the globe in a particular epoch will, through the miracle of genius, be able to generalize his experience for all time and all space. It says in effect that there is never anything essentially new under the sun, that any moment of experience sufficiently understood would be seen to contain all history and all destiny—that the intellect reasoning on one piece of experience could know what all the rest of experience was like. Looked at more closely this philosophy means that novelty is an illusion of ignorance, that life is an endless repetition, that when you know one revolution of it, you know all the rest. In a very real sense the world has no history and no future, the race has no career. At any moment everything is given: our reason could know that moment so thoroughly that all the rest of life would be like the commuter's who travels back and forth on the same line every day. There would be no inventions and no discoveries, for in the instant that reason had found the key of experience everything would be unfolded. The present would not be the womb of the future: nothing would be embryonic, nothing would grow. Experience would cease to be an adventure in order to become the monotonous fulfilment of a perfect prophecy.

This omniscience of the human intellect is one of the commonest assumptions in the world. Although when you state the belief as I have, it sounds absurdly pretentious, yet the boastfulness is closer to the child's who stretches out its hand for the moon than the romantic egotist's who thinks he has created the moon and all the stars. Whole systems of philosophy have claimed such an eternal and absolute validity; the nineteenth century produced a bumper crop of so-called atheists, materialists and determinists who believed in all sincerity that "Science" was capable of a complete truth and unfailing prediction. If you want to see this faith in all its naïveté go into those quaint rationalist circles where Herbert Spencer's ghost announces the "laws of life," with only a few inessential details omitted.

The Walter Lippmann Reader

Now, of course, no philosophy of this sort has ever realized such hopes. Mankind has certainly come nearer to justifying Mr. Chesterton's observation that one of its favorite games is called "Cheat the Prophet."... "The players listen very carefully and respectfully to all that the clever men have to say about what is to happen in the next generation. The players then wait until all the clever men are dead, and bury them nicely. They then go and do something else." Now this weakness is not, as Mr. Chesterton would like to believe, confined to the clever men. But it is a weakness, and many people have speculated about it. Why in the face of hundreds of philosophies wrecked on the rocks of the unexpected do men continue to believe that the intellect can transcend the vicissitudes of experience?

For they certainly do believe it, and generally the more parochial their outlook, the more cosmic their pretensions. All of us at times yearn for the comfort of an absolute philosophy. We try to believe that, however finite we may be, our intellect is something apart from the cycle of our life, capable by an Olympian detachment from human interests of a divine thoroughness. Even our evolutionist philosophy, as Bergson shows, "begins by showing us in the intellect a local effect of evolution, a flame, perhaps accidental, which lights up the coming and going of living things in the narrow passage open to their action; and lo! forgetting what it has just told us, makes of this lantern glimmering in a tunnel a Sun which can illuminate the world."

This is what most of us do in our search for a philosophy of politics. We forget that the big systems of theory are much more like village lamp-posts than they are like the sun, that they were made to light up a particular path, obviate certain dangers, and aid a peculiar mode of life. The understanding of the place of theory in life is a comparatively new one. We are just beginning to see how creeds are made. And the insight is enormously fertile. Thus Mr. Alfred Zimmern in his fine study of "The Greek Commonwealth" says of Plato and Aristotle that no interpretation can be satisfactory which does not take into account the impression left upon their minds by the social development which made the age of these philosophers a period of Athenian decline. Mr. Zimmern's approach is common enough in modern scholarship, but the full significance of it for the creeds we ourselves are making is still something of a novelty. When we are asked to think of the "Republic" as the reaction of decadent Greece upon the conservative temperament of Plato, the function of theory is given a new illumination. Political

106

philosophy at once appears as a human invention in a particular crisis—an instrument to fit a need. The pretension to finality falls away.

This is a great emancipation. Instead of clinging to the naïve belief that Plato was legislating for all mankind, you can discuss his plans as a temporary superstructure made for an historical purpose. You are free then to appreciate the more enduring portions of his work, to understand Santayana when he says of the Platonists, "their theories are so extravagant, yet their wisdom seems so great. Platonism is a very refined and beautiful expression of our natural instincts, it embodies conscience and utters our inmost hopes." This insight into the values of human life, partial though it be, is what constitutes the abiding monument of Plato's genius. His constructions, his formal creeds, his law-making and social arrangements are local and temporary—for us they can have only an antiquarian interest.

In some such way as this the sophomoric riddle is answered: no thinker can lay down a course of action for all mankind—programs if they are useful at all are useful for some particular historical period. But if the thinker sees at all deeply into the life of his own time, his theoretical system will rest upon observation of human nature. That remains as a residue of wisdom long after his reasoning and his concrete program have passed into limbo. For human nature in all its profounder aspects changes very little in the few generations since our Western wisdom has come to be recorded. These *aperçus* left over from the great speculations are the golden threads which successive thinkers weave into the pattern of their thought. Wisdom remains; theory passes.

If that is true of Plato with his ample vision how much truer is it of the theories of the littler men—politicians, courtiers and propagandists who make up the academy of politics. Machiavelli will, of course, be remembered at once as a man, whose speculations were fitted to an historical crisis. His advice to the Prince was real advice, not a sermon. A boss was telling a governor how to extend his power. The wealth of Machiavelli's learning and the splendid penetration of his mind are used to interpret experience for a particular purpose. I have always thought that Machiavelli derives his bad name from a too transparent honesty. Less direct minds would have found high-sounding ethical sanctions in which to conceal the real intent. That was the nauseating method of nineteenth century economists when they tried to identify the brutal practices of capitalism with the beneficence of nature and the Will of God. Not so Machiavelli. He could write without a blush that "a prince, especially a new one, cannot observe all those things for which men are esteemed, being often forced, in order to maintain the state, to act contrary to fidelity, friendship, humanity, and religion." The apologists of business also justified a rupture with human decencies. They too fitted their theory to particular purposes, but they had not the courage to avow it even to themselves.

The rare value of Machiavelli is just this lack of self-deception. You may think his morals devilish, but you cannot accuse him of quoting scripture. I certainly do not admire the end he serves: the extension of an autocrat's power is a frivolous perversion of government. His ideal happens, however, to be the aim of most foreign offices, politicians and "princes of finance." Machiavelli's morals are not one bit worse than the practices of the men who rule the world to-day. An American Senate tore up the Hay-Pauncefote treaty, and with the approval of the President acted "contrary to fidelity" and friendship too; Austria violated the Treaty of Berlin by annexing Bosnia and Herzegovina. Machiavelli's ethics are commonplace enough. His head is clearer than the average. He let the cat out of the bag and showed in the boldest terms how theory becomes an instrument of practice. You may take him as a symbol of the political theorist. You may say that all the thinkers of influence have been writing advice to the Prince. Machiavelli recognized Lorenzo the Magnificent; Marx, the proletariat of Europe.

At first this sounds like standing the world on its head, denying reason and morality, and exalting practice over righteousness. That is neither here nor there. I am simply trying to point out an illuminating fact whose essential truth can hardly be disputed. The important social philosophies are consciously or otherwise the servants of men's purposes. Good or bad, that it seems to me is the way we work. We find reasons for what we want to do. The big men from Machiavelli through Rousseau to Karl Marx brought history, logic, science and philosophy to prop up and strengthen their deepest desires. The followers, the epigones, may accept the reasons of Rousseau and Marx and deduce rules of action from them. But the original genius sees the dynamic purpose first, finds reasons afterward. This amounts to saying that man when he is most creative is not a rational, but a wilful animal.

The political thinker who to-day exercises the greatest influence on the Western World is, I suppose, Karl Marx. The socialist movement calls him its prophet, and, while many socialists say he is superseded, no one disputes his historical importance. Now Marx embalmed his thinking in the language of the Hegelian school. He founded it on a general philosophy of society which is known as the materialistic conception of history. Moreover, Marx put forth the claim that he had made socialism "scientific"—had shown that it was woven into the texture of natural phenomena. The Marxian paraphernalia crowds three heavy volumes, so elaborate and difficult that socialists rarely read them. I have known one socialist who lived leisurely on his country estate and claimed to have "looked" at every page of Marx. Most socialists, including the leaders, study selected passages and let it go at that. This is a wise economy based on a good instinct. For all the parade of learning and dialectic is an after-thought—an accident from the fact that the prophetic genius of Marx appeared in Germany under the incubus of Hegel. Marx saw what he wanted to do long before he wrote three volumes to justify it. Did not the Communist Manifesto appear many years before "Das Kapital"?

Nothing is more instructive than a socialist "experience" meeting at which everyone tries to tell how he came to be converted. These gatherings are notoriously untruthful—in fact, there is a genial pleasure in not telling the truth about one's salad days in the socialist movement. The prevalent lie is to explain how the new convert, standing upon a mountain of facts, began to trace out the highways that led from hell to heaven. Everybody knows that no such process was actually lived through, and almost without exception the real story can be discerned: a man was dissatisfied, he wanted a new condition of life, he embraced a theory that would justify his hopes and his discontent. For once you touch the biographies of human beings, the notion that political beliefs are logically determined collapses like a pricked balloon. In the language of philosophers, socialism as a living force is a product of the will—a will to beauty, order, neighborliness, not infrequently a will to health. Men desire first, then they reason; fascinated by the future, they invent a "scientific socialism" to get there.

Many people don't like to admit this. Or if they admit it, they do so with a sigh. Their minds construct a utopia—one in which all judgments are based on logical inference from syllogisms built on the law of mathematical probabilities. If you quote David Hume at them, and say that reason itself is an irrational impulse they think you are indulging in a silly paradox. I shall not pursue this point very far, but I believe it could be shown without too much difficulty that the rationalists are fascinated by a certain kind of thinking—logical and orderly thinking—and that it is their will to impose that method upon other men.

For fear that somebody may regard this as a play on words drawn from some ultra-modern "anti-intellectualist" source, let me quote Santayana. This is what the author of that masterly series "The Life of Reason" wrote in one of his earlier books: "The ideal of rationality is itself as arbitrary, as much dependent on the needs of a finite organization, as any other ideal. Only as ultimately securing tranquillity of mind, which the philosopher instinctively pursues, has it for him any necessity. In spite of the verbal propriety of saying that reason demands rationality, what really demands rationality, what makes it a good and indispensable thing and gives it all its authority, is not its own nature, but our need of it both in safe and economical action and in the pleasures of comprehension." Because rationality itself is a wilful exercise one hears Hymns to Reason and sees it personified as an extremely dignified goddess. For all the light and shadow of sentiment and passion play even about the syllogism.

The attempts of theorists to explain man's successes as rational acts and his failures as lapses of reason have always ended in a dismal and misty unreality. No genuine politician ever treats his constituents as reasoning animals. This is as true of the high politics of Isaiah as it is of the ward boss. Only the pathetic amateur deludes himself into thinking that, if he presents the major and minor premise, the voter will automatically draw the conclusion on election day. The successful politician—good or bad—deals with the dynamics—with the will, the hopes, the needs and the visions of men.

It isn't sentimentality which says that where there is no vision the people perisheth. Every time Tammany Hall sets off fireworks and oratory on the Fourth of July; every time the picture of Lincoln is displayed at a political convention; every red bandanna of the Progressives and red flag of the socialists; every song from "The Battle Hymn of the Republic" to the "International"; every metrical conclusion to a great speech—whether we stand at Armageddon, refuse to press upon the brow of labor another crown of thorns, or call upon the workers of the world to unite—every one of these slogans is an incitement of the will—an effort to energize politics. They are attempts to harness blind impulses to particular purposes. They are tributes to the sound practical sense of a vision in politics. No cause can succeed without them: so long as you rely on the efficacy of "scientific" demonstration and logical proof you can hold your conventions in anybody's back parlor and have room to spare.

I remember an observation that Lincoln Steffens made in a speech about Mayor Tom Johnson. "Tom failed," said Mr. Steffens, "because he was too practical." Coming from a man who had seen as much of actual politics as Mr. Steffens, it puzzled me a great deal. I taxed him with it later and he explained somewhat as follows: "Tom Johnson had a vision of Cleveland which he called The City on the Hill. He pictured the town emancipated from its ugliness and its cruelty—a beautiful city for free men and women. He used to talk of that vision to the 'cabinet' of political lieutenants which met every Sunday night at his house. He had all his appointees working for the City on the Hill. But when he went out campaigning before the people he talked only of three-cent fares and the tax outrages. Tom Johnson didn't show the people the City on the Hill. He didn't take them into his confidence. They never really saw what it was all about. And they went back on Tom Johnson."

That is one of Mr. Steffens's most acute observations. What makes it doubly interesting is that Tom Johnson confirmed it a few months before he died. His friends were telling him that his defeat was temporary, that the work he had begun was unchecked. It was plain that in the midst of his suffering, with death close by, he found great comfort in that assurance. But his mind was so realistic, his integrity so great that he could not blink the fact that there had been a defeat. Steffens was pointing out the explanation: "you did not show the people what you saw, you gave them the details, you fought their battles, you started to build, but you left them in darkness as to the final goal."

I wish I could recall the exact words in which Tom Johnson replied. For in them the greatest of the piecemeal reformers admitted the practical weakness of opportunist politics.

There is a type of radical who has an idea that he can insinuate advanced ideas into legislation without being caught. His plan of action is to keep his real program well concealed and to dole out sections of it to the public from time to time. John A. Hobson in "The Crisis of Liberalism" describes the "practical reformer" so that anybody can recognize him: "This revolt against ideas is carried so far that able men have come seriously to look upon progress as a matter for the manipulation of wire-pullers, something to be 'jobbed' in committee by sophistical notions or other clever trickery." Lincoln Steffens calls these people "our damned rascals." Mr. Hobson continues, "The attraction of some obvious gain, the suppression of some scandalous abuse of monopolist power by a private company, some needed enlargement of existing Municipal or State enterprise by lateral expansion—such are the sole springs of action." Well may Mr. Hobson inquire, "Now, what provision is made for generating the motor power of progress in Collectivism?"

The Walter Lippmann Reader

No amount of architect's plans, bricks and mortar will build a house. Someone must have the wish to build it. So with the modern democratic state. Statesmanship cannot rest upon the good sense of its program. It must find popular feeling, organize it, and make that the motive power of government. If you study the success of Roosevelt the point is re-enforced. He is a man of will in whom millions of people have felt the embodiment of their own will. For a time Roosevelt was a man of destiny in the truest sense. He wanted what a nation wanted: his own power radiated power; he embodied a vision; Tom, Dick and Harry moved with his movement.

No use to deplore the fact. You cannot stop a living body with nothing at all. I think we may picture society as a compound of forces that are always changing. Put a vision in front of one of these currents and you can magnetize it in that direction. For visions alone organize popular passions. Try to ignore them or box them up, and they will burst forth destructively. When Haywood dramatizes the class struggle he uses class resentment for a social purpose. You may not like his purpose, but unless you can gather proletarian power into some better vision, you have no grounds for resenting Haywood. I fancy that the demonstration of King Canute settled once and for all the stupid attempt to ignore a moving force.

A dynamic conception of society always frightens a great number of people. It gives politics a restless and intractable quality. Pure reason is so gentlemanly, but will and the visions of a people—these are adventurous and incalculable forces. Most politicians living for the day prefer to ignore them. If only society will stand fairly still while their career is in the making they are content to avoid the actualities. But a politician with some imaginative interest in genuine affairs need not be seduced into the learned folly of pretending that reality is something else than it is. If he is to influence life he must deal with it. A deep respect is due the Schopenhauerian philosopher who looks upon the world, finds that its essence is evil, and turns towards insensitive calm. But no respect is due to anyone who sets out to reform the world by ignoring its quality. Whoever is bent upon shaping politics to better human uses must accept freely as his starting point the impulses that agitate human beings. If observation shows that reason is an instrument of will, then only confusion can result from pretending that it isn't.

I have called this misplaced "rationality" a piece of learned folly, because it shows itself most dangerously among those thinkers about politics who are divorced from action. In the Universities political movements are generally regarded as essentially

112

static, cut and dried solids to be judged by their logical consistency. It is as if the stream of life had to be frozen before it could be studied. The socialist movement was given a certain amount of attention when I was an undergraduate. The discussion turned principally on two points: were rent, interest and dividends *earned?* Was collective ownership of capital a feasible scheme? And when the professor, who was a good dialectician, had proved that interest was a payment for service ("saving") and that public ownership was not practicable, it was assumed that socialism was disposed of. The passions, the needs, the hopes that generate this world-wide phenomenon were, I believe, pocketed and ignored under the pat saying: "Of course, socialism is not an economic policy, it's a religion." That was the end of the matter for the students of politics. It was then a matter for the divinity schools. If the same scholastic method is in force there, all that would be needed to crush socialism is to show its dogmatic inconsistencies.

The theorist is incompetent when he deals with socialism just because he assumes that men are determined by logic and that a false conclusion will stop a moving, creative force. Occasionally he recognizes the wilful character of politics: then he shakes his head, climbs into an ivory tower and deplores the moonshine, the religious manias and the passions of the mob. Real life is beyond his control and influence because real life is largely agitated by impulses and habits, unconscious needs, faith, hope and desire. With all his learning he is ineffective because, instead of trying to use the energies of men, he deplores them.

Suppose we recognize that creeds are instruments of the will, how would it alter the character of our thinking? Take an ancient quarrel like that over determinism. Whatever your philosophy, when you come to the test of actual facts you find, I think, all grades of freedom and determinism. For certain purposes you believe in free will, for others you do not. Thus, as Mr. Chesterton suggests, no determinist is prevented from saying "if you please" to the housemaid. In love, in your career, you have no doubt that "if" is a reality. But when you are engaged in scientific investigation, you try to reduce the spontaneous in life to a minimum. Mr. Arnold Bennett puts forth a rather curious hybrid when he advises us to treat ourselves as free agents and everyone else as an automaton. On the other hand Prof. Münsterberg has always insisted that in social relations we must always treat everyone as a purposeful, integrated character.

Your doctrine, in short, depends on your purpose: a theory by itself is neither moral nor immoral, its value is conditioned by the purpose it serves. In any accurate sense theory is to be judged only as an effective or ineffective instrument of a desire: the discussion of doctrines is technical and not moral. A theory has no intrinsic value: that is why the devil can talk theology.

No creed possesses any final sanction. Human beings have desires that are far more important than the tools and toys and churches they make to satisfy them. It is more penetrating, in my opinion, to ask of a creed whether it served than whether it was "true." Try to judge the great beliefs that have swayed mankind by their inner logic or their empirical solidity and you stand forever, a dull pedant, apart from the interests of men. The Christian tradition did not survive because of Aquinas or fall before the Higher Criticism, nor will it be revived because someone proves the scientific plausibility of its doctrine. What we need to know about the Christian epic is the effect it had on men—true or false, they have believed in it for nineteen centuries. Where has it helped them, where hindered? What needs did it answer? What energies did it transmute? And what part of mankind did it neglect? Where did it begin to do violence to human nature?

Political creeds must receive the same treatment. The doctrine of the "social contract" formulated by Hobbes and made current by Rousseau can no longer be accepted as a true account of the origin of society. Jean-Jacques is in fact a supreme case—perhaps even a slight caricature—of the way in which formal creeds bolster up passionate wants. I quote from Prof. Walter's introduction in which he says that "The Social Contract *showed to those who were eager to be convinced* that no power was legitimate which was guilty of abuses. It is no wonder that its author was buried in the Pantheon with pompous procession, that the framers of the new Constitution, Thouret and Lièyes and La Fayette, did not forget and dared not forget its doctrines, that it was the text-book and the delight of Camille Desmoulins and Danton and St. Just, that Robespierre read it through once every day." In the perspective of history, no one feels that he has said the last word about a philosophy like Rousseau's after demonstrating its "untruth." Good or bad, it has meant too much for any such easy disposal. What shall we call an idea, objectively untrue, but practically of the highest importance?

The thinker who has faced this difficulty most radically is Georges Sorel in the "Reflexions sur la Violence." His doctrine of the "social myth" has seemed to many commentators one of those silly paradoxes that only a revolutionary syndicalist and Frenchman could have put forward. M. Sorel is engaged in presenting the General Strike as the decisive battle of the class struggle and the core of the socialist movement. Now whatever else he may be, M. Sorel is not naïve: the sharp criticism of other socialists was something he could not peacefully ignore. They told him that the General Strike was an idle dream, that it could never take place, that, even if it could, the results would not be very significant. Sidney Webb, in the customary Fabian fashion, had dismissed the General Strike as a sign of socialist immaturity. There is no doubt that M. Sorel felt the force of these attacks. But he was not ready to abandon his favorite idea because it had been shown to be unreasonable and impossible. Just the opposite effect showed itself and he seized the opportunity of turning an intellectual defeat into a spiritual triumph. This performance must have delighted him to the very bottom of his soul, for he has boasted that his task in life is to aid in ruining "le prestige de la culture bourgeoise."

M. Sorel's defence of the General Strike is very startling. He admits that it may never take place, that it is not a true picture of the goal of the socialist movement. Without a blush he informs us that this central gospel of the working class is simply a "myth." The admission frightens M. Sorel not at all. "It doesn't matter much," he remarks, "whether myths contain details actually destined to realization in the scheme of an historical future; they are not astrological almanacks; it may even be that nothing of what they express will actually happen—as in the case of that catastrophe which the early Christians expected. Are we not accustomed in daily life to recognizing that the reality differs very greatly from the ideas of it that we made before we acted? Yet that doesn't hinder us from making resolutions.... Myths must be judged as instruments for acting upon present conditions; all discussion about the manner of applying them concretely to the course of history is senseless. *The entire myth is what counts*.... There is no use then in reasoning about details which might arise in the midst of the class struggle ... even though the revolutionists should be deceiving themselves through and through in making a fantastic picture of the general strike, this picture would still have been a power of the highest order in preparing for revolution, so long as it expressed completely all the aspirations of socialism and bound together revolutionary ideas with a precision and firmness that no other methods of thought could have given."

It may well be imagined that this highly sophisticated doctrine was regarded as perverse. All the ordinary prejudices of thought are irritated by a thinker who frankly advises masses of his fellow-men to hold fast to a belief which by all the canons of common sense is nothing but an illusion. M. Sorel must have felt the need of closer statement, for in a letter to Daniel Halèvy, published in the second edition, he makes his position much clearer. "Revolutionary myths ..." we read, "enable us to understand the activity, the feelings, and the ideas of a populace preparing to enter into a decisive struggle; *they are not descriptions of things, but expressions of will.*" The italics are mine: they set in relief the insight that makes M. Sorel so important to our discussion. I do not know whether a quotation torn from its context can possibly do justice to its author. I do know that for any real grasp of this point it is necessary to read M. Sorel with great sympathy.

One must grant at least that he has made an accurate observation. The history of the world is full of great myths which have had the most concrete results. M. Sorel cites primitive Christianity, the Reformation, the French Revolution and the Mazzini campaign. The men who took part in those great social movements summed up their aspiration in pictures of decisive battles resulting in the ultimate triumph of their cause. We in America might add an example from our own political life. For it is Theodore Roosevelt who is actually attempting to make himself and his admirers the heroes of a new social myth. Did he not announce from the platform at Chicago—"we stand at Armageddon and we battle for the Lord"?

Let no one dismiss M. Sorel then as an empty paradoxer. The myth is not one of the outgrown crudities of our pagan ancestors. We, in the midst of our science and our rationalism, are still making myths, and their force is felt in the actual affairs of life. They convey an impulse, not a program, nor a plan of reconstruction. Their practical value cannot be ignored, for they embody the motor currents in social life.

Myths are to be judged, as M. Sorel says, by their ability to express aspiration. They stand or fall by that. In such a test the Christian myth, for example, would be valued for its power of incarnating human desire. That it did not do so completely is the cause of its decline. From Aucassin to Nietzsche men have resented it as a partial and stunting dream. It had too little room for profane love, and only by turning the Church of Christ into the Church Militant could the essential Christian passivity obtain the assent of aggressive and masculine races. To-day traditional Christianity has weakened in the face of man's interest in the conquest of this world. The liberal and advanced churches recognize this fact by exhibiting a great preoccupation with everyday affairs. Now they may be doing important service—I have no wish to deny that—but when the Christian Churches turn to civics, to reformism or socialism, they are in fact announcing that the Christian dream is dead. They may continue to practice some of its moral teachings and hold

The Walter Lippmann Reader

to some of its creed, but the Christian impulse is for them no longer active. A new dream, which they reverently call Christian, has sprung from their desires.

During their life these social myths contain a nation's finest energy. It is just because they are "not descriptions of things, but expressions of will" that their influence is so great. Ignore what a man desires and you ignore the very source of his power; run against the grain of a nation's genius and see where you get with your laws. Robert Burns was right when he preferred poetry to charters. The recognition of this truth by Sorel is one of the most impressive events in the revolutionary movement. Standing as a spokesman of an actual social revolt, he has not lost his vision because he understands its function. If Machiavelli is a symbol of the political theorist making reason an instrument of purpose, we may take Sorel as a self-conscious representative of the impulses which generate purpose.

It must not be supposed that respect for the myth is a discovery of Sorel's. He is but one of a number of contemporary thinkers who have reacted against a very stupid prejudice of nineteenth century science to the effect that the mental habits of human beings were not "facts." Unless ideas mirrored external nature they were regarded as beneath the notice of the scientific mind. But in more recent years we have come to realize that, in a world so full of ignorance and mistake, error itself is worthy of study. Our untrue ideas are significant because they influence our lives enormously. They are "facts" to be investigated. One might point to the great illumination that has resulted from Freud's analysis of the abracadabra of our dreams. No one can any longer dismiss the fantasy because it is logically inconsistent, superficially absurd, or objectively untrue. William James might also be cited for his defense of those beliefs that are beyond the realm of proof. His essay, "The Will to Believe," is a declaration of independence, which says in effect that scientific demonstration is not the only test of ideas. He stated the case for those beliefs which influence life so deeply, though they fail to describe it. James himself was very disconcerting to many scientists because he insisted on expressing his aspirations about the universe in what his colleague Santayana calls a "romantic cosmology": "I am far from wishing to suggest that such a view seems to me more probable than conventional idealism or the Christian Orthodoxy. All three are in the region of dramatic system-making and myth, to which probabilities are irrelevant."

It is impossible to leave this point without quoting Nietzsche, who had this insight and stated it most provocatively. In "Beyond Good and Evil" Nietzsche says flatly that "the falseness of an opinion is not for us any objection to it: it is here, perhaps, that our new language sounds most strangely. The question is, how far an opinion is life-furthering, life-preserving, species-preserving, perhaps species-rearing...." Then he comments on the philosophers. "They all pose as though their real opinions had been discovered and attained through the self-evolving of a cold, pure, divinely indifferent dialectic...; whereas, in fact, a prejudiced proposition, idea, or 'suggestion,' which is generally their heart's desire abstracted and refined, is defended by them with arguments sought out after the event. They are all advocates who do not wish to be regarded as such, generally astute defenders, also, of their prejudices, which they dub 'truths'—and very far from having the conscience which bravely admits this to itself; very far from having the good taste or the courage which goes so far as to let this be understood, perhaps to warn friend or foe, or in cheerful confidence and self-ridicule.... It has gradually become clear to me what every great philosophy up till now has consisted of—namely, the confession of its originator, and a species of involuntary and unconscious autobiography, and, moreover, that the moral (or immoral) purpose in every philosophy has constituted the true vital germ out of which the entire plant has always grown.... Whoever considers the fundamental impulses of man with a view to determining how far they may have acted as *inspiring* genii (or as demons and cobolds) will find that they have all practiced philosophy at one time or another, and that each one of them would have been only too glad to look upon itself as the ultimate end of existence and the legitimate *lord* over all the other impulses. For every impulse is imperious, and, as such, attempts to philosophize."

What Nietzsche has done here is, in his swashbuckling fashion, to cut under the abstract and final pretensions of creeds. Difficulties arise when we try to apply this wisdom in the present. That dogmas were instruments of human purposes is not so incredible; that they still are instruments is not so clear to everyone; and that they will be, that they should be—this seems a monstrous attack on the citadel of truth. It is possible to believe that other men's theories were temporary and merely useful; we like to believe that ours will have a greater authority.

It seems like topsy-turvyland to make reason serve the irrational. Yet that is just what it has always done, and ought always to do. Many of us are ready to grant that in the past men's motives were deeper than their intellects: we forgive them with a kind of self-righteousness which says that they knew not what they did. But to follow the great tradition of human wisdom deliberately, with our eyes open in the manner of Sorel, that seems a crazy procedure. A notion of intellectual honor fights against it: we think we must aim at final truth, and not allow autobiography to creep into speculation.

Now the trouble with such an idol is that autobiography creeps in anyway. The more we censor it, the more likely it is to appear disguised, to fool us subtly and perhaps dangerously. The men like Nietzsche and James who show the wilful origin of creeds are in reality the best watchers of the citadel of truth. For there is nothing disastrous in the temporary nature of our ideas. They are always that. But there may very easily be a train of evil in the self-deception which regards them as final. I think God will forgive us our skepticism sooner than our Inquisitions.

From the political point of view, another observation is necessary. The creed of a Rousseau, for example, is active in politics, not for what it says, but for what people think it says. I have urged that Marx found scientific reasons for what he wanted to do. It is important to add that the people who adopted his reasons for what they wanted to do were not any too respectful of Marx's reasons. Thus the so-called materialistic philosophy of Karl Marx is not by any means identical with the theories one hears among Marxian socialists. There is a big distortion in the transmitting of ideas. A common purpose, far more than common ideas, binds Marx to his followers. And when a man comes to write about his philosophy he is confronted with a choice: shall the creed described be that of Marx or of the Marxians?

For the study of politics I should say unhesitatingly that it is more important to know what socialist leaders, stump speakers, pamphleteers, think Marx meant, than to know what he said. For then you are dealing with living ideas: to search his text has its uses, but compared with the actual tradition of Marx it is the work of pedantry. I say this here for two reasons—because I hope to avoid the critical attack of the genuine Marxian specialist, and because the observation is, I believe, relevant to our subject.

Relevant it is in that it suggests the importance of style, of propaganda, the popularization of ideas. The host of men who stand between a great thinker and the average man are not automatic transmitters. They work on the ideas; perhaps that is why a genius usually hates his disciples. It is interesting to notice the explanation given by Frau Förster-Nietzsche for her brother's quarrel with Wagner. She dates it from the time when Nietzsche, under the guise of Wagnerian propaganda, began to expound himself. The critics and interpreters are themselves creative. It is really unfair to speak of the Marxian philosophy as a political force. It is juster to speak of the Marxian tradition.

So when I write of Marx's influence I have in mind what men and women in socialist meetings, in daily life here in America, hold as a faith and attribute to Marx. There is no pretension whatever to any critical study of "Das Kapital" itself. I am thinking rather of stuffy halls in which an earnest voice is expounding "the evolution of capitalism," of little groups, curious and bewildered, listening in the streets of New York to the story of the battle between the "master class" and the "working class," of little red pamphlets, of newspapers, and cartoons—awkward, badly printed and not very genial, a great stream of spellbinding and controversy through which the aspirations of millions are becoming articulate:

The tradition is saying that "the system" and not the individual is at fault. It describes that system as one in which a small class owns the means of production and holds the rest of mankind in bondage. Arts, religions, laws, as well as vice and crime and degradation, have their source in this central economic condition. If you want to understand our life you must see that it is determined by the massing of capital in the hands of a few. All epochs are determined by economic arrangements. But a system of property always contains within itself "the seeds of its own destruction." Mechanical inventions suggest a change: a dispossessed class compels it. So mankind has progressed through savagery, chattel slavery, serfdom, to "wage slavery" or the capitalism of to-day. This age is pregnant with the socialism of to-morrow.

So roughly the tradition is handed on. Two sets of idea seem to dominate it: we are creatures of economic conditions; a war of classes is being fought everywhere in which the proletariat will ultimately capture the industrial machinery and produce a sound economic life as the basis of peace and happiness for all. The emphasis on environment is insistent. Facts are marshaled, the news of the day is interpreted to show that men are determined by economic conditions. This fixation has brought down upon the socialists a torrent of abuse in which "atheism" and "materialism" are prevailing epithets. But the propaganda continues and the philosophy spreads, penetrating reform groups, social workers, historians, and sociologists.

It has served the socialist purpose well. To the workingmen it has brought home the importance of capturing the control of industry. Economic determinism has been an antidote to mere preaching of goodness, to hero-worship and political quackery. Socialism to succeed had to concentrate attention on the ownership of capital: whenever any other interest like religion or patriotism threatened to diffuse that attention, socialist leaders have always been ready to show that the economic fact is more central. Dignity and prestige were supplied by making economics the key of history; passion was chained by building paradise upon it.

In all the political philosophies there is none so adapted to its end. Every sanction that mankind respects has been grouped about this one purpose—the control of capital. It is as if all history converged upon the issue, and the workers in the cause feel that they carry within them the destiny of the race. Start anywhere, with an orthodox socialist and he will lead you to this supreme economic situation. Tyrannies and race hatred, national rivalries, sex problems, the difficulties of artistic endeavor, all failures, crimes, vices—there is not one which he will not relate to private capitalism. Nor is there anything disingenuous about this focusing of the attention: a real belief is there. Of course you will find plenty of socialists who see other issues and who smile a bit at the rigors of economic determinism. In these later days there is in fact, a decided loosening in the creed. But it is fair to say that the mass of socialists hold this philosophy with as much solemnity as a reformer held his when he wrote to me that the cure for obscenity was the taxation of land values and absolute free trade.

Singlemindedness has done good service. It has bound the world together and has helped men to think socially. Turning their attention away from the romanticism of history, the materialistic philosophy has helped them to look at realities. It has engendered a fine concern about average people, about the voiceless multitudes who have been left to pass unnoticed. Not least among the blessings is a shattering of the good-and-bad-man theory: the assassination of tyrants or the adoration of saviors. A shallow and specious other-worldliness has been driven out: an other-worldliness which is really nothing but laziness about this one. And if from a speculative angle the Marxian tradition has shaded too heavily the economic facts, it was at least a plausible and practical exaggeration.

But the drawbacks are becoming more and more evident as socialism approaches nearer to power and responsibility. The feeling that man is a creature and not a creator is disastrous as a personal creed when you come to act. If you insist upon being "determined by conditions" you do hesitate about saying "I shall." You are likely to wait for something to determine you. Personal initiative and individual genius are poorly regarded: many socialists are suspicious of originality. This philosophy, so useful in propaganda, is becoming a burden in action. That is another way of saying that the instrument has turned into an idol.

For while it is illuminating to see how environment moulds men, it is absolutely essential that men regard themselves as moulders of their environment. A new philosophical basis is becoming increasingly necessary to socialism—one that may not be "truer" than the old materialism but that shall simply be more useful. Having learned for a long time what is done to us, we are now faced with the task of doing. With this changed purpose goes a change of instruments. All over the world socialists are breaking away from the stultifying influence of the outworn determinism. For the time is at hand when they must cease to look upon socialism as inevitable in order to make it so.

Nor will the philosophy of class warfare serve this new need. That can be effective only so long as the working-class is without sovereignty. But no sooner has it achieved power than a new outlook is needed in order to know what to do with it. The tactics of the battlefield are of no use when the battle is won.

I picture this philosophy as one of deliberate choices. The underlying tone of it is that society is made by man for man's uses, that reforms are inventions to be applied when by experiment they show their civilizing value. Emphasis is placed upon the devising, adapting, constructing faculties. There is no reason to believe that this view is any colder than that of the war of class against class. It will generate no less energy. Men to-day can feel almost as much zest in the building of the Panama Canal as they did in a military victory. Their domineering impulses find satisfaction in conquering things, in subjecting brute forces to human purposes. This sense of mastery in a winning battle against the conditions of our life is, I believe, the social myth that will inspire our reconstructions. We shall feel free to choose among alternatives—to take this much of socialism, insert so much syndicalism, leave standing what of capitalism seems worth conserving. We shall be making our own house for our own needs, cities to suit ourselves, and we shall believe ourselves capable of moving mountains, as engineers do, when mountains stand in their way.

And history, science, philosophy will support our hopes. What will fascinate us in the past will be the records of inventions, of great choices, of those alternatives on which destiny seems to hang. The splendid epochs will be interpreted as monuments of man's creation, not of his propulsion. We shall be interested primarily in the way nations established their civilization in spite of hostile conditions. Admiration will go out to the men who did not submit, who bent things to human use. We may see the entire tragedy of life in being driven.

Half-truths and illusions, if you like, but tonic. This view will suit our mood. For we shall be making and the makers of history will become more real to us. Instead of urging that issues are inevitable, instead of being swamped by problems that are unavoidable, we may stand up and affirm the issues we propose to handle. Perhaps we shall say with Nietzsche:

"Let the value of everything be determined afresh by you."

The Red Herring

At the beginning of every campaign the newspapers tell about secret conferences in which the candidate and his managers decide upon "the line of attack." The approach to issues, the way in which they shall be stressed, what shall be put forward in one part of the country and what in another, are discussed at these meetings. Here is where the real program of a party is worked out. The document produced at the convention is at its best nothing but a suggestive formality. It is not until the speakers and the publicity agents have actually begun to animate it that the country sees what the party is about. It is as if the convention adopted the Decalogue, while these secret conferences decided which of the Commandments was to be made the issue. Almost always, of course, the decision is entirely a "practical" one, which means that each section of people is exhorted to practice the commandment it likes the most. Thus for the burglars is selected, not the eighth tablet, but the one on which is recommended a day of rest from labor; to the happily married is preached the seventh commandment.

These conferences are decisive. On them depends the educational value of a campaign, and the men who participate in them, being in a position to state the issues and point them, determine the political interests of the people for a considerable period of time. To-day in America, for example, no candidate can escape entirely that underlying irritation which socialists call poverty and some call the high cost of living. But the conspicuous candidates do decide what direction thought shall take about this condition. They can center it upon the tariff or the trusts or even the currency.

Thus Mr. Roosevelt has always had a remarkable power of diverting the country from the tariff to the control of the trusts. His Democratic opponents, especially Woodrow Wilson, are, as I write, in the midst of the Presidential campaign of 1912, trying to focus attention on the tariff. In a way the battle resembles a tug-of-war in which each of the two leading candidates is trying to pull the nation over to his favorite issue. On the side you can see the Prohibitionists endeavoring to make the country see drink as a central problem; the emerging socialists insisting that not the tariff, or liquor, or the control of trusts, but the ownership of capital should be the heart of the discussion. Electoral campaigns do not resemble debates so much as they do competing amusement shows where, with bright lights, gaudy posters and persuasive, insistent voices, each booth is trying to collect a crowd; The victory in a campaign is far more likely to go to the most plausible diagnosis than to the most convincing method of cure. Once a party can induce the country to see its issue as supreme the greater part of its task is done.

The clever choice of issues influences all politics from the petty manœuvers of a ward leader to the most brilliant creative statesmanship. I remember an instance that happened at the beginning of the first socialist administration in Schenectady: The officials had out of the goodness of their hearts suspended a city ordinance which forbade coasting with bob-sleds on the hills of the city. A few days later one of the sleds ran into a wagon and a little girl was killed. The opposition papers put the accident into scareheads with the result that public opinion became very bitter. It looked like a bad crisis at the very beginning and the old ring politicians made the most of it. But they had reckoned without the political shrewdness of the socialists. For in the second day of excitement, the mayor made public a plan by which the main business street of the town was to be lighted with high-power lamps and turned into a "brilliant white way of Schenectady." The swiftness with which the papers displaced the gruesome details of the little girl's death by exultation over the business future of the city was a caution. Public attention was shifted and a political crisis avoided. I tell this story simply as a suggestive fact. The ethical considerations do not concern us here.

There is nothing exceptional about the case. Whenever governments enter upon foreign invasions in order to avoid civil wars, the same trick is practiced. In the Southern States the race issue has been thrust forward persistently to prevent an economic alignment. Thus you hear from Southerners that unless socialism gives up its demand for racial equality, the propaganda cannot go forward. How often in great strikes have riots been started in order to prevent the public from listening to the workers' demands! It is an old story—the red herring dragged across the path in order to destroy the scent.

Having seen the evil results we have come to detest a conscious choice of issues, to feel that it smacks of sinister plotting. The vile practice of yellow newspapers and chauvinistic politicians is almost the only experience of it we have. Religion, patriotism, race, and sex are the favorite red herrings of foul political method—they are the most successful because they explode so easily and flood the mind with those unconscious prejudices which make critical thinking difficult. Yet for all its abuse the deliberate choice of issues is one of the high selective arts of the statesman. In the debased form we know it there is little encouragement. But the

The Walter Lippmann Reader

devil is merely a fallen angel, and when God lost Satan he lost one of his best lieutenants. It is always a pretty good working rule that whatever is a great power of evil may become a great power for good. Certainly nothing so effective in the art of politics can be left out of the equipment of the statesman.

Looked at closely, the deliberate making of issues is very nearly the core of the statesman's task. His greatest wisdom is required to select a policy that will fertilize the public mind. He fails when the issue he sets is sterile; he is incompetent if the issue does not lead to the human center of a problem; whenever the statesman allows the voters to trifle with taboos and by-products, to wander into blind alleys like "16 to 1," his leadership is a public calamity. The newspaper or politician which tries to make an issue out of a supposed "prosperity" or out of admiration for the mere successes of our ancestors is doing its best to choke off the creative energies in politics. All the stultification of the stand-pat mind may be described as inability, and perhaps unwillingness, to nourish a fruitful choice of issues.

That choice is altogether too limited in America, anyway. Political discussion, whether reactionary or radical, is monotonously confined to very few issues. It is as if social life were prevented from irrigating political thought. A subject like the tariff, for example, has absorbed an amount of attention which would justify an historian in calling it the incubus of American politics. Now the exaltation of one issue like that is obviously out of all proportion to its significance. A contributory factor it certainly is, but the country's destiny is not bound up finally with its solution. The everlasting reiterations about the tariff take up altogether too much time. To any government that was clear about values, that saw all problems in their relation to human life, the tariff would be an incident, a mechanical device and little else. High protectionist and free trader alike fall under the indictment—for a tariff wall is neither so high as heaven nor so broad as the earth. It may be necessary to have dykes on portions of the seashore; they may be superfluous elsewhere. But to concentrate nine-tenths of your attention on the subject of dykes is to forget the civilization they are supposed to protect. A wall is a wall: the presence of it will not do the work of civilization—the absence of it does not absolve anyone from the tasks of social life. That a statecraft might deal with the tariff as an aid to its purposes is evident. But anyone who makes the tariff the principal concern of statecraft is, I believe, mistaking the hedge for the house.

The tariff controversy is almost as old as the nation. A more recent one is what Senator La Follette calls "The great issue before the American people to-day, ... the

126

control of their own government." It has taken the form of an attack on corruption, on what is vaguely called "special privilege" and of a demand for a certain amount of political machinery such as direct primaries, the initiative, referendum, and recall. The agitation has a curious sterility: the people are exhorted to control their own government, but they are given very little advice as to what they are to do with it when they control it. Of course, the leaders who spend so much time demanding these mechanical changes undoubtedly see them as a safeguard against corrupt politicians and what Roosevelt calls "their respectable allies and figureheads, who have ruled and legislated and decided as if in some way the vested rights of privilege had a first mortgage on the whole United States." But look at the way these innovations are presented and I think the feeling is unavoidable that the control of government is emphasized as an end in itself. Now an observation of this kind is immediately open to dispute: it is not a clear-cut distinction but a rather subtle matter of stress—an impression rather than a definite conviction.

Yet when you look at the career of Judge Lindsey in Denver the impression is sharpened by contrast. What gave his exposure of corruption a peculiar vitality was that it rested on a very positive human ideal: the happiness of children in a big city. Lindsey's attack on vice and financial jobbery was perhaps the most convincing piece of muckraking ever done in this country for the very reason that it sprang from a concern about real human beings instead of abstractions about democracy or righteousness. From the point of view of the political hack, Judge Lindsey made a most distressing use of the red herring. He brought the happiness of childhood into political discussion, and this opened up a new source of political power. By touching something deeply instinctive in millions of people, Judge Lindsey animated dull proposals with human interest. The pettifogging objections to some social plan had very little chance of survival owing to the dynamic power of the reformers. It was an excellent example of the creative results that come from centering a political problem on human nature.

If you move only from legality to legality, you halt and hesitate, each step is a monstrous task. If the reformer is a pure opportunist, and lays out only "the next step," that step will be very difficult. But if he aims at some real human end, at the genuine concerns of men, women, and children, if he can make the democracy see and feel that end, the little mechanical devices of suffrage and primaries and tariffs will be dealt with as a craftsman deals with his tools. But to say that we must make tools first, and then begin, is to invert the process of life. Men did not agree to refrain from travel until a railroad was built. To make the manufacture of instruments an ideal is to lose much of their ideal value. A nation bent upon a policy of social invention would make its tools an incident. But just this perception is lacking in many propagandists. That is why their issues are so sterile; that is why the absorption in "next steps" is a diversion from statesmanship.

The narrowness of American political issues is a fixation upon instruments. Tradition has centered upon the tariff, the trusts, the currency, and electoral machinery as the items of consideration. It is the failure to go behind them—to see them as the pale servants of a vivid social life—that keeps our politics in bondage to a few problems. It is a common experience repeated in you and me. Once our profession becomes all absorbing it hardens into pedantry. "A human being," says Wells, "who is a philosopher in the first place, a teacher in the first place, or a statesman in the first place is thereby and inevitably, though he bring God-like gifts to the pretense—a quack."

Reformers particularly resent the enlargement of political issues. I have heard socialists denounce other socialists for occupying themselves with the problems of sex. The claim was that these questions should be put aside so as not to disturb the immediate program. The socialists knew from experience that sex views cut across economic ones—that a new interest breaks up the alignment. Woodrow Wilson expressed this same fear in his views on the liquor question: after declaring for local option he went on to say that "the questions involved are social and moral and are not susceptible of being made part of a party program. Whenever they have been made the subject matter of party contests they have cut the lines of party organization and party action athwart, to the utter confusion of political action in every other field.... I do not believe party programs of the highest consequence to the political life of the State and of the nation ought to be thrust on one side and hopelessly embarrassed for long periods together by making a political issue of a great question which is essentially non-political, non-partisan, moral and social in its nature."

That statement was issued at the beginning of a campaign in which Woodrow Wilson was the nominee of a party that has always been closely associated with the liquor interests. The bogey of the saloon had presented itself early: it was very clear that an affirmative position by the candidate was sure to alienate either the temperance or the "liquor vote." No doubt a sense of this dilemma is partly responsible for Wilson's earnest plea that the question of liquor be left out of the campaign. He saw the confusion and embarrassment he speaks of as an immediate danger. Like his views on immigration and Chinese labor it was a red herring across his path. It would, if brought into prominence, cut the lines of party action athwart.

His theoretical grounds for ignoring the question in politics are very interesting just because they are vitalized by this practical difficulty which he faced. Like all party men Woodrow Wilson had thrust upon him here a danger that haunts every political program. The more issues a party meets the less votes it is likely to poll. And for a very simple reason: you cannot keep the citizenship of a nation like this bound in its allegiance to two large parties unless you make the grounds of allegiance very simple and very obvious. If you are to hold five or six million voters enlisted under one emblem the less specific you are and the fewer issues you raise the more probable it is that you can stop this host from quarreling within the ranks.

No doubt this is a partial explanation of the bareness of American politics. The two big parties have had to preserve a superficial homogeneity; and a platitude is more potent than an issue. The minor parties—Populist, Prohibition, Independence League and Socialist—have shown a much greater willingness to face new problems. Their view of national policy has always been more inclusive, perhaps for the very reason that their membership is so much more exclusive. But if anyone wishes a smashing illustration of this paradox let him consider the rapid progress of Roosevelt's philosophy in the very short time between the Republican Convention in June to the Progressive Convention in August, 1912. As soon as Roosevelt had thrown off the burden of preserving a false harmony among irreconcilable Republicans, he issued a platform full of definiteness and square dealing with many issues. He was talking to a minority party. But Roosevelt's genius is not that of group leadership. He longs for majorities. He set out to make the campaign a battle between the Progressives and the Democrats—the old discredited Republicans fell back into a rather dead conservative minority. No sooner did Roosevelt take the stump than the paradox loomed up before him. His speeches began to turn on platitudes—on the vague idealism and indisputable moralities of the Decalogue and the Sermon on the Mount. The fearlessness of the Chicago confession was melted down into a featureless alloy.

The embarrassment from the liquor question which Woodrow Wilson feared does not arise because teetotaler and drunkard both become intoxicated when they discuss the saloon. It would come just as much from a radical program of land taxation, factory reform, or trust control. Let anyone of these issues be injected into his campaign and the lines of party action would be cut "athwart." For Woodrow Wilson was dealing with the inevitable embarrassment of a party system dependent on an inexpressive homogeneity. The grouping of the voters into two large herds costs a large price: it means that issues must be so simplified and selected that the real demands of the nation rise only now and then to the level of political discussion. The more people a party contains the less it expresses their needs.

Woodrow Wilson's diagnosis of the red herring in politics is obviously correct. A new issue does embarrass a wholesale organization of the voters. His desire to avoid it in the midst of a campaign is understandable. His urgent plea that the liquor question be kept a local issue may be wise. But the general philosophy which says that the party system should not be cut athwart is at least open to serious dispute. Instead of an evil, it looks to me like progress towards greater responsiveness of parties to popular need. It is good to disturb alignments: to break up a superficial unanimity. The masses of people held together under the name Democratic are bound in an enervating communion. The real groups dare not speak their convictions for fear the crust will break. It is as if you had thrown a large sheet over a mass of men and made them anonymous.

The man who raises new issues has always been distasteful to politicians. He musses up what had been so tidily arranged. I remember once speaking to a local boss about woman suffrage. His objections were very simple: "We've got the organization in fine shape now—we know where every voter in the district stands. But you let all the women vote and we'll be confused as the devil. It'll be an awful job keeping track of them." He felt what many a manufacturer feels when somebody has the impertinence to invent a process which disturbs the routine of business.

Hard as it is upon the immediate plans of the politician, it is a national blessing when the lines of party action are cut athwart by new issues. I recognize that the red herring is more often frivolous and personal—a matter of misrepresentation and spite—than an honest attempt to enlarge the scope of politics. However, a fine thing must not be deplored because it is open to vicious caricature. To the party worker the petty and the honest issue are equally disturbing. The break-up of the parties into expressive groups would be a ventilation of our national life. No use to cry peace when there is no peace. The false bonds are best broken: with their collapse would come a release of social energy into political discussion. For every country is a mass of minorities which should find a voice in public affairs. Any device like proportional representation and preferential voting which facilitates the political expression of group interests is worth having. The objection that popular government cannot be conducted without the two party system is, I believe, refuted by the experience of Europe. If I had to choose between a Congressional caucus and a coalition ministry, I should not have to hesitate very long. But no one need go abroad for actual experience: in the United States Senate during the Taft administration there were really three parties—Republicans, Insurgents and Democrats. Public business went ahead with at least as much effectiveness as under the old Aldrich ring.

There are deeper reasons for urging a break-up of herd-politics. It is not only desirable that groups should be able to contribute to public discussion: it is absolutely essential if the parliamentary method is not to be superseded by direct and violent action. The two party system chokes off the cry of a minority—perhaps the best way there is of precipitating an explosion. An Englishman once told me that the utter freedom of speech in Hyde Park was the best safeguard England had against the doctrines that were propounded there. An anarchist who was invited to address Congress would be a mild person compared to the man forbidden to speak in the streets of San Diego. For many a bomb has exploded into rhetoric.

The rigidity of the two-party system is, I believe, disastrous: it ignores issues without settling them, dulls and wastes the energies of active groups, and chokes off the protests which should find a civilized expression in public life. A recognition of what an incubus it is should make us hospitable to all those devices which aim at making politics responsive by disturbing the alignments of habit. The initiative and referendum will help: they are a method of voting on definite issues instead of electing an administration in bulk. If cleverly handled these electoral devices should act as a check on a wholesale attitude toward politics. Men could agree on a candidate and disagree on a measure. Another device is the separation of municipal, state and national elections: to hold them all at the same time is an inducement to prevent the voter from splitting his allegiance. Proportional representation and preferential voting I have mentioned. The short ballot is a psychological principle which must be taken into account wherever there is voting: it will help the differentiation of political groups by concentrating the attention on essential choices. The recall of public officials is in part a policeman's club, in part a clumsy way of getting around the American prejudice for a fixed term of office. That rigidity which by the mere movement of the calendar throws an official out of office in the midst of his work or compels him to go campaigning is merely the

The Walter Lippmann Reader

crude method of a democracy without confidence in itself. The recall is a half-hearted and negative way of dealing with this difficulty. It does enable us to rid ourselves of an officer we don't like instead of having to wait until the earth has revolved to a certain place about the sun. But we still have to vote on a fixed date whether we have anything to vote upon or not. If a recall election is held when the people petition for it, why not all elections?

In ways like these we shall go on inventing methods by which the fictitious party alignments can be dissolved. There is one device suggested now and then, tried, I believe, in a few places, and vaguely championed by some socialists. It is called in German an "Interessenvertrag"—a political representation by trade interests as well as by geographical districts. Perhaps this is the direction towards which the bi-cameral legislature will develop. One chamber would then represent a man's sectional interests as a consumer: the other his professional interests as a producer. The railway workers, the miners, the doctors, the teachers, the retail merchants would have direct representation in the "Interessenvertrag." You might call it a Chamber of Special Interests. I know how that phrase "Special Interests" hurts. In popular usage we apply it only to corrupting businesses. But our feeling against them should not blind us to the fact that every group in the community has its special interests. They will always exist until mankind becomes a homogeneous jelly. The problem is to find some social adjustment for all the special interests of a nation. That is best achieved by open recognition and clear representation. Let no one then confuse the "Interessenvertrag" with those existing legislatures which are secret Chambers of Special Privilege.

The scheme is worth looking at for it does do away with the present dilemma of the citizen in which he wonders helplessly whether he ought to vote as a consumer or as a producer. I believe he should have both votes, and the "Interessenvertrag" is a way.

These devices are mentioned here as illustrations and not as conclusions. You can think of them as arrangements by which the red herring is turned from a pest into a benefit. I grant that in the rigid political conditions prevailing to-day a new issue is an embarrassment, perhaps a hindrance to the procedure of political life. But instead of narrowing the scope of politics, to avoid it, the only sensible thing to do is to invent methods which will allow needs and problems and group interests avenues into politics.

The Walter Lippmann Reader

But a suggestion like this is sure to be met with the argument which Woodrow Wilson has in mind when he says that the "questions involved are social and moral and are not susceptible of being made parts of a party program." He voices a common belief when he insists that there are moral and social problems, "essentially non-political." Innocent as it looks at first sight this plea by Woodrow Wilson is weighted with the tradition of a century and a half. To my mind it symbolizes a view of the state which we are outgrowing, and throws into relief the view towards which we are struggling. Its implications are well worth tracing, for through them I think we can come to understand better the method of Twentieth Century politics.

It is perfectly true that that government is best which governs least. It is equally true that that government is best which provides most. The first truth belongs to the Eighteenth Century: the second to the Twentieth. Neither of them can be neglected in our attitude towards the state. Without the Jeffersonian distrust of the police we might easily grow into an impertinent and tyrannous collectivism: without a vivid sense of the possibilities of the state we abandon the supreme instrument of civilization. The two theories need to be held together, yet clearly distinguished.

Government has been an exalted policeman: it was there to guard property and to prevent us from quarreling too violently. That was about all it was good for. Yet society found problems on its hands—problems which Woodrow Wilson calls moral and social in their nature. Vice and crime, disease, and grinding poverty forced themselves on the attention of the community. A typical example is the way the social evil compelled the city of Chicago to begin an investigation. Yet when government was asked to handle the question it had for wisdom an ancient conception of itself as a policeman. Its only method was to forbid, to prosecute, to jail—in short, to use the taboo. But experience has shown that the taboo will not solve "moral and social questions"—that nine times out of ten it aggravates the disease. Political action becomes a petty, futile, mean little intrusion when its only method is prosecution.

No wonder then that conservatively-minded men pray that moral and social questions be kept out of politics; no wonder that more daring souls begin to hate the whole idea of government and take to anarchism. So long as the state is conceived merely as an agent of repression, the less it interferes with our lives, the better. Much of the horror of socialism comes from a belief that by increasing the functions of government its regulating power over our daily lives will grow into a tyranny. I share this horror when certain socialists begin to propound their schemes. There is a dreadful amount of forcible scrubbing and arranging and pocketing implied in some socialisms. There is a wish to have the state use its position as general employer to become a censor of morals and arbiter of elegance, like the benevolent employers of the day who take an impertinent interest in the private lives of their workers. Without any doubt socialism has within it the germs of that great bureaucratic tyranny which Chesterton and Belloc have named the Servile State.

So it is a wise instinct that makes men jealous of the policeman's power. Far better we may say that moral and social problems be left to private solution than that they be subjected to the clumsy method of the taboo. When Woodrow Wilson argues that social problems are not susceptible to treatment in a party program, he must mean only one thing: that they cannot be handled by the state as he conceives it. He is right. His attitude is far better than that of the Vice Commission: it too had only a policeman's view of government, but it proceeded to apply it to problems that are not susceptible to such treatment. Wilson, at least, knows the limitations of his philosophy.

But once you see the state as a provider of civilizing opportunities, his whole objection collapses. As soon as government begins to supply services, it is turning away from the sterile tyranny of the taboo. The provision of schools, streets, plumbing, highways, libraries, parks, universities, medical attention, post-offices, a Panama Canal, agricultural information, fire protection—is a use of government totally different from the ideal of Jefferson. To furnish these opportunities is to add to the resources of life, and only a doctrinaire adherence to a misunderstood ideal will raise any objection to them.

When an anarchist says that the state must be abolished he does not mean what he says. What he wants to abolish is the repressive, not the productive state. He cannot possibly object to being furnished with the opportunity of writing to his comrade three thousand miles away, of drinking pure water, or taking a walk in the park. Of course when he finds the post-office opening his mail, or a law saying that he must drink nothing but water, he begins to object even to the services of the government. But that is a confusion of thought, for these tyrannies are merely intrusions of the eighteenth century upon the twentieth. The postmaster is still something of a policeman.

The Walter Lippmann Reader

Once you realize that moral and social problems must be treated to fine opportunities, that the method of the future is to compete with the devil rather than to curse him; that the furnishing of civilized environments is the goal of statecraft, then there is no longer any reason for keeping social and moral questions out of politics. They are what politics must deal with essentially, now that it has found a way. The policeman with his taboo did make moral and social questions insusceptible to treatment in party platforms. He kept the issues of politics narrow and irrelevant, and just because these really interesting questions could not be handled, politics was an over-advertised hubbub. But the vision of the new statecraft in centering politics upon human interests becomes a creator of opportunities instead of a censor of morals, and deserves a fresh and heightened regard.

The party platform will grow ever more and more into a program of services. In the past it has been an armory of platitudes or a forecast of punishments. It promised that it would stop this evil practice, drive out corruption here, and prosecute this-and-that offense. All that belongs to a moribund tradition. Abuse and disuse characterize the older view of the state: guardian and censor it has been, provider but grudgingly. The proclamations of so-called progressives that they will jail financiers, or "wage relentless warfare" upon social evils, are simply the reiterations of men who do not understand the uses of the state.

A political revolution is in progress: the state as policeman is giving place to the state as producer.

Revolution and Culture

There is a legend of a peasant who lived near Paris through the whole Napoleonic era without ever having heard of the name of Bonaparte. A story of that kind is enough to make a man hesitate before he indulges in a flamboyant description of social changes. That peasant is more than a symbol of the privacy of human interest: he is a warning against the incurable romanticism which clings about the idea of a revolution. Popular history is deceptive if it is used to furnish a picture for coming events. Like drama which compresses the tragedy of a lifetime into a unity of time, place, and action, history foreshortens an epoch into an episode. It gains in poignancy, but loses reality. Men grew from infancy to old age, their children's children had married and loved and worked while the social change we speak of as the industrial revolution was being consummated. That is why it is so difficult for living people to believe that they too are in the midst of great transformations. What looks to us like an incredible rush of events sloping towards a great historical crisis was to our ancestors little else than the occasional punctuation of daily life with an exciting incident. Even to-day when we have begun to speak of our age as a transition, there are millions of people who live in an undisturbed routine. Even those of us who regard ourselves as active in mothering the process and alert in detecting its growth are by no means constantly aware of any great change. For even the fondest mother cannot watch her child grow.

I remember how tremendously surprised I was in visiting Russia several years ago to find that in Moscow or St. Petersburg men were interested in all sorts of things besides the revolution. I had expected every Russian to be absorbed in the struggle. It seemed at first as if my notions of what a revolution ought to be were contradicted everywhere. And I assure you it wrenched the imagination to see tidy nursemaids wheeling perambulators and children playing diavolo on the very square where Bloody Sunday had gone into history. It takes a long perspective and no very vivid acquaintance with revolution to be melodramatic about it. So much is left out of history and biography which would spoil the effect. The anti-climax is almost always omitted.

Perhaps that is the reason why Arnold Bennett's description of the siege of Paris in "The Old Wives' Tale" is so disconcerting to many people. It is hard to believe that daily life continues with its stretches of boredom and its personal interests even while the enemy is bombarding a city. How much more difficult is it to imagine a revolution that is to come—to space it properly through a long period of time, to conceive what it will be like to the people who live through it. Almost all social prediction is catastrophic and absurdly simplified. Even those who talk of the slow "evolution" of society are likely to think of it as a series of definite changes easily marked and well known to everybody. It is what Bernard Shaw calls the reformer's habit of mistaking his private emotions for a public movement.

Even though the next century is full of dramatic episodes—the collapse of governments and labor wars—these events will be to the social revolution what the smashing of machines in Lancashire was to the industrial revolution. The reality that is worthy of attention is a change in the very texture and quality of millions of lives—a change that will be vividly perceptible only in the retrospect of history.

The conservative often has a sharp sense of the complexity of revolution: not desiring change, he prefers to emphasize its difficulties, whereas the reformer is enticed into a faith that the intensity of desire is a measure of its social effect. Yet just because no reform is in itself a revolution, we must not jump to the assurance that no revolution can be accomplished. True as it is that great changes are imperceptible, it is no less true that they are constantly taking place. Moreover, for the very reason that human life changes its quality so slowly, the panic over political proposals is childish.

It is obvious, for instance, that the recall of judges will not revolutionize the national life. That is why the opposition generated will seem superstitious to the next generation. As I write, a convention of the Populist Party has just taken place. Eight delegates attended the meeting, which was held in a parlor. Even the reactionary press speaks in a kindly way about these men. Twenty years ago the Populists were hated and feared as if they practiced black magic. What they wanted is on the point of realization. To some of us it looks like a drop in the bucket—a slight part of vastly greater plans. But how stupid was the fear of Populism, what unimaginative nonsense it was to suppose twenty years ago that the program was the road to the end of the world.

One good deed or one bad one is no measure of a man's character: the Last Judgment let us hope will be no series of decisions as simple as that. "The soul survives its adventures," says Chesterton with a splendid sense of justice. A country survives its legislation. That truth should not comfort the conservative nor depress the radical. For it means that public policy can enlarge its scope and increase its audacity, can try big experiments without trembling too much over the result. This

The Walter Lippmann Reader

nation could enter upon the most radical experiments and could afford to fail in them. Mistakes do not affect us so deeply as we imagine. Our prophecies of change are subjective wishes or fears that never come to full realization.

Those socialists are confused who think that a new era can begin by a general strike or an electoral victory. Their critics are just a bit more confused when they become hysterical over the prospect. Both of them over-emphasize the importance of single events. Yet I do not wish to furnish the impression that crises are negligible. They are extremely important as symptoms, as milestones, and as instruments. It is simply that the reality of a revolution is not in a political decree or the scarehead of a newspaper, but in the experiences, feelings, habits of myriads of men.

No one who watched the textile strike at Lawrence, Massachusetts, in the winter of 1912 can forget the astounding effect it had on the complacency of the public. Very little was revealed that any well-informed social worker does not know as a commonplace about the mill population. The wretchedness and brutality of Lawrence conditions had been described in books and magazines and speeches until radicals had begun to wonder at times whether the power of language wasn't exhausted. The response was discouragingly weak—an occasional government investigation, an impassioned protest from a few individuals, a placid charity, were about all that the middle-class public had to say about factory life. The cynical indifference of legislatures and the hypocrisy of the dominant parties were all that politics had to offer. The Lawrence strike touched the most impervious: story after story came to our ears of hardened reporters who suddenly refused to misrepresent the strikers, of politicians aroused to action, of social workers become revolutionary. Daily conversation was shocked into some contact with realities—the newspapers actually printed facts about the situation of a working class population.

And why? The reason is not far to seek. The Lawrence strikers did something more than insist upon their wrongs; they showed a disposition to right them. That is what scared public opinion into some kind of truth-telling. So long as the poor are docile in their poverty, the rest of us are only too willing to satisfy our consciences by pitying them. But when the downtrodden gather into a threat as they did at Lawrence, when they show that they have no stake in civilization and consequently no respect for its institutions, when the object of pity becomes the avenger of its own miseries, then the middle-class public begins to look at the problem more intelligently.

The Walter Lippmann Reader

We are not civilized enough to meet an issue before it becomes acute. We were not intelligent enough to free the slaves peacefully—we are not intelligent enough to-day to meet the industrial problem before it develops a crisis. That is the hard truth of the matter. And that is why no honest student of politics can plead that social movements should confine themselves to argument and debate, abandoning the militancy of the strike, the insurrection, the strategy of social conflict.

Those who deplore the use of force in the labor struggle should ask themselves whether the ruling classes of a country could be depended upon to inaugurate a program of reconstruction which would abolish the barbarism that prevails in industry. Does anyone seriously believe that the business leaders, the makers of opinion and the politicians will, on their own initiative, bring social questions to a solution? If they do it will be for the first time in history. The trivial plans they are introducing to-day—profit-sharing and welfare work—are on their own admission an attempt to quiet the unrest and ward off the menace of socialism.

No, paternalism is not dependable, granting that it is desirable. It will do very little more than it feels compelled to do. Those who to-day bear the brunt of our evils dare not throw themselves upon the mercy of their masters, not though there are bread and circuses as a reward. From the groups upon whom the pressure is most direct must come the power to deal with it. We are not all immediately interested in all problems: our attention wanders unless the people who are interested compel us to listen.

Social movements are at once the symptoms and the instruments of progress. Ignore them and statesmanship is irrelevant; fail to use them and it is weak. Often in the course of these essays I have quoted from H. G. Wells. I must do so again: "Every party stands essentially for the interests and mental usages of some definite class or group of classes in the exciting community, and every party has its scientific minded and constructive leading section, with well defined hinterlands formulating its social functions in a public spirited form, and its superficial-minded following confessing its meannesses and vanities and prejudices. No class will abolish itself, materially alter its way of living, or drastically reconstruct itself, albeit no class is indisposed to co-operate in the unlimited socialization of any other class. In that capacity for aggression upon other classes lies the essential driving force of modern affairs."

The truth of this can be tested in the socialist movement. There is a section among the socialists which regards the class movement of labor as a driving force in the socialization of industry. This group sees clearly that without the threat of aggression no settlement of the issues is possible. Ordinarily such socialists say that the class struggle is a movement which will end classes. They mean that the self-interest of labor is identical with the interests of a community—that it is a kind of social selfishness. But there are other socialists who speak constantly of "working-class government" and they mean just what they say. It is their intention to have the community ruled in the interests of labor. Probe their minds to find out what they mean by labor and in all honesty you cannot escape the admission that they mean industrial labor alone. These socialists think entirely in terms of the factory population of cities: the farmers, the small shop-keepers, the professional classes have only a perfunctory interest for them. I know that no end of phrases could be adduced to show the inclusiveness of the word labor. But their intention is what I have tried to describe: they are thinking of government by a factory population.

They appeal to history for confirmation: have not all social changes, they ask, meant the emergence of a new economic class until it dominated society? Did not the French Revolution mean the conquest of the feudal landlord by the middle-class merchant? Why should not the Social Revolution mean the victory of the proletariat over the bourgeoisie? That may be true, but it is no reason for being bullied by it into a tame admission that what has always been must always be. I see no reason for exalting the unconscious failures of other revolutions into deliberate models for the next one. Just because the capacity of aggression in the middle class ran away with things, and failed to fuse into any decent social ideal, is not ground for trying as earnestly as possible to repeat the mistake.

The lesson of it all, it seems to me, is this: that class interests are the driving forces which keep public life centered upon essentials. They become dangerous to a nation when it denies them, thwarts them and represses them so long that they burst out and become dominant. Then there is no limit to their aggression until another class appears with contrary interests. The situation might be compared to those hysterias in which a suppressed impulse flares up and rules the whole mental life.

Social life has nothing whatever to fear from group interests so long as it doesn't try to play the ostrich in regard to them. So the burden of national crises is squarely upon the dominant classes who fight so foolishly against the emergent ones. That is what precipitates violence, that is what renders social co-operation impossible, that is what makes catastrophes the method of change.

The Walter Lippmann Reader

The wisest rulers see this. They know that the responsibility for insurrections rests in the last analysis upon the unimaginative greed and endless stupidity of the dominant classes. There is something pathetic in the blindness of powerful people when they face a social crisis. Fighting viciously every readjustment which a nation demands, they make their own overthrow inevitable. It is they who turn opposing interests into a class war. Confronted with the deep insurgency of labor what do capitalists and their spokesmen do? They resist every demand, submit only after a struggle, and prepare a condition of war to the death. When far-sighted men appear in the ruling classes—men who recognize the need of a civilized answer to this increasing restlessness, the rich and the powerful treat them to a scorn and a hatred that are incredibly bitter. The hostility against men like Roosevelt, La Follette, Bryan, Lloyd-George is enough to make an observer believe that the rich of to-day are as stupid as the nobles of France before the Revolution.

It seems to me that Roosevelt never spoke more wisely or as a better friend of civilization than the time when he said at New York City on March 20, 1912, that "the woes of France for a century and a quarter have been due to the folly of her people in splitting into the two camps of unreasonable conservatism and unreasonable radicalism. Had pre-Revolutionary France listened to men like Turgot and backed them up all would have gone well. But the beneficiaries of privilege, the Bourbon reactionaries, the short-sighted ultra-conservatives, turned down Turgot; and then found that instead of him they had obtained Robespierre. They gained twenty years' freedom from all restraint and reform at the cost of the whirlwind of the red terror; and in their turn the unbridled extremists of the terror induced a blind reaction; and so, with convulsion and oscillation from one extreme to another, with alterations of violent radicalism and violent Bourbonism, the French people went through misery to a shattered goal."

Profound changes are not only necessary, but highly desirable. Even if this country were comfortably well-off, healthy, prosperous, and educated, men would go on inventing and creating opportunities to amplify the possibilities of life. These inventions would mean radical transformations. For we are bent upon establishing more in this nation than a minimum of comfort. A liberal people would welcome social inventions as gladly as we do mechanical ones. What it would fear is a hard-shell resistance to change which brings it about explosively.

Catastrophes are disastrous to radical and conservative alike: they do not preserve what was worth maintaining; they allow a deformed and often monstrous

141

The Walter Lippmann Reader

perversion of the original plan. The emancipation of the slaves might teach us the lesson that an explosion followed by reconstruction is satisfactory to nobody.

Statesmanship would go out to meet a crisis before it had become acute. The thing it would emphatically not do is to dam up an insurgent current until it overflowed the countryside. Fight labor's demands to the last ditch and there will come a time when it seizes the whole of power, makes itself sovereign, and takes what it used to ask. That is a poor way for a nation to proceed. For the insurgent become master is a fanatic from the struggle, and as George Santayana says, he is only too likely to redouble his effort after he has forgotten his aim.

Nobody need waste his time debating whether or not there are to be great changes. That is settled for us whether we like it or not. What is worth debating is the method by which change is to come about. Our choice, it seems to me, lies between a blind push and a deliberate leadership, between thwarting movements until they master us, and domesticating them until they are answered.

When Roosevelt formed the Progressive Party on a platform of social reform he crystallized a deep unrest, brought it out of the cellars of resentment into the agora of political discussion. He performed the real task of a leader—a task which has essentially two dimensions. By becoming part of the dynamics of unrest he gathered a power of effectiveness: by formulating a program for insurgency he translated it into terms of public service.

What Roosevelt did at the middle-class level, the socialists have done at the proletarian. The world has been slow to recognize the work of the Socialist Party in transmuting a dumb muttering into a civilized program. It has found an intelligent outlet for forces that would otherwise be purely cataclysmic. The truth of this has been tested recently in the appearance of the "direct actionists."

They are men who have lost faith in political socialism. Why? Because, like all other groups, the socialists tend to become routineers, to slip into an easy reiteration. The direct actionists are a warning to the Socialist Party that its tactics and its program are not adequate to domesticating the deepest unrest of labor. Within that party, therefore, a leadership is required which will ride the forces of "syndicalism" and use them for a constructive purpose. The brilliant writer of the "Notes of the Week" in the English New Age has shown how this might be done. He has fused the insight of the syndicalist with the plans of the collectivists under the name of Guild Socialism.

142

The Walter Lippmann Reader

His plan calls for co-management of industry by the state and the labor union. It steers a course between exploitation by a bureaucracy in the interests of the consumer—the socialist danger—and oppressive monopolies by industrial unions—the syndicalist danger. I shall not attempt to argue here either for or against the scheme. My concern is with method rather than with special pleadings. The Guild Socialism of the "New Age" is merely an instance of statesmanlike dealing with a new social force. Instead of throwing up its hands in horror at one over-advertised tactical incident like sabotage, the "New Age" went straight to the creative impulse of the syndicalist movement.

Every true craftsman, artist or professional man knows and sympathizes with that impulse: you may call it a desire for self-direction in labor. The deepest revolt implied in the term syndicalism is against the impersonal, driven quality of modern industry—against the destruction of that pride which alone distinguishes work from slavery. Some such impulse as that is what marks off syndicalism from the other revolts of labor. Our suspicion of the collectivist arrangement is aroused by the picture of a vast state machine so horribly well-regulated that human impulse is utterly subordinated. I believe too that the fighting qualities of syndicalism are kept at the boiling point by a greater sense of outraged human dignity than can be found among mere socialists or unionists. The imagination is more vivid: the horror of capitalism is not alone in the poverty and suffering it entails, but in its ruthless denial of life to millions of men. The most cruel of all denials is to deprive a human being of joyous activity. Syndicalism is shot through with the assertion that an imposed drudgery is intolerable—that labor at a subsistence wage as a cog in a meaningless machine is no condition upon which to found civilization. That is a new kind of revolt—more dangerous to capitalism than the demand for higher wages. You can not treat the syndicalists like cattle because forsooth they have ceased to be cattle. "The damned wantlessness of the poor," about which Oscar Wilde complained, the cry for a little more fodder, gives way to an insistence upon the chance to be interested in life.

To shut the door in the face of such a current of feeling because it is occasionally exasperated into violence would be as futile as locking up children because they get into mischief. The mind which rejects syndicalism entirely because of the by-products of its despair has had pearls cast before it in vain. I know that syndicalism means a revision of some of our plans—that it is an intrusion upon many a glib prejudice. But a human impulse is more important than any existing

143

theory. We must not throw an unexpected guest out of the window because no place is set for him at table. For we lose not only the charm of his company: he may in anger wreck the house.

Yet the whole nation can't sit at one table: the politician will object that all human interests can't be embodied in a party program. That is true, truer than most politicians would admit in public. No party can represent a whole nation, although, with the exception of the socialists, all of them pretend to do just that. The reason is very simple: a platform is a list of performances that are possible within a few years. It is concerned with more or less immediate proposals, and in a nation split up by class, sectional and racial interests, these proposals are sure to arouse hostility. No definite industrial and political platform, for example, can satisfy rich and poor, black and white, Eastern creditor and Western farmer. A party that tried to answer every conflicting interest would stand still because people were pulling in so many different directions. It would arouse the anger of every group and the approval of its framers. It would have no dynamic power because the forces would neutralize each other.

One comprehensive party platform fusing every interest is impossible and undesirable. What is both possible and desirable is that every group interest should be represented in public life—that it should have spokesmen and influence in public affairs. This is almost impossible to-day. Our blundering political system is pachydermic in its irresponsiveness. The methods of securing representation are unfit instruments for any flexible use. But the United States is evidently not exceptional in this respect. England seems to suffer in the same way. In May, 1912, the "Daily Mail" published a series of articles by H. G. Wells on "The Labour Unrest." Is he not describing almost any session of Congress when he says that "to go into the House of Commons is to go aside out of the general stream of the community's vitality into a corner where little is learnt and much is concocted, into a specialized Assembly which is at once inattentive to and monstrously influential in our affairs?" Further on Wells remarks that "this diminishing actuality of our political life is a matter of almost universal comment to-day.... In Great Britain we do not have Elections any more; we have Rejections. What really happens at a general election is that the party organizations—obscure and secretive conclaves with entirely mysterious funds—appoint about 1200 men to be our rulers, and all that we, we so-called self-governing people, are permitted to do is, in a muddled angry way, to strike off the names of about half these selected gentlemen."

A cynic might say that the people can't go far wrong in politics because they can't be very right. Our so-called representative system is unrepresentative in a deeper way than the reformers who talk about the money power imagine. It is empty and thin: a stifling of living currents in the interest of a mediocre regularity.

But suppose that politics were made responsive—suppose that the forces of the community found avenues of expression into public life. Would not our legislatures be cut up into antagonistic parties, would not the conflicts of the nation be concentrated into one heated hall? If you really represented the country in its government, would you not get its partisanship in a quintessential form? After all group interests in the nation are diluted by space and time: the mere separation in cities and country prevents them from falling into the psychology of the crowd. But let them all be represented in one room by men who are professionally interested in their constituency's prejudices and what would you accomplish but a deepening of the cleavages? Would the session not become an interminable wrangle?

Nobody can answer these questions with any certainty. Most prophecies are simply the masquerades of prejudice, and the people who love stability and prefer to let their own well-being alone will see in a sensitive political system little but an invitation to chaos. They will choose facts to adorn their fears. History can be all things to all men: nothing is easier than to summon the Terror, the Commune, lynchings in the Southern States, as witnesses to the excesses and hysterias of the mob. Those facts will prove the case conclusively to anyone who has already made up his mind on the subject. Absolute democrats can also line up their witnesses: the conservatism of the Swiss, Wisconsin's successful experiments, the patience and judgment of the Danes. Both sides are remarkably sure that the right is with them, whereas the only truth about which an observer can be entirely certain is that in some places and in certain instances democracy is admittedly successful.

There is no absolute case one way or the other. It would be silly from the experience we have to make a simple judgment about the value of direct expression. You cannot lump such a mass of events together and come to a single conclusion about them. It is a crude habit of mind that would attempt it. You might as well talk abstractly about the goodness or badness of this universe which contains happiness, pain, exhilaration and indifference in a thousand varying grades and quantities. There is no such thing as Democracy; there are a number of more or less

The Walter Lippmann Reader

democratic experiments which are not subject to wholesale eulogy or condemnation.

The questions about the success of a truly representative system are pseudo-questions. And for this reason: success is not due to the system; it does not flow from it automatically. The source of success is in the people who use the system: as an instrument it may help or hinder them, but they must operate it. Government is not a machine running on straight tracks to a desired goal. It is a human work which may be facilitated by good tools.

That is why the achievements of the Swiss may mean nothing whatever when you come to prophesy about the people of New York. Because Wisconsin has made good use of the direct primary it does not follow that it will benefit the Filipino. It always seems curious to watch the satisfaction of some reform magazines when China or Turkey or Persia imitates the constitutional forms of Western democracies. Such enthusiasts postulate a uniformity of human ability which every fact of life contradicts.

Present-day reform lays a great emphasis upon instruments and very little on the skilful use of them. It says that human nature is all right, that what is wrong is the "system." Now the effect of this has been to concentrate attention on institutions and to slight men. A small step further, institutions become an end in themselves. They may violate human nature as the taboo does. That does not disturb the interest in them very much, for by common consent reformers are to fix their minds upon the "system."

A machine should be run by men for human uses. The preoccupation with the "system" lays altogether too little stress on the men who operate it and the men for whom it is run. It is as if you put all your effort into the working of a plough and forgot the farmer and the consumer. I state the case baldly and contradiction would be easy. The reformer might point to phrases like "human welfare" which appear in his writings. And yet the point stands, I believe. The emphasis which directs his thinking bears most heavily upon the mechanics of life—only perfunctorily upon the ability of the men who are to use them.

Even an able reformer like Mr. Frederic C. Howe does not escape entirely. A recent book is devoted to a glowing eulogy of "Wisconsin, an Experiment in Democracy." In a concluding chapter Mr. Howe states the philosophy of the experiment. "What is the explanation of Wisconsin?" he asks. "Why has it been able to eliminate corruption, machine politics, and rid itself of the boss? What is the

146

The Walter Lippmann Reader

cause of the efficiency, the thoroughness, the desire to serve which animate the state? Why has Wisconsin succeeded where other states have uniformly failed? I think the explanation is simple. It is also perfectly natural. It is traceable to democracy, to the political freedom which had its beginning in the direct primary law, and which has been continuously strengthened by later laws"; some pages later, "Wisconsin assumed that the trouble with our politics is not with our people, but with the machinery with which the people work.... It has established a line of vision as direct as possible between the people and the expression of their will." The impression Mr. Howe evidently wishes to leave with his readers is that the success of the experiment is due to the instruments rather than to the talent of the people of Wisconsin. That would be a valuable and comforting assurance to propagandists, for it means that other states with the same instruments can achieve the same success. But the conclusion seems to me utterly unfounded. The reasoning is perilously like that of the gifted lady amateur who expects to achieve greatness by imitating the paint box and palette, oils and canvases of an artist.

Mr. Howe's own book undermines his conclusions. He begins with an account of La Follette—of a man with initiative and a constructive bent. The forces La Follette set in motion are commented upon. The work of Van Hise is shown. What Wisconsin had was leadership and a people that responded, inventors, and constructive minds. They forged the direct primary and the State University out of the impetus within themselves. No doubt they were fortunate in their choice of instruments. They made the expression of the people's will direct, yet that will surely is the more primary thing. It makes and uses representative systems: but you cannot reverse the process. A man can manufacture a plough and operate it, but no amount of ploughs will create a man and endow him with skill.

All sorts of observers have pointed out that the Western States adopt reform legislation more quickly than the Eastern. Yet no one would seriously maintain that the West is more progressive because it has progressive laws. The laws are a symptom and an aid but certainly not the cause. Constitutions do not make people; people make constitutions. So the task of reform consists not in presenting a state with progressive laws, but in getting the people to want them.

The practical difference is extraordinary. I insist upon it so much because the tendency of political discussion is to regard government as automatic: a device that is sure to fail or sure to succeed. It is sure of nothing. Effort moves it, intelligence directs it; its fate is in human hands.

The Walter Lippmann Reader

The politics I have urged in these chapters cannot be learned by rote. What can be taught by rule of thumb is the administration of precedents. That is at once the easiest and the most fruitless form of public activity. Only a low degree of intelligence is required and of effort merely a persistent repetition. Men fall into a routine when they are tired and slack: it has all the appearance of activity with few of its burdens. It was a profound observation when Bernard Shaw said that men dread liberty because of the bewildering responsibility it imposes and the uncommon alertness it demands. To do what has always been done, to think in well-cut channels, to give up "the intolerable disease of thought," is an almost constant demand of our natures. That is perhaps why so many of the romantic rebels of the Nineteenth Century sank at last into the comforting arms of Mother Church. That is perhaps the reason why most oldish men acquire information, but learn very little. The conservative who loves his routine is in nine cases out of ten a creature too lazy to change its habits.

Confronted with a novelty, the first impulse is to snub it, and send it into exile. When it becomes too persistent to be ignored a taboo is erected and threats of fines and condign punishment are made if it doesn't cease to appear. This is the level of culture at which Sherman Anti-Trust acts are passed, brothels are raided, and labor agitators are thrown into jail. If the taboo is effective it drives the evil under cover, where it festers and emits a slow poison. This is the price we pay for the appearance of suppression. But if the problem is more heavily charged with power, the taboo irritates the force until it explodes. Not infrequently what was once simply a factor of life becomes the dominating part of it. At this point the whole routineer scheme of things collapses, there is a period of convulsion and Cæsarean births, and men weary of excitement sink back into a newer routine. Thus the cycle of futility is completed.

The process bears as much resemblance to statecraft as sitting backward on a runaway horse does to horsemanship. The ordinary politician has no real control, no direction, no insight into the power he rides. What he has is an elevated, though temporary seat. Real statesmanship has a different ambition. It begins by accepting human nature. No routine has ever done that in spite of the conservative patter about "human nature"; mechanical politics has usually begun by ignoring and ended by violating the nature of men.

To accept that nature does not mean that we accept its present character. It is probably true that the impulses of men have changed very little within recorded

148

history. What has changed enormously from epoch to epoch is the character in which these impulses appear. The impulses that at one period work themselves out into cruelty and lust may at another produce the richest values of civilized life. The statesman can affect that choice. His business is to provide fine opportunities for the expression of human impulses—to surround childhood, youth and age with homes and schools, cities and countryside that shall be stocked with interest and the chance for generous activity.

Government can play a leading part in this work, for with the decadence of the church it has become the only truly catholic organization in the land. Its task is essentially to carry out programs of service, to add and build and increase the facilities of life. Repression is an insignificant part of its work; the use of the club can never be applauded, though it may be tolerated *faute de mieux*. Its use is a confession of ignorance.

A sensitively representative machinery will probably serve such statesmanship best. For the easy expression of public opinion in government is a clue to what services are needed and a test of their success. It keeps the processes of politics well ventilated and reminds politicians of their excuse for existence.

In that kind of statesmanship there will be a premium on inventiveness, on the ingenuity to devise and plan. There will be much less use for lawyers and a great deal more for scientists. The work requires industrial organizers, engineers, architects, educators, sanitists to achieve what leadership brings into the program of politics.

This leadership is the distinctive fact about politics. The statesman acts in part as an intermediary between the experts and his constituency. He makes social movements conscious of themselves, expresses their needs, gathers their power and then thrusts them behind the inventor and the technician in the task of actual achievement. What Roosevelt did in the conservation movement was typical of the statesman's work. He recognized the need of attention to natural resources, made it public, crystallized its force and delegated the technical accomplishment to Pinchot and his subordinates.

But creative statesmanship requires a culture to support it. It can neither be taught by rule nor produced out of a vacuum. A community that clatters along with its rusty habits of thought unquestioned, making no distinction between instruments and idols, with a dull consumption of machine-made romantic fiction,

The Walter Lippmann Reader

no criticism, an empty pulpit and an unreliable press, will find itself faithfully mirrored in public affairs. The one thing that no democrat may assume is that the people are dear good souls, fully competent for their task. The most valuable leaders never assume that. No one, for example, would accuse Karl Marx of disloyalty to workingmen. Yet in 1850 he could write at the demagogues among his friends: "While we draw the attention of the German workman to the *undeveloped state* of the proletariat in Germany, you flatter the national spirit and the guild prejudices of the German artisans in the grossest manner, a method of procedure without doubt the more popular of the two. Just as the democrats made a sort of fetich of the words, 'the people,' so you make one of the word 'proletariat.'" John Spargo quotes this statement in his "Life." Marx, we are told, could use phrases like "democratic miasma." He never seems to have made the mistake of confusing democracy with demolatry. Spargo is perfectly clear about this characteristic of Marx: "He admired most of all, perhaps, that fine devotion to truth as he understood it, and disregard of popularity which marked Owen's life. Contempt for popular opinion was one of his most strongly developed characteristics. He was fond, says Liebknecht, of quoting as his motto the defiant line of Dante, with which he afterwards concluded his preface to 'Das Kapital':

'Segui il tuo corso e lascia dir le genti.'"

It is to Marx's everlasting credit that he set the intellectual standard of socialism on the most vigorous intellectual basis he could find. He knew better than to be satisfied with loose thinking and fairly good intentions. He knew that the vast change he contemplated needed every ounce of intellectual power that the world possessed. A fine boast it was that socialism was equipped with all the culture of the age. I wonder what he would have thought of an enthusiastic socialist candidate for Governor of New York who could write that "until men are free the world has no need of any more literary efforts, of any more paintings, of any more poems. It is better to have said one word for the emancipation of the race than to have written the greatest novel of the times.... The world doesn't need any more literature."

I will not venture a guess as to what Marx would have said, but I know what we must say: "Without a literature the people is dumb, without novels and poems, plays and criticism, without books of philosophy, there is neither the intelligence to plan, the imagination to conceive, nor the understanding of a common purpose. Without culture you can knock down governments, overturn property relations, you can create excitement, but you cannot create a genuine revolution in the lives of

150

The Walter Lippmann Reader

men." The reply of the workingmen in 1847 to Cabet's proposal that they found Icaria, "a new terrestrial Paradise," in Texas if you please, contains this interesting objection: "Because although those comrades who intend to emigrate with Cabet may be eager Communists, yet they still possess too many of the faults and prejudices of present-day society by reason of their past education to be able to get rid of them at once by joining Icaria."

That simple statement might be taken to heart by all the reformers and socialists who insist that the people are all right, that only institutions are wrong. The politics of reconstruction require a nation vastly better educated, a nation freed from its slovenly ways of thinking, stimulated by wider interests, and jacked up constantly by the sharpest kind of criticism. It is puerile to say that institutions must be changed from top to bottom and then assume that their victims are prepared to make the change. No amount of charters, direct primaries, or short ballots make a democracy out of an illiterate people. Those portions of America where there are voting booths but no schools cannot possibly be described as democracies. Nor can the person who reads one corrupt newspaper and then goes out to vote make any claim to having registered his will. He may have a will, but he has not used it.

For politics whose only ideal is the routine, it is just as well that men shouldn't know what they want or how to express it. Education has always been a considerable nuisance to the conservative intellect. In the Southern States, culture among the negroes is openly deplored, and I do not blame any patriarch for dreading the education of women. It is out of culture that the substance of real revolutions is made. If by some magic force you could grant women the vote and then keep them from schools and colleges, newspapers and lectures, the suffrage would be no more effective than a Blue Law against kissing your wife on Sunday. It is democratic machinery with an educated citizenship behind it that embodies all the fears of the conservative and the hopes of the radical.

Culture is the name for what people are interested in, their thoughts, their models, the books they read and the speeches they hear, their table-talk, gossip, controversies, historical sense and scientific training, the values they appreciate, the quality of life they admire. All communities have a culture. It is the climate of their civilization. Without a favorable culture political schemes are a mere imposition. They will not work without a people to work them.

The real preparation for a creative statesmanship lies deeper than parties and legislatures. It is the work of publicists and educators, scientists, preachers and artists. Through all the agents that make and popularize thought must come a bent of mind interested in invention and freed from the authority of ideas. The democratic culture must, with critical persistence, make man the measure of all things. I have tried again and again to point out the iconoclasm that is constantly necessary to avoid the distraction that comes of idolizing our own methods of thought. Without an unrelaxing effort to center the mind upon human uses, human purposes, and human results, it drops into idolatry and becomes hostile to creation.

The democratic experiment is the only one that requires this wilful humanistic culture. An absolutism like Russia's is served better when the people accept their ideas as authoritative and piously sacrifice humanity to a non-human purpose. An aristocracy flourishes where the people find a vicarious enjoyment in admiring the successes of the ruling class. That prevents men from developing their own interests and looking for their own successes. No doubt Napoleon was well content with the philosophy of those guardsmen who drank his health before he executed them.

But those excellent soldiers would make dismal citizens. A view of life in which man obediently allows himself to be made grist for somebody else's mill is the poorest kind of preparation for the work of self-government. You cannot long deny external authorities in government and hold to them for the rest of life, and it is no accident that the nineteenth century questioned a great deal more than the sovereignty of kings. The revolt went deeper and democracy in politics was only an aspect of it. The age might be compared to those years of a boy's life when he becomes an atheist and quarrels with his family. The nineteenth century was a bad time not only for kings, but for priests, the classics, parental autocrats, indissoluble marriage, Shakespeare, the Aristotelian Poetics and the validity of logic. If disobedience is man's original virtue, as Oscar Wilde suggested, it was an extraordinarily virtuous century. Not a little of the revolt was an exuberant rebellion for its own sake. There were also counter-revolutions, deliberate returns to orthodoxy, as in the case of Chesterton. The transvaluation of values was performed by many hands into all sorts of combinations.

There have been other periods of revolution. Heresy is just a few hours younger than orthodoxy. Disobedience is certainly not the discovery of the nineteenth century. But the quality of it is. I believe Chesterton has hold of an essential truth when he says that this is the first time men have boasted of their heresy. The older rebels claimed to be more orthodox than the Church, to have gone back to the true authorities. The radicals of recent times proclaim that there is no orthodoxy, no doctrine that men must accept without question.

Without doubt they deceive themselves mightily. They have their invisible popes, called Art, Nature, Science, with regalia and ritual and a catechism. But they don't mean to have them. They mean to be self-governing in their spiritual lives. And this intention is the half-perceived current which runs through our age and galvanizes so many queer revolts. It would be interesting to trace out the forms it has taken, the abortive cults it has tried and abandoned. In another connection I pointed to autonomy as the hope of syndicalism. It would not be difficult to find a similar assertion in the feminist agitation. From Mrs. Gilman's profound objections against a "man-made" world to the lady who would like to vote about her taxes, there is a feeling that woman must be something more than a passive creature. Walter Pater might be quoted in his conclusion to the effect that "the theory or idea or system which requires of us the sacrifice of any part of experience, in consideration of some interest into which we cannot enter, or some abstract theory we have not identified with ourselves, or what is only conventional, has no real claim upon us." The desire for self-direction has made a thousand philosophies as contradictory as the temperaments of the thinkers. A storehouse of illustration is at hand: Nietzsche advising the creative man to bite off the head of the serpent which is choking him and become "a transfigured being, a light-surrounded being, that laughed!" One might point to Stirner's absolute individualism or turn to Whitman's wholehearted acceptance of every man with his catalogue of defects and virtues. Some of these men have cursed each other roundly: Georges Sorel, for example, who urges workingmen to accept none of the bourgeois morality, and becomes most eloquent when he attacks other revolutionists.

I do not wish to suggest too much unanimity in the hundreds of artists and thinkers that are making the thought of our times. There is a kind of "professional reconciler" of opposites who likes to lump all the prominent rebels together and refer to them affectionately as "us radicals." Yet that there is a common impulse in modern thought which strives towards autonomy is true and worth remarking. In some men it is half-conscious, in others a minor influence, but almost no one of weight escapes the contagion of it entirely. It is a new culture that is being prepared. Without it there would to-day be no demand for a creative statesmanship which turns its back upon the routine and the taboo, kings and idols, and non-human purposes. It does more. It is making the atmosphere in which a humanly centered

The Walter Lippmann Reader

politics can flourish. The fact that this culture is multiform and often contradictory is a sign that more and more of the interests of life are finding expression. We should rejoice at that, for profusion means fertility; where a dead uniformity ceases, invention and ingenuity flourish.

Perhaps the insistence on the need of a culture in statecraft will seem to many people an old-fashioned delusion. Among the more rigid socialists and reformers it is not customary to spend much time discussing mental habits. That, they think, was made unnecessary by the discovery of an economic basis of civilization. The destinies of society are felt to be too solidly set in industrial conditions to allow any cultural direction. Where there is no choice, of what importance is opinion?

All propaganda is, of course, a practical tribute to the value of culture. However inevitable the process may seem, all socialists agree that its inevitability should be fully realized. They teach at one time that men act from class interests: but they devote an enormous amount of energy to making men conscious of their class. It evidently matters to that supposedly inevitable progress whether men are aware of it. In short, the most hardened socialist admits choice and deliberation, culture and ideals into his working faith. He may talk as if there were an iron determinism, but his practice is better than his preachment.

Yet there are necessities in social life. To all the purposes of politics it is settled, for instance, that the trust will never be "unscrambled" into small competing businesses. We say in our argument that a return to the days of the stage-coach is impossible or that "you cannot turn back the hands of the clock." Now man might return to the stage-coach if that seemed to him the supreme goal of all his effort, just as anyone can follow Chesterton's advice to turn back the hands of the clock if he pleases. But nobody can recover his yesterdays no matter how much he abuses the clock, and no man can expunge the memory of railroads though all the stations and engines were dismantled.

"From this survival of the past," says Bergson, "it follows that consciousness cannot go through the same state twice." This is the real necessity that makes any return to the imagined glories of other days an idle dream. Graham Wallas remarks that those who have eaten of the tree of knowledge cannot forget—"Mr. Chesterton cries out, like the Cyclops in the play, against those who complicate the life of man, and tells us to eat 'caviare on impulse,' instead of 'grapenuts on principle.' But since we cannot unlearn our knowledge, Mr. Chesterton is only telling us to eat caviare on principle." The binding fact we must face in all our calculations, and so in

154

politics too, is that you cannot recover what is passed. That is why educated people are not to be pressed into the customs of their ignorance, why women who have reached out for more than "Kirche, Kinder und Küche" can never again be entirely domestic and private in their lives. Once people have questioned an authority their faith has lost its naïveté. Once men have tasted inventions like the trust they have learned something which cannot be annihilated. I know of one reformer who devotes a good deal of his time to intimate talks with powerful conservatives. He explains them to themselves: never after do they exercise their power with the same unquestioning ruthlessness.

Life is an irreversible process and for that reason its future can never be a repetition of the past. This insight we owe to Bergson. The application of it to politics is not difficult because politics is one of the interests of life. We can learn from him in what sense we are bound. "The finished portrait is explained by the features of the model, by the nature of the artist, by colors spread out on the palette; but even with the knowledge of what explains it, no one, not even the artist, could have foreseen exactly what the portrait would be, for to predict it would have been to produce it before it was produced...." The future is explained by the economic and social institutions which were present at its birth: the trust and the labor union, all the "movements" and institutions, will condition it. "Just as the talent of the painter is formed or deformed—in any case, is modified—under the very influence of the work he produces, so each of our states, at the moment of its issue, modifies our personality, being indeed the new form we are just assuming. It is then right to say that what we do depends on what we are; but it is necessary to add also, that we are, to a certain extent, what we do, and that we are creating ourselves continually."

What I have called culture enters into political life as a very powerful condition. It is a way of creating ourselves. Make a blind struggle luminous, drag an unconscious impulse into the open day, see that men are aware of their necessities, and the future is in a measure controlled. The culture of to-day is for the future an historical condition. That is its political importance. The mental habits we are forming, our philosophies and magazines, theaters, debates, schools, pulpits and newspapers become part of an active past which as Bergson says "follows us at every instant; all that we have felt, thought, and willed from our earliest infancy is there, leaning over the present which is about to join it, pressing against the portals of consciousness that would fain leave it outside."

155

The Walter Lippmann Reader

Socialists claim that because the McNamara brothers had no "class-consciousness," because they were without a philosophy of society and an understanding of the labor movement their sense of wrong was bound to seek out dynamite. That is a profound truth backed by abundant evidence. If you turn, for example, to Spargo's Life of Karl Marx you see that all through his career Marx struggled with the mere insurrectionists. It was the men without the Marxian vision of growth and discipline who were forever trying to lead little marauding bands against the governments of Europe. The fact is worth pondering: the Marxian socialists, openly declaring that all authority is a temporary manifestation of social conditions, have waged what we must call a war of culture against the powers of the world. They have tried to arouse in workingmen the consciousness of an historical mission—the patience of that labor is one of the wonders of the age. But the McNamaras had a culture that could help them not at all. They were Catholics, Democrats and old-fashioned trade-unionists. Religion told them that authority was absolute and eternal, politics that Jefferson had said about all there was to say, economics insisted that the struggle between labor and capital was an everlasting see-saw. But life told them that society was brutal: an episode like the shirtwaist factory fire drove them to blasphemy and dynamite.

Those bombs at Los Angeles, assassination and terrorism, are compounded of courage, indignation and ignorance. Civilization has much to fear from the blind class antagonisms it fosters; but the preaching of "class consciousness," far from being a fomenter of violence, must be recognized as the civilizing influence of culture upon economic interests.

Thoughts and feelings count. We live in a revolutionary period and nothing is so important as to be aware of it. The measure of our self-consciousness will more or less determine whether we are to be the victims or the masters of change. Without philosophy we stumble along. The old routines and the old taboos are breaking up anyway, social forces are emerging which seek autonomy and struggle against slavery to non-human purposes. We seem to be moving towards some such statecraft as I have tried to suggest. But without knowledge of it that progress will be checkered and perhaps futile. The dynamics for a splendid human civilization are all about us. They need to be used. For that there must be a culture practiced in seeking the inwardness of impulses, competent to ward off the idols of its own thought, hospitable to novelty and sufficiently inventive to harness power.

The Walter Lippmann Reader

Why this age should have come to be what it is, why at this particular time the whole drift of thought should be from authority to autonomy would be an interesting speculation. It is one of the ultimate questions of politics. It is like asking why Athens in the Fifth Century B. C. was singled out as the luminous point of the Western World. We do not know enough to cut under such mysteries. We can only begin to guess why there was a Renaissance, why in certain centuries man seems extraordinarily creative. Perhaps the Modern Period with its flexibility, sense of change, and desire for self-direction is a liberation due to the great surplus of wealth. Perhaps the ease of travel, the popularizing of knowledge, the break-down of frontiers have given us a new interest in human life by showing how temporary are all its instruments. Certainly placid or morose acceptance is undermined. If men remain slaves either to ideas or to other men, it will be because they do not know they are slaves. Their intention is to be free. Their desire is for a full and expressive life and they do not relish a lop-sided and lamed humanity. For the age is rich with varied and generous passions.

Liberty and the News

Table of Contents

In writing this tract I have dared to believe that many things were possible because of the personal example offered to all who practice journalism by Mr. C. P. Scott, for over forty-five years editor-in-chief of the *Manchester Guardian*. In the light of his career it cannot seem absurd or remote to think of freedom and truth in relation to the news.

Two of the essays in this volume, "What Modern Liberty Means" and "Liberty and the News," were published originally in the *Atlantic Monthly*. I wish to thank Mr. Ellery Sedgwick for the encouragement he gave me while writing them, and for permission to reprint them.

W.L.
New York City

Journalism and the Higher Law

Volume I, Number I, of the first American newspaper was published in Boston on September 25, 1690. It was called *Publick Occurrences*. The second issue did not appear because the Governor and Council suppressed it. They found that Benjamin Harris, the editor, had printed "reflections of a very high nature."1 Even today some of his reflections seem very high indeed. In his prospectus he had written:

> "That something may be done toward the Curing, or at least the Charming of that Spirit of Lying, which prevails amongst us, wherefore nothing shall be entered, but what we have reason to believe is true, repairing to the best fountains for our Information. And when there appears any material mistake in anything that is collected, it shall be corrected in the next. Moreover, the Publisher of these Occurrences is willing to engage, that whereas, there are many False Reports, maliciously made, and spread among us, if any well-minded person will be at the pains to trace any such false Report, so far as to find out and Convict the First Raiser of it, he will in this Paper (unless just Advice be given to the contrary) expose the Name of such Person, as A malicious Raiser of a false Report. It is suppos'd that none will dislike this Proposal, but such as intend to be guilty of so villainous a Crime." ("History of American Journalism," James Melvin Lee, Houghton Mifflin Co., 1917, p. 10.)

Everywhere today men are conscious that somehow they must deal with questions more intricate than any that church or school had prepared them to understand. Increasingly they know that they cannot understand them if the facts are not quickly and steadily available. Increasingly they are baffled because the facts are not available; and they are wondering whether government by consent can survive in a time when the manufacture of consent is an unregulated private enterprise. For in an exact sense the present crisis of western democracy is a crisis in journalism.

I do not agree with those who think that the sole cause is corruption. There is plenty of corruption, to be sure, moneyed control, caste pressure, financial and social bribery, ribbons, dinner parties, clubs, petty politics. The speculators in Russian rubles who lied on the Paris Bourse about the capture of Petrograd are not the only example of their species. And yet corruption does not explain the condition of modern journalism.

Mr. Franklin P. Adams wrote recently: "Now there is much pettiness—and almost incredible stupidity and ignorance—in the so-called free press; but it is the pettiness, etc., common to the so-called human race—a pettiness found in musicians, steamfitters, landlords, poets, and waiters. And when Miss Lowell [who had made the usual aristocratic complaint] speaks of the incurable desire in all American newspapers to make fun of everything in season and out, we quarrel again. There is an incurable desire in American newspapers to take things much more seriously than they deserve. Does Miss Lowell read the ponderous news from Washington? Does she read the society news? Does she, we wonder, read the newspapers?"

Mr. Adams does read them, and when he writes that the newspapers take things much more seriously than they deserve, he has, as the mayor's wife remarked to the queen, said a mouthful. Since the war, especially, editors have come to believe that their highest duty is not to report but to instruct, not to print news but to save civilization, not to publish what Benjamin Harris calls "the Circumstances of Publique Affairs, both abroad and at home," but to keep the nation on the straight and narrow path. Like the Kings of England, they have elected themselves Defenders of the Faith.

"For five years," says Mr. Cobb of the *New York World*, "there has been no free play of public opinion in the world. Confronted by the inexorable necessities of war, governments conscripted public opinion....They goose-stepped it. They taught it to stand at attention and salute.... It sometimes seems that after the armistice was signed, millions of Americans must have taken a vow that they would never again do any thinking for themselves. They were willing to die for their country, but not willing to think for it." That minority, which is proudly prepared to think for it, and not only prepared, but cocksure that it alone knows how to think for it, has adopted the theory that the public should know what is good for it.

The work of reporters has thus become confused with the work of preachers, revivalists, prophets and agitators. The current theory of American newspaperdom is that an abstraction like the truth and a grace like fairness must be sacrificed whenever anyone thinks the necessities of civilization require the sacrifice. To Archbishop Whately's dictum that it matters greatly whether you put truth in the first place or the second, the candid expounder of modern journalism would reply that he put truth second to what he conceived to be the national interest. Judged simply by their product, men like Mr. Ochs or Viscount Northcliffe believe that their respective nations will perish and civilization decay unless their idea of what is patriotic is permitted to temper the curiosity of their readers.

They believe that edification is more important than veracity. They believe it profoundly, violently, relentlessly. They preen themselves upon it. To patriotism, as they define it from day to day, all other considerations must yield. That is their pride. And yet what is this but one more among myriad examples of the doctrine that the end justifies the means. A more insidiously misleading rule of conduct was, I believe, never devised among men. It was a plausible rule as long as men believed that an omniscient and benevolent Providence taught them what end to seek. But now that men are critically aware of how their purposes are special to their age, their locality, their interests, and their limited knowledge, it is blazing arrogance to sacrifice hard-won standards of credibility to some special purpose. It is nothing but the doctrine that I want what I want when I want it. Its monuments are the Inquisition and the invasion of Belgium. It is the reason given for almost every act of unreason, the law invoked whenever lawlessness justifies itself. At bottom it is nothing but the anarchical nature of man imperiously hacking its way through.

Just as the most poisonous form of disorder is the mob incited from high places, the most immoral act the immorality of a government, so the most destructive form of untruth is sophistry and propaganda by those whose profession it is to report the news. The news columns are common carriers. When those who control them arrogate to themselves the right to determine by their own consciences what shall be reported and for what purpose, democracy is unworkable. Public opinion is blockaded. For when a people can no longer confidently repair 'to the best fountains for their information,' then anyone's guess and anyone's rumor, each man's hope and each man's whim becomes the basis of government. All that the sharpest critics of democracy have alleged is true, if there is no steady supply of trustworthy and relevant news. Incompetence and aimlessness, corruption and disloyalty, panic and ultimate disaster, must come to any people which is denied an assured access to the facts. No one can manage anything on pap. Neither can a people.

Statesmen may devise policies; they will end in futility, as so many have recently ended, if the propagandists and censors can put a painted screen where there should be a window to the world. Few episodes in recent history are more poignant than that of the British Prime Minister, sitting at the breakfast table with that morning's paper before him protesting that he cannot do the sensible thing in regard to Russia because a powerful newspaper proprietor has drugged the public. That incident is a photograph of the supreme danger which confronts popular government. All other dangers are contingent upon it, for the news is the chief source of the opinion by which government now proceeds. So long as there is interposed between the ordinary citizen and the facts a news organization determining by entirely private and unexamined standards, no matter how lofty, what he shall know, and hence what he shall believe, no one will be able to say that the substance of democratic government is secure. The theory of our constitution, says Mr. Justice Holmes, is that truth is the only ground upon which men's wishes safely can be carried out. (Supreme Court of the United States, No. 316, October term, 1919, Jacob Abrams et al., Plaintiffs in Error vs. the United States.) In so far as those who purvey the news make of their own beliefs a higher law than truth, they are attacking the foundations of our constitutional system. There can be no higher law in journalism than to tell the truth and shame the devil.

That I have few illusions as to the difficulty of truthful reporting anyone can see who reads these pages. If truthfulness were simply a matter of sincerity the future would be rather simple. But the modern news problem is not solely a question of the newspaperman's morals. It is, as I have tried to show in what follows, the intricate result of a civilization too extensive for any man's personal observation. As the problem is manifold, so must be the remedy. There is no panacea. But however puzzling the matter may be, there are some things that anyone may assert about it, and assert without fear of contradiction. They are that there is a problem of the news which is of absolutely basic importance to the survival of popular government, and that the importance of that problem is not vividly realized nor sufficiently considered.

In a few generations it will seem ludicrous to historians that a people professing government by the will of the people should have made no serious effort to guarantee the news without which a governing opinion cannot exist. "Is it possible," they will ask, "that at the beginning of the Twentieth Century nations calling themselves democracies were content to act on what happened to drift across their doorsteps; that apart from a few sporadic exposures and outcries they made no plans to bring these common carriers under social control; that they provided no genuine training schools for the men upon whose sagacity they were dependent;

The Walter Lippmann Reader

above all that their political scientists went on year after year writing and lecturing about government without producing one, one single, significant study of the process of public opinion?" And then they will recall the centuries in which the Church enjoyed immunity from criticism, and perhaps they will insist that the news structure of secular society was not seriously examined for analogous reasons.

When they search into the personal records they will find that among journalists, as among the clergy, institutionalism had induced the usual prudence. I have made no criticism in this book which is not the shoptalk of reporters and editors. But only rarely do newspapermen take the general public into their confidence. They will have to sooner or later. It is not enough for them to struggle against great odds, as many of them are doing, wearing out their souls to do a particular assignment well. The philosophy of the work itself needs to be discussed; the news about the news needs to be told. For the news about the government of the news structure touches the center of all modern government.

They need not be much concerned if leathery-minded individuals ask What is Truth of all who plead for the effort of truth in modern journalism. Jesting Pilate asked the same question, and he also would not stay for an answer. No doubt an organon of news reporting must wait upon the development of psychology and political science. But resistance to the inertias of the profession, heresy to the institution, and the willingness to be fired rather than write what you do not believe, these wait on nothing but personal courage. And without the assistance which they will bring from within the profession itself, democracy through it will deal with the problem somehow, will deal with it badly.

The essays which follow are an attempt to describe the character of the problem, and to indicate headings under which it may be found useful to look for remedies.

What Modern Liberty Means

From our recent experience it is clear that the traditional liberties of speech and opinion rest on no solid foundation. At a time when the world needs above all other things the activity of generous imaginations and the creative leadership of planning and inventive minds, our thinking is shriveled with panic. Time and energy that should go to building and restoring are instead consumed in warding off the pinpricks of prejudice and fighting a guerilla war against misunderstanding and intolerance. For suppression is felt, not simply by the scattered individuals who are actually suppressed. It reaches back into the steadiest minds, creating tension everywhere; and the tension of fear produces sterility. Men cease to say what they think; and when they cease to say it, they soon cease to think it. They think in reference to their critics and not in reference to the facts. For when thought becomes socially hazardous, men spend more time wondering about the hazard than they do in cultivating their thought. Yet nothing is more certain than that mere bold resistance will not permanently liberate men's minds. The problem is not only greater than that, but different, and the time is ripe for reconsideration. We have learned that many of the hard-won rights of man are utterly insecure. It may be that we cannot make them secure simply by imitating the earlier champions of liberty.

Something important about the human character was exposed by Plato when, with the spectacle of Socrates's death before him, he founded Utopia on a censorship stricter than any which exists on this heavily censored planet. His intolerance seems strange. But it is really the logical expression of an impulse that most of us have not the candor to recognize. It was the service of Plato to formulate the dispositions of men in the shape of ideals, and the surest things we can learn from him are not what we ought to do, but what we are inclined to do. We are peculiarly inclined to suppress whatever impugns the security of that to which we have given our allegiance. If our loyalty is turned to what exists, intolerance begins at its frontiers; if it is turned, as Plato's was, to Utopia, we shall find Utopia defended with intolerance.

There are, so far as I can discover, no absolutists of liberty; I can recall no doctrine of liberty, which, under the acid test, does not become contingent upon some other ideal. The goal is never liberty, but liberty for something or other. For liberty is a condition under which activity takes place, and men's interests attach themselves primarily to their activities and what is necessary to fulfill them, not to the abstract requirements of any activity that might be conceived.

And yet controversialists rarely take this into account. The battle is fought with banners on which are inscribed absolute and universal ideals. They are not absolute and universal in fact. No man has ever thought out an absolute or a universal ideal in politics, for the simple reason that nobody knows enough, or can know enough, to do it. But we all use absolutes, because an ideal which seems to exist apart from time, space, and circumstance has a prestige that no candid avowal of special purpose can ever have. Looked at from one point of view universals are part of the fighting apparatus in men. What they desire enormously they easily come to call God's will, or their nation's purpose. Looked at genetically, these idealizations are probably born in that spiritual reverie where all men live most of the time. In reverie there is neither time, space, nor particular reference, and hope is omnipotent. This omnipotence, which is denied to them in action, nevertheless illuminates activity with a sense of utter and irresistible value.

The classic doctrine of liberty consists of absolutes. It consists of them except at the critical points where the author has come into contact with objective difficulties. Then he introduces into the argument, somewhat furtively, a reservation which liquidates its universal meaning and reduces the exalted plea for liberty in general to a special argument for the success of a special purpose.

There are at the present time, for instance, no more fervent champions of liberty than the western sympathizers with the Russian Soviet government. Why is it that they are indignant when Mr. Burleson suppresses a newspaper and complacent when Lenin does? And, *vice versa*, why is it that the anti-Bolshevist forces in the world are in favor of restricting constitutional liberty as a preliminary to establishing genuine liberty in Russia? Clearly the argument about liberty has little actual relation to the existence of it. It is the purpose of the social conflict, not the freedom of opinion, that lies close to the heart of the partisans. The word liberty is a weapon and an advertisement, but certainly not an ideal which transcends all special aims.

If there were any man who believed in liberty apart from particular purposes, that man would be a hermit contemplating all existence with a hopeful and neutral eye. For him, in the last analysis, there could be nothing worth resisting, nothing particularly worth attaining, nothing particularly worth defending, not even the right of hermits to contemplate existence with a cold and neutral eye. He would be loyal simply to the possibilities of the human spirit, even to those possibilities which most seriously impair its variety and its health. No such man has yet counted much in the history of politics. For what every theorist of liberty has meant is that certain types of behavior and classes of opinion hitherto regulated should be somewhat differently regulated in the future. What each seems to say is that opinion and action should be free; that liberty is the highest and most sacred interest of life. But somewhere each of them inserts a weasel clause to the effect that "of course" the freedom granted shall not be employed too destructively. It is this clause which checks exuberance and reminds us that, in spite of appearances, we are listening to finite men pleading a special cause.

Among the English classics none are more representative than Milton's *Areopagitica* and the essay *On Liberty* by John Stuart Mill. Of living men Mr. Bertrand Russell is perhaps the most outstanding advocate of liberty. The three together are a formidable set of witnesses. Yet nothing is easier than to draw texts from each which can be cited either as an argument for absolute liberty or as an excuse for as much repression as seems desirable at the moment. Says Milton:

> Yet if all cannot be of one mind, as who looks they should be? this doubtles is more wholsome, more prudent, and more Christian that many be tolerated, rather than all compell'd.

So much for the generalization. Now for the qualification which follows immediately upon it.

> I mean not tolerated Popery, and open superstition, which as it extirpats all religions and civill supremacies, so itself should be extirpat, provided first that all charitable and compassionat means be used to win and regain the weak and misled: that also which is impious or evil absolutely either against faith or maners no law can possibly permit, that intends not to unlaw it self: but those neighboring differences, or rather *indifferences*, are what I speak of, whether in some point of doctrine or of discipline, which though they may be many, yet need not interrupt the unity of spirit, if we could but find among us the bond of peace.

The Walter Lippmann Reader

With this as a text one could set up an inquisition. Yet it occurs in the noblest plea for liberty that exists in the English language. The critical point in Milton's thought is revealed by the word "indifferences." The area of opinion which he wished to free comprised the "neighboring differences" of certain Protestant sects, and only these where they were truly ineffective in manners and morals. Milton, in short, had come to the conclusion that certain conflicts of doctrine were sufficiently insignificant to be tolerated. The conclusion depended far less upon his notion of the value of liberty than upon his conception of God and human nature and the England of his time. He urged indifference to things that were becoming indifferent.

If we substitute the word indifference for the word liberty, we shall come much closer to the real intention that lies behind the classic argument. Liberty is to be permitted where differences are of no great moment. It is this definition which has generally guided practice. In times when men feel themselves secure, heresy is cultivated as the spice of life. During a war liberty disappears as the community feels itself menaced. When revolution seems to be contagious, heresy-hunting is a respectable occupation. In other words, when men are not afraid, they are not afraid of ideas; when they are much afraid, they are afraid of anything that seems, or can even be made to appear, seditious. That is why nine-tenths of the effort to live and let live consists in proving that the thing we wish to have tolerated is really a matter of indifference.

In Mill this truth reveals itself still more clearly. Though his argument is surer and completer than Milton's, the qualification is also surer and completer.

> Such being the reasons which make it imperative that human beings should be free to form opinions, and to express their opinions without reserve; and such the baneful consequences to the intellectual and through that to the moral nature of man, unless this liberty is either conceded or asserted in spite of prohibition, let us next examine whether the same reasons do not require that men should be free to act upon their opinions, to carry these out in their lives, without hindrance, either moral or physical, from their fellow men, so long as it is at their own risk and peril. *This last proviso is of course indispensable.* No one pretends that actions should be as free as opinions. On the contrary, *even*

168

opinions lose their immunity when the circumstances in which they are expressed are such as to constitute their expression a positive instigation to some mischievous act.

"At their own risk and peril." In other words, at the risk of eternal damnation. The premise from which Mill argued was that many opinions then under the ban of society were of no interest to society, and ought therefore not to be interfered with. The orthodoxy with which he was at war was chiefly theocratic. It assumed that a man's opinions on cosmic affairs might endanger his personal salvation and make him a dangerous member of society. Mill did not believe in the theological view, did not fear damnation, and was convinced that morality did not depend upon the religious sanction. In fact, he was convinced that a more reasoned morality could be formed by laying aside theological assumptions. "But no one pretends that actions should be as free as opinions." The plain truth is that Mill did not believe that much action would result from the toleration of those opinions in which he was most interested.

Political heresy occupied the fringe of his attention, and he uttered only the most casual comments. So incidental are they, so little do they impinge on his mind, that the arguments of this staunch apostle of liberty can be used honestly, and in fact are used, to justify the bulk of the suppressions which have recently occurred. "Even opinions lose their immunity, *when the circumstances* in which they are expressed are such as to constitute their expression a positive instigation to some mischievous act." Clearly there is no escape here for Debs or Haywood or obstructors of Liberty Loans. The argument used is exactly the one employed in sustaining the conviction of Debs.

In corroboration Mill's single concrete instance may be cited: "An opinion that corn dealers are starvers of the poor, or that private property is robbery, ought to be unmolested when simply circulated through the press, but may justly incur punishment when delivered orally to an excited mob assembled before the house of a corn dealer, or when handed about among the same mob in the form of a placard."

Clearly Mill's theory of liberty wore a different complexion when he considered opinions which might directly affect social order. Where the stimulus of opinion upon action was effective he could say with entire complacency, "The liberty of the individual must be thus far limited; he must not make himself a nuisance to other people." Because Mill believed this, it is entirely just to infer that the distinction drawn between a speech or placard and publication in the press would soon have broken down for Mill had he lived at a time when the press really circulated and the art of type-display had made a newspaper strangely like a placard.

On first acquaintance no man would seem to go further than Mr. Bertrand Russell in loyalty to what he calls "the unfettered development of all the instincts that build up life and fill it with mental delights." He calls these instincts "creative"; and against them he sets off the "possessive impulses." These, he says, should be restricted by "a public authority, a repository of practically irresistible force whose function should be primarily to repress the private use of force." Where Milton said no "tolerated Popery," Mr. Russell says, no tolerated "possessive impulses." Surely he is open to the criticism that, like every authoritarian who has preceded him, he is interested in the unfettered development of only that which seems good to him. Those who think that "enlightened selfishness" produces social harmony will tolerate more of the possessive impulses, and will be inclined to put certain of Mr. Russell's creative impulses under lock and key.

The moral is, not that Milton, Mill, and Bertrand Russell are inconsistent, or that liberty is to be obtained by arguing for it without qualifications. The impulse to what we call liberty is as strong in these three men as it is ever likely to be in our society. The moral is of another kind. It is that the traditional core of liberty, namely, the notion of indifference, is too feeble and unreal a doctrine to protect the purpose of liberty, which is the furnishing of a healthy environment in which human judgment and inquiry can most successfully organize human life. Too feeble, because in time of stress nothing is easier than to insist, and by insistence to convince, that tolerated indifference is no longer tolerable because it has ceased to be indifferent..

It is clear that in a society where public opinion has become decisive, nothing that counts in the formation of it can really be a matter of indifference. When I say "can be," I am speaking literally. What men believed about the constitution of heaven became a matter of indifference when heaven disappeared in metaphysics; but what they believe about property, government, conscription, taxation, the origins of the late war, or the origins of the Franco-Prussian War, or the distribution of Latin culture in the vicinity of copper mines, constitutes the difference between life and death, prosperity and misfortune, and it will never on this earth be tolerated as indifferent, or not interfered with, no matter how many noble arguments are made for liberty, or how many martyrs give their lives for it. If widespread tolerance of opposing views is to be achieved in modern society, it will not be simply by fighting the Debs' cases through the courts, and certainly not by threatening to upset those courts if they do not yield to the agitation. The task is fundamentally of another order, requiring other methods and other theories.

The world about which each man is supposed to have opinions has become so complicated as to defy his powers of understanding. What he knows of events that matter enormously to him, the purposes of governments, the aspirations of peoples, the struggle of classes, he knows at second, third, or fourth hand. He cannot go and see for himself. Even the things that are near to him have become too involved for his judgment. I know of no man, even among those who devote all of their time to watching public affairs, who can even pretend to keep track, at the same time, of his city government, his state government, Congress, the departments, the industrial situation, and the rest of the world. What men who make the study of politics a vocation cannot do, the man who has an hour a day for newspapers and talk cannot possibly hope to do. He must seize catchwords and headlines or nothing.

This vast elaboration of the subject-matter of politics is the root of the whole problem. News comes from a distance; it comes helter-skelter, in inconceivable confusion; it deals with matters that are not easily understood; it arrives and is assimilated by busy and tired people who must take what is given to them. Any lawyer with a sense of evidence knows how unreliable such information must necessarily be.

The taking of testimony in a trial is hedged about with a thousand precautions derived from long experience of the fallibility of the witness and the prejudices of the jury. We call this, and rightly, a fundamental phase of human liberty. But in public affairs the stake is infinitely greater. It involves the lives of millions, and the fortune of everybody. The jury is the whole community, not even the qualified voters alone. The jury is everybody who creates public sentiment— chattering gossips, unscrupulous liars, congenital liars, feeble-minded people, prostitute corrupting agents. To this jury any testimony is submitted, is submitted in any form, by any anonymous person, with no test of reliability, no test of credibility, and no penalty for perjury. If I lie in a lawsuit involving the fate of my neighbor's cow, I can go to jail. But if I lie to a million readers in a matter involving war and peace, I can lie my head off, and, if I choose the right series of lies, be entirely irresponsible. Nobody will punish me if I lie about Japan, for example. I can announce that every

171

The Walter Lippmann Reader

Japanese valet is a reservist, and every Japanese art store a mobilization center. I am immune. And if there should be hostilities with Japan, the more I lied the more popular I should be. If I asserted that the Japanese secretly drank the blood of children, that Japanese women were unchaste, that the Japanese were really not a branch of the human race after all, I guarantee that most of the newspapers would print it eagerly, and that I could get a hearing in churches all over the country. And all this for the simple reason that the public, when it is dependent on testimony and protected by no rules of evidence, can act only on the excitement of its pugnacities and its hopes.

The mechanism of the news-supply has developed without plan, and there is no one point in it at which one can fix the responsibility for truth. The fact is that the subdivision of labor is now accompanied by the subdivision of the news-organization. At one end of it is the eye-witness, at the other, the reader. Between the two is a vast, expensive transmitting and editing apparatus. This machine works marvelously well at times, particularly in the rapidity with which it can report the score of a game or a transatlantic flight, or the death of a monarch, or the result of an election. But where the issue is complex, as for example in the matter of the success of a policy, or the social conditions among a foreign people—that is to say, where the real answer is neither yes or no, but subtle, and a matter of balanced evidence—the subdivision of the labor involved in the report causes no end of derangement, misunderstanding, and even misrepresentation.

Thus the number of eye-witnesses capable of honest statement is inadequate and accidental. Yet. the reporter making up his news is dependent upon the eye-witnesses. They may be actors in the event. Then they can hardly be expected to have perspective. Who, for example, if he put aside his own likes and dislikes would trust a Bolshevik's account of what exists in Soviet Russia or an exiled Russian prince's story of what exists in Siberia? Sitting just across the frontier, say in Stockholm, how is a reporter to write dependable news when his witnesses consist of *emigrés* or Bolshevist agents?

At the Peace Conference, news was given out by the agents of the conferees and the rest leaked through those who were clamoring at the doors of the Conference. Now the reporter, if he is to earn his living, must nurse his personal contacts with the eye-witnesses and privileged informants. If he is openly hostile to those in authority, he will cease to be a reporter unless there is an opposition party in the inner circle who can feed him news. Failing that, he will know precious little of what is going on.

Most people seem to believe that, when they meet a war correspondent or a special writer from the Peace Conference, they have seen a man who has seen the things he wrote about. Far from it. Nobody, for example, saw this war. Neither the men in the trenches nor the commanding general. The men saw their trenches, their billets, sometimes they saw an enemy trench, but nobody, unless it be the aviators, saw a battle. What the correspondents saw, occasionally, was the terrain over which a battle had been fought; but what they reported day by day was what they were told at press headquarters, and of that only what they were allowed to tell.

At the Peace Conference the reporters were allowed to meet periodically the four least important members of the Commission, men who themselves had considerable difficulty in keeping track of things, as any reporter who was present will testify. This was supplemented by spasmodic personal interviews with the commissioners, their secretaries, their secretaries' secretaries, other newspaper men, and confidential representatives of the President, who stood between him and the impertinences of curiosity. This and the French press, than which there is nothing more censored and inspired, a local English trade-journal of the expatriates, the gossip of the Grillon lobby, the Majestic, and the other official hotels, constituted the source of the news upon which American editors and the American people have had to base one of the most difficult judgments of their history. I should perhaps add that there were a few correspondents occupying privileged positions with foreign governments. They wore ribbons in their button-holes to prove it. They were in many ways the most useful correspondents because they always revealed to the trained reader just what it was that their governments wished America to believe.

The news accumulated by the reporter from his witnesses has to be selected, if for no other reason than that the cable facilities are limited. At the cable office several varieties of censorship intervene. The legal censorship in Europe is political as well as military, and both words are elastic. It has been applied, not only to the substance of the news, but to the mode of presentation, and even to the character of the type and the position on the page. But the real censorship on the wires is the cost of transmission. This in itself is enough to limit any expensive competition or any significant independence. The big Continental news agencies are subsidized. Censorship operates also through congestion and the resultant need of a system of priority. Congestion makes possible good and bad service, and undesirable messages are not infrequently served badly.

When the report does reach the editor, another series of interventions occurs. The editor is a man who may know all about something, but he can hardly be expected to know all about everything. Yet he has to decide the question which is of more importance than any other in the formation of opinions, the question where attention is to be directed. In a newspaper the heads are the foci of attention, the odd corners the fringe; and whether one aspect of the news or another appears in the center or at the periphery makes all the difference in the world. The news of the day as it reaches the newspaper office is an incredible medley of fact, propaganda, rumor, suspicion, clues, hopes, and fears, and the task of selecting and ordering that news is one of the truly sacred and priestly offices in a democracy. For the newspaper, is in all literalness the bible of democracy, the book out of which a people determines its conduct. It is the only serious book most people read. It is the only book they read every day. Now the power to determine each day what shall seem important and what shall be neglected is a power unlike any that has been exercised since the Pope lost his hold on the secular mind.

The ordering is not done by one man, but by a host of men, who are on the whole curiously unanimous in their selection and in their emphasis. Once you know the party and social affiliations of a newspaper, you can predict with considerable certainty the perspective in which the news will be displayed. This perspective is by no means altogether deliberate. Though the editor is ever so much more sophisticated than all but a minority of his readers, his own sense of relative importance is determined by rather standardized constellations of ideas. He very soon comes to believe that his habitual emphasis is the only possible one.

Why the editor is possessed by a particular set of ideas is a difficult question in social psychology, of which no adequate analysis has been made. But we shall not be far wrong if we say that he deals with the news in reference to the prevailing mores of his social group. These mores are of course in a large measure the product of what previous newspapers have said; and experience shows that, in order to break out of this circle, it has been necessary at various times to create new forms of journalism, such as the national monthly, the critical weekly, the circular, the paid advertisements of ideas, in order to change the emphasis which had become obsolete and habit-ridden.

The Walter Lippmann Reader

Into this extremely refractory, and I think increasingly disserviceable mechanism, there has been thrown, especially since the outbreak of war, another monkey-wrench—propaganda. The word, of course, covers a multitude of sins and a few virtues. The virtues can be easily separated out, and given another name, either advertisement or advocacy. Thus, if the National Council of Belgravia wishes to publish a magazine out of its own funds, under its own imprint, advocating the annexation of Thrums, no one will object. But if, in support of that advocacy, it gives to the press stories that are lies about the atrocities committed in Thrums; or, worse still, if those stories seem to come from Geneva, or Amsterdam, not from the press-service of the National Council of Belgravia, then Belgravia is conducting propaganda. If, after arousing a certain amount of interest in itself, Belgravia then invites a carefully selected correspondent, or perhaps a labor leader, to its capital, puts him up at the best hotel, rides him around in limousines, fawns on him at banquets, lunches with him very confidentially, and then puts him through a conducted tour so that he shall see just what will create the desired impression, then again Belgravia is conducting propaganda. Or if Belgravia happens to possess the greatest trombone-player in the world, and if she sends him over to charm the wives of influential husbands, Belgravia is, in a less objectionable way, perhaps, committing propaganda, and making fools of the husbands.

Now, the plain fact is that out of the troubled areas of the world the public receives practically nothing that is not propaganda. Lenin and his enemies control all the news there is of Russia, and no court of law would accept any of the testimony as valid in a suit to determine the possession of a donkey. I am writing many months after the Armistice. The Senate is at this moment engaged in debating the question whether it will guarantee the frontiers of Poland; but what we learn of Poland we learn from the Polish Government and the Jewish Committee. Judgment on the vexed issues of Europe is simply out of the question for the average American; and the more cocksure he is, the more certainly is he the victim of some propaganda.

These instances are drawn from foreign affairs, but the difficulty at home, although less flagrant, is nevertheless real. Theodore Roosevelt, and Leonard Wood after him, have told us to think nationally. It is not easy. It is easy to parrot what those people say who live in a few big cities and who have constituted themselves the only true and authentic voice of America. But beyond that it is difficult. I live in New York and I have not the vaguest idea what Brooklyn is interested in. It is possible, with effort, much more effort than most people can afford to give, for me to know what a few organized bodies like the NonPartisan League, the National Security League, the American Federation of Labor, and the Republican National Committee are up to; but what the unorganized workers, and the unorganized farmers, the shopkeepers, the local bankers and boards of trade are thinking and feeling, no one has any means of knowing, except perhaps in a vague way at election time. To think nationally means, at least, to take into account the major interests and needs and desires of this continental population; and for that each man would need a staff of secretaries, traveling agents, and a very expensive press-clipping bureau.

We do not think nationally because the facts that count are not systematically reported and presented in a form we can digest. Our most abysmal ignorance occurs where we deal with the immigrant. If we read his press at all, it is to discover "Bolshevism" in it and to blacken all immigrants with suspicion. For his culture and his aspirations, for his high gifts of hope and variety, we have neither eyes nor ears. The immigrant colonies are like holes in the road which we never notice until we trip over them. Then, because we have no current information and no background of facts, we are, of course, the undiscriminating objects of any agitator who chooses to rant against "foreigners."

Now, men who have lost their grip upon the relevant facts of their environment are the inevitable victims of agitation and propaganda. The quack, the charlatan, the jingo, and the terrorist, can flourish only where the audience is deprived of independent access to information. But where all news comes at second-hand, where all the testimony is uncertain, men cease to respond to truths, and respond simply to opinions. The environment in which they act is not the realities themselves, but the pseudo-environment of reports, rumors, and guesses. The whole reference of thought comes to be what somebody asserts, not what actually is. Men ask, not whether such and such a thing occurred in Russia, but whether Mr. Raymond Robins is at heart more friendly to the Bolsheviki than Mr. Jerome Landfield. And so, since they are deprived of any trustworthy means of knowing what is really going on, since everything is on the plane of assertion and propaganda, they believe whatever fits most comfortably with their prepossessions.

That this breakdown of the means of public knowledge should occur at a time of immense change is a compounding of the difficulty. From bewilderment to panic is a short step, as everyone knows who has watched a crowd when danger

176

threatens.At the present time a nation easily acts like a crowd. Under the influence of headlines and panicky print, the contagion of unreason can easily spread through a settled community. For when the comparatively recent and unstable nervous organization which makes us capable of responding to reality as it is, and not as we should wish it, is baffled over a continuing period of time, the more primitive but much stronger instincts are let loose.

War and Revolution, both of them founded on censorship and propaganda, are the supreme destroyers of realistic thinking, because the excess of danger and the fearful overstimulation of passion unsettle disciplined behavior. Both breed fanatics of all kinds, men who, in the words of Mr. Santayana, have redoubled their effort when they have forgotten their aim.The effort itself has become the aim. Men live in their effort, and for a time find great exaltation. They seek stimulation of their effort rather than direction of it. That is why both in war and revolution there seems to operate a kind of Gresham's Law of the emotions, in which leadership passes by a swift degradation from a Mirabeau to a Robespierre; and in war, from a high-minded statesmanship to the depths of virulent, hating jingoism.

The cardinal fact always is the loss of contact with objective information. Public as well as private reason depends upon it. Not what somebody says, not what somebody wishes were true, but what is so beyond all our opining, constitutes the touchstone of our sanity. And a society which lives at second-hand will commit incredible follies and countenance inconceivable brutalities if that contact is intermittent and untrustworthy. Demagoguery is a parasite that flourishes where discrimination fails, and only those who are at grips with things themselves are impervious to it. For, in the last analysis, the demagogue, whether of the Right or the Left, is, consciously or unconsciously an undetected liar.

Many students of politics have concluded that, because public opinion was unstable, the remedy lay in making government as independent of it as possible. The theorists of representative government have argued persistently from this premise against the believers in direct legislation. But it appears now that, while they have been making their case against direct legislation, rather successfully it seems to me, they have failed sufficiently to notice the increasing malady of representative government.

Parliamentary action is becoming notoriously ineffective. In America certainly the concentration of power in the Executive is out of all proportion either to the intentions of the Fathers or to the orthodox theory of representative government.

The Walter Lippmann Reader

The cause is fairly clear. Congress is an assemblage of men selected for local reasons from districts. It brings to Washington a more or less accurate sense of the superficial desires of its constituency. In Washington it is supposed to think nationally and internationally. But for that task its equipment and its sources of information are hardly better than that of any other reader of the newspaper. Except for its spasmodic investigating committees, Congress has no particular way of informing itself. But the Executive has. The Executive is an elaborate hierarchy reaching to every part of the nation and to all parts of the world. It has an independent machinery, fallible and not too truthworthy, of course, but nevertheless a machinery of intelligence. It can be informed and it can act, whereas Congress is not informed and cannot act.

Now the popular theory of representative government is that the representatives have the information and therefore create the policy which the executive administers. The more subtle theory is that the executive initiates the policy which the legislature corrects in accordance with popular wisdom. But when the legislature is haphazardly informed, this amounts to very little, and the people themselves prefer to trust the executive which knows, rather than the Congress which is vainly trying to know. The result has been the development of a kind of government which has been harshly described as plebiscite autocracy, or government by newspapers. Decisions in the modern state tend to be made by the interaction, not of Congress and the executive, but of public opinion and the executive.

Public opinion for this purpose finds itself collected about special groups which act as extralegal organs of government. There is a labor nucleus, a farmers' nucleus, a prohibition nucleus, a National Security League nucleus, and so on. These groups conduct a continual electioneering campaign upon the unformed, exploitable mass of public opinion. Being special groups, they have special sources of information, and what they lack in the way of information is often manufactured. These conflicting pressures beat upon the executive departments and upon Congress, and formulate the conduct of the government. The government itself acts in reference to these groups far more than in reference to the district congressmen. So politics as it is now played consists in coercing and seducing the representative by the threat and the appeal of these unofficial groups. Sometimes they are the allies, sometimes the enemies, of the party in power, but more and more they are the energy of public affairs. Government tends to operate by the impact of controlled opinion upon administration. This shift in the locus of sovereignty has placed a premium upon the manufacture of what is usually called consent. No wonder that the most powerful newspaper proprietor in the English-speaking world declined a mere government post.

No wonder, too, that the protection of the sources of its opinion is the basic problem of democracy. Everything else depends upon it. Without protection against propaganda, without standards of evidence, without criteria of emphasis, the living substance of all popular decision is exposed to every prejudice and to infinite exploitation. That is why I have argued that the older doctrine of liberty was misleading. It did not assume a public opinion that governs. Essentially it demanded toleration of opinions that were, as Milton said, indifferent. It can guide us little in a world where opinion is sensitive and decisive.

The axis of the controversy needs to be shifted. The attempt to draw fine distinctions between "liberty" and "license" is no doubt part of the day's work, but it is fundamentally a negative part. It consists in trying to make opinion responsible to prevailing social standards, whereas the really important thing is to try and make opinion increasingly responsible to the facts. There can be no liberty for a community which lacks the information by which to detect lies. Trite as the conclusion may at first seem, it has, I believe, immense practical consequences, and may perhaps offer an escape from the logomachy into which the contests of liberty so easily degenerate.

It may be bad to suppress a particular opinion, but the really deadly thing is to suppress the news. In time of great insecurity, certain opinions acting on unstable minds may cause infinite disaster. Knowing that such opinions necessarily originate in slender evidence, that they are propelled more by prejudice from the rear than by reference to realities, it seems to me that to build the case for liberty upon the dogma of their unlimited prerogatives is to build it upon the poorest foundation. For, even though we grant that the world is best served by the liberty of all opinion, the plain fact is that men are too busy and too much concerned to fight more than spasmodically for such liberty. When freedom of opinion is revealed as freedom of error, illusion, and misinterpretation, it is virtually impossible to stir up much interest in its behalf. It is the thinnest of all abstractions and an over-refinement of mere intellectualism. But people, wide circles of people, are aroused when their curiosity is baulked. The desire to know, the dislike of being deceived and made game of, is a really powerful motive, and it is that motive that can best be enlisted in the cause of freedom.

The Walter Lippmann Reader

What, for example, was the one most general criticism of the work of the Peace Conference? It was that the covenants were not openly arrived at. This fact stirred Republican Senators, British Labor, the whole gamut of parties from the Right to the Left. And in the last analysis lack of parties from the Right to the Left. And in the last analysis lack of information about the Conference was the origin of its difficulties. Because of the secrecy endless suspicion was aroused; because of it the world seemed to be presented with a series of accomplished facts which it could not reject and did not wish altogether to accept. It was lack of information which kept public opinion from affecting the negotiations at the time when intervention would have counted most and cost least. Publicity occurred when the covenants were arrived at, with all the emphasis on the at. This is what the Senate objected to, and this is what alienated much more liberal opinion than the Senate represents.

In a passage quoted previously in this essay, Milton said that differences of opinion, "which though they may be many, yet need not interrupt the unity of spirit, if we could but find among us the bond of peace." There is but one kind of unity possible in a world as diverse as ours. It is unity of method, rather than of aim; the unity of the disciplined experiment. There is but one bond of peace that is both permanent and enriching: the increasing knowledge of the world in which experiment occurs. With a common intellectual method and a common area of valid fact, differences may become a form of co-operation and cease to be an irreconcilable antagonism.

That, I think, constitutes the meaning of freedom for us. We cannot successfully define liberty, or accomplish it, by a series of permissions and prohibitions. For that is to ignore the content of opinion in favor of its form. Above all, it is an attempt to define liberty of opinion in terms of opinion. It is a circular and sterile logic. A useful definition of liberty is obtainable only by seeking the principle of liberty in the main business of human life, that is to say, in the process by which men educate their response and learn to control their environment. In this view liberty is the name we give to measures by which we protect and increase the veracity of the information upon which we act.

Liberty and the News

The debates about liberty have hitherto all been attempts to determine just when in the series from Right to Left the censorship should intervene. In the preceding paper I ventured to ask whether these attempts do not turn on a misconception of the problem. The conclusion reached was that, in dealing with liberty of opinion, we were dealing with a subsidiary phase of the whole matter; that, so long as we were content to argue about the privileges and immunities of opinion, we were missing the point and trying to make bricks without straw. We should never succeed even in fixing a standard of tolerance for opinions, if we concentrated all our attention on the opinions. For they are derived, not necessarily by reason, to be sure, but somehow, from the stream of news that reaches the public, and the protection of that stream is the critical interest in a modern state. In going behind opinion to the information which it exploits, and in making the validity of the news our ideal, we shall be fighting the battle where it is really being fought. We shall be protecting for the public interest that which all the special interests in the world are most anxious to corrupt.

As the sources of the news are protected, as the information they furnish becomes accessible and usable, as our capacity to read that information is educated, the old problem of tolerance will wear a new aspect. Many questions which seem hopelessly insoluble now will cease to seem important enough to be worth solving. Thus the advocates of a larger freedom always argue that true opinions will prevail over error; their opponents always claim that you can fool most of the people most of the time. Both statements are true, but both are half-truths. True opinions can prevail only if the facts to which they refer are known; if they are not known, false ideas are just as effective as true ones, if not a little more effective.

The sensible procedure in matters affecting the liberty of opinion would be to ensure as impartial an investigation of the facts as is humanly possible. But it is just this investigation that is denied us. It is denied us, because we are dependent upon the testimony of anonymous and untrained and prejudiced witnesses; because the complexity of the relevant facts is beyond the scope of our hurried understanding; and finally, because the process we call education fails so lamentably to educate the sense of evidence or the power of penetrating to the controlling center of a situation. The task of liberty, therefore, falls roughly under three heads, protection of the sources of the news, organization of the news so as to make it comprehensible, and education of human response.

We need, first, to know what can be done with the existing news-structure, in order to correct its grosser evils. How far is it useful to go in fixing personal responsibility for the truthfulness of news? Much further, I am inclined to think, than we have ever gone. We ought to know the names of the whole staff of every periodical. While it is not necessary, or even desirable, that each article should be signed, each article should be documented, and false documentation should be illegal. An item of news should always state whether it is received from one of the great news-agencies, or from a reporter, or from a press bureau. Particular emphasis should be put on marking news supplied by press bureaus, whether they are labeled "Geneva," or "Stockholm," or "El Paso."

One wonders next whether anything can be devised to meet that great evil of the press, the lie which, once under way, can never be tracked down. The more scrupulous papers will, of course, print a retraction when they have unintentionally injured someone; but the retraction rarely compensates the victim. The law of libel is a clumsy and expensive instrument, and rather useless to private individuals or weak organizations because of the gentlemen's agreement which obtains in the newspaper world. After all; the remedy for libel is not money damages, but an undoing of the injury. Would it be possible then to establish courts of honor in which publishers should be compelled to meet their accusers and, if found guilty of misrepresentation, ordered to publish the correction in the particular form and with the prominence specified by the finding of the court? I do not know. Such courts might prove to be a great nuisance, consuming time and energy and attention; and offering too free a field for individuals with a persecution mania.

Perhaps a procedure could be devised which would eliminate most of these inconveniences. Certainly it would be a great gain if the accountability of publishers could be increased. They exercise more power over the individual than is healthy, as everybody knows who has watched the yellow press snooping at keyholes and invading the privacy of helpless men and women. Even more important than this, is the utterly reckless power of the press in dealing with news vitally affecting the friendship of peoples. In a Court of Honor, possible perhaps only in Utopia, voluntary associations working for decent relations with other peoples might hale the jingo and the subtle propagandist before a tribunal, to prove the reasonable truth of his assertion or endure the humiliation of publishing prominently a finding against his character.

This whole subject is immensely difficult, and full of traps. It would be well worth an intensive investigation by a group of publishers, lawyers, and students of public affairs. Because in some form or other the next generation will attempt to bring the publishing business under greater social control. There is everywhere an increasingly angry disillusionment about the press, a growing sense of being baffled and misled; and wise publishers will not pooh-pooh these omens. They might well note the history of prohibition, where a failure to work out a programme of temperance brought about an undiscriminating taboo. The regulation of the publishing business is a subtle and elusive matter, and only by an early and sympathetic effort to deal with great evils can the more sensible minds retain their control. If publishers and authors themselves do not face the facts and attempt to deal with them, some day Congress, in a fit of temper, egged on by an outraged public opinion, will operate on the press with an ax. For somehow the community must find a way of making the men who publish news accept responsibility for an honest effort not to misrepresent the facts.

But the phrase "honest effort" does not take us very far. The problem here is not different from that which we begin dimly to apprehend in the field of government and business administration. The untrained amateur may mean well, but he knows not how to do well. Why should he? What are the qualifications for being a surgeon? A certain minimum of special training. What are the qualifications for operating daily on the brain and heart of a nation? None. Go some time and listen to the average run of questions asked in interviews with Cabinet officers—or anywhere else.

I remember one reporter who was detailed to the Peace Conference by a leading news-agency He came around every day for "news." It was a time when Central Europe seemed to be disintegrating, and great doubt existed as to whether governments would be found with which to sign a peace. But all that this "reporter" wanted to know was whether the German fleet, then safely interned at Scapa Flow, was going to be sunk in the North Sea. He insisted every day on knowing that. For him it was the German fleet or nothing. Finally, he could endure it ho longer. So he anticipated Admiral Reuther and announced, in a dispatch to his home papers, that the fleet would be sunk. And when I say that a million American adults learned all that they ever learned about the Peace Conference through this reporter, I am stating a very moderate figure.

He suggests the delicate question raised by the schools of journalism: how far can we go in turning newspaper enterprise from a haphazard trade into a disciplined profession? Quite far, I imagine, for it is altogether unthinkable that a society like ours should remain forever dependent upon untrained accidental witnesses. It is no answer to say that there have been in the past, and that there are now, first-rate correspondents. Of course there are. Men like Brailsford, Oulahan, Gibbs, Lawrence, Swope, Strunsky, Draper, Hard, Dillon, Lowry, Levine, Ackerman, Ray Stannard Baker, Frank Cobb, and William Allen White, know their way about in this world. But they are eminences on a rather flat plateau. The run of the news is handled by men of much smaller caliber. It is handled by such men because reporting is not a dignified profession for which men will invest the time and cost of an education, but an underpaid, insecure, anonymous form of drudgery, conducted on catch-as-catch-can principles. Merely to talk about the reporter in terms of his real importance to civilization will make newspaper men laugh. Yet reporting is a post of peculiar honor. Observation must precede every other activity, and the public observer (that is, the reporter) is a man of critical value. No amount of money or effort spent in fitting the right men for this work could possibly be wasted, for the health of society depends upon the quality of the information it receives.

Do our schools of journalism, the few we have, make this kind of training their object, or are they trade-schools designed to fit men for higher salaries in the existing structure? I do not presume to answer the question, nor is the answer of great moment when we remember how small a part these schools now play in actual journalism. But it is important to know whether it would be worth while to endow large numbers of schools on the model of those now existing, and make their diplomas a necessary condition for the practice of reporting. It is worth considering. Against the idea lies the fact that it is difficult to decide just what reporting is—where in the whole mass of printed matter it begins and ends. No one would wish to set up a closed guild of reporters and thus exclude invaluable casual reporting and writing. If there is anything in the idea at all, it would apply only to the routine service of the news through large organizations.

Personally I should distrust too much ingenuity of this kind, on the ground that, while it might correct certain evils, the general tendency would be to turn the control of the news over to unenterprising stereotyped minds soaked in the traditions of a journalism always ten years out of date. The better course is to avoid the deceptive short cuts, and make up our minds to send out into reporting a generation of men who will by sheer superiority, drive the incompetents out of business. That means two things. It means a public recognition of the dignity of such a career, so that it will cease to be the refuge of the vaguely talented. With this increase of prestige must go a professional training in journalism in which the ideal of objective testimony is cardinal. The cynicism of the trade needs to be abandoned, for the true patterns of the journalistic apprentice are not the slick persons who scoop the news, but the patient and fearless men of science who have labored to see what the world really is. It does not matter that the news is not susceptible of mathematical statement. In fact, just because news is complex and slippery, good reporting requires the exercise of the highest of the scientific virtues. They are the habits of ascribing no more credibility to a statement than it warrants, a nice sense of the probabilities, and a keen understanding of the quantitative importance of particular facts. You can judge the general reliability of any observer most easily by the estimate he puts upon the reliability of his own report. If you have no facts of your own with which to check him, the best rough measurement is to wait and see whether he is aware of any limitations in himself; whether he knows that he saw only part of the event he describes; and whether he has any background of knowledge against which he can set what he thinks he has seen.

This kind of sophistication is, of course, necessary for the merest pretense to any education. But for different professions it needs to be specialized in particular ways. A sound legal training is pervaded by it, but the skepticism is pointed to the type of case with which the lawyer deals. The reporter's work is not carried on under the same conditions, and therefore requires a different specialization. How he is to acquire it is, of course, a pedagogical problem requiring an inductive study of the types of witness and the sources of information with whom the reporter is in contact.

Some time in the future, when men have thoroughly grasped the role of public opinion in society, scholars will not hesitate to write treatises on evidence for the use of news-gathering services. No such treatise exists today, because political science has suffered from that curious prejudice of the scholar which consists in regarding an irrational phenomenon as not quite worthy of serious study.

The Walter Lippmann Reader

Closely akin to an education in the tests of credibility is rigorous discipline in the use of words. It is almost impossible to overestimate the confusion in daily life caused by sheer inability to use language with intention. We talk scornfully of "mere .words." Yet through words the whole vast process of human .communication takes place. The sights and sounds and meanings of nearly all that we deal with as "politics," we learn, not by our own experience, but through the words of others. If those words are meaningless lumps charged with emotion, instead of the messengers of fact, all sense of evidence breaks down. Just so long as big words like Bolshevism, Americanism, patriotism, pro-Germanism, are used by reporters to cover anything and anybody that the biggest fool at large wishes to include, just so long shall we be seeking our course through a fog so dense that we cannot tell whether we fly upside-down or right-side-up. It is a measure of our education as a people that so many of us are perfectly content to live our political lives in this fraudulent environment of unanalyzed words. For the reporter, abracadabra is fatal. So long as he deals in it, he is gullibility itself, seeing nothing of the world, and living, as it were, in a hall of crazy mirrors.

Only the discipline of a modernized logic can open the door to reality. An overwhelming part of the dispute about "freedom of opinion" turns on words which mean different things to the censor and the agitator. So long as the meanings of the words are not dissociated, the dispute will remain a circular wrangle. Education that shall make men masters of their vocabulary is one of the central interests of liberty. For such an education alone can transform the dispute into debate from similar premises.

A sense of evidence and a power to define words must for the modern reporter be accompanied by a working knowledge of the main stratifications and currents of interest. Unless he knows that "news" of society almost always starts from a special group, he is doomed to report the surface of events. He will report the ripples of a passing steamer, and forget the tides and the currents and the ground-swell. He will report what Kolchak or Lenin says, and see what they do only when it confirms what he thinks they said. He will deal with the flicker of events and not with their motive. There are ways of reading that flicker so as to discern the motive, but they have not been formulated in the light of recent knowledge. Here is big work for the student of politics. The good reporter reads events with an intuition trained by wide personal experience. The poor reporter cannot read them, because he is not even aware that there is anything in particular to read.

The Walter Lippmann Reader

And then the reporter needs a general sense of what the world is doing. Emphatically he ought not to be serving a cause, no matter how good. In his professional activity it is no business of his to care whose ox is gored. To be sure, when so much reporting is ex parte, and hostile to insurgent forces, the insurgents in self-defense send out ex parte reporters of their own. But a community cannot rest content to learn the truth about the Democrats by reading the Republican papers, and the truth about the Republicans by reading the Democratic papers. There is room, and there is need, for disinterested reporting; and if this sounds like a counsel of perfection now, it is only because the science of public opinion is still at the point where astronomy was when theological interests proclaimed the conclusions that all research must vindicate.

While the reporter will serve no cause, he will possess a steady sense that the chief purpose of "news" is to enable mankind to live successfully toward the future. He will know that the world is a process, not by any means always onward and upward, but never quite the same. As the observer of the signs of change, his value to society depends upon the prophetic discrimination with which he selects those signs.

But the news from which he must pick and choose has long since become too complicated even for the most highly trained reporter. The work, say, of the government is really a small part of the day's news, yet even the wealthiest and most resourceful newspapers fail in their efforts to report "Washington." The high lights and the disputes and sensational incidents are noted, but no one can keep himself informed about his Congressman or about the individual departments, by reading the daily press. This failure in no way reflects on the newspapers. It results from the intricacy and unwieldiness of the subject-matter. Thus, it is easier to report Congress than it is to report the departments, because the work of Congress crystallizes crudely every so often in a roll-call. But administration, although it has become more important than legislation, is hard to follow, because its results are spread over a longer period of time, and its effects are felt in ways that no reporter can really measure.

Theoretically Congress is competent to act as the critical eye on administration. Actually, the investigations of Congress are almost always plan-less raids, conducted by men too busy and too little informed to do more than catch the grosser evils, or intrude upon good work that is not understood. It was a recognition of these difficulties that was the cause of two very interesting experiments in late years. One was the establishment of more or less semi-official institutes of government research; the other, the growth of specialized private agencies which attempt to give

187

technical summaries of the work of various branches of the government. Neither experiment has created much commotion: yet together they illustrate an idea which, properly developed, will be increasingly valuable to an enlightened public opinion.

Their principle is simple. They are expert organized reporters. Having no horror of dullness, no interest in being dramatic, they can study statistics and orders and reports which are beyond the digestive powers of a newspaper man or of his readers. The lines of their growth would seem to be threefold: to make a current record, to make a running analysis of it, and on the basis of both, to suggest plans.

Record and analysis require an experimental formulation of standards by which the work of government can be tested. Such standards are not to be evolved off-hand out of anyone's consciousness. Some have already been worked out experimentally, others still need to be discovered; all need to be refined and brought into perspective by the wisdom of experience. Carried out competently, the public would gradually learn to substitute objective criteria for gossip and intuitions. One can imagine a public-health service subjected to such expert criticism. The institute of research publishes the death-rate as a whole for a period of years. It seems that for a particular season the rate is bad in certain maladies, that in others the rate of improvement is not sufficiently rapid. These facts are compared with the expenditures of the service, and with the main lines of its activity. Are the bad results due to the causes beyond the control of the service? Do they indicate a lack of foresight in asking appropriations for special work? Or in the absence of novel phenomena, do they point to a decline of the personnel, or in its morale? If the latter, further analysis may reveal that salaries are too low to attract men of ability, or that the head of the service by bad management has weakened the interest of his staff.

When the work of government is analyzed in some such way as this, the reporter deals with a body of knowledge that has been organized for his apprehension. In other words, he is able to report the "news," because between him and the raw material of government there has been interposed a more or less expert political intelligence. He ceases to be the ant, described by William James, whose view of a building was obtained by crawling over the cracks in the walls.

These political observatories will, I think, be found useful in all branches of government, national, state, municipal, industrial and even in foreign affairs. They should be clearly out of reach either of the wrath or of the favor of the office-holders. They must, of course, be endowed, but the endowment should be beyond the immediate control of the legislature and of the rich patron. Their independence can be partially protected by the terms of the trust; the rest must be defended by the ability of the institute to make itself so much the master of the facts as to be impregnably based on popular confidence.

One would like to think that the universities could be brought into such a scheme. Were they in close contact with the current record and analysis, there might well be a genuine "field work" in political science for the students; and there could be no better directing idea for their more advanced researches than the formulation of the intellectual methods by which the experience of government could be brought to usable control. After all, the purpose of studying "political science" is to be able to act more effectively in politics, the word effectively being understood in the largest and, therefore, the ideal sense. In the universities men should be able to think patiently and generously for the good of society. If they do not, surely one of the reasons is that thought terminates in doctor's theses and brown quarterlies, and not in the critical issues of politics.

On first thought, all this may seem rather a curious direction for an inquiry into the substance of liberty. Yet we have always known, as a matter of common sense, that there was an intimate connection between "liberty" and the use of liberty. Every one who has examined the subject at all has had to conclude that tolerance per se is an arbitrary line, and that, in practice, the determining factor is the significance of the opinion to be tolerated. This study is based on an avowal of that fact. Once it is avowed, there seems to be no way of evading the conclusion that liberty is not so much permission as it is the construction of a system of information increasingly independent of opinion. In the long run it looks as if opinion could be made at once free and enlightening only by transferring our interest from "opinion" to the objective realities from which it springs. This thought has led us to speculations on ways of protecting and organizing the stream of news as the source of all opinion that matters. Obviously these speculations do not pretend to offer a fully considered or a completed scheme. Their nature forbids it, and I should be guilty of the very opinionativeness I have condemned, did these essays claim to be anything more than tentative indications of the more important phases of the problem.

Yet I can well imagine their causing a considerable restlessness in the minds I of some readers. Standards, institutes, university research, schools of journalism, they will argue, may be all right, but they are a gray business in a vivid world. They blunt the edge of life; they leave out of account the finely irresponsible opinion thrown out by the creative mind; they do not protect the indispensable novelty from

The Walter Lippmann Reader

philistinism and oppression. These proposals of yours, they will say, ignore the fact that such an apparatus of knowledge will in the main be controlled by the complacent and the traditional, and the execution will inevitably be illiberal.

There is force in the indictment. And yet I am convinced that we shall accomplish more by fighting for truth than by fighting for our theories. It is a better loyalty. It is a humble one, but it is also more irresistible. Above all it is educative. For the real enemy is ignorance, from which all of us, conservative, liberal, and revolutionary, suffer. If our effort is concentrated on our desires—be it our desire to have and to hold what is good, our desire to remake peacefully, or our desire to transform suddenly—we shall divide hopelessly and irretrievably. We must go back of our opinions to the neutral facts for unity and refreshment of spirit. To deny this, it seems to me, is to claim that the mass of men is impervious to education, and to deny that, is to deny the postulate of democracy and to seek salvation in a dictatorship. There is, I am convinced, nothing. but misery and confusion that way. But I am equally convinced that democracy will degenerate into this dictatorship either of the Right or of the Left, if it does not become genuinely self-governing. That means, in terms of public opinion, a resumption of that contact between beliefs and realities which we have been losing steadily since the small-town democracy was absorbed into the Great Society.

The administration of public information toward greater accuracy and more successful analysis is the highway of liberty. It is, I believe, a matter of first-rate importance that we should fix this in our minds. Having done so, we may be able to deal more effectively with the traps and the lies and the special interests which obstruct the road and drive us astray. Without a clear conception of what the means of liberty are, the struggle for free speech and free opinion easily . degenerates into a mere contest of opinion.

But realization is not the last step, though it is the first. We need be under no illusion that the stream of news can be purified simply by pointing out the value of purity. The existing news-structure may be made serviceable to democracy along the general lines suggested, by the training of the journalist, and by the development of expert record and analysis. But while it may be, it will not be, simply by saying that it ought to be. Those who are now in control have too much at stake, and they control the source of reform itself.

Change will come only by the drastic competition of those whose interest are not represented in the existing news-organization. It will come only if organized labor and militant liberalism set a pace which cannot be ignored. Our sanity and, therefore, our safety depend upon this competition, upon fearless and relentless exposure conducted by self-conscious groups that are now in a minority. It is for these groups to understand that the satisfaction of advertising a pet theory is as nothing compared to the publication of the news. And having realized it, it is for them to combine their resources and their talent for the development of an authentic news-service which is invincible because it supplies what the community is begging for and cannot get.

All the gallant little sheets expressing particular programmes are at bottom vanity, and in the end, futility, so long as the reporting of daily news is left in untrained and biased hands. If we are to move ahead, we must see a great independent journalism, setting standards for commercial journalism, like those which the splendid English cooperative societies are setting for commercial business. An enormous amount of money is dribbled away in one fashion or another on little papers, mass-meetings, and what not. If only some considerable portion of it could be set aside to establish a central international news-agency, we should make progress. We cannot fight the untruth which envelops us by parading out opinions. We can do if only by reporting the facts, and we do not deserve to win if the facts are against us.

The country is spotted with benevolent foundations of one kind or another, many of them doing nothing but pay the upkeep of fine buildings and sinecures. Organized labor spends large sums of money on politics and strikes which fail because it is impossible to secure a genuine hearing in public opinion. Could there be a pooling of money for a news-agency? Not, I imagine, if its object were to further a cause. But suppose the plan were for a news-service in which editorial matter was rigorously excluded, and the work was done by men who had already won the confidence of the public by their independence? Then, perhaps.

At any rate, our salvation lies in two things: ultimately, in the infusion of the news-structure by men with a new training and outlook; immediately, in the concentration of the independent forces against the complacency and bad service of the routineers. We shall advance when we have learned humility; when we have learned to seek the truth, to reveal it and publish it; when we care more for that than for the privilege of arguing about ideas in a fog of uncertainty.

Public Opinion

"Behold! human beings living in a sort of underground den, which has a mouth open towards the light and reaching all across the den; they have been here from their childhood, and have their legs and necks chained so that they cannot move, and can only see before them; for the chains are arranged in such a manner as to prevent them from turning round their heads. At a distance above and behind them the light of a fire is blazing, and between the fire and the prisoners there is a raised way; and you will see, if you look, a low wall built along the way, like the screen which marionette players have before them, over which they show the puppets.

I see, he said.

And do you see, I said, men passing along the wall carrying vessels, which appear over the wall; also figures of men and animals, made of wood and stone and various materials; and some of the prisoners, as you would expect, are talking, and some of them are silent?

This is a strange image, he said, and they are strange prisoners.

Like ourselves, I replied; and they see only their own shadows, or the shadows of one another, which the fire throws on the opposite wall of the cave?

True, he said: how could they see anything but the shadows if they were never allowed to move their heads?

And of the objects which are being carried in like manner they would see only the shadows?

Yes, he said.

And if they were able to talk with one another, would they not suppose that they were naming what was actually before them?" —The Republic of Plato, Book Seven. (Jowett Translation.)

Contents

PART VI. THE IMAGE OF DEMOCRACY

PART VII. NEWSPAPERS

PART VIII. ORGANIZED INTELLIGENCE

PART I
INTRODUCTION

CHAPTER I
The World Outside and the Pictures in Our Heads

There is an island in the ocean where in 1914 a few Englishmen, Frenchmen, and Germans lived. No cable reaches that island, and the British mail steamer comes but once in sixty days. In September it had not yet come, and the islanders were still talking about the latest newspaper which told about the approaching trial of Madame Caillaux for the shooting of Gaston Calmette. It was, therefore, with more than usual eagerness that the whole colony assembled at the quay on a day in mid-September to hear from the captain what the verdict had been. They learned that for over six weeks now those of them who were English and those of them who were French had been fighting in behalf of the sanctity of treaties against those of them who were Germans. For six strange weeks they had acted as if they were friends, when in fact they were enemies.

But their plight was not so different from that of most of the population of Europe. They had been mistaken for six weeks, on the continent the interval may have been only six days or six hours. There was an interval. There was a moment when the picture of Europe on which men were conducting their business as usual, did not in any way correspond to the Europe which was about to make a jumble of their lives. There was a time for each man when he was still adjusted to an environment that no longer existed. All over the world as late as July 25th men were making goods that they would not be able to ship, buying goods they would not be able to import, careers were being planned, enterprises contemplated, hopes and expectations entertained, all in the belief that the world as known was the world as it was. Men were writing books describing that world. They trusted the picture in their heads. And then over four years later, on a Thursday morning, came the news of an armistice, and people gave vent to their unutterable relief that the slaughter was over. Yet in the five days before the

195

The Walter Lippmann Reader

real armistice came, though the end of the war had been celebrated, several thousand young men died on the battlefields.

Looking back we can see how indirectly we know the environment in which nevertheless we live. We can see that the news of it comes to us now fast, now slowly; but that whatever we believe to be a true picture, we treat as if it were the environment itself. It is harder to remember that about the beliefs upon which we are now acting, but in respect to other peoples and other ages we flatter ourselves that it is easy to see when they were in deadly earnest about ludicrous pictures of the world. We insist, because of our superior hindsight, that the world as they needed to know it, and the world as they did know it, were often two quite contradictory things. We can see, too, that while they governed and fought, traded and reformed in the world as they imagined it to be, they produced results, or failed to produce any, in the world as it was. They started for the Indies and found America. They diagnosed evil and hanged old women. They thought they could grow rich by always selling and never buying. A caliph, obeying what he conceived to be the Will of Allah, burned the library at Alexandria.

Writing about the year 389, St. Ambrose stated the case for the prisoner in Plato's cave who resolutely declines to turn his head. "To discuss the nature and position of the earth does not help us in our hope of the life to come. It is enough to know what Scripture states. 'That He hung up the earth upon nothing' (Job xxvi. 7). Why then argue whether He hung it up in air or upon the water, and raise a controversy as to how the thin air could sustain the earth; or why, if upon the waters, the earth does not go crashing down to the bottom?... Not because the earth is in the middle, as if suspended on even balance, but because the majesty of God constrains it by the law of His will, does it endure stable upon the unstable and the void." [Footnote: Hexaemeron, i. cap 6, quoted in *The Mediæval Mind*, by Henry Osborn Taylor, Vol. i, p. 73.]

It does not help us in our hope of the life to come. It is enough to know what Scripture states. Why then argue? But a century and a half after St. Ambrose, opinion was still troubled, on this occasion by the problem of the antipodes. A monk named Cosmas, famous for his scientific attainments, was therefore deputed to write a Christian Topography, or "Christian Opinion concerning the World." [Footnote: Lecky, *Rationalism in Europe*, Vol. I, pp. 276-8.] It is clear that he knew exactly what was expected of him, for he based all his conclusions on

The Walter Lippmann Reader

the Scriptures as he read them. It appears, then, that the world is a flat parallelogram, twice as broad from east to west as it is long from north to south., In the center is the earth surrounded by ocean, which is in turn surrounded by another earth, where men lived before the deluge. This other earth was Noah's port of embarkation. In the north is a high conical mountain around which revolve the sun and moon. When the sun is behind the mountain it is night. The sky is glued to the edges of the outer earth. It consists of four high walls which meet in a concave roof, so that the earth is the floor of the universe. There is an ocean on the other side of the sky, constituting the "waters that are above the firmament." The space between the celestial ocean and the ultimate roof of the universe belongs to the blest. The space between the earth and sky is inhabited by the angels. Finally, since St. Paul said that all men are made to live upon the "face of the earth" how could they live on the back where the Antipodes are supposed to be? With such a passage before his eyes, a Christian, we are told, should not 'even speak of the Antipodes.'" [Footnote: *Id.*]

Far less should he go to the Antipodes; nor should any Christian prince give him a ship to try; nor would any pious mariner wish to try. For Cosmas there was nothing in the least absurd about his map. Only by remembering his absolute conviction that this was the map of the universe can we begin to understand how he would have dreaded Magellan or Peary or the aviator who risked a collision with the angels and the vault of heaven by flying seven miles up in the air. In the same way we can best understand the furies of war and politics by remembering that almost the whole of each party believes absolutely in its picture of the opposition, that it takes as fact, not what is, but what it supposes to be the fact. And that therefore, like Hamlet, it will stab Polonius behind the rustling curtain, thinking him the king, and perhaps like Hamlet add:

"Thou wretched, rash, intruding fool, farewell!
I took thee for thy better; take thy fortune."

2

Great men, even during their lifetime, are usually known to the public only through a fictitious personality. Hence the modicum of truth in the old saying that no man is a hero to his valet. There is only a modicum of truth, for the valet, and the private secretary, are often immersed in the fiction themselves. Royal personages are, of course, constructed personalities. Whether they themselves believe in their public character, or whether they merely permit the chamberlain to stage-manage it, there are at least two distinct selves, the public and regal self, the private and human. The biographies of great people fall more or less readily into the histories of these two selves. The official biographer reproduces the public life, the revealing memoir the other. The Charnwood Lincoln, for example, is a noble portrait, not of an actual human being, but of an epic figure, replete with significance, who moves on much the same level of reality as Aeneas or St. George. Oliver's Hamilton is a majestic abstraction, the sculpture of an idea, "an essay" as Mr. Oliver himself calls it, "on American union." It is a formal monument to the state-craft of federalism, hardly the biography of a person. Sometimes people create their own facade when they think they are revealing the interior scene. The Repington diaries and Margot Asquith's are a species of self-portraiture in which the intimate detail is most revealing as an index of how the authors like to think about themselves.

But the most interesting kind of portraiture is that which arises spontaneously in people's minds. When Victoria came to the throne, says Mr. Strachey, [Footnote: Lytton Strachey, *Queen Victoria*, p. 72.] "among the outside public there was a great wave of enthusiasm. Sentiment and romance were coming into fashion; and the spectacle of the little girl-queen, innocent, modest, with fair hair and pink cheeks, driving through her capital, filled the hearts of the beholders with raptures of affectionate loyalty. What, above all, struck everybody with overwhelming force was the contrast between Queen Victoria and her uncles. The nasty old men, debauched and selfish, pigheaded and ridiculous, with their perpetual burden of debts, confusions, and disreputabilities—they had vanished like the snows of winter and here at last, crowned and radiant, was the spring."

M. Jean de Pierrefeu [Footnote: Jean de Pierrefeu, G. Q. G. *Trois ans au Grand Quartier General*, pp 94-95.] saw hero-worship at first hand, for he was an officer on Joffre's staff at the moment of that soldier's greatest fame:

"For two years, the entire world paid an almost divine homage to the victor of the Marne. The baggage-master literally bent under the weight of the boxes, of the packages and letters which unknown people sent him with a frantic testimonial of their admiration. I think that outside of General Joffre, no commander in the war has been able to realize a comparable idea of what glory is. They sent him boxes of candy from all the great confectioners of the world, boxes of champagne, fine wines of every vintage, fruits, game, ornaments and utensils, clothes, smoking materials, inkstands, paperweights. Every territory sent its specialty. The painter sent his picture, the sculptor his statuette, the dear old lady a comforter or socks, the shepherd in his hut carved a pipe for his sake. All the manufacturers of the world who were hostile to Germany shipped their products, Havana its cigars, Portugal its port wine. I have known a hairdresser who had nothing better to do than to make a portrait of the General out of hair belonging to persons who were dear to him; a professional penman had the same idea, but the features were composed of thousands of little phrases in tiny characters which sang the praise of the General. As to letters, he had them in all scripts, from all countries, written in every dialect, affectionate letters, grateful, overflowing with love, filled with adoration. They called him Savior of the World, Father of his Country, Agent of God, Benefactor of Humanity, etc.... And not only Frenchmen, but Americans, Argentinians, Australians, etc. etc.... Thousands of little children, without their parents' knowledge, took pen in hand and wrote to tell him their love: most of them called him Our Father. And there was poignancy about their effusions, their adoration, these sighs of deliverance that escaped from thousands of hearts at the defeat of barbarism. To all these naif little souls, Joffre seemed like St. George crushing the dragon. Certainly he incarnated for the conscience of mankind the victory of good over evil, of light over darkness.

Lunatics, simpletons, the half-crazy and the crazy turned their darkened brains toward him as toward reason itself. I have read the letter of a person living in Sydney, who begged the General to save him from his enemies; another, a New Zealander, requested him to send some soldiers to the house of a gentleman who owed him ten pounds and would not pay.

Finally, some hundreds of young girls, overcoming the timidity of their sex, asked for engagements, their families not to know about it; others wished only to serve him."

This ideal Joffre was compounded out of the victory won by him, his staff and his troops, the despair of the war, the personal sorrows, and the hope of future victory. But beside hero-worship there is the exorcism of devils. By the same mechanism through which heroes are incarnated, devils are made. If everything good was to come from Joffre, Foch, Wilson, or Roosevelt, everything evil originated in the Kaiser Wilhelm, Lenin and Trotsky. They were as omnipotent for evil as the heroes were omnipotent for good. To many simple and frightened minds there was no political reverse, no strike, no obstruction, no mysterious death or mysterious conflagration anywhere in the world of which the causes did not wind back to these personal sources of evil.

3

Worldwide concentration of this kind on a symbolic personality is rare enough to be clearly remarkable, and every author has a weakness for the striking and irrefutable example. The vivisection of war reveals such examples, but it does not make them out of nothing. In a more normal public life, symbolic pictures are no less governant of behavior, but each symbol is far less inclusive because there are so many competing ones. Not only is each symbol charged with less feeling because at most it represents only a part of the population, but even within that part there is infinitely less suppression of individual difference. The symbols of public opinion, in times of moderate security, are subject to check and comparison and argument. They come and go, coalesce and are forgotten, never organizing perfectly the emotion of the whole group. There is, after all, just one human activity left in which whole populations accomplish the union sacrée. It occurs in those middle phases of a war when fear, pugnacity, and hatred have secured complete dominion of the spirit, either to crush every other instinct or to enlist it, and before weariness is felt.

At almost all other times, and even in war when it is deadlocked, a sufficiently greater range of feelings is aroused to establish conflict, choice, hesitation, and compromise. The symbolism of public opinion usually bears, as we shall see, [Footnote: Part V.] the marks of this balancing of interest. Think, for example, of how rapidly, after the armistice, the precarious and by no means successfully established symbol of Allied Unity disappeared, how it was followed almost immediately by the breakdown of each nation's symbolic picture of the other: Britain the Defender of Public Law, France watching at the Frontier of Freedom, America the Crusader. And think then of how within each nation the symbolic picture of itself frayed out, as party and class conflict and personal ambition began to stir postponed issues. And then of how the symbolic pictures of the leaders gave way, as one by one, Wilson, Clemenceau, Lloyd George, ceased to be the incarnation of human hope, and became merely the negotiators and administrators for a disillusioned world.

Whether we regret this as one of the soft evils of peace or applaud it as a return to sanity is obviously no matter here. Our first concern with fictions and symbols is to forget their value to the existing social order, and to think of them simply as an important part of the machinery of human communication. Now in any society that is not completely self-contained in its interests and so small that everyone can know all about everything that happens, ideas deal with events that are out of sight and hard to grasp. Miss Sherwin of Gopher Prairie, [Footnote: See Sinclair Lewis, *Main Street*.] is aware that a war is raging in France and tries to conceive it. She has never been to France, and certainly she has never been along what is now the battlefront.

Pictures of French and German soldiers she has seen, but it is impossible for her to imagine three million men. No one, in fact, can imagine them, and the professionals do not try. They think of them as, say, two hundred divisions. But Miss Sherwin has no access to the order of battle maps, and so if she is to think about the war, she fastens upon Joffre and the Kaiser as if they were engaged in a personal duel. Perhaps if you could see what she sees with her mind's eye, the image in its composition might be not unlike an Eighteenth Century engraving of a great soldier. He stands there boldly unruffled and more than life size, with a shadowy army of tiny little figures winding off into the landscape behind. Nor it seems are great men oblivious to these expectations. M. de Pierrefeu tells of a photographer's visit to Joffre. The General was in his "middle class office, before the worktable without papers, where he sat down to write his signature. Suddenly it was noticed that there were no maps on the walls. But since according to popular ideas it is not possible to think of a general without maps, a few were placed in position for the picture, and removed soon afterwards." [Footnote: *Op. cit.*, p. 99.]

The only feeling that anyone can have about an event he does not experience is the feeling aroused by his mental image of that event. That is why until we know what others think they know, we cannot truly understand their acts. I have seen a young girl, brought up in a Pennsylvania mining town, plunged suddenly from entire cheerfulness into a paroxysm of grief when a gust of wind cracked the kitchen window-pane. For hours she was inconsolable, and to me incomprehensible. But when she was able to talk, it transpired that if a window-

The Walter Lippmann Reader

pane broke it meant that a close relative had died. She was, therefore, mourning for her father, who had frightened her into running away from home. The father was, of course, quite thoroughly alive as a telegraphic inquiry soon proved. But until the telegram came, the cracked glass was an authentic message to that girl. Why it was authentic only a prolonged investigation by a skilled psychiatrist could show. But even the most casual observer could see that the girl, enormously upset by her family troubles, had hallucinated a complete fiction out of one external fact, a remembered superstition, and a turmoil of remorse, and fear and love for her father.

Abnormality in these instances is only a matter of degree. When an Attorney-General, who has been frightened by a bomb exploded on his doorstep, convinces himself by the reading of revolutionary literature that a revolution is to happen on the first of May 1920, we recognize that much the same mechanism is at work. The war, of course, furnished many examples of this pattern: the casual fact, the creative imagination, the will to believe, and out of these three elements, a counterfeit of reality to which there was a violent instinctive response. For it is clear enough that under certain conditions men respond as powerfully to fictions as they do to realities, and that in many cases they help to create the very fictions to which they respond. Let him cast the first stone who did not believe in the Russian army that passed through England in August, 1914, did not accept any tale of atrocities without direct proof, and never saw a plot, a traitor, or a spy where there was none. Let him cast a stone who never passed on as the real inside truth what he had heard someone say who knew no more than he did.

In all these instances we must note particularly one common factor. It is the insertion between man and his environment of a pseudo-environment. To that pseudo-environment his behavior is a response. But because it is behavior, the consequences, if they are acts, operate not in the pseudo-environment where the behavior is stimulated, but in the real environment where action eventuates. If the behavior is not a practical act, but what we call roughly thought and emotion, it may be a long time before there is any noticeable break in the texture of the fictitious world. But when the stimulus of the pseudo-fact results in action on things or other people, contradiction soon develops. Then comes the sensation of butting one's head against a stone wall, of learning by experience, and witnessing Herbert Spencer's tragedy of the murder of a Beautiful Theory by

202

a Gang of Brutal Facts, the discomfort in short of a maladjustment. For certainly, at the level of social life, what is called the adjustment of man to his environment takes place through the medium of fictions.

By fictions I do not mean lies. I mean a representation of the environment which is in lesser or greater degree made by man himself. The range of fiction extends all the way from complete hallucination to the scientists' perfectly self-conscious use of a schematic model, or his decision that for his particular problem accuracy beyond a certain number of decimal places is not important. A work of fiction may have almost any degree of fidelity, and so long as the degree of fidelity can be taken into account, fiction is not misleading. In fact, human culture is very largely the selection, the rearrangement, the tracing of patterns upon, and the stylizing of, what William James called "the random irradiations and resettlements of our ideas." [Footnote: James, *Principles of Psychology*, Vol. II, p. 638] The alternative to the use of fictions is direct exposure to the ebb and flow of sensation. That is not a real alternative, for however refreshing it is to see at times with a perfectly innocent eye, innocence itself is not wisdom, though a source and corrective of wisdom. For the real environment is altogether too big, too complex, and too fleeting for direct acquaintance. We are not equipped to deal with so much subtlety, so much variety, so many permutations and combinations. And although we have to act in that environment, we have to reconstruct it on a simpler model before we can manage with it. To traverse the world men must have maps of the world. Their persistent difficulty is to secure maps on which their own need, or someone else's need, has not sketched in the coast of Bohemia.

4

The analyst of public opinion must begin then, by recognizing the triangular relationship between the scene of action, the human picture of that scene, and the human response to that picture working itself out upon the scene of action. It is like a play suggested to the actors by their own experience, in which the plot is transacted in the real lives of the actors, and not merely in their stage parts. The moving picture often emphasizes with great skill this double drama of interior motive and external behavior. Two men are quarreling, ostensibly about some money, but their passion is inexplicable. Then the picture fades out and what one or the other of the two men sees with his mind's eye is reënacted.

The Walter Lippmann Reader

Across the table they were quarreling about money. In memory they are back in their youth when the girl jilted him for the other man. The exterior drama is explained: the hero is not greedy; the hero is in love.

A scene not so different was played in the United States Senate. At breakfast on the morning of September 29, 1919, some of the Senators read a news dispatch in the *Washington Post* about the landing of American marines on the Dalmatian coast. The newspaper said:

FACTS NOW ESTABLISHED

"The following important facts appear already *established*. The orders to Rear Admiral Andrews commanding the American naval forces in the Adriatic, came from the British Admiralty via the War Council and Rear Admiral Knapps in London. The approval or disapproval of the American Navy Department was not asked...

WITHOUT DANIELS' KNOWLEDGE

"Mr. Daniels was admittedly placed in a peculiar position when cables reached here stating that the forces over which he is presumed to have exclusive control were carrying on what amounted to naval warfare without his knowledge. It was fully realized that the *British Admiralty might desire to issue orders to Rear Admiral Andrews* to act on behalf of Great Britain and her Allies, because the situation required sacrifice on the part of some nation if D'Annunzio's followers were to be held in check.

"It was further realized that *under the new league of nations plan foreigners would be in a position to direct American Naval forces in emergencies* with or without the consent of the American Navy Department...." etc. (Italics mine).

The first Senator to comment is Mr. Knox of Pennsylvania. Indignantly he demands investigation. In Mr. Brandegee of Connecticut, who spoke next, indignation has already stimulated credulity. Where Mr. Knox indignantly wishes to know if the report is true, Mr. Brandegee, a half a minute later, would like to know what would have happened if marines had been killed. Mr. Knox, interested in the question, forgets that he asked for an inquiry, and replies. If American marines had been killed, it would be war. The mood of the debate is still conditional. Debate proceeds. Mr. McCormick of Illinois reminds the

Senate that the Wilson administration is prone to the waging of small unauthorized wars. He repeats Theodore Roosevelt's quip about "waging peace." More debate. Mr. Brandegee notes that the marines acted "under orders of a Supreme Council sitting somewhere," but he cannot recall who represents the United States on that body. The Supreme Council is unknown to the Constitution of the United States. Therefore Mr. New of Indiana submits a resolution calling for the facts.

So far the Senators still recognize vaguely that they are discussing a rumor. Being lawyers they still remember some of the forms of evidence. But as red-blooded men they already experience all the indignation which is appropriate to the fact that American marines have been ordered into war by a foreign government and without the consent of Congress. Emotionally they want to believe it, because they are Republicans fighting the League of Nations. This arouses the Democratic leader, Mr. Hitchcock of Nebraska. He defends the Supreme Council: it was acting under the war powers. Peace has not yet been concluded because the Republicans are delaying it. Therefore the action was necessary and legal. Both sides now assume that the report is true, and the conclusions they draw are the conclusions of their partisanship. Yet this extraordinary assumption is in a debate over a resolution to investigate the truth of the assumption. It reveals how difficult it is, even for trained lawyers, to suspend response until the returns are in. The response is instantaneous. The fiction is taken for truth because the fiction is badly needed.

A few days later an official report showed that the marines were not landed by order of the British Government or of the Supreme Council. They had not been fighting the Italians. They had been landed at the request of the Italian Government to protect Italians, and the American commander had been officially thanked by the Italian authorities. The marines were not at war with Italy. They had acted according to an established international practice which had nothing to do with the League of Nations.

The scene of action was the Adriatic. The picture of that scene in the Senators' heads at Washington was furnished, in this case probably with intent to deceive, by a man who cared nothing about the Adriatic, but much about defeating the League. To this picture the Senate responded by a strengthening of its partisan differences over the League.

5

Whether in this particular case the Senate was above or below its normal standard, it is not necessary to decide. Nor whether the Senate compares favorably with the House, or with other parliaments. At the moment, I should like to think only about the world-wide spectacle of men acting upon their environment, moved by stimuli from their pseudo-environments. For when full allowance has been made for deliberate fraud, political science has still to account for such facts as two nations attacking one another, each convinced that it is acting in self-defense, or two classes at war each certain that it speaks for the common interest. They live, we are likely to say, in different worlds. More accurately, they live in the same world, but they think and feel in different ones.

It is to these special worlds, it is to these private or group, or class, or provincial, or occupational, or national, or sectarian artifacts, that the political adjustment of mankind in the Great Society takes place. Their variety and complication are impossible to describe. Yet these fictions determine a very great part of men's political behavior. We must think of perhaps fifty sovereign parliaments consisting of at least a hundred legislative bodies. With them belong at least fifty hierarchies of provincial and municipal assemblies, which with their executive, administrative and legislative organs, constitute formal authority on earth. But that does not begin to reveal the complexity of political life. For in each of these innumerable centers of authority there are parties, and these parties are themselves hierarchies with their roots in classes, sections, cliques and clans; and within these are the individual politicians, each the personal center of a web of connection and memory and fear and hope.

Somehow or other, for reasons often necessarily obscure, as the result of domination or compromise or a logroll, there emerge from these political bodies commands, which set armies in motion or make peace, conscript life, tax, exile, imprison, protect property or confiscate it, encourage one kind of enterprise and discourage another, facilitate immigration or obstruct it, improve communication or censor it, establish schools, build navies, proclaim "policies," and "destiny," raise economic barriers, make property or unmake it, bring one people under the rule of another, or favor one class as against another. For each of these decisions some view of the facts is taken to be conclusive, some view of the circumstances is accepted as the basis of inference and as the stimulus of feeling. What view of the facts, and why that one?

The Walter Lippmann Reader

And yet even this does not begin to exhaust the real complexity. The formal political structure exists in a social environment, where there are innumerable large and small corporations and institutions, voluntary and semi-voluntary associations, national, provincial, urban and neighborhood groupings, which often as not make the decision that the political body registers. On what are these decisions based?

"Modern society," says Mr. Chesterton, "is intrinsically insecure because it is based on the notion that all men will do the same thing for different reasons.... And as within the head of any convict may be the hell of a quite solitary crime, so in the house or under the hat of any suburban clerk may be the limbo of a quite separate philosophy. The first man may be a complete Materialist and feel his own body as a horrible machine manufacturing his own mind. He may listen to his thoughts as to the dull ticking of a clock. The man next door may be a Christian Scientist and regard his own body as somehow rather less substantial than his own shadow. He may come almost to regard his own arms and legs as delusions like moving serpents in the dream of delirium tremens. The third man in the street may not be a Christian Scientist but, on the contrary, a Christian. He may live in a fairy tale as his neighbors would say; a secret but solid fairy tale full of the faces and presences of unearthly friends. The fourth man may be a theosophist, and only too probably a vegetarian; and I do not see why I should not gratify myself with the fancy that the fifth man is a devil worshiper.... Now whether or not this sort of variety is valuable, this sort of unity is shaky. To expect that all men for all time will go on thinking different things, and yet doing the same things, is a doubtful speculation. It is not founding society on a communion, or even on a convention, but rather on a coincidence. Four men may meet under the same lamp post; one to paint it pea green as part of a great municipal reform; one to read his breviary in the light of it; one to embrace it with accidental ardour in a fit of alcoholic enthusiasm; and the last merely because the pea green post is a conspicuous point of rendezvous with his young lady. But to expect this to happen night after night is unwise...." [Footnote: G. K. Chesterton, "The Mad Hatter and the Sane Householder," *Vanity Fair*, January, 1921, p. 54]

For the four men at the lamp post substitute the governments, the parties, the corporations, the societies, the social sets, the trades and professions, universities, sects, and nationalities of the world. Think of the legislator voting a statute that will affect distant peoples, a statesman coming to a decision. Think of the Peace Conference reconstituting the frontiers of Europe, an ambassador in a foreign country trying to discern the intentions of his own government and of the foreign government, a promoter working a concession in a backward country, an editor demanding a war, a clergyman calling on the police to regulate amusement, a club lounging-room making up its mind about a strike, a sewing circle preparing to regulate the schools, nine judges deciding whether a legislature in Oregon may fix the working hours of women, a cabinet meeting to decide on the recognition of a government, a party convention choosing a candidate and writing a platform, twenty-seven million voters casting their ballots, an Irishman in Cork thinking about an Irishman in Belfast, a Third International planning to reconstruct the whole of human society, a board of directors confronted with a set of their employees' demands, a boy choosing a career, a merchant estimating supply and demand for the coming season, a speculator predicting the course of the market, a banker deciding whether to put credit behind a new enterprise, the advertiser, the reader of advertisments.... Think of the different sorts of Americans thinking about their notions of "The British Empire" or "France" or "Russia" or "Mexico." It is not so different from Mr. Chesterton's four men at the pea green lamp post.

6

And so before we involve ourselves in the jungle of obscurities about the innate differences of men, we shall do well to fix our attention upon the extraordinary differences in what men know of the world. [Footnote: *Cf.* Wallas, *Our Social Heritage*, pp. 77 *et seq.*] I do not doubt that there are important biological differences. Since man is an animal it would be strange if there were not. But as rational beings it is worse than shallow to generalize at all about comparative behavior until there is a measurable similarity between the environments to which behavior is a response.

The pragmatic value of this idea is that it introduces a much needed refinement into the ancient controversy about nature and nurture, innate quality and environment. For the pseudo-environment is a hybrid compounded of "human nature" and "conditions." To my mind it shows the uselessness of pontificating about what man is and always will be from what we observe man to be doing, or about what are the necessary conditions of society. For we do not know how men would behave in response to the facts of the Great Society. All that we really know is how they behave in response to what can fairly be called a most inadequate picture of the Great Society. No conclusion about man or the Great Society can honestly be made on evidence like that.

This, then, will be the clue to our inquiry. We shall assume that what each man does is based not on direct and certain knowledge, but on pictures made by himself or given to him. If his atlas tells him that the world is flat he will not sail near what he believes to be the edge of our planet for fear of falling off. If his maps include a fountain of eternal youth, a Ponce de Leon will go in quest of it. If someone digs up yellow dirt that looks like gold, he will for a time act exactly as if he had found gold. The way in which the world is imagined determines at any particular moment what men will do. It does not determine what they will achieve. It determines their effort, their feelings, their hopes, not their accomplishments and results. The very men who most loudly proclaim their "materialism" and their contempt for "ideologues," the Marxian communists, place their entire hope on what? On the formation by propaganda of a class-conscious group. But what is propaganda, if not the effort to alter the picture to which men respond, to substitute one social pattern for another? What is class consciousness but a way of realizing the world? National consciousness but another way? And Professor Giddings' consciousness of kind, but a process of believing that we recognize among the multitude certain ones marked as our kind?

Try to explain social life as the pursuit of pleasure and the avoidance of pain. You will soon be saying that the hedonist begs the question, for even supposing that man does pursue these ends, the crucial problem of why he thinks one course rather than another likely to produce pleasure, is untouched. Does the guidance of man's conscience explain? How then does he happen to have the particular conscience which he has? The theory of economic self-interest? But how do men come to conceive their interest in one way rather than another? The desire for security, or prestige, or domination, or what is vaguely called self-realization? How do men conceive their security, what do they consider prestige, how do they figure out the means of domination, or what is the notion of self which they wish to realize? Pleasure, pain, conscience, acquisition, protection, enhancement, mastery, are undoubtedly names for some of the ways people act. There may be instinctive dispositions which work toward such ends. But no

The Walter Lippmann Reader

statement of the end, or any description of the tendencies to seek it, can explain the behavior which results. The very fact that men theorize at all is proof that their pseudo-environments, their interior representations of the world, are a determining element in thought, feeling, and action. For if the connection between reality and human response were direct and immediate, rather than indirect and inferred, indecision and failure would be unknown, and (if each of us fitted as snugly into the world as the child in the womb), Mr. Bernard Shaw would not have been able to say that except for the first nine months of its existence no human being manages its affairs as well as a plant.

The chief difficulty in adapting the psychoanalytic scheme to political thought arises in this connection. The Freudians are concerned with the maladjustment of distinct individuals to other individuals and to concrete circumstances. They have assumed that if internal derangements could be straightened out, there would be little or no confusion about what is the obviously normal relationship. But public opinion deals with indirect, unseen, and puzzling facts, and there is nothing obvious about them. The situations to which public opinions refer are known only as opinions. The psychoanalyst, on the other hand, almost always assumes that the environment is knowable, and if not knowable then at least bearable, to any unclouded intelligence. This assumption of his is the problem of public opinion. Instead of taking for granted an environment that is readily known, the social analyst is most concerned in studying how the larger political environment is conceived, and how it can be conceived more successfully. The psychoanalyst examines the adjustment to an X, called by him the environment; the social analyst examines the X, called by him the pseudo-environment.

He is, of course, permanently and constantly in debt to the new psychology, not only because when rightly applied it so greatly helps people to stand on their own feet, come what may, but because the study of dreams, fantasy and rationalization has thrown light on how the pseudo-environment is put together. But he cannot assume as his criterion either what is called a "normal biological career" [Footnote: Edward J. Kempf, *Psychopathology*, p. 116.] within the existing social order, or a career "freed from religious suppression and dogmatic conventions" outside. [Footnote: *Id.*, p. 151.] What for a sociologist is a normal social career? Or one freed from suppressions and conventions? Conservative critics do, to be sure, assume the first, and romantic ones the second. But in assuming them they are taking the whole world for granted. They are saying in effect either that society is the sort of thing which corresponds to their idea of what is normal, or the sort of thing which corresponds to their idea of what is free. Both ideas are merely public opinions, and while the psychoanalyst as physician may perhaps assume them, the sociologist may not take the products of existing public opinion as criteria by which to study public opinion.

7

The world that we have to deal with politically is out of reach, out of sight, out of mind. It has to be explored, reported, and imagined. Man is no Aristotelian god contemplating all existence at one glance. He is the creature of an evolution who can just about span a sufficient portion of reality to manage his survival, and snatch what on the scale of time are but a few moments of insight and happiness. Yet this same creature has invented ways of seeing what no naked eye could see, of hearing what no ear could hear, of weighing immense masses and infinitesimal ones, of counting and separating more items than he can individually remember. He is learning to see with his mind vast portions of the world that he could never see, touch, smell, hear, or remember. Gradually he makes for himself a trustworthy picture inside his head of the world beyond his reach.

Those features of the world outside which have to do with the behavior of other human beings, in so far as that behavior crosses ours, is dependent upon us, or is interesting to us, we call roughly public affairs. The pictures inside the heads of these human beings, the pictures of themselves, of others, of their needs, purposes, and relationship, are their public opinions. Those pictures which are acted upon by groups of people, or by individuals acting in the name of groups, are Public Opinion with capital letters. And so in the chapters which follow we shall inquire first into some of the reasons why the picture inside so often misleads men in their dealings with the world outside. Under this heading we shall consider first the chief factors which limit their access to the facts. They are the artificial censorships, the limitations of social contact, the comparatively meager time available in each day for paying attention to public affairs, the distortion arising because events have to be compressed into very short messages, the difficulty of making a small vocabulary express a complicated world, and finally the fear of facing those facts which would seem to threaten the established routine of men's lives.

211

The Walter Lippmann Reader

The analysis then turns from these more or less external limitations to the question of how this trickle of messages from the outside is affected by the stored up images, the preconceptions, and prejudices which interpret, fill them out, and in their turn powerfully direct the play of our attention, and our vision itself. From this it proceeds to examine how in the individual person the limited messages from outside, formed into a pattern of stereotypes, are identified with his own interests as he feels and conceives them. In the succeeding sections it examines how opinions are crystallized into what is called Public Opinion, how a National Will, a Group Mind, a Social Purpose, or whatever you choose to call it, is formed.

The first five parts constitute the descriptive section of the book. There follows an analysis of the traditional democratic theory of public opinion. The substance of the argument is that democracy in its original form never seriously faced the problem which arises because the pictures inside people's heads do not automatically correspond with the world outside. And then, because the democratic theory is under criticism by socialist thinkers, there follows an examination of the most advanced and coherent of these criticisms, as made by the English Guild Socialists. My purpose here is to find out whether these reformers take into account the main difficulties of public opinion. My conclusion is that they ignore the difficulties, as completely as did the original democrats, because they, too, assume, and in a much more complicated civilization, that somehow mysteriously there exists in the hearts of men a knowledge of the world beyond their reach.

I argue that representative government, either in what is ordinarily called politics, or in industry, cannot be worked successfully, no matter what the basis of election, unless there is an independent, expert organization for making the unseen facts intelligible to those who have to make the decisions. I attempt, therefore, to argue that the serious acceptance of the principle that personal representation must be supplemented by representation of the unseen facts would alone permit a satisfactory decentralization, and allow us to escape from the intolerable and unworkable fiction that each of us must acquire a competent opinion about all public affairs. It is argued that the problem of the press is confused because the critics and the apologists expect the press to realize this fiction, expect it to make up for all that was not foreseen in the theory of democracy, and that the readers expect this miracle to be performed at no cost

The Walter Lippmann Reader

or trouble to themselves. The newspapers are regarded by democrats as a panacea for their own defects, whereas analysis of the nature of news and of the economic basis of journalism seems to show that the newspapers necessarily and inevitably reflect, and therefore, in greater or lesser measure, intensify, the defective organization of public opinion. My conclusion is that public opinions must be organized for the press if they are to be sound, not by the press as is the case today. This organization I conceive to be in the first instance the task of a political science that has won its proper place as formulator, in advance of real decision, instead of apologist, critic, or reporter after the decision has been made. I try to indicate that the perplexities of government and industry are conspiring to give political science this enormous opportunity to enrich itself and to serve the public. And, of course, I hope that these pages will help a few people to realize that opportunity more vividly, and therefore to pursue it more consciously.

PART II
APPROACHES TO THE
WORLD OUTSIDE

CHAPTER II
Censorship and Privacy

1

The picture of a general presiding over an editorial conference at the most terrible hour of one of the great battles of history seems more like a scene from The Chocolate Soldier than a page from life. Yet we know at first hand from the officer who edited the French communiqués that these conferences were a regular part of the business of war; that in the worst moment of Verdun, General Joffre and his cabinet met and argued over the nouns, adjectives, and verbs that were to be printed in the newspapers the next morning.

"The evening communiqué of the twenty-third (February 1916)" says M. de Pierrefeu, [Footnote: G. Q. G., pp. 126-129.] "was edited in a dramatic atmosphere. M. Berthelot, of the Prime Minister's office, had just telephoned by order of the minister asking General Pellé to strengthen the report and to emphasize the proportions of the enemy's attack. It was necessary to prepare the public for the worst outcome in case the affair turned into a catastrophe. This anxiety showed clearly that neither at G. H. Q. nor at the Ministry of War had the Government found reason for confidence. As M. Berthelot spoke, General Pellé made notes. He handed me the paper on which he had written the Government's wishes, together with the order of the day issued by General von Deimling and found on some prisoners, in which it was stated that this attack was the supreme offensive to secure peace. Skilfully used, all this was to demonstrate that Germany was letting loose a gigantic effort, an effort without precedent, and that from its success she hoped for the end of the war. The logic of this was that nobody need be surprised at our withdrawal. When, a half hour later, I went down with my manuscript, I found gathered together in Colonel Claudel's office, he being away, the major-general, General Janin, Colonel Dupont, and Lieutenant-Colonel Renouard. Fearing that I would not succeed in

214

giving the desired impression, General Pellé had himself prepared a proposed communiqué. I read what I had just done. It was found to be too moderate. General Pellé's, on the other hand, seemed too alarming. I had purposely omitted von Deimling's order of the day. To put it into the communiqué *would be to break with the formula to which the public was accustomed*, would be to transform it into a kind of pleading. It would seem to say: 'How do you suppose we can resist?' There was reason to fear that the public would be distracted by this change of tone and would believe that everything was lost. I explained my reasons and suggested giving Deimling's text to the newspapers in the form of a separate note.

"Opinion being divided, General Pellé went to ask General de Castelnau to come and decide finally. The General arrived smiling, quiet and good humored, said a few pleasant words about this new kind of literary council of war, and looked at the texts. He chose the simpler one, gave more weight to the first phrase, inserted the words 'as had been anticipated,' which supply a reassuring quality, and was flatly against inserting von Deimling's order, but was for transmitting it to the press in a special note ... " General Joffre that evening read the communiqué carefully and approved it.

Within a few hours those two or three hundred words would be read all over the world. They would paint a picture in men's minds of what was happening on the slopes of Verdun, and in front of that picture people would take heart or despair. The shopkeeper in Brest, the peasant in Lorraine, the deputy in the Palais Bourbon, the editor in Amsterdam or Minneapolis had to be kept in hope, and yet prepared to accept possible defeat without yielding to panic. They are told, therefore, that the loss of ground is no surprise to the French Command. They are taught to regard the affair as serious, but not strange. Now, as a matter of fact, the French General Staff was not fully prepared for the German offensive. Supporting trenches had not been dug, alternative roads had not been built, barbed wire was lacking. But to confess that would have aroused images in the heads of civilians that might well have turned a reverse into a disaster. The High Command could be disappointed, and yet pull itself together; the people at home and abroad, full of uncertainties, and with none of the professional man's singleness of purpose, might on the basis of a complete story have lost sight of the war in a melee of faction and counter-faction about the competence of the officers. Instead, therefore, of letting the public act on all the facts which the generals knew, the authorities presented only certain facts, and these only in such a way as would be most likely to steady the people.

In this case the men who arranged the pseudo-environment knew what the real one was. But a few days later an incident occurred about which the French Staff did not know the truth. The Germans announced [Footnote: On February 26, 1916. Pierrefeu, G. Q. G., pp. 133 *et seq.*] that on the previous afternoon they had taken Fort Douaumont by assault. At French headquarters in Chantilly no one could understand this news. For on the morning of the twenty-fifth, after the engagement of the XXth corps, the battle had taken a turn for the better. Reports from the front said nothing about Douaumont. But inquiry showed that the German report was true, though no one as yet knew how the fort had been taken. In the meantime, the German communiqué was being flashed around the world, and the French had to say something. So headquarters explained. "In the midst of total ignorance at Chantilly about the way the attack had taken place, we imagined, in the evening communiqué of the 26th, a plan of the attack which certainly had a thousand to one chance of being true." The communiqué of this imaginary battle read:

"A bitter struggle is taking place around Fort de Douaumont which is an advanced post of the old defensive organization of Verdun. The position taken this morning by the enemy, *after several unsuccessful assaults that cost him very heavy losses,* has been reached again and passed by our troops whom the enemy has not been able to drive back." [Footnote: This is my own translation: the English translation from London published in the New York Times of Sunday, Feb. 27, is as follows:

London, Feb. 26 (1916). A furious struggle has been in progress around Fort de Douaumont which is an advance element of the old defensive organization of Verdun fortresses. The position captured this morning by the enemy after several fruitless assaults which cost him extremely heavy losses, [Footnote: The French text says "pertes tres elevees." Thus the English translation exaggerates the original text.] was reached again and gone beyond by our troops, which all the attempts of the enemy have not been able to push back."]

What had actually happened differed from both the French and German accounts. While changing troops in the line, the position had somehow been forgotten in a confusion of orders. Only a battery commander and a few men remained in the fort. Some German soldiers, seeing the door open, had crawled into the fort, and taken everyone inside prisoner. A little later the French who were on the slopes of the hill were horrified at being shot at from the fort. There had been no battle at Douaumont and no losses. Nor had the French troops advanced beyond it as the communiqués seemed to say. They were beyond it on either side, to be sure, but the fort was in enemy hands.

Yet from the communiqué everyone believed that the fort was half surrounded. The words did not explicitly say so, but "the press, as usual, forced the pace." Military writers concluded that the Germans would soon have to surrender. In a few days they began to ask themselves why the garrison, since it lacked food, had not yet surrendered. "It was necessary through the press bureau to request them to drop the encirclement theme." [Footnote: Pierrefeu, *op. cit.*, pp. 134-5.]

2

The editor of the French communiqué tells us that as the battle dragged out, his colleagues and he set out to neutralize the pertinacity of the Germans by continual insistence on their terrible losses. It is necessary to remember that at this time, and in fact until late in 1917, the orthodox view of the war for all the Allied peoples was that it would be decided by "attrition." Nobody believed in a war of movement. It was insisted that strategy did not count, or diplomacy. It was simply a matter of killing Germans. The general public more or less believed the dogma, but it had constantly to be reminded of it in face of spectacular German successes.

"Almost no day passed but the communiqué.... ascribed to the Germans with some appearance of justice heavy losses, extremely heavy, spoke of bloody sacrifices, heaps of corpses, hecatombs. Likewise the wireless constantly used the statistics of the intelligence bureau at Verdun, whose chief, Major Cointet, had invented a method of calculating German losses which obviously produced marvelous results. Every fortnight the figures increased a hundred thousand or so. These 300,000, 400,000, 500,000 casualties put out, divided into daily, weekly, monthly losses, repeated in all sorts of ways, produced a striking effect. Our formulae varied little: 'according to prisoners the German losses in the course of the attack have been considerable' ... 'it is proved that the losses' ... 'the enemy exhausted by his losses has not renewed the attack' ... Certain formulae, later abandoned because they had been overworked, were used each day: 'under

217

our artillery and machine gun fire' ... 'mowed down by our artillery and machine gun fire' ... Constant repetition impressed the neutrals and Germany itself, and helped to create a bloody background in spite of the denials from Nauen (the German wireless) which tried vainly to destroy the bad effect of this perpetual repetition." [Footnote: *Op. cit.*, pp. 138-139.]

The thesis of the French Command, which it wished to establish publicly by these reports, was formulated as follows for the guidance of the censors:

"This offensive engages the active forces of our opponent whose manpower is declining. We have learned that the class of 1916 is already at the front. There will remain the 1917 class already being called up, and the resources of the third category (men above forty-five, or convalescents). In a few weeks, the German forces exhausted by this effort, will find themselves confronted with all the forces of the coalition (ten millions against seven millions)." [Footnote: *Op. cit.*, p. 147.]

According to M. de Pierrefeu, the French command had converted itself to this belief. "By an extraordinary aberration of mind, only the attrition of the enemy was seen; it appeared that our forces were not subject to attrition. General Nivelle shared these ideas. We saw the result in 1917."

We have learned to call this propaganda. A group of men, who can prevent independent access to the event, arrange the news of it to suit their purpose. That the purpose was in this case patriotic does not affect the argument at all. They used their power to make the Allied publics see affairs as they desired them to be seen. The casualty figures of Major Cointet which were spread about the world are of the same order. They were intended to provoke a particular kind of inference, namely that the war of attrition was going in favor of the French. But the inference is not drawn in the form of argument. It results almost automatically from the creation of a mental picture of endless Germans slaughtered on the hills about Verdun. By putting the dead Germans in the focus of the picture, and by omitting to mention the French dead, a very special view of the battle was built up. It was a view designed to neutralize the effects of German territorial advances and the impression of power which the persistence of the offensive was making. It was also a view that tended to make the public acquiesce in the demoralizing defensive strategy imposed upon the Allied armies. For the public, accustomed to the idea that war consists of great strategic movements, flank attacks, encirclements, and dramatic surrenders, had gradually to forget that picture in favor of the terrible idea that by matching lives the war would be won. Through its control over all news from the front, the General Staff substituted a view of the facts that comported with this strategy.

The General Staff of an army in the field is so placed that within wide limits it can control what the public will perceive. It controls the selection of correspondents who go to the front, controls their movements at the front, reads and censors their messages from the front, and operates the wires. The Government behind the army by its command of cables and passports, mails and custom houses and blockades increases the control. It emphasizes it by legal power over publishers, over public meetings, and by its secret service. But in the case of an army the control is far from perfect. There is always the enemy's communiqué, which in these days of wireless cannot be kept away from neutrals. Above all there is the talk of the soldiers, which blows back from the front, and is spread about when they are on leave. [Footnote: For weeks prior to the American attack at St. Mihiel and in the Argonne-Meuse, everybody in France told everybody else the deep secret.] An army is an unwieldy thing. And that is why the naval and diplomatic censorship is almost always much more complete. Fewer people know what is going on, and their acts are more easily supervised.

3

Without some form of censorship, propaganda in the strict sense of the word is impossible. In order to conduct a propaganda there must be some barrier between the public and the event. Access to the real environment must be limited, before anyone can create a pseudo-environment that he thinks wise or desirable. For while people who have direct access can misconceive what they see, no one else can decide how they shall misconceive it, unless he can decide where they shall look, and at what. The military censorship is the simplest form of barrier, but by no means the most important, because it is known to exist, and is therefore in certain measure agreed to and discounted.

At different times and for different subjects some men impose and other men accept a particular standard of secrecy. The frontier between what is concealed because publication is not, as we say, "compatible with the public interest" fades gradually into what is concealed because it is believed to be none of the public's business. The notion of what constitutes a person's private affairs is elastic. Thus the amount of a man's fortune is considered a private affair, and careful provision is made in the income tax law to keep it as private as possible. The sale

The Walter Lippmann Reader

of a piece of land is not private, but the price may be. Salaries are generally treated as more private than wages, incomes as more private than inheritances. A person's credit rating is given only a limited circulation. The profits of big corporations are more public than those of small firms. Certain kinds of conversation, between man and wife, lawyer and client, doctor and patient, priest and communicant, are privileged. Directors' meetings are generally private. So are many political conferences. Most of what is said at a cabinet meeting, or by an ambassador to the Secretary of State, or at private interviews, or dinner tables, is private. Many people regard the contract between employer and employee as private. There was a time when the affairs of all corporations were held to be as private as a man's theology is to-day. There was a time before that when his theology was held to be as public a matter as the color of his eyes. But infectious diseases, on the other hand, were once as private as the processes of a man's digestion. The history of the notion of privacy would be an entertaining tale. Sometimes the notions violently conflict, as they did when the bolsheviks published the secret treaties, or when Mr. Hughes investigated the life insurance companies, or when somebody's scandal exudes from the pages of Town Topics to the front pages of Mr. Hearst's newspapers.

Whether the reasons for privacy are good or bad, the barriers exist. Privacy is insisted upon at all kinds of places in the area of what is called public affairs. It is often very illuminating, therefore, to ask yourself how you got at the facts on which you base your opinion. Who actually saw, heard, felt, counted, named the thing, about which you have an opinion? Was it the man who told you, or the man who told him, or someone still further removed? And how much was he permitted to see? When he informs you that France thinks this and that, what part of France did he watch? How was he able to watch it? Where was he when he watched it? What Frenchmen was he permitted to talk to, what newspapers did he read, and where did they learn what they say? You can ask yourself these questions, but you can rarely answer them. They will remind you, however, of the distance which often separates your public opinion from the event with which it deals. And the reminder is itself a protection.

CHAPTER III
Contact and Opportunity

1

While censorship and privacy intercept much information at its source, a very much larger body of fact never reaches the whole public at all, or only very slowly. For there are very distinct limits upon the circulation of ideas.

A rough estimate of the effort it takes to reach "everybody" can be had by considering the Government's propaganda during the war. Remembering that the war had run over two years and a half before America entered it, that millions upon millions of printed pages had been circulated and untold speeches had been delivered, let us turn to Mr. Creel's account of his fight "for the minds of men, for the conquest of their convictions" in order that "the gospel of Americanism might be carried to every corner of the globe." [Footnote: George Creel, *How We Advertised America.*]

Mr. Creel had to assemble machinery which included a Division of News that issued, he tells us, more than six thousand releases, had to enlist seventy-five thousand Four Minute Men who delivered at least seven hundred and fifty-five thousand, one hundred and ninety speeches to an aggregate of over three hundred million people. Boy scouts delivered annotated copies of President Wilson's addresses to the householders of America. Fortnightly periodicals were sent to six hundred thousand teachers. Two hundred thousand lantern slides were furnished for illustrated lectures. Fourteen hundred and thirty-eight different designs were turned out for posters, window cards, newspaper advertisements, cartoons, seals and buttons. The chambers of commerce, the churches, fraternal societies, schools, were used as channels of distribution. Yet Mr. Creel's effort, to which I have not begun to do justice, did not include Mr. McAdoo's stupendous organization for the Liberty Loans, nor Mr. Hoover's far reaching propaganda about food, nor the campaigns of the Red Cross, the Y. M. C. A., Salvation Army, Knights of Columbus, Jewish Welfare Board, not to mention the independent work of patriotic societies, like the League to Enforce Peace, the League of Free Nations Association, the National Security League, nor the activity of the publicity bureaus of the Allies and of the submerged nationalities.

221

The Walter Lippmann Reader

Probably this is the largest and the most intensive effort to carry quickly a fairly uniform set of ideas to all the people of a nation. The older proselyting worked more slowly, perhaps more surely, but never so inclusively. Now if it required such extreme measures to reach everybody in time of crisis, how open are the more normal channels to men's minds? The Administration was trying, and while the war continued it very largely succeeded, I believe, in creating something that might almost be called one public opinion all over America. But think of the dogged work, the complicated ingenuity, the money and the personnel that were required. Nothing like that exists in time of peace, and as a corollary there are whole sections, there are vast groups, ghettoes, enclaves and classes that hear only vaguely about much that is going on.

They live in grooves, are shut in among their own affairs, barred out of larger affairs, meet few people not of their own sort, read little. Travel and trade, the mails, the wires, and radio, railroads, highways, ships, motor cars, and in the coming generation aeroplanes, are, of course, of the utmost influence on the circulation of ideas. Each of these affects the supply and the quality of information and opinion in a most intricate way. Each is itself affected by technical, by economic, by political conditions. Every time a government relaxes the passport ceremonies or the customs inspection, every time a new railway or a new port is opened, a new shipping line established, every time rates go up or down, the mails move faster or more slowly, the cables are uncensored and made less expensive, highways built, or widened, or improved, the circulation of ideas is influenced. Tariff schedules and subsidies affect the direction of commercial enterprise, and therefore the nature of human contracts. And so it may well happen, as it did for example in the case of Salem, Massachusetts, that a change in the art of shipbuilding will reduce a whole city from a center where international influences converge to a genteel provincial town. All the immediate effects of more rapid transit are not necessarily good. It would be difficult to say, for example, that the railroad system of France, so highly centralized upon Paris, has been an unmixed blessing to the French people.

It is certainly true that problems arising out of the means of communication are of the utmost importance, and one of the most constructive features of the program of the League of Nations has been the study given to railroad transit and access to the sea. The monopolizing of cables, [Footnote: Hence the wisdom of taking Yap seriously.] of ports, fuel stations, mountain passes, canals, straits, river courses, terminals, market places means a good deal more than the enrichment of a group of business men, or the prestige of a government. It means a barrier upon the exchange of news and opinion. But monopoly is not the only barrier. Cost and available supply are even greater ones, for if the cost of travelling or trading is prohibitive, if the demand for facilities exceeds the supply, the barriers exist even without monopoly.

2

The size of a man's income has considerable effect on his access to the world beyond his neighborhood. With money he can overcome almost every tangible obstacle of communication, he can travel, buy books and periodicals, and bring within the range of his attention almost any known fact of the world. The income of the individual, and the income of the community determine the amount of communication that is possible. But men's ideas determine how that income shall be spent, and that in turn affects in the long run the amount of income they will have. Thus also there are limitations, none the less real, because they are often self-imposed and self-indulgent.

There are portions of the sovereign people who spend most of their spare time and spare money on motoring and comparing motor cars, on bridge-whist and post-mortems, on moving-pictures and potboilers, talking always to the same people with minute variations on the same old themes. They cannot really be said to suffer from censorship, or secrecy, the high cost or the difficulty of communication. They suffer from anemia, from lack of appetite and curiosity for the human scene. Theirs is no problem of access to the world outside. Worlds of interest are waiting for them to explore, and they do not enter.

They move, as if on a leash, within a fixed radius of acquaintances according to the law and the gospel of their social set. Among men the circle of talk in business and at the club and in the smoking car is wider than the set to which they belong. Among women the social set and the circle of talk are frequently almost identical. It is in the social set that ideas derived from reading and lectures and from the circle of talk converge, are sorted out, accepted, rejected, judged and sanctioned. There it is finally decided in each phase of a discussion which authorities and which sources of information are admissible, and which not.

The Walter Lippmann Reader

Our social set consists of those who figure as people in the phrase "people are saying"; they are the people whose approval matters most intimately to us. In big cities among men and women of wide interests and with the means for moving about, the social set is not so rigidly defined. But even in big cities, there are quarters and nests of villages containing self-sufficing social sets. In smaller communities there may exist a freer circulation, a more genuine fellowship from after breakfast to before dinner. But few people do not know, nevertheless, which set they really belong to, and which not.

Usually the distinguishing mark of a social set is the presumption that the children may intermarry. To marry outside the set involves, at the very least, a moment of doubt before the engagement can be approved. Each social set has a fairly clear picture of its relative position in the hierarchy of social sets. Between sets at the same level, association is easy, individuals are quickly accepted, hospitality is normal and unembarrassed. But in contact between sets that are "higher" or "lower," there is always reciprocal hesitation, a faint malaise, and a consciousness of difference. To be sure in a society like that of the United States, individuals move somewhat freely out of one set into another, especially where there is no racial barrier and where economic position changes so rapidly.

Economic position, however, is not measured by the amount of income. For in the first generation, at least, it is not income that determines social standing, but the character of a man's work, and it may take a generation or two before this fades out of the family tradition. Thus banking, law, medicine, public utilities, newspapers, the church, large retailing, brokerage, manufacture, are rated at a different social value from salesmanship, superintendence, expert technical work, nursing, school teaching, shop keeping; and those, in turn, are rated as differently from plumbing, being a chauffeur, dressmaking, subcontracting, or stenography, as these are from being a butler, lady's maid, a moving picture operator, or a locomotive engineer. And yet the financial return does not necessarily coincide with these gradations.

3

Whatever the tests of admission, the social set when formed is not a mere economic class, but something which more nearly resembles a biological clan. Membership is intimately connected with love, marriage and children, or, to speak more exactly, with the attitudes and desires that are involved. In the social set, therefore, opinions encounter the canons of Family Tradition, Respectability, Propriety, Dignity, Taste and Form, which make up the social set's picture of itself, a picture assiduously implanted in the children. In this picture a large space is tacitly given to an authorized version of what each set is called upon inwardly to accept as the social standing of the others. The more vulgar press for an outward expression of the deference due, the others are decently and sensitively silent about their own knowledge that such deference invisibly exists. But that knowledge, becoming overt when there is a marriage, a war, or a social upheaval, is the nexus of a large bundle of dispositions classified by Trotter [Footnote: W. Trotter, Instincts of the Herd in War and Peace.] under the general term instinct of the herd.

Within each social set there are augurs like the van der Luydens and Mrs. Manson Mingott in "The Age of Innocence," [Footnote: Edith Wharton, *The Age of Innocence*.] who are recognized as the custodians and the interpreters of its social pattern. You are made, they say, if the van der Luydens take you up. The invitations to their functions are the high sign of arrival and status. The elections to college societies, carefully graded and the gradations universally accepted, determine who is who in college. The social leaders, weighted with the ultimate eugenic responsibility, are peculiarly sensitive. Not only must they be watchfully aware of what makes for the integrity of their set, but they have to cultivate a special gift for knowing what other social sets are doing. They act as a kind of ministry of foreign affairs. Where most of the members of a set live complacently within the set, regarding it for all practical purposes as the world, the social leaders must combine an intimate knowledge of the anatomy of their own set with a persistent sense of its place in the hierarchy of sets.

The hierarchy, in fact, is bound together by the social leaders. At any one level there is something which might almost be called a social set of the social leaders. But vertically the actual binding together of society, in so far as it is bound together at all by social contact, is accomplished by those exceptional people, frequently suspect, who like Julius Beaufort and Ellen Olenska in "The Age of Innocence" move in and out. Thus there come to be established personal channels from one set to another, through which Tarde's laws of imitation operate. But for large sections of the population there are no such channels. For them the patented accounts of society and the moving pictures of high life have to serve. They may develop a social hierarchy of their own, almost unnoticed, as have the Negroes and the "foreign element," but among that assimilated mass which always considers itself the "nation," there is in spite of the great separateness of sets, a variety of personal contacts through which a circulation of standards takes place.

Some of the sets are so placed that they become what Professor Ross has called "radiant points of conventionality." [Footnote: Ross, *Social Psychology*, Ch. IX, X, XI.] Thus the social superior is likely to be imitated by the social inferior, the holder of power is imitated by subordinates, the more successful by the less successful, the rich by the poor, the city by the country. But imitation does not stop at frontiers. The powerful, socially superior, successful, rich, urban social set is fundamentally international throughout the western hemisphere, and in many ways London is its center. It counts among its membership the most influential people in the world, containing as it does the diplomatic set, high finance, the upper circles of the army and the navy, some princes of the church, a few great newspaper proprietors, their wives and mothers and daughters who wield the scepter of invitation. It is at once a great circle of talk and a real social set. But its importance comes from the fact that here at last the distinction between public and private affairs practically disappears. The private affairs of this set are public matters, and public matters are its private, often its family affairs. The confinements of Margot Asquith like the confinements of royalty are, as the philosophers say, in much the same universe of discourse as a tariff bill or a parliamentary debate.

There are large areas of governments in which this social set is not interested, and in America, at least, it has exercised only a fluctuating control over the national government. But its power in foreign affairs is always very great, and in war time its prestige is enormously enhanced. That is natural enough because these cosmopolitans have a contact with the outer world that most people do not possess. They have dined with each other in the capitals, and their sense of national honor is no mere abstraction; it is a concrete experience of being snubbed or approved by their friends. To Dr. Kennicott of Gopher Prairie it matters mighty little what Winston thinks and a great deal what Ezra Stowbody thinks, but to Mrs. Mingott with a daughter married to the Earl of Swithin it matters a lot when she visits her daughter, or entertains Winston himself. Dr. Kennicott and Mrs. Mingott are both socially sensitive, but Mrs. Mingott is sensitive to a social set that governs the world, while Dr. Kennicott's social set governs only in Gopher Prairie. But in matters that effect the larger relationships of the Great Society, Dr. Kennicott will often be found holding what he thinks is purely his own opinion, though, as a matter of fact, it has trickled down to Gopher Prairie from High Society, transmuted on its passage through the provincial social sets.

4

It is no part of our inquiry to attempt an account of the social tissue. We need only fix in mind how big is the part played by the social set in our spiritual contact with the world, how it tends to fix what is admissible, and to determine how it shall be judged. Affairs within its immediate competence each set more or less determines for itself. Above all it determines the detailed administration of the judgment. But the judgment itself is formed on patterns [Footnote: *Cf.* Part III] that may be inherited from the past, transmitted or imitated from other social sets. The highest social set consists of those who embody the leadership of the Great Society. As against almost every other social set where the bulk of the opinions are first hand only about local affairs, in this Highest Society the big decisions of war and peace, of social strategy and the ultimate distribution of political power, are intimate experiences within a circle of what, potentially at least, are personal acquaintances.

Since position and contact play so big a part in determining what can be seen, heard, read, and experienced, as well as what it is permissible to see, hear, read, and know, it is no wonder that moral judgment is so much more common than constructive thought. Yet in truly effective thinking the prime necessity is to liquidate judgments, regain an innocent eye, disentangle feelings, be curious and open-hearted. Man's history being what it is, political opinion on the scale of the Great Society requires an amount of selfless equanimity rarely attainable by any one for any length of time. We are concerned in public affairs, but immersed in our private ones. The time and attention are limited that we can spare for the labor of not taking opinions for granted, and we are subject to constant interruption.

CHAPTER IV
Time and Attention

NATURALLY it is possible to make a rough estimate only of the amount of attention people give each day to informing themselves about public affairs. Yet it is interesting that three estimates that I have examined agree tolerably well, though they were made at different times, in different places, and by different methods. [Footnote: July, 1900. D. F. Wilcox, *The American Newspaper: A Study in Social Psychology*, Annals of the American Academy of Political and Social Science, vol. xvi, p. 56. (The statistical tables are reproduced in James Edward Rogers, *The American Newspaper.*)

1916 (?) W. D. Scott, *The Psychology of Advertising*, pp. 226-248. See also Henry Foster Adams, *Advertising and its Mental Laws*, Ch. IV.

1920 *Newspaper Reading Habits of College Students*, by Prof.

George Burton Hotchkiss and Richard B. Franken, published by the

Association of National Advertisers, Inc., 15 East 26th Street, New

York City.]

A questionnaire was sent by Hotchkiss and Franken to 1761 men and women college students in New York City, and answers came from all but a few. Scott used a questionnaire on four thousand prominent business and professional men in Chicago and received replies from twenty-three hundred. Between seventy and seventy-five percent of all those who replied to either inquiry thought they spent a quarter of an hour a day reading newspapers. Only four percent of the Chicago group guessed at less than this and twenty-five percent guessed at more. Among the New Yorkers a little over eight percent figured their newspaper reading at less than fifteen minutes, and seventeen and a half at more.

Very few people have an accurate idea of fifteen minutes, so the figures are not to be taken literally. Moreover, business men, professional people, and college students are most of them liable to a curious little bias against appearing to spend too much time over the newspapers, and perhaps also to a faint suspicion of a desire to be known as rapid readers. All that the figures can justly be taken to mean is that over three quarters of those in the selected groups rate rather low the attention they give to printed news of the outer world.

The Walter Lippmann Reader

These time estimates are fairly well confirmed by a test which is less subjective. Scott asked his Chicagoans how many papers they read each day, and was told that

14 percent read but one paper			
46	"	"	two papers
21	"	"	three papers
10	"	"	four papers
3	"	"	five papers
2	"	"	six papers
3	"	"	all the papers (eight at the time of this inquiry).

The two- and three-paper readers are sixty-seven percent, which comes fairly close to the seventy-one percent in Scott's group who rate themselves at fifteen minutes a day. The omnivorous readers of from four to eight papers coincide roughly with the twenty-five percent who rated themselves at more than fifteen minutes.

2

It is still more difficult to guess how the time is distributed. The college students were asked to name "the five features which interest you most." Just under twenty percent voted for "general news," just under fifteen for editorials, just under twelve for "politics," a little over eight for finance, not two years after the armistice a little over six for foreign news, three and a half for local, nearly three for business, and a quarter of one percent for news about "labor." A scattering said they were most interested in sports, special articles, the theatre, advertisements, cartoons, book reviews, "accuracy," music, "ethical tone," society, brevity, art, stories, shipping, school news, "current news," print. Disregarding these, about sixty-seven and a half percent picked as the most interesting features news and opinion that dealt with public affairs.

This was a mixed college group. The girls professed greater interest than the boys in general news, foreign news, local news, politics, editorials, the theatre, music, art, stories, cartoons, advertisements, and "ethical tone." The boys on the other hand were more absorbed in finance, sports, business page, "accuracy" and "brevity." These discriminations correspond a little too closely with the ideals of what is cultured and moral, manly and decisive, not to make one suspect the utter objectivity of the replies.

Yet they agree fairly well with the replies of Scott's Chicago business and professional men. They were asked, not what features interested them most, but why they preferred one newspaper to another. Nearly seventy-one percent based their conscious preference on local news (17.8%), or political (15.8%) or financial (11.3%), or foreign (9.5%), or general (7.2%), or editorials (9%). The other thirty percent decided on grounds not connected with public affairs. They ranged from not quite seven who decided for ethical tone, down to one twentieth of one percent who cared most about humor.

How do these preferences correspond with the space given by newspapers to various subjects? Unfortunately there are no data collected on this point for the newspapers read by the Chicago and New York groups at the time the questionnaires were made. But there is an interesting analysis made over twenty years ago by Wilcox. He studied one hundred and ten newspapers in fourteen large cities, and classified the subject matter of over nine thousand columns.

Averaged for the whole country the various newspaper matter was found to fill:

```
                { (a) War News  17.9
                {                              { Foreign 1.2
                { (b) General "  21.8          { Politics 6.4
  I. News 55.3  {                              { Crime 3.1
                {                              { Misc. 11.1
                {
                {                              { Business 8.2
                { (c) Special "  15.6          { Sport 5.1
                                               { Society 2.3
```

II. Illustrations 3.1
III. Literature 2.4
IV. Opinion 7.1   { (a) Editorials 3.9
                 { (b) Letters & Exchange 3.2
V. Advertisements 32.1

The Walter Lippmann Reader

In order to bring this table into a fair comparison, it is necessary to exclude the space given to advertisements, and recompute the percentages. For the advertisements occupied only an infinitesimal part of the conscious preference of the Chicago group or the college group. I think this is justifiable for our purposes because the press prints what advertisements it can get, [Footnote: Except those which it regards as objectionable, and those which, in rare instances, are crowded out.] whereas the rest of the paper is designed to the taste of its readers. The table would then read:

```
                            {War News           26.4-
                            {                    {Foreign     1.8-
I. News 81.4+{General News 32.0+  {Political   9.4+
                            {                    {Crime       4.6-
                            {                    {Misc.      16.3+
                            {
                            {                    {Business 12.1-
                            {Special  "   23.0-  {Sporting 7.5+
                                                 {Society 3.3-
II. Illustrations 4.6-
III. Literature 3.5+
IV. Opinion 10.5-    {Editorials 5.8-
                     {Letters 4.7+
```

In this revised table if you add up the items which may be supposed to deal with public affairs, that is to say war, foreign, political, miscellaneous, business news, and opinion, you find a total of 76.5% of the edited space devoted in 1900 to the 70.6% of reasons given by Chicago business men in 1916 for preferring a particular newspaper, and to the five features which most interested 67.5% of the New York College students in 1920.

This would seem to show that the tastes of business men and college students in big cities to-day still correspond more or less to the averaged judgments of newspaper editors in big cities twenty years ago. Since that time the proportion of features to news has undoubtedly increased, and so has the circulation and the size of newspapers. Therefore, if to-day you could secure accurate replies from more typical groups than college students or business and professional men, you would expect to find a smaller percentage of time devoted to public affairs, as well as a smaller percentage of space. On the other hand you would expect to find that the average man spends more than the quarter of an hour on his newspaper, and that while the percentage of space given to public affairs is less than twenty years ago the net amount is greater.

No elaborate deductions are to be drawn from these figures. They help merely to make somewhat more concrete our notions of the effort that goes day by day into acquiring the data of our opinions. The newspapers are, of course, not the only means, but they are certainly the principal ones. Magazines, the public forum, the chautauqua, the church, political gatherings, trade union meetings, women's clubs, and news serials in the moving picture houses supplement the press. But taking it all at the most favorable estimate, the time each day is small when any of us is directly exposed to information from our unseen environment.

CHAPTER V

Speed, Words, and Clearness

1

The unseen environment is reported to us chiefly by words. These words are transmitted by wire or radio from the reporters to the editors who fit them into print. Telegraphy is expensive, and the facilities are often limited. Press service news is, therefore, usually coded. Thus a dispatch which reads,—

"Washington, D. C. June I.—The United States regards the question of German shipping seized in this country at the outbreak of hostilities as a closed incident,"

may pass over the wires in the following form:

"Washn i. The Uni Stas rgds tq of Ger spg seized in ts cou at t outbk o hox as a clod incident." [Footnote: Phillip's Code.]

A news item saying:

"Berlin, June 1, Chancellor Wirth told the Reichstag to-day in outlining the Government's program that 'restoration and reconciliation would be the keynote of the new Government's policy.' He added that the Cabinet was determined disarmament should be carried out loyally and that disarmament would not be the occasion of the imposition of further penalties by the Allies."

may be cabled in this form:

"Berlin 1. Chancellor Wirth told t Reichstag tdy in outlining the gvts pgn tt qn restoration & reconciliation wd b the keynote f new gvts policy. qj He added ttt cabinet ws dtmd disarmament sd b carried out loyally & tt disarmament wd n b. the ocan f imposition of further penalties bi t alis."

In this second item the substance has been culled from a long speech in a foreign tongue, translated, coded, and then decoded. The operators who receive the messages transcribe them as they go along, and I am told that a good operator can write fifteen thousand or even more words per eight hour day, with a half an hour out for lunch and two ten minute periods for rest.

2

A few words must often stand for a whole succession of acts, thoughts, feelings and consequences. We read:

233

The Walter Lippmann Reader

"Washington, Dec. 23—A statement charging Japanese military authorities with deeds more 'frightful and barbarous' than anything ever alleged to have occurred in Belgium during the war was issued here to-day by the Korean Commission, based, the Commission said, on authentic reports received by it from Manchuria."

Here eyewitnesses, their accuracy unknown, report to the makers of 'authentic reports'; they in turn transmit these to a commission five thousand miles away. It prepares a statement, probably much too long for publication, from which a correspondent culls an item of print three and a half inches long. The meaning has to be telescoped in such a way as to permit the reader to judge how much weight to give to the news.

It is doubtful whether a supreme master of style could pack all the elements of truth that complete justice would demand into a hundred word account of what had happened in Korea during the course of several months. For language is by no means a perfect vehicle of meanings. Words, like currency, are turned over and over again, to evoke one set of images to-day, another to-morrow. There is no certainty whatever that the same word will call out exactly the same idea in the reader's mind as it did in the reporter's. Theoretically, if each fact and each relation had a name that was unique, and if everyone had agreed on the names, it would be possible to communicate without misunderstanding. In the exact sciences there is an approach to this ideal, and that is part of the reason why of all forms of world-wide cooperation, scientific inquiry is the most effective.

Men command fewer words than they have ideas to express, and language, as Jean Paul said, is a dictionary of faded metaphors. [Footnote: Cited by White, *Mechanisms of Character Formation*.] The journalist addressing half a million readers of whom he has only a dim picture, the speaker whose words are flashed to remote villages and overseas, cannot hope that a few phrases will carry the whole burden of their meaning. "The words of Lloyd George, badly understood and badly transmitted," said M. Briand to the Chamber of Deputies, [Footnote: Special Cable to *The New York Times*, May 25, 1921, by Edwin L, James.] "seemed to give the Pan-Germanists the idea that the time had come to start something." A British Prime Minister, speaking in English to the whole attentive world, speaks his own meaning in his own words to all kinds of people who will see their meaning in those words. No matter how rich or subtle—or rather the more rich and the more subtle that which he has to say, the more his

234

meaning will suffer as it is sluiced into standard speech and then distributed again among alien minds. [Footnote: In May of 1921, relations between England and France were strained by the insurrection of M. Korfanty in Upper Silesia. The London Correspondence of the *Manchester Guardian* (May 20, 1921), contained the following item:

"The Franco-English Exchange in Words.

"In quarters well acquainted with French ways and character I find a tendency to think that undue sensibility has been shown by our press and public opinion in the lively and at times intemperate language of the French press through the present crisis. The point was put to me by a well-informed neutral observer in the following manner.

"Words, like money, are tokens of value. They represent meaning, therefore, and just as money, their representative value goes up and down. The French word 'etonnant' was used by Bossuet with a terrible weight of meaning which it has lost to-day. A similar thing can be observed with the English word 'awful.' Some nations constitutionally tend to understate, others to overstate. What the British Tommy called an unhealthy place could only be described by an Italian soldier by means of a rich vocabulary aided with an exuberant mimicry. Nations that understate keep their word-currency sound. Nations that overstate suffer from inflation in their language.

"Expressions such as 'a distinguished scholar,' 'a clever writer,' must be translated into French as 'a great savant,' 'an exquisite master.' It is a mere matter of exchange, just as in France one pound pays 46 francs, and yet one knows that that does not increase its value at home. Englishmen reading the French press should endeavour to work out a mental operation similar to that of the banker who puts back francs into pounds, and not forget in so doing that while in normal times the change was 25 it is now 46 on account of the war. For there is a war fluctuation on word exchanges as well as on money exchanges.

"The argument, one hopes, works both ways, and Frenchmen do not fail to realize that there is as much value behind English reticence as behind their own exuberance of expression."]

Millions of those who are watching him can read hardly at all. Millions more can read the words but cannot understand them. Of those who can both read and understand, a good three-quarters we may assume have some part of half an hour a day to spare for the subject. To them the words so acquired are the cue for a whole train of ideas on which ultimately a vote of untold consequences may be based. Necessarily the ideas which we allow the words we read to evoke form the biggest part of the original data of our opinions. The world is vast, the situations that concern us are intricate, the messages are few, the biggest part of opinion must be constructed in the imagination.

When we use the word "Mexico" what picture does it evoke in a resident of New York? Likely as not, it is some composite of sand, cactus, oil wells, greasers, rum-drinking Indians, testy old cavaliers flourishing whiskers and sovereignty, or perhaps an idyllic peasantry à la Jean Jacques, assailed by the prospect of smoky industrialism, and fighting for the Rights of Man. What does the word "Japan" evoke? Is it a vague horde of slant-eyed yellow men, surrounded by Yellow Perils, picture brides, fans, Samurai, banzais, art, and cherry blossoms? Or the word "alien"? According to a group of New England college students, writing in the year 1920, an alien was the following: [Footnote: *The New Republic*: December 29, 1920, p. 142.]

"A person hostile to this country."

"A person against the government."

"A person who is on the opposite side."

"A native of an unfriendly country."

"A foreigner at war."

"A foreigner who tries to do harm to the country he is in."

"An enemy from a foreign land."

"A person against a country." etc....

Yet the word alien is an unusually exact legal term, far more exact than words like sovereignty, independence, national honor, rights, defense, aggression, imperialism, capitalism, socialism, about which we so readily take sides "for" or "against."

3

The power to dissociate superficial analogies, attend to differences and appreciate variety is lucidity of mind. It is a relative faculty. Yet the differences in lucidity are extensive, say as between a newly born infant and a botanist examining a flower. To the infant there is precious little difference between his own toes, his father's watch, the lamp on the table, the moon in the sky, and a nice bright yellow edition of Guy de Maupassant. To many a member of the

The Walter Lippmann Reader

Union League Club there is no remarkable difference between a Democrat, a Socialist, an anarchist, and a burglar, while to a highly sophisticated anarchist there is a whole universe of difference between Bakunin, Tolstoi, and Kropotkin. These examples show how difficult it might be to secure a sound public opinion about de Maupassant among babies, or about Democrats in the Union League Club.

A man who merely rides in other people's automobiles may not rise to finer discrimination than between a Ford, a taxicab, and an automobile. But let that same man own a car and drive it, let him, as the psychoanalysts would say, project his libido upon automobiles, and he will describe a difference in carburetors by looking at the rear end of a car a city block away. That is why it is often such a relief when the talk turns from "general topics" to a man's own hobby. It is like turning from the landscape in the parlor to the ploughed field outdoors. It is a return to the three dimensional world, after a sojourn in the painter's portrayal of his own emotional response to his own inattentive memory of what he imagines he ought to have seen.

We easily identify, says Ferenczi, two only partially similar things: [Footnote: Internat. Zeitschr, f. Arztl. Psychoanalyse, 1913. Translated and republished by Dr. Ernest Jones in S. Ferenczi, *Contributions to Psychoanalysis*, Ch. VIII, *Stages in the Development of the Sense of Reality*.] the child more easily than the adult, the primitive or arrested mind more readily than the mature. As it first appears in the child, consciousness seems to be an unmanageable mixture of sensations. The child has no sense of time, and almost none of space, it reaches for the chandelier with the same confidence that it reaches for its mother's breast, and at first with almost the same expectation. Only very gradually does function define itself. To complete inexperience this is a coherent and undifferentiated world, in which, as someone has said of a school of philosophers, all facts are born free and equal. Those facts which belong together in the world have not yet been separated from those which happen to lie side by side in the stream of consciousness.

At first, says Ferenczi, the baby gets some of the things it wants by crying for them. This is "the period of magical hallucinatory omnipotence." In its second phase the child points to the things it wants, and they are given to it. "Omnipotence by the help of magic gestures." Later, the child learns to talk, asks for what it wishes, and is partially successful. "The period of magic thoughts and magic words." Each phase may persist for certain situations, though overlaid and only visible at times, as for example, in the little harmless superstitions from which few of us are wholly free. In each phase, partial success tends to confirm that way of acting, while failure tends to stimulate the development of another. Many individuals, parties, and even nations, rarely appear to transcend the magical organization of experience. But in the more advanced sections of the most advanced peoples, trial and error after repeated failure has led to the invention of a new principle. The moon, they learn, is not moved by baying at it. Crops are not raised from the soil by spring festivals or Republican majorities, but by sunlight, moisture, seeds, fertilizer, and cultivation. [Footnote: Ferenczi, being a pathologist, does not describe this maturer period where experience is organized as equations, the phase of realism on the basis of science.]

Allowing for the purely schematic value of Ferenczi's categories of response, the quality which we note as critical is the power to discriminate among crude perceptions and vague analogies. This power has been studied under laboratory conditions. [Footnote: See, for example, Diagnostische Assoziation Studien, conducted at the Psychiatric University Clinic in Zurich under the direction of Dr. C. G. Jung. These tests were carried on principally under the so-called Krapelin-Aschaffenburg classification. They show reaction time, classify response to the stimulant word as inner, outer, and clang, show separate results for the first and second hundred words, for reaction time and reaction quality when the subject is distracted by holding an idea in mind, or when he replies while beating time with a metronome. Some of the results are summarized in Jung, *Analytical Psychology*, Ch. II, transl. by Dr. Constance E. Long.] The Zurich Association Studies indicate clearly that slight mental fatigue, an inner disturbance of attention or an external distraction, tend to "flatten" the quality of the response. An example of the very "flat" type is the clang association (cat-hat), a reaction to the sound and not to the sense of the stimulant word. One test, for example, shows a 9% increase of clang in the second series of a hundred reactions. Now the clang is almost a repetition, a very primitive form of analogy.

4

If the comparatively simple conditions of a laboratory can so readily flatten out discrimination, what must be the effect of city life? In the laboratory the fatigue is slight enough, the distraction rather trivial. Both are balanced in measure by the subject's interest and self-consciousness. Yet if the beat of a metronome will depress intelligence, what do eight or twelve hours of noise, odor, and heat in a factory, or day upon day among chattering typewriters and telephone bells and slamming doors, do to the political judgments formed on the basis of newspapers read in street-cars and subways? Can anything be heard in the hubbub that does not shriek, or be seen in the general glare that does not flash like an electric sign? The life of the city dweller lacks solitude, silence, ease. The nights are noisy and ablaze. The people of a big city are assaulted by incessant sound, now violent and jagged, now falling into unfinished rhythms, but endless and remorseless. Under modern industrialism thought goes on in a bath of noise. If its discriminations are often flat and foolish, here at least is some small part of the reason. The sovereign people determines life and death and happiness under conditions where experience and experiment alike show thought to be most difficult. "The intolerable burden of thought" is a burden when the conditions make it burdensome. It is no burden when the conditions are favorable. It is as exhilarating to think as it is to dance, and just as natural.

Every man whose business it is to think knows that he must for part of the day create about himself a pool of silence. But in that helter-skelter which we flatter by the name of civilization, the citizen performs the perilous business of government under the worst possible conditions. A faint recognition of this truth inspires the movement for a shorter work day, for longer vacations, for light, air, order, sunlight and dignity in factories and offices. But if the intellectual quality of our life is to be improved that is only the merest beginning. So long as so many jobs are an endless and, for the worker, an aimless routine, a kind of automatism using one set of muscles in one monotonous pattern, his whole life will tend towards an automatism in which nothing is particularly to be distinguished from anything else unless it is announced with a thunderclap. So long as he is physically imprisoned in crowds by day and even by night his attention will flicker and relax. It will not hold fast and define clearly where he is the victim of all sorts of pother, in a home which needs to be ventilated of its welter of drudgery, shrieking children, raucous assertions, indigestible food, bad air, and suffocating ornament.

Occasionally perhaps we enter a building which is composed and spacious; we go to a theatre where modern stagecraft has cut away distraction, or go to sea, or into a quiet place, and we remember how cluttered, how capricious, how superfluous and clamorous is the ordinary urban life of our time. We learn to understand why our addled minds seize so little with precision, why they are caught up and tossed about in a kind of tarantella by headlines and catch-words, why so often they cannot tell things apart or discern identity in apparent differences.

5

But this external disorder is complicated further by internal. Experiment shows that the speed, the accuracy, and the intellectual quality of association is deranged by what we are taught to call emotional conflicts. Measured in fifths of a second, a series of a hundred stimuli containing both neutral and hot words may show a variation as between 5 and 32 or even a total failure to respond at all. [Footnote: Jung, *Clark Lectures*.] Obviously our public opinion is in intermittent contact with complexes of all sorts; with ambition and economic interest, personal animosity, racial prejudice, class feeling and what not. They distort our reading, our thinking, our talking and our behavior in a great variety of ways.

And finally since opinions do not stop at the normal members of society, since for the purposes of an election, a propaganda, a following, numbers constitute power, the quality of attention is still further depressed. The mass of absolutely illiterate, of feeble-minded, grossly neurotic, undernourished and frustrated individuals, is very considerable, much more considerable there is reason to think than we generally suppose. Thus a wide popular appeal is circulated among persons who are mentally children or barbarians, people whose lives are a morass of entanglements, people whose vitality is exhausted, shut-in people, and people whose experience has comprehended no factor in the problem under discussion. The stream of public opinion is stopped by them in little eddies of misunderstanding, where it is discolored with prejudice and far fetched analogy.

A "broad appeal" takes account of the quality of association, and is made to those susceptibilities which are widely distributed. A "narrow" or a "special" appeal is one made to those susceptibilities which are uncommon. But the same individual may respond with very different quality to different stimuli, or to the same stimuli at different times. Human susceptibilities are like an alpine country. There are isolated peaks, there are extensive but separated plateaus, and there are deeper strata which are quite continuous for nearly all mankind. Thus the individuals whose susceptibilities reach the rarefied atmosphere of those peaks where there exists an exquisitive difference between Frege and Peano, or between Sassetta's earlier and later periods, may be good stanch Republicans at another level of appeal, and when they are starving and afraid, indistinguishable from any other starving and frightened person. No wonder that the magazines with the large circulations prefer the face of a pretty girl to any other trade mark, a face, pretty enough to be alluring, but innocent enough to be acceptable. For the "psychic level" on which the stimulus acts determines whether the public is to be potentially a large or a small one.

6

Thus the environment with which our public opinions deal is refracted in many ways, by censorship and privacy at the source, by physical and social barriers at the other end, by scanty attention, by the poverty of language, by distraction, by unconscious constellations of feeling, by wear and tear, violence, monotony. These limitations upon our access to that environment combine with the obscurity and complexity of the facts themselves to thwart clearness and justice of perception, to substitute misleading fictions for workable ideas, and to deprive us of adequate checks upon those who consciously strive to mislead.

PART III
STEREOTYPES

CHAPTER VI

Stereotypes

1

Each of us lives and works on a small part of the earth's surface, moves in a small circle, and of these acquaintances knows only a few intimately. Of any public event that has wide effects we see at best only a phase and an aspect. This is as true of the eminent insiders who draft treaties, make laws, and issue orders, as it is of those who have treaties framed for them, laws promulgated to them, orders given at them. Inevitably our opinions cover a bigger space, a longer reach of time, a greater number of things, than we can directly observe. They have, therefore, to be pieced together out of what others have reported and what we can imagine.

Yet even the eyewitness does not bring back a naéve picture of the scene. [Footnote: *E. g. cf.* Edmond Locard, *L'Enquête Criminelle et les Méthodes Scientifiques.* A great deal of interesting material has been gathered in late years on the credibility of the witness, which shows, as an able reviewer of Dr. Locard's book says in *The Times* (London) Literary Supplement (August 18, 1921), that credibility varies as to classes of witnesses and classes of events, and also as to type of perception. Thus, perceptions of touch, odor, and taste have low evidential value. Our hearing is defective and arbitrary when it judges the source and direction of sound, and in listening to the talk of other people "words which are not heard will be supplied by the witness in all good faith. He will have a theory of the purport of the conversation, and will arrange the sounds he heard to fit it." Even visual perceptions are liable to great error, as in identification, recognition, judgment of distance, estimates of numbers, for example, the size of a crowd. In the untrained observer, the sense of time is highly variable. All these original weaknesses are complicated by tricks of memory, and the incessant creative quality of the imagination. *Cf.* also Sherrington, *The Integrative Action of the Nervous System*, pp. 318-327.

The Walter Lippmann Reader

The late Professor Hugo Münsterberg wrote a popular book on this subject called *On the Witness Stand*.] For experience seems to show that he himself brings something to the scene which later he takes away from it, that oftener than not what he imagines to be the account of an event is really a transfiguration of it. Few facts in consciousness seem to be merely given. Most facts in consciousness seem to be partly made. A report is the joint product of the knower and known, in which the role of the observer is always selective and usually creative. The facts we see depend on where we are placed, and the habits of our eyes.

An unfamiliar scene is like the baby's world, "one great, blooming, buzzing confusion." [Footnote: Wm. James, *Principles of Psychology*, Vol. I, p. 488.] This is the way, says Mr. John Dewey, [Footnote: John Dewey, *How We Think*, pg 121.] that any new thing strikes an adult, so far as the thing is really new and strange. "Foreign languages that we do not understand always seem jibberings, babblings, in which it is impossible to fix a definite, clear-cut, individualized group of sounds. The countryman in the crowded street, the landlubber at sea, the ignoramus in sport at a contest between experts in a complicated game, are further instances. Put an inexperienced man in a factory, and at first the work seems to him a meaningless medley. All strangers of another race proverbially look alike to the visiting stranger. Only gross differences of size or color are perceived by an outsider in a flock of sheep, each of which is perfectly individualized to the shepherd. A diffusive blur and an indiscriminately shifting suction characterize what we do not understand. The problem of the acquisition of meaning by things, or (stated in another way) of forming habits of simple apprehension, is thus the problem of introducing (1) *definiteness* and *distinction* and (2) *consistency* or *stability* of meaning into what is otherwise vague and wavering."

But the kind of definiteness and consistency introduced depends upon who introduces them. In a later passage [Footnote: *op. cit.*, p. 133.] Dewey gives an example of how differently an experienced layman and a chemist might define the word metal. "Smoothness, hardness, glossiness, and brilliancy, heavy weight for its size ... the serviceable properties of capacity for being hammered and pulled without breaking, of being softened by heat and hardened by cold, of retaining the shape and form given, of resistance to pressure and decay, would probably be included" in the layman's definition. But the chemist would likely as not ignore these esthetic and utilitarian qualities, and define a metal as "any

243

chemical element that enters into combination with oxygen so as to form a base."

For the most part we do not first see, and then define, we define first and then see. In the great blooming, buzzing confusion of the outer world we pick out what our culture has already defined for us, and we tend to perceive that which we have picked out in the form stereotyped for us by our culture. Of the great men who assembled at Paris to settle the affairs of mankind, how many were there who were able to see much of the Europe about them, rather than their commitments about Europe? Could anyone have penetrated the mind of M. Clemenceau, would he have found there images of the Europe of 1919, or a great sediment of stereotyped ideas accumulated and hardened in a long and pugnacious existence? Did he see the Germans of 1919, or the German type as he had learned to see it since 1871? He saw the type, and among the reports that came to him from Germany, he took to heart those reports, and, it seems, those only, which fitted the type that was in his mind. If a junker blustered, that was an authentic German; if a labor leader confessed the guilt of the empire, he was not an authentic German.

At a Congress of Psychology in Göttingen an interesting experiment was made with a crowd of presumably trained observers. [Footnote: A. von Gennep, *La formation des légendes*, pp. 158-159. Cited F. van Langenhove, *The Growth of a Legend*, pp. 120-122.]

"Not far from the hall in which the Congress was sitting there was a public fete with a masked ball. Suddenly the door of the hall was thrown open and a clown rushed in madly pursued by a negro, revolver in hand. They stopped in the middle of the room fighting; the clown fell, the negro leapt upon him, fired, and then both rushed out of the hall. The whole incident hardly lasted twenty seconds.

"The President asked those present to write immediately a report since there was sure to be a judicial inquiry. Forty reports were sent in. Only one had less than 20% of mistakes in regard to the principal facts; fourteen had 20% to 40% of mistakes; twelve from 40% to 50%; thirteen more than 50%. Moreover in twenty-four accounts 10% of the details were pure inventions and this proportion was exceeded in ten accounts and diminished in six. Briefly a quarter of the accounts were false.

The Walter Lippmann Reader

"It goes without saying that the whole scene had been arranged and even photographed in advance. The ten false reports may then be relegated to the category of tales and legends; twenty-four accounts are half legendary, and six have a value approximating to exact evidence."

Thus out of forty trained observers writing a responsible account of a scene that had just happened before their eyes, more than a majority saw a scene that had not taken place. What then did they see? One would suppose it was easier to tell what had occurred, than to invent something which had not occurred. They saw their stereotype of such a brawl. All of them had in the course of their lives acquired a series of images of brawls, and these images flickered before their eyes. In one man these images displaced less than 20% of the actual scene, in thirteen men more than half. In thirty-four out of the forty observers the stereotypes preempted at least one-tenth of the scene.

A distinguished art critic has said [Footnote: Bernard Berenson, *The Central Italian Painters of the Renaissance*, pp. 60, *et seq.*] that "what with the almost numberless shapes assumed by an object. ... What with our insensitiveness and inattention, things scarcely would have for us features and outlines so determined and clear that we could recall them at will, but for the stereotyped shapes art has lent them." The truth is even broader than that, for the stereotyped shapes lent to the world come not merely from art, in the sense of painting and sculpture and literature, but from our moral codes and our social philosophies and our political agitations as well. Substitute in the following passage of Mr. Berenson's the words 'politics,' 'business,' and 'society,' for the word 'art' and the sentences will be no less true: "... unless years devoted to the study of all schools of art have taught us also to see with our own eyes, we soon fall into the habit of moulding whatever we look at into the forms borrowed from the one art with which we are acquainted. There is our standard of artistic reality. Let anyone give us shapes and colors which we cannot instantly match in our paltry stock of hackneyed forms and tints, and we shake our heads at his failure to reproduce things as we know they certainly are, or we accuse him of insincerity."

Mr. Berenson speaks of our displeasure when a painter "does not visualize objects exactly as we do," and of the difficulty of appreciating the art of the Middle Ages because since then "our manner of visualizing forms has changed in a thousand ways." [Footnote: *Cf.* also his comment on *Dante's Visual Images, and*

245

his Early Illustrators in *The Study and Criticism of Italian Art* (First Series), p. 13. "We cannot help dressing Virgil as a Roman, and giving him a 'classical profile' and 'statuesque carriage,' but Dante's visual image of Virgil was probably no less mediaeval, no more based on a critical reconstruction of antiquity, than his entire conception of the Roman poet. Fourteenth Century illustrators make Virgil look like a mediaeval scholar, dressed in cap and gown, and there is no reason why Dante's visual image of him should have been other than this."] He goes on to show how in regard to the human figure we have been taught to see what we do see. "Created by Donatello and Masaccio, and sanctioned by the Humanists, the new canon of the human figure, the new cast of features ... presented to the ruling classes of that time the type of human being most likely to win the day in the combat of human forces... Who had the power to break through this new standard of vision and, out of the chaos of things, to select shapes more definitely expressive of reality than those fixed by men of genius? No one had such power. People had perforce to see things in that way and in no other, and to see only the shapes depicted, to love only the ideals presented...." [Footnote: *The Central Italian Painters*, pp. 66-67.]

2

If we cannot fully understand the acts of other people, until we know what they think they know, then in order to do justice we have to appraise not only the information which has been at their disposal, but the minds through which they have filtered it. For the accepted types, the current patterns, the standard versions, intercept information on its way to consciousness. Americanization, for example, is superficially at least the substitution of American for European stereotypes. Thus the peasant who might see his landlord as if he were the lord of the manor, his employer as he saw the local magnate, is taught by Americanization to see the landlord and employer according to American standards. This constitutes a change of mind, which is, in effect, when the inoculation succeeds, a change of vision. His eye sees differently. One kindly gentlewoman has confessed that the stereotypes are of such overweening importance, that when hers are not indulged, she at least is unable to accept the brotherhood of man and the fatherhood of God: "we are strangely affected by the clothes we wear. Garments create a mental and social atmosphere. What can be hoped for the Americanism of a man who insists on employing a London

The Walter Lippmann Reader

tailor? One's very food affects his Americanism. What kind of American consciousness can grow in the atmosphere of sauerkraut and Limburger cheese? Or what can you expect of the Americanism of the man whose breath always reeks of garlic?" [Footnote: Cited by Mr. Edward Hale Bierstadt, *New Republic*, June 1 1921 p. 21.]

This lady might well have been the patron of a pageant which a friend of mine once attended. It was called the Melting Pot, and it was given on the Fourth of July in an automobile town where many foreign-born workers are employed. In the center of the baseball park at second base stood a huge wooden and canvas pot. There were flights of steps up to the rim on two sides. After the audience had settled itself, and the band had played, a procession came through an opening at one side of the field. It was made up of men of all the foreign nationalities employed in the factories. They wore their native costumes, they were singing their national songs; they danced their folk dances, and carried the banners of all Europe. The master of ceremonies was the principal of the grade school dressed as Uncle Sam. He led them to the pot. He directed them up the steps to the rim, and inside. He called them out again on the other side. They came, dressed in derby hats, coats, pants, vest, stiff collar and polka-dot tie, undoubtedly, said my friend, each with an Eversharp pencil in his pocket, and all singing the Star-Spangled Banner.

To the promoters of this pageant, and probably to most of the actors, it seemed as if they had managed to express the most intimate difficulty to friendly association between the older peoples of America and the newer. The contradiction of their stereotypes interfered with the full recognition of their common humanity. The people who change their names know this. They mean to change themselves, and the attitude of strangers toward them.

There is, of course, some connection between the scene outside and the mind through which we watch it, just as there are some long-haired men and short-haired women in radical gatherings. But to the hurried observer a slight connection is enough. If there are two bobbed heads and four beards in the audience, it will be a bobbed and bearded audience to the reporter who knows beforehand that such gatherings are composed of people with these tastes in the management of their hair. There is a connection between our vision and the facts, but it is often a strange connection. A man has rarely looked at a landscape, let us say, except to examine its possibilities for division into building

247

lots, but he has seen a number of landscapes hanging in the parlor. And from them he has learned to think of a landscape as a rosy sunset, or as a country road with a church steeple and a silver moon. One day he goes to the country, and for hours he does not see a single landscape. Then the sun goes down looking rosy. At once he recognizes a landscape and exclaims that it is beautiful. But two days later, when he tries to recall what he saw, the odds are that he will remember chiefly some landscape in a parlor.

Unless he has been drunk or dreaming or insane he did see a sunset, but he saw in it, and above all remembers from it, more of what the oil painting taught him to observe, than what an impressionist painter, for example, or a cultivated Japanese would have seen and taken away with him. And the Japanese and the painter in turn will have seen and remembered more of the form they had learned, unless they happen to be the very rare people who find fresh sight for mankind. In untrained observation we pick recognizable signs out of the environment. The signs stand for ideas, and these ideas we fill out with our stock of images. We do not so much see this man and that sunset; rather we notice that the thing is man or sunset, and then see chiefly what our mind is already full of on those subjects.

3

There is economy in this. For the attempt to see all things freshly and in detail, rather than as types and generalities, is exhausting, and among busy affairs practically out of the question. In a circle of friends, and in relation to close associates or competitors, there is no shortcut through, and no substitute for, an individualized understanding. Those whom we love and admire most are the men and women whose consciousness is peopled thickly with persons rather than with types, who know us rather than the classification into which we might fit. For even without phrasing it to ourselves, we feel intuitively that all classification is in relation to some purpose not necessarily our own; that between two human beings no association has final dignity in which each does not take the other as an end in himself. There is a taint on any contact between two people which does not affirm as an axiom the personal inviolability of both.

But modern life is hurried and multifarious, above all physical distance separates men who are often in vital contact with each other, such as employer and employee, official and voter. There is neither time nor opportunity for intimate acquaintance. Instead we notice a trait which marks a well known type, and fill in the rest of the picture by means of the stereotypes we carry about in our heads. He is an agitator. That much we notice, or are told. Well, an agitator is this sort of person, and so *he* is this sort of person. He is an intellectual. He is a plutocrat. He is a foreigner. He is a "South European." He is from Back Bay. He is a Harvard Man. How different from the statement: he is a Yale Man. He is a regular fellow. He is a West Pointer. He is an old army sergeant. He is a Greenwich Villager: what don't we know about him then, and about her? He is an international banker. He is from Main Street.

The subtlest and most pervasive of all influences ere those which create and maintain the repertory of stereotypes. We are told about the world before we see it. We imagine most things before we experience them. And those preconceptions, unless education has made us acutely aware, govern deeply the whole process of perception. They mark out certain objects as familiar or strange, emphasizing the difference, so that the slightly familiar is seen as very familiar, and the somewhat strange as sharply alien. They are aroused by small signs, which may vary from a true index to a vague analogy. Aroused, they flood fresh vision with older images, and project into the world what has been resurrected in memory. Were there no practical uniformities in the environment, there would be no economy and only error in the human habit of accepting foresight for sight. But there are uniformities sufficiently accurate, and the need of economizing attention is so inevitable, that the abandonment of all stereotypes for a wholly innocent approach to experience would impoverish human life.

What matters is the character of the stereotypes, and the gullibility with which we employ them. And these in the end depend upon those inclusive patterns which constitute our philosophy of life. If in that philosophy we assume that the world is codified according to a code which we possess, we are likely to make our reports of what is going on describe a world run by our code. But if our philosophy tells us that each man is only a small part of the world, that his intelligence catches at best only phases and aspects in a coarse net of ideas, then, when we use our stereotypes, we tend to know that they are only stereotypes, to hold them lightly, to modify them gladly. We tend, also, to realize more and more clearly when our ideas started, where they started, how they came to us, why we accepted them. All useful history is antiseptic in this fashion. It enables us to know what fairy tale, what school book, what tradition, what novel, play, picture, phrase, planted one preconception in this mind, another in that mind.

4

Those who wish to censor art do not at least underestimate this influence. They generally misunderstand it, and almost always they are absurdly bent on preventing other people from discovering anything not sanctioned by them. But at any rate, like Plato in his argument about the poets, they feel vaguely that the types acquired through fiction tend to be imposed on reality. Thus there can be little doubt that the moving picture is steadily building up imagery which is then evoked by the words people read in their newspapers. In the whole experience of the race there has been no aid to visualization comparable to the cinema. If a Florentine wished to visualize the saints, he could go to the frescoes in his church, where he might see a vision of saints standardized for his time by Giotto. If an Athenian wished to visualize the gods he went to the temples. But the number of objects which were pictured was not great. And in the East, where the spirit of the second commandment was widely accepted, the portraiture of concrete things was even more meager, and for that reason perhaps the faculty of practical decision was by so much reduced. In the western world, however, during the last few centuries there has been an enormous increase in the volume and scope of secular description, the word picture, the narrative, the illustrated narrative, and finally the moving picture and, perhaps, the talking picture.

Photographs have the kind of authority over imagination to-day, which the printed word had yesterday, and the spoken word before that. They seem utterly real. They come, we imagine, directly to us without human meddling, and they are the most effortless food for the mind conceivable. Any description in words, or even any inert picture, requires an effort of memory before a picture exists in the mind. But on the screen the whole process of observing, describing, reporting, and then imagining, has been accomplished for you. Without more trouble than is needed to stay awake the result which your imagination is always aiming at is reeled off on the screen. The shadowy idea becomes vivid; your hazy notion, let us say, of the Ku Klux Klan, thanks to Mr. Griffiths, takes vivid shape when you see the Birth of a Nation. Historically it may be the wrong shape, morally it may be a pernicious shape, but it is a shape, and I doubt whether anyone who has seen the film and does not know more about the Ku Klux Klan than Mr. Griffiths, will ever hear the name again without seeing those white horsemen.

5

And so when we speak of the mind of a group of people, of the French mind, the militarist mind, the bolshevik mind, we are liable to serious confusion unless we agree to separate the instinctive equipment from the stereotypes, the patterns, and the formulae which play so decisive a part in building up the mental world to which the native character is adapted and responds. Failure to make this distinction accounts for oceans of loose talk about collective minds, national souls, and race psychology. To be sure a stereotype may be so consistently and authoritatively transmitted in each generation from parent to child that it seems almost like a biological fact. In some respects, we may indeed have become, as Mr. Wallas says, [Footnote: Graham Wallas, *Our Social Heritage*, p. 17.] biologically parasitic upon our social heritage. But certainly there is not the least scientific evidence which would enable anyone to argue that men are born with the political habits of the country in which they are born. In so far as political habits are alike in a nation, the first places to look for an explanation are the nursery, the school, the church, not in that limbo inhabited by Group Minds and National Souls. Until you have thoroughly failed to see tradition being handed on from parents, teachers, priests, and uncles, it is a solecism of the worst order to ascribe political differences to the germ plasm.

It is possible to generalize tentatively and with a decent humility about comparative differences within the same category of education and experience. Yet even this is a tricky enterprise. For almost no two experiences are exactly alike, not even of two children in the same household. The older son never does have the experience of being the younger. And therefore, until we are able to discount the difference in nurture, we must withhold judgment about differences of nature. As well judge the productivity of two soils by comparing their yield before you know which is in Labrador and which in Iowa, whether they have been cultivated and enriched, exhausted, or allowed to run wild.

CHAPTER VII
Stereotypes as Defense

1

THERE is another reason, besides economy of effort, why we so often hold to our stereotypes when we might pursue a more disinterested vision. The systems of stereotypes may be the core of our personal tradition, the defenses of our position in society.

They are an ordered, more or less consistent picture of the world, to which our habits, our tastes, our capacities, our comforts and our hopes have adjusted themselves. They may not be a complete picture of the world, but they are a picture of a possible world to which we are adapted. In that world people and things have their well-known places, and do certain expected things. We feel at home there. We fit in. We are members. We know the way around. There we find the charm of the familiar, the normal, the dependable; its grooves and shapes are where we are accustomed to find them. And though we have abandoned much that might have tempted us before we creased ourselves into that mould, once we are firmly in, it fits as snugly as an old shoe.

No wonder, then, that any disturbance of the stereotypes seems like an attack upon the foundations of the universe. It is an attack upon the foundations of *our* universe, and, where big things are at stake, we do not readily admit that there is any distinction between our universe and the universe. A world which turns out to be one in which those we honor are unworthy, and those we despise are noble, is nerve-racking. There is anarchy if our order of precedence is not the only possible one. For if the meek should indeed inherit the earth, if the first should be last, if those who are without sin alone may cast a stone, if to Caesar you render only the things that are Caesar's, then the foundations of self-respect would be shaken for those who have arranged their lives as if these maxims were not true. A pattern of stereotypes is not neutral. It is not merely a way of substituting order for the great blooming, buzzing confusion of reality. It is not merely a short cut. It is all these things and something more. It is the guarantee of our self-respect; it is the projection upon the world of our own sense of our own value, our own position and our own rights. The stereotypes are, therefore, highly charged with the feelings that are attached to them. They are the fortress of our tradition, and behind its defenses we can continue to feel ourselves safe in the position we occupy.

2

When, for example, in the fourth century B. C., Aristotle wrote his defense of slavery in the face of increasing skepticism, [Footnote: Zimmern: *Greek Commonwealth*. See his footnote, p. 383.] the Athenian slaves were in great part indistinguishable from free citizens Mr. Zimmern quotes an amusing passage from the Old Oligarch explaining the good treatment of the slaves. "Suppose it were legal for a slave to be beaten by a citizen, it would frequently happen that an Athenian might be mistaken for a slave or an alien and receive a beating;—since the Athenian people is not better clothed than the slave or alien, nor in personal appearance is there any superiority." This absence of distinction would naturally tend to dissolve the institution. If free men and slaves looked alike, what basis was there for treating them so differently? It was this confusion which Aristotle set himself to clear away in the first book of his Politics. With unerring instinct he understood that to justify slavery he must teach the Greeks a way of *seeing* their slaves that comported with the continuance of slavery.

So, said Aristotle, there are beings who are slaves by nature. [Footnote: *Politics*, Bk. 1, Ch. 5.] "He then is by nature formed a slave, who is fitted to become the chattel of another person, *and on that account is so*." All this really says is that whoever happens to be a slave is by nature intended to be one. Logically the statement is worthless, but in fact it is not a proposition at all, and logic has nothing to do with it. It is a stereotype, or rather it is part of a stereotype. The rest follows almost immediately. After asserting that slaves perceive reason, but are not endowed with the use of it, Aristotle insists that "it is the intention of nature to make the bodies of slaves and free men different from each other, that the one should be robust for their necessary purposes, but the other erect; useless indeed for such servile labours, but fit for civil life... It is clear then that some men are free by nature, and others are slaves. ...."

If we ask ourselves what is the matter with Aristotle's argument, we find that he has begun by erecting a great barrier between himself and the facts. When he had said that those who are slaves are by nature intended to be slaves, he at one stroke excluded the fatal question whether those particular men who happened to be slaves were the particular men intended by nature to be slaves. For that

253

question would have tainted each case of slavery with doubt. And since the fact of being a slave was not evidence that a man was destined to be one, no certain test would have remained. Aristotle, therefore, excluded entirely that destructive doubt. Those who are slaves are intended to be slaves. Each slave holder was to look upon his chattels as natural slaves. When his eye had been trained to see them that way, he was to note as confirmation of their servile character the fact that they performed servile work, that they were competent to do servile work, and that they had the muscles to do servile work.

This is the perfect stereotype. Its hallmark is that it precedes the use of reason; is a form of perception, imposes a certain character on the data of our senses before the data reach the intelligence. The stereotype is like the lavender window-panes on Beacon Street, like the door-keeper at a costume ball who judges whether the guest has an appropriate masquerade. There is nothing so obdurate to education or to criticism as the stereotype. It stamps itself upon the evidence in the very act of securing the evidence. That is why the accounts of returning travellers are often an interesting tale of what the traveller carried abroad with him on his trip. If he carried chiefly his appetite, a zeal for tiled bathrooms, a conviction that the Pullman car is the acme of human comfort, and a belief that it is proper to tip waiters, taxicab drivers, and barbers, but under no circumstances station agents and ushers, then his Odyssey will be replete with good meals and bad meals, bathing adventures, compartment-train escapades, and voracious demands for money. Or if he is a more serious soul he may while on tour have found himself at celebrated spots. Having touched base, and cast one furtive glance at the monument, he buried his head in Baedeker, read every word through, and moved on to the next celebrated spot; and thus returned with a compact and orderly impression of Europe, rated one star, or two.

In some measure, stimuli from the outside, especially when they are printed or spoken words, evoke some part of a system of stereotypes, so that the actual sensation and the preconception occupy consciousness at the same time. The two are blended, much as if we looked at red through blue glasses and saw green. If what we are looking at corresponds successfully with what we anticipated, the stereotype is reinforced for the future, as it is in a man who knows in advance that the Japanese are cunning and has the bad luck to run across two dishonest Japanese.

The Walter Lippmann Reader

If the experience contradicts the stereotype, one of two things happens. If the man is no longer plastic, or if some powerful interest makes it highly inconvenient to rearrange his stereotypes, he pooh- poohs the contradiction as an exception that proves the rule, discredits the witness, finds a flaw somewhere, and manages to forget it. But if he is still curious and open-minded, the novelty is taken into the picture, and allowed to modify it. Sometimes, if the incident is striking enough, and if he has felt a general discomfort with his established scheme, he may be shaken to such an extent as to distrust all accepted ways of looking at life, and to expect that normally a thing will not be what it is generally supposed to be. In the extreme case, especially if he is literary, he may develop a passion for inverting the moral canon by making Judas, Benedict Arnold, or Caesar Borgia the hero of his tale.

3

The role played by the stereotype can be seen in the German tales about Belgian snipers. Those tales curiously enough were first refuted by an organization of German Catholic priests known as Pax. [Footnote: Fernand van Langenhove, *The Growth of a Legend*. The author is a Belgian sociologist.] The existence of atrocity stories is itself not remarkable, nor that the German people gladly believed them. But it is remarkable that a great conservative body of patriotic Germans should have set out as early as August 16, 1914, to contradict a collection of slanders on the enemy, even though such slanders were of the utmost value in soothing the troubled conscience of their fellow countrymen. Why should the Jesuit order in particular have set out to destroy a fiction so important to the fighting morale of Germany?

I quote from M. van Langenhove's account:

"Hardly had the German armies entered Belgium when strange rumors began to circulate. They spread from place to place, they were reproduced by the press, and they soon permeated the whole of Germany. It was said that the Belgian people, *instigated by the clergy*, had intervened perfidiously in the hostilities; had attacked by surprise isolated detachments; had indicated to the enemy the positions occupied by the troops; that old men, and even children, had been guilty of horrible atrocities upon wounded and defenseless German soldiers, tearing out their eyes and cutting off fingers, nose or ears; *that the priests from their*

255

The Walter Lippmann Reader

pulpits had exhorted the people to commit these crimes, promising them as a reward the kingdom of heaven, and had even taken the lead in this barbarity.

"Public credulity accepted these stories. The highest powers in the state welcomed them without hesitation and endorsed them with their authority...

"In this way public opinion in Germany was disturbed and a lively indignation manifested itself, *directed especially against the priests* who were held responsible for the barbarities attributed to the Belgians... By a natural diversion *the anger* to which they were a prey *was directed* by the Germans *against the Catholic clergy generally.* Protestants allowed the old religious hatred to be relighted in their minds and delivered themselves to attacks against Catholics. A new *Kulturkampf* was let loose.

"The Catholics did not delay in taking action against this hostile attitude." (Italics mine) [Footnote: *Op. cit.*, pp. 5-7]

There may have been some sniping. It would be extraordinary if every angry Belgian had rushed to the library, opened a manual of international law, and had informed himself whether he had a right to take potshot at the infernal nuisance tramping through his streets. It would be no less extraordinary if an army that had never been under fire, did not regard every bullet that came its way as unauthorized, because it was inconvenient, and indeed as somehow a violation of the rules of the Kriegspiel, which then constituted its only experience of war. One can imagine the more sensitive bent on convincing themselves that the people to whom they were doing such terrible things must be terrible people. And so the legend may have been spun until it reached the censors and propagandists, who, whether they believed it or not, saw its value, and let it loose on the German civilians. They too were not altogether sorry to find that the people they were outraging were sub-human. And, above all, since the legend came from their heroes, they were not only entitled to believe it, they were unpatriotic if they did not.

But where so much is left to the imagination because the scene of action is lost in the fog of war, there is no check and no control. The legend of the ferocious Belgian priests soon tapped an old hatred. For in the minds of most patriotic protestant Germans, especially of the upper classes, the picture of Bismarck's victories included a long quarrel with the Roman Catholics. By a process of association, Belgian priests became priests, and hatred of Belgians a vent for all their hatreds. These German protestants did what some Americans did when

256

under the stress of war they created a compound object of hatred out of the enemy abroad and all their opponents at home. Against this synthetic enemy, the Hun in Germany and the Hun within the Gate, they launched all the animosity that was in them.

The Catholic resistance to the atrocity tales was, of course, defensive. It was aimed at those particular fictions which aroused animosity against all Catholics, rather than against Belgian Catholics alone. The *Informations Pax*, says M. van Langenhove, had only an ecclesiastical bearing and "confined their attention almost exclusively to the reprehensible acts attributed to the priests." And yet one cannot help wondering a little about what was set in motion in the minds of German Catholics by this revelation of what Bismarck's empire meant in relation to them; and also whether there was any obscure connection between that knowledge and the fact that the prominent German politician who was willing in the armistice to sign the death warrant of the empire was Erzberger, [Footnote: Since this was written, Erzberger has been assassinated.] the leader of the Catholic Centre Party.

CHAPTER VIII
Blind Spots and Their Value

1

I HAVE been speaking of stereotypes rather than ideals, because the word ideal is usually reserved for what we consider the good, the true and the beautiful. Thus it carries the hint that here is something to be copied or attained. But our repertory of fixed impressions is wider than that. It contains ideal swindlers, ideal Tammany politicians, ideal jingoes, ideal agitators, ideal enemies. Our stereotyped world is not necessarily the world we should like it to be. It is simply the kind of world we expect it to be. If events correspond there is a sense of familiarity, and we feel that we are moving with the movement of events. Our slave must be a slave by nature, if we are Athenians who wish to have no qualms. If we have told our friends that we do eighteen holes of golf in 95, we tell them after doing the course in 110, that we are not ourselves to-day. That is to say, we are not acquainted with the duffer who foozled fifteen strokes.

Most of us would deal with affairs through a rather haphazard and shifting assortment of stereotypes, if a comparatively few men in each generation were not constantly engaged in arranging, standardizing, and improving them into logical systems, known as the Laws of Political Economy, the Principles of Politics, and the like. Generally when we write about culture, tradition, and the group mind, we are thinking of these systems perfected by men of genius. Now there is no disputing the necessity of constant study and criticism of these idealized versions, but the historian of people, the politician, and the publicity man cannot stop there. For what operates in history is not the systematic idea as a genius formulated it, but shifting imitations, replicas, counterfeits, analogies, and distortions in individual minds.

Thus Marxism is not necessarily what Karl Marx wrote in Das Kapital, but whatever it is that all the warring sects believe, who claim to be the faithful. From the gospels you cannot deduce the history of Christianity, nor from the Constitution the political history of America. It is Das Kapital as conceived, the gospels as preached and the preachment as understood, the Constitution as interpreted and administered, to which you have to go. For while there is a reciprocating influence between the standard version and the current versions, it is these current versions as distributed among men which affect their behavior.

258

The Walter Lippmann Reader

[Footnote: But unfortunately it is ever so much harder to know this actual culture than it is to summarize and to comment upon the works of genius. The actual culture exists in people far too busy to indulge in the strange trade of formulating their beliefs. They record them only incidentally, and the student rarely knows how typical are his data. Perhaps the best he can do is to follow Lord Bryce's suggestion [*Modern Democracies*, Vol. i, p. 156] that he move freely "among all sorts and conditions of men," to seek out the unbiassed persons in every neighborhood who have skill in sizing up. "There is a *flair* which long practise and 'sympathetic touch' bestow. The trained observer learns how to profit by small indications, as an old seaman discerns, sooner than the landsman, the signs of coming storm." There is, in short, a vast amount of guess work involved, and it is no wonder that scholars, who enjoy precision, so often confine their attentions to the neater formulations of other scholars.]

"The theory of Relativity," says a critic whose eyelids, like the Lady Lisa's, are a little weary, "promises to develop into a principle as adequate to universal application as was the theory of Evolution. This latter theory, from being a technical biological hypothesis, became an inspiring guide to workers in practically every branch of knowledge: manners and customs, morals, religions, philosophies, arts, steam engines, electric tramways—everything had 'evolved.' 'Evolution' became a very general term; it also became imprecise until, in many cases, the original, definite meaning of the word was lost, and the theory it had been evoked to describe was misunderstood. We are hardy enough to prophesy a similar career and fate for the theory of Relativity. The technical physical theory, at present imperfectly understood, will become still more vague and dim. History repeats itself, and Relativity, like Evolution, after receiving a number of intelligible but somewhat inaccurate popular expositions in its scientific aspect, will be launched on a world-conquering career. We suggest that, by that time, it will probably be called *Relativismus*. Many of these larger applications will doubtless be justified; some will be absurd and a considerable number will, we imagine, reduce to truisms. And the physical theory, the mere seed of this mighty growth, will become once more the purely technical concern of scientific men." [Footnote: *The Times* (London), *Literary Supplement*, June 2, 1921, p. 352. Professor Einstein said when he was in America in 1921 that people tended to overestimate the influence of his theory, and to under-estimate its certainty.]

The Walter Lippmann Reader

But for such a world-conquering career an idea must correspond, however imprecisely, to something. Professor Bury shows for how long a time the idea of progress remained a speculative toy. "It is not easy," he writes, [Footnote: J. B. Bury, *The Idea of Progress*, p. 324.] "for a new idea of the speculative order to penetrate and inform the general consciousness of a community until it has assumed some external and concrete embodiment, or is recommended by some striking material evidence. In the case of Progress both these conditions were fulfilled (in England) in the period 1820-1850." The most striking evidence was furnished by the mechanical revolution. "Men who were born at the beginning of the century had seen, before they had passed the age of thirty, the rapid development of steam navigation, the illumination of towns and houses by gas, the opening of the first railway." In the consciousness of the average householder miracles like these formed the pattern of his belief in the perfectibility of the human race.

Tennyson, who was in philosophical matters a fairly normal person, tells us that when he went by the first train from Liverpool to Manchester (1830) he thought that the wheels ran in grooves. Then he wrote this line:

"Let the great world spin forever down the ringing grooves of change." [Footnote: 2 Tennyson, *Memoir by his Son*, Vol. I, p. 195. Cited by Bury, *op. cit.*, p. 326.]

And so a notion more or less applicable to a journey between Liverpool and Manchester was generalized into a pattern of the universe "for ever." This pattern, taken up by others, reinforced by dazzling inventions, imposed an optimistic turn upon the theory of evolution. That theory, of course, is, as Professor Bury says, neutral between pessimism and optimism. But it promised continual change, and the changes visible in the world marked such extraordinary conquests of nature, that the popular mind made a blend of the two. Evolution first in Darwin himself, and then more elaborately in Herbert Spencer, was a "progress towards perfection."

2

The stereotype represented by such words as "progress" and "perfection" was composed fundamentally of mechanical inventions. And mechanical it has remained, on the whole, to this day. In America more than anywhere else, the spectacle of mechanical progress has made so deep an impression, that it has suffused the whole moral code. An American will endure almost any insult except the charge that he is not progressive. Be he of long native ancestry, or a recent immigrant, the aspect that has always struck his eye is the immense physical growth of American civilization. That constitutes a fundamental stereotype through which he views the world: the country village will become the great metropolis, the modest building a skyscraper, what is small shall be big; what is slow shall be fast; what is poor shall be rich; what is few shall be many; whatever is shall be more so.

Not every American, of course, sees the world this way. Henry Adams didn't, and William Allen White doesn't. But those men do, who in the magazines devoted to the religion of success appear as Makers of America. They mean just about that when they preach evolution, progress, prosperity, being constructive, the American way of doing things. It is easy to laugh, but, in fact, they are using a very great pattern of human endeavor. For one thing it adopts an impersonal criterion; for another it adopts an earthly criterion; for a third it is habituating men to think quantitatively. To be sure the ideal confuses excellence with size, happiness with speed, and human nature with contraption. Yet the same motives are at work which have ever actuated any moral code, or ever will. The desire for the biggest, the fastest, the highest, or if you are a maker of wristwatches or microscopes the smallest; the love in short of the superlative and the "peerless," is in essence and possibility a noble passion.

Certainly the American version of progress has fitted an extraordinary range of facts in the economic situation and in human nature. It turned an unusual amount of pugnacity, acquisitiveness, and lust of power into productive work. Nor has it, until more recently perhaps, seriously frustrated the active nature of the active members of the community. They have made a civilization which provides them who made it with what they feel to be ample satisfaction in work, mating and play, and the rush of their victory over mountains, wildernesses, distance, and human competition has even done duty for that part of religious feeling which is a sense of communion with the purpose of the universe. The pattern has been a success so nearly perfect in the sequence of ideals, practice, and results, that any challenge to it is called un-American.

And yet, this pattern is a very partial and inadequate way of representing the world. The habit of thinking about progress as "development" has meant that many aspects of the environment were simply neglected. With the stereotype of "progress" before their eyes, Americans have in the mass seen little that did not accord with that progress. They saw the expansion of cities, but not the accretion of slums; they cheered the census statistics, but refused to consider overcrowding; they pointed with pride to their growth, but would not see the drift from the land, or the unassimilated immigration. They expanded industry furiously at reckless cost to their natural resources; they built up gigantic corporations without arranging for industrial relations. They grew to be one of the most powerful nations on earth without preparing their institutions or their minds for the ending of their isolation. They stumbled into the World War morally and physically unready, and they stumbled out again, much disillusioned, but hardly more experienced.

In the World War the good and the evil influence of the American stereotype was plainly visible. The idea that the war could be won by recruiting unlimited armies, raising unlimited credits, building an unlimited number of ships, producing unlimited munitions, and concentrating without limit on these alone, fitted the traditional stereotype, and resulted in something like a physical miracle. [Footnote: I have in mind the transportation and supply of two million troops overseas. Prof. Wesley Mitchell points out that the total production of goods after our entrance into the war did not greatly increase in volume over that of the year 1916; but that production for war purposes did increase.] But among those most affected by the stereotype, there was no place for the consideration of what the fruits of victory were, or how they were to be attained. Therefore, aims were ignored, or regarded as automatic, and victory was conceived, because the stereotype demanded it, as nothing but an annihilating victory in the field. In peace time you did not ask what the fastest motor car was for, and in war you did not ask what the completest victory was for. Yet in Paris the pattern did not fit the facts. In peace you can go on endlessly supplanting small things with big ones, and big ones with bigger ones; in war when you have won absolute victory, you cannot go on to a more absolute victory. You have to do something on an entirely different pattern. And if you lack such a pattern, the end of the war is to you what it was to so many good people, an anticlimax in a dreary and savorless world.

This marks the point where the stereotype and the facts, that cannot be ignored, definitely part company. There is always such a point, because our images of how things behave are simpler and more fixed than the ebb and flow of affairs. There comes a time, therefore, when the blind spots come from the edge of vision into the center. Then unless there are critics who have the courage to sound an alarm, and leaders capable of understanding the change, and a people tolerant by habit, the stereotype, instead of economizing effort, and focussing energy as it did in 1917 and 1918, may frustrate effort and waste men's energy by blinding them, as it did for those people who cried for a Carthaginian peace in 1919 and deplored the Treaty of Versailles in 1921.

3

Uncritically held, the stereotype not only censors out much that needs to be taken into account, but when the day of reckoning comes, and the stereotype is shattered, likely as not that which it did wisely take into account is ship-wrecked with it. That is the punishment assessed by Mr. Bernard Shaw against Free Trade, Free Contract, Free Competition, Natural Liberty, Laissez-faire, and Darwinism. A hundred years ago, when he would surely have been one of the tartest advocates of these doctrines, he would not have seen them as he sees them to-day, in the Infidel Half Century, [Footnote: *Back to Methuselah*. Preface.] to be excuses for "'doing the other fellow down' with impunity, all interference by a guiding government, all organization except police organization to protect legalized fraud against fisticuffs, all attempt to introduce human purpose and design and forethought into the industrial welter being 'contrary to the laws of political economy'" He would have seen, then, as one of the pioneers of the march to the plains of heaven [Footnote: *The Quintessence of Ibsenism*] that, of the kind of human purpose and design and forethought to be found in a government like that of Queen Victoria's uncles, the less the better. He would have seen, not the strong doing the weak down, but the foolish doing the strong down. He would have seen purposes, designs and forethoughts at work, obstructing invention, obstructing enterprise, obstructing what he would infallibly have recognized as the next move of Creative Evolution.

Even now Mr. Shaw is none too eager for the guidance of any guiding government he knows, but in theory he has turned a full loop against laissez-faire. Most advanced thinking before the war had made the same turn against the established notion that if you unloosed everything, wisdom would bubble up, and establish harmony. Since the war, with its definite demonstration of guiding

The Walter Lippmann Reader

governments, assisted by censors, propagandists, and spies, Roebuck Ramsden and Natural Liberty have been readmitted to the company of serious thinkers.

One thing is common to these cycles. There is in each set of stereotypes a point where effort ceases and things happen of their own accord, as you would like them to. The progressive stereotype, powerful to incite work, almost completely obliterates the attempt to decide what work and why that work. Laissez-faire, a blessed release from stupid officialdom, assumes that men will move by spontaneous combustion towards a pre-established harmony. Collectivism, an antidote to ruthless selfishness, seems, in the Marxian mind, to suppose an economic determinism towards efficiency and wisdom on the part of socialist officials. Strong government, imperialism at home and abroad, at its best deeply conscious of the price of disorder, relies at last on the notion that all that matters to the governed will be known by the governors. In each theory there is a spot of blind automatism.

That spot covers up some fact, which if it were taken into account, would check the vital movement that the stereotype provokes. If the progressive had to ask himself, like the Chinaman in the joke, what he wanted to do with the time he saved by breaking the record, if the advocate of laissez-faire had to contemplate not only free and exuberant energies of men, but what some people call their human nature, if the collectivist let the center of his attention be occupied with the problem of how he is to secure his officials, if the imperialist dared to doubt his own inspiration, you would find more Hamlet and less Henry the Fifth. For these blind spots keep away distracting images, which with their attendant emotions, might cause hesitation and infirmity of purpose. Consequently the stereotype not only saves time in a busy life and is a defense of our position in society, but tends to preserve us from all the bewildering effect of trying to see the world steadily and see it whole.

CHAPTER IX

Codes and Their Enemies

ANYONE who has stood at the end of a railroad platform waiting for a friend, will recall what queer people he mistook for him. The shape of a hat, a slightly characteristic gait, evoked the vivid picture in his mind's eye. In sleep a tinkle may sound like the pealing of a great bell; the distant stroke of a hammer like a thunderclap. For our constellations of imagery will vibrate to a stimulus that is perhaps but vaguely similar to some aspect of them. They may, in hallucination, flood the whole consciousness. They may enter very little into perception, though I am inclined to think that such an experience is extremely rare and highly sophisticated, as when we gaze blankly at a familiar word or object, and it gradually ceases to be familiar. Certainly for the most part, the way we see things is a combination of what is there and of what we expected to find. The heavens are not the same to an astronomer as to a pair of lovers; a page of Kant will start a different train of thought in a Kantian and in a radical empiricist; the Tahitian belle is a better looking person to her Tahitian suitor than to the readers of the *National Geographic Magazine*.

Expertness in any subject is, in fact, a multiplication of the number of aspects we are prepared to discover, plus the habit of discounting our expectations. Where to the ignoramus all things look alike, and life is just one thing after another, to the specialist things are highly individual. For a chauffeur, an epicure, a connoisseur, a member of the President's cabinet, or a professor's wife, there are evident distinctions and qualities, not at all evident to the casual person who discusses automobiles, wines, old masters, Republicans, and college faculties.

But in our public opinions few can be expert, while life is, as Mr. Bernard Shaw has made plain, so short. Those who are expert are so on only a few topics. Even among the expert soldiers, as we learned during the war, expert cavalrymen were not necessarily brilliant with trench-warfare and tanks. Indeed, sometimes a little expertness on a small topic may simply exaggerate our normal human habit of trying to squeeze into our stereotypes all that can be squeezed, and of casting into outer darkness that which does not fit.

Whatever we recognize as familiar we tend, if we are not very careful, to visualize with the aid of images already in our mind. Thus in the American view of Progress and Success there is a definite picture of human nature and of society. It is the kind of human nature and the kind of society which logically produce the kind of progress that is regarded as ideal. And then, when we seek to describe or explain actually successful men, and events that have really happened, we read back into them the qualities that are presupposed in the stereotypes.

These qualities were standardized rather innocently by the older economists. They set out to describe the social system under which they lived, and found it too complicated for words. So they constructed what they sincerely hoped was a simplified diagram, not so different in principle and in veracity from the parallelogram with legs and head in a child's drawing of a complicated cow. The scheme consisted of a capitalist who had diligently saved capital from his labor, an entrepreneur who conceived a socially useful demand and organized a factory, a collection of workmen who freely contracted, take it or leave it, for their labor, a landlord, and a group of consumers who bought in the cheapest market those goods which by the ready use of the pleasure-pain calculus they knew would give them the most pleasure. The model worked. The kind of people, which the model assumed, living in the sort of world the model assumed, invariably coöperated harmoniously in the books where the model was described.

With modification and embroidery, this pure fiction, used by economists to simplify their thinking, was retailed and popularized until for large sections of the population it prevailed as the economic mythology of the day. It supplied a standard version of capitalist, promoter, worker and consumer in a society that was naturally more bent on achieving success than on explaining it. The buildings which rose, and the bank accounts which accumulated, were evidence that the stereotype of how the thing had been done was accurate. And those who benefited most by success came to believe they were the kind of men they were supposed to be. No wonder that the candid friends of successful men, when they read the official biography and the obituary, have to restrain themselves from asking whether this is indeed their friend.

2

To the vanquished and the victims, the official portraiture was, of course, unrecognizable. For while those who exemplified progress did not often pause to inquire whether they had arrived according to the route laid down by the

The Walter Lippmann Reader

economists, or by some other just as creditable, the unsuccessful people did inquire. "No one," says William James, [Footnote: *The Letters of William James*, Vol. I, p.65] "sees further into a generalization than his own knowledge of detail extends." The captains of industry saw in the great trusts monuments of (their) success; their defeated competitors saw the monuments of (their) failure. So the captains expounded the economies and virtues of big business, asked to be let alone, said they were the agents of prosperity, and the developers of trade. The vanquished insisted upon the wastes and brutalities of the trusts, and called loudly upon the Department of Justice to free business from conspiracies. In the same situation one side saw progress, economy, and a splendid development; the other, reaction, extravagance, and a restraint of trade. Volumes of statistics, anecdotes about the real truth and the inside truth, the deeper and the larger truth, were published to prove both sides of the argument.

For when a system of stereotypes is well fixed, our attention is called to those facts which support it, and diverted from those which contradict. So perhaps it is because they are attuned to find it, that kindly people discover so much reason for kindness, malicious people so much malice. We speak quite accurately of seeing through rose-colored spectacles, or with a jaundiced eye. If, as Philip Littell once wrote of a distinguished professor, we see life as through a class darkly, our stereotypes of what the best people and the lower classes are like will not be contaminated by understanding. What is alien will be rejected, what is different will fall upon unseeing eyes. We do not see what our eyes are not accustomed to take into account. Sometimes consciously, more often without knowing it, we are impressed by those facts which fit our philosophy.

3

This philosophy is a more or less organized series of images for describing the unseen world. But not only for describing it. For judging it as well. And, therefore, the stereotypes are loaded with preference, suffused with affection or dislike, attached to fears, lusts, strong wishes, pride, hope. Whatever invokes the stereotype is judged with the appropriate sentiment. Except where we deliberately keep prejudice in suspense, we do not study a man and judge him to be bad. We see a bad man. We see a dewy morn, a blushing maiden, a sainted priest, a humorless Englishman, a dangerous Red, a carefree bohemian, a lazy Hindu, a wily Oriental, a dreaming Slav, a volatile Irishman, a greedy Jew, a

The Walter Lippmann Reader

100% American. In the workaday world that is often the real judgment, long in advance of the evidence, and it contains within itself the conclusion which the evidence is pretty certain to confirm. Neither justice, nor mercy, nor truth, enter into such a judgment, for the judgment has preceded the evidence. Yet a people without prejudices, a people with altogether neutral vision, is so unthinkable in any civilization of which it is useful to think, that no scheme of education could be based upon that ideal. Prejudice can be detected, discounted, and refined, but so long as finite men must compress into a short schooling preparation for dealing with a vast civilization, they must carry pictures of it around with them, and have prejudices. The quality of their thinking and doing will depend on whether those prejudices are friendly, friendly to other people, to other ideas, whether they evoke love of what is felt to be positively good, rather than hatred of what is not contained in their version of the good.

Morality, good taste and good form first standardize and then emphasize certain of these underlying prejudices. As we adjust ourselves to our code, we adjust the facts we see to that code. Rationally, the facts are neutral to all our views of right and wrong. Actually, our canons determine greatly what we shall perceive and how.

For a moral code is a scheme of conduct applied to a number of typical instances. To behave as the code directs is to serve whatever purpose the code pursues. It may be God's will, or the king's, individual salvation in a good, solid, three dimensional paradise, success on earth, or the service of mankind. In any event the makers of the code fix upon certain typical situations, and then by some form of reasoning or intuition, deduce the kind of behavior which would produce the aim they acknowledge. The rules apply where they apply.

But in daily living how does a man know whether his predicament is the one the law-giver had in mind? He is told not to kill. But if his children are attacked, may he kill to stop a killing? The Ten Commandments are silent on the point. Therefore, around every code there is a cloud of interpreters who deduce more specific cases. Suppose, then, that the doctors of the law decide that he may kill in self-defense. For the next man the doubt is almost as great; how does he know that he is defining self-defense correctly, or that he has not misjudged the facts, imagined the attack, and is really the aggressor? Perhaps he has provoked the attack. But what is a provocation? Exactly these confusions infected the minds of most Germans in August, 1914.

The Walter Lippmann Reader

Far more serious in the modern world than any difference of moral code is the difference in the assumptions about facts to which the code is applied. Religious, moral and political formulae are nothing like so far apart as the facts assumed by their votaries. Useful discussion, then, instead of comparing ideals, reexamines the visions of the facts. Thus the rule that you should do unto others as you would have them do unto you rests on the belief that human nature is uniform. Mr. Bernard Shaw's statement that you should not do unto others what you would have them do unto you, because their tastes may be different, rests on the belief that human nature is not uniform. The maxim that competition is the life of trade consists of a whole tome of assumptions about economic motives, industrial relations, and the working of a particular commercial system. The claim that America will never have a merchant marine, unless it is privately owned and managed, assumes a certain proved connection between a certain kind of profit-making and incentive. The justification by the bolshevik propagandist of the dictatorship, espionage, and the terror, because "every state is an apparatus of violence" [Footnote: See *Two Years of Conflict on the Internal Front*, published by the Russian Socialist Federated Soviet Republic, Moscow, 1920. Translated by Malcolm W. Davis for the *New York Evening Post*, January 15, 1921.] is an historical judgment, the truth of which is by no means self-evident to a non-communist.

At the core of every moral code there is a picture of human nature, a map of the universe, and a version of history. To human nature (of the sort conceived), in a universe (of the kind imagined), after a history (so understood), the rules of the code apply. So far as the facts of personality, of the environment and of memory are different, by so far the rules of the code are difficult to apply with success. Now every moral code has to conceive human psychology, the material world, and tradition some way or other. But in the codes that are under the influence of science, the conception is known to be an hypothesis, whereas in the codes that come unexamined from the past or bubble up from the caverns of the mind, the conception is not taken as an hypothesis demanding proof or contradiction, but as a fiction accepted without question. In the one case, man is humble about his beliefs, because he knows they are tentative and incomplete; in the other he is dogmatic, because his belief is a completed myth. The moralist who submits to the scientific discipline knows that though he does not know everything, he is in the way of knowing something; the dogmatist, using a myth,

269

believes himself to share part of the insight of omniscience, though he lacks the criteria by which to tell truth from error. For the distinguishing mark of a myth is that truth and error, fact and fable, report and fantasy, are all on the same plane of credibility.

The myth is, then, not necessarily false. It might happen to be wholly true. It may happen to be partly true. If it has affected human conduct a long time, it is almost certain to contain much that is profoundly and importantly true. What a myth never contains is the critical power to separate its truths from its errors. For that power comes only by realizing that no human opinion, whatever its supposed origin, is too exalted for the test of evidence, that every opinion is only somebody's opinion. And if you ask why the test of evidence is preferable to any other, there is no answer unless you are willing to use the test in order to test it.

4

The statement is, I think, susceptible of overwhelming proof, that moral codes assume a particular view of the facts. Under the term moral codes I include all kinds: personal, family, economic, professional, legal, patriotic, international. At the center of each there is a pattern of stereotypes about psychology, sociology, and history. The same view of human nature, institutions or tradition rarely persists through all our codes. Compare, for example, the economic and the patriotic codes. There is a war supposed to affect all alike. Two men are partners in business. One enlists, the other takes a war contract. The soldier sacrifices everything, perhaps even his life. He is paid a dollar a day, and no one says, no one believes, that you could make a better soldier out of him by any form of economic incentive. That motive disappears out of his human nature. The contractor sacrifices very little, is paid a handsome profit over costs, and few say or believe that he would produce the munitions if there were no economic incentive. That may be unfair to him. The point is that the accepted patriotic code assumes one kind of human nature, the commercial code another. And the codes are probably founded on true expectations to this extent, that when a man adopts a certain code he tends to exhibit the kind of human nature which the code demands.

That is one reason why it is so dangerous to generalize about human nature. A loving father can be a sour boss, an earnest municipal reformer, and a rapacious jingo abroad. His family life, his business career, his politics, and his foreign

270

policy rest on totally different versions of what others are like and of how he should act. These versions differ by codes in the same person, the codes differ somewhat among persons in the same social set, differ widely as between social sets, and between two nations, or two colors, may differ to the point where there is no common assumption whatever. That is why people professing the same stock of religious beliefs can go to war. The element of their belief which determines conduct is that view of the facts which they assume.

That is where codes enter so subtly and so pervasively into the making of public opinion. The orthodox theory holds that a public opinion constitutes a moral judgment on a group of facts. The theory I am suggesting is that, in the present state of education, a public opinion is primarily a moralized and codified version of the facts. I am arguing that the pattern of stereotypes at the center of our codes largely determines what group of facts we shall see, and in what light we shall see them. That is why, with the best will in the world, the news policy of a journal tends to support its editorial policy; why a capitalist sees one set of facts, and certain aspects of human nature, literally sees them; his socialist opponent another set and other aspects, and why each regards the other as unreasonable or perverse, when the real difference between them is a difference of perception. That difference is imposed by the difference between the capitalist and socialist pattern of stereotypes. "There are no classes in America," writes an American editor. "The history of all hitherto existing society is the history of class struggles," says the Communist Manifesto. If you have the editor's pattern in your mind, you will see vividly the facts that confirm it, vaguely and ineffectively those that contradict. If you have the communist pattern, you will not only look for different things, but you will see with a totally different emphasis what you and the editor happen to see in common.

5

And since my moral system rests on my accepted version of the facts, he who denies either my moral judgments or my version of the facts, is to me perverse, alien, dangerous. How shall I account for him? The opponent has always to be explained, and the last explanation that we ever look for is that he sees a different set of facts. Such an explanation we avoid, because it saps the very foundation of our own assurance that we have seen life steadily and seen it whole. It is only when we are in the habit of recognizing our opinions as a partial experience seen through our stereotypes that we become truly tolerant of an opponent. Without that habit, we believe in the absolutism of our own vision, and consequently in the treacherous character of all opposition. For while men are willing to admit that there are two sides to a "question," they do not believe that there are two sides to what they regard as a "fact." And they never do believe it until after long critical education, they are fully conscious of how second-hand and subjective is their apprehension of their social data.

So where two factions see vividly each its own aspect, and contrive their own explanations of what they see, it is almost impossible for them to credit each other with honesty. If the pattern fits their experience at a crucial point, they no longer look upon it as an interpretation. They look upon it as "reality." It may not resemble the reality, except that it culminates in a conclusion which fits a real experience. I may represent my trip from New York to Boston by a straight line on a map, just as a man may regard his triumph as the end of a straight and narrow path. The road by which I actually went to Boston may have involved many detours, much turning and twisting, just as his road may have involved much besides pure enterprise, labor and thrift. But provided I reach Boston and he succeeds, the airline and the straight path will serve as ready made charts. Only when somebody tries to follow them, and does not arrive, do we have to answer objections. If we insist on our charts, and he insists on rejecting them, we soon tend to regard him as a dangerous fool, and he to regard us as liars and hypocrites. Thus we gradually paint portraits of each other. For the opponent presents himself as the man who says, evil be thou my good. He is an annoyance who does not fit into the scheme of things. Nevertheless he interferes. And since that scheme is based in our minds on incontrovertible fact fortified by irresistible logic, some place has to be found for him in the scheme. Rarely in politics or industrial disputes is a place made for him by the simple admission that he has looked upon the same reality and seen another aspect of it. That would shake the whole scheme.

Thus to the Italians in Paris Fiume was Italian It was not merely a city that it would be desirable to include within the Italian kingdom. It was Italian. They fixed their whole mind upon the Italian majority within the legal boundaries of the city itself. The American delegates, having seen more Italians in New York than there are in Fiume, without regarding New York as Italian, fixed their eyes on Fiume as a central European port of entry. They saw vividly the Jugoslavs in the suburbs and the non-Italian hinterland. Some of the Italians in Paris were therefore in need of a convincing explanation of the American perversity. They found it in a rumor which started, no one knows where, that an influential American diplomat was in the snares of a Jugoslav mistress. She had been seen.... He had been seen.... At Versailles just off the boulevard. ... The villa with the large trees.

This is a rather common way of explaining away opposition. In their more libelous form such charges rarely reach the printed page, and a Roosevelt may have to wait years, or a Harding months, before he can force an issue, and end a whispering campaign that has reached into every circle of talk. Public men have to endure a fearful amount of poisonous clubroom, dinner table, boudoir slander, repeated, elaborated, chuckled over, and regarded as delicious. While this sort of thing is, I believe, less prevalent in America than in Europe, yet rare is the American official about whom somebody is not repeating a scandal.

Out of the opposition we make villains and conspiracies. If prices go up unmercifully the profiteers have conspired; if the newspapers misrepresent the news, there is a capitalist plot; if the rich are too rich, they have been stealing; if a closely fought election is lost, the electorate was corrupted; if a statesman does something of which you disapprove, he has been bought or influenced by some discreditable person. If workingmen are restless, they are the victims of agitators; if they are restless over wide areas, there is a conspiracy on foot. If you do not produce enough aeroplanes, it is the work of spies; if there is trouble in Ireland, it is German or Bolshevik "gold." And if you go stark, staring mad looking for plots, you see all strikes, the Plumb plan, Irish rebellion, Mohammedan unrest, the restoration of King Constantine, the League of Nations, Mexican disorder, the movement to reduce armaments, Sunday movies, short skirts, evasion of the liquor laws, Negro self-assertion, as sub-plots under some grandiose plot engineered either by Moscow, Rome, the Free Masons, the Japanese, or the Elders of Zion.

CHAPTER X

The Detection of Stereotypes

1

Skilled diplomatists, compelled to talk out loud to the warring peoples, learned how to use a large repertory of stereotypes. They were dealing with a precarious alliance of powers, each of which was maintaining its war unity only by the most careful leadership. The ordinary soldier and his wife, heroic and selfless beyond anything in the chronicles of courage, were still not heroic enough to face death gladly for all the ideas which were said by the foreign offices of foreign powers to be essential to the future of civilization. There were ports, and mines, rocky mountain passes, and villages that few soldiers would willingly have crossed No Man's Land to obtain for their allies.

Now it happened in one nation that the war party which was in control of the foreign office, the high command, and most of the press, had claims on the territory of several of its neighbors. These claims were called the Greater Ruritania by the cultivated classes who regarded Kipling, Treitschke, and Maurice Barres as one hundred percent Ruritanian. But the grandiose idea aroused no enthusiasm abroad. So holding this finest flower of the Ruritanian genius, as their poet laureate said, to their hearts, Ruritania's statesmen went forth to divide and conquer. They divided the claim into sectors. For each piece they invoked that stereotype which some one or more of their allies found it difficult to resist, because that ally had claims for which it hoped to find approval by the use of this same stereotype.

The first sector happened to be a mountainous region inhabited by alien peasants. Ruritania demanded it to complete her natural geographical frontier. If you fixed your attention long enough on the ineffable value of what is natural, those alien peasants just dissolved into fog, and only the slope of the mountains was visible. The next sector was inhabited by Ruritanians, and on the principle that no people ought to live under alien rule, they were re-annexed. Then came a city of considerable commercial importance, not inhabited by Ruritanians. But until the Eighteenth Century it had been part of Ruritania, and on the principle of Historic Right it was annexed. Farther on there was a splendid mineral deposit owned by aliens and worked by aliens. On the principle of reparation for damage it was annexed. Beyond this there was a territory inhabited 97% by aliens, constituting the natural geographical frontier of another nation, never historically a part of Ruritania. But one of the provinces which had been federated into Ruritania had formerly traded in those markets, and the upper class culture was Ruritanian. On the principle of cultural superiority and the necessity of defending civilization, the lands were claimed. Finally, there was a port wholly disconnected from Ruritania geographically, ethnically, economically, historically, traditionally. It was demanded on the ground that it was needed for national defense.

In the treaties that concluded the Great War you can multiply examples of this kind. Now I do not wish to imply that I think it was possible to resettle Europe consistently on any one of these principles. I am certain that it was not. The very use of these principles, so pretentious and so absolute, meant that the spirit of accommodation did not prevail and that, therefore, the substance of peace was not there. For the moment you start to discuss factories, mines, mountains, or even political authority, as perfect examples of some eternal principle or other, you are not arguing, you are fighting. That eternal principle censors out all the objections, isolates the issue from its background and its context, and sets going in you some strong emotion, appropriate enough to the principle, highly inappropriate to the docks, warehouses, and real estate. And having started in that mood you cannot stop. A real danger exists. To meet it you have to invoke more absolute principles in order to defend what is open to attack. Then you have to defend the defenses, erect buffers, and buffers for the buffers, until the whole affair is so scrambled that it seems less dangerous to fight than to keep on talking.

There are certain clues which often help in detecting the false absolutism of a stereotype. In the case of the Ruritanian propaganda the principles blanketed each other so rapidly that one could readily see how the argument had been constructed. The series of contradictions showed that for each sector that stereotype was employed which would obliterate all the facts that interfered with the claim. Contradiction of this sort is often a good clue.

2

Inability to take account of space is another. In the spring of 1918, for example, large numbers of people, appalled by the withdrawal of Russia, demanded the "reestablishment of an Eastern Front." The war, as they had conceived it, was on two fronts, and when one of them disappeared there was an instant demand that it be recreated. The unemployed Japanese army was to man the front, substituting for the Russian. But there was one insuperable obstacle. Between Vladivostok and the eastern battleline there were five thousand miles of country, spanned by one broken down railway. Yet those five thousand miles would not stay in the minds of the enthusiasts. So overwhelming was their conviction that an eastern front was needed, and so great their confidence in the valor of the Japanese army, that, mentally, they had projected that army from Vladivostok to Poland on a magic carpet. In vain our military authorities argued that to land troops on the rim of Siberia had as little to do with reaching the Germans, as climbing from the cellar to the roof of the Woolworth building had to do with reaching the moon.

The stereotype in this instance was the war on two fronts. Ever since men had begun to imagine the Great War they had conceived Germany held between France and Russia. One generation of strategists, and perhaps two, had lived with that visual image as the starting point of all their calculations. For nearly four years every battle-map they saw had deepened the impression that this was the war. When affairs took a new turn, it was not easy to see them as they were then. They were seen through the stereotype, and facts which conflicted with it, such as the distance from Japan to Poland, were incapable of coming vividly into consciousness.

It is interesting to note that the American authorities dealt with the new facts more realistically than the French. In part, this was because (previous to 1914) they had no preconception of a war upon the continent; in part because the Americans, engrossed in the mobilization of their forces, had a vision of the western front which was itself a stereotype that excluded from *their* consciousness any very vivid sense of the other theatres of war. In the spring of 1918 this American view could not compete with the traditional French view, because while the Americans believed enormously in their own powers, the French at that time (before Cantigny and the Second Marne) had the gravest doubts. The American confidence suffused the American stereotype, gave it that power to possess consciousness, that liveliness and sensible pungency, that stimulating effect upon the will, that emotional interest as an object of desire, that congruity with the activity in hand, which James notes as characteristic of what we regard as "real." [Footnote: *Principles of Psychology*, Vol. II, p. 300.] The French in despair remained fixed on their accepted image. And when facts, gross geographical facts, would not fit with the preconception, they were either censored out of mind, or the facts were themselves stretched out of shape. Thus the difficulty of the Japanese reaching the Germans five thousand miles away was, in measure, overcome by bringing the Germans more than half way to meet them. Between March and June 1918, there was supposed to be a German army operating in Eastern Siberia. This phantom army consisted of some German prisoners actually seen, more German prisoners thought about, and chiefly of the delusion that those five thousand intervening miles did not really exist. [Footnote: See in this connection Mr. Charles Grasty's interview with Marshal Foch, *New York Times*, February 26, 1918. "Germany is walking through Russia. America and Japan, who are in a position to do so, should go to meet her in Siberia." See also the resolution by Senator King of Utah, June 10, 1918, and Mr. Taft's statement in the *New York Times*, June 11, 1918, and the appeal to America on May 5, 1918, by Mr. A. J. Sack, Director of the Russian Information Bureau: "If Germany were in the Allied place... she would have 3,000,000 fighting on the East front within a year."]

3

A true conception of space is not a simple matter. If I draw a straight line on a map between Bombay and Hong Kong and measure the distance, I have learned nothing whatever about the distance I should have to cover on a voyage. And even if I measure the actual distance that I must traverse, I still know very little until I know what ships are in the service, when they run, how fast they go, whether I can secure accommodation and afford to pay for it. In practical life space is a matter of available transportation, not of geometrical planes, as the old railroad magnate knew when he threatened to make grass grow in the streets of a city that had offended him. If I am motoring and ask how far it is to my destination, I curse as an unmitigated booby the man who tells me it is three miles, and does not mention a six mile detour. It does me no good to be told that it is three miles if you walk. I might as well be told it is one mile as the crow flies. I do not fly like a crow, and I am not walking either. I must know that it is nine miles for a motor car, and also, if that is the case, that six of them are ruts and puddles. I call the pedestrian a nuisance who tells me it is three miles and think evil of the aviator who told me it was one mile. Both of them are talking about the space they have to cover, not the space I must cover.

In the drawing of boundary lines absurd complications have arisen through failure to conceive the practical geography of a region. Under some general formula like self-determination statesmen have at various times drawn lines on maps, which, when surveyed on the spot, ran through the middle of a factory, down the center of a village street, diagonally across the nave of a church, or between the kitchen and bedroom of a peasant's cottage. There have been frontiers in a grazing country which separated pasture from water, pasture from market, and in an industrial country, railheads from railroad. On the colored ethnic map the line was ethnically just, that is to say, just in the world of that ethnic map.

4

But time, no less than space, fares badly. A common example is that of the man who tries by making an elaborate will to control his money long after his death. "It had been the purpose of the first William James," writes his great-grandson Henry James, [Footnote: *The Letters of William James*, Vol. I, p. 6.] "to provide that his children (several of whom were under age when he died) should qualify themselves by industry and experience to enjoy the large patrimony which he expected to bequeath to them, and with that in view he left a will which was a voluminous compound of restraints and instructions. He showed thereby how great were both his confidence in his own judgment and his solicitude for the moral welfare of his descendants." The courts upset the will. For the law in its objection to perpetuities recognizes that there are distinct limits to the usefulness of allowing anyone to impose his moral stencil upon an unknown future. But the desire to impose it is a very human trait, so human that the law permits it to operate for a limited time after death.

The amending clause of any constitution is a good index of the confidence the authors entertained about the reach of their opinions in the succeeding generations. There are, I believe, American state constitutions which are almost incapable of amendment. The men who made them could have had but little sense of the flux of time: to them the Here and Now was so brilliantly certain, the Hereafter so vague or so terrifying, that they had the courage to say how life should run after they were gone. And then because constitutions are difficult to amend, zealous people with a taste for mortmain have loved to write on this imperishable brass all kinds of rules and restrictions that, given any decent humility about the future, ought to be no more permanent than an ordinary statute.

A presumption about time enters widely into our opinions. To one person an institution which has existed for the whole of his conscious life is part of the permanent furniture of the universe: to another it is ephemeral. Geological time is very different from biological time. Social time is most complex. The statesman has to decide whether to calculate for the emergency or for the long run. Some decisions have to be made on the basis of what will happen in the next two hours; others on what will happen in a week, a month, a season, a decade, when the children have grown up, or their children's children. An important part of wisdom is the ability to distinguish the time-conception that properly belongs to the thing in hand. The person who uses the wrong time-conception ranges from the dreamer who ignores the present to the philistine who can see nothing else. A true scale of values has a very acute sense of relative time.

Distant time, past and future, has somehow to be conceived. But as James says, "of the longer duration we have no direct 'realizing' sense." [Footnote: *Principles of Psychology*, Vol. I, p. 638.] The longest duration which we immediately feel is what is called the "specious present." It endures, according to Titchener, for about six seconds. [Footnote: Cited by Warren, *Human Psychology*, p. 255.] "All impressions within this period of time are present to us *at once*. This makes it possible for us to perceive changes and events as well as stationary objects. The perceptual present is supplemented by the ideational present. Through the combination of perceptions with memory images, entire days, months, and even years of the past are brought together into the present."

In this ideational present, vividness, as James said, is proportionate to the number of discriminations we perceive within it. Thus a vacation in which we were bored with nothing to do passes slowly while we are in it, but seems very short in memory. Great activity kills time rapidly, but in memory its duration is long. On the relation between the amount we discriminate and our time perspective James has an interesting passage: [Footnote: *Op. cit.*, Vol. I, p. 639.]

"We have every reason to think that creatures may possibly differ enormously in the amounts of duration which they intuitively feel, and in the fineness of the events that may fill it. Von Baer has indulged in some interesting computations

The Walter Lippmann Reader

of the effect of such differences in changing the aspect of Nature. Suppose we were able, within the length of a second, to note 10,000 events distinctly, instead of barely 10 as now; [Footnote: In the moving picture this effect is admirably produced by the ultra-rapid camera.] if our life were then destined to hold the same number of impressions, it might be 1000 times as short. We should live less than a month, and personally know nothing of the change of seasons. If born in winter, we should believe in summer as we now believe in the heats of the carboniferous era. The motions of organic beings would be so slow to our senses as to be inferred, not seen. The sun would stand still in the sky, the moon be almost free from change, and so on. But now reverse the hypothesis and suppose a being to get only one 1000th part of the sensations we get in a given time, and consequently to live 1000 times as long. Winters and summers will be to him like quarters of an hour. Mushrooms and the swifter growing plants will shoot into being so rapidly as to appear instantaneous creations; annual shrubs will rise and fall from the earth like restless boiling water springs; the motions of animals will be as invisible as are to us the movements of bullets and cannon-balls; the sun will scour through the sky like a meteor, leaving a fiery trail behind him, etc."

5

In his Outline of History Mr. Wells has made a gallant effort to visualize "the true proportions of historical to geological time" [Footnote: 1 Vol. II, p. 605. See also James Harvey Robinson, *The New History*, p. 239.] On a scale which represents the time from Columbus to ourselves by three inches of space, the reader would have to walk 55 feet to see the date of the painters of the Altamara caves, 550 feet to see the earlier Neanderthalers, a mile or so to the last of the dinosaurs. More or less precise chronology does not begin until after 1000 B.C., and at that time "Sargon I of the Akkadian-Sumerian Empire was a remote memory,... more remote than is Constantine the Great from the world of the present day.... Hammurabi had been dead a thousand years... Stonehedge in England was already a thousand years old."

Mr. Wells was writing with a purpose. "In the brief period of ten thousand years these units (into which men have combined) have grown from the small family tribe of the early neolithic culture to the vast united realms—vast yet still too small and partial—of the present time." Mr. Wells hoped by changing the time perspective on our present problems to change the moral perspective. Yet the astronomical measure of time, the geological, the biological, any telescopic measure which minimizes the present is not "more true" than a microscopic. Mr. Simeon Strunsky is right when he insists that "if Mr. Wells is thinking of his subtitle, The Probable Future of Mankind, he is entitled to ask for any number of centuries to work out his solution. If he is thinking of the salvaging of this western civilization, reeling under the effects of the Great War, he must think in decades and scores of years." [Footnote: In a review of *The Salvaging of Civilization*, *The Literary Review of the N. Y. Evening Post*, June 18, 1921, p. 5.] It all depends upon the practical purpose for which you adopt the measure. There are situations when the time perspective needs to be lengthened, and others when it needs to be shortened.

The man who says that it does not matter if 15,000,000 Chinese die of famine, because in two generations the birthrate will make up the loss, has used a time perspective to excuse his inertia. A person who pauperizes a healthy young man because he is sentimentally overimpressed with an immediate difficulty has lost sight of the duration of the beggar's life. The people who for the sake of an immediate peace are willing to buy off an aggressive empire by indulging its appetite have allowed a specious present to interfere with the peace of their children. The people who will not be patient with a troublesome neighbor, who want to bring everything to a "showdown" are no less the victims of a specious present.

6

Into almost every social problem the proper calculation of time enters. Suppose, for example, it is a question of timber. Some trees grow faster than others. Then a sound forest policy is one in which the amount of each species and of each age cut in each season is made good by replanting. In so far as that calculation is correct the truest economy has been reached. To cut less is waste, and to cut more is exploitation. But there may come an emergency, say the need for aeroplane spruce in a war, when the year's allowance must be exceeded. An alert government will recognize that and regard the restoration of the balance as a charge upon the future.

Coal involves a different theory of time, because coal, unlike a tree, is produced on the scale of geological time. The supply is limited. Therefore a correct social policy involves intricate computation of the available reserves of the world, the indicated possibilities, the present rate of use, the present economy of use, and the alternative fuels. But when that computation has been reached it must finally be squared with an ideal standard involving time. Suppose, for example, that engineers conclude that the present fuels are being exhausted at a certain rate; that barring new discoveries industry will have to enter a phase of contraction at some definite time in the future. We have then to determine how much thrift and self-denial we will use, after all feasible economies have been exercised, in order not to rob posterity. But what shall we consider posterity? Our grandchildren? Our great grandchildren? Perhaps we shall decide to calculate on a hundred years, believing that to be ample time for the discovery of alternative fuels if the necessity is made clear at once. The figures are, of course, hypothetical. But in calculating that way we shall be employing what reason we have. We shall be giving social time its place in public opinion. Let us now imagine a somewhat different case: a contract between a city and a trolley-car company. The company says that it will not invest its capital unless it is granted a monopoly of the main highway for ninety-nine years. In the minds of the men who make that demand ninety-nine years is so long as to mean "forever." But suppose there is reason to think that surface cars, run from a central power plant on tracks, are going out of fashion in twenty years. Then it is a most unwise contract to make, for you are virtually condemning a future generation to inferior transportation. In making such a contract the city officials lack a realizing sense of ninety-nine years. Far better to give the company a subsidy now in order to attract capital than to stimulate investment by indulging a fallacious sense of eternity. No city official and no company official has a sense of real time when he talks about ninety-nine years.

Popular history is a happy hunting ground of time confusions. To the average Englishman, for example, the behavior of Cromwell, the corruption of the Act of Union, the Famine of 1847 are wrongs suffered by people long dead and done by actors long dead with whom no living person, Irish or English, has any real connection. But in the mind of a patriotic Irishman these same events are almost contemporary. His memory is like one of those historical paintings, where Virgil and Dante sit side by side conversing. These perspectives and foreshortenings are a great barrier between peoples. It is ever so difficult for a person of one tradition to remember what is contemporary in the tradition of another.

The Walter Lippmann Reader

Almost nothing that goes by the name of Historic Rights or Historic Wrongs can be called a truly objective view of the past. Take, for example, the Franco-German debate about Alsace-Lorraine. It all depends on the original date you select. If you start with the Rauraci and Sequani, the lands are historically part of Ancient Gaul. If you prefer Henry I, they are historically a German territory; if you take 1273 they belong to the House of Austria; if you take 1648 and the Peace of Westphalia, most of them are French; if you take Louis XIV and the year 1688 they are almost all French. If you are using the argument from history you are fairly certain to select those dates in the past which support your view of what should be done now.

Arguments about "races" and nationalities often betray the same arbitrary view of time. During the war, under the influence of powerful feeling, the difference between "Teutons" on the one hand, and "Anglo-Saxons" and French on the other, was popularly believed to be an eternal difference. They had always been opposing races. Yet a generation ago, historians, like Freeman, were emphasizing the common Teutonic origin of the West European peoples, and ethnologists would certainly insist that the Germans, English, and the greater part of the French are branches of what was once a common stock. The general rule is: if you like a people to-day you come down the branches to the trunk; if you dislike them you insist that the separate branches are separate trunks. In one case you fix your attention on the period before they were distinguishable; in the other on the period after which they became distinct. And the view which fits the mood is taken as the "truth."

An amiable variation is the family tree. Usually one couple are appointed the original ancestors, if possible, a couple associated with an honorific event like the Norman Conquest. That couple have no ancestors. They are not descendants. Yet they were the descendants of ancestors, and the expression that So-and-So was the founder of his house means not that he is the Adam of his family, but that he is the particular ancestor from whom it is desirable to start, or perhaps the earliest ancestor of which there is a record. But genealogical tables exhibit a deeper prejudice. Unless the female line happens to be especially remarkable descent is traced down through the males. The tree is male. At various moments females accrue to it as itinerant bees light upon an ancient apple tree.

283

7

But the future is the most illusive time of all. Our temptation here is to jump over necessary steps in the sequence; and as we are governed by hope or doubt, to exaggerate or to minimize the time required to complete various parts of a process. The discussion of the role to be exercised by wage-earners in the management of industry is riddled with this difficulty. For management is a word that covers many functions. [Footnote: Cf. Carter L. Goodrich, The Frontier of Control.] Some of these require no training; some require a little training; others can be learned only in a lifetime. And the truly discriminating program of industrial democratization would be one based on the proper time sequence, so that the assumption of responsibility would run parallel to a complementary program of industrial training. The proposal for a sudden dictatorship of the proletariat is an attempt to do away with the intervening time of preparation; the resistance to all sharing of responsibility an attempt to deny the alteration of human capacity in the course of time. Primitive notions of democracy, such as rotation in office, and contempt for the expert, are really nothing but the old myth that the Goddess of Wisdom sprang mature and fully armed from the brow of Jove. They assume that what it takes years to learn need not be learned at all.

Whenever the phrase "backward people" is used as the basis of a policy, the conception of time is a decisive element. The Covenant of the League of Nations says, [Footnote: Article XIX.] for example, that "the character of the mandate must differ according to the stage of the development of the people," as well as on other grounds. Certain communities, it asserts, "have reached a stage of development" where their independence can be provisionally recognized, subject to advice and assistance "until such time as they are able to stand alone." The way in which the mandatories and the mandated conceive that time will influence deeply their relations. Thus in the case of Cuba the judgment of the American government virtually coincided with that of the Cuban patriots, and though there has been trouble, there is no finer page in the history of how strong powers have dealt with the weak. Oftener in that history the estimates have not coincided. Where the imperial people, whatever its public expressions, has been deeply convinced that the backwardness of the backward was so hopeless as not to be worth remedying, or so profitable that it was not desirable to remedy it, the tie has festered and poisoned the peace of the world. There have been a few cases, very few, where backwardness has meant to the ruling power the need for a program of forwardness, a program with definite standards and definite estimates of time. Far more frequently, so frequently in fact as to seem the rule, backwardness has been conceived as an intrinsic and eternal mark of inferiority. And then every attempt to be less backward has been frowned upon as the sedition, which, under these conditions, it undoubtedly is. In our own race wars we can see some of the results of the failure to realize that time would gradually obliterate the slave morality of the Negro, and that social adjustment based on this morality would begin to break down.

It is hard not to picture the future as if it obeyed our present purposes, to annihilate whatever delays our desire, or immortalize whatever stands between us and our fears.

8

In putting together our public opinions, not only do we have to picture more space than we can see with our eyes, and more time than we can feel, but we have to describe and judge more people, more actions, more things than we can ever count, or vividly imagine. We have to summarize and generalize. We have to pick out samples, and treat them as typical.

To pick fairly a good sample of a large class is not easy. The problem belongs to the science of statistics, and it is a most difficult affair for anyone whose mathematics is primitive, and mine remain azoic in spite of the half dozen manuals which I once devoutly imagined that I understood. All they have done for me is to make me a little more conscious of how hard it is to classify and to sample, how readily we spread a little butter over the whole universe.

Some time ago a group of social workers in Sheffield, England, started out to substitute an accurate picture of the mental equipment of the workers of that city for the impressionistic one they had. [Footnote: *The Equipment of the Worker.*] They wished to say, with some decent grounds for saying it, how the workers of Sheffield were equipped. They found, as we all find the moment we refuse to let our first notion prevail, that they were beset with complications. Of the test they employed nothing need be said here except that it was a large questionnaire. For the sake of the illustration, assume that the questions were a fair test of mental equipment for English city life. Theoretically, then, those questions should have been put to every member of the working class. But it is not so easy to know who are the working class. However, assume again that the census knows how to classify them. Then there were roughly 104,000 men and 107,000 women who ought to have been questioned. They possessed the answers which would justify or refute the casual phrase about the "ignorant workers" or the "intelligent workers." But nobody could think of questioning the whole two hundred thousand.

So the social workers consulted an eminent statistician, Professor Bowley. He advised them that not less than 408 men and 408 women would prove to be a fair sample. According to mathematical calculation this number would not show a greater deviation from the average than 1 in 22. [Footnote: *Op. cit.*, p. 65.] They had, therefore, to question at least 816 people before they could pretend to talk about the average workingman. But which 816 people should they approach? "We might have gathered particulars concerning workers to whom one or another of us had a pre-inquiry access; we might have worked through philanthropic gentlemen and ladies who were in contact with certain sections of workers at a club, a mission, an infirmary, a place of worship, a settlement. But such a method of selection would produce entirely worthless results. The workers thus selected would not be in any sense representative of what is popularly called 'the average run of workers;' they would represent nothing but the little coteries to which they belonged.

"The right way of securing 'victims,' to which at immense cost of time and labour we rigidly adhered, is to get hold of your workers by some 'neutral' or 'accidental' or 'random' method of approach." This they did. And after all these precautions they came to no more definite conclusion than that on their classification and according to their questionnaire, among 200,000 Sheffield workers "about one quarter" were "well equipped," "approaching three-quarters" were "inadequately equipped" and that "about one-fifteenth" were "mal-equipped."

Compare this conscientious and almost pedantic method of arriving at an opinion, with our usual judgments about masses of people, about the volatile Irish, and the logical French, and the disciplined Germans, and the ignorant Slavs, and the honest Chinese, and the untrustworthy Japanese, and so on and so on. All these are generalizations drawn from samples, but the samples are selected by a method that statistically is wholly unsound. Thus the employer will judge labor by the most troublesome employee or the most docile that he knows, and many a radical group has imagined that it was a fair sample of the working class. How many women's views on the "servant question" are little more than the reflection of their own treatment of their servants? The tendency of the casual mind is to pick out or stumble upon a sample which supports or defies its prejudices, and then to make it the representative of a whole class.

A great deal of confusion arises when people decline to classify themselves as we have classified them. Prophecy would be so much easier if only they would stay where we put them. But, as a matter of fact, a phrase like the working class will cover only some of the truth for a part of the time. When you take all the people, below a certain level of income, and call them the working class, you cannot help assuming that the people so classified will behave in accordance with your stereotype. Just who those people are you are not quite certain. Factory hands and mine workers fit in more or less, but farm hands, small farmers, peddlers, little shop keepers, clerks, servants, soldiers, policemen, firemen slip out of the net. The tendency, when you are appealing to the "working class," is to fix your attention on two or three million more or less confirmed trade unionists, and treat them as Labor; the other seventeen or eighteen million, who might qualify statistically, are tacitly endowed with the point of view ascribed to the organized nucleus. How very misleading it was to impute to the British working class in 1918-1921 the point of view expressed in the resolutions of the Trades Union Congress or in the pamphlets written by intellectuals.

The stereotype of Labor as Emancipator selects the evidence which supports itself and rejects the other. And so parallel with the real movements of working men there exists a fiction of the Labor Movement, in which an idealized mass moves towards an ideal goal. The fiction deals with the future. In the future possibilities are almost indistinguishable from probabilities and probabilities from certainties. If the future is long enough, the human will might turn what is just conceivable into what is very likely, and what is likely into what is sure to happen. James called this the faith ladder, and said that "it is a slope of goodwill on which in the larger questions of life men habitually live." [Footnote: William James, *Some Problems of Philosophy*, p. 224.]

"1. There is nothing absurd in a certain view of the world being true, nothing contradictory;

2. It *might* have been true under certain conditions;

3. It *may* be true even now;

4. It is *fit* to be true;

5. It *ought* to be true;

6. It *must* be true;

7. It *shall* be true, at any rate true for me."

And, as he added in another place, [Footnote: A *Pluralistic Universe*, p. 329.] "your acting thus may in certain special cases be a means of making it securely true in the end." Yet no one would have insisted more than he, that, so far as we know how, we must avoid substituting the goal for the starting point, must avoid reading back into the present what courage, effort and skill might create in the future. Yet this truism is inordinately difficult to live by, because every one of us is so little trained in the selection of our samples.

If we believe that a certain thing ought to be true, we can almost always find either an instance where it is true, or someone who believes it ought to be true. It is ever so hard when a concrete fact illustrates a hope to weigh that fact properly. When the first six people we meet agree with us, it is not easy to remember that they may all have read the same newspaper at breakfast. And yet we cannot send out a questionnaire to 816 random samples every time we wish to estimate a probability. In dealing with any large mass of facts, the presumption is against our having picked true samples, if we are acting on a casual impression.

9

And when we try to go one step further in order to seek the causes and effects of unseen and complicated affairs, haphazard opinion is very tricky. There are few big issues in public life where cause and effect are obvious at once. They are not obvious to scholars who have devoted years, let us say, to studying business cycles, or price and wage movements, or the migration and the assimilation of peoples, or the diplomatic purposes of foreign powers. Yet somehow we are all supposed to have opinions on these matters, and it is not surprising that the commonest form of reasoning is the intuitive, post hoc ergo propter hoc.

The more untrained a mind, the more readily it works out a theory that two things which catch its attention at the same time are causally connected. We have already dwelt at some length on the way things reach our attention. We have seen that our access to information is obstructed and uncertain, and that our apprehension is deeply controlled by our stereotypes; that the evidence available to our reason is subject to illusions of defense, prestige, morality, space, time, and sampling. We must note now that with this initial taint, public opinions are still further beset, because in a series of events seen mostly through stereotypes, we readily accept sequence or parallelism as equivalent to cause and effect.

This is most likely to happen when two ideas that come together arouse the same feeling. If they come together they are likely to arouse the same feeling; and even when they do not arrive together a powerful feeling attached to one is likely to suck out of all the corners of memory any idea that feels about the same. Thus everything painful tends to collect into one system of cause and effect, and likewise everything pleasant.

"IId IIm (1675) This day I hear that G[od] has shot an arrow into the midst of this Town. The small pox is in an ordinary ye sign of the Swan, the ordinary Keepers name is Windsor. His daughter is sick of the disease. It is observable that this disease begins at an alehouse, to testify God's displeasure agt the sin of drunkenness & yt of multiplying alehouses!" [Footnote: *The Heart of the Puritan*, p. 177, edited by Elizabeth Deering Hanscom.]

Thus Increase Mather, and thus in the year 1919 a distinguished Professor of Celestial Mechanics discussing the Einstein theory:

"It may well be that.... Bolshevist uprisings are in reality the visible objects of some underlying, deep, mental disturbance, world-wide in character.... This same spirit of unrest has invaded science." [Footnote: Cited in *The New Republic*, Dec. 24, 1919, p. 120.]

In hating one thing violently, we readily associate with it as cause or effect most of the other things we hate or fear violently. They may have no more connection than smallpox and alehouses, or Relativity and Bolshevism, but they are bound together in the same emotion. In a superstitious mind, like that of the Professor of Celestial Mechanics, emotion is a stream of molten lava which catches and imbeds whatever it touches. When you excavate in it you find, as in a buried city, all sorts of objects ludicrously entangled in each other. Anything can be related to anything else, provided it feels like it. Nor has a mind in such a state any way of knowing how preposterous it is. Ancient fears, reinforced by more recent fears, coagulate into a snarl of fears where anything that is dreaded is the cause of anything else that is dreaded.

10

Generally it all culminates in the fabrication of a system of all evil, and of another which is the system of all good. Then our love of the absolute shows itself. For we do not like qualifying adverbs. [Footnote: *Cf.* Freud's discussion of absolutism in dreams, *Interpretation of Dreams*, Chapter VI, especially pp. 288, *et seq.*] They clutter up sentences, and interfere with irresistible feeling. We prefer most to more, least to less, we dislike the words rather, perhaps, if, or, but, toward, not quite, almost, temporarily, partly. Yet nearly every opinion about public affairs needs to be deflated by some word of this sort. But in our free moments everything tends to behave absolutely,—one hundred percent, everywhere, forever.

It is not enough to say that our side is more right than the enemy's, that our victory will help democracy more than his. One must insist that our victory will end war forever, and make the world safe for democracy. And when the war is over, though we have thwarted a greater evil than those which still afflict us, the relativity of the result fades out, the absoluteness of the present evil overcomes our spirit, and we feel that we are helpless because we have not been irresistible. Between omnipotence and impotence the pendulum swings.

Real space, real time, real numbers, real connections, real weights are lost. The perspective and the background and the dimensions of action are clipped and frozen in the stereotype.

PART IV
INTERESTS

CHAPTER XI

The Enlisting of Interest

1

BUT the human mind is not a film which registers once and for all each impression that comes through its shutters and lenses. The human mind is endlessly and persistently creative. The pictures fade or combine, are sharpened here, condensed there, as we make them more completely our own. They do not lie inert upon the surface of the mind, but are reworked by the poetic faculty into a personal expression of ourselves. We distribute the emphasis and participate in the action.

In order to do this we tend to personalize quantities, and to dramatize relations. As some sort of allegory, except in acutely sophisticated minds, the affairs of the world are represented. Social Movements, Economic Forces, National Interests, Public Opinion are treated as persons, or persons like the Pope, the President, Lenin, Morgan or the King become ideas and institutions. The deepest of all the stereotypes is the human stereotype which imputes human nature to inanimate or collective things.

The bewildering variety of our impressions, even after they have been censored in all kinds of ways, tends to force us to adopt the greater economy of the allegory. So great is the multitude of things that we cannot keep them vividly in mind. Usually, then, we name them, and let the name stand for the whole impression. But a name is porous. Old meanings slip out and new ones slip in, and the attempt to retain the full meaning of the name is almost as fatiguing as trying to recall the original impressions. Yet names are a poor currency for thought. They are too empty, too abstract, too inhuman. And so we begin to see the name through some personal stereotype, to read into it, finally to see in it the incarnation of some human quality.

Yet human qualities are themselves vague and fluctuating. They are best remembered by a physical sign. And therefore, the human qualities we tend to ascribe to the names of our impressions, themselves tend to be visualized in physical metaphors. The people of England, the history of England, condense

The Walter Lippmann Reader

into England, and England becomes John Bull, who is jovial and fat, not too clever, but well able to take care of himself. The migration of a people may appear to some as the meandering of a river, and to others like a devastating flood. The courage people display may be objectified as a rock; their purpose as a road, their doubts as forks of the road, their difficulties as ruts and rocks, their progress as a fertile valley. If they mobilize their dread-naughts they unsheath a sword. If their army surrenders they are thrown to earth. If they are oppressed they are on the rack or under the harrow.

When public affairs are popularized in speeches, headlines, plays, moving pictures, cartoons, novels, statues or paintings, their transformation into a human interest requires first abstraction from the original, and then animation of what has been abstracted. We cannot be much interested in, or much moved by, the things we do not see. Of public affairs each of us sees very little, and therefore, they remain dull and unappetizing, until somebody, with the makings of an artist, has translated them into a moving picture. Thus the abstraction, imposed upon our knowledge of reality by all the limitations of our access and of our prejudices, is compensated. Not being omnipresent and omniscient we cannot see much of what we have to think and talk about. Being flesh and blood we will not feed on words and names and gray theory. Being artists of a sort we paint pictures, stage dramas and draw cartoons out of the abstractions.

Or, if possible, we find gifted men who can visualize for us. For people are not all endowed to the same degree with the pictorial faculty. Yet one may, I imagine, assert with Bergson that the practical intelligence is most closely adapted to spatial qualities. [Footnote: *Creative Evolution*, Chs. III, IV.] A "clear" thinker is almost always a good visualizer. But for that same reason, because he is "cinematographic," he is often by that much external and insensitive. For the people who have intuition, which is probably another name for musical or muscular perception, often appreciate the quality of an event and the inwardness of an act far better than the visualizer. They have more understanding when the crucial element is a desire that is never crudely overt, and appears on the surface only in a veiled gesture, or in a rhythm of speech. Visualization may catch the stimulus and the result. But the intermediate and internal is often as badly caricatured by a visualizer, as is the intention of the composer by an enormous soprano in the sweet maiden's part.

The Walter Lippmann Reader

Nevertheless, though they have often a peculiar justice, intuitions remain highly private and largely incommunicable. But social intercourse depends on communication, and while a person can often steer his own life with the utmost grace by virtue of his intuitions, he usually has great difficulty in making them real to others. When he talks about them they sound like a sheaf of mist. For while intuition does give a fairer perception of human feeling, the reason with its spatial and tactile prejudice can do little with that perception. Therefore, where action depends on whether a number of people are of one mind, it is probably true that in the first instance no idea is lucid for practical decision until it has visual or tactile value. But it is also true, that no visual idea is significant to us until it has enveloped some stress of our own personality. Until it releases or resists, depresses or enhances, some craving of our own, it remains one of the objects which do not matter.

2

Pictures have always been the surest way of conveying an idea, and next in order, words that call up pictures in memory. But the idea conveyed is not fully our own until we have identified ourselves with some aspect of the picture. The identification, or what Vernon Lee has called empathy, [Footnote: *Beauty and Ugliness*.] may be almost infinitely subtle and symbolic. The mimicry may be performed without our being aware of it, and sometimes in a way that would horrify those sections of our personality which support our self-respect. In sophisticated people the participation may not be in the fate of the hero, but in the fate of the whole idea to which both hero and villain are essential. But these are refinements.

In popular representation the handles for identification are almost always marked. You know who the hero is at once. And no work promises to be easily popular where the marking is not definite and the choice clear. [Footnote: A fact which bears heavily on the character of news. *Cf*. Part VII.] But that is not enough. The audience must have something to do, and the contemplation of the true, the good and the beautiful is not something to do. In order not to sit inertly in the presence of the picture, and this applies as much to newspaper stories as to fiction and the cinema, the audience must be exercised by the image. Now there are two forms of exercise which far transcend all others, both as to ease with which they are aroused, and eagerness with which stimuli for

293

them are sought. They are sexual passion and fighting, and the two have so many associations with each other, blend into each other so intimately, that a fight about sex outranks every other theme in the breadth of its appeal. There is none so engrossing or so careless of all distinctions of culture and frontiers.

The sexual motif figures hardly at all in American political imagery. Except in certain minor ecstasies of war, in an occasional scandal, or in phases of the racial conflict with Negroes or Asiatics, to speak of it at all would seem far-fetched. Only in moving pictures, novels, and some magazine fiction are industrial relations, business competition, politics, and diplomacy tangled up with the girl and the other woman. But the fighting motif appears at every turn. Politics is interesting when there is a fight, or as we say, an issue. And in order to make politics popular, issues have to be found, even when in truth and justice, there are none,—none, in the sense that the differences of judgment, or principle, or fact, do not call for the enlistment of pugnacity. [Footnote: *Cf.* Frances Taylor Patterson, *Cinema Craftsmanship*, pp. 31-32. "III. If the plot lacks suspense: 1. Add an antagonist, 2. Add an obstacle, 3. Add a problem, 4. Emphasize one of the questions in the minds of the spectator.,.."]

But where pugnacity is not enlisted, those of us who are not directly involved find it hard to keep up our interest. For those who are involved the absorption may be real enough to hold them even when no issue is involved. They may be exercised by sheer joy in activity, or by subtle rivalry or invention. But for those to whom the whole problem is external and distant, these other faculties do not easily come into play. In order that the faint image of the affair shall mean something to them, they must be allowed to exercise the love of struggle, suspense, and victory.

Miss Patterson [Footnote: *Op. cit.*, pp. 6-7.] insists that "suspense... constitutes the difference between the masterpieces in the Metropolitan Museum of Art and the pictures at the Rivoli or the Rialto Theatres." Had she made it clear that the masterpieces lack either an easy mode of identification or a theme popular for this generation, she would be wholly right in saying that this "explains why the people straggle into the Metropolitan by twos and threes and struggle into the Rialto and Rivoli by hundreds. The twos and threes look at a picture in the Art Museum for less than ten minutes—unless they chance to be art students, critics, or connoisseurs. The hundreds in the Rivoli or the Rialto look at the picture for more than an hour. As far as beauty is concerned there can be no comparison of the merits of the two pictures. Yet the motion picture draws more people and holds them at attention longer than do the masterpieces, not through any intrinsic merit of its own, but because it depicts unfolding events, the outcome of which the audience is breathlessly waiting. It possesses the element of struggle, which never fails to arouse suspense."

In order then that the distant situation shall not be a gray flicker on the edge of attention, it should be capable of translation into pictures in which the opportunity for identification is recognizable. Unless that happens it will interest only a few for a little while. It will belong to the sights seen but not felt, to the sensations that beat on our sense organs, and are not acknowledged. We have to take sides. We have to be able to take sides. In the recesses of our being we must step out of the audience on to the stage, and wrestle as the hero for the victory of good over evil. We must breathe into the allegory the breath of our life.

3

And so, in spite of the critics, a verdict is rendered in the old controversy about realism and romanticism. Our popular taste is to have the drama originate in a setting realistic enough to make identification plausible and to have it terminate in a setting romantic enough to be desirable, but not so romantic as to be inconceivable. In between the beginning and the end the canons are liberal, but the true beginning and the happy ending are landmarks. The moving picture audience rejects fantasy logically developed, because in pure fantasy there is no familiar foothold in the age of machines. It rejects realism relentlessly pursued because it does not enjoy defeat in a struggle that has become its own.

What will be accepted as true, as realistic, as good, as evil, as desirable, is not eternally fixed. These are fixed by stereotypes, acquired from earlier experiences and carried over into judgment of later ones. And, therefore, if the financial investment in each film and in popular magazines were not so exorbitant as to require instant and widespread popularity, men of spirit and imagination would be able to use the screen and the periodical, as one might dream of their being used, to enlarge and to refine, to verify and criticize the repertory of images with which our imaginations work. But, given the present costs, the men who make moving pictures, like the church and the court painters of other ages, must adhere to the stereotypes that they find, or pay the price of frustrating expectation. The stereotypes can be altered, but not in time to guarantee success when the film is released six months from now.

The men who do alter the stereotypes, the pioneering artists and critics, are naturally depressed and angered at managers and editors who protect their investments. They are risking everything, then why not the others? That is not quite fair, for in their righteous fury they have forgotten their own rewards, which are beyond any that their employers can hope to feel. They could not, and would not if they could, change places. And they have forgotten another thing in the unceasing war with Philistia. They have forgotten that they are measuring their own success by standards that artists and wise men of the past would never have dreamed of invoking. They are asking for circulations and audiences that were never considered by any artist until the last few generations. And when they do not get them, they are disappointed.

Those who catch on, like Sinclair Lewis in "Main Street," are men who have succeeded in projecting definitely what great numbers of other people were obscurely trying to say inside their heads. "You have said it for me." They establish a new form which is then endlessly copied until it, too, becomes a stereotype of perception. The next pioneer finds it difficult to make the public see Main Street any other way. And he, like the forerunners of Sinclair Lewis, has a quarrel with the public.

This quarrel is due not only to the conflict of stereotypes, but to the pioneering artist's reverence for his material. Whatever the plane he chooses, on that plane he remains. If he is dealing with the inwardness of an event he follows it to its conclusion regardless of the pain it causes. He will not tag his fantasy to help anyone, or cry peace where there is no peace. There is his America. But big audiences have no stomach for such severity. They are more interested in themselves than in anything else in the world. The selves in which they are interested are the selves that have been revealed by schools and by tradition. They insist that a work of art shall be a vehicle with a step where they can climb aboard, and that they shall ride, not according to the contours of the country, but to a land where for an hour there are no clocks to punch and no dishes to wash. To satisfy these demands there exists an intermediate class of artists who are able and willing to confuse the planes, to piece together a realistic-romantic compound out of the inventions of greater men, and, as Miss Patterson advises, give "what real life so rarely does-the triumphant resolution of a set of difficulties; the anguish of virtue and the triumph of sin... changed to the glorifications of virtue and the eternal punishment of its enemy." [Footnote: *Op. cit.*, p. 46. "The hero and heroine must in general possess youth, beauty, goodness, exalted self-sacrifice, and unalterable constancy."]

4

The ideologies of politics obey these rules. The foothold of realism is always there. The picture of some real evil, such as the German threat or class conflict, is recognizable in the argument. There is a description of some aspect of the world which is convincing because it agrees with familiar ideas. But as the ideology deals with an unseen future, as well as with a tangible present, it soon crosses imperceptibly the frontier of verification. In describing the present you are more or less tied down to common experience. In describing what nobody has experienced you are bound to let go. You stand at Armageddon, more or less, but you battle for the Lord, perhaps.... A true beginning, true according to the standards prevailing, and a happy ending. Every Marxist is hard as nails about the brutalities of the present, and mostly sunshine about the day after the dictatorship. So were the war propagandists: there was not a bestial quality in human nature they did not find everywhere east of the Rhine, or west of it if they were Germans. The bestiality was there all right. But after the victory, eternal peace. Plenty of this is quite cynically deliberate. For the skilful propagandist knows that while you must start with a plausible analysis, you must not keep on analyzing, because the tedium of real political accomplishment will soon destroy interest. So the propagandist exhausts the interest in reality by a tolerably plausible beginning, and then stokes up energy for a long voyage by brandishing a passport to heaven.

The formula works when the public fiction enmeshes itself with a private urgency. But once enmeshed, in the heat of battle, the original self and the original stereotype which effected the junction may be wholly lost to sight.

CHAPTER XII
Self-Interest Reconsidered

1

THEREFORE, the identical story is not the same story to all who hear it. Each will enter it at a slightly different point, since no two experiences are exactly alike; he will reenact it in his own way, and transfuse it with his own feelings. Sometimes an artist of compelling skill will force us to enter into lives altogether unlike our own, lives that seem at first glance dull, repulsive, or eccentric. But that is rare. In almost every story that catches our attention we become a character and act out the role with a pantomime of our own. The pantomime may be subtle or gross, may be sympathetic to the story, or only crudely analogous; but it will consist of those feelings which are aroused by our conception of the role. And so, the original theme as it circulates, is stressed, twisted, and embroidered by all the minds through which it goes. It is as if a play of Shakespeare's were rewritten each time it is performed with all the changes of emphasis and meaning that the actors and audience inspired.

Something very like that seems to have happened to the stories in the sagas before they were definitively written down. In our time the printed record, such as it is, checks the exuberance of each individual's fancy. But against rumor there is little or no checks and the original story, true or invented, grows wings and horns, hoofs and beaks, as the artist in each gossip works upon it. The first narrator's account does not keep its shape and proportions. It is edited and revised by all who played with it as they heard it, used it for day dreams, and passed it on. [Footnote: For an interesting example, see the case described by C. J. Jung, *Zentralblatt für Psychoanalyse*, 1911, Vol. I, p. 81. Translated by Constance Long, in *Analytical Psychology*, Ch. IV.]

Consequently the more mixed the audience, the greater will be the variation in the response. For as the audience grows larger, the number of common words diminishes. Thus the common factors in the story become more abstract. This story, lacking precise character of its own, is heard by people of highly varied character. They give it their own character.

2

The character they give it varies not only with sex and age, race and religion and social position, but within these cruder classifications, according to the inherited and acquired constitution of the individual, his faculties, his career, the progress of his career, an emphasized aspect of his career, his moods and tenses, or his place on the board in any of the games of life that he is playing. What reaches him of public affairs, a few lines of print, some photographs, anecdotes, and some casual experience of his own, he conceives through his set patterns and recreates with his own emotions. He does not take his personal problems as partial samples of the greater environment. He takes his stories of the greater environment as a mimic enlargement of his private life.

But not necessarily of that private life as he would describe it to himself. For in his private life the choices are narrow, and much of himself is squeezed down and out of sight where it cannot directly govern his outward behavior. And thus, beside the more average people who project the happiness of their own lives into a general good will, or their unhappiness into suspicion and hate, there are the outwardly happy people who are brutal everywhere but in their own circle, as well as the people who, the more they detest their families, their friends, their jobs, the more they overflow with love for mankind.

As you descend from generalities to detail, it becomes more apparent that the character in which men deal with their affairs is not fixed. Possibly their different selves have a common stem and common qualities, but the branches and the twigs have many forms. Nobody confronts every situation with the same character. His character varies in some degree through the sheer influence of time and accumulating memory, since he is not an automaton. His character varies, not only in time, but according to circumstance. The legend of the solitary Englishman in the South Seas, who invariably shaves and puts on a black tie for dinner, bears witness to his own intuitive and civilized fear of losing the character which he has acquired. So do diaries, and albums, and souvenirs, old letters, and old clothes, and the love of unchanging routine testify to our sense of how hard it is to step twice in the Heraclitan river.

There is no one self always at work. And therefore it is of great importance in the formation of any public opinion, what self is engaged. The Japanese ask the right to settle in California. Clearly it makes a whole lot of difference whether you conceive the demand as a desire to grow fruit or to marry the white man's

The Walter Lippmann Reader

daughter. If two nations are disputing a piece of territory, it matters greatly whether the people regard the negotiations as a real estate deal, an attempt to humiliate them, or, in the excited and provocative language which usually enclouds these arguments, as a rape. For the self which takes charge of the instincts when we are thinking about lemons or distant acres is very different from the self which appears when we are thinking even potentially as the outraged head of a family. In one case the private feeling which enters into the opinion is tepid, in the other, red hot. And so while it is so true as to be mere tautology that "self-interest" determines opinion, the statement is not illuminating, until we know which self out of many selects and directs the interest so conceived.

Religious teaching and popular wisdom have always distinguished several personalities in each human being. They have been called the Higher and Lower, the Spiritual and the Material, the Divine and the Carnal; and although we may not wholly accept this classification, we cannot fail to observe that distinctions exist. Instead of two antithetic selves, a modern man would probably note a good many not so sharply separated. He would say that the distinction drawn by theologians was arbitrary and external, because many different selves were grouped together as higher provided they fitted into the theologian's categories, but he would recognize nevertheless that here was an authentic clue to the variety of human nature.

We have learned to note many selves, and to be a little less ready to issue judgment upon them. We understand that we see the same body, but often a different man, depending on whether he is dealing with a social equal, a social inferior, or a social superior; on whether he is making love to a woman he is eligible to marry, or to one whom he is not; on whether he is courting a woman, or whether he considers himself her proprietor; on whether he is dealing with his children, his partners, his most trusted subordinates, the boss who can make him or break him; on whether he is struggling for the necessities of life, or successful; on whether he is dealing with a friendly alien, or a despised one; on whether he is in great danger, or in perfect security; on whether he is alone in Paris or among his family in Peoria.

People differ widely, of course, in the consistency of their characters, so widely that they may cover the whole gamut of differences between a split soul like Dr. Jekyll's and an utterly singleminded Brand, Parsifal, or Don Quixote. If the selves are too unrelated, we distrust the man; if they are too inflexibly on one track we find him arid, stubborn, or eccentric. In the repertory of characters, meager for the isolated and the self-sufficient, highly varied for the adaptable, there is a whole range of selves, from that one at the top which we should wish God to see, to those at the bottom that we ourselves do not dare to see. There may be octaves for the family,—father, Jehovah, tyrant,—husband, proprietor, male,—lover, lecher,—for the occupation,—employer, master, exploiter,—competitor, intriguer, enemy,—subordinate, courtier, snob. Some never come out into public view. Others are called out only by exceptional circumstances. But the characters take their form from a man's conception of the situation in which he finds himself. If the environment to which he is sensitive happens to be the smart set, he will imitate the character he conceives to be appropriate. That character will tend to act as modulator of his bearing, his speech, his choice of subjects, his preferences. Much of the comedy of life lies here, in the way people imagine their characters for situations that are strange to them: the professor among promoters, the deacon at a poker game, the cockney in the country, the paste diamond among real diamonds.

3

Into the making of a man's characters there enters a variety of influences not easily separated. [Footnote: For an interesting sketch of the more noteworthy early attempts to explain character, see the chapter called "The Antecedents of the Study of Character and Temperament," in Joseph Jastrow's *The Psychology of Conviction*.] The analysis in its fundamentals is perhaps still as doubtful as it was in the fifth century B. C. when Hippocrates formulated the doctrine of the humors, distinguished the sanguine, the melancholic, the choleric, and the phlegmatic dispositions, and ascribed them to the blood, the black bile, the yellow bile, and the phlegm. The latest theories, such as one finds them in Cannon, [Footnote: *Bodily Changes in Pleasure, Pain and Anger*.] Adler, [Footnote: *The Neurotic Constitution*.] Kempf, [Footnote: *The Autonomic Functions and the Personality; Psychopathology*. Cf. also Louis Berman: *The Glands Regulating Personality*.] appear to follow much the same scent, from the outward behavior and the inner consciousness to the physiology of the body. But in spite of an immensely improved technique, no one would be likely to claim that there are settled conclusions which enable us to set apart nature from nurture, and abstract the native character from the acquired. It is only in what Joseph Jastrow has called the slums of psychology that the explanation of character is regarded as a fixed system to be applied by phrenologists, palmists, fortune-tellers, mind-readers, and a few political professors. There you will still find it asserted that "the Chinese are fond of colors, and have their eyebrows much vaulted" while "the heads of the Calmucks are depressed from above, but very large laterally, about the organ which gives the inclination to acquire; and this nation's propensity to steal, etc., is admitted." [Footnote: *Jastrow, op. cit.*, p. 156.]

The modern psychologists are disposed to regard the outward behavior of an adult as an equation between a number of variables, such as the resistance of the environment, repressed cravings of several maturities, and the manifest personality. [Footnote: Formulated by Kempf, *Psychopathology*, p. 74, as follows:

Manifest wishes } over } Later Repressed Wishes } Over } opposed by the resistance of the Adolescent Repressed Wishes } environment=Behavior Over } Preadolescent Repressed Wishes }] They permit us to suppose, though I have not seen the notion formulated, that the repression or control of cravings is fixed not in relation to the whole person all the time, but more or less in respect to his various selves. There are things he will not do as a patriot that he will do when he is not thinking of himself as a patriot. No doubt there are impulses, more or less incipient in childhood, that are never exercised again in the whole of a man's life, except as they enter obscurely and indirectly into combination with other impulses. But even that is not certain, since repression is not irretrievable. For just as psychoanalysis can bring to the surface a buried impulse, so can social situations. [Footnote: *Cf.* the very interesting book of Everett Dean Martin, *The Behavior of Crowds.*

Also Hobbes, *Leviathan*, Part II, Ch. 25. "For the passions of men, which asunder are moderate, as the heat of one brand, in an assembly are like many brands, that inflame one another, especially when they blow one another with orations...."

LeBon, *The Crowd*, elaborates this observation of Hobbes's.] It is only when our surroundings remain normal and placid, when what is expected of us by those we meet is consistent, that we live without knowledge of many of our dispositions. When the unexpected occurs, we learn much about ourselves that we did not know.

The Walter Lippmann Reader

The selves, which we construct with the help of all who influence us, prescribe which impulses, how emphasized, how directed, are appropriate to certain typical situations for which we have learned prepared attitudes. For a recognizable type of experience, there is a character which controls the outward manifestations of our whole being. Murderous hate is, for example, controlled in civil life. Though you choke with rage, you must not display it as a parent, child, employer, politician. You would not wish to display a personality that exudes murderous hate. You frown upon it, and the people around you also frown. But if a war breaks out, the chances are that everybody you admire will begin to feel the justification of killing and hating. At first the vent for these feelings is very narrow. The selves which come to the front are those which are attuned to a real love of country, the kind of feeling that you find in Rupert Brooke, and in Sir Edward Grey's speech on August 3, 1914, and in President Wilson's address to Congress on April 2, 1917. The reality of war is still abhorred, and what war actually means is learned but gradually. For previous wars are only transfigured memories. In that honeymoon phase, the realists of war rightly insist that the nation is not yet awake, and reassure each other by saying: "Wait for the casualty lists." Gradually the impulse to kill becomes the main business, and all those characters which might modify it, disintegrate. The impulse becomes central, is sanctified, and gradually turns unmanageable. It seeks a vent not alone on the idea of the enemy, which is all the enemy most people actually see during the war, but upon all the persons and objects and ideas that have always been hateful. Hatred of the enemy is legitimate. These other hatreds have themselves legitimized by the crudest analogy, and by what, once having cooled off, we recognize as the most far-fetched analogy. It takes a long time to subdue so powerful an impulse once it goes loose. And therefore, when the war is over in fact, it takes time and struggle to regain self-control, and to deal with the problems of peace in civilian character.

Modern war, as Mr. Herbert Croly has said, is inherent in the political structure of modern society, but outlawed by its ideals. For the civilian population there exists no ideal code of conduct in war, such as the soldier still possesses and chivalry once prescribed. The civilians are without standards, except those that the best of them manage to improvise. The only standards they possess make war an accursed thing. Yet though the war may be a necessary one, no moral training has prepared them for it. Only their higher selves have a code and patterns, and when they have to act in what the higher regards as a lower character profound disturbance results.

The preparation of characters for all the situations in which men may find themselves is one function of a moral education. Clearly then, it depends for its success upon the sincerity and knowledge with which the environment has been explored. For in a world falsely conceived, our own characters are falsely conceived, and we misbehave. So the moralist must choose: either he must offer a pattern of conduct for every phase of life, however distasteful some of its phases may be, or he must guarantee that his pupils will never be confronted by the situations he disapproves. Either he must abolish war, or teach people how to wage it with the greatest psychic economy; either he must abolish the economic life of man and feed him with stardust and dew, or he must investigate all the perplexities of economic life and offer patterns of conduct which are applicable in a world where no man is self-supporting. But that is just what the prevailing moral culture so generally refuses to do. In its best aspects it is diffident at the awful complication of the modern world. In its worst, it is just cowardly. Now whether the moralists study economics and politics and psychology, or whether the social scientists educate the moralists is no great matter. Each generation will go unprepared into the modern world, unless it has been taught to conceive the kind of personality it will have to be among the issues it will most likely meet.

4

Most of this the naive view of self-interest leaves out of account. It forgets that self and interest are both conceived somehow, and that for the most part they are conventionally conceived. The ordinary doctrine of self-interest usually omits altogether the cognitive function. So insistent is it on the fact that human beings finally refer all things to themselves, that it does not stop to notice that men's ideas of all things and of themselves are not instinctive. They are acquired.

Thus it may be true enough, as James Madison wrote in the tenth paper of the Federalist, that "a landed interest, a manufacturing interest, a mercantile interest, a moneyed interest, with many lesser interests, grow up of necessity in civilized nations, and divide them into different classes, actuated by different sentiments and views." But if you examine the context of Madison's paper, you discover something which I think throws light upon that view of instinctive

The Walter Lippmann Reader

fatalism, called sometimes the economic interpretation of history. Madison was arguing for the federal constitution, and "among the numerous advantages of the union" he set forth "its tendency to break and control the violence of faction." Faction was what worried Madison. And the causes of faction he traced to "the nature of man," where latent dispositions are "brought into different degrees of activity, according to the different circumstances of civil society. A zeal for different opinions concerning religion, concerning government and many other points, as well of speculation as of practice; an attachment to different leaders ambitiously contending for preeminence and power, or to persons of other descriptions whose fortunes have been interesting to the human passions, have, in turn, divided mankind into parties, inflamed them with mutual animosity, and rendered them much more disposed to vex and oppress each other, than to coöperate for their common good. So strong is this propensity of mankind to fall into mutual animosities, that where no substantial occasion presents itself, the most frivolous and fanciful distinctions have been sufficient to kindle their unfriendly passions and excite their most violent conflicts. But the *most common* and *durable* source of factions has been the various and unequal distribution of property."

Madison's theory, therefore, is that the propensity to faction may be kindled by religious or political opinions, by leaders, but most commonly by the distribution of property. Yet note that Madison claims only that men are divided by their relation to property. He does not say that their property and their opinions are cause and effect, but that differences of property are the causes of differences of opinion. The pivotal word in Madison's argument is "different." From the existence of differing economic situations you can tentatively infer a probable difference of opinions, but you cannot infer what those opinions will necessarily be.

This reservation cuts radically into the claims of the theory as that theory is usually held. That the reservation is necessary, the enormous contradiction between dogma and practice among orthodox socialists bears witness. They argue that the next stage in social evolution is the inevitable result of the present stage. But in order to produce that inevitable next stage they organize and agitate to produce "class consciousness." Why, one asks, does not the economic situation produce consciousness of class in everybody? It just doesn't, that is all. And therefore the proud claim will not stand that the socialist philosophy rests

305

on prophetic insight into destiny. It rests on an hypothesis about human nature. [Footnote: *Cf.* Thorstein Veblen, "The Socialist Economics of Karl Marx and His Followers," in *The Place of Science in Modern Civilization*, esp. pp. 413-418.]

The socialist practice is based on a belief that if men are economically situated in different ways, they can then be induced to hold certain views. Undoubtedly they often come to believe, or can be induced to believe different things, as they are, for example, landlords or tenants, employees or employers, skilled or unskilled laborers, wageworkers or salaried men, buyers or sellers, farmers or middle-men, exporters or importers, creditors or debtors. Differences of income make a profound difference in contact and opportunity. Men who work at machines will tend, as Mr. Thorstein Veblen has so brilliantly demonstrated, [Footnote: *The Theory of Business Enterprise*.] to interpret experience differently from handicraftsmen or traders. If this were all that the materialistic conception of politics asserted, the theory would be an immensely valuable hypothesis that every interpreter of opinion would have to use. But he would often have to abandon the theory, and he would always have to be on guard. For in trying to explain a certain public opinion, it is rarely obvious which of a man's many social relations is effecting a particular opinion. Does Smith's opinion arise from his problems as a landlord, an importer, an owner of railway shares, or an employer? Does Jones's opinion, Jones being a weaver in a textile mill, come from the attitude of his boss, the competition of new immigrants, his wife's grocery bills, or the ever present contract with the firm which is selling him a Ford car and a house and lot on the instalment plan? Without special inquiry you cannot tell. The economic determinist cannot tell.

A man's various economic contacts limit or enlarge the range of his opinions. But which of the contacts, in what guise, on what theory, the materialistic conception of politics cannot predict. It can predict, with a high degree of probability, that if a man owns a factory, his ownership will figure in those opinions which seem to have some bearing on that factory. But how the function of being an owner will figure, no economic determinist as such, can tell you. There is no fixed set of opinions on any question that go with being the owner of a factory, no views on labor, on property, on management, let alone views on less immediate matters. The determinist can predict that in ninety-nine cases out of a hundred the owner will resist attempts to deprive him of ownership, or that he will favor legislation which he thinks will increase his

The Walter Lippmann Reader

profits. But since there is no magic in ownership which enables a business man to know what laws will make him prosper, there is no chain of cause and effect described in economic materialism which enables anyone to prophesy whether the owner will take a long view or a short one, a competitive or a cooperative.

Did the theory have the validity which is so often claimed for it, it would enable us to prophesy. We could analyze the economic interests of a people, and deduce what the people was bound to do. Marx tried that, and after a good guess about the trusts, went wholly wrong. The first socialist experiment came, not as he predicted, out of the culmination of capitalist development in the West, but out of the collapse of a pre-capitalist system in the East. Why did he go wrong? Why did his greatest disciple, Lenin, go wrong? Because the Marxians thought that men's economic position would irresistibly produce a clear conception of their economic interests. They thought they themselves possessed that clear conception, and that what they knew the rest of mankind would learn. The event has shown, not only that a clear conception of interest does not arise automatically in everyone, but that it did not arise even in Marx and Lenin themselves. After all that Marx and Lenin have written, the social behavior of mankind is still obscure. It ought not to be, if economic position alone determined public opinion. Position ought, if their theory were correct, not only to divide mankind into classes, but to supply each class with a view of its interest and a coherent policy for obtaining it. Yet nothing is more certain than that all classes of men are in constant perplexity as to what their interests are. [Footnote: As a matter of fact, when it came to the test, Lenin completely abandoned the materialistic interpretation of politics. Had he held sincerely to the Marxian formula when he seized power in 1917, he would have said to himself: according to the teachings of Marx, socialism will develop out of a mature capitalism... here am I, in control of a nation that is only entering upon a capitalist development... it is true that I am a socialist, but I am a scientific socialist... it follows that for the present all idea of a socialist republic is out of the question... we must advance capitalism in order that the evolution which Marx predicted may take place. But Lenin did nothing of the sort. Instead of waiting for evolution to evolve, he tried by will, force, and education, to defy the historical process which his philosophy assumed.

Since this was written Lenin has abandoned communism on the ground that Russia does not possess the necessary basis in a mature capitalism. He now says

307

that Russia must create capitalism, which will create a proletariat, which will some day create communism. This is at least consistent with Marxist dogma. But it shows how little determinism there is in the opinions of a determinist.]

This dissolves the impact of economic determinism. For if our economic interests are made up of our variable concepts of those interests, then as the master key to social processes the theory fails. That theory assumes that men are capable of adopting only one version of their interest, and that having adopted it, they move fatally to realize it. It assumes the existence of a specific class interest. That assumption is false. A class interest can be conceived largely or narrowly, selfishly or unselfishly, in the light of no facts, some facts, many facts, truth and error. And so collapses the Marxian remedy for class conflicts. That remedy assumes that if all property could be held in common, class differences would disappear. The assumption is false. Property might well be held in common, and yet not be conceived as a whole. The moment any group of people failed to see communism in a communist manner, they would divide into classes on the basis of what they saw.

In respect to the existing social order Marxian socialism emphasizes property conflict as the maker of opinion, in respect to the loosely defined working class it ignores property conflict as the basis of agitation, in respect to the future it imagines a society without property conflict, and, therefore, without conflict of opinion. Now in the existing social order there may be more instances where one man must lose if another is to gain, than there would be under socialism, but for every case where one must lose for another to gain, there are endless cases where men simply imagine the conflict because they are uneducated. And under socialism, though you removed every instance of absolute conflict, the partial access of each man to the whole range of facts would nevertheless create conflict. A socialist state will not be able to dispense with education, morality, or liberal science, though on strict materialistic grounds the communal ownership of properties ought to make them superfluous. The communists in Russia would not propagate their faith with such unflagging zeal if economic determinism were alone determining the opinion of the Russian people.

5

The socialist theory of human nature is, like the hedonistic calculus, an example of false determinism. Both assume that the unlearned dispositions

The Walter Lippmann Reader

fatally but intelligently produce a certain type of behavior. The socialist believes that the dispositions pursue the economic interest of a class; the hedonist believes that they pursue pleasure and avoid pain. Both theories rest on a naive view of instinct, a view, defined by James, [Footnote: *Principles of Psychology*, Vol. II, p. 383.] though radically qualified by him, as "the faculty of acting in such a way as to produce certain ends, without foresight of the ends and without previous education in the performance."

It is doubtful whether instinctive action of this sort figures at all in the social life of mankind. For as James pointed out: [Footnote: *Op. cit.*, Vol. II, p. 390.] "every instinctive act in an animal with memory must cease to be 'blind' after being once repeated." Whatever the equipment at birth, the innate dispositions are from earliest infancy immersed in experience which determines what shall excite them as stimulus. "They become capable," as Mr. McDougall says, [Footnote: Introduction to *Social Psychology*, Fourth Edition, pp. 31-32.] "of being initiated, not only by the perception of objects of the kind which directly excite the innate disposition, the natural or native excitants of the instinct, but also by ideas of such objects, and by perceptions and by ideas of objects of other kinds." [Footnote: "Most definitions of instincts and instinctive actions take account only of their conative aspects... and it is a common mistake to ignore the cognitive and affective aspects of the instinctive mental process." Footnote *op. cit.*, p. 29.]

It is only the "central part of the disposition" [Footnote: p. 34.] says Mr. McDougall further, "that retains its specific character and remains common to all individuals and all situations in which the instinct is excited." The cognitive processes, and the actual bodily movements by which the instinct achieves its end may be indefinitely complicated. In other words, man has an instinct of fear, but what he will fear and how he will try to escape, is determined not from birth, but by experience.

If it were not for this variability, it would be difficult to conceive the inordinate variety of human nature. But when you consider that all the important tendencies of the creature, his appetites, his loves, his hates, his curiosity, his sexual cravings, his fears, and pugnacity, are freely attachable to all sorts of objects as stimulus, and to all kinds of objects as gratification, the complexity of human nature is not so inconceivable. And when you think that each new generation is the casual victim of the way a previous generation was conditioned, as well as the inheritor of the environment that resulted, the possible combinations and permutations are enormous.

There is no prima facie case then for supposing that because persons crave some particular thing, or behave in some particular way, human nature is fatally constituted to crave that and act thus. The craving and the action are both learned, and in another generation might be learned differently. Analytic psychology and social history unite in supporting this conclusion. Psychology indicates how essentially casual is the nexus between the particular stimulus and the particular response. Anthropology in the widest sense reinforces the view by demonstrating that the things which have excited men's passions, and the means which they have used to realize them, differ endlessly from age to age and from place to place.

Men pursue their interest. But how they shall pursue it is not fatally determined, and, therefore, within whatever limits of time this planet will continue to support human life, man can set no term upon the creative energies of men. He can issue no doom of automatism. He can say, if he must, that for his life there will be no changes which he can recognize as good. But in saying that he will be confining his life to what he can see with his eye, rejecting what he might see with his mind; he will be taking as the measure of good a measure which is only the one he happens to possess. He can find no ground for abandoning his highest hopes and relaxing his conscious effort unless he chooses to regard the unknown as the unknowable, unless he elects to believe that what no one knows no one will know, and that what someone has not yet learned no one will ever be able to teach.

PART V
THE MAKING OF A
COMMON WILL

CHAPTER XIII

The Transfer of Interest

This goes to show that there are many variables in each man's impressions of the invisible world. The points of contact vary, the stereotyped expectations vary, the interest enlisted varies most subtly of all. The living impressions of a large number of people are to an immeasurable degree personal in each of them, and unmanageably complex in the mass. How, then, is any practical relationship established between what is in people's heads and what is out there beyond their ken in the environment? How in the language of democratic theory, do great numbers of people feeling each so privately about so abstract a picture, develop any common will? How does a simple and constant idea emerge from this complex of variables? How are those things known as the Will of the People, or the National Purpose, or Public Opinion crystallized out of such fleeting and casual imagery?

That there is a real difficulty here was shown by an angry tilt in the spring of 1921 between the American Ambassador to England and a very large number of other Americans. Mr. Harvey, speaking at a British dinner table, had assured the world without the least sign of hesitancy what were the motives of Americans in 1917. [Footnote: *New York Times*, May 20, 1921.] As he described them, they were not the motives which President Wilson had insisted upon when *he* enunciated the American mind. Now, of course, neither Mr. Harvey nor Mr. Wilson, nor the critics and friends of either, nor any one else, can know quantitatively and qualitatively what went on in thirty or forty million adult minds. But what everybody knows is that a war was fought and won by a multitude of efforts, stimulated, no one knows in what proportion, by the motives of Wilson and the motives of Harvey and all kinds of hybrids of the two. People enlisted and fought, worked, paid taxes, sacrificed to a common end, and yet no one can begin to say exactly what moved each person to do each thing that he did. It is no use, then, Mr. Harvey telling a soldier who thought this was a war to end war that the soldier did not think any such thing. The soldier who thought that *thought that*. And Mr. Harvey, who thought something else, thought *something else*.

In the same speech Mr. Harvey formulated with equal clarity what the voters of 1920 had in their minds. That is a rash thing to do, and, if you simply assume that all who voted your ticket voted as you did, then it is a disingenuous thing to do. The count shows that sixteen millions voted Republican, and nine millions Democratic. They voted, says Mr. Harvey, for and against the League of Nations, and in support of this claim, he can point to Mr. Wilson's request for a referendum, and to the undeniable fact that the Democratic party and Mr. Cox insisted that the League was the issue. But then, saying that the League was the issue did not make the League the issue, and by counting the votes on election day you do not know the real division of opinion about the League. There were, for example, nine million Democrats. Are you entitled to believe that all of them are staunch supporters of the League? Certainly you are not. For your knowledge of American politics tells you that many of the millions voted, as they always do, to maintain the existing social system in the South, and that whatever their views on the League, they did not vote to express their views. Those who wanted the League were no doubt pleased that the Democratic party wanted it too. Those who disliked the League may have held their noses as they voted. But both groups of Southerners voted the same ticket.

Were the Republicans more unanimous? Anybody can pick Republican voters enough out of his circle of friends to cover the whole gamut of opinion from the irreconcilability of Senators Johnson and Knox to the advocacy of Secretary Hoover and Chief Justice Taft. No one can say definitely how many people felt in any particular way about the League, nor how many people let their feelings on that subject determine their vote. When there are only two ways of expressing a hundred varieties of feeling, there is no certain way of knowing what the decisive combination was. Senator Borah found in the Republican ticket a reason for voting Republican, but so did President Lowell. The Republican majority was composed of men and women who thought a Republican victory would kill the League, plus those who thought it the most practical way to secure the League, plus those who thought it the surest way offered to obtain an amended League. All these voters were inextricably entangled with their own desire, or the desire of other voters to improve business, or put labor in its place,

The Walter Lippmann Reader

or to punish the Democrats for going to war, or to punish them for not having gone sooner, or to get rid of Mr. Burleson, or to improve the price of wheat, or to lower taxes, or to stop Mr. Daniels from outbuilding the world, or to help Mr. Harding do the same thing.

And yet a sort of decision emerged; Mr. Harding moved into the White House. For the least common denominator of all the votes was that the Democrats should go and the Republicans come in. That was the only factor remaining after all the contradictions had cancelled each other out. But that factor was enough to alter policy for four years. The precise reasons why change was desired on that November day in 1920 are not recorded, not even in the memories of the individual voters. The reasons are not fixed. They grow and change and melt into other reasons, so that the public opinions Mr. Harding has to deal with are not the opinions that elected him. That there is no inevitable connection between an assortment of opinions and a particular line of action everyone saw in 1916. Elected apparently on the cry that he kept us out of war, Mr. Wilson within five months led the country into war.

The working of the popular will, therefore, has always called for explanation. Those who have been most impressed by its erratic working have found a prophet in M. LeBon, and have welcomed generalizations about what Sir Robert Peel called "that great compound of folly, weakness, prejudice, wrong feeling, right feeling, obstinacy and newspaper paragraphs which is called public opinion." Others have concluded that since out of drift and incoherence, settled aims do appear, there must be a mysterious contrivance at work somewhere over and above the inhabitants of a nation. They invoke a collective soul, a national mind, a spirit of the age which imposes order upon random opinion. An oversoul seems to be needed, for the emotions and ideas in the members of a group do not disclose anything so simple and so crystalline as the formula which those same individuals will accept as a true statement of their Public Opinion.

2

But the facts can, I think, be explained more convincingly without the help of the oversoul in any of its disguises. After all, the art of inducing all sorts of people who think differently to vote alike is practiced in every political campaign. In 1916, for example, the Republican candidate had to produce Republican votes out of many different kinds of Republicans. Let us look at Mr.

Hughes' first speech after accepting the nomination. [Footnote: Delivered at Carnegie Hall, New York City, July 31, 1916.] The context is still clear enough in our minds to obviate much explanation; yet the issues are no longer contentious. The candidate was a man of unusually plain speech, who had been out of politics for several years and was not personally committed on the issues of the recent past. He had, moreover, none of that wizardry which popular leaders like Roosevelt, Wilson, or Lloyd George possess, none of that histrionic gift by which such men impersonate the feelings of their followers. From that aspect of politics he was by temperament and by training remote. But yet he knew by calculation what the politician's technic is. He was one of those people who know just how to do a thing, but who can not quite do it themselves. They are often better teachers than the virtuoso to whom the art is so much second nature that he himself does not know how he does it. The statement that those who can, do; those who cannot, teach, is not nearly so much of a reflection on the teacher as it sounds.

Mr. Hughes knew the occasion was momentous, and he had prepared his manuscript carefully. In a box sat Theodore Roosevelt just back from Missouri. All over the house sat the veterans of Armageddon in various stages of doubt and dismay. On the platform and in the other boxes the ex-whited sepulchres and ex-second-story men of 1912 were to be seen, obviously in the best of health and in a melting mood. Out beyond the hall there were powerful pro-Germans and powerful pro-Allies; a war party in the East and in the big cities; a peace party in the middle and far West. There was strong feeling about Mexico. Mr. Hughes had to form a majority against the Democrats out of people divided into all sorts of combinations on Taft vs. Roosevelt, pro-Germans vs. pro-Allies, war vs. neutrality, Mexican intervention vs. non-intervention.

About the morality or the wisdom of the affair we are, of course, not concerned here. Our only interest is in the method by which a leader of heterogeneous opinion goes about the business of securing a homogeneous vote.

"This *representative* gathering is a happy augury. It means the strength of *reunion*. It means that the party of *Lincoln* is restored...."

The italicized words are binders: *Lincoln* in such a speech has of course, no relation to Abraham Lincoln. It is merely a stereotype by which the piety which surrounds that name can be transferred to the Republican candidate who now stands in his shoes. Lincoln reminds the Republicans, Bull Moose and Old Guard, that before the schism they had a common history. About the schism no one can afford to speak. But it is there, as yet unhealed.

The speaker must heal it. Now the schism of 1912 had arisen over domestic questions; the reunion of 1916 was, as Mr. Roosevelt had declared, to be based on a common indignation against Mr. Wilson's conduct of international affairs. But international affairs were also a dangerous source of conflict. It was necessary to find an opening subject which would not only ignore 1912 but would avoid also the explosive conflicts of 1916. The speaker skilfully selected the spoils system in diplomatic appointments. "Deserving Democrats" was a discrediting phrase, and Mr. Hughes at once evokes it. The record being indefensible, there is no hesitation in the vigor of the attack. Logically it was an ideal introduction to a common mood.

Mr. Hughes then turns to Mexico, beginning with an historical review. He had to consider the general sentiment that affairs were going badly in Mexico; also, a no less general sentiment that war should be avoided; and two powerful currents of opinion, one of which said President Wilson was right in not recognizing Huerta, the other which preferred Huerta to Carranza, and intervention to both. Huerta was the first sore spot in the record...

"He was certainly in fact the head of the Government in Mexico."

But the moralists who regarded Huerta as a drunken murderer had to be placated.

"Whether or not he should be recognized was a question to be determined in the exercise of a sound discretion, but according to correct principles."

So instead of saying that Huerta should have been recognized, the candidate says that correct principles ought to be applied. Everybody believes in correct principles, and everybody, of course, believes he possesses them. To blur the issue still further President Wilson's policy is described as "intervention." It was that in law, perhaps, but not in the sense then currently meant by the word. By stretching the word to cover what Mr. Wilson had done, as well as what the real interventionists wanted, the issue between the two factions was to be repressed.

Having got by the two explosive points "*Huerta*" and "*intervention*" by letting the words mean all things to all men, the speech passes for a while to safer ground. The candidate tells the story of Tampico, Vera Cruz, Villa, Santa Ysabel, Columbus and Carrizal. Mr. Hughes is specific, either because the facts as known from the newspapers are irritating, or because the true explanation is, as for example in regard to Tampico, too complicated. No contrary passions could be aroused by such a record. But at the end the candidate had to take a position. His audience expected it. The indictment was Mr. Roosevelt's. Would Mr. Hughes adopt his remedy, intervention?

"The nation has no policy of aggression toward Mexico. We have no desire for any part of her territory. We wish her to have peace, stability and prosperity. We should be ready to aid her in binding up her wounds, in relieving her from starvation and distress, in giving her in every practicable way the benefits of our disinterested friendship. The conduct of this administration has created difficulties which we shall have to surmount.... *We shall have to adopt a new policy*, a policy of *firmness* and consistency through which alone we can promote an enduring *friendship*."

The theme friendship is for the non-interventionists, the theme "new policy" and "firmness" is for the interventionists. On the non-contentious record, the detail is overwhelming; on the issue everything is cloudy.

Concerning the European war Mr. Hughes employed an ingenious formula:

"I stand for the unflinching maintenance of *all* American rights on land and sea."

In order to understand the force of that statement at the time it was spoken, we must remember how each faction during the period of neutrality believed that the nations it opposed in Europe were alone violating American rights. Mr. Hughes seemed to say to the pro-Allies: I would have coerced Germany. But the pro-Germans had been insisting that British sea power was violating most of our rights. The formula covers two diametrically opposed purposes by the symbolic phrase "American rights."

But there was the Lusitania. Like the 1912 schism, it was an invincible obstacle to harmony.

"... I am confident that there would have been no destruction of American lives by the sinking of the Lusitania."

Thus, what cannot be compromised must be obliterated, when there is a question on which we cannot all hope to get together, let us pretend that it does not exist. About the future of American relations with Europe Mr. Hughes was silent. Nothing he could say would possibly please the two irreconcilable factions for whose support he was bidding.

It is hardly necessary to say that Mr. Hughes did not invent this technic and did not employ it with the utmost success. But he illustrated how a public opinion constituted out of divergent opinions is clouded; how its meaning approaches the neutral tint formed out of the blending of many colors. Where superficial harmony is the aim and conflict the fact, obscurantism in a public appeal is the usual result. Almost always vagueness at a crucial point in public debate is a symptom of cross-purposes.

3

But how is it that a vague idea so often has the power to unite deeply felt opinions? These opinions, we recall, however deeply they may be felt, are not in continual and pungent contact with the facts they profess to treat. On the unseen environment, Mexico, the European war, our grip is slight though our feeling may be intense. The original pictures and words which aroused it have not anything like the force of the feeling itself. The account of what has happened out of sight and hearing in a place where we have never been, has not and never can have, except briefly as in a dream or fantasy, all the dimensions of reality. But it can arouse all, and sometimes even more emotion than the reality. For the trigger can be pulled by more than one stimulus.

The stimulus which originally pulled the trigger may have been a series of pictures in the mind aroused by printed or spoken words. These pictures fade and are hard to keep steady; their contours and their pulse fluctuate. Gradually the process sets in of knowing what you feel without being entirely certain why you feel it. The fading pictures are displaced by other pictures, and then by names or symbols. But the emotion goes on, capable now of being aroused by the substituted images and names. Even in severe thinking these substitutions take place, for if a man is trying to compare two complicated situations, he soon finds exhausting the attempt to hold both fully in mind in all their detail. He employs a shorthand of names and signs and samples. He has to do this if he is to advance at all, because he cannot carry the whole baggage in every phrase through every step he takes. But if he forgets that he has substituted and simplified, he soon lapses into verbalism, and begins to talk about names regardless of objects. And then he has no way of knowing when the name divorced from its first thing is carrying on a misalliance with some other thing. It is more difficult still to guard against changelings in casual politics.

For by what is known to psychologists as conditioned response, an emotion is not attached merely to one idea. There are no end of things which can arouse the emotion, and no end of things which can satisfy it. This is particularly true where the stimulus is only dimly and indirectly perceived, and where the objective is likewise indirect. For you can associate an emotion, say fear, first with something immediately dangerous, then with the idea of that thing, then with something similar to that idea, and so on and on. The whole structure of human culture is in one respect an elaboration of the stimuli and responses of which the original emotional capacities remain a fairly fixed center. No doubt the quality of emotion has changed in the course of history, but with nothing like the speed, or elaboration, that has characterized the conditioning of it.

People differ widely in their susceptibility to ideas. There are some in whom the idea of a starving child in Russia is practically as vivid as a starving child within sight. There are others who are almost incapable of being excited by a distant idea. There are many gradations between. And there are people who are insensitive to facts, and aroused only by ideas. But though the emotion is aroused by the idea, we are unable to satisfy the emotion by acting ourselves upon the scene itself. The idea of the starving Russian child evokes a desire to feed the child. But the person so aroused cannot feed it. He can only give money to an impersonal organization, or to a personification which he calls Mr. Hoover. His money does not reach that child. It goes to a general pool from which a mass of children are fed. And so just as the idea is second hand, so are the effects of the action second hand. The cognition is indirect, the conation is indirect, only the effect is immediate. Of the three parts of the process, the stimulus comes from somewhere out of sight, the response reaches somewhere out of sight, only the emotion exists entirely within the person. Of the child's hunger he has only an idea, of the child's relief he has only an idea, but of his own desire to help he has a real experience. It is the central fact of the business, the emotion within himself, which is first hand.

Within limits that vary, the emotion is transferable both as regards stimulus and response. Therefore, if among a number of people, possessing various tendencies to respond, you can find a stimulus which will arouse the same emotion in many of them, you can substitute it for the original stimuli. If, for example, one man dislikes the League, another hates Mr. Wilson, and a third fears labor, you may be able to unite them if you can find some symbol which is the antithesis of what they all hate. Suppose that symbol is Americanism. The first man may read it as meaning the preservation of American isolation, or as he may call it, independence; the second as the rejection of a politician who clashes with his idea of what an American president should be, the third as a call to resist revolution. The symbol in itself signifies literally no one thing in particular, but it can be associated with almost anything. And because of that it can become the common bond of common feelings, even though those feelings were originally attached to disparate ideas.

When political parties or newspapers declare for Americanism, Progressivism, Law and Order, Justice, Humanity, they hope to amalgamate the emotion of conflicting factions which would surely divide, if, instead of these symbols, they were invited to discuss a specific program. For when a coalition around the symbol has been effected, feeling flows toward conformity under the symbol rather than toward critical scrutiny of the measures. It is, I think, convenient and technically correct to call multiple phrases like these symbolic. They do not stand for specific ideas, but for a sort of truce or junction between ideas. They are like a strategic railroad center where many roads converge regardless of their ultimate origin or their ultimate destination. But he who captures the symbols by which public feeling is for the moment contained, controls by that much the approaches of public policy. And as long as a particular symbol has the power of coalition, ambitious factions will fight for possession. Think, for example, of Lincoln's name or of Roosevelt's. A leader or an interest that can make itself master of current symbols is master of the current situation. There are limits, of course. Too violent abuse of the actualities which groups of people think the symbol represents, or too great resistance in the name of that symbol to new purposes, will, so to speak, burst the symbol. In this manner, during the year

1917, the imposing symbol of Holy Russia and the Little Father burst under the impact of suffering and defeat.

4

The tremendous consequences of Russia's collapse were felt on all the fronts and among all the peoples. They led directly to a striking experiment in the crystallization of a common opinion out of the varieties of opinion churned up by the war. The Fourteen Points were addressed to all the governments, allied, enemy, neutral, and to all the peoples. They were an attempt to knit together the chief imponderables of a world war. Necessarily this was a new departure, because this was the first great war in which all the deciding elements of mankind could be brought to think about the same ideas, or at least about the same names for ideas, simultaneously. Without cable, radio, telegraph, and daily press, the experiment of the Fourteen Points would have been impossible. It was an attempt to exploit the modern machinery of communication to start the return to a "common consciousness" throughout the world.

But first we must examine some of the circumstances as they presented themselves at the end of 1917. For in the form which the document finally assumed, all these considerations are somehow represented. During the summer and autumn a series of events had occurred which profoundly affected the temper of the people and the course of the war. In July the Russians had made a last offensive, had been disastrously beaten, and the process of demoralization which led to the Bolshevik revolution of November had begun. Somewhat earlier the French had suffered a severe and almost disastrous defeat in Champagne which produced mutinies in the army and a defeatist agitation among the civilians. England was suffering from the effects of the submarine raids, from the terrible losses of the Flanders battles, and in November at Cambrai the British armies met a reverse that appalled the troops at the front and the leaders at home. Extreme war weariness pervaded the whole of western Europe.

In effect, the agony and disappointment had jarred loose men's concentration on the accepted version of the war. Their interests were no longer held by the ordinary official pronouncements, and their attention began to wander, fixing now upon their own suffering, now upon their party and class purposes, now upon general resentments against the governments. That more or less perfect organization of perception by official propaganda, of interest and attention by

320

the stimuli of hope, fear, and hatred, which is called morale, was by way of breaking down. The minds of men everywhere began to search for new attachments that promised relief.

Suddenly they beheld a tremendous drama. On the Eastern front there was a Christmas truce, an end of slaughter, an end of noise, a promise of peace. At Brest-Litovsk the dream of all simple people had come to life: it was possible to negotiate, there was some other way to end the ordeal than by matching lives with the enemy. Timidly, but with rapt attention, people began to turn to the East. Why not, they asked? What is it all for? Do the politicians know what they are doing? Are we really fighting for what they say? Is it possible, perhaps, to secure it without fighting? Under the ban of the censorship, little of this was allowed to show itself in print, but, when Lord Lansdowne spoke, there was a response from the heart. The earlier symbols of the war had become hackneyed, and had lost their power to unify. Beneath the surface a wide schism was opening up in each Allied country.

Something similar was happening in Central Europe. There too the original impulse of the war was weakened; the union sacrée was broken. The vertical cleavages along the battle front were cut across by horizontal divisions running in all kinds of unforeseeable ways. The moral crisis of the war had arrived before the military decision was in sight. All this President Wilson and his advisers realized. They had not, of course, a perfect knowledge of the situation, but what I have sketched they knew.

They knew also that the Allied Governments were bound by a series of engagements that in letter and in spirit ran counter to the popular conception of what the war was about. The resolutions of the Paris Economic Conference were, of course, public property, and the network of secret treaties had been published by the Bolsheviks in November of 1917. [Footnote: President Wilson stated at his conference with the Senators that he had never heard of these treaties until he reached Paris. That statement is perplexing. The Fourteen Points, as the text shows, could not have been formulated without a knowledge of the secret treaties. The substance of those treaties was before the President when he and Colonel House prepared the final published text of the Fourteen Points.] Their terms were only vaguely known to the peoples, but it was definitely believed that they did not comport with the idealistic slogan of self-determination, no annexations and no indemnities. Popular questioning took the form of asking how many thousand English lives Alsace-Lorraine or Dalmatia were worth, how many French lives Poland or Mesopotamia were worth. Nor was such questioning entirely unknown in America. The whole Allied cause had been put on the defensive by the refusal to participate at Brest-Litovsk.

Here was a highly sensitive state of mind which no competent leader could fail to consider. The ideal response would have been joint action by the Allies. That was found to be impossible when it was considered at the Interallied Conference of October. But by December the pressure had become so great that Mr. George and Mr. Wilson were moved independently to make some response. The form selected by the President was a statement of peace terms under fourteen heads. The numbering of them was an artifice to secure precision, and to create at once the impression that here was a business-like document. The idea of stating "peace terms" instead of "war aims" arose from the necessity of establishing a genuine alternative to the Brest-Litovsk negotiations. They were intended to compete for attention by substituting for the spectacle of Russo-German parleys the much grander spectacle of a public world-wide debate.

Having enlisted the interest of the world, it was necessary to hold that interest unified and flexible for all the different possibilities which the situation contained. The terms had to be such that the majority among the Allies would regard them as worth while. They had to meet the national aspirations of each people, and yet to limit those aspirations so that no one nation would regard itself as a catspaw for another. The terms had to satisfy official interests so as not to provoke official disunion, and yet they had to meet popular conceptions so as to prevent the spread of demoralization. They had, in short, to preserve and confirm Allied unity in case the war was to go on.

But they had also to be the terms of a possible peace, so that in case the German center and left were ripe for agitation, they would have a text with which to smite the governing class. The terms had, therefore, to push the Allied governors nearer to their people, drive the German governors away from their people, and establish a line of common understanding between the Allies, the non-official Germans, and the subject peoples of Austria-Hungary. The Fourteen Points were a daring attempt to raise a standard to which almost everyone might repair. If a sufficient number of the enemy people were ready there would be peace; if not, then the Allies would be better prepared to sustain the shock of war.

The Walter Lippmann Reader

All these considerations entered into the making of the Fourteen Points. No one man may have had them all in mind, but all the men concerned had some of them in mind. Against this background let us examine certain aspects of the document. The first five points and the fourteenth deal with "open diplomacy," "freedom of the seas," "equal trade opportunities," "reduction of armaments," no imperialist annexation of colonies, and the League of Nations. They might be described as a statement of the popular generalizations in which everyone at that time professed to believe. But number three is more specific. It was aimed consciously and directly at the resolutions of the Paris Economic Conference, and was meant to relieve the German people of their fear of suffocation.

Number six is the first point dealing with a particular nation. It was intended as a reply to Russian suspicion of the Allies, and the eloquence of its promises was attuned to the drama of Brest-Litovsk. Number seven deals with Belgium, and is as unqualified in form and purpose as was the conviction of practically the whole world, including very large sections of Central Europe. Over number eight we must pause. It begins with an absolute demand for evacuation and restoration of French territory, and then passes on to the question of Alsace-Lorraine. The phrasing of this clause most perfectly illustrates the character of a public statement which must condense a vast complex of interests in a few words. "And the wrong done to France by Prussia in 1871 in the matter of Alsace-Lorraine, which has unsettled the peace of the world for nearly fifty years, should be righted. ..." Every word here was chosen with meticulous care. The wrong done should be righted; why not say that Alsace-Lorraine should be restored? It was not said, because it was not certain that all of the French *at that time* would fight on indefinitely for reannexation if they were offered a plebiscite; and because it was even less certain whether the English and Italians would fight on. The formula had, therefore, to cover both contingencies. The word "righted" guaranteed satisfaction to France, but did not read as a commitment to simple annexation. But why speak of the wrong done by *Prussia* in *1871*? The word Prussia was, of course, intended to remind the South Germans that Alsace-Lorraine belonged not to them but to Prussia. Why speak of peace unsettled for "fifty years," and why the use of "1871"? In the first place, what the French and the rest of the world remembered was 1871. That was the nodal point of their grievance. But the formulators of the Fourteen Points knew that French officialdom planned for more than the Alsace-Lorraine of 1871. The secret memoranda that had passed between the Czar's ministers and French officials in 1916 covered the annexation of the Saar Valley and some sort of dismemberment of the Rhineland. It was planned to include the Saar Valley under the term "Alsace-Lorraine" because it had been part of Alsace-Lorraine in 1814, though it had been detached in 1815, and was no part of the territory at the close of the Franco-Prussian war. The official French formula for annexing the Saar was to subsume it under "Alsace-Lorraine" meaning the Alsace-Lorraine of 1814-1815. By insistence on "1871" the President was really defining the ultimate boundary between Germany and France, was adverting to the secret treaty, and was casting it aside.

Number nine, a little less subtly, does the same thing in respect to Italy. "Clearly recognizable lines of nationality" are exactly what the lines of the Treaty of London were not. Those lines were partly strategic, partly economic, partly imperialistic, partly ethnic. The only part of them that could possibly procure allied sympathy was that which would recover the genuine Italia Irredenta. All the rest, as everyone who was informed knew, merely delayed the impending Jugoslav revolt.

5

It would be a mistake to suppose that the apparently unanimous enthusiasm which greeted the Fourteen Points represented agreement on a program. Everyone seemed to find something that he liked and stressed this aspect and that detail. But no one risked a discussion. The phrases, so pregnant with the underlying conflicts of the civilized world, were accepted. They stood for opposing ideas, but they evoked a common emotion. And to that extent they played a part in rallying the western peoples for the desperate ten months of war which they had still to endure.

As long as the Fourteen Points dealt with that hazy and happy future when the agony was to be over, the real conflicts of interpretation were not made manifest. They were plans for the settlement of a wholly invisible environment, and because these plans inspired all groups each with its own private hope, all hopes ran together as a public hope. For harmonization, as we saw in Mr. Hughes's speech, is a hierarchy of symbols. As you ascend the hierarchy in order to include more and more factions you may for a time preserve the emotional connection though you lose the intellectual. But even the emotion becomes thinner. As you go further away from experience, you go higher into generalization or subtlety. As you go up in the balloon you throw more and more concrete objects overboard, and when you have reached the top with some phrase like the Rights of Humanity or the World Made Safe for Democracy, you see far and wide, but you see very little. Yet the people whose emotions are entrained do not remain passive. As the public appeal becomes more and more all things to all men, as the emotion is stirred while the meaning is dispersed, their very private meanings are given a universal application. Whatever you want badly is the Rights of Humanity. For the phrase, ever more vacant, capable of meaning almost anything, soon comes to mean pretty nearly everything. Mr. Wilson's phrases were understood in endlessly different ways in every corner of the earth. No document negotiated and made of public record existed to correct the confusion. [Footnote: The American interpretation of the fourteen points was explained to the allied statesmen just before the armistice.] And so, when the day of settlement came, everybody expected everything. The European authors of the treaty had a large choice, and they chose to realize those expectations which were held by those of their countrymen who wielded the most power at home.

They came down the hierarchy from the Rights of Humanity to the Rights of France, Britain and Italy. They did not abandon the use of symbols. They abandoned only those which after the war had no permanent roots in the imagination of their constituents. They preserved the unity of France by the use of symbolism, but they would not risk anything for the unity of Europe. The symbol France was deeply attached, the symbol Europe had only a recent history. Nevertheless the distinction between an omnibus like Europe and a symbol like France is not sharp. The history of states and empires reveals times when the scope of the unifying idea increases and also times when it shrinks. One cannot say that men have moved consistently from smaller loyalties to larger ones, because the facts will not bear out the claim. The Roman Empire and the Holy Roman Empire bellied out further than those national unifications in the Nineteenth Century from which believers in a World State argue by analogy. Nevertheless, it is probably true that the real integration has increased regardless of the temporary inflation and deflation of empires.

The Walter Lippmann Reader

Such a real integration has undoubtedly occurred in American history. In the decade before 1789 most men, it seems, felt that their state and their community were real, but that the confederation of states was unreal. The idea of their state, its flag, its most conspicuous leaders, or whatever it was that represented Massachusetts, or Virginia, were genuine symbols. That is to say, they were fed by actual experiences from childhood, occupation, residence, and the like. The span of men's experience had rarely traversed the imaginary boundaries of their states. The word Virginian was related to pretty nearly everything that most Virginians had ever known or felt. It was the most extensive political idea which had genuine contact with their experience.

Their experience, not their needs. For their needs arose out of their real environment, which in those days was at least as large as the thirteen colonies. They needed a common defense. They needed a financial and economic regime as extensive as the Confederation. But as long as the pseudo-environment of the state encompassed them, the state symbols exhausted their political interest. An interstate idea, like the Confederation, represented a powerless abstraction. It was an omnibus, rather than a symbol, and the harmony among divergent groups, which the omnibus creates, is transient.

I have said that the idea of confederation was a powerless abstraction. Yet the need of unity existed in the decade before the Constitution was adopted. The need existed, in the sense that affairs were askew unless the need of unity was taken into account. Gradually certain classes in each colony began to break through the state experience. Their personal interests led across the state lines to interstate experiences, and gradually there was constructed in their minds a picture of the American environment which was truly national in scope. For them the idea of federation became a true symbol, and ceased to be an omnibus. The most imaginative of these men was Alexander Hamilton. It happened that he had no primitive attachment to any one state, for he was born in the West Indies, and had, from the very beginning of his active life, been associated with the common interests of all the states. Thus to most men of the time the question of whether the capital should be in Virginia or in Philadelphia was of enormous importance, because they were locally minded. To Hamilton this question was of no emotional consequence; what he wanted was the assumption of the state debts because they would further nationalize the proposed union. So he gladly traded the site of the capitol for two necessary votes from men who represented the Potomac district. To Hamilton the Union was a symbol that represented all his interests and his whole experience; to White and Lee from the Potomac, the symbol of their province was the highest political entity they served, and they served it though they hated to pay the price. They agreed, says Jefferson, to change their votes, "White with a revulsion of stomach almost convulsive." [Footnote: *Works*, Vol. IX, p. 87. Cited by Beard, *Economic Origins of Jeffersonian Democracy*, p. 172.]

In the crystallizing of a common will, there is always an Alexander Hamilton at work.

CHAPTER XIV

Yes or No

1

Symbols are often so useful and so mysteriously powerful that the word itself exhales a magical glamor. In thinking about symbols it is tempting to treat them as if they possessed independent energy. Yet no end of symbols which once provoked ecstasy have quite ceased to affect anybody. The museums and the books of folklore are full of dead emblems and incantations, since there is no power in the symbol, except that which it acquires by association in the human mind. The symbols that have lost their power, and the symbols incessantly suggested which fail to take root, remind us that if we were patient enough to study in detail the circulation of a symbol, we should behold an entirely secular history.

In the Hughes campaign speech, in the Fourteen Points, in Hamilton's project, symbols are employed. But they are employed by somebody at a particular moment. The words themselves do not crystallize random feeling. The words must be spoken by people who are strategically placed, and they must be spoken at the opportune moment. Otherwise they are mere wind. The symbols must be earmarked. For in themselves they mean nothing, and the choice of possible symbols is always so great that we should, like the donkey who stood equidistant between two bales of hay, perish from sheer indecision among the symbols that compete for our attention.

Here, for example, are the reasons for their vote as stated by certain private citizens to a newspaper just before the election of 1920.

For Harding:

"The patriotic men and women of to-day, who cast their ballots for Harding and Coolidge will be held by posterity to have signed our Second Declaration of Independence."
Mr. Wilmot—, inventor.

"He will see to it that the United States does not enter into 'entangling alliances,' Washington as a city will benefit by changing the control of the government from the Democrats to the Republicans."

The Walter Lippmann Reader

Mr. Clarence—, salesman.

For Cox:
"The people of the United States realize that it is our duty pledged on the fields of France, to join the League of Nations. We must shoulder our share of the burden of enforcing peace throughout the world."
Miss Marie—, stenographer.

"We should lose our own respect and the respect of other nations were we to refuse to enter the League of Nations in obtaining international peace."
Mr. Spencer—, statistician.
The two sets of phrases are equally noble, equally true, and almost reversible. Would Clarence and Wilmot have admitted for an instant that they intended to default in our duty pledged on the fields of France; or that they did not desire international peace? Certainly not. Would Marie and Spencer have admitted that they were in favor of entangling alliances or the surrender of American independence? They would have argued with you that the League was, as President Wilson called it, a disentangling alliance, as well as a Declaration of Independence for all the world, plus a Monroe Doctrine for the planet.

2

Since the offering of symbols is so generous, and the meaning that can be imputed is so elastic, how does any particular symbol take root in any particular person's mind? It is planted there by another human being whom we recognize as authoritative. If it is planted deeply enough, it may be that later we shall call the person authoritative who waves that symbol at us. But in the first instance symbols are made congenial and important because they are introduced to us by congenial and important people.

For we are not born out of an egg at the age of eighteen with a realistic imagination; we are still, as Mr. Shaw recalls, in the era of Burge and Lubin, where in infancy we are dependent upon older beings for our contacts. And so we make our connections with the outer world through certain beloved and authoritative persons. They are the first bridge to the invisible world. And though we may gradually master for ourselves many phases of that larger environment, there always remains a vaster one that is unknown. To that we still relate ourselves through authorities. Where all the facts are out of sight a true report and a plausible error read alike, sound alike, feel alike.

Except on a few subjects where our own knowledge is great, we cannot choose between true and false accounts. So we choose between trustworthy and untrustworthy reporters. [Footnote: See an interesting, rather quaint old book: George Cornewall Lewis, *An Essay on the Influence of Authority in Matters of Opinion.*]

Theoretically we ought to choose the most expert on each subject. But the choice of the expert, though a good deal easier than the choice of truth, is still too difficult and often impracticable. The experts themselves are not in the least certain who among them is the most expert. And at that, the expert, even when we can identify him, is, likely as not, too busy to be consulted, or impossible to get at. But there are people whom we can identify easily enough because they are the people who are at the head of affairs. Parents, teachers, and masterful friends are the first people of this sort we encounter. Into the difficult question of why children trust one parent rather than another, the history teacher rather than the Sunday school teacher, we need not try to enter. Nor how trust gradually spreads through a newspaper or an acquaintance who is interested in public affairs to public personages. The literature of psychoanalysis is rich in suggestive hypothesis.

At any rate we do find ourselves trusting certain people, who constitute our means of junction with pretty nearly the whole realm of unknown things. Strangely enough, this fact is sometimes regarded as inherently undignified, as evidence of our sheep-like, ape-like nature. But complete independence in the universe is simply unthinkable. If we could not take practically everything for granted, we should spend our lives in utter triviality. The nearest thing to a wholly independent adult is a hermit, and the range of a hermit's action is very short. Acting entirely for himself, he can act only within a tiny radius and for simple ends. If he has time to think great thoughts we can be certain that he has accepted without question, before he went in for being a hermit, a whole repertory of painfully acquired information about how to keep warm and how to keep from being hungry, and also about what the great questions are.

On all but a very few matters for short stretches in our lives, the utmost independence that we can exercise is to multiply the authorities to whom we give a friendly hearing. As congenital amateurs our quest for truth consists in stirring

The Walter Lippmann Reader

up the experts, and forcing them to answer any heresy that has the accent of conviction. In such a debate we can often judge who has won the dialectical victory, but we are virtually defenseless against a false premise that none of the debaters has challenged, or a neglected aspect that none of them has brought into the argument. We shall see later how the democratic theory proceeds on the opposite assumption and assumes for the purposes of government an unlimited supply of self-sufficient individuals.

The people on whom we depend for contact with the outer world are those who seem to be running it. [Footnote: *Cf.* Bryce, *Modern Democracies* Vol. II, pp. 544-545.] They may be running only a very small part of the world. The nurse feeds the child, bathes it, and puts it to bed. That does not constitute the nurse an authority on physics, zoology, and the Higher Criticism. Mr. Smith runs, or at least hires, the man who runs the factory. That does not make him an authority on the Constitution of the United States, nor on the effects \of the Fordney tariff. Mr. Smoot runs the Republican party in the State of Utah. That in itself does not prove he is the best man to consult about taxation. But the nurse may nevertheless determine for a while what zoology the child shall learn, Mr. Smith will have much to say on what the Constitution shall mean to his wife, his secretary, and perhaps even to his parson, and who shall define the limits of Senator Smoot's authority?

The priest, the lord of the manor, the captains and the kings, the party leaders, the merchant, the boss, however these men are chosen, whether by birth, inheritance, conquest or election, they and their organized following administer human affairs. They are the officers, and although the same man may be field marshal at home, second lieutenant at the office, and scrub private in politics, although in many institutions the hierarchy of rank is vague or concealed, yet in every institution that requires the cooperation of many persons, some such hierarchy exists. [Footnote: *Cf.* M. Ostrogorski, *Democracy and the Organization of Political Parties, passim*; R. Michels, *Political Parties, passim*; and Bryce, *Modern Democracies*, particularly Chap. LXXV; also Ross, *Principles of Sociology*, Chaps. XXII-XXIV.] In American politics we call it a machine, or "the organization."

3

There are a number of important distinctions between the members of the machine and the rank and file. The leaders, the steering committee and the inner circle, are in direct contact with their environment. They may, to be sure, have a very limited notion of what they ought to define as the environment, but they are not dealing almost wholly with abstractions. There are particular men they hope to see elected, particular balance sheets they wish to see improved, concrete objectives that must be attained. I do not mean that they escape the human propensity to stereotyped vision. Their stereotypes often make them absurd routineers. But whatever their limitations, the chiefs are in actual contact with some crucial part of that larger environment. They decide. They give orders. They bargain. And something definite, perhaps not at all what they imagined, actually happens.

Their subordinates are not tied to them by a common conviction. That is to say the lesser members of a machine do not dispose their loyalty according to independent judgment about the wisdom of the leaders. In the hierarchy each is dependent upon a superior and is in turn superior to some class of his dependents. What holds the machine together is a system of privileges. These may vary according to the opportunities and the tastes of those who seek them, from nepotism and patronage in all their aspects to clannishness, hero-worship or a fixed idea. They vary from military rank in armies, through land and services in a feudal system, to jobs and publicity in a modern democracy. That is why you can breakup a particular machine by abolishing its privileges. But the machine in every coherent group is, I believe, certain to reappear. For privilege is entirely relative, and uniformity is impossible. Imagine the most absolute communism of which your mind is capable, where no one possessed any object that everyone else did not possess, and still, if the communist group had to take any action whatever, the mere pleasure of being the friend of the man who was going to make the speech that secured the most votes, would, I am convinced, be enough to crystallize an organization of insiders around him.

It is not necessary, then, to invent a collective intelligence in order to explain why the judgments of a group are usually more coherent, and often more true to form than the remarks of the man in the street. One mind, or a few can pursue a train of thought, but a group trying to think in concert can as a group do little more than assent or dissent. The members of a hierarchy can have a corporate tradition. As apprentices they learn the trade from the masters, who in turn learned it when they were apprentices, and in any enduring society, the change of personnel within the governing hierarchies is slow enough to permit the transmission of certain great stereotypes and patterns of behavior. From father to son, from prelate to novice, from veteran to cadet, certain ways of seeing and doing are taught. These ways become familiar, and are recognized as such by the mass of outsiders.

4

Distance alone lends enchantment to the view that masses of human beings ever coöperate in any complex affair without a central machine managed by a very few people. "No one," says Bryce, [Footnote: *Op. cit.*, Vol. II, p. 542.] "can have had some years' experience of the conduct of affairs in a legislature or an administration without observing how extremely small is the number of persons by whom the world is governed." He is referring, of course, to affairs of state. To be sure if you consider all the affairs of mankind the number of people who govern is considerable, but if you take any particular institution, be it a legislature, a party, a trade union, a nationalist movement, a factory, or a club, the number of those who govern is a very small percentage of those who are theoretically supposed to govern.

Landslides can turn one machine out and put another in; revolutions sometimes abolish a particular machine altogether. The democratic revolution set up two alternating machines, each of which in the course of a few years reaps the advantage from the mistakes of the other. But nowhere does the machine disappear. Nowhere is the idyllic theory of democracy realized. Certainly not in trades unions, nor in socialist parties, nor in communist governments. There is an inner circle, surrounded by concentric circles which fade out gradually into the disinterested or uninterested rank and file.

Democrats have never come to terms with this commonplace of group life. They have invariably regarded it as perverse. For there are two visions of democracy: one presupposes the self-sufficient individual; the other an Oversoul regulating everything.

Of the two the Oversoul has some advantage because it does at least recognize that the mass makes decisions that are not spontaneously born in the breast of every member. But the Oversoul as presiding genius in corporate behavior is a superfluous mystery if we fix our attention upon the machine. The machine is a quite prosaic reality. It consists of human beings who wear clothes and live in houses, who can be named and described. They perform all the duties usually assigned to the Oversoul.

5

The reason for the machine is not the perversity of human nature. It is that out of the private notions of any group no common idea emerges by itself. For the number of ways is limited in which a multitude of people can act directly upon a situation beyond their reach. Some of them can migrate, in one form or another, they can strike or boycott, they can applaud or hiss. They can by these means occasionally resist what they do not like, or coerce those who obstruct what they desire. But by mass action nothing can be constructed, devised, negotiated, or administered. A public as such, without an organized hierarchy around which it can gather, may refuse to buy if the prices are too high, or refuse to work if wages are too low. A trade union can by mass action in a strike break an opposition so that the union officials can negotiate an agreement. It may win, for example, the *right* to joint control. But it cannot exercise the right except through an organization. A nation can clamor for war, but when it goes to war it must put itself under orders from a general staff.

The limit of direct action is for all practical purposes the power to say Yes or No on an issue presented to the mass. [Footnote: *Cf.* James, *Some Problems of Philosophy*, p. 227. "But for most of our emergencies, fractional solutions are impossible. Seldom can we act fractionally." *Cf.* Lowell, *Public Opinion and Popular Government*, pp. 91, 92.] For only in the very simplest cases does an issue present itself in the same form spontaneously and approximately at the same time to all the members of a public. There are unorganized strikes and boycotts, not merely industrial ones, where the grievance is so plain that virtually without leadership the same reaction takes place in many people. But even in these rudimentary cases there are persons who know what they want to do more quickly than the rest, and who become impromptu ringleaders. Where they do not appear a crowd will mill about aimlessly beset by all its private aims, or stand by fatalistically, as did a crowd of fifty persons the other day, and watch a man commit suicide.

For what we make out of most of the impressions that come to us from the invisible world is a kind of pantomime played out in revery. The number of times is small that we consciously decide anything about events beyond our sight,

334

and each man's opinion of what he could accomplish if he tried, is slight. There is rarely a practical issue, and therefore no great habit of decision. This would be more evident were it not that most information when it reaches us carries with it an aura of suggestion as to how we ought to feel about the news. That suggestion we need, and if we do not find it in the news we turn to the editorials or to a trusted adviser. The revery, if we feel ourselves implicated, is uncomfortable until we know where we stand, that is, until the facts have been formulated so that we can feel Yes or No in regard to them.

When a number of people all say Yes they may have all kinds of reasons for saying it. They generally do. For the pictures in their minds are, as we have already noted, varied in subtle and intimate ways. But this subtlety remains within their minds; it becomes represented publicly by a number of symbolic phrases which carry the individual emotion after evacuating most of the intention. The hierarchy, or, if it is a contest, then the two hierarchies, associate the symbols with a definite action, a vote of Yes or No, an attitude pro or con. Then Smith who was against the League and Jones who was against Article X, and Brown who was against Mr. Wilson and all his works, each for his own reason, all in the name of more or less the same symbolic phrase, register a vote *against* the Democrats by voting for the Republicans. A common will has been expressed.

A concrete choice had to be presented, the choice had to be connected, by the transfer of interest through the symbols, with individual opinion. The professional politicians learned this long before the democratic philosophers. And so they organized the caucus, the nominating convention, and the steering committee, as the means of formulating a definite choice. Everyone who wishes to accomplish anything that requires the cooperation of a large number of people follows their example. Sometimes it is done rather brutally as when the Peace Conference reduced itself to the Council of Ten, and the Council of Ten to the Big Three or Four; and wrote a treaty which the minor allies, their own constituents, and the enemy were permitted to take or leave. More consultation than that is generally possible and desirable. But the essential fact remains that a small number of heads present a choice to a large group.

The Walter Lippmann Reader

6

The abuses of the steering committee have led to various proposals such as the initiative, referendum and direct primary. But these merely postponed or obscured the need for a machine by complicating the elections, or as H. G. Wells once said with scrupulous accuracy, the selections. For no amount of balloting can obviate the need of creating an issue, be it a measure or a candidate, on which the voters can say Yes, or No. There is, in fact, no such thing as "direct legislation." For what happens where it is supposed to exist? The citizen goes to the polls, receives a ballot on which a number of measures are printed, almost always in abbreviated form, and, if he says anything at all, he says Yes or No. The most brilliant amendment in the world may occur to him. He votes Yes or No on that bill and no other. You have to commit violence against the English language to call that legislation. I do not argue, of course, that there are no benefits, whatever you call the process. I think that for certain kinds of issues there are distinct benefits. But the necessary simplicity of any mass decision is a very important fact in view of the inevitable complexity of the world in which those decisions operate. The most complicated form of voting that anyone proposes is, I suppose, the preferential ballot. Among a number of candidates presented the voter under that system, instead of saying yes to one candidate and no to all the others, states the order of his choice. But even here, immensely more flexible though it is, the action of the mass depends upon the quality of the choices presented. [Footnote: Cf. H. J. Laski, *Foundations of Sovereignty*, p. 224. "... proportional representation... by leading, as it seems to lead, to the group system... may deprive the electors of their choice of leaders." The group system undoubtedly tends, as Mr. Laski says, to make the selection of the executive more indirect, but there is no doubt also that it tends to produce legislative assemblies in which currents of opinion are more fully represented. Whether that is good or bad cannot be determined a priori. But one can say that successful cooperation and responsibility in a more accurately representative assembly require a higher organization of political intelligence and political habit, than in a rigid two-party house. It is a more complex political form and may therefore work less well.] And those choices are presented by the energetic coteries who hustle about with petitions and round up the delegates. The Many can elect after the Few have nominated.

CHAPTER XV

Leaders and the Rank and File

1

BECAUSE of their transcendent practical importance, no successful leader has ever been too busy to cultivate the symbols which organize his following. What privileges do within the hierarchy, symbols do for the rank and file. They conserve unity. From the totem pole to the national flag, from the wooden idol to God the Invisible King, from the magic word to some diluted version of Adam Smith or Bentham, symbols have been cherished by leaders, many of whom were themselves unbelievers, because they were focal points where differences merged. The detached observer may scorn the "star-spangled" ritual which hedges the symbol, perhaps as much as the king who told himself that Paris was worth a few masses. But the leader knows by experience that only when symbols have done their work is there a handle he can use to move a crowd. In the symbol emotion is discharged at a common target, and the idiosyncrasy of real ideas blotted out. No wonder he hates what he calls destructive criticism, sometimes called by free spirits the elimination of buncombe. "Above all things," says Bagehot, "our royalty is to be reverenced, and if you begin to poke about it you cannot reverence it." [Footnote: *The English Constitution*, p. 127. D. Appleton & Company, 1914.] For poking about with clear definitions and candid statements serves all high purposes known to man, except the easy conservation of a common will. Poking about, as every responsible leader suspects, tends to break the transference of emotion from the individual mind to the institutional symbol. And the first result of that is, as he rightly says, a chaos of individualism and warring sects. The disintegration of a symbol, like Holy Russia, or the Iron Diaz, is always the beginning of a long upheaval.

These great symbols possess by transference all the minute and detailed loyalties of an ancient and stereotyped society. They evoke the feeling that each individual has for the landscape, the furniture, the faces, the memories that are his first, and in a static society, his only reality. That core of images and devotions without which he is unthinkable to himself, is nationality. The great symbols take up these devotions, and can arouse them without calling forth the primitive images. The lesser symbols of public debate, the more casual chatter of politics, are always referred back to these proto-symbols, and if possible associated with them. The question of a proper fare on a municipal subway is symbolized as an issue between the People and the Interests, and then the People is inserted in the symbol American, so that finally in the heat of a campaign, an eight cent fare becomes unAmerican. The Revolutionary fathers died to prevent it. Lincoln suffered that it might not come to pass, resistance to it was implied in the death of those who sleep in France.

Because of its power to siphon emotion out of distinct ideas, the symbol is both a mechanism of solidarity, and a mechanism of exploitation. It enables people to work for a common end, but just because the few who are strategically placed must choose the concrete objectives, the symbol is also an instrument by which a few can fatten on many, deflect criticism, and seduce men into facing agony for objects they do not understand.

Many aspects of our subjection to symbols are not flattering if we choose to think of ourselves as realistic, self-sufficient, and self-governing personalities. Yet it is impossible to conclude that symbols are altogether instruments of the devil. In the realm of science and contemplation they are undoubtedly the tempter himself. But in the world of action they may be beneficent, and are sometimes a necessity. The necessity is often imagined, the peril manufactured. But when quick results are imperative, the manipulation of masses through symbols may be the only quick way of having a critical thing done. It is often more important to act than to understand. It is sometimes true that the action would fail if everyone understood it. There are many affairs which cannot wait for a referendum or endure publicity, and there are times, during war for example, when a nation, an army, and even its commanders must trust strategy to a very few minds; when two conflicting opinions, though one happens to be right, are more perilous than one opinion which is wrong. The wrong opinion may have bad results, but the two opinions may entail disaster by dissolving unity. [Footnote: Captain Peter S. Wright, Assistant Secretary of the Supreme War Council, *At the Supreme War Council,* is well worth careful reading on secrecy and unity of command, even though in respect to the allied leaders he wages a passionate polemic.]

Thus Foch and Sir Henry Wilson, who foresaw the impending disaster to Cough's army, as a consequence of the divided and scattered reserves, nevertheless kept their opinions well within a small circle, knowing that even the risk of a smashing defeat was less certainly destructive, than would have been an excited debate in the newspapers. For what matters most under the kind of tension which prevailed in March, 1918, is less the rightness of a particular move than the unbroken expectation as to the source of command. Had Foch "gone to the people" he might have won the debate, but long before he could have won it, the armies which he was to command would have dissolved. For the spectacle of a row on Olympus is diverting and destructive.

But so also is a conspiracy of silence. Says Captain Wright: "It is in the High Command and not in the line, that the art of camouflage is most practiced, and reaches to highest flights. All chiefs everywhere are now kept painted, by the busy work of numberless publicists, so as to be mistaken for Napoleons—at a distance....It becomes almost impossible to displace these Napoleons, whatever their incompetence, because of the enormous public support created by hiding or glossing failure, and exaggerating or inventing success.... But the most insidious and worst effect of this so highly organized falsity is on the generals themselves: modest and patriotic as they mostly are, and as most men must be to take up and follow the noble profession of arms, they themselves are ultimately affected by these universal illusions, and reading it every morning in the paper, they also grow persuaded they are thunderbolts of war and infallible, however much they fail, and that their maintenance in command is an end so sacred that it justifies the use of any means.... These various conditions, of which this great deceit is the greatest, at last emancipate all General Staffs from all control. They no longer live for the nation: the nation lives, or rather dies, for them. Victory or defeat ceases to be the prime interest. What matters to these semi-sovereign corporations is whether dear old Willie or poor old Harry is going to be at their head, or the Chantilly party prevail over the Boulevard des Invalides party." [Footnote: *Op. cit.*, pp. 98, 101-105.]

Yet Captain Wright who can be so eloquent and so discerning about the dangers of silence is forced nevertheless to approve the silence of Foch in not publicly destroying the illusions. There is here a complicated paradox, arising as we shall see more fully later on, because the traditional democratic view of life is conceived, not for emergencies and dangers, but for tranquillity and harmony. And so where masses of people must coöperate in an uncertain and eruptive environment, it is usually necessary to secure unity and flexibility without real consent. The symbol does that. It obscures personal intention, neutralizes discrimination, and obfuscates individual purpose. It immobilizes personality, yet at the same time it enormously sharpens the intention of the group and welds that group, as nothing else in a crisis can weld it, to purposeful action. It renders the mass mobile though it immobilizes personality. The symbol is the instrument by which in the short run the mass escapes from its own inertia, the inertia of indecision, or the inertia of headlong movement, and is rendered capable of being led along the zigzag of a complex situation.

2

But in the longer run, the give and take increases between the leaders and the led. The word most often used to describe the state of mind in the rank and file about its leaders is morale. That is said to be good when the individuals do the part allotted to them with all their energy; when each man's whole strength is evoked by the command from above. It follows that every leader must plan his policy with this in mind. He must consider his decision not only on "the merits," but also in its effect on any part of his following whose continued support he requires. If he is a general planning an attack, he knows that his organized military units will scatter into mobs if the percentage of casualties rises too high.

In the Great War previous calculations were upset to an extraordinary degree, for "out of every nine men who went to France five became casualties." [Footnote: *Op. cit.*, p. 37. Figures taken by Captain Wright from the statistical abstract of the war in the Archives of the War Office. The figures refer apparently to the English losses alone, possibly to the English and French.] The limit of endurance was far greater than anyone had supposed. But there was a limit somewhere. And so, partly because of its effect on the enemy, but also in great measure because of its effect on the troops and their families, no command in this war dared to publish a candid statement of its losses. In France the casualty lists were never published. In England, America, and Germany publication of the losses of a big battle were spread out over long periods so as to destroy a unified impression of the total. Only the insiders knew until long afterwards what the Somme had cost, or the Flanders battles; [Footnote: *Op cit.*, p. 34, the Somme cost nearly 500,000 casualties; the Arras and Flanders offensives of 1917 cost 650,000 British casualties.] and Ludendorff undoubtedly had a very much more accurate idea of these casualties than any private person in London, Paris or Chicago. All the leaders in every camp did their best to limit the amount of actual war which any one soldier or civilian could vividly

The Walter Lippmann Reader

conceive. But, of course, among old veterans like the French troops of 1917, a great deal more is known about war than ever reaches the public. Such an army begins to judge its commanders in terms of its own suffering. And then, when another extravagant promise of victory turns out to be the customary bloody defeat, you may find that a mutiny breaks out over some comparatively minor blunder, [Footnote: The Allies suffered many bloodier defeats than that on the Chemin des Dames.] like Nivelle's offensive of 1917, because it is a cumulative blunder. Revolutions and mutinies generally follow a small sample of a big series of evils. [Footnote: Cf. Pierrefeu's account, op. cit., on the causes of the Soissons mutinies, and the method adopted by Pétain to deal with them. Vol. I, Part III, et seq.]

The incidence of policy determines the relation between leader and following. If those whom he needs in his plan are remote from the place where the action takes place, if the results are hidden or postponed, if the individual obligations are indirect or not yet due, above all if assent is an exercise of some pleasurable emotion, the leader is likely to have a free hand. Those programs are immediately most popular, like prohibition among teetotalers, which do not at once impinge upon the private habits of the followers. That is one great reason why governments have such a free hand in foreign affairs. Most of the frictions between two states involve a series of obscure and long-winded contentions, occasionally on the frontier, but far more often in regions about which school geographies have supplied no precise ideas. In Czechoslovakia America is regarded as the Liberator; in American newspaper paragraphs and musical comedy, in American conversation by and large, it has never been finally settled whether the country we liberated is Czechoslavia or Jugoslovakia.

In foreign affairs the incidence of policy is for a very long time confined to an unseen environment. Nothing that happens out there is felt to be wholly real. And so, because in the ante-bellum period, nobody has to fight and nobody has to pay, governments go along according to their lights without much reference to their people. In local affairs the cost of a policy is more easily visible. And therefore, all but the most exceptional leaders prefer policies in which the costs are as far as possible indirect.

They do not like direct taxation. They do not like to pay as they go. They like long term debts. They like to have the voters believe that the foreigner will pay. They have always been compelled to calculate prosperity in terms of the producer rather than in terms of the consumer, because the incidence on the consumer is distributed over so many trivial items. Labor leaders have always preferred an increase of money wages to a decrease in prices. There has always been more popular interest in the profits of millionaires, which are visible but comparatively unimportant, than in the wastes of the industrial system, which are huge but elusive. A legislature dealing with a shortage of houses, such as exists when this is written, illustrates this rule, first by doing nothing to increase the number of houses, second by smiting the greedy landlord on the hip, third by investigating the profiteering builders and working men. For a constructive policy deals with remote and uninteresting factors, while a greedy landlord, or a profiteering plumber is visible and immediate.

But while people will readily believe that in an unimagined future and in unseen places a certain policy will benefit them, the actual working out of policy follows a different logic from their opinions. A nation may be induced to believe that jacking up the freight rates will make the railroads prosperous. But that belief will not make the roads prosperous, if the impact of those rates on farmers and shippers is such as to produce a commodity price beyond what the consumer can pay. Whether the consumer will pay the price depends not upon whether he nodded his head nine months previously at the proposal to raise rates and save business, but on whether he now wants a new hat or a new automobile enough to pay for them.

3

Leaders often pretend that they have merely uncovered a program which existed in the minds of their public. When they believe it, they are usually deceiving themselves. Programs do not invent themselves synchronously in a multitude of minds. That is not because a multitude of minds is necessarily inferior to that of the leaders, but because thought is the function of an organism, and a mass is not an organism.

This fact is obscured because the mass is constantly exposed to suggestion. It reads not the news, but the news with an aura of suggestion about it, indicating the line of action to be taken. It hears reports, not objective as the facts are, but already stereotyped to a certain pattern of behavior. Thus the ostensible leader often finds that the real leader is a powerful newspaper proprietor. But if, as in a laboratory, one could remove all suggestion and leading from the experience of a multitude, one would, I think, find something like this: A mass exposed to the same stimuli would develop responses that could theoretically be charted in a polygon of error. There would be a certain group that felt sufficiently alike to be classified together. There would be variants of feeling at both ends. These classifications would tend to harden as individuals in each of the classifications made their reactions vocal. That is to say, when the vague feelings of those who felt vaguely had been put into words, they would know more definitely what they felt, and would then feel it more definitely.

Leaders in touch with popular feeling are quickly conscious of these reactions. They know that high prices are pressing upon the mass, or that certain classes of individuals are becoming unpopular, or that feeling towards another nation is friendly or hostile. But, always barring the effect of suggestion which is merely the assumption of leadership by the reporter, there would be nothing in the feeling of the mass that fatally determined the choice of any particular policy. All that the feeling of the mass demands is that policy as it is developed and exposed shall be, if not logically, then by analogy and association, connected with the original feeling.

So when a new policy is to be launched, there is a preliminary bid for community of feeling, as in Mark Antony's speech to the followers of Brutus. [Footnote: Excellently analyzed in Martin, *The Behavior of Crowds*, pp. 130-132.] In the first phase, the leader vocalizes the prevalent opinion of the mass. He identifies himself with the familiar attitudes of his audience, sometimes by telling a good story, sometimes by brandishing his patriotism, often by pinching a grievance. Finding that he is trustworthy, the multitude milling hither and thither may turn in towards him. He will then be expected to set forth a plan of campaign. But he will not find that plan in the slogans which convey the feelings of the mass. It will not even always be indicated by them. Where the incidence of policy is remote, all that is essential is that the program shall be verbally and emotionally connected at the start with what has become vocal in the multitude. Trusted men in a familiar role subscribing to the accepted symbols can go a very long way on their own initiative without explaining the substance of their programs.

But wise leaders are not content to do that. Provided they think publicity will not strengthen opposition too much, and that debate will not delay action too long, they seek a certain measure of consent. They take, if not the whole mass, then the subordinates of the hierarchy sufficiently into their confidence to prepare them for what might happen, and to make them feel that they have freely willed the result. But however sincere the leader may be, there is always, when the facts are very complicated, a certain amount of illusion in these consultations. For it is impossible that all the contingencies shall be as vivid to the whole public as they are to the more experienced and the more imaginative. A fairly large percentage are bound to agree without having taken the time, or without possessing the background, for appreciating the choices which the leader presents to them. No one, however, can ask for more. And only theorists do. If we have had our day in court, if what we had to say was heard, and then if what is done comes out well, most of us do not stop to consider how much our opinion affected the business in hand.

And therefore, if the established powers are sensitive and well-informed, if they are visibly trying to meet popular feeling, and actually removing some of the causes of dissatisfaction, no matter how slowly they proceed, provided they are seen to be proceeding, they have little to fear. It takes stupendous and persistent blundering, plus almost infinite tactlessness, to start a revolution from below. Palace revolutions, interdepartmental revolutions, are a different matter. So, too, is demagogy. That stops at relieving the tension by expressing the feeling. But the statesman knows that such relief is temporary, and if indulged too often, unsanitary. He, therefore, sees to it that he arouses no feeling which he cannot sluice into a program that deals with the facts to which the feelings refer.

But all leaders are not statesmen, all leaders hate to resign, and most leaders find it hard to believe that bad as things are, the other fellow would not make them worse. They do not passively wait for the public to feel the incidence of policy, because the incidence of that discovery is generally upon their own heads. They are, therefore, intermittently engaged in mending their fences and consolidating their position.

The mending of fences consists in offering an occasional scapegoat, in redressing a minor grievance affecting a powerful individual or faction, rearranging certain jobs, placating a group of people who want an arsenal in their home town, or a law to stop somebody's vices. Study the daily activity of any public official who depends on election and you can enlarge this list. There are Congressmen elected year after year who never think of dissipating their energy on public affairs. They prefer to do a little service for a lot of people on a lot of little subjects, rather than to engage in trying to do a big service out there in the void. But the number of people to whom any organization can be a successful valet is limited, and shrewd politicians take care to attend either the influential, or somebody so blatantly uninfluential that to pay any attention to him is a mark of sensational magnanimity. The far greater number who cannot be held by favors, the anonymous multitude, receive propaganda.

The established leaders of any organization have great natural advantages. They are believed to have better sources of information. The books and papers are in their offices. They took part in the important conferences. They met the important people. They have responsibility. It is, therefore, easier for them to secure attention and to speak in a convincing tone. But also they have a very great deal of control over the access to the facts. Every official is in some degree a censor. And since no one can suppress information, either by concealing it or forgetting to mention it, without some notion of what he wishes the public to know, every leader is in some degree a propagandist. Strategically placed, and compelled often to choose even at the best between the equally cogent though conflicting ideals of safety for the institution, and candor to his public, the official finds himself deciding more and more consciously what facts, in what setting, in what guise he shall permit the public to know.

4

That the manufacture of consent is capable of great refinements no one, I think, denies. The process by which public opinions arise is certainly no less intricate than it has appeared in these pages, and the opportunities for manipulation open to anyone who understands the process are plain enough.

The creation of consent is not a new art. It is a very old one which was supposed to have died out with the appearance of democracy. But it has not died out. It has, in fact, improved enormously in technic, because it is now based on analysis rather than on rule of thumb. And so, as a result of psychological research, coupled with the modern means of communication, the practice of democracy has turned a corner. A revolution is taking place, infinitely more significant than any shifting of economic power.

Within the life of the generation now in control of affairs, persuasion has become a self-conscious art and a regular organ of popular government. None of us begins to understand the consequences, but it is no daring prophecy to say that the knowledge of how to create consent will alter every political calculation and modify every political premise. Under the impact of propaganda, not necessarily in the sinister meaning of the word alone, the old constants of our thinking have become variables. It is no longer possible, for example, to believe in the original dogma of democracy; that the knowledge needed for the management of human affairs comes up spontaneously from the human heart. Where we act on that theory we expose ourselves to self-deception, and to forms of persuasion that we cannot verify. It has been demonstrated that we cannot rely upon intuition, conscience, or the accidents of casual opinion if we are to deal with the world beyond our reach.

PART VI
THE IMAGE OF DEMOCRACY

"I confess that in America I saw more than America;
I sought the image of democracy itself."
Alexis de Tocqueville.

CHAPTER XVI
The Self-Centered Man

1

SINCE Public Opinion is supposed to be the prime mover in democracies, one might reasonably expect to find a vast literature. One does not find it. There are excellent books on government and parties, that is, on the machinery which in theory registers public opinions after they are formed. But on the sources from which these public opinions arise, on the processes by which they are derived, there is relatively little. The existence of a force called Public Opinion is in the main taken for granted, and American political writers have been most interested either in finding out how to make government express the common will, or in how to prevent the common will from subverting the purposes for which they believe the government exists. According to their traditions they have wished either to tame opinion or to obey it. Thus the editor of a notable series of text-books writes that "the most difficult and the most momentous question of government (is) how to transmit the force of individual opinion into public action." [Footnote: Albert Bushnell Hart in the Introductory note to A. Lawrence Lowell's *Public Opinion and Popular Government.*]

But surely there is a still more momentous question, the question of how to validate our private versions of the political scene. There is, as I shall try to indicate further on, the prospect of radical improvement by the development of principles already in operation. But this development will depend on how well we learn to use knowledge of the way opinions are put together to watch over our own opinions when they are being put together. For casual opinion, being the product of partial contact, of tradition, and personal interests, cannot in the nature of things take kindly to a method of political thought which is based on exact record, measurement, analysis and comparison. Just those qualities of the

347

mind which determine what shall seem interesting, important, familiar, personal, and dramatic, are the qualities which in the first instance realistic opinion frustrates. Therefore, unless there is in the community at large a growing conviction that prejudice and intuition are not enough, the working out of realistic opinion, which takes time, money, labor, conscious effort, patience, and equanimity, will not find enough support. That conviction grows as self-criticism increases, and makes us conscious of buncombe, contemptuous of ourselves when we employ it, and on guard to detect it. Without an ingrained habit of analyzing opinion when we read, talk, and decide, most of us would hardly suspect the need of better ideas, nor be interested in them when they appear, nor be able to prevent the new technic of political intelligence from being manipulated.

Yet democracies, if we are to judge by the oldest and most powerful of them, have made a mystery out of public opinion. There have been skilled organizers of opinion who understood the mystery well enough to create majorities on election day. But these organizers have been regarded by political science as low fellows or as "problems," not as possessors of the most effective knowledge there was on how to create and operate public opinion. The tendency of the people who have voiced the ideas of democracy, even when they have not managed its action, the tendency of students, orators, editors, has been to look upon Public Opinion as men in other societies looked upon the uncanny forces to which they ascribed the last word in the direction of events.

For in almost every political theory there is an inscrutable element which in the heyday of that theory goes unexamined. Behind the appearances there is a Fate, there are Guardian Spirits, or Mandates to a Chosen People, a Divine Monarchy, a Vice-Regent of Heaven, or a Class of the Better Born. The more obvious angels, demons, and kings are gone out of democratic thinking, but the need for believing that there are reserve powers of guidance persists. It persisted for those thinkers of the Eighteenth Century who designed the matrix of democracy. They had a pale god, but warm hearts, and in the doctrine of popular sovereignty they found the answer to their need of an infallible origin for the new social order. There was the mystery, and only enemies of the people touched it with profane and curious hands.

The Walter Lippmann Reader

They did not remove the veil because they were practical politicians in a bitter and uncertain struggle. They had themselves felt the aspiration of democracy, which is ever so much deeper, more intimate and more important than any theory of government. They were engaged, as against the prejudice of ages, in the assertion of human dignity. What possessed them was not whether John Smith had sound views on any public question, but that John Smith, scion of a stock that had always been considered inferior, would now bend his knee to no other man. It was this spectacle that made it bliss "in that dawn to be alive." But every analyst seems to degrade that dignity, to deny that all men are reasonable all the time, or educated, or informed, to note that people are fooled, that they do not always know their own interests, and that all men are not equally fitted to govern.

The critics were about as welcome as a small boy with a drum. Every one of these observations on the fallibility of man was being exploited ad nauseam. Had democrats admitted there was truth in any of the aristocratic arguments they would have opened a breach in the defenses. And so just as Aristotle had to insist that the slave was a slave by nature, the democrats had to insist that the free man was a legislator and administrator by nature. They could not stop to explain that a human soul might not yet have, or indeed might never have, this technical equipment, and that nevertheless it had an inalienable right not to be used as the unwilling instrument of other men. The superior people were still too strong and too unscrupulous to have refrained from capitalizing so candid a statement.

So the early democrats insisted that a reasoned righteousness welled up spontaneously out of the mass of men. All of them hoped that it would, many of them believed that it did, although the cleverest, like Thomas Jefferson, had all sorts of private reservations. But one thing was certain: if public opinion did not come forth spontaneously, nobody in that age believed it would come forth at all. For in one fundamental respect the political science on which democracy was based was the same science that Aristotle formulated. It was the same science for democrat and aristocrat, royalist and republican, in that its major premise assumed the art of government to be a natural endowment. Men differed radically when they tried to name the men so endowed; but they agreed in thinking that the greatest question of all was to find those in whom political wisdom was innate. Royalists were sure that kings were born to govern. Alexander Hamilton thought that while "there are strong minds in every walk of life... the representative body, with too few exceptions to have any influence on the spirit of the government, will be composed of landholders, merchants, and men of the learned professions." [Footnote: *The Federalist*, Nos. 35, 36. *Cf.* comment by Henry Jones Ford in his *Rise and Growth of American Politics*. Ch. V.] Jefferson thought the political faculties were deposited by God in farmers and planters, and sometimes spoke as if they were found in all the people. [Footnote: See below p. 268.] The main premise was the same: to govern was an instinct that appeared, according to your social preferences, in one man or a chosen few, in all males, or only in males who were white and twenty-one, perhaps even in all men and all women.

In deciding who was most fit to govern, knowledge of the world was taken for granted. The aristocrat believed that those who dealt with large affairs possessed the instinct, the democrats asserted that all men possessed the instinct and could therefore deal with large affairs. It was no part of political science in either case to think out how knowledge of the world could be brought to the ruler. If you were for the people you did not try to work out the question of how to keep the voter informed. By the age of twenty-one he had his political faculties. What counted was a good heart, a reasoning mind, a balanced judgment. These would ripen with age, but it was not necessary to consider how to inform the heart and feed the reason. Men took in their facts as they took in their breath.

3

But the facts men could come to possess in this effortless way were limited. They could know the customs and more obvious character of the place where they lived and worked. But the outer world they had to conceive, and they did not conceive it instinctively, nor absorb trustworthy knowledge of it just by living. Therefore, the only environment in which spontaneous politics were possible was one confined within the range of the ruler's direct and certain knowledge. There is no escaping this conclusion, wherever you found government on the natural range of men's faculties. "If," as Aristotle said, [Footnote: *Politics*, Bk. VII, Ch. 4.] "the citizens of a state are to judge and distribute offices according to merit, then they must know each other's characters; where they do not possess this knowledge, both the election to offices and the decision of law suits will go wrong."

The Walter Lippmann Reader

Obviously this maxim was binding upon every school of political thought. But it presented peculiar difficulties to the democrats. Those who believed in class government could fairly claim that in the court of the king, or in the country houses of the gentry, men did know each other's characters, and as long as the rest of mankind was passive, the only characters one needed to know were the characters of men in the ruling class. But the democrats, who wanted to raise the dignity of all men, were immediately involved by the immense size and confusion of their ruling class—the male electorate. Their science told them that politics was an instinct, and that the instinct worked in a limited environment. Their hopes bade them insist that all men in a very large environment could govern. In this deadly conflict between their ideals and their science, the only way out was to assume without much discussion that the voice of the people was the voice of God.

The paradox was too great, the stakes too big, their ideal too precious for critical examination. They could not show how a citizen of Boston was to stay in Boston and conceive the views of a Virginian, how a Virginian in Virginia could have real opinions about the government at Washington, how Congressmen in Washington could have opinions about China or Mexico. For in that day it was not possible for many men to have an unseen environment brought into the field of their judgment. There had been some advances, to be sure, since Aristotle. There were a few newspapers, and there were books, better roads perhaps, and better ships. But there was no great advance, and the political assumptions of the Eighteenth Century had essentially to be those that had prevailed in political science for two thousand years. The pioneer democrats did not possess the material for resolving the conflict between the known range of man's attention and their illimitable faith in his dignity.

Their assumptions antedated not only the modern newspaper, the world-wide press services, photography and moving pictures, but, what is really more significant, they antedated measurement and record, quantitative and comparative analysis, the canons of evidence, and the ability of psychological analysis to correct and discount the prejudices of the witness. I do not mean to say that our records are satisfactory, our analysis unbiased, our measurements sound. I do mean to say that the key inventions have been made for bringing the unseen world into the field of judgment. They had not been made in the time of Aristotle, and they were not yet important enough to be visible for political theory in the age of Rousseau, Montesquieu, or Thomas Jefferson. In a later chapter I think we shall see that even in the latest theory of human reconstruction, that of the English Guild Socialists, all the deeper premises have been taken over from this older system of political thought.

That system, whenever it was competent and honest, had to assume that no man could have more than a very partial experience of public affairs. In the sense that he can give only a little time to them, that assumption is still true, and of the utmost consequence. But ancient theory was compelled to assume, not only that men could give little attention to public questions, but that the attention available would have to be confined to matters close at hand. It would have been visionary to suppose that a time would come when distant and complicated events could conceivably be reported, analyzed, and presented in such a form that a really valuable choice could be made by an amateur. That time is now in sight. There is no longer any doubt that the continuous reporting of an unseen environment is feasible. It is often done badly, but the fact that it is done at all shows that it can be done, and the fact that we begin to know how badly it is often done, shows that it can be done better. With varying degrees of skill and honesty distant complexities are reported every day by engineers and accountants for business men, by secretaries and civil servants for officials, by intelligence officers for the General Staff, by some journalists for some readers. These are crude beginnings but radical, far more radical in the literal meaning of that word than the repetition of wars, revolutions, abdications and restorations; as radical as the change in the scale of human life which has made it possible for Mr. Lloyd George to discuss Welsh coal mining after breakfast in London, and the fate of the Arabs before dinner in Paris.

For the possibility of bringing any aspect of human affairs within the range of judgment breaks the spell which has lain upon political ideas. There have, of course, been plenty of men who did not realize that the range of attention was the main premise of political science. They have built on sand. They have demonstrated in their own persons the effects of a very limited and self-centered knowledge of the world. But for the political thinkers who have counted, from Plato and Aristotle through Machiavelli and Hobbes to the democratic theorists, speculation has revolved around the self-centered man who had to see the whole world by means of a few pictures in his head.

CHAPTER XVII
The Self-Contained Community

1

THAT groups of self-centered people would engage in a struggle for existence if they rubbed against each other has always been evident. This much truth there is at any rate in that famous passage in the Leviathan where Hobbes says that "though there had never been any time wherein particular men were in a condition of war one against another, yet at all times kings and *persons* of *sovereign authority because* of their *independency*, are in continual jealousies and in the state and posture of gladiators, having their weapons pointing, and their eyes fixed on one another..." [Footnote: *Leviathan*, Ch. XIII. Of the Natural Condition of Mankind as concerning their Felicity and Misery.]

2

To circumvent this conclusion one great branch of human thought, which had and has many schools, proceeded in this fashion: it conceived an ideally just pattern of human relations in which each person had well defined functions and rights. If he conscientiously filled the role allotted to him, it did not matter whether his opinions were right or wrong. He did his duty, the next man did his, and all the dutiful people together made a harmonious world. Every caste system illustrates this principle; you find it in Plato's Republic and in Aristotle, in the feudal ideal, in the circles of Dante's Paradise, in the bureaucratic type of socialism, and in laissez-faire, to an amazing degree in syndicalism, guild socialism, anarchism, and in the system of international law idealized by Mr. Robert Lansing. All of them assume a pre-established harmony, inspired, imposed, or innate, by which the self-opinionated person, class, or community is orchestrated with the rest of mankind. The more authoritarian imagine a conductor for the symphony who sees to it that each man plays his part; the anarchistic are inclined to think that a more divine concord would be heard if each player improvised as he went along.

But there have also been philosophers who were bored by these schemes of rights and duties, took conflict for granted, and tried to see how their side might come out on top. They have always seemed more realistic, even when they seemed alarming, because all they had to do was to generalize the experience that nobody could escape. Machiavelli is the classic of this school, a man most mercilessly maligned, because he happened to be the first naturalist who used plain language in a field hitherto preempted by supernaturalists. [Footnote: F. S. Oliver in his *Alexander Hamilton*, says of Machiavelli (p. 174): "Assuming the conditions which exist—the nature of man and of things—to be unchangeable, he proceeds in a calm, unmoral way, like a lecturer on frogs, to show how a valiant and sagacious ruler can best turn events to his own advantage and the security of his dynasty."] He has a worse name and more disciples than any political thinker who ever lived. He truly described the technic of existence for the self-contained state. That is why he has the disciples. He has the bad name chiefly because he cocked his eye at the Medici family, dreamed in his study at night where he wore his "noble court dress" that Machiavelli was himself the Prince, and turned a pungent description of the way things are done into an eulogy on that way of doing them.

In his most infamous chapter [Footnote: *The Prince*, Ch. XVIII. "Concerning the way in which Princes should keep faith." Translation by W. K. Marriott.] he wrote that "a prince ought to take care that he never lets anything slip from his lips that is not replete with the above-named five qualities, that he may appear to him who hears and sees him altogether merciful, faithful, humane, upright, and religious. There is nothing more necessary to appear to have than this last quality, inasmuch as men judge generally more by the eye than by the hand, because it belongs to everybody to see you, to few to come in touch with you. Everyone sees what you appear to be, few really know what you are, and those few dare not oppose themselves to the opinion of the many, who have the majesty of the state to defend them; and in the actions of all men, and especially of princes, which it is not prudent to challenge, one judges by the result.... One prince of the present time, whom it is not well to name, never preaches anything else but peace and good faith, and to both he is most hostile, and either, if he had kept it, would have deprived him of reputation and kingdom many a time."

That is cynical. But it is the cynicism of a man who saw truly without knowing quite why he saw what he saw. Machiavelli is thinking of the run of men and princes "who judge generally more by the eye than by the hand," which is his way of saying that their judgments are subjective. He was too close to earth to pretend that the Italians of his day saw the world steadily and saw it whole. He would not indulge in fantasies, and he had not the materials for imagining a race of men that had learned how to correct their vision.

The world, as he found it, was composed of people whose vision could rarely be corrected, and Machiavelli knew that such people, since they see all public relations in a private way, are involved in perpetual strife. What they see is their own personal, class, dynastic, or municipal version of affairs that in reality extend far beyond the boundaries of their vision. They see their aspect. They see it as right. But they cross other people who are similarly self-centered. Then their very existence is endangered, or at least what they, for unsuspected private reasons, regard as their existence and take to be a danger. The end, which is impregnably based on a real though private experience justifies the means. They will sacrifice any one of these ideals to save all of them,... "one judges by the result..."

3

These elemental truths confronted the democratic philosophers. Consciously or otherwise, they knew that the range of political knowledge was limited, that the area of self-government would have to be limited, and that self-contained states when they rubbed against each other were in the posture of gladiators. But they knew just as certainly, that there was in men a will to decide their own fate, and to find a peace that was not imposed by force. How could they reconcile the wish and the fact?

They looked about them. In the city states of Greece and Italy they found a chronicle of corruption, intrigue and war. [Footnote: "Democracies have ever been spectacles of turbulence and contention... and have in general been as short in their lives as they have been violent in their deaths." Madison, *Federalist*, No. 10.] In their own cities they saw faction, artificiality, fever. This was no environment in which the democratic ideal could prosper, no place where a group of independent and equally competent people managed their own affairs spontaneously. They looked further, guided somewhat perhaps by Jean Jacques Rousseau, to remote, unspoiled country villages. They saw enough to convince themselves that there the ideal was at home. Jefferson in particular felt this, and Jefferson more than any other man formulated the American image of democracy. From the townships had come the power that had carried the American Revolution to victory. From the townships were to come the votes that carried Jefferson's party to power. Out there in the farming communities of Massachusetts and Virginia, if you wore glasses that obliterated the slaves, you could see with your mind's eye the image of what democracy was to be.

"The American Revolution broke out," says de Tocqueville, [Footnote: *Democracy in America*, Vol. I, p. 51. Third Edition] "and the doctrine of the sovereignty of the people, which had been nurtured in the townships, took possession of the state." It certainly took possession of the minds of those men who formulated and popularized the stereotypes of democracy. "The cherishment of the people was our principle," wrote Jefferson. [Footnote: Cited in Charles Beard, *Economic Origins of Jeffersonian Democracy*. Ch. XIV.] But the people he cherished almost exclusively were the small landowning farmers: "Those who labor in the earth are the chosen people of God, if ever He had a chosen people, whose breasts He has made his peculiar deposit for substantial and genuine virtue. It is the focus in which He keeps alive that sacred fire, which otherwise might escape from the face of the earth. Corruption of morals in the mass of cultivators is a phenomenon of which no age nor nation has furnished an example."

However much of the romantic return to nature may have entered into this exclamation, there was also an element of solid sense. Jefferson was right in thinking that a group of independent farmers comes nearer to fulfilling the requirements of spontaneous democracy than any other human society. But if you are to preserve the ideal, you must fence off these ideal communities from the abominations of the world. If the farmers are to manage their own affairs, they must confine affairs to those they are accustomed to managing. Jefferson drew all these logical conclusions. He disapproved of manufacture, of foreign commerce, and a navy, of intangible forms of property, and in theory of any form of government that was not centered in the small self-governing group. He had critics in his day: one of them remarked that "wrapt up in the fullness of self-consequence and strong enough, in reality, to defend ourselves against every invader, we might enjoy an eternal rusticity and live, forever, thus apathized and vulgar under the shelter of a selfish, satisfied indifference." [Footnote: *Op. cit.*, p. 426.]

The Walter Lippmann Reader

The democratic ideal, as Jefferson moulded it, consisting of an ideal environment and a selected class, did not conflict with the political science of his time. It did conflict with the realities. And when the ideal was stated in absolute terms, partly through exuberance and partly for campaign purposes, it was soon forgotten that the theory was originally devised for very special conditions. It became the political gospel, and supplied the stereotypes through which Americans of all parties have looked at politics.

That gospel was fixed by the necessity that in Jefferson's time no one could have conceived public opinions that were not spontaneous and subjective. The democratic tradition is therefore always trying to see a world where people are exclusively concerned with affairs of which the causes and effects all operate within the region they inhabit. Never has democratic theory been able to conceive itself in the context of a wide and unpredictable environment. The mirror is concave. And although democrats recognize that they are in contact with external affairs, they see quite surely that every contact outside that self-contained group is a threat to democracy as originally conceived. That is a wise fear. If democracy is to be spontaneous, the interests of democracy must remain simple, intelligible, and easily managed. Conditions must approximate those of the isolated rural township if the supply of information is to be left to casual experience. The environment must be confined within the range of every man's direct and certain knowledge.

The democrat has understood what an analysis of public opinion seems to demonstrate: that in dealing with an unseen environment decisions "are manifestly settled at haphazard, which clearly they ought not to be." [Footnote: Aristotle, *Politics*, Bk. VII, Ch. IV.] So he has always tried in one way or another to minimize the importance of that unseen environment. He feared foreign trade because trade involves foreign connections; he distrusted manufactures because they produced big cities and collected crowds; if he had nevertheless to have manufactures, he wanted protection in the interest of self-sufficiency. When he could not find these conditions in the real world, he went passionately into the wilderness, and founded Utopian communities far from foreign contacts. His slogans reveal his prejudice. He is for Self-Government, Self-Determination, Independence. Not one of these ideas carries with it any notion of consent or community beyond the frontiers of the self-governing groups. The field of democratic action is a circumscribed area. Within protected boundaries the aim has been to achieve self-sufficiency and avoid entanglement. This rule is not confined to foreign policy, but it is plainly evident there, because life outside the national boundaries is more distinctly alien than any life within. And as history shows, democracies in their foreign policy have had generally to choose between splendid isolation and a diplomacy that violated their ideals. The most successful democracies, in fact, Switzerland, Denmark, Australia, New Zealand, and America until recently, have had no foreign policy in the European sense of that phrase. Even a rule like the Monroe Doctrine arose from the desire to supplement the two oceans by a glacis of states that were sufficiently republican to have no foreign policy.

Whereas danger is a great, perhaps an indispensable condition of autocracy, [Footnote: Fisher Ames, frightened by the democratic revolution of 1800, wrote to Rufus King in 1802: "We need, as all nations do, the compression on the outside of our circle of a formidable neighbor, whose presence shall at all times excite stronger fears than demagogues can inspire the people with towards their government." Cited by Ford, *Rise and Growth of American Politics*, p. 69.] security was seen to be a necessity if democracy was to work. There must be as little disturbance as possible of the premise of a self-contained community. Insecurity involves surprises. It means that there are people acting upon your life, over whom you have no control, with whom you cannot consult. It means that forces are at large which disturb the familiar routine, and present novel problems about which quick and unusual decisions are required. Every democrat feels in his bones that dangerous crises are incompatible with democracy, because he knows that the inertia of masses is such that to act quickly a very few must decide and the rest follow rather blindly. This has not made non-resistants out of democrats, but it has resulted in all democratic wars being fought for pacifist aims. Even when the wars are in fact wars of conquest, they are sincerely believed to be wars in defense of civilization.

These various attempts to enclose a part of the earth's surface were not inspired by cowardice, apathy, or, what one of Jefferson's critics called a willingness to live under monkish discipline. The democrats had caught sight of a dazzling possibility, that every human being should rise to his full stature, freed from man-made limitations. With what they knew of the art of government, they could, no more than Aristotle before them, conceive a society of autonomous individuals, except an enclosed and simple one. They could, then, select no other premise if they were to reach the conclusion that all the people could spontaneously manage their public affairs.

5

Having adopted the premise because it was necessary to their keenest hope, they drew other conclusions as well. Since in order to have spontaneous self-government, you had to have a simple self-contained community, they took it for granted that one man was as competent as the next to manage these simple and self-contained affairs. Where the wish is father to the thought such logic is convincing. Moreover, the doctrine of the omnicompetent citizen is for most practical purposes true in the rural township. Everybody in a village sooner or later tries his hand at everything the village does. There is rotation in office by men who are jacks of all trades. There was no serious trouble with the doctrine of the omnicompetent citizen until the democratic stereotype was universally applied, so that men looked at a complicated civilization and saw an enclosed village.

Not only was the individual citizen fitted to deal with all public affairs, but he was consistently public-spirited and endowed with unflagging interest. He was public-spirited enough in the township, where he knew everybody and was interested in everybody's business. The idea of enough for the township turned easily into the idea of enough for any purpose, for as we have noted, quantitative thinking does not suit a stereotype. But there was another turn to the circle. Since everybody was assumed to be interested enough in important affairs, only those affairs came to seem important in which everybody was interested.

This meant that men formed their picture of the world outside from the unchallenged pictures in their heads. These pictures came to them well stereotyped by their parents and teachers, and were little corrected by their own experience. Only a few men had affairs that took them across state lines. Even fewer had reason to go abroad. Most voters lived their whole lives in one environment, and with nothing but a few feeble newspapers, some pamphlets, political speeches, their religious training, and rumor to go on, they had to conceive that larger environment of commerce and finance, of war and peace. The number of public opinions based on any objective report was very small in proportion to those based on casual fancy.

359

The Walter Lippmann Reader

And so for many different reasons, self-sufficiency was a spiritual ideal in the formative period. The physical isolation of the township, the loneliness of the pioneer, the theory of democracy, the Protestant tradition, and the limitations of political science all converged to make men believe that out of their own consciences they must extricate political wisdom. It is not strange that the deduction of laws from absolute principles should have usurped so much of their free energy. The American political mind had to live on its capital. In legalism it found a tested body of rules from which new rules could be spun without the labor of earning new truths from experience. The formulae became so curiously sacred that every good foreign observer has been amazed at the contrast between the dynamic practical energy of the American people and the static theorism of their public life. That steadfast love of fixed principles was simply the only way known of achieving self-sufficiency. But it meant that the public opinions of any one community about the outer world consisted chiefly of a few stereotyped images arranged in a pattern deduced from their legal and their moral codes, and animated by the feeling aroused by local experiences.

Thus democratic theory, starting from its fine vision of ultimate human dignity, was forced by lack of the instruments of knowledge for reporting its environment, to fall back upon the wisdom and experience which happened to have accumulated in the voter. God had, in the words of Jefferson, made men's breasts "His peculiar deposit for substantial and genuine virtue." These chosen people in their self-contained environment had all the facts before them. The environment was so familiar that one could take it for granted that men were talking about substantially the same things. The only real disagreements, therefore, would be in judgments about the same facts. There was no need to guarantee the sources of information. They were obvious, and equally accessible to all men. Nor was there need to trouble about the ultimate criteria. In the self-contained community one could assume, or at least did assume, a homogeneous code of morals. The only place, therefore, for differences of opinion was in the logical application of accepted standards to accepted facts. And since the reasoning faculty was also well standardized, an error in reasoning would be quickly exposed in a free discussion. It followed that truth could be obtained by liberty within these limits. The community could take its supply of information for granted; its codes it passed on through school, church, and family, and the power to draw deductions from a premise, rather than the ability to find the premise, was regarded as the chief end of intellectual training.

CHAPTER XVIII

The Role of Force, Patronage and Privilege

1

"IT has happened as was to have been foreseen," wrote Hamilton, [Footnote: *Federalist,* No. 15] "the measures of the Union have not been executed; the delinquencies of the States have, step by step, matured themselves to an extreme which has at length arrested all the wheels of the national government and brought them to an awful stand."... For "in our case the concurrence of thirteen distinct sovereign wills is requisite, under the confederation, to the complete execution of every important measure that proceeds from the Union." How could it be otherwise, he asked: "The rulers of the respective members... will undertake to judge of the propriety of the measures themselves. They will consider the conformity of the thing proposed or required to their immediate interests or aims; the momentary conveniences or inconveniences that would attend its adoption. All this will be done, and in a spirit of interested and suspicious scrutiny, without that knowledge of national circumstances and reasons of state which is essential to right judgment, and with that strong predilection in favor of local objects which can hardly fail to mislead the decision. The same process must be repeated in every member of which the body is constituted; and the execution of the plans framed by the councils of the whole, will always fluctuate on the discretion of the ill-informed and prejudiced opinion of every part. Those who have been conversant in the proceedings of popular assemblies, who have seen how difficult it often is, when there is no exterior pressure of circumstances, to bring them to harmonious resolutions on important points, will readily conceive how impossible it must be to induce a number of such assemblies, deliberating at a distance from each other, at different times, and under different impressions, long to coöperate in the same views and pursuits."

Over ten years of storm and stress with a congress that was, as John Adams said, [Footnote: Ford, *op. cit.*, p. 36.] "only a diplomatic assembly," had furnished the leaders of the revolution "with an instructive but afflicting lesson" [Footnote: *Federalist,* No. 15.] in what happens when a number of self-centered communities are entangled in the same environment. And so, when they went to Philadelphia in May of 1787, ostensibly to revise the Articles of Confederation, they were really in full reaction against the fundamental premise of Eighteenth Century democracy. Not only were the leaders consciously opposed to the democratic spirit of the time, feeling, as Madison said, that "democracies have ever been spectacles of turbulence and contention," but within the national frontiers they were determined to offset as far as they could the ideal of self-governing communities in self-contained environments. The collisions and failures of concave democracy, where men spontaneously managed all their own affairs, were before their eyes. The problem as they saw it, was to restore government as against democracy. They understood government to be the power to make national decisions and enforce them throughout the nation; democracy they believed was the insistence of localities and classes upon self-determination in accordance with their immediate interests and aims.

They could not consider in their calculations the possibility of such an organization of knowledge that separate communities would act simultaneously on the same version of the facts. We just begin to conceive this possibility for certain parts of the world where there is free circulation of news and a common language, and then only for certain aspects of life. The whole idea of a voluntary federalism in industry and world politics is still so rudimentary, that, as we see in our own experience, it enters only a little, and only very modestly, into practical politics. What we, more than a century later, can only conceive as an incentive to generations of intellectual effort, the authors of the Constitution had no reason to conceive at all. In order to set up national government, Hamilton and his colleagues had to make plans, not on the theory that men would coöperate because they had a sense of common interest, but on the theory that men could be governed, if special interests were kept in equilibrium by a balance of power. "Ambition," Madison said, [Footnote: *Federalist*, No. 51, cited by Ford, *op. cit.*, p. 60.] "must be made to counteract ambition."

They did not, as some writers have supposed, intend to balance every interest so that the government would be in a perpetual deadlock. They intended to deadlock local and class interest to prevent these from obstructing government. "In framing a government which is to be administered by men over men," wrote Madison, [Footnote: *Id.*] "the great difficulty lies in this: *you must first enable the government to control the governed*, and in the next place, oblige it to control itself."

The Walter Lippmann Reader

In one very important sense, then, the doctrine of checks and balances was the remedy of the federalist leaders for the problem of public opinion. They saw no other way to substitute "the mild influence of the magistracy" for the "sanguinary agency of the sword" [Footnote: *Federalist*, No. 15.] except by devising an ingenious machine to neutralize local opinion. They did not understand how to manipulate a large electorate, any more than they saw the possibility of common consent upon the basis of common information. It is true that Aaron Burr taught Hamilton a lesson which impressed him a good deal when he seized control of New York City in 1800 by the aid of Tammany Hall. But Hamilton was killed before he was able to take account of this new discovery, and, as Mr. Ford says, [Footnote: Ford, *op. cit.*, p. 119.] Burr's pistol blew the brains out of the Federal party.

2

When the constitution was written, "politics could still be managed by conference and agreement among gentlemen" [Footnote: *Op. cit.*, p. 144] and it was to the gentry that Hamilton turned for a government. It was intended that they should manage national affairs when local prejudice had been brought into equilibrium by the constitutional checks and balances. No doubt Hamilton, who belonged to this class by adoption, had a human prejudice in their favor. But that by itself is a thin explanation of his statecraft. Certainly there can be no question of his consuming passion for union, and it is, I think, an inversion of the truth to argue that he made the Union to protect class privileges, instead of saying that he used class privileges to make the Union. "We must take man as we find him," Hamilton said, "and if we expect him to serve the public we must interest his passions in doing so." [Footnote: *Op. cit.*, p. 47] He needed men to govern, whose passions could be most quickly attached to a national interest. These were the gentry, the public creditors, manufacturers, shippers, and traders, [Footnote: Beard, *Economic Interpretation of the Constitution, passim.*] and there is probably no better instance in history of the adaptation of shrewd means to clear ends, than in the series of fiscal measures, by which Hamilton attached the provincial notables to the new government.

Although the constitutional convention worked behind closed doors, and although ratification was engineered by "a vote of probably not more than one-sixth of the adult males," [Footnote: Beard, *op. cit.*, p. 325.] there was little or no pretence. The Federalists argued for union, not for democracy, and even the word republic had an unpleasant sound to George Washington when he had been for more than two years a republican president. The constitution was a candid attempt to limit the sphere of popular rule; the only democratic organ it was intended the government should possess was the House, based on a suffrage highly limited by property qualifications. And even at that, the House, it was believed, would be so licentious a part of the government, that it was carefully checked and balanced by the Senate, the electoral college, the Presidential veto, and by judicial interpretation.

Thus at the moment when the French Revolution was kindling popular feeling the world over, the American revolutionists of 1776 came under a constitution which went back, as far as it was expedient, to the British Monarchy for a model. This conservative reaction could not endure. The men who had made it were a minority, their motives were under suspicion, and when Washington went into retirement, the position of the gentry was not strong enough to survive the inevitable struggle for the succession. The anomaly between the original plan of the Fathers and the moral feeling of the age was too wide not to be capitalized by a good politician.

3

Jefferson referred to his election as "the great revolution of 1800," but more than anything else it was a revolution in the mind. No great policy was altered, but a new tradition was established. For it was Jefferson who first taught the American people to regard the Constitution as an instrument of democracy, and he stereotyped the images, the ideas, and even many of the phrases, in which Americans ever since have described politics to each other. So complete was the mental victory, that twenty-five years later de Tocqueville, who was received in Federalist homes, noted that even those who were "galled by its continuance"—were not uncommonly heard to "laud the delights of a republican government, and the advantages of democratic institutions when they are in public." [Footnote: *Democracy in America*, Vol. I, Ch. X (Third Edition, 1838), p. 216.]

The Constitutional Fathers with all their sagacity had failed to see that a frankly undemocratic constitution would not long be tolerated. The bold denial of popular rule was bound to offer an easy point of attack to a man, like

The Walter Lippmann Reader

Jefferson, who so far as his constitutional opinions ran, was not a bit more ready than Hamilton to turn over government to the "unrefined" will of the people. [Footnote: *Cf.* his plan for the Constitution of Virginia, his ideas for a senate of property holders, and his views on the judicial veto. Beard, *Economic Origins of Jeffersonian Democracy*, pp. 450 *et seq.*] The Federalist leaders had been men of definite convictions who stated them bluntly. There was little real discrepancy between their public and their private views. But Jefferson's mind was a mass of ambiguities, not solely because of its defects, as Hamilton and his biographers have thought, but because he believed in a union and he believed in spontaneous democracies, and in the political science of his age there was no satisfactory way to reconcile the two. Jefferson was confused in thought and action because he had a vision of a new and tremendous idea that no one had thought out in all its bearings. But though popular sovereignty was not clearly understood by anybody, it seemed to imply so great an enhancement of human life, that no constitution could stand which frankly denied it. The frank denials were therefore expunged from consciousness, and the document, which is on its face an honest example of limited constitutional democracy, was talked and thought about as an instrument for direct popular rule. Jefferson actually reached the point of believing that the Federalists had perverted the Constitution, of which in his fancy they were no longer the authors. And so the Constitution was, in spirit, rewritten. Partly by actual amendment, partly by practice, as in the case of the electoral college, but chiefly by looking at it through another set of stereotypes, the facade was no longer permitted to look oligarchic.

The American people came to believe that their Constitution was a democratic instrument, and treated it as such. They owe that fiction to the victory of Thomas Jefferson, and a great conservative fiction it has been. It is a fair guess that if everyone had always regarded the Constitution as did the authors of it, the Constitution would have been violently overthrown, because loyalty to the Constitution and loyalty to democracy would have seemed incompatible. Jefferson resolved that paradox by teaching the American people to read the Constitution as an expression of democracy. He himself stopped there. But in the course of twenty-five years or so social conditions had changed so radically, that Andrew Jackson carried out the political revolution for which Jefferson had prepared the tradition. [Footnote: The reader who has any doubts as to the extent of the revolution that separated Hamilton's opinions from Jackson's practice should turn to Mr. Henry Jones Ford's *Rise and Growth of American Politics.*]

4

The political center of that revolution was the question of patronage. By the men who founded the government public office was regarded as a species of property, not lightly to be disturbed, and it was undoubtedly their hope that the offices would remain in the hands of their social class. But the democratic theory had as one of its main principles the doctrine of the omnicompetent citizen. Therefore, when people began to look at the Constitution as a democratic instrument, it was certain that permanence in office would seem undemocratic. The natural ambitions of men coincided here with the great moral impulse of their age. Jefferson had popularized the idea without carrying it ruthlessly into practice, and removals on party grounds were comparatively few under the Virginian Presidents. It was Jackson who founded the practice of turning public office into patronage.

Curious as it sounds to us, the principle of rotation in office with short terms was regarded as a great reform. Not only did it acknowledge the new dignity of the average man by treating him as fit for any office, not only did it destroy the monopoly of a small social class and appear to open careers to talent, but "it had been advocated for centuries as a sovereign remedy for political corruption," and as the one way to prevent the creation of a bureaucracy. [Footnote: Ford, *op. cit.,* p. 169.] The practice of rapid change in public office was the application to a great territory of the image of democracy derived from the self-contained village.

Naturally it did not have the same results in the nation that it had in the ideal community on which the democratic theory was based. It produced quite unexpected results, for it founded a new governing class to take the place of the submerged federalists. Unintentionally, patronage did for a large electorate what Hamilton's fiscal measures had done for the upper classes. We often fail to realize how much of the stability of our government we owe to patronage. For it was patronage that weaned natural leaders from too much attachment to the self-centered community, it was patronage that weakened the local spirit and brought together in some kind of peaceful cooperation, the very men who, as

366

provincial celebrities, would, in the absence of a sense of common interest, have torn the union apart.

But of course, the democratic theory was not supposed to produce a new governing class, and it has never accommodated itself to the fact. When the democrat wanted to abolish monopoly of offices, to have rotation and short terms, he was thinking of the township where anyone could do a public service, and return humbly to his own farm. The idea of a special class of politicians was just what the democrat did not like. But he could not have what he did like, because his theory was derived from an ideal environment, and he was living in a real one. The more deeply he felt the moral impulse of democracy, the less ready he was to see the profound truth of Hamilton's statement that communities deliberating at a distance and under different impressions could not long coöperate in the same views and pursuits. For that truth postpones anything like the full realization of democracy in public affairs until the art of obtaining common consent has been radically improved. And so while the revolution under Jefferson and Jackson produced the patronage which made the two party system, which created a substitute for the rule of the gentry, and a discipline for governing the deadlock of the checks and balances, all that happened, as it were, invisibly.

Thus, rotation in office might be the ostensible theory, in practice the offices oscillated between the henchmen. Tenure might not be a permanent monopoly, but the professional politician was permanent. Government might be, as President Harding once said, a simple thing, but winning elections was a sophisticated performance. The salaries in office might be as ostentatiously frugal as Jefferson's home-spun, but the expenses of party organization and the fruits of victory were in the grand manner. The stereotype of democracy controlled the visible government; the corrections, the exceptions and adaptations of the American people to the real facts of their environment have had to be invisible, even when everybody knew all about them. It was only the words of the law, the speeches of politicians, the platforms, and the formal machinery of administration that have had to conform to the pristine image of democracy.

5

If one had asked a philosophical democrat how these self-contained communities were to coöperate, when their public opinions were so self-centered, he would have pointed to representative government embodied in the Congress. And nothing would surprise him more than the discovery of how steadily the prestige of representative government has declined, while the power of the Presidency has grown.

Some critics have traced this to the custom of sending only local celebrities to Washington. They have thought that if Congress could consist of the nationally eminent men, the life of the capital would be more brilliant. It would be, of course, and it would be a very good thing if retiring Presidents and Cabinet officers followed the example of John Quincy Adams. But the absence of these men does not explain the plight of Congress, for its decline began when it was relatively the most eminent branch of the government. Indeed it is more probable that the reverse is true, and that Congress ceased to attract the eminent as it lost direct influence on the shaping of national policy.

The main reason for the discredit, which is world wide, is, I think, to be found in the fact that a congress of representatives is essentially a group of blind men in a vast, unknown world. With some exceptions, the only method recognized in the Constitution or in the theory of representative government, by which Congress can inform itself, is to exchange opinions from the districts. There is no systematic, adequate, and authorized way for Congress to know what is going on in the world. The theory is that the best man of each district brings the best wisdom of his constituents to a central place, and that all these wisdoms combined are all the wisdom that Congress needs. Now there is no need to question the value of expressing local opinions and exchanging them. Congress has great value as the market-place of a continental nation. In the coatrooms, the hotel lobbies, the boarding houses of Capitol Hill, at the tea-parties of the Congressional matrons, and from occasional entries into the drawing rooms of cosmopolitan Washington, new vistas are opened, and wider horizons. But even if the theory were applied, and the districts always sent their wisest men, the sum or a combination of local impressions is not a wide enough base for national policy, and no base at all for the control of foreign policy. Since the real effects of most laws are subtle and hidden, they cannot be understood by filtering local experiences through local states of mind. They can be known only by controlled reporting and objective analysis. And just as the head of a large factory cannot know how efficient it is by talking to the foreman, but must examine cost sheets and data that only an accountant can dig out for him, so the lawmaker does not

The Walter Lippmann Reader

arrive at a true picture of the state of the union by putting together a mosaic of local pictures. He needs to know the local pictures, but unless he possesses instruments for calibrating them, one picture is as good as the next, and a great deal better.

The President does come to the assistance of Congress by delivering messages on the state of the Union. He is in a position to do that because he presides over a vast collection of bureaus and their agents, which report as well as act. But he tells Congress what he chooses to tell it. He cannot be heckled, and the censorship as to what is compatible with the public interest is in his hands. It is a wholly one-sided and tricky relationship, which sometimes reaches such heights of absurdity, that Congress, in order to secure an important document has to thank the enterprise of a Chicago newspaper, or the calculated indiscretion of a subordinate official. So bad is the contact of legislators with necessary facts that they are forced to rely either on private tips or on that legalized atrocity, the Congressional investigation, where Congressmen, starved of their legitimate food for thought, go on a wild and feverish man-hunt, and do not stop at cannibalism.

Except for the little that these investigations yield, the occasional communications from the executive departments, interested and disinterested data collected by private persons, such newspapers, periodicals, and books as Congressmen read, and a new and excellent practice of calling for help from expert bodies like the Interstate Commerce Commission, the Federal Trade Commission, and the Tariff Commission, the creation of Congressional opinion is incestuous. From this it follows either that legislation of a national character is prepared by a few informed insiders, and put through by partisan force; or that the legislation is broken up into a collection of local items, each of which is enacted for a local reason. Tariff schedules, navy yards, army posts, rivers and harbors, post offices and federal buildings, pensions and patronage: these are fed out to concave communities as tangible evidence of the benefits of national life. Being concave, they can see the white marble building which rises out of federal funds to raise local realty values and employ local contractors more readily than they can judge the cumulative cost of the pork barrel. It is fair to say that in a large assembly of men, each of whom has practical knowledge only of his own district, laws dealing with translocal affairs are rejected or accepted by the mass of Congressmen without creative participation of any kind. They participate only in making those laws that can be treated as a bundle of local issues. For a legislature without effective means of information and analysis must oscillate between blind regularity, tempered by occasional insurgency, and logrolling. And it is the logrolling which makes the regularity palatable, because it is by logrolling that a Congressman proves to his more active constituents that he is watching their interests as they conceive them.

This is no fault of the individual Congressman's, except when he is complacent about it. The cleverest and most industrious representative cannot hope to understand a fraction of the bills on which he votes. The best he can do is to specialize on a few bills, and take somebody's word about the rest. I have known Congressmen, when they were boning up on a subject, to study as they had not studied since they passed their final examinations, many large cups of black coffee, wet towels and all. They had to dig for information, sweat over arranging and verifying facts, which, in any consciously organized government, should have been easily available in a form suitable for decision. And even when they really knew a subject, their anxieties had only begun. For back home the editors, the board of trade, the central federated union, and the women's clubs had spared themselves these labors, and were prepared to view the Congressman's performance through local spectacles.

6

What patronage did to attach political chieftains to the national government, the infinite variety of local subsidies and privileges do for self-centered communities. Patronage and pork amalgamate and stabilize thousands of special opinions, local discontents, private ambitions. There are but two other alternatives. One is government by terror and obedience, the other is government based on such a highly developed system of information, analysis, and self-consciousness that "the knowledge of national circumstances and reasons of state" is evident to all men. The autocratic system is in decay, the voluntary system is in its very earliest development; and so, in calculating the prospects of association among large groups of people, a League of Nations, industrial government, or a federal union of states, the degree to which the material for a common consciousness exists, determines how far cooperation will depend upon force, or upon the milder alternative to force, which is patronage and privilege. The secret of great state-builders, like Alexander Hamilton, is that they know how to calculate these principles.

CHAPTER XIX
The Old Image in a New Form: Guild Socialism.

Whenever the quarrels of self-centered groups become unbearable, reformers in the past found themselves forced to choose between two great alternatives. They could take the path to Rome and impose a Roman peace upon the warring tribes. They could take the path to isolation, to autonomy and self-sufficiency. Almost always they chose that path which they had least recently travelled. If they had tried out the deadening monotony of empire, they cherished above all other things the simple freedom of their own community. But if they had seen this simple freedom squandered in parochial jealousies they longed for the spacious order of a great and powerful state.

Whichever choice they made, the essential difficulty was the same. If decisions were decentralized they soon floundered in a chaos of local opinions. If they were centralized, the policy of the state was based on the opinions of a small social set at the capital. In any case force was necessary to defend one local right against another, or to impose law and order on the localities, or to resist class government at the center, or to defend the whole society, centralized or decentralized, against the outer barbarian.

Modern democracy and the industrial system were both born in a time of reaction against kings, crown government, and a regime of detailed economic regulation. In the industrial sphere this reaction took the form of extreme devolution, known as laissez-faire individualism. Each economic decision was to be made by the man who had title to the property involved. Since almost everything was owned by somebody, there would be somebody to manage everything. This was plural sovereignty with a vengeance.

It was economic government by anybody's economic philosophy, though it was supposed to be controlled by immutable laws of political economy that must in the end produce harmony. It produced many splendid things, but enough sordid and terrible ones to start counter-currents. One of these was the trust, which established a kind of Roman peace within industry, and a Roman predatory imperialism outside. People turned to the legislature for relief. They invoked representative government, founded on the image of the township farmer, to

371

regulate the semi-sovereign corporations. The working class turned to labor organization. There followed a period of increasing centralization and a sort of race of armaments. The trusts interlocked, the craft unions federated and combined into a labor movement, the political system grew stronger at Washington and weaker in the states, as the reformers tried to match its strength against big business.

In this period practically all the schools of socialist thought from the Marxian left to the New Nationalists around Theodore Roosevelt, looked upon centralization as the first stage of an evolution which would end in the absorption of all the semi-sovereign powers of business by the political state. The evolution never took place, except for a few months during the war. That was enough, and there was a turn of the wheel against the omnivorous state in favor of several new forms of pluralism. But this time society was to swing back not to the atomic individualism of Adam Smith's economic man and Thomas Jefferson's farmer, but to a sort of molecular individualism of voluntary groups.

One of the interesting things about all these oscillations of theory is that each in turn promises a world in which no one will have to follow Machiavelli in order to survive. They are all established by some form of coercion, they all exercise coercion in order to maintain themselves, and they are all discarded as a result of coercion. Yet they do not accept coercion, either physical power or special position, patronage, or privilege, as part of their ideal. The individualist said that self-enlightened self-interest would bring internal and external peace. The socialist is sure that the motives to aggression will disappear. The new pluralist hopes they will. [Footnote: See G. D. H. Cole, *Social Theory*, p. 142.] Coercion is the surd in almost all social theory, except the Machiavellian. The temptation to ignore it, because it is absurd, inexpressible, and unmanageable, becomes overwhelming in any man who is trying to rationalize human life.

2

The lengths to which a clever man will sometimes go in order to escape a full recognition of the role of force is shown by Mr. G. D. H. Cole's book on Guild Socialism. The present state, he says, "is primarily an instrument of coercion;" [Footnote: Cole, *Guild Socialism*, p. 107.] in a guild socialist society there will be no sovereign power, though there will be a coordinating body. He calls this body the Commune.

He then begins to enumerate the powers of the Commune, which, we recall, is to be primarily not an instrument of coercion. [Footnote: *Op. cit.* Ch. VIII.] It settles price disputes. Sometimes it fixes prices, allocates the surplus or distributes the loss. It allocates natural resources, and controls the issue of credit. It also "allocates communal labor-power." It ratifies the budgets of the guilds and the civil services. It levies taxes. "All questions of income" fall within its jurisdiction. It "allocates" income to the non-productive members of the community. It is the final arbiter in all questions of policy and jurisdiction between the guilds. It passes constitutional laws fixing the functions of the functional bodies. It appoints the judges. It confers coercive powers upon the guilds, and ratifies their by-laws wherever these involve coercion. It declares war and makes peace. It controls the armed forces. It is the supreme representative of the nation abroad. It settles boundary questions within the national state. It calls into existence new functional bodies, or distributes new functions to old ones. It runs the police. It makes whatever laws are necessary to regulate personal conduct and personal property.

These powers are exercised not by one commune, but by a federal structure of local and provincial communes with a National commune at the top. Mr. Cole is, of course, welcome to insist that this is not a sovereign state, but if there is a coercive power now enjoyed by any modern government for which he has forgotten to make room, I cannot think of it.

He tells us, however, that Guild society will be non-coercive: "we want to build a new society which will be conceived in the spirit, not of coercion, but of free service." [Footnote: *Op. cit.*, p. 141.] Everyone who shares that hope, as most men and women do, will therefore look closely to see what there is in the Guild Socialist plan which promises to reduce coercion to its lowest limits, even though the Guildsmen of to-day have already reserved for their communes the widest kind of coercive power. It is acknowledged at once that the new society cannot be brought into existence by universal consent. Mr. Cole is too honest to shirk the element of force required to make the transition. [Footnote: *Cf. op. cit.*, Ch. X.] And while obviously he cannot predict how much civil war there might be, he is quite clear that there would have to be a period of direct action by the trade unions.

The Walter Lippmann Reader

But leaving aside the problems of transition, and any consideration of what the effect is on their future action, when men have hacked their way through to the promised land, let us imagine the Guild Society in being. What keeps it running as a non-coercive society?

Mr. Cole has two answers to this question. One is the orthodox Marxian answer that the abolition of capitalist property will remove the motive to aggression. Yet he does not really believe that, because if he did, he would care as little as does the average Marxian how the working class is to run the government, once it is in control. If his diagnosis were correct, the Marxian would be quite right: if the disease were the capitalist class and only the capitalist class, salvation would automatically follow its extinction. But Mr. Cole is enormously concerned about whether the society which follows the revolution is to be run by state collectivism, by guilds or cooperative societies, by a democratic parliament or by functional representation. In fact, it is as a new theory of representative government that guild socialism challenges attention.

The guildsmen do not expect a miracle to result from the disappearance of capitalist property rights. They do expect, and of course quite rightly, that if equality of income were the rule, social relations would be profoundly altered. But they differ, as far as I can make out, from the orthodox Russian communist in this respect: The communist proposes to establish equality by force of the dictatorship of the proletariat, believing that if once people were equalized both in income and in service, they would then lose the incentives to aggression. The guildsmen also propose to establish equality by force, but are shrewd enough to see that if an equilibrium is to be maintained they have to provide institutions for maintaining it. Guildsmen, therefore, put their faith in what they believe to be a new theory of democracy.

Their object, says Mr. Cole, is "to get the mechanism right, and to adjust it as far as possible to the expression of men's social wills." [Reference: *Op. cit.*, p. 16.] These wills need to be given opportunity for self-expression in self-government "in any and every form of social action." Behind these words is the true democratic impulse, the desire to enhance human dignity, as well as the traditional assumption that this human dignity is impugned, unless each person's will enters into the management of everything that affects him. The guildsman, like the earlier democrat therefore, looks about him for an

374

environment in which this ideal of self-government can be realized. A hundred years and more have passed since Rousseau and Jefferson, and the center of interest has shifted from the country to the city. The new democrat can no longer turn to the idealized rural township for the image of democracy. He turns now to the workshop. "The spirit of association must be given free play in the sphere in which it is best able to find expression. This is manifestly the factory, in which men have the habit and tradition of working together. The factory is the natural and fundamental unit of industrial democracy. This involves, not only that the factory must be free, as far as possible, to manage its own affairs, but also that the democratic unit of the factory must be made the basis of the larger democracy of the Guild, and that the larger organs of Guild administration and government must be based largely on the principle of factory representation." [Footnote: *Op. cit.*, p. 40.]

Factory is, of course, a very loose word, and Mr. Cole asks us to take it as meaning mines, shipyards, docks, stations, and every place which is "a natural center of production." [Footnote: *Op. cit.*, p. 41] But a factory in this sense is quite a different thing from an industry. The factory, as Mr. Cole conceives it, is a work place where men are really in personal contact, an environment small enough to be known directly to all the workers. "This democracy if it is to be real, must come home to, and be exercisable directly by, every individual member of the Guild." [Footnote: *Op. cit.*, p. 40.] This is important, because Mr. Cole, like Jefferson, is seeking a natural unit of government. The only natural unit is a perfectly familiar environment. Now a large plant, a railway system, a great coal field, is not a natural unit in this sense. Unless it is a very small factory indeed, what Mr. Cole is really thinking about is the shop. That is where men can be supposed to have "the habit and tradition of working together." The rest of the plant, the rest of the industry, is an inferred environment.

4

Anybody can see, and almost everybody will admit, that self-government in the purely internal affairs of the shop is government of affairs that "can be taken in at a single view." [Footnote: Aristotle, *Politics*, Bk. VII, Ch. IV.] But dispute would arise as to what constitute the internal affairs of a shop. Obviously the biggest interests, like wages, standards of production, the purchase of supplies, the marketing of the product, the larger planning of work, are by no means purely internal. The shop democracy has freedom, subject to enormous limiting conditions from the outside. It can deal to a certain extent with the arrangement of work laid out for the shop, it can deal with the temper and temperament of individuals, it can administer petty industrial justice, and act as a court of first instance in somewhat larger individual disputes. Above all it can act as a unit in dealing with other shops, and perhaps with the plant as a whole. But isolation is impossible. The unit of industrial democracy is thoroughly entangled in foreign affairs. And it is the management of these external relations that constitutes the test of the guild socialist theory.

They have to be managed by representative government arranged in a federal order from the shop to the plant, the plant to the industry, the industry to the nation, with intervening regional grouping of representatives. But all this structure derives from the shop, and all its peculiar virtues are ascribed to this source. The representatives who choose the representatives who choose the representatives who finally "coordinate" and "regulate" the shops are elected, Mr. Cole asserts, by a true democracy. Because they come originally from a self-governing unit, the whole federal organism will be inspired by the spirit and the reality of self-government. Representatives will aim to carry out the workers' "actual will as understood by themselves," [Footnote: *Op. cit.*, p. 42.] that is, as understood by the individual in the shops.

A government run literally on this principle would, if history is any guide, be either a perpetual logroll, or a chaos of warring shops. For while the worker in the shop can have a real opinion about matters entirely within the shop, his "will" about the relation of that shop to the plant, the industry, and the nation is subject to all the limitations of access, stereotype, and self-interest that surround any other self-centered opinion. His experience in the shop at best brings only aspects of the whole to his attention. His opinion of what is right within the shop he can reach by direct knowledge of the essential facts. His opinion of what is right in the great complicated environment out of sight is more likely to be wrong than right if it is a generalization from the experience of the individual shop. As a matter of experience, the representatives of a guild society would find, just as the higher trade union officials find today, that on a great number of questions which they have to decide there is no "actual will as understood" by the shops.

The Walter Lippmann Reader

The guildsmen insist, however, that such criticism is blind because it ignores a great political discovery. You may be quite right, they would say, in thinking that the representatives of the shops would have to make up their own minds on many questions about which the shops have no opinion. But you are simply entangled in an ancient fallacy: you are looking for somebody to represent a group of people. He cannot be found. The only representative possible is one who acts for "some particular function," [Footnote: *Op. cit.*, pp. 23-24.] and therefore each person must help choose as many representatives "as there are distinct essential groups of functions to be performed."

Assume then that the representatives speak, not for the men in the shops, but for certain functions in which the men are interested. They are, mind you, disloyal if they do not carry out the will of the group about the function, as understood by the group. [Footnote: *Cf.* Part V, "The Making of a Common Will."] These functional representatives meet. Their business is to coordinate and regulate. By what standard does each judge the proposals of the other, assuming, as we must, that there is conflict of opinion between the shops, since if there were not, there would be no need to coordinate and regulate?

Now the peculiar virtue of functional democracy is supposed to be that men vote candidly according to their own interests, which it is assumed they know by daily experience. They can do that within the self-contained group. But in its external relations the group as a whole, or its representative, is dealing with matters that transcend immediate experience. The shop does not arrive spontaneously at a view of the whole situation. Therefore, the public opinions of a shop about its rights and duties in the industry and in society, are matters of education or propaganda, not the automatic product of shop-consciousness. Whether the guildsmen elect a delegate, or a representative, they do not escape the problem of the orthodox democrat. Either the group as a whole, or the elected spokesman, must stretch his mind beyond the limits of direct experience. He must vote on questions coming up from other shops, and on matters coming from beyond the frontiers of the whole industry. The primary interest of the shop does not even cover the function of a whole industrial vocation. The function of a vocation, a great industry, a district, a nation is a concept, not an experience, and has to be imagined, invented, taught and believed. And even though you define function as carefully as possible, once you admit that the view of each shop on that function will not necessarily coincide with the view of other shops, you are saying that the representative of one interest is concerned in the proposals made by other interests. You are saying that he must conceive a common interest. And in voting for him you are choosing a man who will not simply represent your view of your function, which is all that you know at first hand, but a man who will represent your views about other people's views of that function. You are voting as indefinitely as the orthodox democrat.

6

The guildsmen in their own minds have solved the question of how to conceive a common interest by playing with the word function. They imagine a society in which all the main work of the world has been analysed into functions, and these functions in turn synthesized harmoniously. [Footnote: *Cf. op. cit.*, Ch. XIX.] They suppose essential agreement about the purposes of society as a whole, and essential agreement about the role of every organized group in carrying out those purposes. It was a nice sentiment, therefore, which led them to take the name of their theory from an institution that arose in a Catholic feudal society. But they should remember that the scheme of function which the wise men of that age assumed was not worked out by mortal man. It is unclear how the guildsmen think the scheme is going to be worked out and made acceptable in the modern world. Sometimes they seem to argue that the scheme will develop from trade union organization, at other times that the communes will define the constitutional function of the groups. But it makes a considerable practical difference whether they believe that the groups define their own functions or not.

In either case, Mr. Cole assumes that society can be carried on by a social contract based on an accepted idea of "distinct essential groups of functions." How does one recognize these distinct essential groups? So far as I can make out, Mr. Cole thinks that a function is what a group of people are interested in. "The essence of functional democracy is that a man should count as many times over as there are functions in which he is interested." [Footnote: *Social Theory*, p. 102 *et seq.*] Now there are at least two meanings to the word interested. You can use it to mean that a man is involved, or that his mind is occupied. John Smith, for example, may have been tremendously interested in the Stillman divorce case. He may have read every word of the news in every lobster edition. On the other hand, young Guy Stillman, whose legitimacy was at stake, probably did not trouble himself at all. John Smith was interested in a suit that did not affect his "interests," and Guy was uninterested in one that would determine the whole course of his life. Mr. Cole, I am afraid, leans towards John Smith. He is answering the "very foolish objection" that to vote by functions is to be voting very often: "If a man is not interested enough to vote, and cannot be aroused to interest enough to make him vote, on, say, a dozen distinct subjects, he waives his right to vote and the result is no less democratic than if he voted blindly and without interest."

Mr. Cole thinks that the uninstructed voter "waives his right to vote." From this it follows that the votes of the instructed reveal their interest, and their interest defines the function. [Footnote: *Cf.* Ch. XVIII of this book. "Since everybody was assumed to be interested enough in important affairs, only those affairs came to seem important in which everybody was interested."] "Brown, Jones, and Robinson must therefore have, not one vote each, but as many different functional votes as there are different questions calling for associative action in which they are interested." [Footnote: *Guild Socialism*, p. 24.] I am considerably in doubt whether Mr. Cole thinks that Brown, Jones and Robinson should qualify in any election where they assert that they are interested, or that somebody else, not named, picks the functions in which they are entitled to be interested. If I were asked to say what I believe Mr. Cole thinks, it would be that he has smoothed over the difficulty by the enormously strange assumption that it is the uninstructed voter who waives his right to vote; and has concluded that whether functional voting is arranged by a higher power, or "from below" on the principle that a man may vote when it interests him to vote, only the instructed will be voting anyway, and therefore the institution will work.

But there are two kinds of uninstructed voter. There is the man who does not know and knows that he does not know. He is generally an enlightened person. He is the man who waives his right to vote. But there is also the man who is uninstructed and does not know that he is, or care. He can always be gotten to the polls, if the party machinery is working. His vote is the basis of the machine. And since the communes of the guild society have large powers over taxation, wages, prices, credit, and natural resources, it would be preposterous to assume that elections will not be fought at least as passionately as our own.

The Walter Lippmann Reader

The way people exhibit their interest will not then delimit the functions of a functional society. There are two other ways that function might be defined. One would be by the trade unions which fought the battle that brought guild socialism into being. Such a struggle would harden groups of men together in some sort of functional relation, and these groups would then become the vested interests of the guild socialist society. Some of them, like the miners and railroad men, would be very strong, and probably deeply attached to the view of their function which they learned from the battle with capitalism. It is not at all unlikely that certain favorably placed trade unions would under a socialist state become the center of coherence and government. But a guild society would inevitably find them a tough problem to deal with, for direct action would have revealed their strategic power, and some of their leaders at least would not offer up this power readily on the altar of freedom. In order to "coordinate" them, guild society would have to gather together its strength, and fairly soon one would find, I think, that the radicals under guild socialism would be asking for communes strong enough to define the functions of the guilds.

But if you are going to have the government (commune) define functions, the premise of the theory disappears. It had to suppose that a scheme of functions was obvious in order that the concave shops would voluntarily relate themselves to society. If there is no settled scheme of functions in every voter's head, he has no better way under guild socialism than under orthodox democracy of turning a self-centered opinion into a social judgment. And, of course, there can be no such settled scheme, because, even if Mr. Cole and his friends devised a good one, the shop democracies from which all power derives, would judge the scheme in operation by what they learn of it and by what they can imagine. The guilds would see the same scheme differently. And so instead of the scheme being the skeleton that keeps guild society together, the attempt to define what the scheme ought to be, would be under guild socialism as elsewhere, the main business of politics. If we could allow Mr. Cole his scheme of functions we could allow him almost everything. Unfortunately he has inserted in his premise what he wishes a guild society to deduce. [Footnote: I have dealt with Mr. Cole's theory rather than with the experience of Soviet Russia because, while the testimony is fragmentary, all competent observers seem to agree that Russia in 1921 does not illustrate a communist state in working order. Russia is in revolution, and what you can learn from Russia is what a revolution is like. You

380

can learn very little about what a communist society would be like. It is, however, immensely significant that, first as practical revolutionists and then as public officials, the Russian communists have relied not upon the spontaneous democracy of the Russian people, but on the discipline, special interest and the noblesse oblige of a specialized class-the loyal and indoctrinated members of the Communist party. In the "transition," on which no time limit has been set, I believe, the cure for class government and the coercive state is strictly homeopathic.

There is also the question of why I selected Mr. Cole's books rather than the much more closely reasoned "Constitution for the Socialist Commonwealth of Great Britain" by Sidney and Beatrice Webb. I admire that book very much; but I have not been able to convince myself that it is not an intellectual tour de force. Mr. Cole seems to me far more authentically in the spirit of the socialist movement, and therefore, a better witness.]

CHAPTER XX

A New Image

1

THE lesson is, I think, a fairly clear one. In the absence of institutions and education by which the environment is so successfully reported that the realities of public life stand out sharply against self-centered opinion, the common interests very largely elude public opinion entirely, and can be managed only by a specialized class whose personal interests reach beyond the locality. This class is irresponsible, for it acts upon information that is not common property, in situations that the public at large does not conceive, and it can be held to account only on the accomplished fact.

The democratic theory by failing to admit that self-centered opinions are not sufficient to procure good government, is involved in perpetual conflict between theory and practice. According to the theory, the full dignity of man requires that his will should be, as Mr. Cole says, expressed "in any and every form of social action." It is supposed that the expression of their will is the consuming passion of men, for they are assumed to possess by instinct the art of government. But as a matter of plain experience, self-determination is only one of the many interests of a human personality. The desire to be the master of one's own destiny is a strong desire, but it has to adjust itself to other equally strong desires, such as the desire for a good life, for peace, for relief from burdens. In the original assumptions of democracy it was held that the expression of each man's will would spontaneously satisfy not only his desire for self-expression, but his desire for a good life, because the instinct to express one's self in a good life was innate.

The emphasis, therefore, has always been on the mechanism for expressing the will. The democratic El Dorado has always been some perfect environment, and some perfect system of voting and representation, where the innate good will and instinctive statesmanship of every man could be translated into action. In limited areas and for brief periods the environment has been so favorable, that is to say so isolated, and so rich in opportunity, that the theory worked well enough to confirm men in thinking that it was sound for all time and everywhere. Then when the isolation ended, and society became complex, and men had to adjust themselves closely to one another, the democrat spent his time trying to devise more perfect units of voting, in the hope that somehow he would, as Mr. Cole says, "get the mechanism right, and adjust it as far as possible to men's social wills." But while the democratic theorist was busy at this, he was far away from the actual interests of human nature. He was absorbed by one interest: self-government. Mankind was interested in all kinds of other things, in order, in its rights, in prosperity, in sights and sounds and in not being bored. In so far as spontaneous democracy does not satisfy their other interests, it seems to most men most of the time to be an empty thing. Because the art of successful self-government is not instinctive, men do not long desire self-government for its own sake. They desire it for the sake of the results. That is why the impulse to self-government is always strongest as a protest against bad conditions.

The democratic fallacy has been its preoccupation with the origin of government rather than with the processes and results. The democrat has always assumed that if political power could be derived in the right way, it would be beneficent. His whole attention has been on the source of power, since he is hypnotized by the belief that the great thing is to express the will of the people, first because expression is the highest interest of man, and second because the will is instinctively good. But no amount of regulation at the source of a river will completely control its behavior, and while democrats have been absorbed in trying to find a good mechanism for originating social power, that is to say a good mechanism of voting and representation, they neglected almost every other interest of men. For no matter how power originates, the crucial interest is in how power is exercised. What determines the quality of civilization is the use made of power. And that use cannot be controlled at the source.

If you try to control government wholly at the source, you inevitably make all the vital decisions invisible. For since there is no instinct which automatically makes political decisions that produce a good life, the men who actually exercise power not only fail to express the will of the people, because on most questions no will exists, but they exercise power according to opinions which are hidden from the electorate.

If, then, you root out of the democratic philosophy the whole assumption in all its ramifications that government is instinctive, and that therefore it can be managed by self-centered opinions, what becomes of the democratic faith in the dignity of man? It takes a fresh lease of life by associating itself with the whole personality instead of with a meager aspect of it. For the traditional democrat risked the dignity of man on one very precarious assumption, that he would exhibit that dignity instinctively in wise laws and good government. Voters did not do that, and so the democrat was forever being made to look a little silly by tough-minded men. But if, instead of hanging human dignity on the one assumption about self-government, you insist that man's dignity requires a standard of living, in which his capacities are properly exercised, the whole problem changes. The criteria which you then apply to government are whether it is producing a certain minimum of health, of decent housing, of material necessities, of education, of freedom, of pleasures, of beauty, not simply whether at the sacrifice of all these things, it vibrates to the self-centered opinions that happen to be floating around in men's minds. In the degree to which these criteria can be made exact and objective, political decision, which is inevitably the concern of comparatively few people, is actually brought into relation with the interests of men.

There is no prospect, in any time which we can conceive, that the whole invisible environment will be so clear to all men that they will spontaneously arrive at sound public opinions on the whole business of government. And even if there were a prospect, it is extremely doubtful whether many of us would wish to be bothered, or would take the time to form an opinion on "any and every form of social action" which affects us. The only prospect which is not visionary is that each of us in his own sphere will act more and more on a realistic picture of the invisible world, and that we shall develop more and more men who are expert in keeping these pictures realistic. Outside the rather narrow range of our own possible attention, social control depends upon devising standards of living and methods of audit by which the acts of public officials and industrial directors are measured. We cannot ourselves inspire or guide all these acts, as the mystical democrat has always imagined. But we can steadily increase our real control over these acts by insisting that all of them shall be plainly recorded, and their results objectively measured. I should say, perhaps, that we can progressively hope to insist. For the working out of such standards and of such audits has only begun.

PART VII
NEWSPAPERS

CHAPTER XXI
The Buying Public

1

THE idea that men have to go forth and study the world in order to govern it, has played a very minor part in political thought. It could figure very little, because the machinery for reporting the world in any way useful to government made comparatively little progress from the time of Aristotle to the age in which the premises of democracy were established.

Therefore, if you had asked a pioneer democrat where the information was to come from on which the will of the people was to be based, he would have been puzzled by the question. It would have seemed a little as if you had asked him where his life or his soul came from. The will of the people, he almost always assumed, exists at all times; the duty of political science was to work out the inventions of the ballot and representative government. If they were properly worked out and applied under the right conditions, such as exist in the self-contained village or the self-contained shop, the mechanism would somehow overcome the brevity of attention which Aristotle had observed, and the narrowness of its range, which the theory of a self-contained community tacitly acknowledged. We have seen how even at this late date the guild socialists are transfixed by the notion that if only you can build on the right unit of voting and representation, an intricate cooperative commonwealth is possible.

Convinced that the wisdom was there if only you could find it, democrats have treated the problem of making public opinions as a problem in civil liberties. [Footnote: The best study is Prof. Zechariah Chafee's, *Freedom of Speech*.] "Who ever knew Truth put to the worse, in a free and open encounter?" [Footnote: Milton, *Areopagitica*, cited at the opening of Mr. Chafee's book. For comment on this classic doctrine of liberty as stated by Milton, John Stuart Mill, and Mr. Bertrand Russel, see my *Liberty and the News*, Ch. II.] Supposing that no one has ever seen it put to the worse, are we to believe then that the truth is generated by the encounter, like fire by rubbing two sticks? Behind this classic doctrine of liberty, which American democrats embodied in their Bill of Rights, there are, in

385

The Walter Lippmann Reader

fact, several different theories of the origin of truth. One is a faith that in the competition of opinions, the truest will win because there is a peculiar strength in the truth. This is probably sound if you allow the competition to extend over a sufficiently long time. When men argue in this vein they have in mind the verdict of history, and they think specifically of heretics persecuted when they lived, canonized after they were dead. Milton's question rests also on a belief that the capacity to recognize truth is inherent in all men, and that truth freely put in circulation will win acceptance. It derives no less from the experience, which has shown that men are not likely to discover truth if they cannot speak it, except under the eye of an uncomprehending policeman.

No one can possibly overestimate the practical value of these civil liberties, nor the importance of maintaining them. When they are in jeopardy, the human spirit is in jeopardy, and should there come a time when they have to be curtailed, as during a war, the suppression of thought is a risk to civilization which might prevent its recovery from the effects of war, if the hysterics, who exploit the necessity, were numerous enough to carry over into peace the taboos of war. Fortunately, the mass of men is too tolerant long to enjoy the professional inquisitors, as gradually, under the criticism of men not willing to be terrorized, they are revealed as mean-spirited creatures who nine-tenths of the time do not know what they are talking about. [Footnote: *Cf.* for example, the publications of the Lusk Committee in New York, and the public statements and prophecies of Mr. Mitchell Palmer, who was Attorney-General of the United States during the period of President Wilson's illness.]

But in spite of its fundamental importance, civil liberty in this sense does not guarantee public opinion in the modern world. For it always assumes, either that truth is spontaneous, or that the means of securing truth exist when there is no external interference. But when you are dealing with an invisible environment, the assumption is false. The truth about distant or complex matters is not self-evident, and the machinery for assembling information is technical and expensive. Yet political science, and especially democratic political science, has never freed itself from the original assumption of Aristotle's politics sufficiently to restate the premises, so that political thought might come to grips with the problem of how to make the invisible world visible to the citizens of a modern state.

386

The Walter Lippmann Reader

So deep is the tradition, that until quite recently, for example, political science was taught in our colleges as if newspapers did not exist. I am not referring to schools of journalism, for they are trade schools, intended to prepare men and women for a career. I am referring to political science as expounded to future business men, lawyers, public officials, and citizens at large. In that science a study of the press and the sources of popular information found no place. It is a curious fact. To anyone not immersed in the routine interests of political science, it is almost inexplicable that no American student of government, no American sociologist, has ever written a book on news-gathering. There are occasional references to the press, and statements that it is not, or that it ought to be, "free" and "truthful." But I can find almost nothing else. And this disdain of the professionals finds its counterpart in public opinions. Universally it is admitted that the press is the chief means of contact with the unseen environment. And practically everywhere it is assumed that the press should do spontaneously for us what primitive democracy imagined each of us could do spontaneously for himself, that every day and twice a day it will present us with a true picture of all the outer world in which we are interested.

2

This insistent and ancient belief that truth is not earned, but inspired, revealed, supplied gratis, comes out very plainly in our economic prejudices as readers of newspapers. We expect the newspaper to serve us with truth however unprofitable the truth may be. For this difficult and often dangerous service, which we recognize as fundamental, we expected to pay until recently the smallest coin turned out by the mint. We have accustomed ourselves now to paying two and even three cents on weekdays, and on Sundays, for an illustrated encyclopedia and vaudeville entertainment attached, we have screwed ourselves up to paying a nickel or even a dime. Nobody thinks for a moment that he ought to pay for his newspaper. He expects the fountains of truth to bubble, but he enters into no contract, legal or moral, involving any risk, cost or trouble to himself. He will pay a nominal price when it suits him, will stop paying whenever it suits him, will turn to another paper when that suits him. Somebody has said quite aptly that the newspaper editor has to be re-elected every day.

This casual and one-sided relationship between readers and press is an anomaly of our civilization. There is nothing else quite like it, and it is,

The Walter Lippmann Reader

therefore, hard to compare the press with any other business or institution. It is not a business pure and simple, partly because the product is regularly sold below cost, but chiefly because the community applies one ethical measure to the press and another to trade or manufacture. Ethically a newspaper is judged as if it were a church or a school. But if you try to compare it with these you fail; the taxpayer pays for the public school, the private school is endowed or supported by tuition fees, there are subsidies and collections for the church. You cannot compare journalism with law, medicine or engineering, for in every one of these professions the consumer pays for the service. A free press, if you judge by the attitude of the readers, means newspapers that are virtually given away.

Yet the critics of the press are merely voicing the moral standards of the community, when they expect such an institution to live on the same plane as that on which the school, the church, and the disinterested professions are supposed to live. This illustrates again the concave character of democracy. No need for artificially acquired information is felt to exist. The information must come naturally, that is to say gratis, if not out of the heart of the citizen, then gratis out of the newspaper. The citizen will pay for his telephone, his railroad rides, his motor car, his entertainment. But he does not pay openly for his news.

He will, however, pay handsomely for the privilege of having someone read about him. He will pay directly to advertise. And he will pay indirectly for the advertisements of other people, because that payment, being concealed in the price of commodities is part of an invisible environment that he does not effectively comprehend. It would be regarded as an outrage to have to pay openly the price of a good ice cream soda for all the news of the world, though the public will pay that and more when it buys the advertised commodities. The public pays for the press, but only when the payment is concealed.

3

Circulation is, therefore, the means to an end. It becomes an asset only when it can be sold to the advertiser, who buys it with revenues secured through indirect taxation of the reader. [Footnote: "An established newspaper is entitled to fix its advertising rates so that its net receipts from circulation may be left on the credit side of the profit and loss account. To arrive at net receipts, I would deduct from the gross the cost of promotion, distribution, and other expenses incidental to circulation." From an address by Mr. Adolph S. Ochs, publisher

388

The Walter Lippmann Reader

of the New York Times, at the Philadelphia Convention of the Associated Advertising Clubs of The World, June 26, 1916. Cited, Elmer Davis, History of The New York Times, 1851-1921, pp. 397-398.] The kind of circulation which the advertiser will buy depends on what he has to sell. It may be "quality" or "mass." On the whole there is no sharp dividing line, for in respect to most commodities sold by advertising, the customers are neither the small class of the very rich nor the very poor. They are the people with enough surplus over bare necessities to exercise discretion in their buying. The paper, therefore, which goes into the homes of the fairly prosperous is by and large the one which offers most to the advertiser. It may also go into the homes of the poor, but except for certain lines of goods, an analytical advertising agent does not rate that circulation as a great asset, unless, as seems to be the case with certain of Mr. Hearst's properties, the circulation is enormous.

A newspaper which angers those whom it pays best to reach through advertisements is a bad medium for an advertiser. And since no one ever claimed that advertising was philanthropy, advertisers buy space in those publications which are fairly certain to reach their future customers. One need not spend much time worrying about the unreported scandals of the dry-goods merchants. They represent nothing really significant, and incidents of this sort are less common than many critics of the press suppose. The real problem is that the readers of a newspaper, unaccustomed to paying the cost of newsgathering, can be capitalized only by turning them into circulation that can be sold to manufacturers and merchants. And those whom it is most important to capitalize are those who have the most money to spend. Such a press is bound to respect the point of view of the buying public. It is for this buying public that newspapers are edited and published, for without that support the newspaper cannot live. A newspaper can flout an advertiser, it can attack a powerful banking or traction interest, but if it alienates the buying public, it loses the one indispensable asset of its existence.

Mr. John L. Given, [Footnote: Making a Newspaper, p. 13. This is the best technical book I know, and should be read by everyone who undertakes to discuss the press. Mr. G. B. Diblee, who wrote the volume on The Newspaper in the Home University Library says (p. 253), that "on the press for pressmen I only know of one good book, Mr. Given's."] formerly of the New York Evening Sun, stated in 1914 that out of over two thousand three hundred dailies published in the United States, there were about one hundred and seventy-five printed in cities having over one hundred thousand inhabitants. These constitute the press for "general news." They are the key papers which collect the news dealing with great events, and even the people who do not read any one of the one hundred and seventy-five depend ultimately upon them for news of the outer world. For they make up the great press associations which coöperate in the exchange of news. Each is, therefore, not only the informant of its own readers, but it is the local reporter for the newspapers of other cities. The rural press and the special press by and large, take their general news from these key papers. And among these there are some very much richer than others, so that for international news, in the main, the whole press of the nation may depend upon the reports of the press associations and the special services of a few metropolitan dailies.

Roughly speaking, the economic support for general news gathering is in the price paid for advertised goods by the fairly prosperous sections of cities with more than one hundred thousand inhabitants. These buying publics are composed of the members of families, who depend for their income chiefly on trade, merchandising, the direction of manufacture, and finance. They are the clientele among whom it pays best to advertise in a newspaper. They wield a concentrated purchasing power, which may be less in volume than the aggregate for farmers and workingmen; but within the radius covered by a daily newspaper they are the quickest assets.

4

They have, moreover, a double claim to attention. They are not only the best customers for the advertiser, they include the advertisers. Therefore the impression made by the newspapers on this public matters deeply. Fortunately this public is not unanimous. It may be "capitalistic" but it contains divergent views on what capitalism is, and how it is to be run. Except in times of danger, this respectable opinion is sufficiently divided to permit of considerable differences of policy. These would be greater still if it were not that publishers are themselves usually members of these urban communities, and honestly see the world through the lenses of their associates and friends.

They are engaged in a speculative business, [Footnote: Sometimes so speculative that in order to secure credit the publisher has to go into bondage to his creditors. Information on this point is very difficult to obtain, and for that

The Walter Lippmann Reader

reason its general importance is often much exaggerated.] which depends on the general condition of trade, and more peculiarly on a circulation based not on a marriage contract with their readers, but on free love. The object of every publisher is, therefore, to turn his circulation from a medley of catch-as-catch-can news stand buyers into a devoted band of constant readers. A newspaper that can really depend upon the loyalty of its readers is as independent as a newspaper can be, given the economics of modern journalism. [Footnote: "It is an axiom in newspaper publishing—'more readers, more independence of the influence of advertisers; fewer readers and more dependence on the advertiser' It may seem like a contradiction (yet it is the truth) to assert: the greater the number of advertisers, the less influence they are individually able to exercise with the publisher." Adolph S. Ochs, *of. supra.*] A body of readers who stay by it through thick and thin is a power greater than any which the individual advertiser can wield, and a power great enough to break up a combination of advertisers. Therefore, whenever you find a newspaper betraying its readers for the sake of an advertiser, you can be fairly certain either that the publisher sincerely shares the views of the advertiser, or that he thinks, perhaps mistakenly, he cannot count upon the support of his readers if he openly resists dictation. It is a question of whether the readers, who do not pay in cash for their news, will pay for it in loyalty.

CHAPTER XXII
The Constant Reader

1

THE loyalty of the buying public to a newspaper is not stipulated in any bond. In almost every other enterprise the person who expects to be served enters into an agreement that controls his passing whims. At least he pays for what he obtains. In the publishing of periodicals the nearest approach to an agreement for a definite time is the paid subscription, and that is not, I believe, a great factor in the economy of a metropolitan daily. The reader is the sole and the daily judge of his loyalty, and there can be no suit against him for breach of promise or nonsupport.

Though everything turns on the constancy of the reader, there does not exist even a vague tradition to call that fact to the reader's mind. His constancy depends on how he happens to feel, or on his habits. And these depend not simply on the quality of the news, but more often on a number of obscure elements that in our casual relation to the press, we hardly take the trouble to make conscious. The most important of these is that each of us tends to judge a newspaper, if we judge it at all, by its treatment of that part of the news in which we feel ourselves involved. The newspaper deals with a multitude of events beyond our experience. But it deals also with some events within our experience. And by its handling of those events we most frequently decide to like it or dislike it, to trust it or refuse to have the sheet in the house. If the newspaper gives a satisfactory account of that which we think we know, our business, our church, our party, it is fairly certain to be immune from violent criticism by us. What better criterion does the man at the breakfast table possess than that the newspaper version checks up with his own opinion? Therefore, most men tend to hold the newspaper most strictly accountable in their capacity, not of general readers, but of special pleaders on matters of their own experience.

Rarely is anyone but the interested party able to test the accuracy of a report. If the news is local, and if there is competition, the editor knows that he will probably hear from the man who thinks his portrait unfair and inaccurate. But if the news is not local, the corrective diminishes as the subject matter recedes into the distance. The only people who can correct what they think is a false picture

392

of themselves printed in another city are members of groups well enough organized to hire publicity men.

Now it is interesting to note that the general reader of a newspaper has no standing in law if he thinks he is being misled by the news. It is only the aggrieved party who can sue for slander or libel, and he has to prove a material injury to himself. The law embodies the tradition that general news is not a matter of common concern, [Footnote: The reader will not mistake this as a plea for censorship. It might, however, be a good thing if there were competent tribunals, preferably not official ones, where charges of untruthfulness and unfairness in the general news could be sifted. *Cf. Liberty and the News*, pp. 73-76.] except as to matter which is vaguely described as immoral or seditious.

But the body of the news, though unchecked as a whole by the disinterested reader, consists of items about which some readers have very definite preconceptions. Those items are the data of his judgment, and news which men read without this personal criterion, they judge by some other standard than their standard of accuracy. They are dealing here with a subject matter which to them is indistinguishable from fiction. The canon of truth cannot be applied. They do not boggle over such news if it conforms to their stereotypes, and they continue to read it if it interests them. [Footnote: Note, for example, how absent is indignation in Mr. Upton Sinclair against socialist papers, even those which are as malignantly unfair to employers as certain of the papers cited by him are unfair to radicals.]

2

There are newspapers, even in large cities, edited on the principle that the readers wish to read about themselves. The theory is that if enough people see their own names in the paper often enough, can read about their weddings, funerals, sociables, foreign travels, lodge meetings, school prizes, their fiftieth birthdays, their sixtieth birthdays, their silver weddings, their outings and clambakes, they will make a reliable circulation.

The classic formula for such a newspaper is contained in a letter written by Horace Greeley on April 3, 1860, to "Friend Fletcher" who was about to start a country newspaper: [Footnote: Cited, James Melvin Lee, *The History of American Journalism*, p. 405.]

The Walter Lippmann Reader

"I. Begin with a clear conception that the subject of deepest interest to an average human being is himself; next to that he is most concerned about his neighbors. Asia and the Tongo Islands stand a long way after these in his regard.... Do not let a new church be organized, or new members be added to one already existing, a farm be sold, a new house raised, a mill set in motion, a store opened, nor anything of interest to a dozen families occur, without having the fact duly, though briefly, chronicled in your columns. If a farmer cuts a big tree, or grows a mammoth beet, or harvests a bounteous yield of wheat or corn, set forth the fact as concisely and unexceptionally as possible."

The function of becoming, as Mr. Lee puts it, "the printed diary of the home town" is one that every newspaper no matter where it is published must in some measure fill. And where, as in a great city like New York, the general newspapers circulated broadcast cannot fill it, there exist small newspapers published on Greeley's pattern for sections of the city. In the boroughs of Manhattan and the Bronx there are perhaps twice as many local dailies as there are general newspapers. [Footnote: Cf. John L. Given, *Making a Newspaper*, p. 13.] And they are supplemented by all kinds of special publications for trades, religions, nationalities.

These diaries are published for people who find their own lives interesting. But there are also great numbers of people who find their own lives dull, and wish, like Hedda Gabler, to live a more thrilling life. For them there are published a few whole newspapers, and sections of others, devoted to the personal lives of a set of imaginary people, with whose gorgeous vices the reader can in his fancy safely identify himself. Mr. Hearst's unflagging interest in high society caters to people who never hope to be in high society, and yet manage to derive some enhancement out of the vague feeling that they are part of the life that they read about. In the great cities "the printed diary of the home town" tends to be the printed diary of a smart set.

And it is, as we have already noted, the dailies of the cities which carry the burden of bringing distant news to the private citizen. But it is not primarily their political and social news which holds the circulation. The interest in that is intermittent, and few publishers can bank on it alone. The newspaper, therefore, takes to itself a variety of other features, all primarily designed to hold a body of readers together, who so far as big news is concerned, are not able to be critical. Moreover, in big news the competition in any one community is not very serious. The press services standardize the main events; it is only once in a while that a great scoop is made; there is apparently not a very great reading public for such massive reporting as has made the New York Times of recent years indispensable to men of all shades of opinion. In order to differentiate themselves and collect a steady public most papers have to go outside the field of general news. They go to the dazzling levels of society, to scandal and crime, to sports, pictures, actresses, advice to the lovelorn, highschool notes, women's pages, buyer's pages, cooking receipts, chess, whist, gardening, comic strips, thundering partisanship, not because publishers and editors are interested in everything but news, but because they have to find some way of holding on to that alleged host of passionately interested readers, who are supposed by some critics of the press to be clamoring for the truth and nothing but the truth.

The newspaper editor occupies a strange position. His enterprises depend upon indirect taxation levied by his advertisers upon his readers; the patronage of the advertisers depends upon the editor's skill in holding together an effective group of customers. These customers deliver judgment according to their private experiences and their stereotyped expectations, for in the nature of things they have no independent knowledge of most news they read. If the judgment is not unfavorable, the editor is at least within range of a circulation that pays. But in order to secure that circulation, he cannot rely wholly upon news of the greater environment. He handles that as interestingly as he can, of course, but the quality of the general news, especially about public affairs, is not in itself sufficient to cause very large numbers of readers to discriminate among the dailies.

This somewhat left-handed relationship between newspapers and public information is reflected in the salaries of newspaper men. Reporting, which theoretically constitutes the foundation of the whole institution, is the most poorly paid branch of newspaper work, and is the least regarded. By and large, able men go into it only by necessity or for experience, and with the definite intention of being graduated as soon as possible. For straight reporting is not a career that offers many great rewards. The rewards in journalism go to specialty work, to signed correspondence which has editorial quality, to executives, and to men with a knack and flavor of their own. This is due, no doubt, to what economists call the rent of ability. But this economic principle operates with such peculiar violence in journalism that newsgathering does not attract to itself anything like the number of trained and able men which its public importance would seem to demand. The fact that the able men take up "straight reporting" with the intention of leaving it as soon as possible is, I think, the chief reason why it has never developed in sufficient measure those corporate traditions that give to a profession prestige and a jealous self-respect. For it is these corporate traditions which engender the pride of craft, which tend to raise the standards of admission, punish breaches of the code, and give men the strength to insist upon their status in society.

3

Yet all this does not go to the root of the matter. For while the economics of journalism is such as to depress the value of news reporting, it is, I am certain, a false determinism which would abandon the analysis at that point. The intrinsic power of the reporter appears to be so great, the number of very able men who pass through reporting is so large, that there must be some deeper reason why, comparatively speaking, so little serious effort has gone into raising the vocation to the level say of medicine, engineering, or law.

Mr. Upton Sinclair speaks for a large body of opinion in America, [Footnote: Mr. Hilaire Belloc makes practically the same analysis for English newspapers. Cf. *The Free Press*.] when he claims that in what he calls "The Brass Check" he has found this deeper reason:

"The Brass Check is found in your pay envelope every week—you who write and print and distribute our newspapers and magazines. The Brass check is the price of your shame—you who take the fair body of truth and sell it in the market place, who betray the virgin hopes of mankind into the loathsome brothel of Big Business." [Footnote: Upton Sinclair, *The Brass Check. A Study of American Journalism*. p. 116.]

It would seem from this that there exists a body of known truth, and a set of well founded hopes, which are prostituted by a more or less conscious conspiracy of the rich owners of newspapers. If this theory is correct, then a certain conclusion follows. It is that the fair body of truth would be inviolate in a press not in any way connected with Big Business. For if it should happen that a press not controlled by, and not even friendly with, Big Business somehow failed to contain the fair body of truth, something would be wrong with Mr. Sinclair's theory.

The Walter Lippmann Reader

There is such a press. Strange to say, in proposing a remedy Mr. Sinclair does not advise his readers to subscribe to the nearest radical newspaper. Why not? If the troubles of American journalism go back to the Brass Check of Big Business why does not the remedy lie in reading the papers that do not in any remote way accept the Brass Check? Why subsidize a "National News" with a large board of directors "of all creeds or causes" to print a paper full of facts "regardless of what is injured, the Steel Trust or the I. W. W., the Standard Oil Company or the Socialist Party?" If the trouble is Big Business, that is, the Steel Trust, Standard Oil and the like, why not urge everybody to read I. W. W. or Socialist papers? Mr. Sinclair does not say why not. But the reason is simple. He cannot convince anybody, not even himself, that the anti-capitalist press is the remedy for the capitalist press. He ignores the anti-capitalist press both in his theory of the Brass Check and in his constructive proposal. But if you are diagnosing American journalism you cannot ignore it. If what you care about is "the fair body of truth," you do not commit the gross logical error of assembling all the instances of unfairness and lying you can find in one set of newspapers, ignore all the instances you could easily find in another set, and then assign as the cause of the lying, the one supposedly common characteristic of the press to which you have confined your investigation. If you are going to blame "capitalism" for the faults of the press, you are compelled to prove that those faults do not exist except where capitalism controls. That Mr. Sinclair cannot do this, is shown by the fact that while in his diagnosis he traces everything to capitalism, in his prescription he ignores both capitalism and anti-capitalism.

One would have supposed that the inability to take any non-capitalist paper as a model of truthfulness and competence would have caused Mr. Sinclair, and those who agree with him, to look somewhat more critically at their assumptions. They would have asked themselves, for example, where is the fair body of truth, that Big Business prostitutes, but anti-Big Business does not seem to obtain? For that question leads, I believe, to the heart of the matter, to the question of what is news.

CHAPTER XXIII

The Nature of News

1

ALL the reporters in the world working all the hours of the day could not witness all the happenings in the world. There are not a great many reporters. And none of them has the power to be in more than one place at a time. Reporters are not clairvoyant, they do not gaze into a crystal ball and see the world at will, they are not assisted by thought-transference. Yet the range of subjects these comparatively few men manage to cover would be a miracle indeed, if it were not a standardized routine.

Newspapers do not try to keep an eye on all mankind. [Footnote: See the illuminating chapter in Mr. John L. Given's book, already cited, on "Uncovering the News," Ch. V.] They have watchers stationed at certain places, like Police Headquarters, the Coroner's Office, the County Clerk's Office, City Hall, the White House, the Senate, House of Representatives, and so forth. They watch, or rather in the majority of cases they belong to associations which employ men who watch "a comparatively small number of places where it is made known when the life of anyone... departs from ordinary paths, or when events worth telling about occur. For example, John Smith, let it be supposed, becomes a broker. For ten years he pursues the even tenor of his way and except for his customers and his friends no one gives him a thought. To the newspapers he is as if he were not. But in the eleventh year he suffers heavy losses and, at last, his resources all gone, summons his lawyer and arranges for the making of an assignment. The lawyer posts off to the County Clerk's office, and a clerk there makes the necessary entries in the official docket. Here in step the newspapers. While the clerk is writing Smith's business obituary a reporter glances over his shoulder and a few minutes later the reporters know Smith's troubles and are as well informed concerning his business status as they would be had they kept a reporter at his door every day for over ten years. [Footnote: Op. cit., p. 57.]

When Mr. Given says that the newspapers know "Smith's troubles" and "his business status," he does not mean that they know them as Smith knows them, or as Mr. Arnold Bennett would know them if he had made Smith the hero of a three volume novel. The newspapers know only "in a few minutes" the bald facts which are recorded in the County Clerk's Office. That overt act "uncovers" the news about Smith. Whether the news will be followed up or not is another matter. The point is that before a series of events become news they have usually to make themselves noticeable in some more or less overt act. Generally too, in a crudely overt act. Smith's friends may have known for years that he was taking risks, rumors may even have reached the financial editor if Smith's friends were talkative. But apart from the fact that none of this could be published because it would be libel, there is in these rumors nothing definite on which to peg a story. Something definite must occur that has unmistakable form. It may be the act of going into bankruptcy, it may be a fire, a collision, an assault, a riot, an arrest, a denunciation, the introduction of a bill, a speech, a vote, a meeting, the expressed opinion of a well known citizen, an editorial in a newspaper, a sale, a wage-schedule, a price change, the proposal to build a bridge.... There must be a manifestation. The course of events must assume a certain definable shape, and until it is in a phase where some aspect is an accomplished fact, news does not separate itself from the ocean of possible truth.

2

Naturally there is room for wide difference of opinion as to when events have a shape that can be reported. A good journalist will find news oftener than a hack. If he sees a building with a dangerous list, he does not have to wait until it falls into the street in order to recognize news. It was a great reporter who guessed the name of the next Indian Viceroy when he heard that Lord So-and-So was inquiring about climates. There are lucky shots but the number of men who can make them is small. Usually it is the stereotyped shape assumed by an event at an obvious place that uncovers the run of the news. The most obvious place is where people's affairs touch public authority. De minimis non curat lex. It is at these places that marriages, births, deaths, contracts, failures, arrivals, departures, lawsuits, disorders, epidemics and calamities are made known.

In the first instance, therefore, the news is not a mirror of social conditions, but the report of an aspect that has obtruded itself. The news does not tell you how the seed is germinating in the ground, but it may tell you when the first sprout breaks through the surface. It may even tell you what somebody says is happening to the seed under ground. It may tell you that the sprout did not come up at the time it was expected. The more points, then, at which any happening can be fixed, objectified, measured, named, the more points there are at which news can occur.

So, if some day a legislature, having exhausted all other ways of improving mankind, should forbid the scoring of baseball games, it might still be possible to play some sort of game in which the umpire decided according to his own sense of fair play how long the game should last, when each team should go to bat, and who should be regarded as the winner. If that game were reported in the newspapers it would consist of a record of the umpire's decisions, plus the reporter's impression of the hoots and cheers of the crowd, plus at best a vague account of how certain men, who had no specified position on the field moved around for a few hours on an unmarked piece of sod. The more you try to imagine the logic of so absurd a predicament, the more clear it becomes that for the purposes of newsgathering, (let alone the purposes of playing the game) it is impossible to do much without an apparatus and rules for naming, scoring, recording. Because that machinery is far from perfect, the umpire's life is often a distracted one. Many crucial plays he has to judge by eye. The last vestige of dispute could be taken out of the game, as it has been taken out of chess when people obey the rules, if somebody thought it worth his while to photograph every play. It was the moving pictures which finally settled a real doubt in many reporters' minds, owing to the slowness of the human eye, as to just what blow of Dempsey's knocked out Carpentier.

Wherever there is a good machinery of record, the modern news service works with great precision. There is one on the stock exchange, and the news of price movements is flashed over tickers with dependable accuracy. There is a machinery for election returns, and when the counting and tabulating are well done, the result of a national election is usually known on the night of the election. In civilized communities deaths, births, marriages and divorces are recorded, and are known accurately except where there is concealment or neglect. The machinery exists for some, and only some, aspects of industry and government, in varying degrees of precision for securities, money and staples, bank clearances, realty transactions, wage scales. It exists for imports and exports because they pass through a custom house and can be directly recorded. It exists in nothing like the same degree for internal trade, and especially for trade over the counter.

The Walter Lippmann Reader

It will be found, I think, that there is a very direct relation between the certainty of news and the system of record. If you call to mind the topics which form the principal indictment by reformers against the press, you find they are subjects in which the newspaper occupies the position of the umpire in the unscored baseball game. All news about states of mind is of this character: so are all descriptions of personalities, of sincerity, aspiration, motive, intention, of mass feeling, of national feeling, of public opinion, the policies of foreign governments. So is much news about what is going to happen. So are questions turning on private profit, private income, wages, working conditions, the efficiency of labor, educational opportunity, unemployment, [Footnote: Think of what guess work went into the Reports of Unemployment in 1921.] monotony, health, discrimination, unfairness, restraint of trade, waste, "backward peoples," conservatism, imperialism, radicalism, liberty, honor, righteousness. All involve data that are at best spasmodically recorded. The data may be hidden because of a censorship or a tradition of privacy, they may not exist because nobody thinks record important, because he thinks it red tape, or because nobody has yet invented an objective system of measurement. Then the news on these subjects is bound to be debatable, when it is not wholly neglected. The events which are not scored are reported either as personal and conventional opinions, or they are not news. They do not take shape until somebody protests, or somebody investigates, or somebody publicly, in the etymological meaning of the word, makes an *issue* of them.

This is the underlying reason for the existence of the press agent. The enormous discretion as to what facts and what impressions shall be reported is steadily convincing every organized group of people that whether it wishes to secure publicity or to avoid it, the exercise of discretion cannot be left to the reporter. It is safer to hire a press agent who stands between the group and the newspapers. Having hired him, the temptation to exploit his strategic position is very great. "Shortly before the war," says Mr. Frank Cobb, "the newspapers of New York took a census of the press agents who were regularly employed and regularly accredited and found that there were about twelve hundred of them. How many there are now (1919) I do not pretend to know, but what I do know is that many of the direct channels to news have been closed and the information for the public is first filtered through publicity agents. The great corporations have them, the banks have them, the railroads have them, all the organizations of business and of social and political activity have them, and they are the media through which news comes. Even statesmen have them." [Footnote: Address before the Women's City Club of New York, Dec. 11, 1919. Reprinted, *New Republic*, Dec. 31, 1919, p. 44.]

Were reporting the simple recovery of obvious facts, the press agent would be little more than a clerk. But since, in respect to most of the big topics of news, the facts are not simple, and not at all obvious, but subject to choice and opinion, it is natural that everyone should wish to make his own choice of facts for the newspapers to print. The publicity man does that. And in doing it, he certainly saves the reporter much trouble, by presenting him a clear picture of a situation out of which he might otherwise make neither head nor tail. But it follows that the picture which the publicity man makes for the reporter is the one he wishes the public to see. He is censor and propagandist, responsible only to his employers, and to the whole truth responsible only as it accords with the employers' conception of his own interests.

The development of the publicity man is a clear sign that the facts of modern life do not spontaneously take a shape in which they can be known. They must be given a shape by somebody, and since in the daily routine reporters cannot give a shape to facts, and since there is little disinterested organization of intelligence, the need for some formulation is being met by the interested parties.

3

The good press agent understands that the virtues of his cause are not news, unless they are such strange virtues that they jut right out of the routine of life. This is not because the newspapers do not like virtue, but because it is not worth while to say that nothing has happened when nobody expected anything to happen. So if the publicity man wishes free publicity he has, speaking quite accurately, to start something. He arranges a stunt: obstructs the traffic, teases the police, somehow manages to entangle his client or his cause with an event that is already news. The suffragists knew this, did not particularly enjoy the knowledge but acted on it, and kept suffrage in the news long after the arguments pro and con were straw in their mouths, and people were about to settle down to thinking of the suffrage movement as one of the established institutions of American life. [Footnote: Cf. Inez Haynes Irwin, *The Story of the*

The Walter Lippmann Reader

Woman's Party. It is not only a good account of a vital part of a great agitation, but a reservoir of material on successful, non-revolutionary, non-conspiring agitation under modern conditions of public attention, public interest, and political habit.]

Fortunately the suffragists, as distinct from the feminists, had a perfectly concrete objective, and a very simple one. What the vote symbolizes is not simple, as the ablest advocates and the ablest opponents knew. But the right to vote is a simple and familiar right. Now in labor disputes, which are probably the chief item in the charges against newspapers, the right to strike, like the right to vote, is simple enough. But the causes and objects of a particular strike are like the causes and objects of the woman's movement, extremely subtle.

Let us suppose the conditions leading up to a strike are bad. What is the measure of evil? A certain conception of a proper standard of living, hygiene, economic security, and human dignity. The industry may be far below the theoretical standard of the community, and the workers may be too wretched to protest. Conditions may be above the standard, and the workers may protest violently. The standard is at best a vague measure. However, we shall assume that the conditions are below par, as par is understood by the editor. Occasionally without waiting for the workers to threaten, but prompted say by a social worker, he will send reporters to investigate, and will call attention to bad conditions. Necessarily he cannot do that often. For these investigations cost time, money, special talent, and a lot of space. To make plausible a report that conditions are bad, you need a good many columns of print. In order to tell the truth about the steel worker in the Pittsburgh district, there was needed a staff of investigators, a great deal of time, and several fat volumes of print. It is impossible to suppose that any daily newspaper could normally regard the making of Pittsburgh Surveys, or even Interchurch Steel Reports, as one of its tasks. News which requires so much trouble as that to obtain is beyond the resources of a daily press. [Footnote: Not long ago Babe Ruth was jailed for speeding. Released from jail just before the afternoon game started, he rushed into his waiting automobile, and made up for time lost in jail by breaking the speed laws on his way to the ball grounds. No policeman stopped him, but a reporter timed him, and published his speed the next morning. Babe Ruth is an exceptional man. Newspapers cannot time all motorists. They have to take their news about speeding from the police.]

The Walter Lippmann Reader

The bad conditions as such are not news, because in all but exceptional cases, journalism is not a first hand report of the raw material. It is a report of that material after it has been stylized. Thus bad conditions might become news if the Board of Health reported an unusually high death rate in an industrial area. Failing an intervention of this sort, the facts do not become news, until the workers organize and make a demand upon their employers. Even then, if an easy settlement is certain the news value is low, whether or not the conditions themselves are remedied in the settlement. But if industrial relations collapse into a strike or lockout the news value increases. If the stoppage involves a service on which the readers of the newspapers immediately depend, or if it involves a breach of order, the news value is still greater.

The underlying trouble appears in the news through certain easily recognizable symptoms, a demand, a strike, disorder. From the point of view of the worker, or of the disinterested seeker of justice, the demand, the strike, and the disorder, are merely incidents in a process that for them is richly complicated. But since all the immediate realities lie outside the direct experience both of the reporter, and of the special public by which most newspapers are supported, they have normally to wait for a signal in the shape of an overt act. When that signal comes, say through a walkout of the men or a summons for the police, it calls into play the stereotypes people have about strikes and disorders. The unseen struggle has none of its own flavor. It is noted abstractly, and that abstraction is then animated by the immediate experience of the reader and reporter. Obviously this is a very different experience from that which the strikers have. They feel, let us say, the temper of the foreman, the nerve-racking monotony of the machine, the depressingly bad air, the drudgery of their wives, the stunting of their children, the dinginess of their tenements. The slogans of the strike are invested with these feelings. But the reporter and reader see at first only a strike and some catchwords. They invest these with their feelings. Their feelings may be that their jobs are insecure because the strikers are stopping goods they need in their work, that there will be shortage and higher prices, that it is all devilishly inconvenient. These, too, are realities. And when they give color to the abstract news that a strike has been called, it is in the nature of things that the workers are at a disadvantage. It is in the nature, that is to say, of the existing system of industrial relations that news arising from grievances or hopes by workers should almost invariably be uncovered by an overt attack on production.

The Walter Lippmann Reader

You have, therefore, the circumstances in all their sprawling complexity, the overt act which signalizes them, the stereotyped bulletin which publishes the signal, and the meaning that the reader himself injects, after he has derived that meaning from the experience which directly affects him. Now the reader's experience of a strike may be very important indeed, but from the point of view of the central trouble which caused the strike, it is eccentric. Yet this eccentric meaning is automatically the most interesting. [Footnote: *Cf.* Ch. XI, "The Enlisting of Interest."] To enter imaginatively into the central issues is for the reader to step out of himself, and into very different lives.

It follows that in the reporting of strikes, the easiest way is to let the news be uncovered by the overt act, and to describe the event as the story of interference with the reader's life. That is where his attention is first aroused, and his interest most easily enlisted. A great deal, I think myself the crucial part, of what looks to the worker and the reformer as deliberate misrepresentation on the part of newspapers, is the direct outcome of a practical difficulty in uncovering the news, and the emotional difficulty of making distant facts interesting unless, as Emerson says, we can "perceive (them) to be only a new version of our familiar experience" and can "set about translating (them) at once into our parallel facts." [Footnote: From his essay entitled *Art and Criticism*. The quotation occurs in a passage cited on page 87 of Professor R. W. Brown's, *The Writer's Art*.]

If you study the way many a strike is reported in the press, you will find, very often, that the issues are rarely in the headlines, barely in the leading paragraphs, and sometimes not even mentioned anywhere. A labor dispute in another city has to be very important before the news account contains any definite information as to what is in dispute. The routine of the news works that way, with modifications it works that way in regard to political issues and international news as well. The news is an account of the overt phases that are interesting, and the pressure on the newspaper to adhere to this routine comes from many sides. It comes from the economy of noting only the stereotyped phase of a situation. It comes from the difficulty of finding journalists who can see what they have not learned to see. It comes from the almost unavoidable difficulty of finding sufficient space in which even the best journalist can make plausible an unconventional view. It comes from the economic necessity of interesting the reader quickly, and the economic risk involved in not interesting him at all, or of offending him by unexpected news insufficiently or clumsily described. All these difficulties combined make for uncertainty in the editor when there are dangerous issues at stake, and cause him naturally to prefer the indisputable fact and a treatment more readily adapted to the reader's interest. The indisputable fact and the easy interest, are the strike itself and the reader's inconvenience.

All the subtler and deeper truths are in the present organization of industry very unreliable truths. They involve judgments about standards of living, productivity, human rights that are endlessly debatable in the absence of exact record and quantitative analysis. And as long as these do not exist in industry, the run of news about it will tend, as Emerson said, quoting from Isocrates, "to make of moles mountains, and of mountains moles." [Footnote: *Id., supra*] Where there is no constitutional procedure in industry, and no expert sifting of evidence and the claims, the fact that is sensational to the reader is the fact that almost every journalist will seek. Given the industrial relations that so largely prevail, even where there is conference or arbitration, but no independent filtering of the facts for decision, the issue for the newspaper public will tend not to be the issue for the industry. And so to try disputes by an appeal through the newspapers puts a burden upon newspapers and readers which they cannot and ought not to carry. As long as real law and order do not exist, the bulk of the news will, unless consciously and courageously corrected, work against those who have no lawful and orderly method of asserting themselves. The bulletins from the scene of action will note the trouble that arose from the assertion, rather than the reasons which led to it. The reasons are intangible.

4

The editor deals with these bulletins. He sits in his office, reads them, rarely does he see any large portion of the events themselves. He must, as we have seen, woo at least a section of his readers every day, because they will leave him without mercy if a rival paper happens to hit their fancy. He works under enormous pressure, for the competition of newspapers is often a matter of minutes. Every bulletin requires a swift but complicated judgment. It must be understood, put in relation to other bulletins also understood, and played up or played down according to its probable interest for the public, as the editor conceives it. Without standardization, without stereotypes, without routine judgments, without a fairly ruthless disregard of subtlety, the editor would soon die of excitement. The final page is of a definite size, must be ready at a precise moment; there can be only a certain number of captions on the items, and in each caption there must be a definite number of letters. Always there is the precarious urgency of the buying public, the law of libel, and the possibility of endless trouble. The thing could not be managed at all without systematization, for in a standardized product there is economy of time and effort, as well as a partial guarantee against failure.

It is here that newspapers influence each other most deeply. Thus when the war broke out, the American newspapers were confronted with a subject about which they had no previous experience. Certain dailies, rich enough to pay cable tolls, took the lead in securing news, and the way that news was presented became a model for the whole press. But where did that model come from? It came from the English press, not because Northcliffe owned American newspapers, but because at first it was easier to buy English correspondence, and because, later, it was easier for American journalists to read English newspapers than it was for them to read any others. London was the cable and news center, and it was there that a certain technic for reporting the war was evolved. Something similar occurred in the reporting of the Russian Revolution. In that instance, access to Russia was closed by military censorship, both Russian and Allied, and closed still more effectively by the difficulties of the Russian language. But above all it was closed to effective news reporting by the fact that the hardest thing to report is chaos, even though it is an evolving chaos. This put the formulating of Russian news at its source in Helsingfors, Stockholm, Geneva, Paris and London, into the hands of censors and propagandists. They were for a long time subject to no check of any kind. Until they had made themselves ridiculous they created, let us admit, out of some genuine aspects of the huge Russian maelstrom, a set of stereotypes so evocative of hate and fear, that the very best instinct of journalism, its desire to go and see and tell, was for a long time crushed. [Footnote: Cf. A Test of the News, by Walter Lippmann and Charles Merz, assisted by Faye Lippmann, New Republic, August 4, 1920.]

5

Every newspaper when it reaches the reader is the result of a whole series of selections as to what items shall be printed, in what position they shall be printed, how much space each shall occupy, what emphasis each shall have.

The Walter Lippmann Reader

There are no objective standards here. There are conventions. Take two newspapers published in the same city on the same morning. The headline of one reads: "Britain pledges aid to Berlin against French aggression; France openly backs Poles." The headline of the second is "Mrs. Stillman's Other Love." Which you prefer is a matter of taste, but not entirely a matter of the editor's taste. It is a matter of his judgment as to what will absorb the half hour's attention a certain set of readers will give to his newspaper. Now the problem of securing attention is by no means equivalent to displaying the news in the perspective laid down by religious teaching or by some form of ethical culture. It is a problem of provoking feeling in the reader, of inducing him to feel a sense of personal identification with the stories he is reading. News which does not offer this opportunity to introduce oneself into the struggle which it depicts cannot appeal to a wide audience. The audience must participate in the news, much as it participates in the drama, by personal identification. Just as everyone holds his breath when the heroine is in danger, as he helps Babe Ruth swing his bat, so in subtler form the reader enters into the news. In order that he shall enter he must find a familiar foothold in the story, and this is supplied to him by the use of stereotypes. They tell him that if an association of plumbers is called a "combine" it is appropriate to develop his hostility; if it is called a "group of leading business men" the cue is for a favorable reaction.

It is in a combination of these elements that the power to create opinion resides. Editorials reinforce. Sometimes in a situation that on the news pages is too confusing to permit of identification, they give the reader a clue by means of which he engages himself. A clue he must have if, as most of us must, he is to seize the news in a hurry. A suggestion of some sort he demands, which tells him, so to speak, where he, a man conceiving himself to be such and such a person, shall integrate his feelings with the news he reads.

"It has been said" writes Walter Bagehot, [Footnote: On the Emotion of Conviction, *Literary Studies*, Vol. III, p. 172.] "that if you can only get a middleclass Englishman to think whether there are 'snails in Sirius,' he will soon have an opinion on it. It will be difficult to make him think, but if he does think, he cannot rest in a negative, he will come to some decision. And on any ordinary topic, of course, it is so. A grocer has a full creed as to foreign policy, a young lady a complete theory of the sacraments, as to which neither has any doubt whatever."

The Walter Lippmann Reader

Yet that same grocer will have many doubts about his groceries, and that young lady, marvelously certain about the sacraments, may have all kinds of doubts as to whether to marry the grocer, and if not whether it is proper to accept his attentions. The ability to rest in the negative implies either a lack of interest in the result, or a vivid sense of competing alternatives. In the case of foreign policy or the sacraments, the interest in the results is intense, while means for checking the opinion are poor. This is the plight of the reader of the general news. If he is to read it at all he must be interested, that is to say, he must enter into the situation and care about the outcome. But if he does that he cannot rest in a negative, and unless independent means of checking the lead given him by his newspaper exists, the very fact that he is interested may make it difficult to arrive at that balance of opinions which may most nearly approximate the truth. The more passionately involved he becomes, the more he will tend to resent not only a different view, but a disturbing bit of news. That is why many a newspaper finds that, having honestly evoked the partisanship of its readers, it can not easily, supposing the editor believes the facts warrant it, change position. If a change is necessary, the transition has to be managed with the utmost skill and delicacy. Usually a newspaper will not attempt so hazardous a performance. It is easier and safer to have the news of that subject taper off and disappear, thus putting out the fire by starving it.

CHAPTER XXIV
News, Truth, and a Conclusion

As we begin to make more and more exact studies of the press, much will depend upon the hypothesis we hold. If we assume with Mr. Sinclair, and most of his opponents, that news and truth are two words for the same thing, we shall, I believe, arrive nowhere. We shall prove that on this point the newspaper lied. We shall prove that on that point Mr. Sinclair's account lied. We shall demonstrate that Mr. Sinclair lied when he said that somebody lied, and that somebody lied when he said Mr. Sinclair lied. We shall vent our feelings, but we shall vent them into air.

The hypothesis, which seems to me the most fertile, is that news and truth are not the same thing, and must be clearly distinguished. [Footnote: When I wrote *Liberty and the News*, I did not understand this distinction clearly enough to state it, but *cf.* p. 89 ff.] The function of news is to signalize an event, the function of truth is to bring to light the hidden facts, to set them into relation with each other, and make a picture of reality on which men can act. Only at those points, where social conditions take recognizable and measurable shape, do the body of truth and the body of news coincide. That is a comparatively small part of the whole field of human interest. In this sector, and only in this sector, the tests of the news are sufficiently exact to make the charges of perversion or suppression more than a partisan judgment. There is no defense, no extenuation, no excuse whatever, for stating six times that Lenin is dead, when the only information the paper possesses is a report that he is dead from a source repeatedly shown to be unreliable. The news, in that instance, is not "Lenin Dead" but "Helsingfors Says Lenin is Dead." And a newspaper can be asked to take the responsibility of not making Lenin more dead than the source of the news is reliable; if there is one subject on which editors are most responsible it is in their judgment of the reliability of the source. But when it comes to dealing, for example, with stories of what the Russian people want, no such test exists.

The absence of these exact tests accounts, I think, for the character of the profession, as no other explanation does. There is a very small body of exact knowledge, which it requires no outstanding ability or training to deal with. The rest is in the journalist's own discretion. Once he departs from the region where

410

it is definitely recorded at the County Clerk's office that John Smith has gone into bankruptcy, all fixed standards disappear. The story of why John Smith failed, his human frailties, the analysis of the economic conditions on which he was shipwrecked, all of this can be told in a hundred different ways. There is no discipline in applied psychology, as there is a discipline in medicine, engineering, or even law, which has authority to direct the journalist's mind when he passes from the news to the vague realm of truth. There are no canons to direct his own mind, and no canons that coerce the reader's judgment or the publisher's. His version of the truth is only his version. How can he demonstrate the truth as he sees it? He cannot demonstrate it, any more than Mr. Sinclair Lewis can demonstrate that he has told the whole truth about Main Street. And the more he understands his own weaknesses, the more ready he is to admit that where there is no objective test, his own opinion is in some vital measure constructed out of his own stereotypes, according to his own code, and by the urgency of his own interest. He knows that he is seeing the world through subjective lenses. He cannot deny that he too is, as Shelley remarked, a dome of many-colored glass which stains the white radiance of eternity.

And by this knowledge his assurance is tempered. He may have all kinds of moral courage, and sometimes has, but he lacks that sustaining conviction of a certain technic which finally freed the physical sciences from theological control. It was the gradual development of an irrefragable method that gave the physicist his intellectual freedom as against all the powers of the world. His proofs were so clear, his evidence so sharply superior to tradition, that he broke away finally from all control. But the journalist has no such support in his own conscience or in fact. The control exercised over him by the opinions of his employers and his readers, is not the control of truth by prejudice, but of one opinion by another opinion that it is not demonstrably less true. Between Judge Gary's assertion that the unions will destroy American institutions, and Mr. Gomper's assertion that they are agencies of the rights of man, the choice has, in large measure, to be governed by the will to believe.

The task of deflating these controversies, and reducing them to a point where they can be reported as news, is not a task which the reporter can perform. It is possible and necessary for journalists to bring home to people the uncertain character of the truth on which their opinions are founded, and by criticism and agitation to prod social science into making more usable formulations of social facts, and to prod statesmen into establishing more visible institutions. The press, in other words, can fight for the extension of reportable truth. But as social truth is organized to-day, the press is not constituted to furnish from one edition to the next the amount of knowledge which the democratic theory of public opinion demands. This is not due to the Brass Check, as the quality of news in radical papers shows, but to the fact that the press deals with a society in which the governing forces are so imperfectly recorded. The theory that the press can itself record those forces is false. It can normally record only what has been recorded for it by the working of institutions. Everything else is argument and opinion, and fluctuates with the vicissitudes, the self-consciousness, and the courage of the human mind.

If the press is not so universally wicked, nor so deeply conspiring, as Mr. Sinclair would have us believe, it is very much more frail than the democratic theory has as yet admitted. It is too frail to carry the whole burden of popular sovereignty, to supply spontaneously the truth which democrats hoped was inborn. And when we expect it to supply such a body of truth we employ a misleading standard of judgment. We misunderstand the limited nature of news, the illimitable complexity of society; we overestimate our own endurance, public spirit, and all-round competence. We suppose an appetite for uninteresting truths which is not discovered by any honest analysis of our own tastes.

If the newspapers, then, are to be charged with the duty of translating the whole public life of mankind, so that every adult can arrive at an opinion on every moot topic, they fail, they are bound to fail, in any future one can conceive they will continue to fail. It is not possible to assume that a world, carried on by division of labor and distribution of authority, can be governed by universal opinions in the whole population. Unconsciously the theory sets up the single reader as theoretically omnicompetent, and puts upon the press the burden of accomplishing whatever representative government, industrial organization, and diplomacy have failed to accomplish. Acting upon everybody for thirty minutes in twenty-four hours, the press is asked to create a mystical force called Public Opinion that will take up the slack in public institutions. The press has often mistakenly pretended that it could do just that. It has at great moral cost to itself, encouraged a democracy, still bound to its original premises, to expect newspapers to supply spontaneously for every organ of government, for every social problem, the machinery of information which these do not normally

The Walter Lippmann Reader

supply themselves. Institutions, having failed to furnish themselves with instruments of knowledge, have become a bundle of "problems," which the population as a whole, reading the press as a whole, is supposed to solve.

The press, in other words, has come to be regarded as an organ of direct democracy, charged on a much wider scale, and from day to day, with the function often attributed to the initiative, referendum, and recall. The Court of Public Opinion, open day and night, is to lay down the law for everything all the time. It is not workable. And when you consider the nature of news, it is not even thinkable. For the news, as we have seen, is precise in proportion to the precision with which the event is recorded. Unless the event is capable of being named, measured, given shape, made specific, it either fails to take on the character of news, or it is subject to the accidents and prejudices of observation.

Therefore, on the whole, the quality of the news about modern society is an index of its social organization. The better the institutions, the more all interests concerned are formally represented, the more issues are disentangled, the more objective criteria are introduced, the more perfectly an affair can be presented as news. At its best the press is a servant and guardian of institutions; at its worst it is a means by which a few exploit social disorganization to their own ends. In the degree to which institutions fail to function, the unscrupulous journalist can fish in troubled waters, and the conscientious one must gamble with uncertainties.

The press is no substitute for institutions. It is like the beam of a searchlight that moves restlessly about, bringing one episode and then another out of darkness into vision. Men cannot do the work of the world by this light alone. They cannot govern society by episodes, incidents, and eruptions. It is only when they work by a steady light of their own, that the press, when it is turned upon them, reveals a situation intelligible enough for a popular decision. The trouble lies deeper than the press, and so does the remedy. It lies in social organization based on a system of analysis and record, and in all the corollaries of that principle; in the abandonment of the theory of the omnicompetent citizen, in the decentralization of decision, in the coordination of decision by comparable record and analysis. If at the centers of management there is a running audit, which makes work intelligible to those who do it, and those who superintend it, issues when they arise are not the mere collisions of the blind. Then, too, the news is uncovered for the press by a system of intelligence that is also a check upon the press.

That is the radical way. For the troubles of the press, like the troubles of representative government, be it territorial or functional, like the troubles of industry, be it capitalist, cooperative, or communist, go back to a common source: to the failure of self-governing people to transcend their casual experience and their prejudice, by inventing, creating, and organizing a machinery of knowledge. It is because they are compelled to act without a reliable picture of the world, that governments, schools, newspapers and churches make such small headway against the more obvious failings of democracy, against violent prejudice, apathy, preference for the curious trivial as against the dull important, and the hunger for sideshows and three legged calves. This is the primary defect of popular government, a defect inherent in its traditions, and all its other defects can, I believe, be traced to this one.

PART VIII
ORGANIZED INTELLIGENCE

CHAPTER XXV
The Entering Wedge

1

If the remedy were interesting, American pioneers like Charles McCarthy, Robert Valentine, and Frederick W. Taylor would not have had to fight so hard for a hearing. But it is clear why they had to fight, and why bureaus of governmental research, industrial audits, budgeting and the like are the ugly ducklings of reform. They reverse the process by which interesting public opinions are built up. Instead of presenting a casual fact, a large screen of stereotypes, and a dramatic identification, they break down the drama, break through the stereotypes, and offer men a picture of facts, which is unfamiliar and to them impersonal. When this is not painful, it is dull, and those to whom it is painful, the trading politician and the partisan who has much to conceal, often exploit the dullness that the public feels, in order to remove the pain that they feel.

2

Yet every complicated community has sought the assistance of special men, of augurs, priests, elders. Our own democracy, based though it was on a theory of universal competence, sought lawyers to manage its government, and to help manage its industry. It was recognized that the specially trained man was in some dim way oriented to a wider system of truth than that which arises spontaneously in the amateur's mind. But experience has shown that the traditional lawyer's equipment was not enough assistance. The Great Society had grown furiously and to colossal dimensions by the application of technical knowledge. It was made by engineers who had learned to use exact measurements and quantitative analysis. It could not be governed, men began to discover, by men who thought deductively about rights and wrongs. It could be brought under human control only by the technic which had created it. Gradually, then, the more enlightened directing minds have called in experts who were trained, or had trained themselves, to make parts of this Great Society intelligible to those who manage it. These men are known by all kinds of names, as statisticians, accountants, auditors, industrial counsellors, engineers of many species, scientific managers, personnel administrators, research men, "scientists," and sometimes just as plain private secretaries. They have brought with them each a jargon of his own, as well as filing cabinets, card catalogues, graphs, loose-leaf contraptions, and above all the perfectly sound ideal of an executive who sits before a flat-top desk, one sheet of typewritten paper before him, and decides on matters of policy presented in a form ready for his rejection or approval.

This whole development has been the work, not so much of a spontaneous creative evolution, as of blind natural selection. The statesman, the executive, the party leader, the head of a voluntary association, found that if he had to discuss two dozen different subjects in the course of the day, somebody would have to coach him. He began to clamor for memoranda. He found he could not read his mail. He demanded somebody who would blue-pencil the interesting sentences in the important letters. He found he could not digest the great stacks of type-written reports that grew mellow on his desk. He demanded summaries. He found he could not read an unending series of figures. He embraced the man who made colored pictures of them. He found that he really did not know one machine from another. He hired engineers to pick them, and tell him how much they cost and what they could do. He peeled off one burden after another, as a man will take off first his hat, then his coat, then his collar, when he is struggling to move an unwieldy load.

3

Yet curiously enough, though he knew that he needed help, he was slow to call in the social scientist. The chemist, the physicist, the geologist, had a much earlier and more friendly reception. Laboratories were set up for them, inducements offered, for there was quick appreciation of the victories over nature. But the scientist who has human nature as his problem is in a different case. There are many reasons for this: the chief one, that he has so few victories to exhibit. He has so few, because unless he deals with the historic past, he cannot prove his theories before offering them to the public. The physical scientist can make an hypothesis, test it, revise the hypothesis hundreds of times, and, if after all that, he is wrong, no one else has to pay the price. But the social scientist cannot begin to offer the assurance of a laboratory test, and if his advice is followed, and he is wrong, the consequences may be incalculable. He is in the nature of things far more responsible, and far less certain.

But more than that. In the laboratory sciences the student has conquered the dilemma of thought and action. He brings a sample of the action to a quiet place, where it can be repeated at will, and examined at leisure. But the social scientist is constantly being impaled on a dilemma. If he stays in his library, where he has the leisure to think, he has to rely upon the exceedingly casual and meager printed record that comes to him through official reports, newspapers, and interviews. If he goes out into "the world" where things are happening, he has to serve a long, often wasteful, apprenticeship, before he is admitted to the sanctum where they are being decided. What he cannot do is to dip into action and out again whenever it suits him. There are no privileged listeners. The man of affairs, observing that the social scientist knows only from the outside what he knows, in part at least, from the inside, recognizing that the social scientist's hypothesis is not in the nature of things susceptible of laboratory proof, and that verification is possible only in the "real" world, has developed a rather low opinion of social scientists who do not share his views of public policy.

In his heart of hearts the social scientist shares this estimate of himself. He has little inner certainty about his own work. He only half believes in it, and being sure of nothing, he can find no compelling reason for insisting on his own freedom of thought. What can he actually claim for it, in the light of his own conscience? [Footnote: Cf. Charles E. Merriam, *The Present State of the Study of Politics, American Political Science Review*, Vol. XV. No. 2, May, 1921.] His data are uncertain, his means of verification lacking. The very best qualities in him are a source of frustration. For if he is really critical and saturated in the scientific spirit, he cannot be doctrinaire, and go to Armageddon against the trustees and the students and the Civic Federation and the conservative press for a theory of which he is not sure. If you are going to Armageddon, you have to battle for the Lord, but the political scientist is always a little doubtful whether the Lord called him.

Consequently if so much of social science is apologetic rather than constructive, the explanation lies in the opportunities of social science, not in "capitalism." The physical scientists achieved their freedom from clericalism by working out a method that produced conclusions of a sort that could not be suppressed or ignored. They convinced themselves and acquired dignity, and knew what they were fighting for. The social scientist will acquire his dignity and his strength when he has worked out his method. He will do that by turning into opportunity the need among directing men of the Great Society for instruments of analysis by which an invisible and made intelligible.

But as things go now, the social scientist assembles his data out of a mass of unrelated material. Social processes are recorded spasmodically, quite often as accidents of administration. A report to Congress, a debate, an investigation, legal briefs, a census, a tariff, a tax schedule; the material, like the skull of the Piltdown man, has to be put together by ingenious inference before the student obtains any sort of picture of the event he is studying. Though it deals with the conscious life of his fellow citizens, it is all too often distressingly opaque, because the man who is trying to generalize has practically no supervision of the way his data are collected. Imagine medical research conducted by students who could rarely go into a hospital, were deprived of animal experiment, and compelled to draw conclusions from the stories of people who had been ill, the reports of nurses, each of whom had her own system of diagnosis, and the statistics compiled by the Bureau of Internal Revenue on the excess profits of druggists. The social scientist has usually to make what he can out of categories that were uncritically in the mind of an official who administered some part of a law, or who was out to justify, to persuade, to claim, or to prove. The student knows this, and, as a protection against it, has developed that branch of scholarship which is an elaborated suspicion about where to discount his information.

That is a virtue, but it becomes a very thin virtue when it is merely a corrective for the unwholesome position of social science. For the scholar is condemned to guess as shrewdly as he can why in a situation not clearly understood something or other may have happened. But the expert who is employed as the mediator among representatives, and as the mirror and measure of administration, has a very different control of the facts. Instead of being the man who generalizes from the facts dropped to him by the men of action, he becomes the man who prepares the facts for the men of action. This is a profound change in his strategic position. He no longer stands outside, chewing the cud provided by busy men of affairs, but he takes his place in front of decision instead of behind it. To-day the sequence is that the man of affairs finds his facts, and decides on the basis of them; then, some time later, the social scientist deduces excellent reasons why he did or did not decide wisely. This ex post facto relationship is academic in the bad sense of that fine word. The real sequence should be one where the disinterested expert first finds and formulates the facts for the man of action, and later makes what wisdom he can out of comparison between the decision, which he understands, and the facts, which he organized.

4

For the physical sciences this change in strategic position began slowly, and then accelerated rapidly. There was a time when the inventor and the engineer were romantic half-starved outsiders, treated as cranks. The business man and the artisan knew all the mysteries of their craft. Then the mysteries grew more mysterious, and at last industry began to depend upon physical laws and chemical combinations that no eye could see, and only a trained mind could conceive. The scientist moved from his noble garret in the Latin Quarter into office buildings and laboratories. For he alone could construct a working image of the reality on which industry rested. From the new relationship he took as much as he gave, perhaps more: pure science developed faster than applied, though it drew its economic support, a great deal of its inspiration, and even more of its relevancy, from constant contact with practical decision. But physical science still labored under the enormous limitation that the men who made decisions had only their commonsense to guide them. They administered without scientific aid a world complicated by scientists. Again they had to deal with facts they could not apprehend, and as once they had to call in engineers, they now have to call in statisticians, accountants, experts of all sorts.

These practical students are the true pioneers of a new social science. They are "in mesh with the driving wheels" [Footnote: Cf. The Address of the President of the American Philosophical Association, Mr. Ralph Barton Perry, Dec. 28, 1920. Published in the Proceedings of the Twentieth Annual Meeting.] and from this practical engagement of science and action, both will benefit radically: action by the clarification of its beliefs; beliefs by a continuing test in action. We are in the earliest beginnings. But if it is conceded that all large forms of human association must, because of sheer practical difficulty, contain men who will come to see the need for an expert reporting of their particular environment, then the imagination has a premise on which to work. In the exchange of technic and result among expert staffs, one can see, I think, the beginning of

419

The Walter Lippmann Reader

experimental method in social science. When each school district and budget, and health department, and factory, and tariff schedule, is the material of knowledge for every other, the number of comparable experiences begins to approach the dimensions of genuine experiment. In forty-eight states, and 2400 cities, and 277,000 school houses, 270,000 manufacturing establishments, 27,000 mines and quarries, there is a wealth of experience, if only it were recorded and available. And there is, too, opportunity for trial and error at such slight risk that any reasonable hypothesis might be given a fair test without shaking the foundations of society.

The wedge has been driven, not only by some directors of industry and some statesmen who had to have help, but by the bureaus of municipal research, [Footnote: The number of these organizations in the United States is very great. Some are alive, some half dead. They are in rapid flux. Lists of them supplied to me by Dr. L. D. Upson of the Detroit Bureau of Governmental Research, Miss Rebecca B. Rankin of the Municipal Reference Library of New York City, Mr. Edward A. Fitzpatrick, Secretary of the State Board of Education (Wisconsin), Mr. Savel Zimand of the Bureau of Industrial Research (New York City), run into the hundreds.] the legislative reference libraries, the specialized lobbies of corporations and trade unions and public causes, and by voluntary organizations like the League of Women Voters, the Consumers' League, the Manufacturers' Associations: by hundreds of trade associations, and citizens' unions; by publications like the *Searchlight on Congress* and the *Survey*; and by foundations like the General Education Board. Not all by any means are disinterested. That is not the point. All of them do begin to demonstrate the need for interposing some form of expertness between the private citizen and the vast environment in which he is entangled.

CHAPTER XXVI
Intelligence Work

1

THE practice of democracy has been ahead of its theory. For the theory holds that the adult electors taken together make decisions out of a will that is in them. But just as there grew up governing hierarchies which were invisible in theory, so there has been a large amount of constructive adaptation, also unaccounted for in the image of democracy. Ways have been found to represent many interests and functions that are normally out of sight.

We are most conscious of this in our theory of the courts, when we explain their legislative powers and their vetoes on the theory that there are interests to be guarded which might be forgotten by the elected officials. But the Census Bureau, when it counts, classifies, and correlates people, things, and changes, is also speaking for unseen factors in the environment. The Geological Survey makes mineral resources evident, the Department of Agriculture represents in the councils of the nation factors of which each farmer sees only an infinitesimal part. School authorities, the Tariff Commission, the consular service, the Bureau of Internal Revenue give representation to persons, ideas, and objects which would never automatically find themselves represented in this perspective by an election. The Children's Bureau is the spokesman of a whole complex of interests and functions not ordinarily visible to the voter, and, therefore, incapable of becoming spontaneously a part of his public opinions. Thus the printing of comparative statistics of infant mortality is often followed by a reduction of the death rate of babies. Municipal officials and voters did not have, before publication, a place in their picture of the environment for those babies. The statistics made them visible, as visible as if the babies had elected an alderman to air their grievances.

In the State Department the government maintains a Division of Far Eastern Affairs. What is it for? The Japanese and the Chinese Governments both maintain ambassadors in Washington. Are they not qualified to speak for the Far East? They are its representatives. Yet nobody would argue that the American Government could learn all that it needed to know about the Far East by consulting these ambassadors. Supposing them to be as candid as they know how to be, they are still limited channels of information. Therefore, to supplement them we maintain embassies in Tokio and Peking, and consular agents at many points. Also, I assume, some secret agents. These people are supposed to send reports which pass through the Division of Far Eastern Affairs to the Secretary of State. Now what does the Secretary expect of the Division? I know one who expected it to spend its appropriation. But there are Secretaries to whom special revelation is denied, and they turn to their divisions for help. The last thing they expect to find is a neat argument justifying the American position.

What they demand is that the experts shall bring the Far East to the Secretary's desk, with all the elements in such relation that it is as if he were in contact with the Far East itself. The expert must translate, simplify, generalize, but the inference from the result must apply in the East, not merely on the premises of the report. If the Secretary is worth his salt, the very last thing he will tolerate in his experts is the suspicion that they have a "policy." He does not want to know from them whether they like Japanese policy in China. He wants to know what different classes of Chinese and Japanese, English, Frenchmen, Germans, and Russians, think about it, and what they are likely to do because of what they think. He wants all that represented to him as the basis of his decision. The more faithfully the Division represents what is not otherwise represented, either by the Japanese or American ambassadors, or the Senators and Congressmen from the Pacific coast, the better Secretary of State he will be. He may decide to take his policy from the Pacific Coast, but he will take his view of Japan from Japan.

2

It is no accident that the best diplomatic service in the world is the one in which the divorce between the assembling of knowledge and the control of policy is most perfect. During the war in many British Embassies and in the British Foreign Office there were nearly always men, permanent officials or else special appointees, who quite successfully discounted the prevailing war mind. They discarded the rigmarole of being pro and con, of having favorite nationalities, and pet aversions, and undelivered perorations in their bosoms. They left that to the political chiefs. But in an American Embassy I once heard an ambassador say that he never reported anything to Washington which would not cheer up the folks at home. He charmed all those who met him, helped many a stranded war worker, and was superb when he unveiled a monument.

The Walter Lippmann Reader

He did not understand that the power of the expert depends upon separating himself from those who make the decisions, upon not caring, in his expert self, what decision is made. The man who, like the ambassador, takes a line, and meddles with the decision, is soon discounted. There he is, just one more on that side of the question. For when he begins to care too much, he begins to see what he wishes to see, and by that fact ceases to see what he is there to see. He is there to represent the unseen. He represents people who are not voters, functions of voters that are not evident, events that are out of sight, mute people, unborn people, relations between things and people. He has a constituency of intangibles. And intangibles cannot be used to form a political majority, because voting is in the last analysis a test of strength, a sublimated battle, and the expert represents no strength available in the immediate. But he can exercise force by disturbing the line up of the forces. By making the invisible visible, he confronts the people who exercise material force with a new environment, sets ideas and feelings at work in them, throws them out of position, and so, in the profoundest way, affects the decision.

Men cannot long act in a way that they know is a contradiction of the environment as they conceive it. If they are bent on acting in a certain way they have to reconceive the environment, they have to censor out, to rationalize. But if in their presence, there is an insistent fact which is so obtrusive that they cannot explain it away, one of three courses is open. They can perversely ignore it, though they will cripple themselves in the process, will overact their part and come to grief. They can take it into account but refuse to act. They pay in internal discomfort and frustration. Or, and I believe this to be the most frequent case, they adjust their whole behavior to the enlarged environment.

The idea that the expert is an ineffectual person because he lets others make the decisions is quite contrary to experience. The more subtle the elements that enter into the decision, the more irresponsible power the expert wields. He is certain, moreover, to exercise more power in the future than ever he did before, because increasingly the relevant facts will elude the voter and the administrator. All governing agencies will tend to organize bodies of research and information, which will throw out tentacles and expand, as have the intelligence departments of all the armies in the world. But the experts will remain human beings. They will enjoy power, and their temptation will be to appoint themselves censors, and so absorb the real function of decision. Unless their function is correctly

423

defined they will tend to pass on the facts they think appropriate, and to pass down the decisions they approve. They will tend, in short, to become a bureaucracy.

The only institutional safeguard is to separate as absolutely as it is possible to do so the staff which executes from the staff which investigates. The two should be parallel but quite distinct bodies of men, recruited differently, paid if possible from separate funds, responsible to different heads, intrinsically uninterested in each other's personal success. In industry, the auditors, accountants, and inspectors should be independent of the manager, the superintendents, foremen, and in time, I believe, we shall come to see that in order to bring industry under social control the machinery of record will have to be independent of the boards of directors and the shareholders.

3

But in building the intelligence sections of industry and politics, we do not start on cleared ground. And, apart from insisting on this basic separation of function, it would be cumbersome to insist too precisely on the form which in any particular instance the principle shall take. There are men who believe in intelligence work, and will adopt it; there are men who do not understand it, but cannot do their work without it; there are men who will resist. But provided the principle has a foothold somewhere in every social agency it will make progress, and the way to begin is to begin. In the federal government, for example, it is not necessary to straighten out the administrative tangle and the illogical duplications of a century's growth in order to find a neat place for the intelligence bureaus which Washington so badly needs. Before election you can promise to rush bravely into the breach. But when you arrive there all out of breath, you find that each absurdity is invested with habits, strong interests, and chummy Congressmen. Attack all along the line and you engage every force of reaction. You go forth to battle, as the poet said, and you always fall. You can lop off an antiquated bureau here, a covey of clerks there, you can combine two bureaus. And by that time you are busy with the tariff and the railroads, and the era of reform is over. Besides, in order to effect a truly logical reorganization of the government, such as all candidates always promise, you would have to disturb more passions than you have time to quell. And any new scheme, supposing you had one ready, would require officials to man it. Say what one will about officeholders, even Soviet Russia was glad to get many of the old ones back; and these old officials, if they are too ruthlessly treated, will sabotage Utopia itself.

No administrative scheme is workable without good will, and good will about strange practices is impossible without education. The better way is to introduce into the existing machinery, wherever you can find an opening, agencies that will hold up a mirror week by week, month by month. You can hope, then, to make the machine visible to those who work it, as well as to the chiefs who are responsible, and to the public outside. When the office-holders begin to see themselves,—or rather when the outsiders, the chiefs, and the subordinates all begin to see the same facts, the same damning facts if you like, the obstruction will diminish. The reformer's opinion that a certain bureau is inefficient is just his opinion, not so good an opinion in the eyes of the bureau, as its own. But let the work of that bureau be analysed and recorded, and then compared with other bureaus and with private corporations, and the argument moves to another plane.

There are ten departments at Washington represented in the Cabinet. Suppose, then, there was a permanent intelligence section for each. What would be some of the conditions of effectiveness? Beyond all others that the intelligence officials should be independent both of the Congressional Committees dealing with that department, and of the Secretary at the head of it; that they should not be entangled either in decision or in action. Independence, then, would turn mainly on three points on funds, tenure, and access to the facts. For clearly if a particular Congress or departmental official can deprive them of money, dismiss them, or close the files, the staff becomes its creature.

4

The question of funds is both important and difficult. No agency of research can be really free if it depends upon annual doles from what may be a jealous or a parsimonious congress. Yet the ultimate control of funds cannot be removed from the legislature. The financial arrangement should insure the staff against left-handed, joker and rider attack, against sly destruction, and should at the same time provide for growth. The staff should be so well entrenched that an attack on its existence would have to be made in the open. It might, perhaps, work behind a federal charter creating a trust fund, and a sliding scale over a period of years based on the appropriation for the department to which the intelligence bureau belonged. No great sums of money are involved anyway. The trust fund might cover the overhead and capital charges for a certain minimum staff, the sliding scale might cover the enlargements. At any rate the appropriation should be put beyond accident, like the payment of any long term obligation. This is a much less serious way of "tying the hands of Congress" than is the passage of a Constitutional amendment or the issuance of government bonds. Congress could repeal the charter. But it would have to repeal it, not throw monkey wrenches into it.

Tenure should be for life, with provision for retirement on a liberal pension, with sabbatical years set aside for advanced study and training, and with dismissal only after a trial by professional colleagues. The conditions which apply to any non-profit-making intellectual career should apply here. If the work is to be salient, the men who do it must have dignity, security, and, in the upper ranks at least, that freedom of mind which you find only where men are not too immediately concerned in practical decision.

Access to the materials should be established in the organic act. The bureau should have the right to examine all papers, and to question any official or any outsider. Continuous investigation of this sort would not at all resemble the sensational legislative inquiry and the spasmodic fishing expedition which are now a common feature of our government. The bureau should have the right to propose accounting methods to the department, and if the proposal is rejected, or violated after it has been accepted, to appeal under its charter to Congress.

In the first instance each intelligence bureau would be the connecting link between Congress and the Department, a better link, in my judgment, than the appearance of cabinet officers on the floor of both House and Senate, though the one proposal in no way excludes the other. The bureau would be the Congressional eye on the execution of its policy. It would be the departmental answer to Congressional criticism. And then, since operation of the Department would be permanently visible, perhaps Congress would cease to feel the need of that minute legislation born of distrust and a false doctrine of the separation of powers, which does so much to make efficient administration difficult.

5

But, of course, each of the ten bureaus could not work in a watertight compartment. In their relation one to another lies the best chance for that "coordination" of which so much is heard and so little seen. Clearly the various staffs would need to adopt, wherever possible, standards of measurement that were comparable. They would exchange their records. Then if the War Department and the Post Office both buy lumber, hire carpenters, or construct brick walls they need not necessarily do them through the same agency, for that might mean cumbersome over-centralization; but they would be able to use the same measure for the same things, be conscious of the comparisons, and be treated as competitors. And the more competition of this sort the better.

For the value of competition is determined by the value of the standards used to measure it. Instead, then, of asking ourselves whether we believe in competition, we should ask ourselves whether we believe in that for which the competitors compete. No one in his senses expects to "abolish competition," for when the last vestige of emulation had disappeared, social effort would consist in mechanical obedience to a routine, tempered in a minority by native inspiration. Yet no one expects to work out competition to its logical conclusion in a murderous struggle of each against all. The problem is to select the goals of competition and the rules of the game. Almost always the most visible and obvious standard of measurement will determine the rules of the game: such as money, power, popularity, applause, or Mr. Veblen's "conspicuous waste." What other standards of measurement does our civilization normally provide? How does it measure efficiency, productivity, service, for which we are always clamoring?

By and large there are no measures, and there is, therefore, not so much competition to achieve these ideals. For the difference between the higher and the lower motives is not, as men often assert, a difference between altruism and selfishness. [Footnote: Cf. Ch. XII] It is a difference between acting for easily understood aims, and for aims that are obscure and vague. Exhort a man to make more profit than his neighbor, and he knows at what to aim. Exhort him to render more social service, and how is he to be certain what service is social? What is the test, what is the measure? A subjective feeling, somebody's opinion. Tell a man in time of peace that he ought to serve his country and you have uttered a pious platitude, Tell him in time of war, and the word service has a meaning; it is a number of concrete acts, enlistment, or buying bonds, or saving food, or working for a dollar a year, and each one of these services he sees definitely as part of a concrete purpose to put at the front an army larger and better armed, than the enemy's.

So the more you are able to analyze administration and work out elements that can be compared, the more you invent quantitative measures for the qualities you wish to promote, the more you can turn competition to ideal ends. If you can contrive the right index numbers [Footnote: I am not using the term index numbers in its purely technical meaning, but to cover any device for the comparative measurement of social phenomena.] you can set up a competition between individual workers in a shop; between shops; between factories; between schools; [Footnote: See, for example, *An Index Number for State School Systems* by Leonard P. Ayres, Russell Sage Foundation, 1920. The principle of the quota was very successfully applied in the Liberty Loan Campaigns, and under very much more difficult circumstances by the Allied Maritime Transport Council.] between government departments; between regiments; between divisions; between ships; between states; counties; cities; and the better your index numbers the more useful the competition.

6

The possibilities that lie in the exchange of material are evident. Each department of government is all the time asking for information that may already have been obtained by another department, though perhaps in a somewhat different form. The State Department needs to know, let us say, the extent of the Mexican oil reserves, their relation to the rest of the world's supply, the present ownership of Mexican oil lands, the importance of oil to warships now under construction or planned, the comparative costs in different fields. How does it secure such information to-day? The information is probably scattered through the Departments of Interior, Justice, Commerce, Labor and Navy. Either a clerk in the State Department looks up Mexican oil in a book of reference, which may or may not be accurate, or somebody's private secretary telephones somebody else's private secretary, asks for a memorandum, and in the course of time a darkey messenger arrives with an armful of unintelligible reports. The Department should be able to call on its own intelligence bureau to assemble the facts in a way suited to the diplomatic problem up for decision.

The Walter Lippmann Reader

And these facts the diplomatic intelligence bureau would obtain from the central clearing house. [Footnote: There has been a vast development of such services among the trade associations. The possibilities of a perverted use were revealed by the New York Building Trades investigation of 1921.]

This establishment would pretty soon become a focus of information of the most extraordinary kind. And the men in it would be made aware of what the problems of government really are. They would deal with problems of definition, of terminology, of statistical technic, of logic; they would traverse concretely the whole gamut of the social sciences. It is difficult to see why all this material, except a few diplomatic and military secrets, should not be open to the scholars of the country. It is there that the political scientist would find the real nuts to crack and the real researches for his students to make. The work need not all be done in Washington, but it could be done in reference to Washington. The central agency would, thus, have in it the makings of a national university. The staff could be recruited there for the bureaus from among college graduates. They would be working on theses selected after consultation between the curators of the national university and teachers scattered over the country. If the association was as flexible as it ought to be, there would be, as a supplement to the permanent staff, a steady turnover of temporary and specialist appointments from the universities, and exchange lecturers called out from Washington. Thus the training and the recruiting of the staff would go together. A part of the research itself would be done by students, and political science in the universities would be associated with politics in America.

7

In its main outlines the principle is equally applicable to state governments, to cities, and to rural counties. The work of comparison and interchange could take place by federations of state and city and county bureaus. And within those federations any desirable regional combination could be organized. So long as the accounting systems were comparable, a great deal of duplication would be avoided. Regional coordination is especially desirable. For legal frontiers often do not coincide with the effective environments. Yet they have a certain basis in custom that it would be costly to disturb. By coordinating their information several administrative areas could reconcile autonomy of decision with cooperation. New York City, for example, is already an unwieldy unit for good

The Walter Lippmann Reader

government from the City Hall. Yet for many purposes, such as health and transportation, the metropolitan district is the true unit of administration. In that district, however, there are large cities, like Yonkers, Jersey City, Paterson, Elizabeth, Hoboken, Bayonne. They could not all be managed from one center, and yet they should act together for many functions. Ultimately perhaps some such flexible scheme of local government as Sidney and Beatrice Webb have suggested may be the proper solution. [Footnote: "The Reorganization of Local Government" (Ch. IV), in A *Constitution for the Socialist Commonwealth of Great Britain.*] But the first step would be a coordination, not of decision and action, but of information and research. Let the officials of the various municipalities see their common problems in the light of the same facts.

8

It would be idle to deny that such a net work of intelligence bureaus in politics and industry might become a dead weight and a perpetual irritation. One can easily imagine its attraction for men in search of soft jobs, for pedants, for meddlers. One can see red tape, mountains of papers, questionnaires ad nauseam, seven copies of every document, endorsements, delays, lost papers, the use of form 136 instead of form 2gb, the return of the document because pencil was used instead of ink, or black ink instead of red ink. The work could be done very badly. There are no fool-proof institutions.

But if one could assume that there was circulation through the whole system between government departments, factories, offices, and the universities; a circulation of men, a circulation of data and of criticism, the risks of dry rot would not be so great. Nor would it be true to say that these intelligence bureaus will complicate life. They will tend, on the contrary, to simplify, by revealing a complexity now so great as to be humanly unmanageable. The present fundamentally invisible system of government is so intricate that most people have given up trying to follow it, and because they do not try, they are tempted to think it comparatively simple. It is, on the contrary, elusive, concealed, opaque. The employment of an intelligence system would mean a reduction of personnel per unit of result, because by making available to all the experience of each, it would reduce the amount of trial and error; and because by making the social process visible, it would assist the personnel to self-criticism. It does not involve a great additional band of officials, if you take into account the time now

430

spent vainly by special investigating committees, grand juries, district attorneys, reform organizations, and bewildered office holders, in trying to find their way through a dark muddle.

If the analysis of public opinion and of the democratic theories in relation to the modern environment is sound in principle, then I do not see how one can escape the conclusion that such intelligence work is the clue to betterment. I am not referring to the few suggestions contained in this chapter. They are merely illustrations. The task of working out the technic is in the hands of men trained to do it, and not even they can to-day completely foresee the form, much less the details. The number of social phenomena which are now recorded is small, the instruments of analysis are very crude, the concepts often vague and uncriticized. But enough has been done to demonstrate, I think, that unseen environments can be reported effectively, that they can be reported to divergent groups of people in a way which is neutral to their prejudice, and capable of overcoming their subjectivism.

If that is true, then in working out the intelligence principle men will find the way to overcome the central difficulty of self-government, the difficulty of dealing with an unseen reality. Because of that difficulty, it has been impossible for any self-governing community to reconcile its need for isolation with the necessity for wide contact, to reconcile the dignity and individuality of local decision with security and wide coordination, to secure effective leaders without sacrificing responsibility, to have useful public opinions without attempting universal public opinions on all subjects. As long as there was no way of establishing common versions of unseen events, common measures for separate actions, the only image of democracy that would work, even in theory, was one based on an isolated community of people whose political faculties were limited, according to Aristotle's famous maxim, by the range of their vision.

But now there is a way out, a long one to be sure, but a way. It is fundamentally the same way as that which has enabled a citizen of Chicago, with no better eyes or ears than an Athenian, to see and hear over great distances. It is possible to-day, it will become more possible when more labor has gone into it, to reduce the discrepancies between the conceived environment and the effective environment. As that is done, federalism will work more and more by consent, less and less by coercion. For while federalism is the only possible method of union among self-governing groups, [Footnote: *Cf.* H. J. Laski, *The*

The Walter Lippmann Reader

Foundations of Sovereignty, and other Essays, particularly the Essay of this name, as well as the Problems of Administrative Areas, The Theory of Popular Sovereignty, and The Pluralistic State.] federalism swings either towards imperial centralization or towards parochial anarchy wherever the union is not based on correct and commonly accepted ideas of federal matters. These ideas do not arise spontaneously. They have to be pieced together by generalization based on analysis, and the instruments for that analysis have to be invented and tested by research.

No electoral device, no manipulation of areas, no change in the system of property, goes to the root of the matter. You cannot take more political wisdom out of human beings than there is in them. And no reform, however sensational, is truly radical, which does not consciously provide a way of overcoming the subjectivism of human opinion based on the limitation of individual experience. There are systems of government, of voting, and representation which extract more than others. But in the end knowledge must come not from the conscience but from the environment with which that conscience deals. When men act on the principle of intelligence they go out to find the facts and to make their wisdom. When they ignore it, they go inside themselves and find only what is there. They elaborate their prejudice, instead of increasing their knowledge.

CHAPTER XXVII
The Appeal to the Public

1

IN real life no one acts on the theory that he can have a public opinion on every public question, though this fact is often concealed where a person thinks there is no public question because he has no public opinion. But in the theory of our politics we continue to think more literally than Lord Bryce intended, that "the action of Opinion is continuous," [Footnote: *Modern Democracies*, Vol. I, p. 159.] even though "its action... deals with broad principles only." [Footnote: Id., footnote, p. 158.] And then because we try to think of ourselves having continuous opinions, without being altogether certain what a broad principle is, we quite naturally greet with an anguished yawn an argument that seems to involve the reading of more government reports, more statistics, more curves and more graphs. For all these are in the first instance just as confusing as partisan rhetoric, and much less entertaining.

The amount of attention available is far too small for any scheme in which it was assumed that all the citizens of the nation would, after devoting themselves to the publications of all the intelligence bureaus, become alert, informed, and eager on the multitude of real questions that never do fit very well into any broad principle. I am not making that assumption. Primarily, the intelligence bureau is an instrument of the man of action, of the representative charged with decision, of the worker at his work, and if it does not help them, it will help nobody in the end. But in so far as it helps them to understand the environment in which they are working, it makes what they do visible. And by that much they become more responsible to the general public.

The purpose, then, is not to burden every citizen with expert opinions on all questions, but to push that burden away from him towards the responsible administrator. An intelligence system has value, of course, as a source of general information, and as a check on the daily press. But that is secondary. Its real use is as an aid to representative government and administration both in politics and industry. The demand for the assistance of expert reporters in the shape of accountants, statisticians, secretariats, and the like, comes not from the public, but from men doing public business, who can no longer do it by rule of thumb.

The Walter Lippmann Reader

It is in origin and in ideal an instrument for doing public business better, rather than an instrument for knowing better how badly public business is done.

2

As a private citizen, as a sovereign voter, no one could attempt to digest these documents. But as one party to a dispute, as a committeeman in a legislature, as an officer in government, business, or a trade union, as a member of an industrial council, reports on the specific matter at issue will be increasingly welcome. The private citizen interested in some cause would belong, as he does now, to voluntary societies which employed a staff to study the documents, and make reports that served as a check on officialdom. There would be some study of this material by newspaper men, and a good deal by experts and by political scientists. But the outsider, and every one of us is an outsider to all but a few aspects of modern life, has neither time, nor attention, nor interest, nor the equipment for specific judgment. It is on the men inside, working under conditions that are sound, that the daily administrations of society must rest.

The general public outside can arrive at judgments about whether these conditions are sound only on the result after the event, and on the procedure before the event. The broad principles on which the action of public opinion can be continuous are essentially principles of procedure. The outsider can ask experts to tell him whether the relevant facts were duly considered; he cannot in most cases decide for himself what is relevant or what is due consideration. The outsider can perhaps judge whether the groups interested in the decision were properly heard, whether the ballot, if there was one, was honestly taken, and perhaps whether the result was honestly accepted. He can watch the procedure when the news indicates that there is something to watch. He can raise a question as to whether the procedure itself is right, if its normal results conflict with his ideal of a good life. [Footnote: *Cf.* Chapter XX.] But if he tries in every case to substitute himself for the procedure, to bring in Public Opinion like a providential uncle in the crisis of a play, he will confound his own confusion. He will not follow any train of thought consecutively.

For the practice of appealing to the public on all sorts of intricate matters means almost always a desire to escape criticism from those who know by enlisting a large majority which has had no chance to know. The verdict is made to depend on who has the loudest or the most entrancing voice, the most skilful

434

or the most brazen publicity man, the best access to the most space in the newspapers. For even when the editor is scrupulously fair to "the other side," fairness is not enough. There may be several other sides, unmentioned by any of the organized, financed and active partisans.

The private citizen, beset by partisan appeals for the loan of his Public Opinion, will soon see, perhaps, that these appeals are not a compliment to his intelligence, but an imposition on his good nature and an insult to his sense of evidence. As his civic education takes account of the complexity of his environment, he will concern himself about the equity and the sanity of procedure, and even this he will in most cases expect his elected representative to watch for him. He will refuse himself to accept the burden of these decisions, and will turn down his thumbs in most cases on those who, in their hurry to win, rush from the conference table with the first dope for the reporters.

Only by insisting that problems shall not come up to him until they have passed through a procedure, can the busy citizen of a modern state hope to deal with them in a form that is intelligible. For issues, as they are stated by a partisan, almost always consist of an intricate series of facts, as he has observed them, surrounded by a large fatty mass of stereotyped phrases charged with his emotion. According to the fashion of the day, he will emerge from the conference room insisting that what he wants is some soulfilling idea like Justice, Welfare, Americanism, Socialism. On such issues the citizen outside can sometimes be provoked to fear or admiration, but to judgment never. Before he can do anything with the argument, the fat has to be boiled out of it for him.

3

That can be done by having the representative inside carry on discussion in the presence of some one, chairman or mediator, who forces the discussion to deal with the analyses supplied by experts. This is the essential organization of any representative body dealing with distant matters. The partisan voices should be there, but the partisans should find themselves confronted with men, not personally involved, who control enough facts and have the dialectical skill to sort out what is real perception from what is stereotype, pattern and elaboration. It is the Socratic dialogue, with all of Socrates's energy for breaking through words to meanings, and something more than that, because the dialectic in modern life must be done by men who have explored the environment as well as the human mind.

There is, for example, a grave dispute in the steel industry. Each side issues a manifesto full of the highest ideals. The only public opinion that is worth respect at this stage is the opinion which insists that a conference be organized. For the side which says its cause is too just to be contaminated by conference there can be little sympathy, since there is no such cause anywhere among mortal men. Perhaps those who object to conference do not say quite that. Perhaps they say that the other side is too wicked; they cannot shake hands with traitors. All that public opinion can do then is to organize a hearing by public officials to hear the proof of wickedness. It cannot take the partisans' word for it. But suppose a conference is agreed to, and suppose there is a neutral chairman who has at his beck and call the consulting experts of the corporation, the union, and, let us say, the Department of Labor.

Judge Gary states with perfect sincerity that his men are well paid and not overworked, and then proceeds to sketch the history of Russia from the time of Peter the Great to the murder of the Czar. Mr. Foster rises, states with equal sincerity that the men are exploited, and then proceeds to outline the history of human emancipation from Jesus of Nazareth to Abraham Lincoln. At this point the chairman calls upon the intelligence men for wage tables in order to substitute for the words "well paid" and "exploited" a table showing what the different classes *are* paid. Does Judge Gary think they are all well paid? He does. Does Mr. Foster think they are all exploited? No, he thinks that groups C, M, and X are exploited. What does he mean by exploited? He means they are not paid a living wage. They are, says Judge Gary. What can a man buy on that wage, asks the chairman. Nothing, says Mr. Foster. Everything he needs, says Judge Gary. The chairman consults the budgets and price statistics of the government. [Footnote: See an article on "The Cost of Living and Wage Cuts," in the *New Republic*, July 27, 1921, by Dr. Leo Wolman, for a brilliant discussion of the naive use of such figures and "pseudo-principles." The warning is of particular importance because it comes from an economist and statistician who has himself done so much to improve the technic of industrial disputes.] He rules that X can meet an average budget, but that C and M cannot. Judge Gary serves notice that he does not regard the official statistics as sound. The budgets are too high, and prices have come down. Mr. Foster also serves notice of exception. The budget is too low, prices have gone up. The chairman rules that this point is not within the jurisdiction of the conference, that the official figures stand, and that Judge Gary's experts and Mr. Foster's should carry their appeals to the standing committee of the federated intelligence bureaus.

Nevertheless, says Judge Gary, we shall be ruined if we change these wage scales. What do you mean by ruined, asks the chairman, produce your books. I can't, they are private, says Judge Gary. What is private does not interest us, says the chairman, and, therefore, issues a statement to the public announcing that the wages of workers in groups C and M are so-and-so much below the official minimum living wage, and that Judge Gary declines to increase them for reasons that he refuses to state. After a procedure of that sort, a public opinion in the eulogistic sense of the term [Footnote: As used by Mr. Lowell in his *Public Opinion and Popular Government*.] can exist.

The value of expert mediation is not that it sets up opinion to coerce the partisans, but that it disintegrates partisanship. Judge Gary and Mr. Foster may remain as little convinced as when they started, though even they would have to talk in a different strain. But almost everyone else who was not personally entangled would save himself from being entangled. For the entangling stereotypes and slogans to which his reflexes are so ready to respond are by this kind of dialectic untangled.

4

On many subjects of great public importance, and in varying degree among different people for more personal matters, the threads of memory and emotion are in a snarl. The same word will connote any number of different ideas: emotions are displaced from the images to which they belong to names which resemble the names of these images. In the uncriticized parts of the mind there is a vast amount of association by mere clang, contact, and succession. There are stray emotional attachments, there are words that were names and are masks. In dreams, reveries, and panic, we uncover some of the disorder, enough to see how the naive mind is composed, and how it behaves when not disciplined by wakeful effort and external resistance. We see that there is no more natural order than in a dusty old attic. There is often the same incongruity between fact, idea, and emotion as there might be in an opera house, if all the wardrobes were dumped in a heap and all the scores mixed up, so that Madame Butterfly in a

The Walter Lippmann Reader

Valkyr's dress waited lyrically for the return of Faust. "At Christmas-tide" says an editorial, "old memories soften the heart. Holy teachings are remembered afresh as thoughts run back to childhood. The world does not seem so bad when seen through the mist of half-happy, half-sad recollections of loved ones now with God. No heart is untouched by the mysterious influence.... The country is honeycombed with red propaganda—but there is a good supply of ropes, muscles and lampposts... while this world moves the spirit of liberty will burn in the breast of man."

The man who found these phrases in his mind needs help. He needs a Socrates who will separate the words, cross-examine him until he has defined them, and made words the names of ideas. Made them mean a particular object and nothing else. For these tense syllables have got themselves connected in his mind by primitive association, and are bundled together by his memories of Christmas, his indignation as a conservative, and his thrills as the heir to a revolutionary tradition. Sometimes the snarl is too huge and ancient for quick unravelling. Sometimes, as in modern psychotherapy, there are layers upon layers of memory reaching back to infancy, which have to be separated and named.

The effect of naming, the effect, that is, of saying that the labor groups C and M, but not X, are underpaid, instead of saying that Labor is Exploited, is incisive. Perceptions recover their identity, and the emotion they arouse is specific, since it is no longer reinforced by large and accidental connections with everything from Christmas to Moscow. The disentangled idea with a name of its own, and an emotion that has been scrutinized, is ever so much more open to correction by new data in the problem. It had been imbedded in the whole personality, had affiliations of some sort with the whole ego: a challenge would reverberate through the whole soul. After it has been thoroughly criticized, the idea is no longer *me* but *that*. It is objectified, it is at arm's length. Its fate is not bound up with my fate, but with the fate of the outer world upon which I am acting.

5

Re-education of this kind will help to bring our public opinions into grip with the environment. That is the way the enormous censoring, stereotyping, and dramatizing apparatus can be liquidated. Where there is no difficulty in knowing what the relevant environment is, the critic, the teacher, the physician, can

438

unravel the mind. But where the environment is as obscure to the analyst as to his pupil, no analytic technic is sufficient. Intelligence work is required. In political and industrial problems the critic as such can do something, but unless he can count upon receiving from expert reporters a valid picture of the environment, his dialectic cannot go far.

Therefore, though here, as in most other matters, "education" is the supreme remedy, the value of this education will depend upon the evolution of knowledge. And our knowledge of human institutions is still extraordinarily meager and impressionistic. The gathering of social knowledge is, on the whole, still haphazard; not, as it will have to become, the normal accompaniment of action. And yet the collection of information will not be made, one may be sure, for the sake of its ultimate use. It will be made because modern decision requires it to be made. But as it is being made, there will accumulate a body of data which political science can turn into generalization, and build up for the schools into a conceptual picture of the world. When that picture takes form, civic education can become a preparation for dealing with an unseen environment.

As a working model of the social system becomes available to the teacher, he can use it to make the pupil acutely aware of how his mind works on unfamiliar facts. Until he has such a model, the teacher cannot hope to prepare men fully for the world they will find. What he can do is to prepare them to deal with that world with a great deal more sophistication about their own minds. He can, by the use of the case method, teach the pupil the habit of examining the sources of his information. He can teach him, for example, to look in his newspaper for the place where the dispatch was filed, for the name of the correspondent, the name of the press service, the authority given for the statement, the circumstances under which the statement was secured. He can teach the pupil to ask himself whether the reporter saw what he describes, and to remember how that reporter described other events in the past. He can teach him the character of censorship, of the idea of privacy, and furnish him with knowledge of past propaganda. He can, by the proper use of history, make him aware of the stereotype, and can educate a habit of introspection about the imagery evoked by printed words. He can, by courses in comparative history and anthropology, produce a life-long realization of the way codes impose a special pattern upon the imagination. He can teach men to catch themselves making allegories, dramatizing relations, and personifying abstractions. He can show the pupil how he identifies himself with these allegories, how he becomes interested, and how he selects the attitude, heroic, romantic, economic which he adopts while holding a particular opinion. The study of error is not only in the highest degree prophylactic, but it serves as a stimulating introduction to the study of truth. As our minds become more deeply aware of their own subjectivism, we find a zest in objective method that is not otherwise there. We see vividly, as normally we should not, the enormous mischief and casual cruelty of our prejudices. And the destruction of a prejudice, though painful at first, because of its connection with our self-respect, gives an immense relief and a fine pride when it is successfully done. There is a radical enlargement of the range of attention. As the current categories dissolve, a hard, simple version of the world breaks up. The scene turns vivid and full. There follows an emotional incentive to hearty appreciation of scientific method, which otherwise it is not easy to arouse, and is impossible to sustain. Prejudices are so much easier and more interesting. For if you teach the principles of science as if they had always been accepted, their chief virtue as a discipline, which is objectivity, will make them dull. But teach them at first as victories over the superstitions of the mind, and the exhilaration of the chase and of the conquest may carry the pupil over that hard transition from his own self-bound experience to the phase where his curiosity has matured, and his reason has acquired passion.

CHAPTER XXVIII

The Appeal to Reason

1

I HAVE written, and then thrown away, several endings to this book. Over all of them there hung that fatality of last chapters, in which every idea seems to find its place, and all the mysteries, that the writer has not forgotten, are unravelled. In politics the hero does not live happily ever after, or end his life perfectly. There is no concluding chapter, because the hero in politics has more future before him than there is recorded history behind him. The last chapter is merely a place where the writer imagines that the polite reader has begun to look furtively at his watch.

2

When Plato came to the point where it was fitting that he should sum up, his assurance turned into stage-fright as he thought how absurd it would sound to say what was in him about the place of reason in politics. Those sentences in book five of the Republic were hard even for Plato to speak; they are so sheer and so stark that men can neither forget them nor live by them. So he makes Socrates say to Glaucon that he will be broken and drowned in laughter for telling "what is the least change which will enable a state to pass into the truer form," [Footnote: *Republic*, Bk. V, 473. Jowett transl.] because the thought he "would fain have uttered if it had not seemed too extravagant" was that "until philosophers are kings, or the kings and princes of this world have the spirit and power of philosophy, and political greatness and wisdom meet in one... cities will never cease from ill,—no, nor the human race..."

Hardly had he said these awful words, when he realized they were a counsel of perfection, and felt embarrassed at the unapproachable grandeur of his idea. So he hastens to add that, of course, "the true pilot" will be called "a prater, a star-gazer, a good-for-nothing." [Footnote: 2 Bk. VI, 488-489.] But this wistful admission, though it protects him against whatever was the Greek equivalent for the charge that he lacked a sense of humor, furnished a humiliating tailpiece to a solemn thought. He becomes defiant and warns Adeimantus that he must "attribute the uselessness" of philosophers "to the fault of those who will not use them, and not to themselves. The pilot should not humbly beg the sailors to be commanded by him—that is not the order of nature." And with this haughty gesture, he hurriedly picked up the tools of reason, and disappeared into the Academy, leaving the world to Machiavelli.

Thus, in the first great encounter between reason and politics, the strategy of reason was to retire in anger. But meanwhile, as Plato tells us, the ship is at sea. There have been many ships on the sea, since Plato wrote, and to-day, whether we are wise or foolish in our belief, we could no longer call a man a true pilot, simply because he knows how to "pay attention to the year and seasons and sky and stars and winds, and whatever else belongs to his art." [Footnote: Bk. VI, 488-489.] He can dismiss nothing which is necessary to make that ship sail prosperously. Because there are mutineers aboard, he cannot say: so much the worse for us all... it is not in the order of nature that I should handle a mutiny... it is not in the order of philosophy that I should consider mutiny... I know how to navigate... I do not know how to navigate a ship full of sailors... and if they do not see that I am the man to steer, I cannot help it. We shall all go on the rocks, they to be punished for their sins; I, with the assurance that I knew better....

3

Whenever we make an appeal to reason in politics, the difficulty in this parable recurs. For there is an inherent difficulty about using the method of reason to deal with an unreasoning world. Even if you assume with Plato that the true pilot knows what is best for the ship, you have to recall that he is not so easy to recognize, and that this uncertainty leaves a large part of the crew unconvinced. By definition the crew does not know what he knows, and the pilot, fascinated by the stars and winds, does not know how to make the crew realize the importance of what he knows. There is no time during mutiny at sea to make each sailor an expert judge of experts. There is no time for the pilot to consult his crew and find out whether he is really as wise as he thinks he is. For education is a matter of years, the emergency a matter of hours. It would be altogether academic, then, to tell the pilot that the true remedy is, for example, an education that will endow sailors with a better sense of evidence. You can tell that only to shipmasters on dry land. In the crisis, the only advice is to use a gun, or make a speech, utter a stirring slogan, offer a compromise, employ any quick means available to quell the mutiny, the sense of evidence being what it is. It is only on shore where men plan for many voyages, that they can afford to, and must for their own salvation, deal with those causes that take a long time to remove. They will be dealing in years and generations, not in emergencies alone. And nothing will put a greater strain upon their wisdom than the necessity of distinguishing false crises from real ones. For when there is panic in the air, with one crisis tripping over the heels of another, actual dangers mixed with imaginary scares, there is no chance at all for the constructive use of reason, and any order soon seems preferable to any disorder.

It is only on the premise of a certain stability over a long run of time that men can hope to follow the method of reason. This is not because mankind is inept, or because the appeal to reason is visionary, but because the evolution of reason on political subjects is only in its beginnings. Our rational ideas in politics are still large, thin generalities, much too abstract and unrefined for practical guidance, except where the aggregates are large enough to cancel out individual peculiarity and exhibit large uniformities. Reason in politics is especially immature in predicting the behavior of individual men, because in human conduct the smallest initial variation often works out into the most elaborate differences. That, perhaps, is why when we try to insist solely upon an appeal to reason in dealing with sudden situations, we are broken and drowned in laughter.

4

For the rate at which reason, as we possess it, can advance itself is slower than the rate at which action has to be taken. In the present state of political science there is, therefore, a tendency for one situation to change into another, before the first is clearly understood, and so to make much political criticism hindsight and little else. Both in the discovery of what is unknown, and in the propagation of that which has been proved, there is a time-differential, which ought to, in a much greater degree than it ever has, occupy the political philosopher. We have begun, chiefly under the inspiration of Mr. Graham Wallas, to examine the effect of an invisible environment upon our opinions. We do not, as yet, understand, except a little by rule of thumb, the element of time in politics, though it bears most directly upon the practicability of any constructive proposal. [Footnote: *Cf.* H. G. Wells in the opening chapters of *Mankind in the Making.*] We can see, for example, that somehow the relevancy of any plan depends upon the length of time the operation requires. Because on the length of time it will depend whether the data which the plan assumes as given, will in truth remain the same. [Footnote: The better the current analysis in the intelligence work of any institution, the less likely, of course, that men will deal with tomorrow's problems in the light of yesterday's facts.] There is a factor here which realistic and experienced men do take into account, and it helps to mark them off somehow from the opportunist, the visionary, the philistine and the pedant. [Footnote: Not all, but some of the differences between reactionaries, conservatives, liberals, and radicals are due, I think, to a different intuitive estimate of the rate of change in social affairs.] But just how the calculation of time enters into politics we do not know at present in any systematic way.

Until we understand these matters more clearly, we can at least remember that there is a problem of the utmost theoretical difficulty and practical consequence. It will help us to cherish Plato's ideal, without sharing his hasty conclusion about the perversity of those who do not listen to reason. It is hard to obey reason in politics, because you are trying to make two processes march together, which have as yet a different gait and a different pace. Until reason is subtle and particular, the immediate struggle of politics will continue to require an amount of native wit, force, and unprovable faith, that reason can neither provide nor control, because the facts of life are too undifferentiated for its powers of understanding. The methods of social science are so little perfected that in many of the serious decisions and most of the casual ones, there is as yet no choice but to gamble with fate as intuition prompts.

But we can make a belief in reason one of those intuitions. We can use our wit and our force to make footholds for reason. Behind our pictures of the world, we can try to see the vista of a longer duration of events, and wherever it is possible to escape from the urgent present, allow this longer time to control our decisions. And yet, even when there is this will to let the future count, we find again and again that we do not know for certain how to act according to the dictates of reason. The number of human problems on which reason is prepared to dictate is small.

5

There is, however, a noble counterfeit in that charity which comes from self-knowledge and an unarguable belief that no one of our gregarious species is alone in his longing for a friendlier world. So many of the grimaces men make at each other go with a flutter of their pulse, that they are not all of them important. And where so much is uncertain, where so many actions have to be carried out on guesses, the demand upon the reserves of mere decency is enormous, and it is necessary to live as if good will would work. We cannot prove in every instance that it will, nor why hatred, intolerance, suspicion, bigotry, secrecy, fear, and lying are the seven deadly sins against public opinion. We can only insist that they have no place in the appeal to reason, that in the longer run they are a poison; and taking our stand upon a view of the world which outlasts our own predicaments, and our own lives, we can cherish a hearty prejudice against them.

We can do this all the better if we do not allow frightfulness and fanaticism to impress us so deeply that we throw up our hands peevishly, and lose interest in the longer run of time because we have lost faith in the future of man. There is no ground for this despair, because all the *ifs* on which, as James said, our destiny hangs, are as pregnant as they ever were. What we have seen of brutality, we have seen, and because it was strange, it was not conclusive. It was only Berlin, Moscow, Versailles in 1914 to 1919, not Armageddon, as we rhetorically said. The more realistically men have faced out the brutality and the hysteria, the more they have earned the right to say that it is not foolish for men to believe, because another great war took place, that intelligence, courage and effort cannot ever contrive a good life for all men.

Great as was the horror, it was not universal. There were corrupt, and there were incorruptible. There was muddle and there were miracles. There was huge lying. There were men with the will to uncover it. It is no judgment, but only a mood, when men deny that what some men have been, more men, and ultimately enough men, might be. You can despair of what has never been. You can despair of ever having three heads, though Mr. Shaw has declined to despair even of that. But you cannot despair of the possibilities that could exist by virtue of any human quality which a human being has exhibited. And if amidst all the evils of this decade, you have not seen men and women, known moments that you would like to multiply, the Lord himself cannot help you.

The Phantom Public

Table of Contents

PART I

Chapter 1
The Disenchanted Man

1

THE private citizen today has come to feel rather like a deaf spectator in the back row, who ought to keep his mind on the mystery off there, but cannot quite manage to keep awake. He knows he is somehow affected by what is going on. Rules and regulations continually, taxes annually and wars occasionally remind him that he is being swept along by great drifts of circumstance.

Yet these public affairs are in no convincing way his affairs. They are for the most part invisible. They are managed, if they are managed at all, at distant centers, from behind the scenes, by unnamed powers. As a private person he does not know for certain what is going on, or who is doing it, or where he is being carried. No newspaper reports his environment so that he can grasp it; no school has taught him how to imagine it; his ideals, often, do not fit with it; listening to speeches, uttering opinions and voting do not, he finds, enable him to govern it. He lives in a world which he cannot see, does not understand and is unable to direct.

In the cold light of experience he knows that his sovereignty is a fiction. He reigns in theory, but in fact he does not govern. Contemplating himself and his actual accomplishments in public affairs, contrasting the influence he exerts with the influence he is supposed according to democratic theory to exert, he must say of his sovereignty what Bismarck said of Napoleon III.: "At a distance it is something, but close to it is nothing at all."[1] When, during an agitation of some sort, say a political campaign, he hears himself and some thirty million others described as the source of all wisdom and power and righteousness, the prime mover and the ultimate goal, the remnants of sanity in him protest. He cannot all the time play Chanticleer who was so dazzled and delighted because he himself had caused the sun to rise.

The Walter Lippmann Reader

For when the private man has lived through the romantic age in politics and is no longer moved by the stale echoes of its hot cries, when he is sober and unimpressed, his own part in public affairs appears to him a pretentious thing, a second rate, an inconsequential. You cannot move him then with a good straight talk about service and civic duty, nor by waving a flag in his face, nor by sending a boy scout after him to make him vote. He is a man back home from a crusade to make the world something or other it did not become; he has been tantalized too often by the foam of events, has seen the gas go out of it, and, with sour derision for the stuff, he is saying with the author of *Trivia:*[2]

"'Self-determination,' one of them insisted.

"'Arbitration,' cried another.

"'Coöperation,' suggested the mildest of the party.

"'Confiscation,' answered an uncompromising female.

"I, too, became intoxicated with the sound of these vocables. And were they not the cure for all our ills?

"'Inoculation!' I chimed in. 'Transubstantiation, alliteration, inundation, flagellation, and afforestation!'"

2

It is well known that nothing like the whole people takes part in public affairs. Of the eligible voters in the United States less than half go to the polls even in a presidential year.[3] During the campaign of 1924 a special effort was made to bring out more voters. They did not come out. The Constitution, the nation, the party system, the presidential succession, private property, all were supposed to be in danger. One party prophesied red ruin, another black corruption, a third tyranny and imperialism if the voters did not go to the polls in greater numbers. Half the citizenship was unmoved.

The students used to write books about voting. They are now beginning to, write books about nonvoting. At the University of Chicago Professor Merriam and Mr. Gosnell have made an elaborate inquiry[4] into the reason

448

why, at the typical Chicago mayoral election of 1923, there were, out of 1,400,000 eligible electors, only 900,000 who registered, and out of those who registered there were only 723,000 who finally managed to vote. Thousands of persons were interviewed. About 30 per cent of the abstainers had, or at least claimed to have had, an insuperable difficulty about going to the polls. They were ill, they were absent from the city, they were women detained at home by a child or an invalid, they had had insufficient legal residence. The other 70 per cent, representing about half a million free and sovereign citizens of this Republic, did not even pretend to have a reason for not voting, which, in effect, was not an admission that they did not care about voting. They were needed at their work, the polls were crowded, the polls were inconveniently located, they were afraid to tell their age, they did not believe in woman suffrage, the husband objected, politics is rotten, elections are rotten, they were afraid to vote, they did not know there was an election. About a quarter of those who were interviewed had the honesty to say they were wholly uninterested.

Yet Bryce is authority for the statement that "the will of the sovereign people is expressed . . . in the United States . . . by as large a proportion of the registered voters as in any other country."[5] And certainly Mr. Lowell's tables on the use of the initiative and referendum in Switzerland in the main support the view that the indifference of the American voter is not unique.[6] In fact, realistic political thinkers in Europe long aga abandoned the notion that the collective mass of the people direct the course of public affairs. Robert Michels, himself a Socialist, says flatly that "the majority is permanently incapable of self-government,"[7] and quotes approvingly the remark of a Swedish Socialist Deputy, Gustaf F. Steffen, that "even after the victory there will always remain in political life the leaders and the led." Michels, who is a political thinker of great penetration, unburdens himself finally on the subject by printing a remark of Hertzen's that the victory of an opposition party amounts to "passing from the sphere of envy to the sphere of avarice."

The Walter Lippmann Reader

There is then nothing particularly new in the disenchantment which the private citizen expresses by not voting at all, by voting only for the head of the ticket, by staying away from the primaries, by not reading speeches and documents, by the whole list of sins of omission for which he is denounced. I shall not denounce him further. My sympathies are with him, for I believe that he has been saddled with an impossible task and that he is asked to practice an unattainable ideal. I find it so myself for, although public business is my main interest and I give most of my time to watching it, I cannot find time to do what is expected of me in the theory of democracy; that is, to know what is going on and to have an opinion worth expressing on every question which confronts a self-governing community. And I have not happened to meet anybody, from a President of the United States to a professor of political science, who came anywhere near to embodying the accepted ideal of the sovereign and omnicompetent citizen.

Chapter 2
The Unattainable Ideal

I HAVE tried to imagine how the perfect citizen could be produced. Some say he will have to be born of the conjunction of the right germ plasms, and, in the pages of books written by Madison Grant, Lothrop Stoddard and other revivalists, I have seen prescriptions as to just who ought to marry whom to produce a great citizenry. Not being a biologist I keep an open but hopeful mind on this point, tempered, however, with the knowledge that certainty about how to breed ability in human beings is on the whole in inverse proportion to the writer's scientific reputation.

It is then to education that logically one turns next, for education has furnished the thesis of the last chapter of every optimistic book on democracy written for one hundred and fifty years. Even Robert Michels stern and unbending antisentimentalist that he is, says in his "final considerations" that "it is the great task of social education to raise the intellectual level of the masses, so that they may be enabled, within the limits of what is possible, to counteract the oligarchical tendencies" of all collective action.

So I have been reading some of the new standard textbooks used to teach citizenship in schools and colleges. After reading them I do not see how any one can escape the conclusion that man must have the appetite of an encyclopedist and infinite time ahead of him. To be sure he no longer is expected to remember the exact salary of the county clerk and the length of the coroner' s term. In the new civics he studies the problems of government, and not the structural detail. He is told, in one textbook of five hundred concise, contentious pages, which I have been reading, about city problems, state problems, national problems, international problems, trust problems, labor problems, transportation problems, banking problems, rural problems, agricultural problems, and so on *ad infinitum*. In the eleven pages devoted to problems of the City there are described twelve sub-problems.

But nowhere in this well-meant book is the sovereign citizen of the future given a hint as to how, while he is earning a living, rearing children and enjoying his life, he is to keep himself informed about the progress of the swarming confusion of problems. He is exhorted to conserve the natural resources of the country because they are limited in quantity, He is advised to watch public expenditures because the taxpayers cannot pay out indefinitely increasing amounts. But he, the voter, the citizen, the sovereign, is apparently expected to yield an unlimited quantity of public spirit, interest, curiosity and effort. The author of the textbook, touching on everything, as he thinks, from city sewers to Indian Opium, misses a decisive fact: the citizen gives but a little of his time to public affairs, has but a casual interest in facts and but a poor appetite for theory.

It never occurs to this preceptor of civic duty to provide the student with a rule by which he can know whether on Thursday it is his duty to consider subways in Brooklyn or the Manchurian Railway, nor how, if he determines on Thursday to express his sovereign will on the subway question, he is to repair those gaps in his knowledge of that question which are due to his having been preoccupied the day before in expressing his sovereign will about rural credits in Montana and the rights of Britain in the Sudan. Yet he cannot know all about everything all the time, and while he is watching one thing a thousand others undergo great changes, Unless he can discover some rational ground for fixing his attention where it will do the most good, and in a way that suits his inherently amateurish equipment, he will be as bewildered as a puppy trying to lick three bones at once.

I do not wish to say that it does the student no good to be taken on a sightseeing tour of the problems of the world. It may teach him that the world is complicated, even if he comes out of the adventure "laden with germs, breathing creeds and convictions on you whenever he opens his mouth."[1] He may learn humility, but most certainly his acquaintance with what a high-minded author thought were American problems in 1925 will not equip him to master American problems ten years later. Unless out of the study of transient issues he acquires an intellectual attitude no education has occurred.

That is why the usual appeal to education as the remedy for the incompetence of democracy is so barren. it is, in effect, a proposal that school teachers shall by some magic of their own fit men to govern after the makers of laws and the preachers of civic ideals have had a free hand in writing the specifications. The reformers do not ask what men can be taught. They say they should be taught whatever may be necessary to fit them to govern the modern world.

The usual appeal to education can bring only disappointment. For the problems of the modern world appear and change faster than any set of teachers can grasp them, much faster than they can convey their substance to a population of children. If the schools attempt to teach children how to solve the problems of the day, they are bound always to be in arrears. The most they can conceivably attempt is the teaching of a pattern of thought and feeling which will enable the citizen to approach a new problem in some useful fashion. But that pattern cannot be invented by the pedagogue. It is the political theorist's business to trace out that pattern. In that task he must not assume that the mass has political genius, but that men even if they had genius, would give only a little time and attention to public affairs.

The moralist, I am afraid, will agree all too readily with the idea that social education must deal primarily not with the elements and solutions of particular phases of transient problems but with the principles that constitute an attitude toward all problems. I warn him off. It will require more than a good conscience to govern modern society, for conscience is no guide in situations where the essence of the difficulty is to find a guide for the conscience.

When I am tempted to think that men can be fitted out to deal with the modern world simply by teaching morals, manners and patriotism, I try to remember the fable of the pensive professor walking in the woods at twilight. He stumbled into a tree. This experience compelled him to act. Being a man of honor and breeding, he raised his hat, bowed deeply to the tree, and exclaimed with sincere regret: "Excuse me, sir, I thought you were a tree."

Is it fair, I ask, as a matter of morality, to chide him for his conduct? If he had encountered a tree, can any one deny his right to collide with it? If he had stumbled into a man, was his apology not sufficient? Here was a moral code in perfect working order, and the only questionable aspect of his conduct turned not on the goodness of his heart or the firmness of his principles but on a point of fact. You may retort that he had a moral obligation to know the difference between a man and a tree. Perhaps so. But suppose that instead of walking in the woods he had been casting a ballot; suppose that instead of a tree he had encountered the Fordney-McCumber tariff. How much more obligation to know the truth would you have imposed on him then? After all, this walker in the woods at twilight with his mind on other things was facing, as all of us think we are, the facts he imagined were there, and was doing his duty as he had learned it.

In some degree the whole animate world seems to share the inexpertness of the thoughtful professor. Pavlov showed by his experiments on dogs that an animal with a false stomach can experience all the pleasures of eating, and the number of mice and monkeys known to have been deceived in laboratories is surpassed only by the hopeful citizens of a democracy. Man's reflexes are, as the psychologists say, conditioned. And, therefore, he responds quite readily to a glass egg, a decoy duck, a stuffed shirt or a political platform. No moral code, as such, will enable him to know whether he is exercising his moral faculties on a real and an important event. For effective virtue, as Socrates pointed out long ago, is knowledge; and a code of the right and the wrong must wait upon a perception of the true and the false.

The Walter Lippmann Reader

But even the successful practice of a moral code would not emancipate democracy. There are too many moral codes. In our immediate lives, within the boundaries of our own society, there may be commonly accepted standards. But a political theorist who asks that a local standard be universally applied is merely begging one of the questions he ought to be trying to solve. For, while possibly it may be an aim of political organization to arrive at a common standard of judgment, one of the conditions which engenders politics and makes political organization necessary is the conflict of standards.

Darwin's story of the cats and clover[2] may be recommended to any one who finds it difficult to free his mind of the assumption that his notions of good and bad are universal. The purple clover is cross-fertilized by the bumblebee, and, therefore, the more bumblebees the better next year's crop of clover. But the nests of bumblebees are rifled by field mice which are fond of the white grubs. Therefore, the more field mice the fewer bumblebees and the poorer the crop. But in the neighborhood of villages the cats hunt down the field mice. And so the more cats the fewer mice, the more bumblebees the better the crop. And the more kindly old ladies there are in the village the more cats there will be.

If you happen not to be a Hindu or a vegetarian and are a beef-eating Occidental you will commend the old ladies who keep the cats who hunt the mice who destroy the bumblebees who make the pasture of clover for the cattle. If you are a cat you also will be in favor of the old ladies. But if you are a field mouse, how different the rights and wrongs of that section of the universe! The old ladies who keep cats will seem about as kindly as witches with pet tigers, and the Old Lady Peril will be debated hysterically by the Field Mouse Security League. For what could a patriotic mouse think of a world in which bumblebees did not exist for the sole purpose of producing white grubs for field mice? There would seem to be no law and order in such a world; and only a highly philosophical mouse would admit with Bergson that "the idea of disorder objectifies for the convenience of language, the disappointment of a mind that finds before it an order different from what it wants."[3] For the order which we recognize as good is an order suited to our needs and hopes and habits.

There is nothing universal or eternal or unchangeable about our expectations. For rhetorical effect we often say there is. But in concrete cases it is not easy to explain why the thing we desire is so righteous. If the farmers are able to buy less than their accustomed amount of manufactured foods there is disorder and a problem. But what absolute standard is there which determines whether a bushel of wheat in 1925 should, as compared with 1913, exchange for more, as many, or less manufactures? Can any one define a principle which shall say whether the standard of living of the farmers or of any other class should rise or fall, and how fast and how much? There may be more jobs than workingmen at the wage offered: the employers will complain and will call it a problem, but who knows any rule which tells how large a surplus of labor there ought to be and at what price? There may be more workingmen than jobs of the kind and at the places and for the wages they will or can take. But, although the problem will be acute, there is no principle which determines how many machinists, clerks, coal miners, bankers, or salesmen it is the duty of society to provide work for.

It requires intense partisanship and much self-deception to argue that some sort of peculiar righteousness adheres to the farmers' claims as against the manufacturers', the employers' against the wage-earners', the creditors' against the debtors', or the other way around. These conflicts of interest are problems. They require solution. But there is no moral pattern available from which the precise nature of the solution can be deduced. If then eugenics cannot produce the ideal democratic citizen, omnicompetent and sovereign, because biology knows neither how to breed political excellence nor what that excellence is; if education cannot equip the citizen, because the school teacher cannot anticipate the issues of the future; if morality cannot direct him, first, because right or wrong in specific cases depends upon the perception of true or false, and, second, on the assumption that there is a universal moral code, which, in fact, does not exist, where else shall we look for the method of making the competent citizen? Democratic theorists in the nineteenth century had several other prescriptions which still influence the thinking of many hopeful persons.

One school based their reforms on the aphorism that the cure for the evils of democracy is more democracy. It was assumed that the popular will was wise and good if only you could get at it. They proposed extensions of the suffrage, and as much voting as possible by means of the initiative, referendum and recall, direct election of Senators, direct primaries, an elected judiciary, and the like. They begged the question, for it has never been proved that there exists the kind of public opinion which they presupposed. Since the Bryan campaign of 1896 this school of thought has made great conquests in most of the states, and has profoundly influenced the federal government. The eligible vote has trebled since 1896; the direct action of the voter has been enormously extended. Yet that same period has seen a decline in the percentage of the popular vote cast at presidential elections from 80.75 per cent in 1896 to 52.36 per cent in 1920. Apparently there is a fallacy in the first assumption of this school that "the whole people" desires to participate actively in government. Nor is there any evidence to show that the persons who do participate are in any real sense directing the course of affairs. The party machines have survived every attack. And why should they not? If the voter cannot grasp the details of the problems of the day because he has not the time, the interest or the knowledge, he will not have a better public opinion because he is asked to express his opinion more often. He will simply be more bewildered, more bored and more ready to follow along.

Another school, calling themselves revolutionary, have ascribed the disenchantment of democracy to the capitalistic system. They have argued that property is power, and that until there is as wide a distribution of economic power as there is of the right to vote the suffrage cannot be more effective. No serious student, I think, would dispute that socialist premise which asserts that the weight of influence on society exercised by an individual is more nearly related to the character of his property than to his abstract legal citizenship. But the socialist conclusion that economic power can be distributed by concentrating the ownership of great utilities in the state, the conclusion that the pervasion of industrial life by voting and referenda will yield competent popular decisions, seems to me again to beg the question. For what reason is there to think that subjecting so many more affairs to the method of the vote will reveal hitherto undiscovered wisdom and technical competence and reservoirs of public interest in men? The socialist scheme has at its root the mystical fallacy of democracy, that the people, all of them, are competent; at its top it suffers from the homeopathic fallacy that adding new tasks to a burden the people will not and cannot carry now will make the burden of citizenship easily borne. The socialist theory presupposes an unceasing, untiring round of civic duties, an enormous complication of the political interests that are already much too complicated.

These various remedies, eugenic, educational, ethical, populist and socialist, all assume that either the voters are inherently competent to direct the course of affairs or that they are making progress toward such an ideal. I think it is a false ideal. I do not mean an undesirable ideal. I mean an unattainable ideal, bad only in the sense that it is bad for a fat man to try to be a ballet dancer. An ideal should express the true possibilities of its subject. When it does not it perverts the true possibilities. The ideal of the omnicompetent, sovereign citizen is, in my opinion, such a false ideal. It is unattainable. The pursuit of it is misleading. The failure to achieve it has produced the current disenchantment.

The individual man does not have opinions on all public affairs. He does not know how to direct public affairs. He does not know what is happening, why it is happening, what ought to happen. I cannot imagine how he could know, and there is not the least reason for thinking, as mystical democrats have thought, that the compounding of individual ignorances in masses of people can produce a continuous directing force in public affairs.

Chapter III
Agents and Bystanders

1

WHEN a citizen has qualified as a voter he finds himself one of the theoretical rulers of a great going concern. He has not made the complicated machine with its five hundred thousand federal officers and its uncounted local offices. He has not seen much of it. He is bound by contracts, by debts, by treaties, by laws, made before he was aware of them. He does not from day to day decide who shall do what in the business of government. Only some small fraction of it comes intermittently to his notice. And in those episodic moments when he stands in the polling booth he is a highly intelligent and public-spirited voter indeed who can discover two real alternatives and enlist his influence for a party which promises something he can understand.

The actual governing is made up of a multitude of arrangements on specific questions by particular individuals. These rarely become visible to the private citizen. Government, in the long intervals between elections, is carried on by politicians, officeholders and influential men who make settlements with other politicians, officeholders and influential men. The mass of people see these settlements, judge them, and affect them only now and then. They are altogether too numerous, too complicated, too obscure in their effects to become the subject of any continuing exercise of public opinion.

Nor in any exact and literal sense are those who conduct the daily business of government accountable after the fact to the great mass of the voters. They are accountable only, except in spectacular cases, to the other politicians, officeholders and influential men directly interested in the particular act. Modern society is not visible to anybody, nor intelligible continuously and as a whole. One section is visible to another section, one series of acts is intelligible to this group and another to that.

459

The Walter Lippmann Reader

Even this degree of responsible understanding is attainable only by the development of fact-finding agencies of great scope and complexity.[1] These agencies give only a remote and incidental assistance to the general public. Their findings are too intricate for the casual reader. They are also almost always much too uninteresting. Indeed the popular boredom and contempt for the expert and for statistical measurement are such that the organization of intelligence to administer modern affairs would probably be entirely neglected were it not that departments of government, corporations, trade unions and trade associations are being compelled by their own internal necessities of administration, and by compulsion of other corporate groups, to record their own acts, measure them, publish them and stand accountable for them.

The need in the Great Society not only for publicity but for uninterrupted publicity is indisputable. But we shall misunderstand the need seriously if we imagine that the purpose of the publication can possibly be the informing of every voter. We live at the mere beginnings of public accounting. Yet the facts far exceed our curiosity. The railroads, for example, make an accounting. Do we read the results? Hardly. A few executives here and there, some bankers, some regulating officials, some representatives of shippers and the like read them. The rest of us ignore them for the good and sufficient reason that we have other things to do.

For the man does not live who can read all the reports that drift across his doorstep or all the dispatches in his newspaper. And if by some development of the radio every man could see and hear all that was happening everywhere, if publicity, in other words, became absolute, how much time could or would he spend watching the Sinking Fund Commission and the Geological Survey? He would probably tune in on the Prince of Wales, or, in desperation, throw off the switch and seek peace in ignorance. It is bad enough today with morning newspapers published in the evening and evening newspapers in the morning, with October magazines in September, with the movies and the radio—to be condemned to live under a barrage of eclectic information, to have one's

460

mind made the receptacle for a hullabaloo of speeches, arguments and unrelated episodes. General information for the informing of public opinion is altogether too general for intellectual decency. And life is too short for the pursuit of omniscience by the counting in a state of nervous excitement of all the leaves on all the trees.

2

If all men had to conceive the whole process of government all the time the world's work would obviously never be carried on. Men make no attempt to consider society as a whole. The farmer decides whether to plant wheat or corn, the mechanic whether to take the job offered at the Pennsylvania or the Erie shops, whether to buy a Ford or a piano, and, if a Ford, whether to buy it from the garage on Elm Street or from the dealer who sent him a circular. These decisions are among fairly narrow choices offered to him; he can no more choose among all the jobs in the world than he can consider marrying any woman in the world. These choices in detail are in their cumulative mass the government of society. They may rest on ignorant or enlightened opinions, but, whether he comes to them by accident or scientific instruction, they are specific and particular among at best a few concrete alternatives and they lead to a definite, visible result.

But men are supposed also to hold public opinions about the general conduct of society. The mechanic is supposed not only to choose between working for the Pennsylvania or the Erie but to decide how in the interests of the nation all the railroads of the country shall be regulated. The two kinds of opinion merge insensibly one into the other; men have general notions which influence their individual decisions and their direct experiences unconsciously govern their general notions. Yet it is useful to distinguish between the two kinds of opinion, the specific and direct, the general and the indirect.

Specific opinions give rise to immediate executive acts; to take a job, to do a particular piece of work, to hire or fire, to buy or sell, to stay here or go there, to accept or refuse, to command or obey. General opinions give rise to delegated, indirect, symbolic, intangible results: to a vote, to a resolution, to applause, to criticism, to praise or dispraise, to audiences, circulations, followings, contentment or discontent. The specific opinion may lead to a decision to act within the area where a man has personal jurisdiction; that is, within the limits set by law and custom, his personal power and his personal desire. But general opinions lead only to some sort of expression, such as voting, and do not result in executive acts except in cooperation with the general opinions of large numbers of other persons.

Since the general opinions of large numbers of persons are almost certain to be a vague and confusing medley, action cannot be taken until these opinions have been factored, down, canalized, compressed and made uniform. The making of one general will out of a multitude of general wishes is not an Hegelian mystery, as so many social philosophers have imagined, but an art well known to leaders, politicians and steering committees.[2] It consists essentially in the use of symbols which assemble emotions after they have been detached from their ideas. Because feelings are much less specific than ideas, and yet more poignant, the leader is able to make a homogeneous will out of a heterogeneous mass of desires. The process, therefore, by which general opinions are brought to cooperation consists of an intensification of feeling and a degradation of significance. Before a mass of general opinions can eventuate in executive action, the choice is narrowed down to a few alternatives. The victorious alternative is executed not by the mass but by individuals in control of its energy.

A private opinion may be quite complicated, and may issue in quite complicated actions, in a whole train of subsidiary opinions, as when a man decides to build a house and then makes a hundred judgments as to how it shall be built. But a public opinion has no such immediate responsibility or continuous result. It leads in politics to the making of a pencil mark on a piece of paper, and then to a period of waiting and watching as to whether one or two years hence the mark shall be made in the same column or in the adjoining one. The decision to make the mark may be for reasons a^1, a^2, a3 . . . a^n: the result, whether an idiot or genius has voted, is A.

For great masses of people, though each of them may have more or less distinct views, must when they act converge to an identical result. And the more complex the collection of men the more ambiguous must be the unity and the simpler the common ideas.

3

In English-speaking countries during the last century the contrast between the action of men individually and in the mass has been much emphasized, and yet greatly misunderstood. Macaulay, for example, speaking on the Reform Bill of 1832, drew the conventional distinction between private enterprise and public action:

"In all those things which depend on the intelligence, the knowledge, the industry, the energy of individuals, this country stands preeminent among all countries of the world ancient and modern. But in those things which it belongs to the state to direct we have no such claim to superiority . . . can there be a stronger contrast than that which exists between the beauty, the completeness, the speed, the precision with which every process is performed in our factories, and the awkwardness, the crudeness, the slowness, the uncertainty of the apparatus by which offenses are punished and rights vindicated? . . . Surely we see the barbarism of the Thirteenth Century and the highest civilization of the Nineteenth Century side by side, and we see that the barbarism belongs to the government, and the civilization to the people."[3]

Macaulay was, of course, thinking of the contrast between factory production and government as it existed in England under Queen Victoria's uncles and the hard-drinking, hard-riding squirearchy. But the Prussian bureaucracy amply demonstrated that there is no such necessary contrast between governmental and private action. There is a contrast between action by and through great masses of people and action that moves without them.

The fundamental contrast is not between public and private enterprises, between "crowd" psychology and individual, but between men doing specific things and men attempting to command general results. The work of the world is carried on by men in their executive capacity, by an infinite number of concrete acts, plowing and planting and reaping, building and destroying, fitting this to that, going from here to there, transforming A into B and moving B from X to Y. The relationships between the individuals doing these specific things are balanced by a most intricate mechanism of exchange, of contract, of custom and of implied promises. Where men are performing their work they must learn to understand the process and the substance of these obligations if they are to do it at all. But in governing the work of other men by votes or by the expression of opinion they can only reward or punish a result, accept or reject alternatives presented to them. They can say yes or no to something which has been done, yes or no to a proposal, but they cannot create, administer and actually perform the act they have in mind. Persons uttering public opinions may now and then be able to define the acts of men, but their opinions do not execute these acts.

4

To the realm of executive acts, each of us, as a member of the public remains always external. Our public opinions are always and forever, by their very nature, an attempt to control the actions of others from the outside. If we can grasp the full significance of that conclusion we shall, I think, have found a way of fixing the role of public opinion in its true perspective; we shall know how to account for the disenchantment of democracy, and we shall begin to see the outline of an ideal of public opinion which, unlike that accepted in the dogma of democracy, may be really attainable.

Chapter IV
What the Public Does

1

I DO not mean to say that there is no other attainable ideal of public opinion but that severely practical one which this essay is meant to disclose. One might aim to enrich the minds of men with charming fantasies, animate nature and society with spirits, set up an Olympus in the skies and an Atlantis at the end of the world. And one might then assert that, so the quality of ideas be fine or give peace, it does not matter how or whether they eventuate in the government of affairs.

Utopia and Nirvana are by definition their own sufficient reason, and it may be that to contemplate them is well worth the abandonment of feeble attempts to control the action of events. Renunciation, however, is a luxury in which all men cannot indulge. They will somehow seek to control the behavior of others, if not by positive law then at least by persuasion. When men are in that posture toward events they are a public, as I am here defining the term; their opinions as to how others ought to behave are public opinions. The more clearly it is understood what the public can do and what it cannot, the more effectively it will do what lies within its power to do well and the less it will interfere with the liberties of men.

The role of public opinion is determined by the fact that its relation to a problem is external. The opinion affects an opinion, but does not itself control the executive act. A public opinion is expressed by a vote, a demonstration of praise or blame, a following or a boycotting. But these manifestations are in themselves nothing. They count only if they influence the course of affairs. They influence it, however, only if they influence an actor in the affair. And it is, I believe, precisely in this secondary, indirect relationship between public opinion and public affairs that we have the clue to the limits and the possibilities of public opinion.

2

It may be objected at once that an election which turns one set of men out of office and installs another is an expression of public opinion which is neither secondary nor indirect. But what in fact is an election? We call it an expression of the popular will. But is it? We go into a polling booth and mark a cross on a piece of paper for one of two, or perhaps three or four names. Have we expressed our thoughts on the public policy of the United States? Presumably we have a number of thoughts on this and that with many buts and ifs and ors. Surely the cross on a piece of paper does not express them. It would take us hours to express our thoughts, and calling a vote the expression of our mind is an empty fiction.

A vote is a promise of support. It is a way of saying: I am lined up with these men, on this side. I enlist with them. I will follow. I will buy. I will boycott. I will strike. I applaud. I jeer. The force I can exert is placed here, not there.

The public does not select the candidate, write the platform, outline the policy any more than it builds the automobile or acts the play. It aligns itself for or against somebody who has offered himself, has made a promise, has produced a play, is selling an automobile. The action of a group as a group is the mobilization of the force it possesses.

The attempt has been made to ascribe some intrinsic moral and intellectual virtue to majority rule. It was said often in the nineteenth century that there was a deep wisdom in majorities which was the voice of God. Sometimes this flattery was a sincere mysticism, sometimes it was the self-deception which always accompanies the idealization of power. In substance it was nothing but a transfer to the new sovereign of the divine attributes of kings. Yet the inherent absurdity of making virtue and wisdom dependent on 51 per cent of any collection of men has always been apparent. The practical realization that the claim was absurd has resulted in a whole code of civil rights to protect minorities and in all sorts of elaborate methods of subsidizing the arts and sciences and other human interests so they might be independent of the operation of majority rule.

The justification of majority rule in politics is not to be found in its ethical superiority. It is to be found in the sheer necessity of finding a place in civilized society for the force which resides in the weight of numbers. I have called voting an act of enlistment, an alignment for or against, a mobilization. These are military metaphors, and rightly so, I think, for an election based on the principle of majority rule is historically and practically a sublimated and denatured civil war, a paper mobilization without physical violence.

Constitutional democrats, in the intervals when they were not idealizing the majority, have acknowledged that a ballot was a civilized substitute for a bullet.

The Walter Lippmann Reader

"The French Revolution," says Bernard Shaw, "overthrew one set of rulers and substituted another with different interests and different views. That is what a general election enables the people to do in England every seven years if they choose. Revolution is therefore a national institution in England; and its advocacy by an Englishman needs no apology."[1] It makes an enormous difference, of course, whether the people fight or vote, but we shall understand the nature of voting better if we recognize it to be a substitute for fighting. "There grew up in the 17th and 18th Centuries in England," says Dwight Morrow in his introduction to Professor Morse's book, "and there has been carried from England to almost every civilized government in the world, a procedure through which party government becomes in large measure a substitute for revolution."[2] Hans Delbrück puts the matter simply when he says that the principle of majority rule is "a purely practical principle. If one wants to avoid a civil war, one lets those rule who in any case would obtain the upper hand if there should be a struggle; and they are the superior numbers."[3]

But, while an election is in essence sublimated warfare, we must take care not to miss the importance of the sublimation. There have been pedantic theorists who wished to disqualify all who could not bear arms, and woman suffrage has been deplored as a falsification of the value of an election in uncovering the alignment of martial force in the community. One can safely ignore such theorizing. For, while the institution of an election is in its historical origins an alignment of the physical force, it has come to be an alignment of all kinds of force. It remains an alignment, though in advanced democracies it has lost most of its primitive association with military combat. It has not lost it in the South where the Negro population is disfranchised by force, and not permitted to make its weight felt in an election. It has not lost it in the unstable Latin American republics where every election is in some measure still an armed revolution. In fact, the United States has officially recognized this truth by proclaiming that the substitution of election for revolution in Central America is the test of political progress.

I do not wish to labor the argument any further than may be necessary to establish the theory that what the public does is not to express its opinions but to align itself for or against a proposal. If that theory is accepted, we must abandon the notion that democratic government can be the direct expression of the will of the people. We must abandon the notion that the people govern.

Instead we must adopt the theory that, by their occasional mobilizations as a majority, people support or oppose the individuals who actually govern. We must say that the popular will does not direct continuously but that it intervenes occasionally.

Chapter V
The Neutralization of Arbitrary Force

1

IF THIS is the nature of public action, what ideal can be formulated which shall conform to it?

We are bound, I think, to express the ideal in its lowest terms, to state it not as an ideal which might conceivably be realized by exceptional groups now and then or in some distant future but as an ideal which normally might be taught and attained. In estimating the burden which a public can carry, a sound political theory must insist upon the largest factor of safety. It must understate the possibilities of public action.

The action of a public, we had concluded, is principally confined to an occasional intervention in affairs by means of an alignment of the force which a dominant section of that public can wield. We must assume, then, that the members of a public will not possess an insider's knowledge of events or share his point of view. They cannot, therefore, construe intent, or appraise the exact circumstances, enter intimately into the minds of the actors or into the details of the argument. They can watch only for coarse signs indicating where their sympathies ought to turn.

We must assume that the members of a public will not anticipate a problem much before its crisis has become obvious, nor stay with the problem long after its crisis is past. They will not know the antecedent events, will not have seen the issue as it developed, will not have thought out or willed a program, and will not be able to predict the consequences of acting on that program. We must assume as a theoretically fixed premise of popular government that normally men as members of a public will not be well informed, continuously interested, nonpartisan, creative or executive. We must assume that a public is inexpert in its curiosity, intermittent, that it discerns only gross distinctions, is slow to be aroused and quickly diverted; that, since it acts by aligning itself, it personalizes whatever it considers, and is interested only when events have been melodramatized as a conflict.

·The public will arrive in the middle of the third act and will leave before the last curtain, having stayed just long enough perhaps to decide who is the hero and who the villain of the piece. Yet usually that judgment will necessarily be made apart from the intrinsic merits, on the basis of a sample of behavior, an aspect of a situation, by very rough external evidence.

We cannot, then, think of public opinion as a conserving or creating force directing society to clearly conceived ends, making deliberately toward socialism or away from it, toward nationalism, an empire, a league of nations or any other doctrinal goal. For men do not agree as to their aims, and it is precisely the lack of agreement which creates the problems that excite public attention. It is idle, then, to argue that though men evidently have conflicting purposes, mankind has some all-embracing purpose of which you or I happen to be the authorized spokesman. We merely should have moved in a circle were we to conclude that the public is in some deep way a messianic force.

2

The work of the world goes on continually without conscious direction from public opinion. At certain junctures problems arise. It is only with the crises of some of these problems that public opinion is concerned. And its object in dealing with a crisis is to help allay that crisis.

I think this conclusion is unescapable. For though we may prefer to believe that the aim of popular action should be to do justice or promote the true, the beautiful and the good, the belief will not maintain itself in the face of plain experience. The public does not know in most crises what specifically is the truth or the justice of the case, and men are not agreed on what is beautiful and good. Nor does the public rouse itself normally at the existence of evil. It is aroused at evil made manifest by the interruption of a habitual process of life. And finally, a problem ceases to occupy attention not when justice, as we happen to define it, has been done but when a workable adjustment that overcomes the crisis has been made. If all this were not the necessary manner of public opinion, if it had seriously to crusade for justice in every issue it touches, the public would have to be dealing with all situations all the time. That is impossible. It is also undesirable. For did justice, truth, goodness and beauty depend on the spasmodic and crude interventions of public opinion there would be little hope for them in this world.

Thus we strip public opinion of any implied duty to deal with the substance of a problem, to make technical decisions, to attempt justice or impose a moral precept. And instead we say that the ideal of public opinion is to align men during the crisis of a problem in such a way as to favor the action of those individuals who may be able to compose the crisis. The power to discern those individuals is the end of the effort to educate public opinion. The aim of research designed to facilitate public action is the discovery of clear signs by which these individuals may be discerned.

The signs are relevant when they reveal by coarse, simple and objective tests which side in a controversy upholds a workable social rule, or which is attacking an unworkable rule, or which proposes a promising new rule. By following such signs the public might know where to align itself. In such an alignment it does not, let us remember, pass judgment on the intrinsic merits. It merely places its force at the disposal of the side which, according to objective signs, seems to be standing for human adjustments according to a clear rule of behavior and against the side which appears to stand for settlement in accordance with its own unaccountable will.

Public opinion, in this theory, is a reserve of force brought into action during a crisis in public affairs. Though it is itself an irrational force, under favorable institutions, sound leadership and decent training the power of public opinion might be placed at the disposal of those who stood for workable law as against brute assertion. In this theory, public opinion does not make the law. But by canceling lawless power it may establish the condition under which law can be made. It does not reason, investigate, invent, persuade, bargain or settle. But, by holding the aggressive party in check, it may liberate intelligence. Public opinion in its highest ideal will defend those who are prepared to act on their reason against the interrupting force of those who merely assert their will.

The action of public opinion at its best would not, let it be noted, be a continual crusade on behalf of reason. When power, however absolute and unaccountable, reigns without provoking a crisis, public opinion does not challenge it. Somebody must challenge arbitrary power first. The public can only come to his assistance.

3

That, I think, is the utmost that public opinion can effectively do. With the substance of the problem it can do nothing usually but meddle ignorantly or tyrannically. It has no need to meddle with it. Men in their active relation to affairs have to deal with the substance, but in that indirect relationship when they can act only through uttering praise or blame, making black crosses on white paper, they have done enough, they have done all they can do if they help to make it possible for the reason of other men to assert itself.

For when public opinion attempts to govern directly it is either a failure or a tyranny. It is not able to master the problem intellectually, nor to deal with it except by wholesale impact. The theory of democracy has not recognized this truth because it has identified the functioning of government with the will of the people. This is a fiction. The intricate business of framing laws and of administering them through several hundred thousand public officials is in no sense the act of the voters nor a translation of their will.

But although the acts of government are not a translation of public opinion, the principal function of government is to do specifically, in greater detail, and more continually what public opinion does crudely, by wholesale, and spasmodically. It enforces some of the working rules of society. It interprets them. It detects and punishes certain kinds of aggression. It presides over the framing of new rules. It has organized force which is used to counteract irregular force.

It is also subject to the same corruption as public opinion. For when government attempts to impose the will of its officials, instead of intervening so as to steady adjustments by consent among the parties directly interested, it becomes heavy-handed, stupid, imperious, even predatory. For the public official, though he is better placed to understand the problem than a reader of newspapers, and though he is much better able to act, is still fundamentally external to the real problems in which he intervenes. Being external, his point of view is indirect, and so his action is most appropriate when it is confined to rendering indirect assistance to those who are directly responsible.

Therefore, instead of describing government as an expression of the people's will, it would seem better to say that government consists of a body of officials, some elected, some appointed, who handle professionally, and in the first instance, problems which come to public opinion spasmodically and on appeal. Where the parties directly responsible do not work out an adjustment, public officials intervene. When the officials fail, public opinion is brought to bear on the issue.

4

This, then, is the ideal of public action which our inquiry suggests. Those who happen in any question to constitute the public should attempt only to create an equilibrium in which settlements can be reached directly and by consent. The burden of carrying on the work of the world, of inventing, creating, executing, of attempting justice, formulating laws and moral codes, of dealing with the technic and the substance, lies not upon public opinion and not upon government but on those who are responsibly concerned as agents in the affair. Where problems arise, the ideal is a settlement by the particular interests involved. They alone know what the trouble really is. No decision by public officials or by commuters reading headlines in the train can usually and in the long run be so good as settlement by consent among the parties at interest. No moral code, no political theory can usually and in the long run be imposed from the heights of public opinion, which will fit a case so well as direct agreement reached where arbitrary power has been disarmed.

It is the function of public opinion to check the use of force in a crisis, so that men, driven to make terms, may live and let live.

PART II

Chapter VI

The Question Aristotle Asked

THESE conclusions are sharply at variance with the accepted theory of popular government. That theory rests upon the belief that there is a public which directs the course of events. I hold that this public is a mere phantom. It is an abstraction. The public in respect to a railroad strike may be the farmers whom the railroad serves; the public in respect to an agricultural tariff may include the very railroad men who were on strike. The public is not, as I see it, a fixed body of individuals. It is merely those persons who are interested in an affair and can affect it only by supporting or opposing the actors.

Since these random publics cannot be expected to deal with the merits of a controversy, they can give their support with reasonable assurance that it will do good only if there are easily recognizable and yet pertinent signs which they can follow. Are there such signs? Can they be discovered? Can they be formulated so they might be learned and used? The chapters of this second part are an attempt to answer these questions.

The signs must be of such a character that they can be recognized without any substantial insight into the substance of a problem. Yet they must be relevant to the solution of the problem. They must be signs which will tell the members of a public where they can best align themselves so as to promote the solution. In short, they must be guides to reasonable action for the use of uninformed people.

The environment is complex. Man's political capacity is simple. Can a bridge be built between them? The question has haunted political science ever since Aristotle first formulated it in the great seventh book of his *Politics*. He answered it by saying that the community must be kept simple and small enough to suit the faculties of its citizens. We who live in the Great Society are unable to follow his advice. The orthodox democrats answered Aristotle's question by assuming that a limitless political capacity resides in public opinion. A century of experience compels us to deny this assumption. For us, then, the old question is unanswered; we can neither reject the Great Society as Aristotle did, nor exaggerate the political capacity of the citizen as the democrats did. We are forced to ask whether it is possible for men to find a way of acting effectively upon highly complex affairs by very simple means.

I venture to think that this problem may be soluble, that principles can be elucidated which might effect a successful junction between the intricacies of the environment and the simplicities of human faculty. It goes without saying that what I shall present here is no final statement of these principles. At most and at best it may be a clue, with some illustrations, that can be developed by research. But even that much assurance seems to me rash in the light of the difficulties which the problem has always presented, and so, following Descartes, I add that "after all, it is possible I may be mistaken; and it is but a little copper and glass I take for gold and diamonds."[1]

Chapter VII
The Nature of a Problem

1

SOMEWHAT in the spirit of Descartes, let us begin by supposing that your whole experience were confined to one glimpse of the world. There would be, I think, no better or worse in your sight, neither good men nor bad, patriots nor profiteers, conservatives nor radicals. You would be a perfect neutral. From such an impression of things, it would never occur to you that the crest of a mountain endured longer than the crest of a wave, that people moved about and that trees did not, or that the roar of an orator would pass sooner than the roar of Niagara.

Lengthen your experience, and you would begin to notice differences in the constancy of things. You would know day and night, perhaps, but not winter and summer, movement in space, but little of age in time. And if you then formulated your social philosophy, would you not almost certainly conclude that the things you saw people doing then it was ordained they should do always, and that their characters as you had seen them that day would be thus and so forever? And would not the resulting treatise pass almost unnoticed in any collection of contemporary disquisitions on the nations, the races, the classes or the sexes?

But the more you lengthened the span of your impression, the more variability you would note, until at last you would say with Heraclitus that all things flow. For when the very stars and the rocks were seen to have a history, men and their institutions and customs, habits and ideals, theories and policies could seem only relatively permanent. And you would have to conclude that what at first glance you had called a constant turns out after you had watched it longer merely to be changing a little more slowly than something else.

With sufficiently long experience you would indeed be bound to conclude that while the diverse elements that bear upon the life of men, including the characters of men themselves, were changing, yet they were not changing at the same pace. Things multiply, they grow, they learn, they age, they wear out and they die at different rates. An individual, his companions, his implements, his institutions, his creeds, his needs, his means of satisfaction, evolve unevenly, and endure unevenly. Events do not concur harmoniously in time. Some hurry, some straggle, some push and some drag. The ranks have always to be reformed.

The Walter Lippmann Reader

Instead of that one grand system of evolution and progress, which the nineteenth century found so reassuring, there would appear to be innumerable systems of evolution, variously affecting each other, some linked, some in collision, but each in some fundamental aspect moving at its own pace and on its own terms.

The disharmonies of this uneven evolution are the problems of mankind.

2

Suppose a man who knew nothing of the history of the nineteenth century were shown the tables compiled in the *Statistical Abstract of the United States* for the period from 1800 to 1918. He would note that the population of the world had multiplied two and a half times; its total commerce 42 times; its shipping tonnage more than 7 times; its railways 3664 times; its telegraphs 317 times; its cotton production 17 times; its coal 113 times; its pig iron 77 times. Could he doubt that in a century of such uneven changes men had faced revolutionary social problems?

Could he not infer from these figures alone that there had been great movements of population, vast changes in men's occupation, in the character of their labor, their wants, their standards of living, their ambitions? Would he not fairly infer that the political system which had existed in 1800 must have altered vastly with these new relationships, that customs, manners and morals appropriate to the settled, small and more or less self-contained communities of 1800 had been subjected to new strains and had probably been thoroughly revised? As he imagined the realities behind the tables, would he not infer that as men lived through the changes which these cold figures summarize they had been in conflict with their old habits and ideals, that the process of making new habits and adjustments must have gone on subject to trial and error with hopefulness over material progress and yet much disorder and confusion of soul?

3

For a more specific illustration of the nature of a problem we may examine the problem of population in its simplest form. When Malthus first stated it he assumed, for the purposes of argument, two elements evolving at different rates. Population, he said, doubled every twenty-five years; the produce of land could be increased in the same time by an amount "equal to what it at present produces."[1] He was writing about the year 1800. The population of England he estimated at seven millions, and the food supply as adequate to that number. There was then, in 1800, no problem. By 1825 the population, according to his estimate of its rate of increase, would have doubled, but the food supply would also have doubled. There would be no problem of population. But by 1850 the population would stand at twenty-eight millions; the food supply would have increased only by an amount to support an additional seven millions. The problem of excess population, or, if you like, of food scarcity, would have appeared. For while in 1800 and in 1825 the food available for each person would be the same, in 1850, owing to the uneven rate of growth, there would be only a three-quarter ration for each person. And this altered relationship Malthus rightly called a problem.

Suppose, now, we complicate Malthus's argument a bit by assuming that in 1850 people had learned to eat less and felt more fit on the three-quarter ration. There would then be no problem in 1850, for the adjustment of the two variables-food and people would be satisfactory. Or, on the contrary, suppose that soon after 1800 people had demanded a higher standard of living and expected more food, though the necessary additional food was not produced. These new demands would create a problem. Or suppose, as was actually the case,[2] the food supply increased faster than Malthus had assumed it could, though population did not. The problem of population would not arise at the date he predicted. Or suppose the increase of population was reduced by birth control. The problem, as Malthus first stated it, would not arise.[3] Or suppose the food supply increased faster than the population could consume it. There would then be a problem not of population but of agricultural surplus.

In an absolutely static society there would be no problems. A problem is the result of change. But not of the change in any self contained element. Change would be unnoticeable unless we could measure it against some other element which did not change at the same pace. If everything in the universe expanded at a mile a minute, or shrank at the same rate, we should never know it. For all we can tell we may be the size of a mosquito one moment in the sight of God, and of an elephant the next; we cannot tell if mosquitoes and elephants and chairs and planets change in proportion. Change is significant only in relation to something else.

The Walter Lippmann Reader

The change which constitutes a problem is an altered relationship between two dependent variables.[4] Thus the automobile is a problem in the city not because there are so many automobiles but because there are too many for the width of the streets, too many for the number of competent drivers, because the too narrow streets are filled with too many cars driven too recklessly for the present ability of the police to control them. Because the automobile is manufactured faster than old city streets can be widened, because some persons acquire cars faster than they acquire prudence and good manners, because automobiles collect in cities faster than policemen can be recruited, trained or paid for by slow yielding taxpayers, there is an automobile problem made evident by crowding, obnoxious fumes and collisions.

But though these evils seem to arise from the automobile, the fault lies not in the automobile but in the relation between the automobile and the city. This may sound like splitting hairs, but unless we insist upon it we never define a problem accurately nor lay it open successfully to solution.

The problem of national defense, for example, can never be stated by a general staff which draws upon its inner consciousness for an estimate of the necessary force. The necessary force can be estimated only in relation to the probable enemy, and the military problem whether of peace or of war lies always in the ratio of forces. Military force is a purely relative conception. The British Navy is helpless as a child against the unarmed mountaineers of Tibet. The French Army has no force as against fishing smacks in the Pacific Ocean. Force has to be measured against its objective: the tiger and the shark are incomparable one with the other.

Now a settled and accepted ratio of forces that might collide is a state of military peace. A competitive and, therefore, constantly unbalanced ratio is a prelude to war. The Canadian border presents no military problem, not because Canada's forces and our own are equal but because, happily, we do not compare them. They are independent variables, having no relation one with the other, and a change in the one does not affect the other. In capital ships we are confronted now with no naval problem in the Atlantic or in the Pacific, because with Britain and Japan, the only two comparable powers, we are agreed on a ratio by treaty.[5] But for all types of ships not subject to the ratio there is a naval problem in both oceans, and if the Washington Treaty should lapse the problem which it settled would recur. It would recur because the synchronized progress of the three navies would be replaced by a relatively uneven progress of each as compared with the others.

4

The field of economic activity is the source of many problems. For, as Cassel says,[6] we include within the meaning of the word economic those means of satisfying human wants which are "usually available only in a limited quantity." Since "the wants of civilized human beings as a whole are, " for all practical purposes, "unlimited," there is in all economic life the constant necessity of reaching "an adjustment between the wants and the means of supplying the wants." This disharmony of supply and demand is the source of an unending series of problems.

We may note at once that the economist does not claim as his province the whole range of adjustments between human wants and the means of satisfying them. He usually omits, for example, the human need to breathe air. For since the air is unlimited in quantity the human need of it is not frustrated, and the surplus air not required by men in no way impinges upon their lives. Yet there may be a scarcity of air, as, for example, in a congested tenement district. Then an economic problem is engendered which has to be met, let us say, by building laws requiring a certain number of cubic feet of air a person. The economist, in other words, takes as his field of interest the maladjustment between human wants and those means of satisfying them which are available, but only in limited quantities. In a world where every want was satisfied there would be no problems for him; nor any in a world where men had no wants; nor any in a world where the only wants men had could be supplied by a change on their part of their own states of consciousness. To create a problem there must be at least two dependent but separated variables: wants and the means of satisfaction; and these two variables must have a disposition to alter so that an antecedent equilibrium is disturbed.

In the measure, says Cassel, in which the economic system succeeds in securing an adjustment between the wants and the means of supplying the wants we speak of it as a sound economy. "This task may be accomplished in three different ways: first, by eliminating the less important wants and so restricting the total wants; secondly, by making the best possible use of the means available for the purposes in question; and, thirdly, by increased personal exertions."[7]

480

The Walter Lippmann Reader

Since the problem arises out of the disharmony of supply and demand, its solution is to be found by increasing the supply or restricting the demand. The choice of method depends first of all on which it is possible in specific cases to follow, and, second, granting the possibility, on which is the easier or the preferred. Either method will give what we acknowledge as a solution. For when two variables are in an adjustment which does not frustrate the expectations of either there is no problem, and none will be felt to exist.

Chapter VIII
Social Contracts

1

IT IS impossible to imagine in the universe a harmony of all things, each with all the others. The only harmonies we know or can conceive, outside of what Mr. Santayana calls the realm of essences, are partial adjustments which sacrifice to some one end all purposes which conflict with it. That the tree may bear fruit for us, we readily kill the insects that eat the fruit. So the fruit will ripen for us, we take no account of the disharmony we create for innumerable flies.

In the light of eternity it may be wholly unimportant whether the harmonies on this earth are suited to men or to insects. For in the light of eternity and from the point of view of the universe as a whole nothing can be what we call good or bad, better or worse. All ideas of value are measurements of some part of this universe with some other part, and it is no more possible to value the universe as a whole than it is to weigh it as a whole. For all scales of value and of weight are contained within it. To judge the whole universe you must, like a god, be outside of it, a point of view no mortal mind can adopt.

Unfortunately for the fly, therefore, we are bound to judge him by human values. In so far as we have power over him, he must submit to the harmonies we seek to establish. We may as a sporting matter admit his theoretical right to establish his own harmonies against us if he can, and to call them better if he likes, but for us that only is good which is good for man. Our universe consists of all that it contains, not as such, not as the fly knows it, but in its relation to us. From any other point of view but man's, his conception of the universe is askew. It has an emphasis and a perspective, it is shaped to a design which is altogether human. The very forms, colors, odors and sound of things are dependent for their quality upon our sense organs. Their relations are seen and understood against the background of our necessities.

In the realm of man's interests and purposes and desires, the perspectives are even narrower. There is no human point of view here, but only the points of view of men. None is valid for all human beings, none for all of human history, none for all corners of the globe. An opinion of the right and the wrong, the good and the bad, the pleasant and the unpleasant, is dated, is localized, is relative. It applies only to some men at some time in some place under some circumstances.

2

Against this deep pluralism thinkers have argued in vain. They have invented social organisms and national souls, and oversouls, and collective souls; they have gone for hopeful analogies to the beehive and the anthill, to the solar system, to the human body; they have gone to Hegel for higher unities and to Rousseau for a general will in an effort to find some basis of union. For though men do not think alike, nor want the same things, though their private interests are so distinct that they do not merge easily in any common interest, yet men cannot live by themselves, nor realize even their private purposes without taking into account the behavior of other people. We, however, no longer expect to find a unity which absorbs diversity. For us the conflicts and differences are so real that we cannot deny them and instead of looking for identity of purpose we look simply for an accommodation of purposes.

When we speak, then, about the solution of a problem in the Great Society, we may mean little more than that two conflicting interests have found a *modus vivendi*. It may be, of course, that they have really removed all their differences, that one interest has yielded to the other, or both to a third. But the solutions of most social problems are not so neat as this; everything does not fit perfectly as in the solution of a puzzle. The conflicting interests merely find a way of giving a little and taking a little, and of existing together without too much bad blood.

They still remain separate interests. The men involved still think differently. They have no union of mind or purpose. But they travel their own ways without collision, and even with some reliance at times upon the others' help. They know their rights and their duties, what to expect and what will be expected. Their rights are usually less than they claim, and their duties heavier than they like, yet, because they are in some degree enforced, conduct is rendered intelligible and predictable, and corporation exists in spite of the conflicting interests of men.

The *modus vivendi* of any particular historical period, the system of rights and duties, has generally acquired some high religious or ideal sanction. The thinkers laureate of the age will generally manage to show that the institutions, the laws, the morality and the custom of that age are divinely inspired. These are tiresome illusions which have been exploded a thousand times. The prevailing system of rights and duties at any time is at bottom a slightly antiquated formulation of the balance of power among the active interests in the community. There is always a certain lag, as Mr. Ogburn calls it, so that the system of rights and duties men are taught is generally a little less contemporary than the system they would find most convenient. But, whether the system is obsolete or not, in its naked origin, a right is a claim somebody was able to assert, and a duty is an obligation somebody was able to impose.

3

The prevailing system of rights and duties is designed to regulate the conflicting purposes of men. An established right is a promise that a certain kind of behavior will be backed by the organized force of the state or at least by the sentiment of the community; a duty is a promise that failure to respect the rights of others in a certain way will be punished. The punishment may be death, imprisonment, loss of property, the nullification of a right, the expression of disapproval. In short, the system of rights and duties is the whole system of promises which the courts and public sentiment will support. It is not a fixed system. It varies from place to place, and from time to time, and with the character of the tribunals and the community. But none the less it makes the conduct of men somewhat rational, and establishes a kind of union in diversity by limiting and defining the freedom with which conflicting purposes can be pursued.

Sometimes the promises are embodied in coercive law: Thou shalt, on penalty of this, do that; thou shalt not do so and so. Sometimes the promise is based on a contract between two parties: there is no obligation to make the contract, but, once made, it must be executed or a certain penalty paid. Sometimes the promise is based on an ecclesiastical code: it must be followed or the wages of sin will be visited either in fact or in anticipation upon the sinner. Sometimes the promise is based on custom: it must be respected or the price of nonconformity, whatever it may happen to be, must be paid. Sometimes the promise is based on habit: it must be executed or the disturbance faced which men feel when they break with their habits.

The question of whether any particular right or duty shall be enforced, the question of how it shall be enforced, whether by the police, by public criticism or private conscience, will not be answered by reasoning *a priori*. It will be answered by the dominant interests in society, each imposing to the limit of its powers the system of rights and duties which most nearly approximates the kind of social harmony it finds convenient and desirable. The system will be a reflection of the power that each interest is able to exert. The interests which find the rule good will defend it; the interests which find it bad will attack it. Their arguments will be weapons of defense and offense; even the most objective appeal to reason will turn out to be an appeal to desert one cause and enlist in another.

4

In the controversies between interests the question will be raised as to the merits of a particular rule; the argument will turn on whether the rule is good, on whether it should be enforced with this penalty or that. And out of those arguments, by persuasion or coercion, the specific rules of society are made, enforced and revised.

It is the thesis of this book that the members of the public, who are the spectators of action, cannot successfully intervene in a controversy on the merits of the case. They must judge eternally, and they can act only by supporting one of the interests directly involved. It follows that the public interest in a controversy cannot turn upon the specific issue. On what, then, does it turn? In what phase of the controversy can the public successfully interest itself?

Only when somebody objects does the public know there is a problem; when nobody any longer objects there is a solution. For the public, then, any rule is right which is agreeable to all concerned. It follows that the public interest in a problem is limited to this: that there shall be rules, which means that the rules which prevail shall be enforced, and that the unenforceable rules shall be changed according to a settled rule. The public's opinion that John Smith should or should not do this or that is immaterial; the public does not know John Smith's motives and needs, and is not concerned with them. But that John Smith shall do what he has promised to do is a matter of public concern, for unless the social contracts of men are made, enforced and revised according to a settled rule, social organization is impossible. Their conflicting purposes will engender unending problems unless they are regulated by some system of rights and duties.

The Walter Lippmann Reader

The interest of the public is not in the rules and contracts and customs themselves but in the maintenance of a regime of rule, contract and custom. The public is interested in law, not in the laws; in the method of law, not in the substance; in the sanctity of contract, not in a particular contract; in understanding based on custom, not in this custom or that. It is concerned in these things to the end that men in their active affairs shall find a *modus vivendi*; its interest is in the workable rule which will define and predict the behavior of men so that they can make their adjustments. The pressure which the public is able to apply through praise and blame, through votes, strikes, boycotts or support can yield results only if it reinforces the men who enforce an old rule or sponsor a new one that is needed.

The public in this theory is not the dispenser of law or morals, but, at best, a reserve force that may be mobilized on behalf of the method and spirit of law and morals. In denying that the public can lay down the rules I have not said that it should abandon any function which the public now exercises. I have merely said that it should abandon a pretense. When the public attempts to deal with the substance it merely becomes the dupe or unconscious ally of a special interest. For there is only one common interest: that all special interests shall act according to settled rule. The moment you ask what rule you invade the realm of competing interests of special points of view, of personal, and class, and sectional, and national bias. The public should not ask what rule because it cannot answer the question. It will contribute its part to the solution of social problems if it recognizes that some system of rights and duties is necessary, but that no particular system is peculiarly sacred.

Chapter IX

The Two Questions Before the Public

THE multitude of untroubled rules that men live by are of no concern to the public. It has to deal only with the failures. Customs that are accepted by all who are expected to follow them, contracts that are carried out peaceably, promises that are kept, expectations fulfilled, raise no issue. Even when there has been a breach of the rule, there is no public question if the breach is clearly established, the aggression clearly identified, the penalty determined and imposed. The aggressor may be identified because he pleads guilty. He may be identified by some due process though he denies his guilt. The rule, a term under which I mean to include the method of detection, interpretation and enforcement, as well as the precept, is in either case intact. The force of the public can be aligned without hesitation on behalf of the authorities who administer the rule.

There is no question for the public unless there is doubt as to the validity of the rule, doubt, that is to say, about its meaning, its soundness or the method of its application. When there is doubt the public requires simple, objective tests to help it decide where it will enlist. These tests must, therefore, answer two questions:

First, Is the rule defective?

Second, How shall the agency be recognized which is most likely to mend it?

These are, I should maintain, the only two questions which the public needs to answer in order to exert the greatest influence it is capable of exerting toward the solution of public problems. They are not, please note, the only questions which anybody has to answer to solve a problem. They are the only questions which a member of the public can usefully concern himself with if he wishes to avoid ignorant meddling.

How then shall he know the rule is defective? How shall he recognize the reformer? If he is to answer those questions at all, he must be able to answer them quickly and without real understanding of the problem. Is it possible for him to do that? Can he act intelligently but in ignorance?

I think this apparently paradoxical thing can be done in some such way as the next four chapters describe.

Chapter X
The Main Value of Public Debate

THE individual whose action is governed by a rule is interested in its substance. But in those rules which do not control his own action his chief interest is that there should be workable rules.

It follows that the membership of the public is not fixed. It changes with the issue: the actors in one affair are the spectators of another, and men are continually passing back and forth between the field where they are executives and the field where they are members of a public. The distinction between the two is not, as I said in Chapter III, an absolute one: there is a twilight zone where it is hard to say whether a man is acting executively on his opinions or merely acting to influence the opinion of some one else who is acting executively. There is often a mixture of the two types of behavior. And it is this mixture, as well as the lack of a clear line of distinction in all cases, which permits a very large confusion in affairs between a public and a private attitude toward them. The public point of view on a question is muddied by the presence in the public of spurious members, persons who are really acting to bend the rule in their favor while pretending or imagining that they are moved only by the common public need that there shall be an acceptable rule.

At the outset it is important, therefore, to detect and to discount the self-interested group. In saying this I do not mean to cast even the slightest reflection on a union of men to promote their self-interest. It would be futile to do so, because we may take it as certain that men will act to benefit themselves whenever they think they conveniently can. A political theory based on the expectation of self-denial and sacrifice by the run of men in any community would not be worth considering. Nor is it at all evident that the work of the world could be done unless men followed their private interest and contributed to affairs that direct inner knowledge which they thus obtain. Moreover, the adjustments are likely to be much more real if they are made from fully conscious and thoroughly explored special points of view.

Thus the genius of any illuminating public discussion is not to obscure and censor private interest but to help it to sail and to make it sail under its own colors. The true public, in my definition of that term, has to purge itself of the self-interested groups who become confused with it. It must purge itself not because private interests are bad but because private interests cannot successfully be adjusted to each other if any one of them acquires a counterfeit strength. If the true public, concerned only in the fact of adjustment, becomes mobilized behind a private interest seeking to prevail, the adjustment is false; it does not represent the real balance of forces in the affair and the solution will break down. It will break down because the true public will not stay mobilized very long for anything, and when it demobilizes the private interest which was falsely exalted will find its privileges unmanageable. It will be like a man placed on Jack Dempsey's chest by six policemen, and then left there after the policemen have gone home to dinner. It will be like France placed by the Allies upon a prostrate Germany and then left there after the Allies have departed from Europe.

The separation of the public from the self-interested group will not be assisted by the self-interested group. We may be sure that any body of farmers, business men, trade unionists will always call themselves the public if they can. How then is their self-interest to be detected? No ordinary bystander is equipped to analyze the propaganda by which a private interest seeks to associate itself with the disinterested public. It is a perplexing matter, perhaps the most perplexing in popular government, and the bystander's only recourse is to insist upon debate. He will not be able, we may assume, to judge the merits of the arguments. But if he does insist upon full freedom of discussion, the advocates are very likely to expose one another. Open debate may lead to no conclusion and throw no light whatever on the problem or its answer, but it will tend to betray the partisan and the advocate. And if it has identified them for the true public, debate will have served its main purpose.

The individual not directly concerned may still choose to join the self-interested group and support its cause. But at least he will know that he has made himself a partisan, and thus perhaps he may be somewhat less likely to mistake a party's purpose for the aim of mankind.

Chapter XI
The Defective Rule

1

A MAN violates a rule and then publicly justifies his action. Here in the simplest form is an attack upon the validity of the rule. It is an appeal for a public judgment.

For he claims to have acted under a new rule which is better than the old one. How shall the public decide as between the two? It cannot, we are assuming, enter into the intrinsic merits of the question. It follows that the public must ask the aggressor why he did not first seek the assent of those concerned before he violated the rule. He may say that he did not have time, that he acted in a crisis. In that event, there is no serious question! for the public, and his associates will either thank him or call him a fool. But since the circumstances were admittedly exceptional they do not really establish a new rule, and the public may be satisfied if the parties at interest peaceably make the best of the result. But suppose there was no emergency. Suppose the innovator had time to seek assent, but did not on the ground that he knew what was best. He may be fairly condemned; the objections of the other parties may be fairly sustained.

For the right of innovation by fiat cannot be defended as a working principle; a new rule, however excellent in intention, cannot be expected to work unless in some degree it has been first understood and approved by all who must live according to it. The innovator may reply, of course, that he is being condemned by a dogma which is not wholly proved. That may be admitted. Against the principle that a new rule requires assent historic experience can be cited. There have been many instances where a regime has been imposed on an unwilling people and admired later by them for its results. The dogma that assent is necessary is imperfect, as are most principles. But, nevertheless, it is a necessary assumption in society. For if no new rule required assent every one could make his own rule, and there would be no rules. The dogma therefore must be maintained, softened by the knowledge that exceptional times and exceptional men of their own force will make way with any dogma. Since the rules of society cannot be based on exceptions the exceptions must justify themselves.

The test, therefore, of whether a rule has been justifiably broken is the test of assent. The question, then, is how in applying the test of assent a member of the public is to determine whether sufficient assent has been given. How is he to know whether the regime has been imposed by arbitrary force or in substance agreed to?

2

We wish to know if assent is lacking. We know it is lacking because there is open protest. Or we know it because there is a widespread refusal to conform. A workable rule, which has assent, will not evoke protest or much disobedience. How shall we, as members of the public, measure the significance of the protest or the extent of the disobedience?

3

Where very few persons are directly involved in the controversy the public does best not to intervene at all. One party may protest, but unless he protests against the public tribunals set up to adjudicate such disputes, his protest may be ignored. The public cannot expect to take part in the minutiae of human adjustments however tragic or important they may be to the individuals concerned. The protest of one individual against another cannot be treated as a public matter. Only if the public tribunal is impugned does it become a public matter, and then only because the case may require investigation by some other tribunal. In such disputes the public must trust the agencies of adjustment acting as checks upon each other. When we remember that the public consist of busy men reading newspapers for half an hour or so a day, it is not heartless but merely prudent to deny that it can do detailed justice.

But where many persons are involved in the controversy there is necessarily a public matter. For when many persons are embroiled the effects not only are likely to be wide but there may be need of all the force the public can exert in order to compel a peaceable adjustment.

The public must take account of a protest voiced on behalf of a relatively large number of persons. But how shall the public know that such a protest has been made? It must look to see whether the spokesman is authorized. How shall it tell if he is authorized? How can it tell, that is to say, whether the representative is able to give assent by committing his constituency to a course of action? Whether the apparent leader is the real leader is a question which the members of a public cannot usually answer directly on the merits. Yet they must answer in some fashion and with some assurance by some rule of thumb.

The rule of thumb is to throw the burden of proof on those who deny that the apparent leader, vested with the external signs of office, is the real leader. As between one nation and another, no matter how obnoxious the other's government may be, if there is no open rebellion, public opinion cannot go behind the returns. For, unless a people is to engage in the hopeless task of playing politics inside another's frontiers, there is no course but to hold that a nation is committed by the officials it fails to discharge. If there is open rebellion, or that milder substitute, an impending election, it may be wise to postpone long term settlements until a firm government has been seated. But settlements, if they are made at all, must be made with the government in office at the other nation's capital.

The same theory holds, with modifications, for large bodies of men within a state. If the officials of the miners' union, for instance, take a position, it is perfectly idle for an employer to deny that they speak for the union miners. He should deny that they speak for the nonunion miners, but if the question at issue requires the assent of the union, then, unless the union itself impeaches the leaders, the public must accept them as authorized.

But suppose the leaders are challenged within the union. How shall the importance of the challenge be estimated by the public? Recall that the object is to find out not whether the objectors are right but simply whether the spokesmen can in fact commit their constituents. In weighing the challenge the public's concern is to know how far the opposition can by virtue of its numbers, or of its strategic importance, or its determination, impair the value of an assent. But if we expected the public to make judgments of this sort we should be asking too much of it. The importance of an opposition can be weighed, if at all, only by rough, external criteria. With an opposition that does not challenge the credentials of the spokesmen, which criticizes but is not in rebellion, the public has no concern. That is an internal affair. It is only an opposition which threatens not to conform that has to be considered.

In such a case, if the spokesmen are elected, they can be held competent to give a reliable assent only until a new election has been held. If the spokesmen are not elective, and a rebellious opposition is evident, their assent can only be taken as tentative. These criteria do not, to be sure, weigh the importance of an opposition, but, by limiting the kind of settlement which can reasonably be made in face of an opposition, they allow for its effect.

They introduce the necessary modification to make workable the general principle that the test of assent by large bodies of men is simply that their spokesmen have agreed.

4

The test of conformity is closely related to the test of assent. For it can be assumed that open criticism of a rule, a custom, a law, an institution, is already accompanied by or will soon be followed by evasion of that rule. It is a fairly safe hypothesis that the run of men wish to conform; that any body of men aroused to the point where they will pay the price of open heresy probably has an arguable case; more certainly that that body will include a considerable number who have passed over the line of criticism into the practice of nonconformity. Their argument may be wrong, the remedy may be foolish, but the fact that they openly criticize at some personal risk is a sign that the rule is not working well. Widespread criticism, therefore, has a significance beyond its intellectual value. It is almost always a symptom on the surface that the rule is unstable.

When a rule is broken not occasionally but very often the rule is defective. It simply does not define the conduct which normally may be expected of men who live under it. It may sound noble. But it does not work. It does not adjust relations. It does not actually organize society.

In what way the rule is defective the public cannot specifically determine. By the two tests I have suggested, of assent and of conformity, the public can determine the presence of a defect in the rule. But whether that defect is due to a false measure of the changing balance of forces involved, or to neglect of an important interest or some relevant circumstance, or to a bad technic of adjustment, or to contradictions in the rule, or to obscurity, or to lack of machinery for its interpretation or for the deduction of specific rules from general ones, the public cannot judge.

It will have gone, I believe, to the limits of its normal powers if it judges the rule to be defective, and turns then to identify the agency most likely to remedy it.

Chapter XII

The Criteria of Reform

1

THE random collections of bystanders who constitute a public could not, even if they had a mind to, intervene in all the problems of the day. They can and must play a part occasionally, I believe, but they cannot take an interest in, they cannot make even the coarsest judgments about, and they will not act even in the most grossly partisan way on; all the questions arising daily in a complex and changing society. Normally they leave their proxies to a kind of professional public consisting of more or less eminent persons. Most issues are never carried beyond this ruling group; the lay publics catch only echoes of the debate.

If, by the push and pull of interested parties and public personages, settlements are made more or less continually the party in power has the confidence of the country. In effect, the outsiders are arrayed behind the dominant insiders. But if the interested parties cannot be made to agree, if, as a result, there is disturbance and chronic crisis, then the opposition among the insiders may come to be considered the hope of the country, and be able to entice the bystanders to its side.

To support the Ins when things are going well; to support the Outs when they seem to be going badly, this, in spite of all that has been said about tweedledum and tweedledee, is the essence of popular government. Even the most intelligent large public of which we have any experience must determine finally who shall wield the organized power of the state, its army and its police, by a choice between the Ins and Outs. A community where there is no choice does not have popular government. It is subject to some form of dictatorship or it is ruled by the intrigues of the politicians in the lobbies.

Although it is the custom of partisans to speak as if there were radical differences between the Ins and the Outs, it could be demonstrated, I believe, that in stable and mature societies the differences are necessarily not profound. If they were profound, the defeated minority would be constantly on the verge of rebellion. An election would be catastrophic, whereas the assumption in every election is that the victors will do nothing to make life intolerable to the vanquished and that the vanquished will endure with good humor policies which they do not approve.

The Walter Lippmann Reader

In the United States, Great Britain, Canada, Australia and in certain of the Continental countries an election rarely means even a fraction of what the campaigners said it would mean. It means some new faces and perhaps a slightly different general tendency in the management of affairs. The Ins may have had a bias toward collectivism; the Outs will lean toward individualism. The Ins may have been suspicious and noncooperative in foreign affairs; the Outs will perhaps be more trusting or entertain another set of suspicions. The Ins may have favored certain manufacturing interests; the Outs may favor agricultural interests. But even these differing tendencies are very small as compared with the immense area of agreement, established habit and unavoidable necessity. In fact, one might say that a nation is politically stable when nothing of radical consequence is determined by its elections.

There is, therefore, a certain mock seriousness about the campaigning for votes in well-established communities. Much of the excitement is not about the fate of the nation but simply about the outcome of the game. Some of the excitement is sincere, like any fervor of intoxication. And much of it is deliberately stoked up by the expenditure of money to overcome the inertia of the mass of the voters. For the most part the real difference between the Ins and the Outs is no more than this: the Ins, after a term of power, become so committed to policies and so entangled with particular interests that they lose their neutral freedom of decision. They cannot then intervene to check the arbitrary movement of the interests with which they have become aligned. Then it is time for the Outs to take power and restore a balance. The virtue of the Outs in this transaction is that they are not committed to those particular policies and those particular interests which have become overweighted.

The test of whether the Ins are handling affairs effectively is the presence or absence of disturbing problems. The need of reform is recognizable, as I pointed out in the chapter before this one, by the test of assent and the test of conformity. But it is my opinion that for the most part the general public cannot back each reformer on each issue. It must choose between the Ins and Outs on the basis of a cumulative judgment as to whether problems are being solved or aggravated. The particular reformers must look for their support normally to the ruling insiders.

If, however, there is to be any refinement of public opinion it must come from the breaking up of these wholesale judgments into somewhat more retail judgments on the major spectacular issues of the day. Not all of the issues which interest the public are within the scope of politics and reachable through the party system. It seems worth while, therefore, to see whether any canons of judgment can be formulated which could guide the bystanders in particular controversies.

The problem is to locate by clear and coarse objective tests the actor in a controversy who is most worthy of public support.

2

When the rule is plain, its validity unchallenged, the breach clear and the aggressor plainly located, the question does not arise. The public supports the agents of the law, though when the law is working well the support of the public is like the gold reserve of a good bank: it is known to be there and need not be drawn upon. But in many fields of controversy the rule is not plain, or its validity is challenged; each party calls the other aggressor, each claims to be acting for the highest ideals of mankind. In disputes between nations, between sectional interests, between classes, between town and country, between churches, the rules of adjustment are lacking and the argument about them is lost in a fog of propaganda.

Yet it is controversies of this kind, the hardest controversies to disentangle, that the public is called in to judge. Where the facts are most obscure, where precedents are lacking, where novelty and confusion pervade everything, the public in all its unfitness is compelled to make its most important decisions. The hardest problems are those which institutions cannot handle. They are the public's problems.

The one test which the members of a public can apply in these circumstances is to note which party to the dispute is least willing to submit its whole claim to inquiry and to abide by the result. This does not mean that experts are always expert or impartial tribunals really impartial. It means simply that where the public is forced to intervene in a strange and complex affair, the test of public inquiry is the surest clue to the sincerity of the claimant, to his confidence in his ability to stand the ordeal of examination, to his willingness to accept risks for the sake of his faith in the possibility of rational human adjustments. He may impugn a particular tribunal. But he must at least propose another. The test is whether, in the absence of an established rule, he is willing to act according to the forms of law and by a process through which law may be made.

Of all the tests which public opinion can employ, the test of inquiry is the most generally useful. If the parties are willing to accept it, there is at once an atmosphere of reason. There is prospect of a settlement. Failing that there is at least a delay of summary action and an opportunity for the clarification of issues. And failing that there is a high probability that the most arbitrary of the disputants will be isolated and clearly identified. It is no wonder that this is the principle invoked for the so-called nonjusticiable questions in all the recent experiments under the covenant of the League of Nations[1] and the Protocol for the Pacific Settlement of International Disputes.[2] For in applying this test of inquiry, what we affirm is this: That there is a dispute. That the merits are not clear. That the policy which ought to be applied is not established. That, nevertheless, we of the public outside say that those who are quarreling must act as if there were law to cover the case. That, even if the material for a reasoned conclusion is lacking, we demand the method and spirit of reason. That we demand any sacrifice that may be necessary, the postponement of satisfaction of their just needs, the risk that one of them will be defeated and that an injustice will be done. These things we affirm because we are maintaining a society based" on the principle that all controversies are soluble by peaceable agreement.

They may not be. But on that dogma our society is founded. And that dogma we are compelled to defend. We can defend it, too, with a good enough conscience, however disconcerting some of its immediate consequences may be. For, by insisting in all disputes upon the spirit of reason, we shall tend in the long run to confirm the habit of reason. And where that habit prevails no point of view can seem absolute to him who holds it, and no problem between men so difficult that there is not at least a *modus vivendi.*

The test of inquiry is the master test by which the public can use its force to extend the frontiers of reason.

3

But while the test of inquiry may distinguish the party which is entitled to initial support, it is of value only where one party refuses inquiry. If all submit to inquiry, it reveals nothing. And in any event it reveals nothing about the prospects of the solution proposed. The party seeking publicity may have less to conceal, and may mean well, but sincerity unfortunately is no index of intelligence. By what criteria are the public then to judge the new rule which is proposed as a solution?

The public cannot tell whether the new rule will, in fact, work. It may assume, however, that in a changing world no rule will always work. A rule, therefore, should be organized so that experience will clearly reveal its defects. The rule should be so clear that a violation is apparent. But since no generality can cover all cases, this means simply that the rule must contain a settled procedure by which it can be interpreted. Thus a treaty which says that a certain territory shall be evacuated when certain conditions are fulfilled is quite defective, and should be condemned, if it does not provide a way of defining exactly what those conditions are and when they have been fulfilled. A rule, in other words, must include the means of its own clarification, so that a breach shall be undeniably overt. Then only does it take account of experience which no human intelligence can foresee.

It follows from this that a rule must be organized so that it can be amended without revolution. Revision must be possible by consent. But assent is not always given, even when the arguments in favor of a change are overwhelming. Men will stand on what they call their rights. Therefore, in order that deadlock should be dissoluble, a rule should provide that subject to a certain formal procedure the controversy over revision shall be public. This will often break up the obstruction. Where it does not, the community is pretty certain to become engaged on behalf of one of the partisans. This is likely to be inconvenient to all concerned, and the inconvenience due to meddling in the substance of a controversy by a crude, violent and badly aimed public opinion at least may teach those directly concerned not to invoke interference the next time.

But although amendment should be possible, it should not be continual or unforeseen. There should be time for habit and custom to form. The pot should not be made to boil all the time, or be stirred up for some comparatively insignificant reason, whenever an orator sees a chance to make himself important. Since the habits and expectations of many different persons are involved in an institution, some way must be found of giving it stability without freezing it in *statu quo*. This can be done by requiring that amendment shall be in order only after due notice.

The Walter Lippmann Reader

What due notice may be in each particular case, the public cannot say. Only the parties at interest are likely to know where the rhythm of their affairs can be interrupted most conveniently. Due notice will be one period of time for men operating on long commitments and another for men operating on short ones. But the public can watch to see whether the principle of due notice is embodied in the proposed settlement.

To judge a new rule, then, the tests proposed here are three: Does it provide for its own clarification? for its own amendment by consent? for due notice that amendment will be proposed? The tests are designed for use in judging the prospects of a settlement not by its substance but by its procedure. Are form which satisfies these tests is normally entitled to public support.

4

This is as far as I know how at present to work out an answer to the question which we inherit from Aristotle: can simple criteria be formulated which will show the bystander where to align himself in complex affairs?

I have suggested that the main value of debate is not that it reveals the truth about the controversy to the audience but that it may identify the partisans. I have suggested further that a problem exists where a rule of action is defective, and that its defectiveness can best be judged by the public through the test of assent and the test of conformity. For remedies I have assumed that normally the public must turn to the Outs as against the Ins, although these wholesale judgments may be refined by more analytical tests for specific issues. As samples of these more analytical tests I have suggested the test of inquiry for confused controversies, and for reforms the test of interpretation, of amendment and of due notice.

These criteria are neither exhaustive nor definitive. Yet, however much tests of this character are improved by practice and reflection, it seems to me there always must remain many public affairs to which they cannot be applied. I do not believe that the public can intervene successfully in all public questions. Many problems cannot be advanced by that obtuse partisanship which is fundamentally all that the public can bring to bear upon them. There is no reason to be surprised, therefore, if the tests I have outlined, or any others that are a vast improvement upon them, are not readily applicable to all questions that are raised in the discussions of the day.

The Walter Lippmann Reader

I should simply maintain that where the members of a public cannot use tests of this sort as a guide to action, the wisest course for them is not to act at all. They had better be neutral, if they can restrain themselves, than blindly partisan. For where events are so confused or so subtly balanced or so hard to understand that they do not yield to judgments of the kind I have been outlining here, the probabilities are very great that the public can produce only muddle if it meddles. For not all problems are soluble in the present state of human knowledge. Many which may be soluble are not soluble with any force the public can exert. Some time alone will cure, and some are the fate of man. It is not essential, therefore, always to do something.

It follows that the proper limits of intervention by the public in affairs are determined by its capacity to make judgments. These limits may be extended as new and better criteria are formulated, or as men become more expert through practice. But where there are no tests, where such tests as these cannot be used, where, in other words, only an opinion on the actual merits of the dispute itself would be of any use, any positive action the bystanders are likely to take is almost certain to be more of a nuisance than a benefit. Their duty is to keep an open mind and wait to see. The existence of a usable test is itself the test of whether the public ought to intervene.

Chapter XIII

The Principles of Public Opinion

1

THE tests outlined in the preceding chapters have certain common characteristics. They all select a few samples of behavior or a few aspects of a proposal. They measure these samples by rough but objective, by highly generalized but definite standards. And they yield a judgment which is to justify the public in aligning itself for or against certain actors in the matter at issue.

I do not, of course, set great store upon my formulation of these tests. That is wholly tentative, being put out merely as a basis of discussion and to demonstrate that the formulation of tests suited to the nature of public opinion is not impracticable. But I do attach great importance to the character of these tests.

The principles underlying them are these:

1. Executive action is not for the public. The public acts only by aligning itself as the partisan of some one in a position to act executively.

2. The intrinsic merits of a question are not for the public. The public intervenes from the outside upon the work of the insiders.

3. The anticipation, the analysis and the solution of a question are not for the public. The public's judgment rests on a small sample of the facts at issue.

4. The specific, technical, intimate criteria required in the handling of a question are not for the public. The public's criteria are generalized for many problems; they turn essentially on procedure and the overt, external forms of behavior.

5. What is left for the public is a judgment as to whether the actors in the controversy are following a settled rule of behavior or their own arbitrary desires. This judgment must be made by sampling an external aspect of the behavior of the insiders.

6. In order that this sampling shall be pertinent, it is necessary to discover criteria, suitable to the nature of public opinion, which can be relied upon to distinguish between reasonable and arbitrary behavior.

7. For the purposes of social action, reasonable behavior is conduct which follows a settled course whether in making a rule, in enforcing it or in amending it.

The Walter Lippmann Reader

*

It is the task of the political scientist to devise the methods of sampling and to define the criteria of judgment. It is the task of civic education in a democracy to train the public in the use of these methods. It is the task of those who build institutions to take them into account.

2

These principles differ radically from those on which democratic reformers have proceeded. At the root of the effort to educate a people for self-government there has, I believe, always been the assumption that the voter should aim to approximate as nearly as he can the knowledge and the point of view of the responsible man. He did not, of course, in the mass, ever approximate it very nearly. But he was supposed to. It was believed that if only he could be taught more facts, if only he would take more interest, if only he would read more and better newspapers, if only he would listen to more lectures and read more reports, he would gradually be trained to direct public affairs. The whole assumption is false. It rests upon a false conception of public opinion and a false conception of the way the public acts. No sound scheme of civic education can come of it. No progress can be made toward this unattainable ideal.

This democratic conception is false because it fails to note the radical difference between the experience of the insider and the outsider; it is fundamentally askew because it asks the outsider to deal as successfully with the substance of a question as the insider. He cannot do it. No scheme of education can equip him in advance for all the problems of mankind; no device of publicity, no machinery of enlightenment, can endow him during a crisis with the antecedent detailed and technical knowledge which is required for executive action.

The democratic ideal has never defined the function of the public. It has treated the public as an immature, shadowy executive of all things. The confusion is deep-seated in a mystical notion of society. "The people" were regarded as a person; their wills as a will; their ideas as a mind; their mass as an organism with an organic unity of which the individual was a cell. Thus the voter identified himself with the officials. He tried to think that their thoughts were his thoughts, that their deeds were his deeds, and even that in some mysterious way they were a part of him. All this confusion of identities led naturally to the theory that everybody was doing everything. I t prevented democracy from arriving at a clear idea of its own limits and attainable ends. It obscured for the purposes of government and social education the separation of function and the specialization in training which have gradually been established in most human activities.

Democracy, therefore, has never developed an education for the public. It has merely given it a smattering of the kind of knowledge which the responsible man requires. It has, in fact, aimed not at making good citizens but at making a mass of amateur executives. It has not taught the child how to act as a member of the public. It has merely given him a hasty, incomplete taste of what he might have to know if he meddled in everything. The result is a bewildered public and a mass of insufficiently trained officials. The responsible men have obtained their training not from the courses in "civics" but in the law schools and law offices and in business. The public at large, which includes everybody outside the field of his own responsible knowledge, has had no coherent political training of any kind. Our civic education does not even begin to tell the voter how he can reduce the maze of public affairs to some intelligible form.

Critics have not been lacking, of course, who pointed out what a hash democracy was making of its pretensions to government. These critics have seen that the important decisions were taken by individuals, and that public opinion was uninformed, irrelevant and meddlesome. They have usually concluded that there was a congenital difference between the masterful few and the ignorant many. They are the victims of a superficial analysis of the evils they see so clearly. The fundamental difference which matters is that between insiders and outsiders. Their relations to a problem are radically different. Only the insider can make decisions, not because he is inherently a better man but because he is so placed that he can understand and can act. The outsider is necessarily ignorant, usually irrelevant and often meddlesome, because he is trying to navigate the ship from dry land. That is why excellent automobile manufacturers, literary critics and scientists often talk such nonsense about politics. Their congenital excellence, if it exists, reveals itself only in their own activity. The aristocratic theorists work from the fallacy of supposing that a sufficiently excellent square peg will also fit a round hole. In short, like the democratic theorists, they miss the essence of the matter, which is, that competence exists only in relation to function; that men are not good, but good for something; that men cannot be educated, but only educated for something.

Education for citizenship, for membership in the public, ought, therefore, to be distinct from education for public office. Citizenship involves a radically different relation to affairs, requires different intellectual habits and different methods of action. The force of public opinion is partisan, spasmodic, simpleminded and external. It needs for its direction, as I have tried to show in these chapters, a new intellectual method which shall provide it with its own usable canons of judgment.

PART III

Chapter XIV
Society in its Place

1

A FALSE ideal of democracy can lead only to disillusionment and to meddlesome tyranny. If democracy cannot direct affairs, then a philosophy which expects it to direct them will encourage the people to attempt the impossible; they will fail, but that will interfere outrageously with the productive liberties of the individual. The public must be put in its place, so that it may exercise its own powers, but no less and perhaps even more, so that each of us may live free of the trampling and the roar of a bewildered herd.

2

The source of that bewilderment lies, I think, in the attempt to ascribe organic unity and purpose to society. We have been taught to think of society as a body, with a mind, a soul and a purpose, not as a collection of men, women and children whose minds, souls and purposes are variously related. Instead of being allowed to think realistically of a complex of social *relations*, we have had foisted upon us by various great propagative movements the notion of a mythical entity, called Society, the Nation, the Community.

In the course of the nineteenth century society was personified under the influence largely of the nationalist and the socialist movements. Each of these doctrinal influences in its own way insisted upon treating the public as the agent of an overmastering social purpose. In point of fact, the real agents were the nationalist leaders and their lieutenants, the social reformers and their lieutenants. But they moved behind a veil of imagery. And the public was habituated to think that any one conforming to the stereotype of nationalism or of social welfare was entitled to support. What the nationalist rulers thought and did was the nation's purpose, and the touchstone for all patriots; what the reformers proposed was the benevolent consciousness of the human race moving mysteriously but progressively toward perfection.

The deception was so generally practiced that it was often practiced sincerely. But to maintain the fiction that their purposes were the spirit of mankind, public men had to accustom themselves to telling the public only a part of what they told themselves. And, incidentally, they confessed to themselves only a part of the truth on which they were acting. Candor in public life became a question of policy and not a rule of life.

"He may judge rightly," Mr. Keynes once said of Mr. Lloyd George,[1] "that this is the best of which a democracy is capable, to be jockeyed, humbugged, cajoled along the right road. A prejudice for truth or for sincerity as a method may be a prejudice based on some aesthetic or personal standard inconsistent, in politics, with practical good. We cannot yet tell."

We do know, as a matter of experience, that all the cards are not laid face up upon the table. For however deep the personal prejudice of the statesman in favor of truth as a method, he is almost certainly forced to treat truth as an element of policy. The evidence on this point is overwhelming. No statesman risks the safety of an army out of sheer devotion to truth. He does not endanger a diplomatic negotiation in order to enlighten everybody. He does not usually forfeit his advantages in an election in order to speak plainly. He does not admit his own mistakes because confession is so good for the soul. In so far as he has power to control the publication of truth, he manipulates it to what he considers the necessities of action, of bargaining, morale and prestige. He may misjudge the necessities. He may exaggerate the goodness of his aims. But where there is a purpose in public affairs there are also apparent necessities which weigh in the balance against the indiscreet expression of belief. The public man does not and cannot act on the fiction that his mind is also the public mind.

You cannot account for this, as angry democrats have done by dismissing all public men as dishonest. It is not a question of personal morals. The business man, the trade-union leader, the college president, the minister of religion, the editor, the critic and the prophet, all feel as Jefferson did when he wrote that "although we often wished to go faster we slackened our pace that our less ardent colleagues might keep pace with us ... [and] by this harmony of the bold with the cautious, we advanced with our constituents in undivided mass."[2]

The necessity for an "undivided mass" makes men put truth in the second place. I do not wish to argue that the necessity is not often a real one. When a statesman tells me that it is not safe for him to disclose all the facts, I am content to trust him in this if I trust him at all. There is nothing misleading in a frank refusal to tell. The mischief comes in the pretense that all is being told, that the public is entirely in the confidence of the public man. And that mischief has its source in the sophistry that the public and all the individuals composing it are one mind, one soul, one purpose. It is seen to be an absurd sophistry, once we look it straight in the face. It is an unnecessary sophistry. For we do well enough with doctors, though we are ignorant of medicine, and with engine drivers, though we cannot drive a locomotive; why not, then, with a Senator, though we cannot pass an examination on the merits of an agricultural bill?

Yet we are so deeply indoctrinated with the notion of union based upon identity, that we are most reluctant to admit that there is room in the world for different and more or less separate purposes. The monistic theory has an air of great stability about it; we are afraid if we do not hang together we shall all hang separately. The pluralistic theory, as its leading advocate, Mr. Laski, has pointed out, seems to carry with it "a hint of anarchy."[3] Yet the suggestion is grossly exaggerated. There is least anarchy precisely in those areas of society where separate functions are most clearly defined and brought into orderly adjustment; there is most anarchy in those twilight zones between nations, between employers and employees, between sections and classes and races, where nothing is clearly defined, where separateness of purpose is covered up and confused, where false unities are worshiped, and each special interest is forever proclaiming itself the voice of the people and attempting to impose its purpose upon everybody as the purpose of all mankind.

3

To this confusion liberalism has with the kindest intentions contributed greatly. Its main insight was into the prejudices of the individual; the liberal discovered a method of proving that men are finite, that they cannot escape from the flesh. From the so called age of enlightenment down to our day the heavy guns of criticism have been used to make men realize that they submit, as Bacon said, the shadows of things to the desires of the mind. Once the resistance was broken by proof that man belonged to the natural world, his pretensions to absolute certainty were attacked from every quarter. He was shown the history of his ideas and of his customs, and he was driven to acknowledge that they were bounded by time and space and circumstance. He was shown that there is a bias in all opinion, even in opinion purged of desire, for the man who holds the opinion must stand at some point in space and time and can see not the whole world but only the world as seen from that point. So men learned that they saw a little through their own eyes, and much more through reports of what other men thought they had seen. They were made to understand that all human eyes have habits of vision, which are often stereotyped, which always throw facts into a perspective; and that the whole of experience is more sophisticated than the naive mind suspects. For its pictures of the world are drawn from things half heard and of things half seen; they deal with the shadows of things unsteadily, and submit unconsciously to the desires of the mind.

It was an amazing and unsettling revelation, and liberalism never quite knew what to do with it. In a theater in Moscow a certain M. Yevreynoff carried the revelation to one of its logical conclusions. He produced the monodrama.[4] This is a play in which the action, the setting and all the characters are seen by the audience through the eyes of one character only, as the hero sees them, and they take on the quality which his mind imagines they possess. Thus in the old theater, if the hero drank too much, he reeled in the midst of a sober environment. But in M. Yevreynoff's supremely liberal theater, if I understand Mr. Macgowan's account of it correctly, the drunkard will not reel about the lamppost; two lampposts will reel about him, and he will be dressed, because that is the way he feels, like Napoleon Bonaparte.

M. Yevreynoff has troubled me a good deal, for he seemed to have finished off the liberal with a fool's cap, and left him sitting in a world that does not exist, except as so many crazy mirrors reflecting his own follies one upon the other. But then I recalled that M. Yevreynoff's logic was defective and make believe. He had all the time stood soberly outside his own drunken hero, and so had his audience; the universe had not after all gone up in the smoke of one fantasy; the drunken hero had his point of view, but, after all, there were others, just as authentic, with which in the course of his career he might collide. There might be a policeman, for example, with fantasies to be sure, but his own, who would break in upon the monodrama and remind the hero, and us, that when we submit the shadows of things to the desires of the mind we do not submit the things themselves.

But while all this does vindicate the sanity of the liberal criticism, it does not answer the question: since every action has to be taken by somebody, since everybody is in some degree a drunken hero with two lampposts teetering about him, how can any common good be furthered by this creature who is dominated by his special purposes ? The answer was that it could be furthered by taming his purposes, enlightening them and fitting them into each other as the violin and the drum are fitted together into the orchestra. The answer was not acceptable in the nineteenth century, when men, in spite of all their iconoclasm, were still haunted by the phantom of identity. So liberals refused to write harmonious but separate parts for the violinist and the drummer. They made, instead, a noble appeal to their highest instincts. They spoke over the heads of men to man.

These general appeals were as vague as they were broad. They gave particular men no clue as to how to behave sincerely, but they furnished them with an excellent masquerade when they behaved arbitrarily. Thus the trappings of liberalism came into the service of commercial exploiters, of profiteers and prohibitionists and jingoes, of charlatans and the makers of buncombe.

For liberalism had burned down the barn to roast the pig. The discovery of prejudice in all particular men gave the liberal a shock from which he never recovered. He was so utterly disconcerted by his own discovery of a necessary but perfectly obvious truth, that he took flight into generalities. The appeal to everybody's conscience gave nobody a clue how to act; the voter, the politician, the laborer, the capitalist had to construct their own codes *ad hoc*, accompanied perhaps by an expansive liberal sentiment, but without intellectual guidance from liberal thought. In time, when liberalism had lost its accidental association with free trade and *laissez faire*, through their abandonment in practice, it sadly justified itself as a necessary and useful spirit, as a kind of genial spook worth having around the place. For when individual men, guided by no philosophy but their own temporary rationalizations, got themselves embroiled, the spook would appear and in a peroration straighten out the more arbitrary biases they displayed.

Yet even in this disembodied state liberalism is important. It tends to awaken a milder spirit; it softens the hardness of action. But it does not dominate action, because it has eliminated the actor from its scheme of things. It cannot say: You do this and you do that, as an ruling philosophies must. It can only say: That isn't fair, that's selfish, that's tyrannical. Liberalism has been, therefore, a defender of the under dog, and his liberator, but not his guide, when he is free. Top dog himself, he easily leaves his liberalism aside, and to liberals the sour reflection that they have forged a weapon of release but not a way of life.

The liberals have misunderstood the nature of the public to which they appealed. The public in any situation is, in fact, merely those persons, indirectly concerned, who might align themselves in support of one of the actors. But the liberal took no such uninflated view of the public. He assumed that all mankind was within hearing, that all mankind when it heard would respond homogeneously because it had a single soul. His appeal to this cosmopolitan, universal, disinterested intuition in everybody was equivalent to an appeal to nobody.

No such fallacy is to be found in the political philosophies which active men have lived by. They have all assumed, as a matter of course, that in the struggle against evil it was necessary to call upon some specific agent to oa the work. Even when the thinker was out of temper with the human race, he had always hitherto made somebody the hero of his campaign. It was the peculiarity of liberalism among theories which have played a great part in the world that it attempted to eliminate the hero entirely.

Plato would certainly have thought this strange: his *Republic* is a tract on the proper education of a ruling class. Dante, in the turmoil of thirteenth century Florence, seeking order and stability, addressed himself not to the conscience of Christendom but to the Imperial Party. The great state builders of modern times, Hamilton, Cavaur, Bismarck, Lenin, each had in mind somebody, some group of real people, who were to realize his program. The agents in the theory have varied, of course; here they are the landlords, then the peasants, or the unions, or the military class, or the manufacturers; there are theories addressed to a church, to the ruling dasses in particular nations, to some nation or race. The theories are always, except in the liberal philosophy, addressed to somebody.

By comparison the liberal philosophy has an air of vague unworldiness. Yet the regard of men for it has been persistent; somehow or other with all the lapses in its logic and with all its practical weaknesses it touches a human need. These appeals from men to man: are they not a way of saying that men desire peace, that there is a harmony attainable in which all men can live and let live? It seems so to me. The attempt to escape from particular purposes into some universal purpose, from personality into something impersonal, is, to be sure, a flight from the human problem, but it is at the same time a demonstration of how we wish to see that problem solved. We seek an adjustment, as perfect as possible, as untroubled as it was before we were born. Even if man were a fighting animal, as some say he is, he would wish for a world in which he could fight perfeetly, with enemies fleet enough to extend him and not too fleet to elude him. All men desire their own perfect adjustment, but they desire it, being finite men, on their own terms.

Because liberalism could not accommodate the universal need of adjustment to the permanence and the reality of individual purpose, it remained an incomplete, a disembodied philosophy. It was frustrated over the ancient problem of the One and the Many. Yet the problem is not so insoluble once we cease to personify society. It is only when we are compelled to personify society that we are puzzled as to how many separate organic individuals can be united in one homogeneous organic individual. This logical underbrush is cleared away. if we think of society not as the name of a thing but as the name of all the adjustments between individuals and their things. Then, we can say without theoretical qualms what common sense plainly tells us is so: it is the individuals who act, not society; it is the individuals who think, not the collective mind; it is the painters who paint, not the artistic spirit of the age; it is the soldiers who fight and are killed, not the nation; it is the merchant who exports, not the country. It is their relations with each other that constitute a society. And it is about the ordering of those relations that the individuals not executively concerned in a specific disorder may have public opinions and may intervene as a public.

Chapter XV
Absentee Rulers

1

THE practical effect of the monistic theories of society has been to rationalize that vast concentrating of political and economic power in the midst of which we live. Since society was supposed to have organic purposes of its own, it came to seem quite reasonable that these purposes should be made manifest to a people by laws and decisions from a central point. Somebody had to have a purpose revealed to him which could be treated as the common purpose; if it was to be accepted it had to be enforced by command; if it was really to look like the national purpose, it had to be handed down as a rule binding upon all. Thus men could say with Goethe:

" And then a mighty work completed stands,
One mind suffices for a thousand hands."[1]

In this fashion the eulogies of the Great Society have been made. Two thousand years ago it was possible for whole civilizations as mature as the Chinese and the Greco-Roman to coexist in total indifference to one another. Today the food supplies, the raw materials, the manufactures, the communications and the peace of the world constitute one great system which cannot be thrown severely out of balance in any part without disturbing the whole.

Looked at from the top, the system in its far-flung and intricate adjustments has a certain grandeur. It might, as some hopeful persons think, even ultimately mean the brotherhood of man since all men living in advanced communities are now in quite obvious fashion dependent upon one another. But the individual man cannot look at the system steadily from the top or see it in its ultimate speculative possibilities. For him it means in practice, along with the rise in certain of his material standards of life, a nerve-wracking increase of the incalculable forces that bear upon his fate. My neighbor in the country who borrowed money to raise potatoes which he cannot sell for cash looks at the bills from the village store asking for immediate cash payments, and does not share the philosophic hopeful view of the interdependence of the world. When unseen commission merchants in New York City refuse his potatoes, the calamity is as dumfounding as a drought or a plague of locusts.

The Walter Lippmann Reader

The harvest in September of the planting in May is now determined not only by wind and weather, which his religion has from time immemorial justified, but by a tangle of distant human arrangements of which only loose threads are in his hands. He may live more richly than his ancestors; he may be wealthier and healthier and, for all he knows, even happier. But he gambles with the behavior of unseen men in a bewildering way. His relations with invisibly managed markets are decisively important for him; his own foresight is not dependable. He is a link in a chain that stretches beyond his horizon.

The role that salesmanship and speculation play is a measure of the spread between the work men do and the results. To market the output of Lancashire, says Dibblee,[2] "the merchants and warehousemen of Manchester and Liverpool, not to mention the marketing organizations in other Lancashire towns, have a greater capital employed than that required in all the manufacturing industries of the cotton trade." And, according to Anderson's calculations,[3] the grain received at Chicago in 1915 was sold sixty-two times in futures, as well as an unknown number of times in spot transactions. Where men produce for invisible and uncertain markets "the initial plans of enterprisers"[4] cannot be adequate. The adjustments, often very crude and costly, are effected by salesmanship and speculation.

Under these conditions neither the discipline of the craftsman who controls his process from beginning to end nor the virtues of thrift, economy and work are a complete guide to a successful career. Defoe in his *Complete English Tradesman*[5] could say that "trade is not a ball where people appear in masque and act apart to make sport . . . but is a plain, visible scene of honest life . . . supported by prudence and frugality" . . . and so "prudent management and frugality will increase any fortune to any degree." Benjamin Franklin might opine that "he that gets all he can honestly, and saves all he gets (necessary expenses excepted) will certainly become rich, if that Being who governs the world, to whom all should look for a blessing on their honest endeavors, doth not in His wise providence, otherwise determine." Young men were until quite recently exhorted in the very words of Defoe and Franklin, though Franklin's rather canny allowance for the whims of the Almighty was not always included. But of late the gospel of success contains less about frugality and more about visions and the message of business. This new gospel, beneath all its highfalutin cant, points dimly though excitedly to the truth that for business success a man must project his mind over an invisible environment.

This need has bred an imperious tendency to organization on a large scale. To defend themselves against the economic powers of darkness, against great monopolies or a devastating competition, the farmers set up great centralized selling agencies. Business men form great trade associations. Everybody organizes, until the number of committees and their paid secretaries cannot be computed. The tendency is pervasive. We have had, if I remember correctly, National Smile Week. At any rate we have had Nebraska which discovered that if you wish to prohibit liquor in Nebraska you must prohibit it everywhere. Nebraska cannot live by itself alone, being too weak to control an international traffic. We have had the socialist who was convinced that socialism can maintain itself only on a socialist planet. We have had Secretary Hughes who was convinced that capitalism could exist only on a capitalist planet. We have had all the imperialists who could not live unless they advanced the backward races. And we have had the Ku Klux Klansmen who were persuaded that if you organized and sold hate on a country-wide scale there would be lots more hate than there was before. We have had the Germans before 1914 who were told they had to choose between "world power or downfall," and the French for some years after 1919 who could not be "secure" in Europe unless every one else was insecure. We have had all conceivable manifestations of the impulse to seek stability in an incalculable environment by standardizing for one's own apparent convenience all those who form the context of one's activity.

It has entailed perpetual effort to bring more and more men under the same law and custom, and then, of course, to assume control of the lawmaking and law-enforcing machinery in this larger area. The effect has been to concentrate decision in central governments, in distant executive offices, in caucuses and in steering committees. Whether this concentration of power is good or bad, permanent or passing, this at least is certain. The men who make the decisions at these central points are remote from the men they govern and the facts with which they deal. Even if they conscientiously regard themselves as agents or trustees, it is a pure fiction to say that they are carrying out the will of the people. They may govern the people wisely. They are not governing with the active consultation of the people. They can at best lay down policy wholesale in response to electorates which judge and act upon only a detail of the result. For the governors see a kind of whole which obscures the infinite varieties of particular interests; their vices are abstraction and generalization which appear in politics as legalism and bureaucracy. The governed, on the contrary, see vivid aspects of a whole which they can rarely imagine, and their prevailing vice is to mistake a local prejudice for a universal truth.

The widening distance between the centers where decisions are taken and the places where the main work of the world is done has undermined the discipline of public opinion upon which all the earlier theorists relied.[6] A century ago the model of popular government was the self-sufficing township in which the voters' opinions were formed and corrected by talk with their neighbors. They might entertain queer opinions about witches and spirits and foreign peoples and other worlds. But about the village itself the facts were not radically in dispute, and nothing was likely to happen that the elders could not with a little ingenuity bring under a well-known precedent of their common law.

But under absentee government these checks upon opinion are lacking. The consequences are often so remote and long delayed that error is not promptly disclosed. The conditioning factors are distant; they do not count vividly in our judgments. The reality is inaccessible; the bounds of subjective opinion are wide. In the interdependent world, desire, rather than custom or objective law, tends to become the criterion of men's conduct. They formulate their demands at large for "security" at the expense of every one else's safety, for "morality" at the expense of other men's tastes and comfort, for the fulfillment of a national destiny that consists in taking what you want when you want it. The lengthening of the interval between conduct and experience, between cause and effect, has nurtured a cult of self-expression in which each thinker thinks about his own thoughts and has subtle feelings about his feelings. That he does not in consequence deeply affect the course of affairs is not surprising.

2

The centralizing tendencies of the Great Society have not been accepted without protest, and the case against them has been stated again and again.[7] Without local institutions, said de Tocqueville, a nation may give itself a free government, but it does not possess the spirit of liberty. To concentrate power at one point is to facilitate the seizure of power. "What are you going to do?" Arthur Young asked some provincials at the time of the French Revolution. "We do not know," they replied; "we must see what Paris is going to do." Local interests handled from a distant central point are roughly handled by busy and inattentive men. And in the meantime the local training and the local winnowing of political talent are neglected. The overburdened central authority expands into a vast hierarchy of bureaucrats and clerks manipulating immense stacks of paper, always dealing with symbols on paper, rarely with things or with people. The genius of centralization reached its climax in the famous boast of a French minister of education, who said: It is three o'clock; all the pupils in the third grade throughout France are now composing a Latin verse.

There is no need to labor the point. The more centralization the less can the people concerned be consulted and give conscious assent. The more extensive the rule laid down the less account it can take of fact and special circumstance. The more it conflicts with local experience, the more distant its source and wholesale its character, the less easily enforceable it is. General rules will tend to violate particular needs. Distantly imposed rules usually lack the sanction of consent. Being less suited to the needs of men, and more external to their minds, they rest on force rather than on custom and on reason.

A centralized society dominated by the fiction that the governors are the spokesmen of a common will tends not only to degrade initiative in the individual but to reduce to insignificance the play of public opinion. For when the action of a whole people is concentrated, the public is so vast that even the crude objective judgments it might make on specific issues cease to be practicable. The tests indicated in preceding chapters by which a public might judge the workability of a rule or the soundness of a new proposal have little value when the public runs into millions and the issues are hopelessly entangled with each other. It is idle under such circumstances to talk about democracy, or about the refinement of public opinion. With such monstrous complications the public can do little more than at intervals to align itself heavily for or against the regime in power, and for the rest to bear with its works, obeying meekly or evading, as seems most convenient. For, in practice, the organic theory of society means a concentration of power; that is, the way the notion of one purpose is actually embodied in affairs. And this in turn means that men must either accept frustration of their own purposes or contrive somehow to frustrate that declared purpose of that central power which pretends it is the purpose of all.

Chapter XVI
The Realms of Disorder

1

YET the practice of centralization and the philosophy which personifies society have acquired a great hold upon men. The dangers are well known. If, nevertheless, the practice and the theory persist, it cannot be merely because men have been led astray by false doctrine.

If you examine the difficulties enumerated by the sponsors of great centralizing measures, such as national prohibition, the national child labor amendment, federal control of education or the nationalization of railroads, they are reducible, I think, to one dominating idea: that it is necessary to extend the area of control over all the factors in a problem or the problem will be insoluble anywhere.

It was to this idea that Mr. Lloyd George appealed when he faced his critics at the end of his administration. While his words are the words of a skillful debater, the idea behind them might almost be called the supreme motive of all the imperial and centralizing tendencies of the Great Society:

"Lord Grey sought to make peace in the Balkans. He made peace. That peace did not stand the jolting of the train that carried it from London to the Balkans. It fell to pieces before it ever reached Sofia. That was not his fault. The plan was good. The intentions were excellent. *But there were factors there which he could not control.* He tried to prevent the Turks from entering the war against us, a most important matter. German diplomacy was too strong for him. He tried to prevent Bulgaria from entering the war against us. There again German diplomacy defeated us. Well, now I have never taunted Lord Grey with that. I do not taunt him now, but what I say is that when you get into the realm of foreign affairs there are things I will not say you cannot visualize, because you do, but there are factors you cannot influence."[1]

Mr. Lloyd George might have said the same of domestic affairs. There, too, factors abound which you cannot influence. And as empires expand to protect their frontiers, and then expand further to protect the protections to their frontiers, so central governments have been led step by step to take one interest after another under their control.

The Walter Lippmann Reader

For the democracies are haunted by this dilemma: they are frustrated unless in the laying down of rules there is a large measure of assent; yet they seem unable to find solutions of their greatest problems except through centralized governing by means of extensive rules which necessarily ignore the principle of assent. The problems that vex democracy seem to be unmanageable by democratic methods.

In supreme crises the dilemma is presented absolutely. Possibly a war can be fought for democracy; it cannot be fought democratically. Possibly a sudden revolution may be made to advance democracy; but the revolution itself will be conducted by a dictatorship. Democracy may be defended against its enemies but it will be defended by a committee of safety. The history of the wars and revolutions since 1914 is ample evidence on this point. In the presence of danger, where swift and concerted action is required, the methods of democracy cannot be employed.

That is understandable enough. But how is it that the democratic method should be abandoned so commonly in more leisurely and less catastrophic times? Why in time of peace should people provoke that centralization of power which deprives them of control over the use of that power? Is it not a probable answer to say that in the presence of certain issues, even in time of peace, the dangers have seemed sufficiently menacing to cause people to seek remedies, regardless of method, by the shortest and easiest way at hand?

It could be demonstrated, I think, that the issues which have seemed so overwhelming were of two kinds: those which turned on the national defense or the public safety and those which turned on the power of modern capitalism. Where the relations of a people to armed enemies are in question or where the relations of employee, customer or farmer to large industry are in question the need for solutions has outweighed all interest in the democratic method.

In the issues engendered by the rise of the national state and the development of large scale industries are to be found the essentially new problems of the modern world. For the solution of these problems there are few precedents. There is no established body of custom and law. The field of international affairs and the field of industrial relations are the two great centers of anarchy in society. It is a pervasive anarchy. Out of the national state with its terrifying military force, and out of great industry with all its elaborate economic compulsion, the threat against personal security always rises. To offset it

518

somehow, to check it and thwart it, seemed more important than any finical regard for the principle of assent.

And so to meet the menace of the national state, its neighbors sought to form themselves into more powerful national states; to tame the power of capitalism they supported the growth of vast bureaucracies. Against powers that were dangerous and uncontrolled they set up powers, nominally their own, which were just as vast and just as uncontrolled.

3

But only for precarious intervals has security been attained by these vast balances of power. From 1870 to 1914 the world was held in equilibrium. It was upset, and the world has not yet found a new order. The balances of power within the nations are no less unsteady. For neither in industry nor in international affairs has it yet been possible to hold any balance long enough to fix it by rule and give it an institutional form. Power has been checked by power here and there and now and then but power has not been adjusted to power and the terms of the adjustment settled and accepted.

The attempt to bring power under control by offsetting it with power was sound enough in intention. The conflicting purposes of men cannot be held under pacific control unless the tendency of all power to become arbitrary is checked by other force. All the machinery of conference, of peaceful negotiation, of law and the rule of reason is workable in large affairs only where the power of the negotiators is neutralized one against the other. It may be neutralized because the parties are in fact equally powerful. It may be neutralized because the weaker has invisible allies among the other powers of the world, or in domestic affairs among other interests in society. But before there can be law there must be order, and an order is an arrangement of power.

The worst that can be said of the nationalists and collectivists is that they attempted to establish balances of power which could not endure. The pluralist at least would say that the end they sought must be attained differently, that in place of vast wholesale balances of power it is necessary to create many detailed balances of power. The people as a whole supporting a centralized government cannot tame capitalism as a whole. For the powers which are summed up in the term capitalism are many. They bear separately upon different groups of people. The nation as a unit does not encounter them all, and cannot deal with them all.

The Walter Lippmann Reader

It is to the different groups of people concerned that we must look for the power which shall offset the arbitrary power that bears upon them. The reduction of capitalism to workable law is no matter of striking at it wholesale by general enactments. It is a matter of defeating its arbitrary power in detail, in every factory, in every office, in every market, and of turning the whole network of relations under which industry operates from the dominion of arbitrary forces into those of settled rules.

And so it is in the anarchy among nations. If all the acts of a citizen are to be treated as organically the actions of that nation, a stable balance of power is impossible. Here also it is necessary to break down the fiction of identity, to insist that the quarrel of one business man with another is their quarrel, and not the nation's, a quarrel in which each is entitled to a vindication of his right to fair adjudication but not to patriotic advocacy of his cause. It is only by this dissociation of private interests that the mass of disputes across frontiers can gradually be brought under an orderly process. For a large part, perhaps the greatest part, of the disputes between nations is an accumulated mass of undetermined disputes between their nationals. If these essentially private disputes could be handled, without patriotic fervor and without confusing an oil prospector with the nation as a whole, with governments acting as friends of the court and not as advocates for a client, the balance of power between governments would be easier to maintain. It would not be subject to constant assault from within each nation by an everlasting propaganda of suspicion by private interests seeking national support. And if only the balance of power between governments could be stabilized long enough to establish a line of precedents for international conference, a longer peace might result.

4

These in roughest outline are some of the conclusions, as they appear to me, of the attempt to bring the theory of democracy into somewhat truer alignment with the nature of public opinion. I have conceived public opinion to be, not the voice of God, nor the voice of society, but the voice of the interested spectators of action. I have, therefore, supposed that the opinions of the spectators must be essentially different from those of the actors, and that the kind of action they were capable of taking was essentially different too. It has seemed to me that the public had a function and must have methods of its own in controversies, qualitatively different from those of the executive men; that it was a dangerous confusion to believe that private purposes were a mere emanation of some common purpose.

This conception of society seems to me truer and more workable than that which endows public opinion with pantheistic powers. It does not assume that men in action have universal purposes; they are denied the fraudulent support of the fiction that they are the agents of a common purpose. They are regarded as the agents of special purposes, without pretense and without embarrassment. They must live in a world with men who have other special purposes. The adjustments which must be made are society, and the best society is the one in which men have purposes which they can realize with the least frustration. When men take a position in respect to the purposes of others they are acting as a public. And the end of their acting in this role is to promote the conditions under which special purposes can be composed.

It is a theory which puts its trust chiefly in the individuals directly concerned. They initiate, they administer, they settle. It would subject them to the least possible interference from ignorant and meddlesome outsiders, for in this theory the public intervenes only when there is a crisis of maladjustment, and then not to deal with the substance of the problem but to neutralize the arbitrary force which prevents adjustment. It is a theory which economizes the attention of men as members of the public, and asks them to do as little as possible in matters' where they can do nothing very well. It confines the effort of men, when they are a public, to a part they might fulfill, to apart which corresponds to their own greatest interest in any social disturbance; that is, to an intervention which may help to allay the disturbance, and thus allow them to return to their own affairs.

For it is the pursuit of their special affairs that they are most interested in. It is by the private labors of individuals that life is enhanced. I set no great store on what can be done by public opinion and the action of masses.

5

I have no legislative program to offer, no new institutions to propose. There are, I believe, immense confusions in the current theory of democracy which frustrate and pervert its action. I have attacked certain of the confusions with no conviction except that a false philosophy tends to stereotype thought against the lessons of experience. I do not know what the lessons will be when we have learned to think of public opinion as it is, and not as the fictitious power we have assumed it to be. It is enough if with Bentham we know that "the perplexity of ambiguous discourse . . . distracts and eludes the apprehension, stimulates and inflames the passions."

Notes

Chapter 1

1 Cited Philip Guedalla, *The Second Empire*.

2 Logan Pearsall Smith, *More Trivia*, p. 41.

3 *Gf.* Simon Michelet, *Stay-at-Home vote and Absentee Voters* pamphlet of the National Get Out the Vote Club; also A. M. Schlesinger and E. M. Erickson, "The Vanishing Voter," *New Republic*, Oct. 15, 1924. The percentage of the popular to the eligible vote from 1865 to 1920 declined from 83.51 per cent to 52.36 per cent.

4 Charles Edward Merriam and Harvey Foote Gosnell. *Non-Voting: Causes and Methods of Control*.

5 James Bryce, *Modern Democracies*, Vol. II, p. 52.

6 A. Lawrence Lowell, *Public Opinion and Popular Government. Cf.* Appendices.

7 Robert Michels, *Political Parties*, p. 390.

Chapter 2

1 Logan Pearsall Smith

2 As told by J. Arthur Thomson, *The Outline of Science*, Vol. III, p 646.

3 *Creative Evolution*, Ch. III.

Chapter 3

1 *Cf.* my *Public Opinion*, Chapters XXV and XXVI.

2 *Cf.* my *Public Opinion*, Chapters XIII and XIV.

3 Speech on the Reform Bill of 1832, quoted in the *Times* (London), July 12, 1923.

Chapter 4

1 Preface to *The Revolutionist's Handbook*, p. 179·

2 *Parties and Party Leaders*, p. xvi.

3 H. Delbrück, *Government and the Will of the People*, p. 15. Translated by Roy S. MacElwee.

The Walter Lippmann Reader

Chapter 6

1 *Discourse on Method,* Part I.

Chapter 7

1 T. R. Malthus, *An Essay on the Principle of Population,* Chapter II.

2 A. M. Carr-Saunders, *The Population Problem,* p. 28.

3 Malthus himself recognized this in a later edition of his book.

4 *Cf.* in this connection W. F. Ogburn, *Social Change, passim,* but particularly Part IV, I, on "The Hypothesis of Cultural Lag."

5 However, the controversy over gun elevation demonstrates how difficult it is to maintain an equilibrium of force where so many factors are variable.

6 Gustav Cassel, A *Theory* of *Social Economy,* Chapter I.

7 *Ibid.,* p. 7.

Chapter 12

1 Articles XIII, XV.

2 Articles 4, 5, 6, 7, 8, 10.

Chapter 14

1 John Maynard Keynes, A *Revision* of the Treaty, p. 4.

2 In a letter to William Wirt, cited by John Sharp Williams, *Thomas Jefferson,* p. 7.

3 Harold J. Laski, *Studies in the Problem* of *Sovereignty,* p. 24.

4 Kenneth Macgowan, *The Theatre of Tomorrow,* pp. 249-50.

Chapter 15

1 *Faust,* Part II, Act v, scene 3.

2 Dibblee, *The Laws of Supply and Demand,* cited by B. M. Anderson, Jr., *The Value of Money,* p. 259·

3 B. M. Anderson, Jr., *The Value of Money,* p. 251.

4 *Ibid.*

5 *Cf.* Werner Lombart, *The Quintessence of Capitalism,* Chapter VII.

6 *Cf.* my *Public Opinion,* Chapters XVI and XVII.

7 In a convenient form by J. Charles Brun, *Le Régionalisme,* pp. 13 *et seq.* Cf. also Walter Thompson, Federal Centralization, Chapter XIX.

Chapter 16
1 Speech at Manchester, October 14., 1922.

CPSIA information can be obtained
at www.ICGtesting.com
Printed in the USA
FSHW012022070921
84615FS